ENDORSEMENTS

Wow! What a massive project! Roger Rapske (Editor)

Reading this book may well, if you let it, liberate you from the frustrating treadmill of fear, guilt, shame, and the uncertainty you're more than likely often overwhelmed with concerning the effectiveness of your efforts to win the approval of God. The main objective of Paul's ministry was to dispel the bewitching notion of self-righteousness in favor of accepting the unmerited favor and acceptance of the love, grace, mercy, and peace of God for "one," well actually, for "all." Roger Rapske (Author)

This is an entirely different perspective on the masterpiece of Paul's writings. It's an insightful and challenging piece of work. This is a commentary alright, an unabashed re-interpretation of the most prolific contributor to the most cherished religious book of all time, the Bible. Roger Rapske (Student)

Did God do "much more" or what? You're about to read what the author has come to understand how to live life to its fullest in the "now," based upon a wonderful appreciation of the "work" of God. It is God's good pleasure to bless you with abundance and liberty beyond your wildest imaginations. Get out your utensils and dig in! Roger Rapske (Theologian)

The author figures the reason so many folks are turned off to religion today is 'cause those who are supposed to have a corner on truth are perhaps the most blind, deaf, and dumb! Like the apostle Paul, Martin Luther, Calvin, Zwingli, among a host of others, the author considers himself a protestant of sorts. He too "protests" the status quo, for it offers little he finds comfort in. Roger Rapske (Religious Speculator)

The secret agenda of this book is not to teach what you need to know about God, rather, what God knows about you! This magnificent revelation will alter the way you think, and more importantly, the way you act. Roger Rapske (Motivational Mentor)

Order this book online at www.trafford.com
or email orders@trafford.com

Most Trafford titles are also available at major online book retailers.

© Copyright 2010 Roger Rapske.

All rights reserved. No part of this publication may be reproduced, stored in a retrieval system, or transmitted, in any form or by any means, electronic, mechanical, photocopying, recording, or otherwise, without the written prior permission of the author.

Printed in Victoria, BC, Canada.

ISBN: 978-1-4269-2793-5 (sc)

Our mission is to efficiently provide the world's finest, most comprehensive book publishing service, enabling every author to experience success. To find out how to publish your book, your way, and have it available worldwide, visit us online at www.trafford.com

Trafford rev. 2/24/2010

 www.trafford.com

North America & international
toll-free: 1 888 232 4444 (USA & Canada)
phone: 250 383 6864 ♦ fax: 812 355 4082

...BUT...

an unauthorized autobiography

of the Apostle Paul

Also by

Roger Rapske, BTh.

More Than Just a Piece of Sky

...But...

an unauthorized autobiography of the Apostle Paul

Roger Rapske
B.Th.

Trafford Publishing
Victoria, British Columbia, Canada

DEDICATION

in loving memory of

my dad

Rev. Rudolph (Rudy) Rapske

whose life was a testimony

of the

gracious and peaceable spirit

of Jesus

PREFACE

January 8, 1988

    That's the momentous date I started tapping the chicklets on my brand new Apple II GS, a limited, special edition computer emblazoned with the signature of no less than the "Woz" himself. Yes, I eventually graduated from the 4 1/2 floppy-disc to the more refined 13" purple i-Mac for over ten years. And now, I'm wrapping this project all up on another Apple beauty, the super-size me 24" i-Mac.
    Twenty-two years and counting!
    How time flies!
    As a teacher of scripture I was often faced with the awareness many folks simply had no contextual concept of Paul's voluminous writings in the New Testament. The general ignorance of Christians regarding the historical foundations of the Biblical books is downright appalling. Where I sit today I'll be the first to confess I accepted hook, line and sinker everything I'd been taught without spending an ounce of diligent effort to seek out information and truth. I blame nobody else other than myself for my own lack of clarity and the toleration of ignorance I perpetuated in my own life for so many years.
    As an example, most commentaries continue to inform us that Paul had four missionary trips. Well, you can lump them all together if you want. I happen to think the nineteen or so different trips Paul actually took were what I would call significant and eventful trips of one kind or another. I think seeing the magnitude of his "on the road again" experiences will hit you between the eyes like never before as we proceed.
    Another example of poor information would be the number of letters he wrote. In my studies I've come across enough strong evidence indicating he wrote a few more letters than we give him credit for. In my version of things I've got four distinct letters to the Corinthians and two to the Philippians. Oh to be sure, it's all there in the original version your familiar with, however, it's quite possible the time line and the sequence of events is quite plausible with what I am presenting. It's another example of how thinking out of the box is perhaps helpful in grasping the context of his information and exhortations.

PREFACE

Never in my wildest dreams did I think this project would transform my life as it has. I had no idea at the start I'd end up writing five complete manuscripts. This monumental project began with my desire to capture the heart and mind of a Biblical hero of mine, the apostle Paul. If I was going to become a better student, a more skillful teacher, and have something worthy of teaching, how better to do it than to walk a mile in his sandals and delve into his psyche. I hoped a chronological and sociological understanding of his tenure on earth might help provide an insight into his understanding of God.

To get into the mind of Paul I figured I'd have to become Paul, think like Paul, talk like Paul, and write like Paul. Therefore, the premise I chose to work with for this project is as follows:

I (Paul) am writing to you, in a language you're hopefully comfortable with, relating my (Paul's) life, ministry, letters, opinions and insights, including historical and sociological contextual information.

Please, while I'm more than comfortable with my work, I claim no sense of infallibility or inerrancy with my conclusions, suppositions, or perceptions. I'm satisfied with the heresy I've adopted, certainly to the chagrin of many of my family and peers. I'm nevertheless a happy camper.

While I intend to challenge your beliefs to the max, I'm not here to tell you I've got the one and only truth out there 'cause I'm coming to discover the truth of God's wisdom isn't contained in a single volume of anyone's creating. What you'll read is what I've come to understand, a wonderful appreciation of the "work" of God I hope you'll find challenging enough to warrant further investigation on your own.

God did way more (Paul said "**much more**") than I ever thought.

Oh, I've got to mention a few titles for this book I thought of as I worked my way through a great number of amazing passages of scripture. In my humble opinion, these are quite clever and imaginative:

- "Oh God, I'm stoned!"
- "Give your head a shake!"
- "What a pile of crap!"
- "You can't handle the truth!"
- "On the road again…"

PREFACE

By now you know you know my safe choice, a choice I'd like to think Paul would approve of in spite of the fact this is an quite naturally an unauthorized accounting of his life and writings.

"BUT," of course, is the minute little word of conjunction Paul used extensively to bridge the gap of human understanding with the perspective and heart of God. The religious world Paul was exposed to had an entrenched systematic theology based squarely upon the shoulders of self-righteousness.

Paul, after an incredible mind blowing experience on one particular trip, got a glimpse of God's perspective, and never looked back. In fact, if you study the context of all he wrote, you'll discover the main objective of his ministry was to dispel the notion of self-righteousness in favor of accepting the unmerited favor and acceptance of the love, grace, mercy, and peace of God, "once," for "one," and for "all!"

Here's a classic example of Paul's insight from his letter to the Galatians as he spoke about the role of a schoolmaster.

BUT now, after you've come to know and appreciate what God has done for you, or rather and more importantly, since you're fully convinced of God's view and opinion of you, how in the world could you turn once again to the weak, the beggarly, the childish, and the elementary systems of laws, rules, and regulations enslaving and entangling you in the chains of bondage to legalistic, self-righteous pursuits of performance?

How indeed?

I feel the enslaving trap the religious world continues to deploy in its attempts to educate and change the world is a sad commentary on how little we've grown in our understanding. I believe the reason so many folks are turned off to religion today is 'cause those who are supposed to have a corner on truth are perhaps the most blind, deaf, and dumb! I'm convinced the hypocrisy of control is losing its appeal.

Like the apostle Paul, Martin Luther, Calvin, Zwingli, among others, I'm a protestant of sorts. I too "protest" the status quo of self-righteousness. It offers nothing I find comfort in. I've resolved to unashamedly proclaim my faith and trust in the One who has redeemed me, who has placed my feet upon the solid rock of salvation based solely upon the work of Jesus on the cross and through His resurrection.

My faith has found a resting place, for my hope is built on nothing less than the blood of Jesus, and His righteousness!

PREFACE

One of the classes I really didn't care for all that much at Bible school was Systematic Theology. Our professor was a brilliant chap by the name of Werner Waitkus, who amazed me that he even remotely understood what he was trying to teach us. I confess I didn't pick up much 'cause I had no idea how it all fit together in the bigger picture. The last time we met at a reunion several years ago I had the humorous nerve to tell him I finally got it after all these years away from school. I took his Germanic chuckle to be a positive response of my admission.

Denominations are formed with the assistance of a systematic theology. Personal understanding, on the other hand, rarely associates or applies a systematic approach to belief. It isn't until I did an in-depth study of Paul's writings did I find an incredible consistency from one end to another of his writings which took decades to record. He didn't just say one thing and another thing somewhere else.

I discovered that if I took a particular theological position I'd better be able to consistently support it. So, if I come to believe (and I have) Paul's assertion that God's grace was a gift, that salvation was purchased on behalf of the whole world through the death and resurrection of Jesus, irregardless of the input of mankind into the equation, oh my, then I have to conclude that even the powerful historically accepted notion that "belief" is a requirement to get into the good book goes out with the bathwater as just another work that doesn't cut it.

If I come to believe (and I have) that Paul's assertion that Jesus is now our High Priest (just wait for the amazing study from Paul's letter to the Hebrews), that sin was dealt with once and for all on the cross, that there's no longer a need for the altar, then my oh my, where does that leave sin.

Oops!

If there's no sin, what happens to confession? Well, didn't the veil get ripped in two?

Gonzo! On and on it goes.

Hey, if God settled the score with His blood what happened to hell?

And what about that devil character?

Happily, my systematic theology is leading me down some incredible paths. The branches are swaying and the roots are being shaken to the core. Yes, I'm not done yet. Donna and I are into some pretty wow stuff like quantum physics and such. And there are no pictures in most of those books. Go figure!

PREFACE

It's amazing how beautifully it's all coming together as pieces of the marvelous tapestry of God's perspective are coming alive before our very eyes.

Understanding has replaced a requirement of belief. Trust and faith in God's ability to complete the task He set out to finish have replaced my self-righteous endeavors. Liberty and abundance in the "now" have superseded my negative hope that I might some day gain the ultimate prize.

Folks, I'm already livin' it!

The secret agenda of my book is not to teach you about what you need to know about God, rather, what God knows about you!

This magnificent revelation alone will alter the way you think, and more importantly, the way you act. It will liberate you from the frustrating treadmill of fear, guilt, shame, and the uncertainty you're often overwhelmed with concerning the effectiveness of your efforts to win the approval of God.

Paul has **"much more"** to share with you.

Let's get it on…

ACKNOWLEDGEMENTS

First of all, I wish to acknowledge the great love and patience of my family. My beloved wife Donna has graciously allowed me the liberty of time and space to pursue this venture at my own pace and in my own creative format. I've no doubt robbed her and our children, Richard and Mandilyn, daughter-in-law Sharla, and our precious grandchildren Ryan and Keira, of many hours of attention as I wandered along on this wonderful journey of spiritual discovery. I'm blessed beyond belief for such a great family. This book is really a legacy for them of my understanding of God's love for all of us.

    My dad gave me a copy of Reese's Chronological Bible back in 1978 during my Bible college days as I studied for my Bachelor of Theology degree. It's been my Bible of choice ever since. I've used the dating of Frank Klassen that forms the basis of the Reese edition as the chronological time line for my manuscript. I have, for the most part, used this point of reference fearing not the margin of error is impossible to guarantee.

    The tremendous historical, sociological, and biographical information that fills the pages of anything William Barclay has written has without question been a favorite and cherished study tool. I also owe a huge debt of gratitude to a host of folks who produce and edit a wide range of scholarly commentaries and works that have done an incredible service in providing linguistic, interpretive, and historical background

    I'm indebted to one of my college professors, Dr. Richard Paetzel, for significantly introducing me to the character of the apostle Paul. I'm grateful for his systematic approach to the teachings of Paul that peaked my interest in pursuing a project of this magnitude. He was truly an example to his students of the character and heart of the Paul.

    Through the years of involvement in church settings I've had the opportunity of sitting under the tutelage of many preachers and teachers. They have all contributed to a great heritage of religious training. Perhaps the one who has helped crystallize the true intent of Paul's writings in my mind has been an itinerant Bible expositor by the name of Mike Williams. I have appreciated and value his insights. I also owe a huge thanks to my best friend Paul, who has opened his heart and understanding with me as we continue to pursue a journey of discovery into the grace and mercy of God.

ACKNOWLEDGEMENT

I'd like to say thanks to Matt Hunckler and all the folks at Trafford Publishing I'd like to meet someday for the great assistance in getting my humble attempts at writing to this point.

I'd also like to extend a big thumbs-up to Jean Lawrence who patiently guided me through the laborious task of preparing the technical aspects enroute to the publishing process, and who given me so many practical, visual suggestions that have greatly added to the presentation.

CONTENTS

Dedication...vi
Preface..vii
Acknowledgments xii
Contents..xiv
Origin of Letters xxii
But Passages xxiii

Introduction... 1

The Early Years
    1.   Hero..4
    2.   Heritage..7
    3.   Tarsus 9
    4.   Just a Kid 10
    5.   Bar Mitzva 14

Trip # 1 Tarsus to Jerusalem
    6.   Ready, Set, Go...17
    7.   Quilt of Education 20
    8.   Caped Crusader...23
    9.   Stone 'm (Acts 6:8-15; 7:1-58) 27
    10.   Nutso (Acts 7:59,60; 8:1-4; 9:1,2).................31

Trip # 2 Jerusalem to Damascas
    11.   Blindsided (Acts 9:3-9)................................34
    12.   Ananias (Acts 9:10-19a) 38
    13.   Three-Year Gap (Acts 9:19b-25; Gal 1:17)...40

Trip # 3 Damascus to Jerusalem
    14.   Not Wanted (Acts 9:26-30; Gal 1:18,19).......44

Trip # 4 Jerusalem to Tarsus
    15.   Home Where I Belong (Acts 11:19-25)..........47

Trip # 5 Tarsus to Antioch
    16.   Antioch (Acts 11:26-30) 49

CONTENTS

Trip # 6 Antioch to Jerusalem
17.   Persecution of Grippa (Acts 12:1-23) 52
18.   John Mark (Acts 12:24,25) 57

Trip # 7 Jerusalem to Antioch
19.   Set Apart (Acts 13:1-3) 60

Trip # 8 Antioch through Cyprus, Pamphylia, Pisidia, and back
20.   Cyprus (Acts 13:4-13a) 62
21.   Perga (Acts 13:13b) 67
22.   Antioch of Pisidia (Acts 13:14,15) 69
23.   Sermon at Antioch (Acts 13:16-41) 71
24.   Dust Up (Acts 13:42-51a) 75
25.   Iconium (Acts 13:15b -14:6a) 78
26.   Lystra (Acts 14:6b-20) 80
27.   Homeward Bound (Acts 14:21-28) 84

Trip # 9 Antioch to Jerusalem
28.   Trouble Makers (Acts 15:1-5) 86
29.   Jerusalem Council (Acts 15:6-21) 90

Trip # 10 Jerusalem to Antioch
30.   Policy (Acts 15:22-35; Gal 2:7-10) 93
31.   Fight with Peter (Gal 2:11-21) 97
32.   High Road (Acts 15:36-39) 101
33.   Silas (Acts 15:40) 103

Trip # 11 Antioch through Asia Minor, Macedonia, Achaia
34.   Timothy (Acts 15:41-16:8) 104
35.   Dr. Luke (Acts 16:9,10) 108
36.   Boat Trip to Macedonia (Acts 16:11) 110
37.   Lydia of Philippi (Acts 16:12-15) 112
38.   Damsel in Distress (Acts 16:16-23) 115
39.   Jailbirds (Acts 16:24-40) 119
40.   Thessalonica (Acts 17:1-10a) 124
41.   Berea (Acts 17:10b-15) 127
42.   Athens (Acts 17:16-18) 128
43.   Mars Hill (Acts 17:19-34) 132

CONTENTS

1 1/2 Years in Corinth
44. Corinth (Acts 18:1) 137
45. Work in Corinth (Acts 18:2-17) 139

First Letter to the Thessalonians
46. Happy Camper (1 Thes 1:1-10) 143
47. Real Deceivers (1 Thes 2:1-16) 146
48. Crown of Rejoicing (1 Thes 2:17-3:12) 149
49. Perfectly Holy (I Thes 3:13-4:11) 151
50. Death (1 Thes 4:12-5:11) 153
51. Live in Harmony (1 Thes 5:1-28) 157

Second Letter to the Thessalonians
52. God's Viewpoint (2 Thes 1:1-12) 159
53. Day of the Lord (2 Thes 2:1-17) 162
54. Live in Peace (2 Thes 3:1-18) 165

Trip # 12 **Corinth to Ephesus, Jerusalem, and back to Antioch**
55. Bald (Acts 18:18-22) 167

Trip # 13 **Antioch through Asia Minor to Ephesus**
56. Apollos (Acts 18:23-19:1) 169

3 Years in Ephesus
57. Ephesus (Acts 19:2-7) 172
58. Divers (Acts 19:8-20) 175
59. Demetrius (Acts 19:21-41) 179

First Letter to the Corinthians
60. Previous Letter (2 Cor 6:13-7:2) 183

Second Letter to the Corinthians
61. God is Faithful (1 Cor 1:1-17) 185
62. Wisdom of God (1 Cor 1:18-31) 188
63. Mind of Jesus (1 Cor 2:1-16) 193
64. Milk and Meat (1 Cor 3:1-23) 196
65. Follow Me (1 Cor 4:1-20) 200
66. Leaven (1 Cor 4:21-5:13) 204
67. Shame On You (1 Cor 6:1-8) 208
68. Temple of God (1 Cor 6:9-20) 211
69. Marriage (1 Cor 7:1-17) 213

CONTENTS

70.	Circumcision (1 Cor 7:18-19)	216
71.	Called of God (1 Cor 7:20-24)	217
72.	Virgins (1 Cor 7:25-40)	219
73.	You Aren't What You Eat (1 Cor 8:1-13)	223
74.	Why I Do What I Do (1 Cor 9:1-23)	228
75.	Run Like Stink (1 Cor 9:24-10:15)	231
76.	Expedient (1 Cor 10:16-11:1)	235
77.	Battle of the Sexes (1 Cor 11:2-16)	238
78.	Piggies (1 Cor 11:17-34)	241
79.	Gift of God (1 Cor 12:1-31)	243
80.	Known of God (1 Cor 13:1-12)	246
81.	Tongue Tied (1 Cor 13:13-14:40)	248
82.	Sting of Death (1 Cor 15:1-58)	253
83.	Conclusion of 2nd Cor (1 Cor 16:1-24)	260

Trip # 14 **Quick trip to Corinth, then back to Ephesus**

Third Letter to the Corinthians

84.	Introduction of the Severe Letter	263
85.	Weapons of Our Warfare (2 Cor 10:1-18)	264
86.	Bragging Rights (2 Cor 11:1-12:10)	267
87.	Conclusion of 3rd Cor (2 Cor 12:11-13:14)	273

Trip # 15 **Ephesus to Philippi**

Fourth Letter to the Corinthians

88.	Introduction of 4th Corinthians	277
89.	Beyond Measure (2 Cor 1:1-2:13)	280
90.	Triumph (2 Cor 2:14-17)	284
91.	Image of God (2 Cor 3:1-8)	287
92.	A Different Perspective (2 Cor 4:1-5:7)	290
93.	Reconciled to God (2 Cor 5:8-21)	293
94.	Day of Salvation (2 Cor 6:1-12; 7:3-16)	296
95.	Challenge to Give (2 Cor 8:1-9:15)	301

Trip # 16 **Philippi to Corinth**

Letter to the Galatians

96.	Introduction of Galatians (Acts 20:2,3a)	305
97.	Gospel of Grace & Peace (Gal 1:1-16a)	307

CONTENTS

98.	Frustrate Grace (Gal 1:16b-2:21)	310
99.	You Fools (Gal 3:1-18)	315
100.	Schoolmaster (Gal 3:19-4:11)	318
101.	Children of the Promise (Gal 4:12-31)	322
102.	Just a Little Snip (Gal 5:1-12)	325
103.	Walk in the Spirit (Gal 5:13-6:10)	328
104.	Conclusion of Galatians (Gal 6:11-18)	331

Letter to the Romans

105.	Introduction of Romans	333
106.	I Am Not Ashamed (Rom 1:1-32)	335
107.	Inexcusable (Rom 2:1-16)	340
108.	Circumcision of the Heart (Rom 2:17-29)	343
109.	Falling Short (Rom 3:1-29)	345
110.	Lessons from Abraham (Rom 3:30-4:25)	349
111.	Much More (Rom 5:1-19)	353
112.	Gift of God (Rom 5:20-6:23)	356
113.	A New Spirit (Rom 7:1-6)	360
114.	War is Over (Rom 7:7-25a)	361
115.	No Condemnation (Rom 7:25b-8:13)	364
116.	Adoption	367
117.	Spirit of Adoption (Rom 8:14-39)	370
118.	Tried, Tested, & True (Rom 9:1-33)	374
119.	End of the Law (Rom 10:1-11:11)	378
120.	Olive Tree (Rom 11:12-36)	383
121.	Transformed (Rom 12:1-21)	387
122.	Higher Power (Rom 13:1-7)	390
123.	Wake Up (Rom 13:8-14)	392
124.	Clean vs Unclean (Rom 14:1-15:7)	394
125.	Root of Jesse (Rom 15:8-33)	398
126.	Conclusion of Romans (Rom 16:1-27)	401

Trip # 17 Corinth through Macedonia, Troas to Jerusalem

127.	Review Time (Acts 20:3b-6)	404
128.	Eutychus (Acts 20:7-12)	407
129.	Farewell at Ephesus (Acts 20:13-38)	409
130.	Don't Cry (Acts 21:1-17)	413

in Jerusalem

131.	Audience with James (Acts 21:18-25)	417
132.	Temple Riot (Acts 21:26-40a)	420

CONTENTS

133.	Appeal to the Mob (Acts 21:40b-22:29)	424
134.	Before the Sanhedrin (Acts 22:30-23:10)	428

Trip # 18 **Jerusalem to Caesarea**
135.	Plot Thickens (Acts 23:11-32)	432
136.	Before Felix (Acts 23:33-24:27a)	436
137.	Festus Takes Over (Acts 24:27b-25:12)	442
138.	Before Agrippa II (Acts 25:13-26:1)	446
139.	Taking the Stand (Acts 26:2-29)	451

Trip # 19 **Caesarea to Rome**
140.	Off to Rome (Acts 26:30-27:26)	456
141.	Shipwrecked (Acts 27:27-44)	462
142.	From Malta to Rome (Acts 28:1-15)	466
143.	Rome! Finally! (Acts 28:16-31)	471

<u>Rome</u>
Letter to Philemon
144.	Introduction of Philemon	475
145.	Profitable (Philemon 1:1-25)	478

Letter to the Colossians
146.	Introduction of Colossians	481
147.	Translated (Col 1:1-22)	484
148.	What Mystery? (Col 1:23-2:15)	488
149.	Don't Go There (Col 2:16-23)	493
150.	Seek Those Things (Col 3:1-15)	495
151.	Walk the Walk (Col 3:16-4:6)	497
152.	Final Greetings (Col 4:7-18)	499

Letter to the Ephesians
153.	Signed, Sealed, Delivered (Eph 1:1-14)	501
154.	In Times Past (Eph 1:15-2:10)	504
155.	Habitation of God (Eph 2:11-22)	506
156.	Full of God (Eph 3:1-19)	509
157.	Crap Shooters (Eph 3:20-4:16)	511
158.	Renew Your Mind (Eph 4:17-32)	513
159.	Get a Life (Eph 5:1-20)	516
160.	Not Even a Zit (Eph 5:21-6:9)	519
161.	Armor of God (Eph 6:10-24)	522

CONTENTS

First Letter to the Philippians
162.	Introduction of the Philippian Letters	524
163.	Dirty dogs (Phil 3:1-4:1)	526

Second Letter to the Philippians
164.	Fruit of Excellence (Phil 1:1-11)	532
165.	I'm a Winner (Phil 1:12-30)	534
166.	Chunk of Godness (Phil 2:1-18)	537
167.	Good on 'im (Phil 2:19-30; 4:2-4a)	541
168.	Whatsoever Things (Phil 4:4b-23)	543

First Letter to Timothy
169.	Introduction of 1st Timothy	546
170.	Immortal, Invisible (1 Tim 1:1-17)	548
171.	One Mediator (1 Tim 1:18-2:7)	551
172.	Goofy Hairdos (1 Tim 2:8-15)	553
173.	Leadership (1 Tim 3:1-13)	554
174.	It's a Good Thing (1 Tim 3:14-4:16)	556
175.	Widows (1Tim 5:1-16)	559
176.	General Counsel (1 Tim 5:17-6:21)	561

Letter to Titus
177.	Pack of Liars (Titus 1:1-14)	566
178.	A Peculiar People (Titus 1:15-2:14)	569
179.	Justified by His Grace (Titus 2:15-3:11)	572
180.	Conclusion of Titus (Titus 3:12-15)	575

Letter to the Hebrews
181.	Introduction of Hebrews	576
182.	Purged (Heb 1:1-3)	580
183.	Angels	583
184.	Bad Mistake (Heb 1:4-2:8)	586
185.	Captain of Salvation (Heb 2:9-15)	589
186.	Set Your Gaze (Heb 2:16-3:6)	591
187.	Rest Up (Heb 3:7-4:13)	593
188.	Great High Priest (Heb 4:14-5:9)	597
189.	Melchizedek (Heb 5:10-6:20)	600
190.	King of Righteousness (Heb 7:1-17)	604
191.	Perfect High Priest (Heb 7:18-28)	608
192.	What Sin? (Heb 8:1-12)	611

CONTENTS

193.	Earthly Tabernacle (Heb 8:13-9:10)	613
194.	Day of Atonement	616
195.	All Cleaned Up (Heb 9:11-26)	621
196.	Re-Destinated (Heb 9:27-10:18)	623
197.	Hang in There (Heb 10:19-39)	626
198.	Faith of God (Heb 11:1-40)	629
199.	Talk about Persecution	634
200.	Race is On (Heb 12:1-3)	640
201.	Fruit of Righteousness (Heb 12:4-13)	641
202.	Unshakeable (Heb 12:14-29)	643
203.	Established With Grace (Heb 13:1-16)	646
204.	Conclusion of Hebrews (Heb 13:17-25)	649

Second Letter to Timothy

205.	Holy Calling (2 Tim 1:1-14)	650
206.	Be Strong in Grace (2 Tim 1:15-2:26)	653
207.	Dirty Rats (2 Tim 3:1-13)	657
208.	Preach It Son (2 Tim 3:14-4:5)	661
209.	As For Me (2 Tim 4:6-22)	663

Paul's Conclusion

210.	That's All Folks	665

Roger's Conclusion

211.	Thanks	669

About the Author ... 671

ORDER OF LETTERS

WHERE THEY WERE WRITTEN

CORINTH
1 Thessalonians
2 Thessalonians

EPHESUS
1 Corinthians
2 Corinthians
3 Corinthians

PHILIPPI
4th Corinthians

CORINTH
Galatians
Romans

ROME
Colossians
Ephesians
1 Philippians
2 Philippians
1 Timothy
Titus
Hebrews
2 Timothy

'BUT' PASSAGES

I consider myself a student of the art and craft of communication. I'd like to think when you conclude this particular book you'll give me at least a little credit for my efforts. Writing this treasure has been an unspeakable blessing for me personally. Speaking and teaching before an audience also gives me great pleasure. Skill to masterfully command the attention of others is almost as daunting a challenge as the concern over the dissemination of the content and context of knowledge and understanding.

Well, there can be no doubt Paul was a master communicator. His skill in the art of comparative teaching is probably unrecognized by most educators. Pity!

Paul thought nothing of speaking and writing his mind. He definitely wasn't ashamed of exposing ignorance and illuminating truth. He would remind people of traditional ways of thinking, and then, promptly proceed to challenge them to wrap their gray matter around a brand new way of thinking. He'd calmly describe what folks considered mysterious and then jump right in to delineate what he considered elementary, fundamental reality. He delighted in shredding apart the wisdom of mankind, then blast into another orbit with overpowering logic to reveal the absolute, unequivocal wisdom of God.

An invaluable weapon in his linguistic arsenal was a marvelous little conjunctive, three-letter word, **"BUT."**

My dictionary says "but" is used to introduce something contrasting with what has already been mentioned. Paul employed this extraordinary tool from his literary workshop with amazing regularity and craftsmanship. His writings are tapestries of insight woven together with majestic creativity.

What a writer! Boy, he not only knew what he taught, he was completely convinced "what" he knew was worth passing on to other folks. What's more, he lived like he believed what he had come to know and understand. He became a consummate model.

Oh, my! If I keep this up, I could end up writing a book about "how" Paul said what he thought. BUT, (and you can assume I just had to slip that in) the focus of this particular masterpiece that you're about to read is intended to draw the bulk of your attention to "what" this master teacher named Paul had to say, in difference to what had previously been spoken and recorded by others before him.

"BUT" PASSAGES

The following list of verses that include Paul's usage of the famous "BUT" word is not only impressive, it's staggering! I simply had to do this list for you 'cause when you see it with your own eyes you may realize the extent Paul used the word. If you're paying attention and read carefully you'll notice Paul even had the fortitude to use the word on more than one occasion in a single verse.

The nerve!

I admit it's possible I've missed a few, or somehow miscounted, however, if my count is correct, the cumulative total is a whopping 640 times!

Incredible! Look 'em up. Study the context. Analyze his methodology of contrasting previous understanding with a fresh, alternative point of view. You'll be as amazed about it as I am. Well, actually, you can read on and I'll shed some light on the context and understanding from my perspective of course.

Acts
13:30, 37, 46
16:37
17:30
18:21
20:20, 24,
21:13
22:9, 28
24:14
25:11
26:16
27:22
28:19

1 Thessalonians
1:5, 8
2:2, 4, 4, 7, 8, 13, 17, 18
3:6
4:7, 8, 9, 10, 13
5:1, 4, 6, 8, 9, 15

2 Thessalonians
2:12, 13
3:3, 8, 9, 11, 13, 15

"BUT" PASSAGES

1 Corinthians (2 Cor 6:13-7:2)

2 Corinthians (1 Cor 1:10-16:24)
1:10, 14, 17, 18, 23, 24, 27, 30
2:4, 7, 9, 10, 11, 12, 13, 14, 15, 16
3:1, 5, 6, 10, 15
4:3, 4, 10, 10, 14, 19, 20
5:3, 8, 11, 13
6:6, 11, 12, 12, 13, 13, 17, 18
7:4, 4, 6, 7, 9, 10, 11, 12, 14, 15, 15, 17, 19, 21, 28, 28, 29, 32, 33, 34
7:35, 36, 37, 38, 39, 40
8:3, 4, 6, 6, 8, 9, 12
9:12, 15, 17, 21, 24, 25, 27
10:5, 13, 13, 20, 23, 23, 24, 28, 29, 33
11:3, 5, 6, 7, 8, 9, 12, 15, 16, 17, 28, 32
12:3, 4, 5, 6, 7, 11, 14, 18, 20, 20, 24, 25, 31
13:6, 8, 10, 11 12, 12, 13
14:1, 2, 3, 4, 5, 14, 17, 20, 22, 22, 22, 24, 28, 33, 34, 38
15:10, 10, 10, 13, 20, 23, 27, 35, 37, 38 39, 40, 46, 51, 57
16:8, 11, 12, 12

3 Corinthians (2 Cor 10:1-13:14)
10:2, 4, 10, 12, 13, 13, 15, 17, 18
11:3, 6, 12, 17
12:5, 6, 14, 14, 16, 19
13:4, 6, 7, 8

4 Corinthians (2 Cor 1:1-6:12; 7:3-9:15)
1:9, 9, 12, 18, 24
2:1, 2, 4, 5, 5, 13, 17, 17
3:3, 3, 5, 6, 6, 7, 14, 15, 18
4:2, 2, 3, 5, 7, 8, 9, 9, 12, 16, 17, 18, 18
5:4, 11, 12, 15
6:4, 12
7:5, 7, 8, 9, 10, 12, 14
8:5, 8, 10, 14, 16, 17, 19, 21, 22
9:6, 12

"BUT" PASSAGES

Galatians
1:1, 8, 11, 12, 15, 23
2:2, 3, 6, 7, 11, 12, 14, 16, 17, 20
3:11, 12, 15, 16, 18, 20, 22, 23, 25
4:2, 4, 7, 9, 14, 17, 18, 23, 23, 26, 29, 31
5:6, 10, 13, 15, 18, 22
6:4, 8, 13, 14, 15

Romans
1:13, 21, 32
2:2, 5, 8, 8, 10, 13, 25, 29, 29
3:5, 21, 2
4:2, 4, 5, 10, 12, 13, 16, 20, 24
5:3, 8, 11, 13, 15, 16, 20
6:10, 11, 13, 14, 15, 17, 17, 22, 23
7:2, 3, 6, 7, 8, 9, 13, 14, 15, 17, 18, 19, 20, 23, 25
8:1, 4, 5, 6, 9, 9, 10, 11, 13, 15, 20, 23, 24, 25, 26
9:7, 8, 10, 11, 13, 16, 20, 24, 31, 32
10:2, 6, 8, 16, 18, 19, 20, 21
11:4, 6, 7, 11, 15, 18, 18, 20, 22, 28
12:2, 3, 16, 19, 21
13:1, 3, 4, 5, 8, 14,
14:1, 10, 13, 14, 15, 17, 20
15:3, 21, 23, 25
16:4, 18, 19, 26

Philemon
1:11, 14, 16, 16, 22

Colossians
1:26
2:17
3:8, 11, 25

Ephesians
1:21
2:4, 13, 19
4:7, 9, 15, 20, 28, 29
5:3, 4, 8, 11, 13, 15, 17, 18, 27, 29
6:4, 6, 12, 21

"BUT" PASSAGES

1 Philippians (Phil 3:1-4:1)
3:1, 7, 8, 8, 9, 12, 13

2 Philippians (Phil 1:1-2:30; 4:2-23)
1:12, 17, 20, 22, 28, 29
2:3, 4, 7, 12, 19, 22, 24, 25, 27, 27
4:10, 10, 15, 17, 18, 19

1 Timothy
1:8, 9, 13
2:10, 12, 12
3:3, 15
4:7, 8, 12
5:1, 4, 6, 8, 11, 13, 19, 23
6:2, 4, 6, 9, 11, 17

Titus
1:3, 8, 15, 15, 16; 2:1
3:2, 4, 5, 9

Hebrews
1:8, 11, 12, 13
2:6, 8, 9, 16
3:4, 6, 13, 17, 18
4:2, 13, 15
5:4, 5, 14
6:8, 9, 12
7:3, 6, 8, 16, 19, 21, 24, 28
8:6
9:7, 11, 12, 23, 24, 26, 27
10:3, 5, 12, 25, 27, 32 38, 39
11:6, 13, 16
12:8, 10, 11, 13, 22, 26, 26
13:4, 14, 16, 19

2 Timothy
1:7, 10, 17
2:9, 14, 16, 20, 20, 22, 23, 24
3:5, 9, 10, 11, 13, 14
4:3, 5, 8, 13, 16, 20

INTRODUCTION

Well, as I mentioned in the preface this is actually the fifth manuscript. Yes, I'm sure if I kept at it for a few more years I could easily get to sixth or seventh and I'd still be making changes to it. I'm sure even Paul would have said things differently a third or fourth time just so there wouldn't be any mistaking his intention.

The first manuscript was very reflective of my religious training from my Baptist roots. I had a great time of studying and developing a writing style. As I did a read through I found a second version taking shape 'cause I actually found myself disagreeing with myself. I was finding holes in my theology and I didn't like it. I could see the beginnings of a different perspective.

By the end of that version I knew I was in for it. God had done way more than I previously thought He had. Donna and I always had a feeling we were somehow missing out on something but we just couldn't put our finger on it. We were becoming exposed to some very interesting books and some very provocative teachings that stirred the void in us that we were experiencing.

We came to the conclusion God's grace and peace was meant for more folks than we'd always believed. So I started all over on the third manuscript from the mindset that God did we would have thought was unthinkable a short time before. He had saved everybody! Yes, whether we believed it or not! Version three wasn't actually that bad in spite of the fact the heretical nature of it was quite exciting for me. Even the third version had its issues.

The fourth manuscript tweaked everything to the place I thought I really had a winner. Then I printed the whole whack of pages (and there were a lot of pages!) off and gave the whole thing to my dear wife to read. Oops! Now, I must tell you that Donna is far more perceptive than I, wise as all get out, and brutally honest with me. Her evaluation was succinct. Like a great three point sermon analyzer she said, "First of all, it's too long. Secondly, it's too repetitive. Thirdly, it sounds like you're angry."

After the words stung in I knew she was absolute right, on all three counts. I knew this was a study of all Paul's writings and it would naturally be quite long, but this manuscript was definite overkill. As I did a quick review I understood what she meant when she said I repeated myself so often it was painful.

INTRODUCTION

It was the last point that really hit the ball out of the park. Anger and frustration were rampant on every page. I had unleashed a kick___ vengeance against a system of religion I thought needed a boot to the posterior. I had filled the pages with repetitive bantering and badgering against the status quo.

Quite bluntly, I was ticked off with myself for not recognizing sooner the reality of God's sovereign activity for His kingdom and His children. I thought I was so caught up in the mind of Paul I had the right to spill my guts. And spill I did, unleashing a verbal diarrhea against the forces of self-righteousness like I thought Paul had done.

Well, I hope you'll find that the venom of Paul's writings is still somewhat intact. I decided that for my final manuscript I'd let his legacy do the talking, and I'd pipe in every once in a while.

Paul's consistent approach throughout his letters was to address his audience like they knew where he was coming from. The folks in Jerusalem, Corinth, Rome, Ephesus, and everywhere else he happened to visit had a very good basis of understanding because they were living in the land of laws, rules, and regulations.

It just so happened he awoke one morning from an eye opening experience and discovered God had a different point of view than He did. From that foundation Paul pulled out his ink and papyrus and laid out for his readers a new and living way. Paul thought he had laid a good foundation as he shuffled around the countryside. On more than one occasion he was very dismayed to discover folks weren't getting the drift.

Paul spent most of his writings counter-balancing the magnetic pull of going backwards to a comfortable theological position. Like the folks of a by-gone era who simply wanted to retreat to the comforts of home in the land of oppression Paul felt those under his charge were dangerously close to giving up all the liberty and abundance God had gained for them in the giving of His precious Son and His sacrifice. He warned them over and over again not to go back.

His theology is shocking! In fact, it's downright revolutionary. To the religious world he addressed it must have been absolutely heretical. I am absolutely convinced he was almost as much of a thorn in the side of the religious connoisseurs as Jesus was. It's no wonder he was stoned, left for dead, got kicked out of more than one city limits, was imprisoned, and that's just for openers!

My obvious opinion is that Paul's writings are still largely misrepresented today.

INTRODUCTION

Let there be no mistake, I've chosen to understand his writings in a somewhat heretical fashion as I believe he wrote. All right, I'm off the deep end, out in left field, and stubbornly in the fold of the black sheep for sure. Well, I can handle it. I'm quite content with the heresy I've adopted 'cause I, like Paul, am convinced God has done "much more" than I ever thought He had in my former understanding.

So here we go. I'm puttin' on my Paul hat as I write. You can follow along with the Bible of your choice, and as we progress you'll find the scripture passages listed as a guide at the beginning of each chapter. I hope you'll enjoy reading things from his perspective, and I trust you'll indulge my occasional bursts of interjectory insights.

It should be quite a ride for you. It sure has been for me.

EARLY YEARS

1. HERO

In some circles I'm considered to be somewhat "famous." Many folks have been kind enough to regard me as the premiere personality of the Biblical "New Testament" era.

Wow! How flattering. I understand there are others who've called me the "greatest" of all the apostles. Oh, my. A "Hebrew of Hebrews" is another term generously applied to me that I can actually handle with little problem.

Well, I did get a chuckle out of those who compared me with that great winged messenger of the gods by the name of "Hermes." Unfortunately unaware of how the term aptly and equally applies to themselves folks have also dared me to call me a "saint."

I admit I've been called a lot of names, not to mention things. I expect in some circles I'm viewed rather negatively, "infamous" shall we say. I'd have to agree during a certain part of my life I could certainly have been regarded as being notorious, driven, ruthless, as well as dangerous. The sad truth is many folks were scared to death of me. Their fears were well founded, for the power and influence I wielded was immense.

Heroes! I'd think most everyone would have a hero. I certainly have mine. Jesus, of course, is at the top of my list. On the human level, there's good ol' Abe, Mo, Ho, Jerry, Isaiah (sorry, no nickname for him) and a batch of other great prophets and spiritual leaders. Oh, I'd better not forget the perennial favorite Davey, the giant slayer.

I ponder from time to time on what it must have been like for them in their day. How'd they get along? What kind of friends did they have? What kinds of aches and pains did they put up with? Did they walk around day by day with their heads so high in the sky they were of very little earthly good on a day-to-day basis? What'd they look like anyway?

No, I can't tell you what I looked like. I wouldn't have won any beauty pageant contests, and that's a for sure! With the passage of time and circumstances, I ended up with a lot less hair, poorer eyesight, a variable sense of hearing, and a different set of taste buds than when I first started out on my little journey through this life. I can also attest to the fact my motor skills weren't as pronounced as they once were either.

Oh, I had my share of toothaches, headaches, and stomach aches too. Man, sometimes my feet just killed me more than softly with blisters. I can't forget to mention the back aches. Hey, I worked hard for my money!

Who said I did't have a sense of humor? I've heard and told my share of "fishy" stories. Yes, I saddled myself around the block a few times you know.

On the other side, heroes come in all shapes and sizes. Most of us who have the great honor of ending up as heroes never started out with that in mind. I certainly didn't. All I can say is I tried my very best at all times. I had a blast as a kid, worked diligently in school (and that's the truth), apprenticed like a journeyman, studied like a gangbuster, rose the corporate ladder with pizzazz, persecuted with zeal, and preached the gospel message of God's grace and peace with all the gusto I could muster.

Perhaps your life would take a different direction if you only knew you were a hero in the eyes of another. Well, I'll tell you right now, whether you know it or not, you "are" a hero. I know there's someone who sees you as the wind beneath their wings. I simply encourage you to fly with them!

There's someone else who thinks the world of you! God does! Did you know "you" are the apple of His eye? Did you know "you" are the very reason He sent His precious Son, Jesus, to this world. He did so in order that you might be adopted into His wonderful family? It's true! His love is as endless as it is boundless.

Oh, I better not get started. That's what the rest of this book's going to be about. One of the unfortunate things of doing an autobiography is not being able to tell you absolutely everything that happened to me. Well, perhaps that's not all bad. Ha. The passage of time dulls the memory bank, erasing details that had so much impact at the point they occurred. Nevertheless, I trust you'll know me a bit better by the time you've finished reading this book. If nothing else you'll know where I stand, theologically speaking.

It's not my intent to teach you everything you need to "know" about God.

It's never been my goal to help you to get "closer" to God.

You'll soon discover just the opposite is true. My objective is to teach you what God "knows" about "you!" I want you to know God sees you as righteous, as holy, and as pure as Jesus!

My desire is for you come to understand you'll never get as "close" to God as you are right now. No amount of "your" belief will achieve the eternal security you so earnestly desire. No amount of "your" faith will help you make a single deposit at the bank of His approval. Last, but certainly not least, no amount of "your" good works will gain you His favor.

Why?

Because He's already gifted you with all of that, and "much more!"

Oh, there I go again, letting the cat out of the bag. Every good book is supposed to have a good measure of suspense, so I'd better bite my tongue. Let me start back at the beginning.

Enjoy!

Here we go...

2. HERITAGE

"In the beginning..."

Isn't that the way it's supposed to go? All good stories have their beginning. So does the story of my life. I had a great start to life with a super mom and dad.

Before you were born your folks probably spent a great deal of time debating about what you'd be called. Would you be a Peter, Mark, Jonathan, Fred, James, or perhaps an Anthony? But then, maybe you might need a name like Linda, Jennifer, Michelle, Lucy, or Elizabeth. Sometimes the decision is made at the last minute. Maybe you were named after a character of the Bible, or after a very important member of your family. Or could your name have been chosen for you because of what the name meant?

The name given to me when I was born was certainly very special. My mom and dad decided to name me "Saul." Saul, of course, is a Hebrew name meaning "asked for." I think it's wonderful my folks discovered I was, at least to them, a special gift they had asked God for.

Later on in life, when my life underwent quite a drastic change in direction, my Roman compatriots decided a new name would be more politically correct, making my life a little easier. They started calling by the name of "Paul." This name happens to mean "little." I don't know if they were picking on my stature or what. Perhaps they were thinking about the amount of hair on my head, or the amount of gray matter underneath it! Ha.

Be sure I'm very proud of my heritage. I'm twice blessed as far as parents are concerned 'cause I really had the best of all worlds. I was raised in the culture and traditions of the Roman empire, and was also fortunate to have grown up under the strict influence of the Jewish culture and traditions.

My parents, you see, were Roman citizens. This isn't something to be taken lightly. This was of supreme importance to me later on in my life. There were several times that my Roman heritage literally saved my bacon. Roman citizenship was something to be coveted. The emperor in Rome often controlled who could become a citizen and who couldn't. Sometimes entire groups of people would become initiated. At other times, a select few, like doctors or great teachers, would become eligible to become Roman citizens.

In some cases, it also took a great deal of money to buy your way into the empire. Couldn't do that to get into the kingdom of God!

Although technically citizens of Rome, we were also citizens of the city of Tarsus. Being a citizen of a provincial city meant you also had to be a member of a tribe. There were many different tribes in those days based upon commonalities such as nationality or religion. It was possible for me to claim membership in the Jewish tribe of Tarsus, in addition, to be a bona fide Roman citizen.

I lay special claim to my Jewish heritage. I wasn't just your average Hebrew offspring either. I came from the cream of the crop. My descendants were of the tribe of Israel, the "pure" ones, the "favorite" children of God. Being of the tribe of Benjamin is something to be very proud of if you are a Jew 'cause the tribe of Benjamin represents a certain standard of living. There's an honor code established through the descendants of Benjamin.

Benjamin, if you don't remember, was the son of Jacob and Rachel. Although the youngest son he was the son "father liked best." He was also favored most by his only full brother, Joseph.

Did you know Ben was the only one of the patriarchs to be born in the chosen land? It's also significant that out of this smallest of the tribes the first king of Israel was chosen.

Can you tell me his name?

"Saul!"

My, oh, my.

What an honor to bear his name. Hey, the people got what they "asked for" didn't they. Ha! Sometimes I just amaze myself with my sense of humor. When the ten tribes decided it was time to take its direction from Jeroboam during the great "church split," only the tribes of Judah and "Benjamin" remained true to the house of David.

The tribe of Benjamin is also known for its place of honor among the military establishment of the Israelites. Time and time again these people defied the odds, remained true to God, and scored resounding victories in the battlegrounds of the day. If you were assigned to be a war correspondent to the front lines of any battle to get a sound bite for the evening news, you'd have no choice but to interview a Benjamite officer. Benjamites had front row seats.

Well, I presume that's where I get it from 'cause I always wanted to be on the front lines. My philosophy was to be where the action was. It's dangerous, it's nerve-racking, but, my goodness, is it ever spontaneous and exciting!

3. TARSUS

I grew up in the city of Tarsus, a great city that sat on the right bank of the Tarsus River, ten miles from the Mediterranean Sea on the south east coast of Asia Minor (Turkey). Records and artifacts have traced its lengthy history through the ages of Persian, Assyrian, and Hittite dominations.

During the days of the Roman Empire Tarsus came into special recognition. In 67 B.C. it became the capital of the province of Cilicia. Cicero ruled the area for a time. The great Caesar visited Tarsus in 47 B.C. after the death of Pompey. It was during this visit Tarsus assumed the title of "Iuliopolis" in honor of Caesar.

Good times turned to bad however. When Tarsus opposed Cassius after the murder of Julius Caesar, Cassius imposed a huge fine upon the city in 43 B.C. It wasn't until 41 B.C. that Mark Anthony finally rescued the city by exempting the citizens from paying the taxes Cassius had initiated.

For all you history buffs out there, here's an interesting bit of trivia. What was the name of the city Mark Anthony was visiting when the love of his life sailed up the river in a magnificent, spectacular event?

If you answered anything other than Tarsus you were wrong. And what was the name of his beloved? I certainly hope you at least got Cleopatra right. Yes, the great Anthony and Cleopatra reunion took place in Tarsus. That must have been quite a sight!

Tarsus did become a pretty important city. Since becoming a free city under the reign of Augustus, the centre became an important commerce and educational success story. Only two other cities, namely Athens and Alexandria, could boast of universities as great as the U. of T. The prosperity of the city was based primarily on the fertility of the plains of Cilicia, supporting industries such as weaving and tent making.

Well, I just loved growing up in the city. As children, we were never without something interesting to do, lots of friends, lots of fun. Isn't that what childhood memories are based on?

Call me a "city-slicker" if you want. Suits me just fine!

4. JUST A KID

I don't think I was really all that different from most of the children of my day. In fact, I was a pretty typical kid, special of course, but typical. No doubt you were just the same.

There are many things I remember about my childhood days, and many things certainly standout. Like most, I tend to remember the good, forgetting things that weren't particularly pleasant. I try to forget about all the times my parents thought they were doing something "spiritual" for "my" benefit! A little swat now and then, accompanied by the occasional "time-out" was pretty much par for the course for me too. Spoiled? Spoiled rotten most of the time.

I confess to being all "boy." We not only played fun games, we invented them. You might even say we "reinvented" the rules as we went along. Ordinary things became objects of attraction and distraction, whether a stick of wood, a tool from my dad's shop, a scrap of leather, a broom stick, or an appropriately sized rock. Creativity is the magic of the mind. Scraps, fights, and disagreements were not uncommon between friends.

My dad was great too. We went lots of places together. He loved sports probably a little more than even I did. What else could a boy ask for? I admit I wasn't too athletically coordinated. I remember when I was just a small kid I ended up running in a race which ended any thoughts I had of becoming a professional athlete. I tripped on the cinder ash track, scraped my knees something fierce. Perhaps the only thing hurt worse than my knee was my dignity and pride.

Occasionally, dad would take me over to the U. of T. where we'd watch the athletes train and compete. Determination, dedication, and persistence were written all over their faces. The muscles on some of them were unbelievable. They strained, they stretched, they ran mile after mile, while others jumped hurdles like horses running wild in the fields. Water rats paddled their boats down the river with intense energy. If you looked deep into the eyes of those engaged in the fierce struggle of their competition you could see all they were focused on was the trophy at the conclusion of the race.

Unfortunately, not everyone could be a winner. Every competition dad and I went to was a confirmation of this reality. There certainly was a winner, but there were also a whole lot more who were losers.

The reward for the winner was always something worth the effort. It may have been a trophy, a parade, a banquet, or some kind of financial gain. The losers weren't treated as kindly. But, you know, many just seemed to come back for more, time and time again.

Do you know something? I decided fairly early in life that winning was much more fun than losing. I determined I wanted to be a "winner." I could taste victory! I dreamt about clutching the trophy! I pondered the idea of a parade just for me! I even contemplated long and hard about stuffing my face at a glorious, scrumptious banquet with none other than the emperor himself sitting right next to me! Little did I know as a child this was to be my eternal destiny!

Can't you dig it?

Sports, contrary to what you might expect, wasn't my whole life as a boy growing up in the big city. Dad took me to other places as well. Sure, the university was a great place for sports, but it was also the home to a wonderful collection of books. Even before I could read my parents would read me whatever they could get their hands on, delighting me with tales of wonderment and excitement. I loved these times together, whether it was on the banks of the river watching the boats go by, on the park bench watching the birds scrounge for scraps, or at home in bed before I went to sleep.

Quite often dad and I would pass by a group of men sittin' on the street corner, thoroughly engrossed in some heavy duty discussion. Tarsus was filled with all kinds of interesting folks from various backgrounds, who loved to talk about themselves and their philosophies about life. Many of them spoke of how wise they were. Ha, if they only knew.

I confess there were very few who made any sense to me at all. To say this form of debate didn't leave an impression on me would be a mistake.

Another interesting place to visit was the grand theater where characters dressed in beautiful costumes dazzled the audiences with their frivolity and drama. Occasionally, a carnival type atmosphere filled the air as a traveling band of artisans amused and entertained. It was always fun to go to these events. When we got home we'd become imitators, I mean actors and actresses, of our own productions. What a blast! We sure could put on a show. It was mandatory for everyone to pay attention when we entertained.

There was one other aspect of growing up you're probably familiar with. "School!"

Riiiiight!

How could anyone forget that? I'm sure my schooling started the day I was born. As early as I can remember mom and dad were teaching me one thing or another. From a very early age I was instructed in the teachings of the Jewish "law." You see, Jewish law and tradition spelled out that a boy child must start his studies of the scriptures when he reached the ripe old age of five. Since my parents were fairly strict, this regulation didn't go unnoticed.

As a youngster I remember the countless hours of memorizing scripture. The process started sometimes before breakfast and continued 'til we went to bed. Often, throughout the day, we were subjected to quiz-like testing as to our skill of remembrance. The significance of us learning scriptures was paramount. It ranked right up there in priority just above work or play. Memorization wasn't just expected, it wasn't just demanded, it was commanded!

Sometimes when I was watching dad make tents he'd test me. "Hey, Saul," he'd query, "what scripture did you learn this morning?" With great pride in my voice I'd loudly respond, "Blessed are those whose lawless deeds have been forgiven, and whose sins have been covered. Blessed is the man whose sin the Lord will not take into account. Psalms 32:1,2." My dad would look at me with such pride. "Great, Saul, that's great. Keep up the good work." Man, would I feel super.

Little did I know how great those verses were at the time! As a kid, it was just another thing to learn. What a difference when you actually know what it means!

Mom would come up to me as I was making my bed and say, "Saul, can you tell me what the Ten Commandments are?" I'd go through the list, naming them one by one. At first, she'd have to help me. She was really special that way. She'd make a game of it. We'd play hide and seek as a family. Whoever was "it" had to stand with eyes closed and repeat one of the Ten Commandments at least three times in a very loud voice, while the rest found hiding places. It was five times on the shorter ones. It sure didn't take very long until we had them all memorized pretty thoroughly.

Learning about God and His word seemed to be a very natural thing in our household, a very big part of our everyday existence. It wasn't something that happened only when we went to the synagogue either. It was a part of our regular routine and activity. It was expected we would learn.

It was never questioned that we would not know about God, or about His dealings with His children, especially since we were a "special" part of His family. We talked about God. We sang songs about God. We were told stories about God, and how He delivered "His people" from those miserable heathens. We were shown God's handiwork in creation. God, God, and more God. Life revolved around God.

As I grew older, things started to become a bit more complex, not to mention a tad more serious. The study of legal traditions within our Jewish race was committed to boys at the mature age of ten! Education was to teach us not only how to think, but, how to act. Dad would say, "Son, there's a difference between knowledge and wisdom. Knowledge is good for you, and don't ever stop getting all you can. When you have knowledge people will call you smart. But, when people call you wise, it means you've put that knowledge to good use for the benefit of yourself and others."

Well, I think my dad was pretty smart. O.K. I think he was a wise guy too!

My dad, as you know, well maybe you don't, was a tent maker. As far as I was concerned, he was the best in town. Tarsus was well known for the tents produced there. You might think making a tent is a very simple thing. I say "Nay, Nay." Actually, it's a lot tougher than it might appear. It took years of apprenticeship and experience to turn a novice canvass cutter into a specialist who could crank out all the differing kinds of tents the market place demands.

Desert tents required a coarse black sackcloth made from goat hair. Other tents were made of a wool fabric, while some were created out of various kinds of animal skins. As I grew up, I watched dad do his thing. The older I got the more he'd trust me to assist him in the delicate, intricate sewing detail he fashioned into every tent he built.

Hey, the cutters needed to be real sharp! And then there were the needles. They all made their point quite often. Get it? They make their point! Ha.

The first tent I made on my own was quite a sight. All right, maybe for sore eyes! It was a little awkward but workable. That one didn't come out exactly as planned but I did get better. They say practice makes perfect. I did come to the place where I could turn out a pretty mean tent. It proved to be a fulfilling vocation to fall back on throughout my life. Mom and dad always told me it would someday pay off. Right again, mom and dad.

5. BAR MITZVA

There's something really special about birthday number thirteen! What an exciting time. Finally, I got to be a teenager! They couldn't call me a kid anymore. I was a "teenager." Oh sure, I still got my share of zits, my voice was becoming deeper and deeper each day, but now I could hold my head up and proclaim, "I'm THIRTEEN!"

For a young buck, Jewish youngster this birthday was even more important than any other. Ever hear of "bar mitzvah?" It means "son of the commandment." At the age of thirteen I became a "bar mitzvah."

Imagine! Me, a son of the commandment!

Man, did we party! It was expected at the age of thirteen a boy would take upon himself the full obligation of the "law." For the more promising students it meant a graduation into a rabbinical school. I was one of those "more promising" students! Or so my parents kept telling me.

There was one present they told me I was to get but couldn't receive 'til the very end of the party where I got to open all my other presents. The suspense was killing me. Dad gave me my very own set of scissors and an incredible set of needles. Mom, of course, got me clothes. Practical or what? I even got a new pair of pants and a shirt from my sister who lived in Jerusalem. Now, it wasn't every kid who had some clothes all the way from the cosmos of Jerusalem you know. I sure had something to show off to all my friends. My best friend even gave me a pair of new sandals.

Suspense continued to build up inside me. Oh, my. We had to eat first! What would this world be like without moms to make food taste so good? We had an absolutely fabulous meal. Dad started the meal with his usual blessing, "Blessed art Thou, Jehovah our God, King of the world, who causes to come forth bread from the earth."

Then we all dug right in. First came the soup. Next, the fresh home made bread. It makes my mouth water just thinking about it. Then came the main course, rack of lamb! I got the biggest piece. Fantastic!

I don't know what your custom is regarding prayer at meal times. For us, we not only prayed before we ate, but also after we enjoyed the food.

Guess what?

Dad asked me to pray the prayer of thanksgiving after we ate. This was the first time I'd been asked to pray this prayer. I was so thrilled to pray in front of my family and friends on this special occasion. To say I was at once honored and scared at the very same time would be an understatement. I was so excited about getting my last present they had promised it was probably one of the shortest prayers they'd ever heard. Loud and proud "AMENS" rang out at my rapid conclusion.

Finally, as was promised, I'd receive the special gift. The suspense was tremendous. What could it possibly be? I was so anxious I could hardly sit still. Dad seemed to take forever. At long last, he got up. He started to say something.

"Loved ones," he stammered, "I...uh, I...uh"

"What? What? Spit it out!" I thought silently.

"Uh, I have to go up to the bedroom to get something."

My brain protested within my noggin, "Get on with it already!"

After what seemed like an hour to me Dad returned to the big family room where everyone was excited beyond measure. Of course, he was probably out of the room for only a couple of minutes. As he returned, I could see he had in his hand something that looked like a rolled up piece of papyrus.

"What the world could that be?" I thought.

"Saul," my dad started, "this is a very great day for all of us. You've made us the proudest parents around. You are a fine son indeed. Here's your present. Happy Birthday Son!"

He handed me the wrapped present and proceeded to bear hug me to the point my ribs felt they cracked in half. I gasped for air as I returned to my chair to discover the hidden treasure. Slowly, I unraveled the mysterious scroll. What I read caught me completely by surprise. Here's what I read:

Hillel Rabbinical School
Jerusalem

Att: Saul

We would like to congratulate you on your thirteenth birthday! We are pleased to confirm your acceptance into the finest learning center in the land.

Your academic records from your schools in Tarsus, together with the highest of recommendations from your parents, friends, and teachers have assured the admissions department that you are truly a fine candidate for our program.

We are obviously proud of our outstanding school and study facilities. No doubt you have heard of our famous professor, Gamaliel. He will be your tutor and instructor. We are excited about having you come to Jerusalem to join him. We anticipate all the necessary arrangements will be completed so you may begin your studies as soon as possible.

Sincerely
President
Rabbinical Studies Department

> Needless to say, I just about fell off my chair!
> "Are you serious? Jerusalem? I'm going to Jerusalem? I'm going to study with Gamaliel?
> Get out of town!

Trip # 1
TARSUS TO JERUSALEM

6. READY, SET, GO

Everybody was shaking, some were jumping around, mom was crying, others were wailing. Pretty soon all of us were wiping our noses and eyes with anything we could get our hands on.

The plans for my trip to Jerusalem were farther along than I could possibly have known. Although a surprise to me, this birthday gift had been in the works by my parents for quite some time. It made things a lot easier for my parents that I'd be staying with my sister and her husband in Jerusalem. It suddenly dawned on me my sister didn't only come to Tarsus for my birthday. She'd come to take me back home with her!

The two weeks until our departure seemed like months. There really wasn't much to do to get me ready. Mom could have thrown a few clothes in a bag, my books in a box, and I'd have been set to go. Well, maybe a lunch for the trip too! But then, you know what moms are like.

Clothes had to be washed first. Then pressed. Then organized properly. Good-byes were in order for all my friends. I was the center of attention at every "get lost" party organized on my behalf. Everyone asked the same questions.

"Will you miss your mom and dad?"

"What will be your first question for Gamaliel?"

"Aren't you scared?"

I know they were all being polite, really anxious and excited for me. Hey, why did I have to worry? There were enough people doing it for me! I have to admit it's truly a very nice feeling to know there are people who do care for you, desiring merely the very best for you.

The night before I left I could hardly sleep. Here I was a boy, no, a "man" who'd made it to the ripe old age of thirteen leaving home to an unknown city, in addition to the possibilities of an unknown future. I was not only departing my home, I was leaving my childhood behind. I was leaving my security blanket to step out boldly into the wild blue yonder to conquer the world! Ever laid awake at night, unable to go to sleep, dreaming up incredible possibilities to every conceivable situation and uncertainty imaginable?

Then you can imagine how I felt that night.

READY, SET, GO   TRIP # 1

Tears. More tears. Some handshakes. Hugs. More hugs. Kisses! Yuck. More kisses. Oh, yuck, yuck.

Then my sister and I were off on the wagon waving like crazy. We waved 'til we couldn't see anybody in the distant. I knew they couldn't hear me but I whispered anyway, "Bye mom. Bye dad."

Thoughts of home started to diminish as the miles evaporated between Tarsus and Jerusalem. The journey itself now seemed to captivate my contemplations. This was my first really big boat trip. Of course, I'd been on the river before, but now we were on open water. All around me was water. Water! I mean no land! The water was a beautiful, powerful color. The huge sails caught the wind and we propelled through the water with amazing speed and agility.

My sister proved to be a great traveling companion. It was rather enjoyable to get to know her a bit better. It definitely showed she'd taken the trip before having already gone through all the stages of fear, anticipation, and excitement. She was a tremendous comfort to me, encouraging me to keep my eyes facing forward.

As we sat out on the deck watching the clouds wave at the ship she told me about all the wonderful things I still had to look forward to. Our first stop would be at Caesarea where we'd continue the land portion of the voyage via a caravan excursion to Jerusalem.

I had heard during my early education about a great teacher named Gamaliel. It seemed he was actually God the way folks spoke of him! Everyone held him in very high regard. I could have only dreamed I'd one day just get to meet this guy, and now, I was on my way to actually study at his feet! Incredible!

My sister started to tell me more about him as the trip went on. She described him as one of the most revered men not only in Jerusalem, but by Jews all over the world. He was a very important member of the Sanhedrin, being a grandson of the very famous Rabbi Hillel. His nickname was "the Elder," the first one to bear the title of "Rabban," which meant "our Master, our Great One." Other teachers were simply called "Rabbi," which meant "my Master."

Sis told me he was a generous hearted man, particularly smart. Strangely enough, he was very tolerant of different ideas, certainly more tolerant than most of his teaching peers. Gamaliel wasn't afraid to incorporate Greek learning into his teaching.

Apparently, this was a no-no to most of the religious community.

READY, SET, GO   TRIP # 1

    The more she talked about this Gamaliel fellow the more anxious I became to meet him. The trip simply couldn't be over fast enough! Man, this was so exciting! The world was taking on a completely new perspective for me.

    Hey, it's a brave new world out there apparently!

7. QUILT OF EDUCATION

Don't let anyone tell you education isn't important. I'm well aware some older folks would prefer to encourage their youngins to let experience get their feet wet over a good dose of classroom education. Certainly, experience can be a great teacher, but there should be no doubt a good education will ensure experience will apply the lessons you've learned.

How do I know this? I had a first class education that shaped and molded me for the remainder of my adult life. My parents started the ball rolling by providing me with great guidance as a toddler. My schoolteachers continued my education by nurturing, sometimes by force I will admit, and guiding me along a well-beaten path of information. And then, there was Gamaliel! My goodness. I could probably write a book just about him and his teaching methods.

I owe so much to Gamaliel for making me learn everything about the sacred books. The methodology of his search and discover techniques steered me to become intimately acquainted with every aspect of the treasured writings. I had to learn all three divisions of the Jewish scriptures. Many of the things I was to speak and write about later in life would be related to the five books of the "Law." Examples from history were extracted from memories of my studies in the writings of the "Prophets." Perhaps my favorite passages from the "Writings," especially from the Psalms, were to prove a comforting influence in many of the situations I'd encounter.

Have you ever noticed how some people tend to place others into certain categories? Some folks get diagnosed as being either "liberal" or "conservatives," as "optimists" or "pessimists," and others get trashed as being pro this, or con that. Labels, labels, labels. Everyone, and everything, seems to need a label so they can be accurately identifiable. I suppose it's just in the nature of humans to be so analytical.

Well, I gather I've been labeled too! Some folks think I spoke and wrote out of my Greek heritage. D'you know what? They're right.

Others tend to think I spoke and wrote from the standpoint of all my Jewish traditions. Do you know what? They're right too.

I'm not really sure how you can separate the two.

I had the great privilege of being brought up in both cultures. The cumulative effect of my heritage and education are forever etched into the fabric of my quilt.

QUILT OF EDUCATION   TRIP # 1

The patterns of my thoughts, as well as the designs of my actions, were established by those who raised and taught me. I always felt I had a tremendous advantage in the duality I inherited.

Gamaliel also helped me to see this. He was indeed a very tolerant teacher who recognized the value in other forms of learning. I was allowed to enhance my studies with the study of Greek authors and literary forms. Without betraying the Hellenistic influences on my life, I was able to employ some of the religious language of the Grecian people to expound the incredible truths of the gospel and grace of God in a way they could relate to it. I was able to quote at will from the greatest of the Greek writers when it was necessary to prove a point or I could argue and debate with the best of them using the "diatribal" form of presentation at will.

Some people, on the other hand, don't seem to recognize the Grecian influence in me at all. They seem to feel most of what I've done and said was because of the Jewish influence. How can I deny this aspect of my upbringing and education?

I've sometimes been called a "Hellenist of the Hellenists." What an honor I must say. Well, I admit it's nice to see some folks take seriously my Hebraic credentials.

I really did understand the Jewish mentality, fully aware of the things that drove the thought patterns of the Jewish religious community.

I guess what I'm trying to say is that I'm a very fortunate man. I've been able to have the best of both worlds. Education has opened for me the cultures of two great societies. I've seen the good, and the not so good, in both.

Perhaps it isn't always wise to toot your own horn but I was a pretty good student!

Man I studied. I'd study, and then I'd study some more. I'd dig every ounce of information I could out of my teachers, many of them belonging to the most elite group of learned men. I poured over the scriptures and sacred writings with uncommon diligence and voracity. My sponge mind sucked in the theology. From my lips poured phraseology so profound even I was baffled by what I could say. In my own mind, I was scaling the heights of scholastic superiority most of my contemporaries could only hope to achieve.

Toot!

Toot!

Along the way, I became a favorite among the ecclesiastical authorities. I had become pre-eminent not only in my scholastic accomplishments, but also in my youthful, energetic, and spontaneous zeal. My time in Jerusalem was increasing filled by tasks that pushed me to excel.

I was fueled by the enticements of rewards and punishment. I climbed the ecclesiastical ladder, rung by rung. Of course, the shape and size of my head grew to match! I'm not sure who said it, but some wise guy once put it this way: "It would be advisable to start living like we think. The alternative is to end up thinking like we live."

Pretty profound I'd say.

So, I made it my ambition to start filling my mind with everything I could to ponder upon to make sure I knew why I was doing things. I wanted to make sure I was absolutely convinced how I lived was a direct result of what I "thought" was the truth. I didn't want to end up living without purpose and direction, having a mind empty and devoid of a challenge to pursue.

Well, down the road I found out the truth of the saying really wasn't in question. What I ended up doing was questioning whether or not what I considered to be the truth was truly the truth! When I was later confronted with the reality of the love of God for the whole world, it not only changed the way I thought, it changed the way I lived! My life was to become a representation of my thoughts. When I lived in the bondage of self-righteousness, I thought I had to "do" something to gain the righteousness of God.

When I discovered and really grabbed hold of the idea God had already given me His righteousness when Jesus rescued me from the slavery of laws, rules, and regulations, I could finally live in peaceful, abundant liberty!

What a difference!

Anyway, we'll get back to some of those concepts as we proceed. Suffice it to say, my education didn't end in Jerusalem under Gamaliel!

8. CAPED CRUSADER

A great education was a necessary ingredient to propel me down the path of life, and let me tell you, I've been on some paths. Ha! Ambition, persistence, and discipline also weighed in pretty heavily. I could mention many other dramatic influences but I'd like to emphasize two.

One is "timing." I often use this saying, "wherever you go there you are." Well, I've come to realize that the "now" is where it's at. I've been the fortunate beneficiary of being at the "right" place at the "right" time and have learned to just make the most of it.

Another factor is "association."

I'm talking about whom you hang with. Perhaps you know this saying: "It isn't so much a matter of how much you know, it's more a matter of who you know!" I've been blessed to hang with many a good folk who have had a deep impact on my life. Oh sure, there have been some rascals in the crowd, but by and large, I've been associated with a colorful cast of characters who've made my life pretty interesting to say the least.

My stint at the rabbinical school was proof of how timing and association can further ones career. As I mentioned previously I was a good student. No, I take it back. Under Gamaliel I took it to a whole other level. I became a greeeeaaaat student!

I simply excelled at my studies. I was so good I eventually was able to tutor others. My leadership skills were being unfurled. I became entrusted with more and more tasks that I completed with speed and accuracy. I hung out with the uppity-ups. I brown nosed to the max. I started attending meetings "ordinary" students were not invited to attend. I went to conferences many folks would have loved to poke their beaks into.

Aggressive?

You bet. I was on the ball, anxious to please, ready to learn, and motivated to rise to the top. I soon realized the ground at the bottom of the ladder was getting further and further away from me. Man, I was in the "in" crowd, in the cream of the crop, in the "upper crust" of the establishment pie, so to speak. I wouldn't have missed this for the world. It was an exciting time for everyone.

The talk of the town, and I'm not just referring to the religious community either, revolved around a character by the name of Jesus. Apparently he'd come from Bethlehem.

Wondered about that. I'd heard not much good of anything came from there. Anyway, he'd stirred up quite a commotion in our parts. We hadn't been exposed to so much controversy for many a year.

Although Jesus had been dead for years now, it seemed like there was no end to the discussion of the things he said and did. Because of who I knew, and because I was an intimate and trusted agent of the Jewish leaders, I came to know everything they had to say about a "new" religion established by this Jesus fellow.

I heard all of the arguments pro and con. I studied all of the scriptures used to support and denounce the teachings of Jesus. I listened to personal testimonies of many of the "believers" who were examined by the Temple and synagogue officials. I found it incredible people were convinced their whole lives had been altered by this guy. I participated in debates and committee meetings that deliberated the accuracy of the statements attributed to this revered, dead dude.

Some folks might question how I could possibly have turned out to be such a rebel after being taught by a very tolerant teacher like Gamaliel to accept a variety of expressions. When did I start to take such an aggressive position against this newly formed religion that seemed to have originated with Jesus as its leader?

Well, at first, there weren't really all that many people who were followers of Jesus. Compared to the number of Jews in our neck of the desert this little band seemed incredibly insignificant. I don't think anyone, initially at least, could have possibly imagined they would create such a stir.

For a while, they seemed to exist in some disarray, so toleration was the appropriate response. Perhaps the problem would just go away. As long as they kept their beliefs and practices to themselves they could be allowed to die out.

To those of us who were more tolerant and noble among the Pharisees, the believers in Jesus were considered to be still within the scope of Judaism and weren't ready to be condemned as heretics. They really didn't give any evidence of becoming lax in the observance of the law just because they believed in Jesus.

The same tolerance, however, was not applied by the Sanhedrin, and especially to those of the Saducean sect and the priestly element. The teachings of these new believers caused so much turmoil to their orderly system of rule.

More importantly, it brought tremendous pressure upon their own authority. They instigated most of the early suppressions against this wayward band.

As time went on, even Pharisees like myself were challenged to consider the strength of these new converts. This new group couldn't simply continue to be ignored merely as a fad soon to disappear. They began to establish their doctrines and theology on a deeper level.

They not only were convincing themselves of some special "truth," they were starting to propagate and enlist other people into their way of thinking. Many of these folks had actually seen or met Jesus and were obviously convinced by his teachings.

The reality of the miracles He performed in addition to the wisdom in his words were still deeply embedded in their hearts and minds. The true dimension of his ministry was becoming clarified and the followers were entering a new phase of expansion.

The status quo was being challenged. We undertook a careful examination and analysis of this growing group. Rumors started flying about like birds.

How could we stop this threat of apostasy? There had to be something we could do.

Most of us were convinced the Messianic age was soon to be upon us. All this activity by these believers could delay the coming. Transgression and apostasy would certainly not speed up the process. We had to build up a wall about the "law" to protect it. We had to spell out in detail the various scriptural prescriptions to keep Israel unified in its worship of God during this all-important time when we anticipated the arrival of the "true" Messiah.

It was for this reason I began my crusade against these "heretics."

Jesus had certainly been discredited by his crucifixion. I didn't think it would be all that difficult of a task to bring this whole matter to a quick and absolute resolution.

Hey, I had scripture to back me up.

"What scripture?"

Well, there are a number of good examples.

Read Numbers 25. You'll find the account of Moses ordering the destruction of the immoral Israelites just before they entered into Canaan. Read how God praised Phinehas for his zeal to put apostasy out of Israel by killing two of the chief offenders himself.

Read 1 Maccabees 2. See how Mattathias and the Hasidim rooted up the apostasy of Israel a couple of centuries ago. I was challenged by the commission in 2 Maccabees 6:13, "For indeed, it is a mark of great kindness when the impious are not let alone for a long time, but punished at once."

How could I be wrong in setting up a campaign against these insolent people? There were merely getting in the way. I took inspiration from my forefathers to wipe out anything that hindered our progress into the Promised Land. Scriptures were on my side. Traditions, laws, rules, and regulations were paramount! Great praise had been poured upon those who worked for God to restore the dignity of the nation.

Hey, there was something in it for me too. Power and control! I was on a quest to get even more of it. The crusade to wipe this faction of dissent was on!

9. STONE 'M
(Acts 6:8-15; 7:1-58)

And then along came Stephen!

This dufus caused me nothing but grief. I was having enough problems already without him having to get involved. We were already pursuing cases against as many of these believers as we could, making life as difficult as we could for them. We did everything to discredit anyone who professed to be a follower of Jesus. We just had to root out this heresy once and for all. It was getting too large to sit by and do nothing about it.

If you want to stop a revolt the best thing to do is try and stop or discredit its leadership. This tactic shouldn't come as a surprise or as some new revelation. It's been a tried and tested procedure throughout history. If you want to cause a division amongst a group, go after the highest face on the hierarchical pole.

Well, we slapped the target on the back of Stephen. I was assigned to the strike force.

The mission?

"Take out Stephen!"

Mission impossible? I said "Nay, Nay. Not for me!" when they handed me the envelope.

I discovered Stephen had been selected as one of seven leaders of the believers. The twelve men who'd been with Jesus realized the numbers were getting too large for them to handle. They had to do something about the crowds so their plan was to divide and conquer. They decided to select seven worthy men and place them in charge of the business affairs of the group. I even found out these seven men were commissioned in a special prayer meeting service.

Go figure!

It was hard to believe one of these leaders wasn't even a Jew. The name of this Gentile was Nicolaos. Boy, they sure had some nerve.

News of what the believers were up to was spreading like wild fire. It was almost impossible to keep it from being the center of attention throughout the entire city of Jerusalem. Like some gigantic sporting activity like the Olympics it became a topic of discussion on the street corner, at the local watering holes, in the market place, in the synagogues, and worst of all, in the Temple area. This nonsense had to be stopped!

Stephen was apparently a man full of a special grace and power. He was able to perform unbelievable signs and wonders before the people. A debate arose in the synagogues. Neither the Libertines, Cyrenians, Alexandrians, Cilician, nor the Asian groups could provide an answer to the wisdom of Stephen, or of the power that enabled him. Apparently, he was the full meal deal.

The mission to entrap Stephen wouldn't be easy. I relished the thought of planning the attack. I suggested to my confederates we find certain men who'd go undercover, then testify they heard Stephen make blasphemous statements not only against Moses, but against God. That should be enough to do him in.

Our plan of attack developed to the point where we really had the crowds stirred up. It was crucial to our plan that the leadership of the Jewish religious establishment be further intimidated to act by enticing a ground swell of anger amongst the population of Jerusalem and its surrounding areas.

The quickest way to get support for our "witch hunt" was to instill a sense of paranoia and fear in the minds of those who had the most to lose.

I had Stephen arrested and brought before the Sanhedrin. We introduced our witnesses against Stephen in this courtroom of religious judgment. This is a part of the testimony we heard.

"This man," and they pointed directly at a nervous Stephen, "never stops saying things against the Temple, and against the law. We have heard him say Jesus of Nazareth will destroy this place, and will change the customs that were handed down to us by Moses."

"Wow! This is great!" I thought to myself. I could only snicker at the great job done by these accusers. Magnificent actors. Dramatic. Stunning. Their presentations had been flawless.

I looked over at Stephen. Man, his face seemed to be glowing. I actually thought I was staring at an angel or something. I couldn't believe my eyes!

The High Priest started to pose some questions to the defendant. Playing up to the assembled crowd of butt kissers, in full and penetrating splendor, our highest ranking religious officer started in on the accused before him.

"Stephen, is this true what these men have said about you?"

Stephen didn't even hesitate to get into his reply. He started to lecture us about history.

Imagine!

He began the lesson with well-known stories about Abraham, Joseph, and Moses. Hey, we knew the stories. We knew how all of the men left behind the inadequacies of their characters and their places in life to follow after the command of God. Stephen was implying we were in direct contrast to the great men of Israel.

Imagine that!

Instead of being adventurous and innovative, we were the ones who were being rigid and unmovable. He implied we wanted merely to keep things the way they are, and that we were mad at the believers in Jesus because He and his followers were dangerous innovators.

Unbelievable!

Stephen continued his lecture stating the Jewish people have always had the most amazing privileges, and yet, they've continually been a disobedient nation. He more or less said we were literally guiltier because we had every chance to know better but we were continuously rebellious.

You gotta know he was starting to hit pretty close to home. He was really treading on dangerous ground when he started talking about the Temple. All of us regarded the Temple as being a very sacred place, perhaps, the most sacred place of all.

Stephen had the audacity to insist we were limiting God. He said we'd become a loathsome people because we'd been worshiping the place, the Temple, rather than God Himself. Stephen insisted that God doesn't live in the Temple.

Man, this guy had plum lost his cookies. He was dangerously close to falling off his rocker. Heresy! Well, this insolent chap might be a pretty good speaker and all, but he sure didn't know how to interpret scripture very well, and more curiously, he certainly didn't know how to size up his audience.

He didn't let up either. He let loose with what most of us considered to be the last straw.

Stephen declared that, since the Jewish people had a history of destroying and persecuting the prophets, abandoning the leaders God had given to His children, it was only natural for the religious establishment were the ones guilty of killing the very person God sent to save us, namely Jesus.

Oops!

Can you imagine?

Stephen accused "us" of murder!

He said we didn't even recognize Jesus was the very Son of God. We had all the information we needed and still we became murderers of the very best God had to give.

Murderers? Did he just call us murderers? You got to be kidding me!

Listen folks, if you've ever been near an angry mob of people you'd have to know something just hit the fan very hard. The temperature of the blood inside of most of people in the stunned audience approached the ever-dangerous boiling point. This guy had some nerve all right. Faces started to distort with anger, no, with rage. You could almost see eyes popping out and teeth separating in preparation for attack.

Incredibly, he wasn't finished. He seemed oblivious to the fact he had a shovel in his hand and was digging his own grave right in front of us. He just kept coming back with more. He peered into the sky like he was in some kind of trance.

"Look, look," he shouted, "now I see the heavens are opened up and the Son of Man is standing at the right hand of God!"

O.K. That does it! This is downright blasphemy! This calls for the death penalty. Stoning is the only appropriate response for blasphemy according to Deuteronomy 13:6ff.

"Let's stone 'im!"

As if one body, the entire gathering rose to its feet in perfect unison. I'd bet the whole city of Jerusalem could hear the shouting and clambering going on behind these hallowed, closed doors. Stephen was apprehended in merciless fashion, definitely destined for the pit. Surrounded by the angry mob, slapped, spit at, kicked repeatedly, Stephen was virtually dragged to the outskirts of town.

We threw him off a steep embankment. If the fall wouldn't kill him, the stones we hurled at Stephen surely would. Lots of folks ripped off their jackets, set them right in front of my feet, and literally just rocked him to death.

I must confess, very sadly from this vantage point, and yet at the time, enthusiastically and with absolute conviction of justification, I whole-heartedly participated in the stoning of Stephen. I might as well have stoned him myself.

10. NUTSO
(Acts 7:59, 60; 8:1-4; 9:1,2)

The cries of agony could be heard at the top of the hill as the rocks wreaked havoc upon our victim.

"Lord Jesus, receive my spirit."

That's what I heard. I could see his body crumble as the rocks continued to pound upon him. Then, in words which would resonate in my memory for a very long time, Stephen uttered his finally plea to God.

"Lord, please forgive my executioners. Don't put this sin on their account."

It seemed like this plea must be a kind of code of honor or something. Even Jesus had been heard to cry out the same thing before he died.

Well, at least this blasphemer was dead. The question was now, "How many more do we have to get rid of?"

My crusade was certainly well on its way. We got our first target. The mission before me to eradicate these believers may just go much better than we first believed. Stephen had literally walked right into the trap we had set for him. We didn't even have to condemn him. He did that pretty much on his own, thank you very much.

Stephen, we hoped, was just the first of many casualties. My rampage continued. It's quite possible I resembled a bull chasing through the market place destroying everything in sight more than a respectable man of the cloth. I simply went ballistic.

Nutso.

I was so utterly determined to wipe out this vile atrocity it consumed me. It didn't surprise me when I heard some spiritual types had taken the body of Stephen to give him a proper burial. I was a bit troubled that the death of Stephen seemed to inspire and egg the believers on to be even more zealous of their beliefs. Rather than slowing down the movement his martyrdom shifted it into high gear. The flames of this Jesus movement were being fanned uncontrollably.

In response all I did was ramp up my efforts and activities as well. I went from house to house to drive out the dirty rats. I arrested anyone I thought was remotely connected to this band of believers. I didn't care whether they were male or female, young or old, good looking or ugly.

No difference to me. A heretic is a heretic. They all had to be silenced. The quicker, the better.

The more I persecuted the more they scattered. Unfortunately, they didn't shut up wherever they went. They just carried the news of Jesus with them. Perhaps Philip was a good example of what I'm talking about. I had heard he'd gone into Samaria to preach the message of Jesus, performing miracles among the people there. I was told the lame and paralyzed would come to him to be healed. I even heard stories of demons coming out of people. Whoa!

Philip, one of the seven leaders chosen with Stephen, was captivating the attention of everyone. In spite of the many illusion tricks he'd played on people even a magician by the name of Simon became a believer. Even though he at one time professed to be a great person possessing unbelievable skills, he gave it all up to become a constant companion of Philip as he preached his way around Samaria.

Can you imagine the people of Samaria receiving this message Philip was teaching? These people weren't even fit to hear anything about God. God was for Jewish people, and nobody else! And yet, it's said they were more than happy to hear about Jesus. This was most incomprehensible.

I was told when the ring leaders in Jerusalem heard about the excitement Philip was creating in Samaria they sent two of their top dogs to help him out. Peter and John, two cronies of Jesus, were whisked off to Samaria themselves to spread the story of Jesus.

My, this was going way too fast and way too far. These "Jesus freaks" had to be stopped. Their numbers were increasing too fast. It became evident my task to eliminate these heretics might take a little longer than originally projected. Nevertheless, I'd continue to explore every avenue open to me.

I determined to go directly to the big guy, none other than the High Priest. We did lunch and I asked him for a special letter of reference I could carry around with me as I scavenged about the territory for believers in Jesus. I knew a letter from the High Priest would gain me entry into any crevice I wanted to crawl into. It would unlock the doors of any synagogue I'd ask for assistance from. As an official ambassador of the highest-ranking religious officer in the land I possessed incredible prestige and authority. His blessing would rubberstamp my every move. I was commissioned to bring the heretics to trial, where a complete examination would decide their fate.

A hot spot of "criminal" behavior, from a variety of accounts, was the city of Damascus. Hey, a change of scenery from Jerusalem is probably exactly what the doctor ordered. The stress and strain had been mounting day by day. I thought getting away from the constant interference of other do-gooders would take some of pressure off of me. Away from the glaring eyes of my superiors and peers where I could carry out my mission in my own way was where I wanted to be.

It might as well be Damascus.

Pack the bags. Get out the whip. Let's get on with it!

My first field trip to the 'burbs!

Trip # 2
JERUSALEM TO DAMASCUS

11. BLINDSIDED
(Acts 9:3-9)

The trip to Damascus wasn't an easy one. The distance between Jerusalem and Damascus was approximately 140 miles, and it was a difficult road to tackle. Getting up and down all the hills was a true test of endurance. However beautiful the scenery appeared, the miles seemed to drag on, and on.

What made the journey a bit lonely was the fact I wanted to be left alone to think creatively about my "plan of attack." Only a few officers of the Sanhedrin religious "police force" accompanied me on this trip. As a top dog Pharisee I had little in common with them so they always kept their distance from me.

To say I had quite a bit of time to connive would be an understatement. I scanned the events of my life and wondered how it was I came to be so fortunate to be me, at the height of my career at my young age. Sure, I thought about my family back in Tarsus. I wondered what they'd think of me. If they only knew about the important task I was engaged in.

I also considered the potential trouble I might be confronted with by the rebellious followers of "the Way." That's the name by which we started identifying those who followed after the teachings of Jesus. I'd heard so much about the area of Galilee and of all the things Jesus accomplished in the territory. Was it possible the things he said were really true? Were the miracles and signs he performed designed to show everyone he was who he claimed to be?

The miles dragged on and on. It seemed I faced a constant battle in my mind to resolve the many questions that were increasingly perplexing to me. The weeklong journey was just about over and I was getting very anxious to reach my destination. The road just before the beautiful city of Damascus winds its way down from the spectacular Mount Hermon. One of the oldest cities in the world lay in the picturesque scope of the mountain. Most of the buildings in Damascus were white and as I looked down over the city the sight of its glimmering landscape radiated against the background of the lush plains surrounding it.

BLINDSIDED TRIP # 2

"Finally, we made it" is what I was thinking when I was suddenly surrounded by an incredible light! It was so intense it was impossible to see what it was. It hit me with so much power it knocked me literally right off my feet! If I were to describe it I'd probably say it was like getting hit with lightning. I'd never bit hit with lightning before but this must rank pretty close to it. The only difference might possibly be that the light didn't seem to diminish or go away.

While blinded, and desperately trying to figure out what was happening to me, I heard a voice as clear as a bell clanging right next to my ear.

"Saul!"

"Man," I exclaimed, "who the heck is that?"

"Saul!" I heard it again. "Saul! Why are you persecuting me?"

"Who is this? Who in the world is talking to me? I can't see you."

"It's all right. It's just me. I'm Jesus. I'm the One you're persecuting."

Shocked. Astonished. Scared spitless. Shaking in my sandals. Bones rattling. All I could do was stammer as I responded to the powerful voice.

"Lord, what do you want me to do?"

"Get up. Dust yourself off. Someone will come and meet you on your way into Damascus. They'll tell you exactly what you're supposed to do."

Alrighty then. As quickly as the invasion of my privacy started, it ended. I don't think I'll ever forget the experience. It only took a minute or so, and yet, the feeling will last forever. I'd been talking to Jesus! But I thought he was dead!

"I talked to HIM!"

"He talked to me!"

"Am I dreaming?"

"Was that really HIM?"

"Nah, maybe it was just one of the policemen trailing me. I must have fallen, hit my head on a rock, and now they're trying to pull a fast one on me. That must be it. Perhaps I really was just struck by lightning. This area is known for its violent electrical storms you know. The hot air of the plains comes up to meet the cold air of the mountain causing wicked storms to erupt out of nowhere. Could I have just been in the "wrong" spot at the "wrong" time?"

My heart was just a tickin'. My mind was playing tricks with me.

"This can't be. Or could it? I know I heard the voice. It was real! I heard it clear as a bell. Hey, I still can't see. Where am I?"

"Hey, I can't see! I'm blind! I can't see a thing! Come quickly, give me a hand!"

Obviously, when the officers heard my screams they came running up beside me. I could sense they were a bit stunned by what they had just witnessed as well. They told me they had heard the voice too, but they didn't see anybody close by.

Now, all of us were confused. I was blind, and they were speechless on Mount Hermon. We didn't even know what to say to one another.

A couple of the guys helped me to my feet while another cautiously dusted me off. I started to grope around trying to find a measure of stability. Realizing I was severely debilitated by whatever it was that struck me they grabbed me by the arms to steady me and had a brief discussion about what to do next. Knowing we weren't all that far from the city they quickly surmised the best course of action was simply to start walking.

According to the message somebody was on their way to meet us. Might as well find out what's up. So, like an injured soldier being carried out of harms way, my compatriots were forced into a situation where they literally had to carry me as we proceeded towards Damascus. Not a word was spoken. Everyone was still stunned, transfixed to figure out what out of this world just happened.

What a freaky experience!

Moments ago I was powerful, ambitious and determined as ever to pursue the challenge just before me in Damascus. Now, I was being carried towards the great city weak, confused, and injured into helplessness. I was like a fish out of water flapping around trying to breathe with normality. This state of being incapacitated was totally foreign to me. Having been immobilized I felt incredibly powerless to understand what had just happened to me, not to mention what was going to happen to me next.

No doubt folks who witnessed the sight of me being carried towards the city saw nothing more into it than a blind man being assisted by some friends. Little did they know I was Saul, an ambassador of the High Priest.

And now, something phenomenal had just happened to me, mere moments before I was to begin another campaign of terror upon some poor, unsuspecting souls. I'm sure they didn't recognize the terror raging within my mind. I was exhausted from thinking. I was puzzled from questioning. I was nervous from fear.

How we ended up where we did is somewhat of a mystery to me. Apparently, my every thought had been focused on what, who, why, and the how. The only other explanation I can give is that I simply drifted off into la-la land. When I finally did acknowledge at least a bit of sensation, I only recognized peace and quiet. Obviously the long trip had ended 'cause I was lying on a soft and comfortable bed rather than in the arms of a couple of husky assistants bumping down the road. Warm, cozy blankets surrounded me as my body felt heavy with exhaustion. Keenly aware of the darkness surrounding me I fell once again into a very deep, restful sleep.

TRIP # 2

12. ANANIAS
(Acts 9:10-19a)

They told me later I was in and out of consciousness for three days. They couldn't even get me to eat or drink because I was so wasted. My first recollections were very dream-like in nature. It seemed so real to me though. I was lying flat on my back, blind as a bat, when I sensed someone come to the side of my bed and gently place their hands on me.

The next thing I knew, I could see! I must have jumped ten feet off the bed. O.K. Maybe it was only one or two feet.
"Hey, what's going on?" I shouted.
"Brother Saul?" responded a grandfatherly, gentle voice.
"Brother Saul."
"Who are you?" "What are you doing here?" I couldn't help but wonder why anybody would call me "brother." My goodness. "Where am I anyway?"
"Well," he replied, "I'm Ananias. The Lord Jesus, the same Jesus who appeared to you on the highway, has sent me to open your eyes, not only to the world in front of you, **but** to the reality of the Holy Spirit of Jesus who dwells in you. He appeared to me as well in a dream and told me to come to this home of Judas on Straight Street to meet with you my friend. I must confess I wasn't all that excited about getting together with you because He told me all about the havoc you've caused in Jerusalem and of the authority and power you possessed to do the same here in Damascus, **but** Jesus insisted I come. He told me you were just as much a chosen one of His as anyone else. He informed me you'd be the one who would take the wonderful message of the gospel of grace and peace to the Gentiles, to the Jews, and even to kings and rulers of the land! He also said you were going to learn a few lessons about suffering for a cause yourself."

Look, I don't mind telling you I prayed to ask God to open my eyes again. At first, I thought what I'd just heard was taking a response just a little out of proportion. Hey, wouldn't you? Sure, it felt like a big chunk of scale had just been removed from both of my eyes. I could see just as clear as I could before I got hit by the bolt of whatever up the road.

Talk about a mountain top experience!

But, you know something, I felt totally different now. I had the sensation of being totally transformed. I could feel it. Not only could I see everything in the crowded room filled with people I didn't even know, I was filled with an awesome sense of calm and security.

Quite often, as I investigated people who had followed in "the Way," I'd heard about a practice they called an "illumination." This ceremony of baptism was a symbolic way for these folks to publicly declare their intention of serving Jesus. It was their way of saying they were being cleansed of an old way of life and being renewed with a different purpose and direction in life.

What a strange twist.

Following a wonderful discussion with Ananias and a few others I found myself in the strange predicament of wanting to declare the change that had taken place in me! You should have seen the looks on the faces of Ananias, Judas, and others who were in the room. I don't think they could believe their ears when they heard me ask if it were possible for me to have this "illumination" thing done to me.

Their mouths simply dropped open. I told them my eyes had been opened in more ways than they could imagine. I got the message!

So, I was baptized!

I also have the wonderful recollection of food tasting a whole lot different. Maybe it was just the home cooked food. Or perhaps it was 'cause I hadn't eaten for days. I was starved. My strength was slowly being renewed by the great food as well as by some terrific fellowship.

13. THREE YEAR GAP
(Galatians 1:17; Acts 9:19b-25)

Hey, there's a three year gap that happened right here.

You might be inclined to think one minute I was in Damascus overcoming my blindness and several days later I was in Jerusalem preaching up a storm. Well, it didn't happen quite that fast.

"Then, where'd you go?" "What'd you do?"

Glad you asked.

Let me tell you I didn't just take a holiday to marinate in the desert sun. I didn't even drop out of sight to participate in some goofy kind of life shattering, metaphysical confrontation with the stars either. Nor did I retreat into some mountainous cave as a means of escaping potential nasty situations I might have faced meeting either my former bosses or unbelieving believers.

On the contrary, this time in my life was probably the most peaceful time in my entire life to this point, with the possible exception of my childhood. Tranquility and serenity are the most appropriate words to describe these three years. It was a time for the new life within me to take root. It was a time to establish the basics of a ministry that was bound to come in the future, based on the news of Ananias. I had a deep sense of conviction things were going to be different from here on out.

I'd been taught a great many things throughout my education stint. It was during this time of renewing my mind that all I had learned came to be challenged. This awakening of the Spirit of Jesus within me took place in what I've called Arabia. Damascus was the main city of the territory ruled by the Nabateans under King Aretas. In a time of relative calm I was able to come to peace with the life of Jesus within me.

The days were filled with revisiting the scriptures and reevaluating all I had come to believe in. Many hours were spent in question and answer sessions. Ananias and many other believers spent a great deal of time with me answering my questions as best they could, often sharing with me the impact Jesus had upon their lives. The encouragement and inspiration these fine folks gave to me was fabulous. They provided me with many opportunities, discreetly at first, to visit the synagogues then gradually exposing me to various crowds so I might share my testimony of my encounter with Jesus.

There were a number of things that became increasingly and unmistakably clear to me. First of all, I became convinced what I had done with my life up until the scales were lifted off my eyes in the home of Judas was nothing more than an exercise in self-righteousness. I'd been involved in nothing less than a self-centered, egotistical rampage. Everything I could accomplish was for my satisfaction alone. All I did was to advance myself in the eyes of others. Oh, of course, my piety allowed me to say "it was all done to bring glory and honor to God!"

Hogwash!

If ever there was a person who attempted to get closer to God through what they had done or would be able to do, it was me. Self-righteous to the hilt.

Secondly, I became convinced Jesus had done something for me completely without my assistance. Coming to this conclusion is not as easy as you might think. Just try to erase all of the teaching you have had and wipe it out in a blink of an eye. I don't think so.

Take all of the memories of your life and cast them out of your thought processes completely. Not so easy to do. The old memory bank is pretty reliable.

Thirdly, my blinders needed to come off. This was probably the hardest thing to understand. I'm referring to my concept of God's love and purpose for the whole world. You see, the Jews were God's "chosen few." That was it. Oh, there may be an outside chance for a few Gentiles to get into God's kingdom but that's really stretching it. I could handle quite easily the intervention of Jesus for me because I was first and foremost a Jew. However, it took me a little longer to understand the amazing truth God loved the "whole" world.

You hear what I'm saying?

God loved the "whole" world.

Everyone! Everything! All! He didn't leave out anyone of His gracious and merciful love.

Cut me some slack. Radical surgery was required to extricate a complete system of theology that ran contrary to God's view and opinion of mankind. The wisdom of mankind had developed laws, rules, regulations, traditions, and sacrifices to govern a relationship with God. Most everything was based on the goodness of human kind. It shouldn't even be called the wisdom of mankind. It should be called the "stupidness" of mankind, or at least the "foolishness" of mankind.

Needless to say, I had to give my head a shake more than a few times. I came to recognize and understand the true righteousness of God was already given to "all" in the person of Jesus. The chains that bound me to laws, rules, and regulations were severed on the cross and my liberty to enjoy the abundance of His Kingdom had been purchased by the blood of the Lamb, Jesus. Now, and forevermore, I had a "great" High Priest who had intervened on my behalf once, and for all time.

Now, let me warn you. Just start talking like this around folks who have their minds made up. You'll soon find out you have enemies. Hey, I know. Who do you think is talking here? I was the prince of enemies. My blood used to boil at the thought of heresy!

But, the more I came to believe in what God had done for the world the bolder I became in proclaiming my understanding of the revelation of God to others. I knew I was starting to have an affect on others because their reactions to me were getting stronger too. I was starting to light some fires under some pious butts and the heat was getting a bit close to home. I began to break down some walls and fences and many folks were afraid I was getting a too close to their house.

Many of my Jewish "friends" were stunned by what I was coming up with. They found it inconceivable I had undergone such a radical change in my understanding. They still perceived me to be the one who was supposed to be capturing the believers rather than setting people free. It was very clear I was getting under their skin too.

I was able to confound most of the Jews in Damascus by proving to them Jesus truly was the Messiah whom they'd been waiting for. They didn't like me all that much. The scriptures were finally starting to make sense to me. I had become intimately acquainted with the good book but it wasn't until now I finally understood the truth they contained.

My life was in apparent danger. I pondered on the warnings of Ananias concerning suffering for the sake of Jesus. Several sources suggested a plot had been hatched to capture me and a contract had been assigned to take me out. A plan of escape would be needed to counter any measure taken against me.

We knew the ticked off Jews had put up around the clock surveillance at each of the city gates in hopes of catching me trying to get out of the city.

Damascus, like many ancient cities, was a walled city. In some areas the walls were wide enough for a chariot to be driven. Houses were literally built into the walls, with windows opening out over the outer wall. One quiet, dark, and lonely night friends took me to the home of a wonderful family who lived in one of these wall condos. Like a convict breaking out of prison I was escaping a prison of my own making. It was a humbling experience to be literally lowered down the side of a city wall in a basket so I could escape from those who wanted to do me in.

What a switch!

I had come to the city of Damascus to take prisoners. I left in danger of being a prisoner myself. I had come to stamp out all of those who would believe in Jesus and I left the city as a believer in Jesus myself.

I had been carried through the city gates in the middle of a hot, blistering day as a blind, sorry excuse for the wisdom (foolishness) of mankind. I was departing in a basket, in the pitch dark of night, in an absolutely clear and focused vision of the wisdom of God's love, grace, mercy, and peace.

Simply amazing!

Trip # 3
DAMASCUS TO JERUSALEM

14. NOT WANTED
(Galatians 1:18,19; Acts 9:26-30)

Thinking of returning to Jerusalem after three years of incognito in the area of Damascus wasn't an easy thing for me. I'd left Jerusalem with the feeling some folks in Damascus weren't going to take too kindly to my arrival. Huh, now, I was having those same feelings as I contemplated my return to Jerusalem.

I purposed to go to Jerusalem not to meet with my old crony, religious friends, but to meet together with my former "enemy" friends. I thought it was high time I got together with the leadership of the believers who gathered together in Jerusalem. I suspect fellows like James, Peter and John were somewhat curious to meet me too. I admit to being a tad nervous.

One thing often preventing progress in one's life is the past. Others also have trouble getting over it. People usually have trouble forgetting what kind of person they knew before. They get very disillusioned when they see the same scenario of disappointment over and over again. People who change expect others to recognize their new leaf. Ultimately many are disillusioned to discover the leaf simply got flipped over. Habits and patterns aren't easily broken. Change is met with suspicion and skepticism. Unfair as it is many folks are not given the luxury of seeing the past disappear. Hey, isn't it a wonderful thing the heart of God is much more gracious!

I had a past that was hard to escape from. I had been more than just an ordinary Joe. Of course, 'cause I was "Saul." Ha! I was a celebrity. I had been a "rising star" on the religious boardwalk. My accomplishments had been emblazoned in the images of my fan club. At one time, I was a hero in the Jewish community, but now, I was a traitor. To the believers, I was once a feared enemy now I was a feared, unknown commodity. They didn't know what to make of me!

When I arrived in Jerusalem, I could feel the tension in the air. Apprehension seemed to cling to me like a nasty rash. I even started to look at my clothes and smell under my armpits just to see if I was emitting a foul odor, or if I was dressed in a fashion faux pas. Nobody had put out the welcome mat for me. Mind you, I wasn't exactly expecting the red carpet treatment, but this was ridiculous.

NOT WANTED   TRIP # 3

I attempted to track down some of the leaders of "the Way." The disciples appeared to be scattered all over the place and it took quite a while for me to finally arrange a meeting with them. Someone must have been sneaking off in front of me to erect roadblock after roadblock to slow me down. It seemed nobody wanted to have anything to do with me.

Finally, my efforts paid off when I met a fellow by the name of Barnabas. He was very kind to me, listening attentively to my life's story. He was a whole lot more interested in my "new" life than he was my "old" life. That was ancient history as far as he was concerned. Barnabas was the one who made the meeting possible, with Peter that is. I came to the conclusion it was Peter's responsibility to check me out. I'm convinced the disciples were a little unsure as to whether they could trust the story of my "captivation."

For fifteen days I was introduced to nobody other than Peter, and, in due time, to James, the brother of Jesus no less. I didn't have to tell them about my days as a persecutor. They knew all too well of my effectiveness in that role. They were much more concerned with the "mountain top" experience and the three years since it occurred. They would listen, then they'd ask more questions. Back and forth it went.

At long last, when these two were convinced of my authenticity, they arranged for a time when I'd be able to meet with others in the movement.

The meeting room was crammed with gawkers. Lucky thing ears and eyes are attached to the rest of the body or else I'm sure there would have been hundreds more people who'd like to have been in there if there only had been room.

Barnabas gave the most flattering introduction I'd ever heard. Barnabas told them all about me, about how I lost my sight up on Mount Hermon near Damascus, about how Ananias had received the vision to come and restore my sight, and also related to them how I had become so fluent and persuasive in spreading the gospel of good news concerning Jesus. He gave my testimony in very convincing fashion. He almost didn't leave anything for me to say other than to fill in the blanks!

The rest of my short stay in Jerusalem was filled with opportunities to share of my new experience in Jesus. I even got into some serious debates with some Greek speaking Jews. You probably don't know this but Stephen was a Grecian too.

I even went to the very same synagogue where once I had argued profusely against the teachings of men like Stephen. Before I went to tear down the name of Jesus and now I had come to lift Him up.

Wow!

Unfortunately, I hit more than a few raw nerves. I've developed a penchant for stepping on people's toes. My life was again in danger. I could just feel it and so did some of my new believing friends. They knew full well my boldness had the potential for bringing some serious harm to me, not to mention what it could bring upon them. I'd been instrumental in the death of Stephen as well as many other believers, but I had no particular interest in becoming a martyr at this point either.

Best case scenario?

Get out of town. And make it snappy!

Once again I was smuggled out of Jerusalem.

The destination this time?

Caesarea.

Why Caesarea? Harbor city with lots of boats going lots of places. Consensus affirmed I needed another break. Tarsus might just be the best place to hide out for a while. Not at all a bad idea. I hadn't been home for many a year.

I parted company with all the wonderful folk from Jerusalem knowing deep down we might just meet up again another day. This little trip to Jerusalem was quite a little adventure I'd say!

Trip # 4
JERUSALEM TO TARSUS

15. HOME WHERE I BELONG
(Acts 11:19-25)

Home comings are a good thing!
My experiences over the past few months had been pretty traumatic. It seemed like I was embroiled in a whirlwind of stress. The boat ride back to Tarsus was nothing short of fantastic. What a time to just relax and unwind. Returning home to see my family and friends was something I eagerly awaited. To tell the truth I'm not sure what I was expecting, unsure as to what kind of reception I'd get there. Most folks would have heard by now about my rise and fall in the religious world. But how would they react to my new understanding of the gospel of Jesus?

Well, without going into a play-by-play account, let's just say I was received like any son who'd been away from home for a long time would be, with open arms. Everyone was so happy to see me again. News does travel fast. Surprisingly, they were very well informed as to what I'd been up to. They were very anxious to hear the story from the horse's mouth. I couldn't resist the opportunities to oblige. Over and over again I would share of the amazing love of God for all.

I spent the days helping my dad in the tent shop just like when I was a kid. We had a great time building tents and awnings in his business. He was very surprised to see how well I could still do the work. Hey, once a tent maker always a tent maker.

I was also able to keep a finger on the pulse of the activities of the new believers. I still had a few friends left within the establishment and they proved to be a good source of information. I was very well aware of the incredible effect I had wasted upon the believers. The persecution I inflicted after the death of Stephen was ruthless. Believers in Jesus were scattered abroad in fear of their very lives. I knew folks had gone into the coastal country of Phoenicia stretching along the sea coast for about one hundred and twenty miles or so as well as to the island of Cyprus, and even as far north as Antioch.

They spread the gospel message as they spread their wings in their flight. Their strategy was limited to sharing the good news of Jesus with only Jews who were able to speak in the Greek tongue.

The positive news was they were extremely effective in helping others believe in the work of God in Jesus because the numbers of believers was increasing by leaps and bounds.

No doubt the reports of this good news was getting back to the leadership of the believing community in Jerusalem. Of course they had to stick their noses into the situation to keep a handle on it. Apparently, they had sent an investigator up to Antioch to determine first hand the scope of the missionary outreach program.

Guess who they sent?

Man, did they ever pick the right guy, at least as far as I was concerned. It was none other than Barnabas, the one who had introduced me to Peter, James, and others while I was in Jerusalem. He'd been told to go no further than Antioch in his assignment.

When he got there, Barnabas became stirred to see the people embracing the grace of God. He was absolutely delighted. He challenged them all to stand firm in their conviction that God's loving grace and peace was sufficient.

He exhorted them to purpose in their hearts to hang on to the understanding Jesus was God's provision of righteousness on their behalf. There was no reason to go back to the slavery of self-righteousness.

Barnabas was one of those good guys you just love to hear about. All who met him were convinced the Spirit of Jesus was evident in his life because he backed up his beliefs with his words and his actions. Many people decided to put their trust in the faith of Jesus because of the integrity of Barnabas.

While in Antioch Barnabas caught wind of the fact I was up in Tarsus lighting up my little corner of the world. Anyway, for whatever reason, Barnabas decided to look me up since he was in the neighborhood, so to speak.

Trip # 5
TARSUS TO ANTIOCH

16. **ANTIOCH**
(Acts 11:26-30)

Well, Barnabas did track me down all right. It was great to see him again. He'd been so kind to me back in Jerusalem and I could tell instantly he hadn't changed a bit. He brought me completely up to date with the happenings both in Jerusalem as well as in Antioch.

It turns out his coming to Tarsus to meet with me was not just to discuss the weather, politics, sports, or religion. He came because he needed help. There was just so much to do. Perhaps he thought I was just sittin' by the riverbanks in Tarsus soakin' up the rays, drinkin' wobbly pops, watching life pass me by.

Ha. Fat chance!

No, he suspected my heart's desire was to spread the gospel of God's love far past the scope of anyone he had ever met. He shared my understanding that God's love stretched out way beyond the borders of our own perceptions. He had become convinced the extent of God's choice was not limited to only the Jews. It had been a big stretch for some to include Greek-speaking Jews into their concept of God's chosen ones however Barnabas knew God's plan of righteousness included the Gentiles too.

Who else could have the influence, not to mention the "guts," to carry off such an endeavor? That's what Barnabas was thinking. His purpose in coming to Tarsus was to conscript me into the "battle!"

No kidding.

I didn't need a whole lot of persuading. I relished a challenge. I finally had another project to sink my teeth into. For some reason, my parents understood. That didn't make the parting once again a very difficult thing.

On the road again...

"To Antioch then!"

Antioch (Antakya, Turkey) was quite a city, situated along the Orontes River at the foot of the towering Mount Silpius. Antioch of Syria was named originally after Antiochus, the father of its founder, Seleucus. In the Greco-Roman world Antioch ranked right up there with Rome (Italy) and Alexandria (Egypt) as one of the greatest cities.

ANTIOCH — TRIP # 5

It became a vital center of trade between the Mediterranean world and the rest of the eastern world by virtue of the fabulous port at Seleucia Pieria, fifteen miles away. In addition to its strategic water route Antioch also lay at the entrance to the best land route between Asia Minor, Syria, and Palestine.

Antioch was not only beautiful she was also very cosmopolitan. She was a world famous city known for a luxurious style of life. In the negative sense, it was decadent and immoral. Chariot racing was the town sport, that's if you didn't include the nightlife in your list of sports. The famous temple of Daphne stood in a laurel grove only five miles out of the city.

Legend had it Daphne was once just a mortal maid until Apollo fell madly in love with her. He pursued her until he caught her. For her protection Apollo changed Daphne into a laurel bush. Can you imagine?

The priestesses of the temple were actually sacred prostitutes, and with the "worshippers," nightly reenacted the pursuit of Apollo for Daphne. "The morals of Daphne." Ever heard that phrase? Well, it's used to describe, let's say, "loose living!"

It was into this type of environment Barney (as I called him to his face) was taking me. Both of us were fully aware of what we were getting ourselves into. Antioch was a melting pot of ideas and customs and into this cauldron we planned on introducing the message of God's grace and peace. The potential for having the gospel message scattered abroad was staggering.

We already had a good base of believers to support us. Obviously, Barney had been there before and had seen first hand what we'd have to work with. Preaching and teaching of the gospel to the Jewish community had already begun. Although the Jews were tough nuts to crack, the believers had succeeded in altering the beliefs many of them clung to.

What was needed, however, was a concerted effort to minister to the Gentile members of the city. Unfortunately, they'd been left to the proverbial scrap heap of a hope-less-ness. That needed to change!

Initially, they mocked and taunted anyone who tried to bring up anything about Jesus. They took great pleasure in nicknaming us "Christians," in obvious reference to the fact we followed after Jesus. Little did they knew they too were "Christ like" themselves because of God's grace. They just needed someone to tell them they were actually "Christians" too, holy and pure in the sight of God!

ANTIOCH   TRIP # 5

Barney and I stayed in Antioch for about a year working to spread the gospel of good news. Whenever we could, to whomever would listen, we shared of God's great love for the whole world. It was an exciting time. We taught and preached the message of the grace and peace of God in such a way that many folks came to believe God had given everyone an incredible gift, His righteousness!

It was during this time the fellowship in Antioch would be visited by itinerant preachers from Jerusalem. These prophets, "fore-tellers" and "forth-tellers," would occasionally show up to exhort and encourage the believers.

Such was a fellow by the name of Agabus. With clarity of purpose and thought he spoke to us of a terrible famine that was terrorizing the whole world during the years of Claudius Caesar's reign. He stirred our hearts to action. Everyone took stock of their own ability to respond and a collection of goods and money was prepared to help in the relief effort for those who lived in desperate conditions in Judaea.

At a specially called meeting it was decided Barney and I should be responsible to take these beneficiary gifts personally to those who needed it most.

Ha, here we go, on the road again…

Trip # 6
ANTIOCH TO JERUSALEM

17. PERSECUTION OF GRIPPA
(Acts 12:1-23)

The road of life certainly has its ups and downs. Natural disasters, sickness, and political unrest unavoidably inflict their share of suffering. Children, family, friends, health, and a host of other great realities counter-balance the negative. Some folks undoubtedly have it a little easier in the pain department.

It was during the reign of Herod Agrippa I those who believed in Jesus saw more than their share of suffering. This Grippa character (as I tagged him) had a real problem. Unfortunately, he took his frustrations out on believers. As Barney and I trekked towards Jerusalem from Antioch we had lots of opportunity to discuss the persecution King Herod was engaged in.

Grippa was the grandson of Herod the Great. He grew up in Rome very close to the imperial family. He'd been a very close friend of Caligula so, when Caligula became the ruler of the Roman Empire, one of the things he did was to give his buddy Grippa the title of "King." Caligula gave him the tetrarchy of Philip, and later, the tetrarchy of Herod Antipas. Grippa was given the rule over Judea and Samaria by Emperor Claudius as a reward for his assistance in helping Claudius succeed Caligula. When Grippa returned to Judea from Rome he took great pains to further his popularity with the Jewish religious leaders.

In spite of the fact he'd been raised in Rome Grippa had learned a great deal about the Jewish people and their customs. He furthered his popularity with the people by meticulously keeping the "law," in addition to all of the Jewish observances. His attack upon the believers in Jesus and their leaders was in large part due to his desire to please the Jewish establishment.

The events of my past activities as a persecutor flashed occasionally across my mind. With great sorrow I reflected upon the turmoil I had created for many people. The intent had been in large part for the furtherance of my career. Grippa was exhibiting many of the same characteristics I had displayed. It was during my persecution a great leader like Stephen was snuffed out. He could take credit for wiping out another great man, namely James, the brother of John.

PERSECUTION OF GRIPPA   TRIP # 6

What a waste of a wonderful life!

As we approached Jerusalem our hearts were stirred with excitement. It had been some time since we were here last. What would we find here now? Would we also find ourselves at risk? Would I still have trouble being accepted by the believers? I took comfort in the fact Barney would be with me to smooth the rough edges.

The other thing that should gain us a greater measure of acceptance would definitely be the offerings of gifts the relief effort had raised. We sought out safe refuge in the home of Mary, the mother of John Mark. Her house was in a very real sense the center of activity for the believers in Jerusalem. She was a real trouper with an incredible, gentle spirit. Could she ever put out a spread! Hospitality was truly her gift for others.

Barney and I took turns sharing with the believers of our experiences and efforts in the city of Antioch. They were blessed and amazed by the generosity of those whom they had never met. They found it difficult believe such kindness should be exhibited by folks they had virtually nothing in common with, other than the common understanding of the gospel of grace and peace of God. We also learnt of the growth and encouragement of the believers in Jerusalem in spite of the wave of suffering they were enduring.

It was John Mark who related the fascinating story of Peter and of his confrontation with the power of "Grippa." He seemed to be tickled pink about the trouble he was causing the fringe groups of believing traitors. At least that's how he viewed them. The Jewish leaders were pretty happy with his actions, especially actions like the removal of James. His killing had received rave reviews from the big chunks of cheese.

"Hey, if the extermination of one of the leaders brings me such adulation, why not take out a few more!" That probably sums up the irrational mind of someone who regards himself a little higher than he should. I suppose that's how he settled on Pete as a target, after all, he was one of the highest ranking leaders in all of the Jerusalem band of believers.

Unfortunately for Grippa, Pete's arrest came during the week of the Passover. Knowing full well the Jewish customs, He couldn't conduct a trial or an execution for that matter during the whole week. These days of unleavened bread were very special to the Jews so it became his mission to have Pete executed at the conclusion of this special week.

Grippa was again confident his stock would rise, that his light would shine even brighter, all because his offensive maneuver was seen in a very positive light by the Jewish religious hierarchy.

Pete was a prized acquisition and the last thing Grippa needed was to have his prize get away. Every possibility of an escape or high-jacking of his plan was to be avoided at any cost. Four quaternions of soldiers were summoned to guard Pete. For those of you who don't know a "quaternion" is a squad of four soldiers. So four times four is sixteen.

Sixteen? Yes, sixteen soldiers were assigned to guard Pete day and night, divided into four shifts of four soldiers on guard for three hours at a time. Customarily, the prisoner had his right hand chained to the left hand of a guard. An extra precaution was taken with Pete. They chained the hand of one guard to his left hand, and the hand of another guard to his right hand. The other two guards were assigned to stand guard at the door.

Security arrangements were set ensuring that Pete's escape would be an impossibility. At the same time preparations were being made for Pete in prison his fellow believers were unceasing in their prayers to God on his behalf.

The very night before Pete was to be brought before Grippa all seemed normal and peaceful. All was quiet, darkness prevailed throughout the dungeon of doom with two soldiers posted dutifully at the door, and Pete slept shackled on either side to the other two guards.

And then all...broke loose!

Pete must have been shocked silly when he felt the slap on his face. When all should have been darkness around him Pete was keenly aware of a light shining in the prison cell. An angel of God lifted him to his feet and told him to "get the lead out!" Perhaps the angel said "get the lead off" 'cause the chains fell off his hands like he'd pulled some escape artist trick on them.

The angel continued, "Pull yourself together. Get your shoes on. Put your coat on and let's get the heck out of here!"

Well, Pete apparently did exactly what the angel instructed him to do. Hey, would you just sit there and argue with an angel of God? I'm sure Pete probably thought he was having some incredible dream. They walked right past the first and second guard, eventually coming to the large iron-gate separating the prison grounds of the captive from the open roads of the free.

The angel simply pushed the gate open and out they went! The angel walked with Pete for a block or so, then just vanished into thin air!

No doubt Pete had to pinch himself a few times just to make sure he was really awake. And out of prison no less! When the pinch actually hurt he realized what had just happened to him. He concluded, "Now I certainly know God sent an angel to deliver me out of the hand of Herod, and from all the high hopes and expectations of the Jewish people."

The next thought he pondered was on what his next move would be. He immediately raced to the home of John Mark's mom, Mary, where comfort and security would be found. He knocked quietly on the door as not to arouse the suspicions of the whole neighborhood. It was Rhoda who happened to hear the knocking first, proceeding to see whom it was. Even though she could hardly see him, Rhoda recognized Pete's voice right away. She was so excited she left him standing outside while she hastened to tell the others who were huddled together in prayer for Pete's sake.

Their first reaction?

"Hey Rhoda, get real. Are you nuts woman? Have you lost all your marbles or something?"

"No! No! It's him. I know it's Peter!" Rhoda insisted.

"Ah, maybe it's his angel," they persisted.

But the knocking resumed. When they finally did get around to opening the door again they were stunned to see it really was Pete. It wasn't until he was able to quiet them down that he could tell them how the angel of God had helped him escape from the prison. He told them to get a hold of James and some of the other leaders to advise them of what was up because some pretty heavy stuff would be coming down the next morning. Pete was then hustled off to another home that wouldn't be an obvious hiding place to search for him.

No kidding!

The escape of Peter caused no small amount of activity the next morning in the prison. His escape was a reality instead of an impossibility! Grippa was furious to say the least. Search parties were initiated and continued without success in tracking down the AWOL prisoner. The quaternion of soldiers was questioned at length. In massive frustration Grippa ordered the whole batch of soldiers responsible for this travesty executed.

Some justice, huh?

PERSECUTION OF GRIPPA — TRIP # 6

Soon after the incident Grippa returned to Caesarea from Judea. It seems he got his reward too. He became very displeased with the people of Tyre and Sidon. The matter was quite serious for the people of Tyre and Sidon had lived in economic prosperity just north of Palestine. Grippa felt he could cut off their sources of income by cutting off the trade links they depended on. He also could cut off all of their food supplies they depended on receiving from Palestine. The people recognized a new peace treaty with Grippa would certainly be in their best interest.

Somehow, with all the intrigue of covert activity, with spies and all, the Tyrenites and Sidonites managed to conspire with Blastus, one of Grip's closest servants. Blastus agreed to make their desire for peace known to the King.

According to the plan a public hearing was scheduled to consider their request. Grippa was dressed to the max in his regal costume. He entered into the theater clad in his robe of silver cloth. It must have been quite a sight. People were so awe struck by the sun glistening off his array of jewelry and the silver in his clothing all the people who saw him started to shout that they were looking at a god rather than a mere mortal.

Wow!

Grippa must have been pretty full of himself by now. He took every bit of credit for the authority and power he could possibly take. Well, this was the very beginning of the end for that poor sucker. Sorry, I don't have too much sympathy for him. A plague of worms is said to have ultimately led to his demise. Couldn't happen to a nicer chap.

His death was a welcome announcement to a whole lot of people including the sturdy band of believers who refused to go away. The terror and grip of Herod Agrippa I's persecution finally came to an end.

18. JOHN MARK
(Acts 12:24,25)

The main reason for our trip to Jerusalem was to take the collection of gifts to those who were having serious difficulties making ends meet. It was a great honor and privilege to do this on behalf of the believers in Antioch. The chance to visit Jerusalem once again was a special highlight for me. I had the chance to get together with some of my old buddies. For most of them, life continued to move along in the treadmill of performance. The more things change, the more they seem to stay the same.

It became evident to us the influence of the believing community was growing by leaps and bounds. They were not only growing in numbers, but also in strength of character and responsibility. The commitment to the message of God's loving grace and peace was heart warming. From personal experience I could share their passion about such a liberating message of good news. Jesus definitely filled the emptiness, guilt, and exhaustion that perplexed and frustrated the hearts of many folks who came to understand God's provision.

In spite of desperate economic times, persecution from political and religious forces, and tensions of their own making, the new believers were making progress in applying the truth of God's love into their lives. The challenge for them was to fan into flame the spark that had been lit inside of them.

Having completed our mission of mercy it was time for Barney and I to head back to Antioch. It was nice to be away, band yet the prospect of getting back closer to home was also appealing. We had spent a great deal of our time in Jerusalem enjoying the hospitality of Mary and her family. Mary, for those of you who don't know, was Barney's sister.

As we discussed our return trip and our plans for the future I noticed her son, John Mark, was paying particular attention to our every word. He took in everything he could. He didn't need to say anything. You could see the look of wonderment in his eyes and the expectation of excitement written all over his face. I couldn't help but wonder how long it would take for him to explode to ask the question he obviously wanted to ask.

It wasn't until the day before we were to leave he finally developed enough courage to pop the question. With this simple question Barney and I were placed in a very awkward position.

"Can I come along?"

How was I to respond?

John Mark was still a mere teenager. A debate raged on in my mind. "Sure he's a very nice kid, polite, and all the rest of it. My, he's still just a kid. Will he be able to handle it? Will we be able to handle it?

But, look at those puppy little eyes so full of excitement.

Did my face light up like that when I had the chance to leave the comfort of home in Tarsus to the unknown of life in Jerusalem?"

The only difference would be that the ball of responsibility would now be in my court. How is it possible to say "No!

Read my lips!

NO!"

But how could you say that to such an inquisitive and longing spirit? Barney and I just looked at each other after we heard the question the first time.

The pause must have been longer than he expected, so John Mark posed the question again.

"Barnabas? Saul? Did you hear me? I asked if I could come along with you guys back to Antioch. I could help! I wouldn't get in the way. Promise!"

I looked over at Barney again, and he returned my indecisive glance. So what's the best response when in trouble?

"What would your mother think?"

Don't lull yourself into thinking we weren't exactly equipped in the smarts or diplomacy department.

Ha. Hope does spring eternal, doesn't it?

John Mark saw the glimmer of hope in our response. Naturally, his first response was to zip out of the room to get his parents.

After discussing all the pros and cons of such a venture we all agreed the experience certainly couldn't hurt him. We weren't exactly sure of what we'd be doing, not to mention where we'd be going, but Barney and I were sure we'd be able to provide for him. In fact, he might even prove to be a valuable assistant to us. His youthful, exuberant company would surely lighten the way.

His parents, while they knew he would be missed around the house, realized the adventure would be just the good kick in the butt he could use to establish himself in life.

Well, I think John Mark jumped about four feet off the floor when his mom and dad told him the good news he could go along with us. I wouldn't be surprised if he already had packed his bags in anticipation of the positive response.

"When do we leave?"

Excited, or what?

It's always hard to say good-bye. I'm not sure it ever gets easy, especially with those whom a special bond has been established. We had come to love and appreciate Mary, her husband, and also many of the other believers we had met in Jerusalem. Our final meal together was an occasion to share our hopes and dreams in Jesus and to give our expressions of encouragement and blessing to one another.

On the road again!

"Antioch, here we come..."

Trip # 7
JERUSALEM TO ANTIOCH

19. SET APART
(Acts 13:1-3)

The group of believers in Antioch was a unique blend of unity and diversity. They were blessed with the wisdom of God as well as the aptitude to express it in their daily lives. Their attentiveness to see a work that needed to be accomplished and doing something about it was a great thing to watch in action.

I'd like to mention just a few of the unique folks who taught and preached in Antioch. Some of us were regulars and then there were some who were itinerant messengers of the gospel message.

Of course, I'd want to include Barney in that group. He was such an inspiration to all, especially to me. He had a practicality about him. Everyone felt comfortable around him 'cause he was so easy going. Perhaps that's the nature of those who come from the solitude of the island of Cyprus.

Another man with a colorful past had to be Simeon. Some folks called him by his Roman name, Niger, which you might surmise, means "black." You may remember him a little more if I would refer to him as Simon, "the Cyrene." Does that help place him? Do you remember the account of the man who was yanked off the street and forced to carry a cross for one who struggled under the load? I thought this might refresh your memory. Well, this chap had a testimony that would knock your sandals off.

Another steadfast champion was a man called Lucius. He happened to be a friend of Simeon. Their friendship had begun many years ago in the city of Cyrene, located on the northern right tip of Africa (Libya).

Manaen was a man with connections. And I mean connections at the top. This guy grew up with the likes of Herod Antipas in the courts of Rome. Even with his colorful background Manaen was a very gentle fellow. When you were with him you could sense the deep peace that enveloped him. His Jewish name Manahem meant "comforter." Boy, talk about a name tailored to perfectly suit a person!

Throw my name into the hat and you had quite a variety of personalities to exhort and inspire the believers of Antioch.

With our different upbringing, our different experiences, our complex characteristics, and with our distinct personalities we pursued the sole ambition of leading people into the liberty of the gospel of Jesus indwelling the hearts and lives of all people.

As time passed by the hearts of the believers were challenged by the necessity of spreading this gospel message far beyond their own safe haven. Perhaps they recognized in Barney and I the vagabond spirit. We had already completed a successful tour of duty to Jerusalem on their behalf, so we were a natural combination to expand the mission field.

I must admit this idea of letting the whole world in on the mystery of God was entirely consistent with the desire of my heart. Barney's too. We both could certainly attest the Holy Spirit of Jesus within us inspired us to share the great news of God's love with the whole world.

It was hardly what I'd call my first missionary adventure. There was a time when I considered my pursuit of "heretic" believers in Jesus as a strategic missionary campaign, albeit, to wipe them out. I'm also inclined to think my little excursion from Damascus to meet with the leaders of the movement in Jerusalem had the markings of a missionary trip. Certainly, the emergency relief trip Barney and I made to Jerusalem on behalf of the believers in Antioch should also be included in any numbering of my missionary trips.

The focus of this missionary trip was solely for the purpose of unlocking the doors of the kingdom of God for those who hadn't heard yet, and unshackling the chains of those who were still bound in the captivity of self-righteousness. There was a big, wide world out there, and our job was to spread the gospel message wherever our travels would take us.

So, Barney, John Mark, and I were set apart to hit the road.

Again!

Telling us to "get lost" was not meant to be a bad thing. Rather, it was their way of saying, "Look, you've been blessed enough by God and by us. Now, get out there and spread the love around!"

How could we refuse such a challenge? Barney hadn't been back to Cyprus for some time. Why not head that way first? Sounded like a good plan to me.

We packed our gear and bought the first tickets we could get on a ship heading for Salamis.

On the water again...

Trip # 8
CYPRUS AND BEYOND

20. **CYPRUS**
(Acts 13:4-13a)

Leaving the pleasant confines of Antioch was a sad moment for us. As we walked up and down the hillside towards the harbor town of Seleucia Pieria, Barney, John Mark, and I felt a strange tinge of sadness. We were uncertain as to when we would get to see our wonderful friends next. For some time we simply walked along in silence, each of us trying to work within the framework of our meandering thoughts.

    The harbor port was situated about five miles north of the mouth of the Orontes River, about fifteen or sixteen miles from Antioch. The town developed there in order to avoid the mud banks deposited by the Orontes as it entered into the Mediterranean Sea. This frontier fortress became a bustling commercial hive of activity because of its docking facilities.

    Barney was undoubtedly more excited about this trip than the rest of us 'cause he still had such fond memories. He was full of facts and figures concerning Cyprus and our trip to the island. He predicted within hours how long the eighty mile journey from the mainland to Cyprus would take. We shared lots of laughter as Barney charmed us with stories of his childhood.

    Traveling southwest, Barney spotted the tip of the beautiful, mountainous island before we did. I guess he knew what he was looking for. Cyprus had been an island overtaken by a variety of foreign powers throughout its history. The Babylonians, Persians, Egyptians, Greeks, and Romans had taken turns ruling this island domain. The big booty for all was the mining and production of copper. Cypriot copper became famous all over the known world.

    The other major manufacturing business contributing to the economy of Cyprus was the ship building industry. Boats of all kinds were constructed there. It only stands to reason. The only way to get on or off Cyprus was by boat!

    Folks sometime called the island by another name, Makaria. That name means "the Happy Isle." Appropriate me thinks. Climate and resources combined to make life very satisfying for its inhabitants. Everything needed to make a person happy and content could be found on this wonderful island in the great Mediterranean.

Once Barney had spotted the northern tip of the island we knew our ambitious project would really start in earnest. Even John Mark was exhibiting signs of excitement. As the ship hugged the shoreline during the last few miles the excitement grew more and more for all of us. Salamis would provide us with the first real opportunities to proclaim the gospel. Our plan was to minister to those who needed to be freed the most.

"Who'd that be?" you ask. Well, they'd be the ones bound up in the slavery of laws, rules, and regulations. If anyone were bound up in the tradition of self-righteousness it would be the Jews. We sought out the synagogue in Salamis as our first point of interaction. It's amazing to me the offer of liberty would be met with such hostility. It just doesn't make sense. Captivity must be a pretty comfortable place.

Well, it's a good thing the revelation of God's love to me included the truth His grace, mercy, and peace were meant for all of mankind, both Jew and Gentile alike. Barney and I were on the same page as far as this was concerned. We also agreed our first stop in any location would be the synagogue, and after that, the door was wide open.

I should also mention, at this point, Barney figured since we were going to start having a more concerted effort to reach out to Gentiles, it would be appropriate, if not more advantageous, for me to start using the name of Paul, instead of Saul.

Hey, I didn't have a problem with that. I could live with it. Others who didn't know me before wouldn't know the difference anyway. Maybe it might even help to avert a possible problem if my former reputation had preceded me.

Salamis was only the starting port of arrival in Cyprus. We continued to travel through the whole island. Wherever we found some Jewish folks gathered we took the opportunity to share with them the gospel message of Jesus. And whenever we could we shared the very same message with the Gentiles we encountered.

Some people listened and some people wouldn't give us the time of day. There were also some folks who believed what we were telling them about God's love. They were very grateful to us for helping them understand the grace of God and were anxious to hear more.

Eventually we made our way to the beautiful city of Paphos. Although Salamis was the largest city on Cyprus, it was Paphos, a hundred miles away, which served as the capital city.

Paphos had many popular tourist attractions which gave it an appeal other cities couldn't match. Being a naval station, it served as a welcome mat for all kinds of military personnel.

Probably the most popular attraction was the Temple of Venus, the goddess of love. It doesn't take too much imagination to surmise the worshipers were very faithful in attending to their "religious" responsibilities. They flocked to their "worship" celebrations whenever they could, day and night!

In 55 B.C. Rome had annexed Cyprus. It became a senatorial province in 22 B.C., and the governor who ruled over Cyprus was given the title of "Proconsul." The Proconsul when we arrived on the scene was Sergius Paulus. He obviously had heard rumors of the message we were spreading around "his" little island. He arranged for us to come and meet with him personally. My first impression was that he was a very sharp individual with an inquisitive nature about him. He politely appeared anxious to hear what any of us could tell him about this message of God's grace and peace.

Hey, if anyone wants to listen, we want to talk!

We were well into a mighty fine presentation when we were rudely interrupted. There was something not quite right with this guy 'cause he seemed just a tad whacked. Some people called him Bar-Jesus, while others referred to him as Elymas. Apparently, skilled like a slick politician, this fellow was bound and determined to screw up our conversation with Serg.

The name Bar-Jesus actually means "son of salvation," while the name Elymas means "the skillful one." He was skillful all right. He was a Jewish false prophet, a specialist in the practice of sorcery, far removed from anything resembling the salvation that God initialized in Jesus.

These kinds of characters really tick me off.

They are able, with cunning deceit, to confuse and distort truth. They are selfishly motivated only to milk the system for whatever they could get out of it. Their magical pronouncements and deeds are merely smokescreens. As soon as the dust settles there's nothing left to see. Elymas was obviously having the time of his life with Serg paying the bills. It's a strange phenomenon to see men of such intellect and power as Sergius sucked in by the likes of a dude like Elymas. It simply goes to show how so many folks get cheated in life because they trust in the folly of the wisdom of mankind.

Anyway, Elymas started interrupting our discussion. His antics were an obvious ploy to prevent Serg from paying too much attention to us. I just couldn't stand it anymore. He was really starting to bug me. I figured the best way to stifle his interference would be to tackle him straight on.

"Hey, buckwheat," I yelled out at him, "knock it off, eh! I've about had enough of you! You are nothing more than a spoiled little child full of mischief and deceit. Your mom and dad must have been quite the parents to put up with you 'cause you ain't good for anything but slandering. Everything you represent runs absolutely contrary to the righteousness God has gifted all mankind with. Look, get with the program! Stop perverting the truth of God!"

"Wanna see something phenomenal?"

"Take a look at the back of your eyelids for a while! Get a real good look at what it's like to be truly blind."

Well, needless to say, that took the cake. God fixed it so Elymas took a back seat for the rest of that meeting. He was blind as a bat in the middle of the day. He just started stumbling around reaching out for someone to help him out, just like a little kid trying to stretch out for security while attempting to take their first step. I personally got quite a chuckle at his confusion. Give him a taste of his own medicine!

Sometimes, I guess it's necessary to take away someone's perception of political correctness before they're willing to see the reality of truth.

How do I know what I am talking about?

I can speak from personal experience. Unfortunately, it took the removal of my physical sight long enough to allow the true Light of this world to illuminate my heart and mind. God knew me well enough to know I needed to get rid of my viewpoint and get a glimpse of His vision for the world!

I suppose I could really relate to a man like Elymas. I, too, had been a magician of sorts, delicately attempting to find the balance between truth and deception as a rabbi. I was entirely dedicated to propagating a message that suited the ambitions and goals of my own life. Well, thankfully there was hope for me and there was for Elymas as well, but certainly not within his capability or sorcery. His only hope was to be found in the One whom we were testifying to Serg about.

Proconsul Serg was impressed! The presentation of God's power in dealing with Elymas was one thing. The logical, rational approach to a God who loved the whole world with so much love is what really did it. It's not like Serg hadn't been impressed before with unusual behavior or powers. He was truly astonished at the simplicity of the gospel message. How could he refuse such an awesome gift that God had so freely given to him? It was our great joy to see him come to understand what God had done for all mankind, including him!

We had a great time on the island of Cyprus that's for sure. It was especially exciting for Barney to see the countryside once again. Paphos proved to be the most interesting spot probably because of our encounter with the top dog on the whole island. This most influential man would definitely make a lasting impact on his little patch of land. Sergius Paulus would be someone we would think of often.

We determined we'd leave Paphos by sailing over to Pamphylia.

TRIP # 8

21. PERGA
(Acts 13:13b)

The boat was pointed northwest. We were on our way back to the mainland where we'd continue to preach the gospel of God's grace and peace to Jew and Gentile alike. We'd be landing in the Roman province of Pamphylia, a tiny strip of land stuck between the openness of the Mediterranean Sea and the towering Taurus Mountain range. Pamphylia lay just to the west of my home province of Cilicia so I felt a little like I was coming back closer to home.

Our first scheduled stop was the city of Perga, situated about eight miles inland from the coastal port of Attalia, five miles west of the Cestrus River. Our boat sailed up to the mouth of the river and we walked the rest of the way to Perga. Her location had a double benefit for the residents of this fine city for it was sheltered from any coastal attacks, and yet, it was on the busy road that passed through the Pamphylian Plain. Its citadel was formed by a naturally rocky hill.

Perga is perhaps best known for its local goddess named "Artemis." Her shrine was on a hill near the city and we had heard the rituals surrounding her worship were quite something. Priests were usually begging throughout the worship ceremonies, if you could call them that!

The sports stadium was also a sight to see. It was built in typical Roman fashion so the action could take place on the ground level and the fans could watch on seats supported by the naturally sloping hill. Apparently, the stadium could hold up to twelve thousand spectators. Wow! Another spectacular building dominated the skyline of the city, the one hundred and sixty foot high Acropolis.

To us Perga was just a stop over before we headed inland to the city of Antioch in Pisidia. Before we could begin this rather dangerous trip north it was determined we would say a sad good-bye to young John Mark.

It's probably natural for some folks to speculate over why John Mark left Barney and I at this point in our travels. Here are some of the excuses I've come across:
- JM got home sick.
- JM was scared spitless to continue because we were about to travel on one of the most dangerous roads in the land.

PERGA — TRIP # 8

- JM was ticked off at me because it appeared more and more I was taking over from Barney as the chief spokesman for our little group.
- JM was content with having spent enough time out in adventure land, satisfied he had been at least to Cyprus.
- JM didn't feel right about preaching to the Gentiles.

I'd like to set the record straight. The three of us had a great time together. We enjoyed the company of one another ever since we'd left Jerusalem way back. We had however reached a point in our journey where a serious decision needed to be made concerning our young protege, John Mark.

The decision wasn't his to make. The decision belonged to Barney and I, and it was a difficult one to make. We both could see evidence of his youthful exuberance waning a bit. All the walking was actually taking a toll on our young compatriot. Considering the potential danger we were about to walk into I was definitely uncomfortable with having him come along.

We had promised his parents we wouldn't compromise his safety. I certainly didn't want to have an unnecessary burden on my shoulder.

If ever there was a good spot to send him home on his own from it was Perga. The sailing route back to Caesarea, then by caravan to Jerusalem, wouldn't be unduly difficult for him. We were confident he'd be safer heading in that direction.

JM agreed with our assessment, albeit with great sadness. His emotions were caught somewhere between disappointment at not being able to stay with us and the happiness of knowing he'd soon be back home, in his own bed, eating mom's home made cooking, and horsing around with his good buddies.

I still think we made the best decision. Barney did too. We set about to arrange for JM to catch the next boat out. He'd set his sights to open water and Barney and I focused our sights on the unknown of the interior.

Handshakes and hugs all around. It was again another sad good-bye. We wished JM all the best, he expressed his great appreciation, and then, he was off.

And so were we.

On the road again...

22. ANTIOCH OF PISIDIA
(Acts 13:14,15)

Antioch of Pisidia wasn't actually in Pisidia. It's best to say it was near Pisidia. The city of Antioch was nestled into a beautiful lake district of southwest Asia Minor, located on a plateau overlooking the plain of Yalvac, very well protected by its natural defenses. It was in 36 B.C. that Antony made the city part of the Galatian empire of King Armyntas. Officially, the name of the city was Colonia Caesarea.

A cult had been established in Antioch to honor Augustus, becoming the center of Roman activity throughout the entire area. Old Roman war veterans were moved there to live with the citizens. Consequently, Antioch had a population comprised of Greeks, Romans, as well as a large community of Jewish folk. This is actually one of the reasons we chose Antioch. It was filled with potential for spreading the gospel message to a great variety of people.

Protecting our health was another reason for traveling up to Antioch. Along the low coastal areas of Asia Minor there was a fever that plagued many of its residents. They say the fever hits you like a red-hot nail hammered right through your forehead. Malarial fever isn't one of those sicknesses you'd want to go out of your way to acquire. Uncomfortable to the max!

Well, guess what? I must have inherited the "bug" either in Perga or just shortly after we left. The discomfort it brought to me was almost beyond my will power to overcome it. It put a tremendous strain on every movement.

To make matters even worse, the stretch of highway between Perga and Antioch wasn't really one of the better roads in the world. "Highway?" Give your head a shake. The road meandered through a climb of some thirty-six hundred feet of elevation. The thought alone of this fact was almost enough to turn back the most hardy of travelers. The only ones who enjoyed the challenge were those who had criminal intentions up their sleeves. The thought of bandits attacking us didn't make the journey any less challenging. The fact I had to stop quite frequently provided the necessity to be even more vigilant than we might normally have been.

Needless to say, we didn't make very good time. For two determined pioneers like Barney and I to concede defeat was unthinkable. I was already exhausted long before we actually arrived in Antioch.

ANTIOCH OF PISIDIA   TRIP # 8

    I even think the strain of travel and of taking care of me finally caught up with good ol' Barney too. It took us several days to recuperate and regain our strength. It was through the network of Jewish hospitality that we found some fine folks who saw to our every need. They were most kind to take us in and nurse us back to health.

    Naturally, on the Sabbath, we all went into the synagogue to worship. Our hosts introduced us to the leadership and we took our place in the midst of a rather large crowd. The room was very quiet during the reading of the passages from the books of the "law" and of the "prophets." As I sat and listened I couldn't help but wonder if all of the people really understood what they were hearing.

    Simple acceptance of what the religious system has developed is a fairly easy trap to fall into. Following the party line is usually the path of least resistance. It isn't easy to buck the system or to challenge what the leaders say 'cause the whole system is perpetuated by a system in which leaders controlling followers. Discipline is maintained when authority is questioned. Hey, been there, done that. I've witnessed this pattern over and over in my travels. It's a sad thing.

    And then it happened! The rulers of the synagogue sent someone over to have a word with us.

        "Brothers, since you are visiting with us today, would like to share a word with us? If you do, then just come right up to the front and say on."

    Music to my ears. Can you imagine? I couldn't have planned it any better myself. Give a speaker a chance to speak and look out!

    With a little hidden giggle in our minds, and a smile on our face Barney and I looked at each other. We knew exactly what the other was thinking. All we had to decide was who was going to say what both of us were holding up inside ourselves. Barney leaned over to me and said, "Go ahead, it's your turn, let'm have it."

    That's all I needed to hear.

23. SERMON AT ANTIOCH
(Acts 13:16-41)

As I walked to the front of the room I figured the best way to tell them the gospel message was to make it as simple as possible for them to understand. I kind of like the three point format.

First, tell them mankind had a problem.

Second, tell them God had the solution.

Third, tell them to get on with living in the grace and peace God has blessed the whole world with.

So I stretched out my arms to gain their attention and started to tell them what I really thought. This is basically what I told them:

"Men of Israel, as well as those of you who have a reverence for God, please give careful attention to what I have to say to you. It was the God of Israel who chose our forefathers to be His special people. It was God who raised up the people of Israel to new heights when they lived as strangers within the land of Egypt. It was God who raised His mighty arm to bring the captives free from the bondage of captivity. In spite of His marvelous works on behalf of His people God had to put up with the poor manners and the insulting behavior of the Israelites for approximately forty years."

"It was God who cleared out the Promised Land by destroying seven nations in the land of Canaan. After giving the land to the people and dividing it up according to their portion, God gave to the people judges to rule over them for about four hundred and fifty years. Samuel was not only the last of the judges, but the first of the prophets."

"And it was God who brought a new King before the people of Israel when they begged for one. God gave them Saul, the son of Cis, a descendant of the tribe of Benjamin. Saul reigned for about forty years until God removed him."

"God then raised up for them another great King. There was something very special about David. God in His own words declared that 'David, the son of Jesse, is a man after my own heart, and he will do everything I ask him to do.' We all know God promised it would be through the lineage of David a Savior would be found for the people of Israel. This Savior's name was to be Jesus."

"Before Jesus would arrive a man named John would preach throughout the land a message of renewal through repentance. People started to think it was John who was the Messiah. He literally had to say to the people, 'who do you think I am? I'm not the Messiah. **But**, pay attention! There's going to come someone right after me who is so great and important I'm not even worthy to untie His sandals.'"

"Men, and brothers, children of the stock of Abraham, and all of those among you who fear God, the good news of this message of salvation is for you!"

"All of the Jews in Jerusalem and those who ruled over them didn't recognize Jesus as the Messiah. When these people condemned Jesus to death they were really fulfilling the words of the prophets long before. It's almost unbelievably they could ignore the prophetic words they read almost every Sabbath."

"In spite of the fact they had absolutely no charge against Jesus which warranted the death penalty, they persuaded Pilate to allow them to put Jesus on the cross. Fulfilling all the prophecies written about Jesus, they took Him down from the cross and placed Him into the tomb."

"**But**, ah, ha! **But**, this isn't where the story ends, my friends! There's more. Lot's more. God wasn't finished with Jesus just yet. He other plans for Him. God raised Jesus from the dead! What? You don't believe it?"

"Well, Jesus was actually seen by many folks after He rose from the dead. Many who traveled with Him from Galilee to Jerusalem had the opportunity to testify they had actually seen Him on a number of occasions over numerous days after His crucifixion. You can be sure all of these folks are accurate and reliable witnesses."

"Furthermore, God had revealed His intentions to our forefathers. This good news we are telling to you is nothing really new at all. You see, the promise of the resurrection of Jesus was given long ago thorough the prophets. God has now allowed us to live in a time when the fulfillment of the prophecies has actually come true. We now know Jesus has in fact been raised from the dead."

"God had spoken in the Psalms about Jesus saying, 'You are my Son, this day I have begotten you' (Psalms 2:7)."

In addition, concerning the fact He had raised Jesus up from the dead, never again to return to corruption God spoke through Isaiah saying He 'will give you the sure and holy blessings of David' (Isaiah 53:3). Psalms also declares God 'will not allow His Holy One, Jesus, to see corruption' (Psalms 16:10)."

"Let me summarize what this means."

"David was a man who belonged to his own generation. He served the people well by the will of God and when his time on earth was done he died. Like his forefathers before him he was laid to rest in the earth. His body was not incorruptible. David understood the promises made to him about a resurrection and incorruptibility were not promises related to himself. **But**, they related to Jesus, God's only begotten Son. It was Jesus who God would raise to new life! It was Jesus who would not see corruption the way every living human would eventually see corruption in the dying of the physical body."

"Friends and brothers, I'd like to make something perfectly clear to all of you. This is a word of victory to those of you who understand and even to those of you who don't. It's through Jesus, and only Jesus, that you are able to receive the forgiveness of your sins."

"Let me repeat this in a different way. Those of you who do understand Jesus is the only way to have your sins forgiven realize the incredible truth you are justified and made righteous by God alone. There's absolutely nothing you could have done or can do to receive righteousness on your own merit! Obeying the Law of Moses can't help you out one iota. If you put all your hopes in obeying laws, rules, and regulations you're wasting your time. They will never justify you!"

"I have a profound warning for you. Beware, lest you fall into the same fate as those who didn't listen to the prophet of old."

"Watch out!"

"I am talking to you despisers and scoffers. You can contemplate your self-righteous achievements all you want. Wasting your life trying to get the favor of God is a tragedy of your own making. You can't get it by what you believe, nor by what you do."

"Why?"

"Get a load of this word from the scripture: 'Because I (God) am accomplishing for you on my own what you could never accomplish. Hey, you probably wouldn't believe it, in the wisdom of mankind, if someone came and told you about it right to your very face' (Habakkuk 1:5)!"

"Yes, God has accomplished, in Jesus, righteousness for the entire world. He has done this without mankind's input, without mankind's approval, without regard to the merit of human accomplishment!"

"I'm telling you this wonderful news right to your face. Don't be so stupid not to recognize God's blessing as our forefathers did!"

TRIP # 8

24. DUST UP
(Acts 13:42-51a)

What? You think I could have been a bit more diplomatic? No way!

    I can tell you the synagogue was certainly a beehive of activity after my little speech. I could tell I had hit a nerve. People were whispering like crazy all around us. Barney and I tried to mingle throughout the congregation as folks filed out of the building. We were standing outside when a number of Gentile brothers approached us. They wanted to know if we could come to their meeting place to tell repeat the same message so they could here it too.

    Wow! Another speaking engagement? Fantastic! Wonderful! No problemo! Just tell us when and where. We'll be there!

    There were also lots of other folks who wanted to talk to us. Many of the Jews who had left the synagogue as well as other interested types started to follow us. They just wanted to hear more about this revolutionary concept. They persuaded us to continue talking about the grace of God for the whole world. Our logical and systematic approach to the revelation of God through the prophets must have convinced many of them. We could only encourage them to shake off the bondage of legalism and self-righteousness and start living in the liberty and abundance of the grace and peace of God.

    Man, the next Sabbath I think almost the whole city showed up to hear the word of God. Unfortunately, the sight of the multitudes touched a raw nerve with some of the leaders of the Jewish religious community. They apparently were choked so many folks were not only interesting in listening to us they were starting to believe what we were telling them.

    In the middle of a speaking engagement some big shot yahoos started to heckle us. If they intended to cause a disturbance, they definitely succeeded. It got personal and ugly as they started mouthing off, yelling out their displeasure, calling us every name under the sun.

    You must understand I'm a man with a relatively short fuse. I'm certainly willing to accept it when folks don't exactly take to what I preach, at least up to a point. I draw the line when folks get rude and nasty. Both Barney and I summoned up all the courage and boldness we could to put our feet down on this unruly batch of hecklers.

    "Hey, you guys, pipe down will you!" I yelled to gain their attention.

"I assume some of you Jewish brothers are having a slight problem with what we're saying. All right. Let me set a few things straight for you. It's been important we preach the message of God's word to the Jews first because you're the ones who should have understood it all along **but** the fact you couldn't, and won't, is your problem. Your very system of laws, rules, and regulations prove you don't consider yourselves worthy to receive the everlasting and abundant life God has given to you so freely."

"Alas, we have turned to our Gentile friends who are much more interested in hearing the truth of God's grace. If you don't accept our word, then accept God's word." He said, 'I've set you to be a light to the Gentiles so you should be the bearers of salvation to the ends of the earth' (Isaiah 49:6)."

"If you're unwilling to accept this task, hey, that's your problem! We intend to honor our commitment to God!"

Well, that about burst their bubble. A huge cheer went up from the Gentile crowd. They were pretty excited to see the Jews humbled by one of their own. They were thrilled mostly because they understood God's loving grace and peace was meant for them too. They had little trouble in accepting the reality and truth of the word of God. We had given them the message God had ordained "all" to receive the gift of His righteousness.

So, everyone got the drift!

What can I say?

Why would you want to argue with God's kind of love?

Why get trapped into the slavery of self-righteousness when the righteousness of God has already been granted to everyone on the basis of the faith of Jesus in the faithfulness of God?

Why indeed?

Let me tell you, word of this message started to spread like wildfire! The whole region heard about the gospel message of Jesus and were flipped out excited about it.

Perhaps I shouldn't have said everybody was happy about it. The Jews were downright perturbed and that's probably putting a mild spin on it. They couldn't seem to get past the jealousy that guarded their erroneous concept that God's privileges were meant exclusively for the Jewish community. They wanted to hog God for themselves. Sharing was a no-no.

DUST UP   TRIP # 8

They set about to stir up some pretty influential people in Antioch. There's nothing like going to the top and, as you might well imagine, many Jews held some rather important posts in the political, social ladder of the city. I find they used quite an interesting tactic of getting to the men in power. They riled up their women-folk.

The heat was getting turned up and we were starting to feel it more and more. Finally, a delegation of the mayor and his pals came to give us our walking papers. They, in unceremonious fashion, convinced us we weren't exactly welcome in their territory. They made their position quite clear.

"GET LOST!"

Hey, we could tell when we weren't wanted. Some problems we can do without.

What'd we do? Right in front of them we shook the dust off of our sandals so the wind would carry it right into their faces. We just couldn't resist the opportunity to bless them one more time. Ha.

Guess what?

On the road again...

25. ICONIUM
(Acts 13:15b-14:6a)

It was about ninety miles from Antioch to Iconium. The main highway from Syria to Ephesus goes right through Iconium, situated right in the heart of beautiful, fertile plains. Fresh streams flow down from the Pisidian Mountains nurturing the orchards of plums and apricots as well as the fields of wheat and flax. The city was as old as they come, many residents asserting Iconium was older than even Damascus.

To Barney and I it was just one more city needing to hear of the good news of Jesus. We were thrilled with how the word of God impacted the residents of Antioch and were hoping for the same results here. We were both completely in tune with the Spirit of Jesus within us. Our plan for this city would be the same as the plan for any other city we would visit. First, we'd go to the Jewish synagogue.

Initially, everything was going great. We had the great opportunity to speak in front of both the Jewish and the Gentile communities. With clarity we presented the gospel message so many of these folks came to understand the word of God.

Sometimes I think life is a bit like a coin, two sided. There's good and bad, happy and sad, well-off and not-so-well-off, acceptance and rejection, and there's belief and unbelief.

Well, Iconium proved my theory had credence once again. We met with great acceptance and also with great resistance. We initially saw great strides of belief until the horde of unbelievers couldn't bear the interference with their agenda of mind and body control. A revolt was provoked by some Jews who refused to understand the truth of God's love for all mankind. They not only stirred up members of their own community, they aggressively targeted the Gentile community as well. Even the minds of the Gentiles were spoiled against us.

For quite a time we were able to continue to speak out boldly about Jesus. We testified of the truth of God's grace and demonstrated the power of His might through the signs and wonders of God's kindness and generosity. Eventually, it became clear that the population of the city was divided in their opinion of us and of our message. Some preferred to believe the pronouncements of the Jewish leaders concerning us. Some, of course, could see through all the smoke of distraction and preferred to accept what we had to say as more legitimate.

ICONIUM　　　　　　　　　　　　　　　TRIP # 8

It came to our attention a plot was being hatched to take us out, literally. Hey, we've heard that one before too. It was true. The Jews hierarchy had resolved to have us exterminated and conscripted their Gentile counterparts to join in the plot. They obviously wanted to use us as guinea pigs to demonstrate to the masses what could happen when one crosses the line of order and authority. A public stoning is what they had in mind.

Well, that's not exactly the way I'd have picked to end my life. I had much better things to do with the time I had remaining. Barney concurred.

We're so out o' here! We're toast! History! Gonzo!

On the road, again…

TRIP # 8

26. LYSTRA
(Acts 14:6b-20)

Our journey would take us twenty miles southeast to the city of Lystra and the surrounding area of Lycaonia. We preached the gospel message to whoever would listen. I'll never forget one particular incident that occurred to us in Lystra.

At one spot Barney and I noticed a poor, lonely, and helpless man. We stopped to talk with him for a while and he told us he couldn't use his feet because he'd been a cripple since birth. This poor fellow had never walked before! Our hearts were definitely touched with compassion for this guy. All I could do was focus in on his gentle spirit. I perceived his faith was very strong, refusing to give up hope he'd someday be able to walk again, even if it took a miracle. I just couldn't pass up this opportunity to minister to his need. So, before I turned to leave, I looked directly at him and spoke to him in a very commanding tone of voice.

"Stand up!"

He was a bit stunned and bewildered by what I said. So I said it again.

"Stand up! Stand up right now! Get up on your feet!"

Wouldn't you know it, the guy just got up and stood there like he couldn't even believe he was actually standing. When he figured out he was it suddenly dawned on him that perhaps he could take a step or sixty-six. Before the victor could spout off "I'm going to Promised Land" he was walking and jumping around like a real trooper. Hey, it was so exciting to see it sent shivers up and down even my spine!

You can well imagine others were watching what happened. Some of them had known this poor chap for most of their lives. One minute the guy could barely move and the next he's jumping up and down like a wild stallion trying to jump an unnatural barrier to his freedom.

Very soon we were being proclaimed as some kind of heroes. The Lycaonians had a dialect all of their own you know. They all started to chant and wail at the top of their lungs. The strangest thing is they figured we were in fact gods who had come down to earth in the form of humans to do this good work to this poor man. "Zeus" is the name they decided to give to Barney. Me? Ha, they called me "Hermes."

Why?

Like most cultures, the people in this neck of the woods had their fables and myths that had been handed down from generation to generation. The people of Lystra were very well acquainted with the tale of Zeus and Hermes. Zeus was known as the "King of the Gods." Hermes was the patron "god of oratory."

Imagine that!

Me, the god of oratory!

Me and my big mouth.

Well, as the story goes Zeus and Hermes decided to come down to earth completely disguised so no one would recognize them. Undetectable, they'd see how mere mortals would react to them and how they would be treated. Unfortunately, they were treated with great unkindness during their stay on earth. They could find almost nobody in the entire land who would display a measure of hospitality towards them.

Finally, two old peasants, Philemon and his wife Baucis, took them in and cared for them. The gods Zeus and Hermes decided to wipe out the entire population because of their unkindness.

Of course there were two notable, hospitable exceptions, Philemon and Baucis, who were rewarded by being made guardians of a beautiful temple. To add a note of melodrama, Philemon and Baucis were turned into two great trees when they died.

The way I figured it, the people of Lystra didn't want to be the focus of another annihilation. They weren't going to take a chance we were just a passin' through with a hidden agenda.

Well, one thing led to another. Pretty soon the people were all worked up into a heavy-duty frenzy. Right at the entrance gates of the city was a temple dedicated to the worship of Zeus. The priest of the shrine decided it was appropriate to perform a ritualistic sacrifice to their great god. They started to bring in the garlands, wreaths, and fillets to decorate the sacrificial oxen.

When we heard of all these elaborate plans to honor us Barney and I got quite upset. Since ripping up your clothes is an appropriate response to blasphemy, we started to rip our clothes right there in the midst of their preparations. I started screaming as loud as I could.

"What in the world are you folks doing? Are you nuts? Just look at us. Look at Barnabas! Look at me! For Pete's sake, do you really think we are gods? Give your head a shake. We're just as human as any of you!"

I think I slowly gained their attention. I must have scared them a bit because they recoiled long enough to stand and stare at me. I caught my breath for a few seconds then continued to let 'em have it.

"We're here for one reason, and for only one reason. We're here to preach to you the best news you will ever hear. Turn from your empty, shallow self-righteous rituals to worship a vibrant, exciting, and living God. Our God has created the heavens, earth, oceans, in addition to everything in them. Throughout the history of mankind God has allowed all of the nations of the earth to go along their own paths."

"**But,** don't let that fool you. God didn't just stay up in heaven and hide Himself from mankind. Many different things prove witness to the fact God exists and cares for the whole world. He has given you rains from heaven, the seasons in order so you might be able to harvest your crops, and the time to enjoy the fruits of your labor. He has filled your hearts with nourishment and has enabled you to enjoy your lives here on this earth."

Well, that impromptu eruption brought a bit of composure to the situation. It took a bit of convincing, but finally we were able to get the crowd dispersed without all the hoopla of a sacrificial ceremony on our behalf. I can only tell you we were grateful to get out of that pickle.

Speaking of pickles. Guess who showed up?

Long before their arrival in Lystra the ambassadors of friendship from the Jewish synagogues of Antioch and Iconium had been planning our demise. The Jewish communications system surely is second to none. They obviously got wind of some success of our mission in the territory and were determined to stop us in our tracks. They really must have some high up connections. A full-scale riot was organized.

Boy, did this bring back memories. I once targeted heretics for this kind of event. Never did I think I'd become the target! Once again, I had to think back to the warning of Ananias that I'd have to learn how to suffer for the sake of Jesus.

Now, I have to tell you, did I ever get stoned! And they used those really big stones too. Man, that hurts. I wouldn't be surprised if they handed more than one rock to each of the citizens to chuck at me. I got just pummeled. It didn't take very long for me to lose consciousness.

The next thing I remember is waking up in some serious pain. Surrounding me was a group of very desperate looking folks who I vaguely remember from some our earlier discussions. Of course Barney was there. Somehow he had escaped the wrath of the people. With a number of other believers he had come to the outskirts of the city to rescue me. I'd been dragged there after the rock concert and left for dead.

Miraculously I survived without too much trauma to my body. Just like the lame man at the gates of Lystra regained his ability and strength to get around normally, I found new strength and energy to flee the coop as fast as we could.

The thought of back tracking didn't take too long to rule out, perhaps a second or two. No, we decided we'd better make our way eastward towards my hometown of Tarsus. The closest city was Derbe, some sixty miles away. So the next day Barney and I made our exit from the interesting city of Lystra.

Yes, on the road, again…

TRIP # 8

27. HOMEWARD BOUND
(Acts 14:21-28)

Barney and I both found the folks in Derbe to be quite receptive to our message. We experienced a great deal of liberty in preaching the good news in the area. I guess our Jewish shadows didn't have the time to pursue us down the highway. They must have been more than just a little ticked off to discover I actually survived their murderous plot. Anyway, our time in Derbe was encouraging to us in that we laid a foundation for these fine folks to believe in. We challenged many people to fellowship and believe together in the goodness of God's grace and peace.

    I have to admit we were getting pretty tired by now. I'd have preferred to head over the mountains to my hometown of Tarsus. However, we were advised against it. The desolate and treacherous mountains would be a formidable foe. Retracing our steps on the well-traveled highway was the only way that made rational sense. We'd just have to been very inconspicuous and stay out of trouble.

    One beneficial result of our retracing route would be the chance to revisit and re-challenge the many who had come to understand the message of Jesus during our initial visit. We exhorted the people with the reality the highway to the Kingdom of God had been paved by the faith of Jesus. Trials and tribulations were not barriers to a citizenship that was guaranteed. Struggles may interfere with the trip but they will never be able to take away the comfort and peace of living in the abundant liberty of the Spirit of Jesus within us.

    It was our joy to help the believers who wished to band together in fellowship to share in worship and service. We provided some assistance to appoint elders within each group to provide guidance and leadership. We always enjoyed special times of prayer and fasting.

    Revisiting the believers in Lystra, Iconium, and Antioch was a great thing to do. We committed them into the care and keeping of Jesus. We were most grateful they has seen the "Light," and decided it really did make sense to believe in God and His grace and peace.

    We made our way right through Pisidia all the way back to Pamphylia without a major incident. We had the privilege again of preaching the word of God in Perga, where we had started the mainland portion of our journey. We then went down to the port of Attalia where we boarded ship.

HOMEWARD BOUND   TRIP # 8

Our heading? Back to the port of Seleucia Pieria and on to Antioch our home base. Finally, we arrived back at the place where we had been set apart to spread the gospel message of the grace of God. The boat trip provided a welcome time of rest and relaxation for both Barney and I.

We were about at the end of our rope by this time. We had incurred blisters and fevers. We had been called names. I'd gotten stoned! But, we also had the joy of seeing many wonderful folks come to understand the works of Jesus. It was all kind of exciting and eventful by most standards.

Back in the safe confines of the fellowship in Antioch Barney and I recounted every detail of our exciting trip. Everyone was amazed at the details of our missionary adventures. They were full of questions about Cyprus, about John Mark, about the sister city of Antioch near Pisidia, about the lame man, and certainly about my rock'n'roll experience in Lystra.

God had opened up the door to His Kingdom to all people because of the faith of Jesus. It was our great honor to bring this message to all people, both Jew and Gentile alike. Our brothers and sisters in Antioch were thrilled with this news.

For the next three years or so we ministered in and around Antioch, teaching and encouraging the believers. We also continued to spread the gospel message of God's love to those who hadn't heard about it.

On top of this, there were so many Jewish brothers and sisters who were bound in the trap of legalism. There were still far too many Gentile folk who were content with the foolishness of self-righteousness at best, and downright ignorance at worst. We were convinced everyone should have at least the chance to alter their way of thinking.

The mission field was wide open.

That's a for sure!

Trip # 9
ANTIOCH TO JERUSALEM

28. TROUBLE MAKERS
(Acts 15:1-5)

Somewhere along the line news of our tremendous outreach program found its way all the way to Jerusalem. Our activities obviously were causing no small amount of controversy. I'm convinced believers in Jerusalem weren't really all that upset that Gentiles were becoming believers too. What they were ticked off with, however, was the fact they weren't becoming believers as per "their" laws, rules, and regulations.

One must keep in mind Jewish folks have always had somewhat of a superiority complex. Unfortunately, this character trait didn't just go away when Jews became believers in Jesus. They persisted in their assessment that God's blessing was, first and foremost, for the "chosen" people of Israel, and secondarily, for the Gentiles. The Gentiles would have to conform to the Jewish pattern if they wanted to participate in this whole thing.

Having heard all the reports, with a few rumors thrown in about the work in Antioch, the leadership was provoked into action. They came up with a very interesting and relatively easy solution to the problem that was becoming larger than they had ever dreamed possible. They chose a number of men as ambassadors to inform us "novices" about the rules of their game. They showed up on our doorstep both uninvited and unannounced.

We felt somewhat obliged to let them address the people. This is basically what they had been ordered to teach the Antioch believers:

"Unless you are circumcised, according to the instructions laid down for the Israelites by Moses, you cannot be saved!"

Well, let me tell you right quickly this whole idea went over like a lead balloon with Barney and I.

The nerve!

"This is ridiculous! Have they fallen off their rockers up there in Jerusalem, or what? Have they gone plum mad? What have they been drinking anyway? They're nuts! This edict is totally absurd and unnecessary!"

That pretty much sums up our initial response.

Needless to say, we ended up having a very heated exchange. It was obvious we were a long way apart in our understanding of the extent of the grace of God. We argued and disputed our positions until we were sick and tired of it.

It became increasingly apparent each of our positions were entrenched and these representatives had no authority to make any decision whatsoever anyway. They were merely ambassadors without any kind of authority to think for themselves. There was only one way to resolve this entire matter. Headquarters would have to make some kind of declaration everyone could live with.

Barney and I were chosen along with a few others to represent the believers of Antioch in a meeting with the apostles and the other leaders in Jerusalem.

Guess what?

You're right.

On the road, again...

The fellowship of Antioch sent us on our way with their blessing.

Our trip through Phoenicia and Samaria gave numerous opportunities to share the gospel message with Gentiles along the way. So much so in fact, all of us who were traveling together could hardly contain our excitement.

Upon our arrival in Jerusalem we were received cordially by all of the people in the fellowship there as well as by the apostles and leaders. It was very noticeable to us they were a bit surprised to see us there as a delegation. There was no mistaking the fact their representatives had failed in their mission to channel our activities to conform to their way of thinking. So, tension and apprehension meshed with anticipation of our report.

Barney and I took turns describing some of the highlights of our missionary trip to Cyprus and to the mainland cities of Antioch, Iconium, Lystra, and Perga. We also fully briefed them on the activities of the believers in our home base of Antioch.

We made no attempts to conceal the fact it was our conviction to carry on preaching the good news of Jesus to whoever would listen to it. That meant anyone, Jew or Gentile, man, woman, or child, young or old, and free or enslaved. Physical capability, mental capacity, race, sex, occupation or social status did not become a qualification for the grace of God.

Why should it become one for us?

People everywhere just need to hear they are loved and redeemed by a loving, gracious, and merciful God! People need to know the God who loved them enough to send His only and precious Son to bring them His righteousness.

Surprise! Surprise!

A group of believers found what we were telling them quite objectionable. They just happened to be Pharisees.

Now, I 'm quite familiar with the mindset of this particular sect of the Jewish people. You may recall I've been called a "Pharisee of the Pharisees." Perhaps I should tell you about this curious group of religious practitioners.

One of the main characteristics of the Pharisees was their legalism or legalistic fanaticism. Another characteristic was their incredible respect for ancestral tradition. What gave this strictest of Jewish sects its force and influence was their scrupulous adherence to their legalistic traditions. An emphasis on ritual purification and separateness, both personal and social, led to a caste-bound system that extolled exclusivity and superiority/inferiority complexes. The canon of scripture went far beyond the five books of Moses to include both the Prophets and the Writings.

It's almost contradictory to suggest that, at the same time they were very exclusive, they were very open to new ideas including those from other religions. Don't regard the Pharisees as quiet, pious, or without significant influence. It would be a mistake not to include them in the power groups who constantly strove to ascend the political and social power ladder of the Jewish people.

They interrupted our debriefing long enough to drive home their theological position.

"Look Paul and Barnabas. We have no problem with people coming to believe in the work of God in Jesus. We are, truth be told, most happy to see this and rejoice with you in your work. However, it is absolutely necessary for you to circumcise those Gentiles who do come into the faith of Jesus. Secondly, it is mandatory you instruct them to keep the Law of Moses."

Oh. Oh.

Now they've got two conditions!

Before, according to the declaration in Antioch, Gentile believers only had to be circumcised. Now, they also have to obey every commandment of Moses too.

What they were really saying was that, if we profess God has included the Gentiles into His plan, then we were obliged to command them to fall in line with the laws, rules, and regulations which bound the traditions of the Jewish believers. They felt they were being kind-hearted enough to allow them into the family of God. The Gentiles would just have to compromise and meet their Jewish brothers and sisters halfway by agreeing to their terms.

My. My. How gracious they were! Sorry to be so cynical. These questions just burned in my heart. Just who the heck do we (humans) think we are to put conditions upon the will and plan of God? It was His decision to love the whole world and His plan to make everyone righteous in His sight! How can we put our qualifying limitations on that?

Let me tell you, this matter was far from over!

TRIP # 9

29. JERUSALEM COUNCIL
(Acts 15:6-21)

I must confess the meeting did get somewhat ugly. It wasn't a pretty sight, or sound, for that matter. The distance between the poles of all-inclusiveness without limitations and all-inclusiveness with laws, rules, and regulations is horrendous. The controversy would not be an easy one to resolve.

    The apostles and elders who had met together were quite divided to put it mildly. The point in time came when someone needed to take command of the situation and bring some sense of order to the debate. Peter seemed to command this kind of respect. He rose to his feet and quietly started to pace back and forth in front of all the others, gently stroking his beard with his nervously shaking head. Turmoil was written all over his face. He motioned for the attention of the noisy, lip-flapping group. When he finally received their full attention he began to offer his opinion.

    "Please, please, gentlemen, lend me your ears. All of us know that a long, long time ago God made a unilateral, conscious decision to choose the whole world to be a part of His family. This good news also included the Gentiles. We all know they'd come to believe in the gospel message of Jesus when told of the good news. God in His wisdom and knowledge of the heart of all mankind gave to the Gentiles the very same Spirit of Jesus He has given to all of us Jews."

    I think you could about hear a needle if it would have dropped on the floor at this point.

    "Yes, God saw to it there would be absolutely no difference in His eyes between the Jew and the Gentile. He purified the hearts of all because of the faith Jesus had in the faithfulness of God."

    "So, why are we trying to change the heart of God? Why should we be placing a yoke of burden upon the necks of those who have come to believe in the graciousness of God? God didn't place any such burdens on our fathers, nor did He place any restrictive measures upon us. We shouldn't saddle the Gentiles with the responsibility and obligation of obeying the wisdom of mankind, with all of the laws and statutes even our own forefathers failed to maintain. The performance of our good works has never, and will never, place God in our debt."

"There is only one condition of our righteousness. The grace of God has been extended to us on the basis of the faith of our Lord Jesus. That's it! The whole world was saved because of Him. We've had the great opportunity and honor of believing this miraculous gospel message, and so do the Gentiles."

The audience was very somber.

Peter had spoken with a clearer understanding of the gospel message than I had given him credit for. I was very pleased to hear him speak his mind so eloquently. He encouraged his compatriots to listen carefully as Barney and I declared all of the miraculous, wondrous things God was doing as we preached the gospel message among the Gentiles.

After listening attentively to all we had to share, James felt it was appropriate he respond to our testimony. Many folks called him "James the Just" because of his reasonable and insightful approach to things.

"Gentlemen, dear friends, please listen to me for just a few moments too. Peter has spoken well of God's intent to declare all people, including the Gentiles, as His beloved children. Peter confirms what the prophets of old have said, for it is written,

'After this I will return and will build again the tabernacle of David which has been destroyed, and I will rebuild the ruins of this tabernacle to restore it to a far greater glory. Why? So all of mankind will search after the goodness of God, including the Gentiles, who also are my children because they bear My name' (Amos 9:11,12)."

"Remember now, this is the word of God. It is God who has done all of these things! God doesn't have to be reminded of what He had in mind from the very beginning of this world. He knows exactly what He purposed in His heart."

James was obviously setting his audience up for his conclusion. Compromise was evidently becoming his objective.

"I've listened carefully to all of your presentations. You all have eloquently spoken of your views and opinions about this very important issue. Here is what I'd like to propose to bridge the gap of our misunderstandings. There is no reason for us to trouble our Gentile brothers and sisters who have come to believe in God **but** we should write to them declaring the following requirements."

"The Gentiles should:"

1. "Abstain from the contaminations of idols."

What the heck is he talking about? Well, the sacrifice of animals in all kinds of religious ceremonies was certainly a very common ritual. However, only a very small portion of the meat of the sacrificed animal was actually used in the ceremony so a portion of the leftover meat was retained by the priest for his own personal use while some of it was probably returned to the offering party to be used as they so chose. It was also possible some of the meat ended up in the public market for sale to the general public. The rationale behind the pronouncement of James was to protect the believers from participating in a ritual that was inconsistent with their worship of the one, the only true God.

2. "Abstain from fornication."

In a world so overwhelmingly corrupt, indecent, and impure, the revolutionary idea of chastity and virtue would be a great model for believers to share with the world.

3. "Abstain from things strangled, and from blood."

I'd better speak about this one for a moment. Sounds gruesome, eh? Blood, if you didn't know, is very important to the Jews. Blood is life. Lose blood, lose life. Life belongs to God. When a Jew killed an animal for food, the meat was always handled in such a way that the blood was allowed to drain off. For Gentiles blood meant quite a different thing. They often time seemed to love blood. Perhaps I should say they were mystified by it. Blood was used extensively in the cults and their rituals. The meat of animals killed by strangulation was considered to be a delicacy. This was a massively repulsive thought to a Jew.

James was obviously expressing his opinion Gentile believers should be careful to show respect to the Jews by refraining from practices which would offend Jewish believers.

"Look," concluded James, "the claims of Moses and other prophets such as Amos, concerning God's love for all mankind are sufficiently safeguarded because the name of God is being preached not only in Jerusalem, **but**, in synagogues all over the world every Sabbath."

Trip # 10
JERUSALEM TO ANTIOCH

30. **POLICY**
(Acts 15:22-35; Galatians 2:7-10; Acts 15:22-29)

This conclusion appeared to resolve this issue for the apostles and most of the elders who were leaders of the Jerusalem believers. They were convinced this compromise should provide satisfactory closure to the whole deal. Consequently, they came up with a plan to get their decision out to the masses.

They chose two men to accompany Barney and I back to Antioch. I guess they figured we might screw up their decision. Maybe that's going a bit too far. I perhaps should say they presumed we might not care to relate the "whole" message. So they chose two men of their leadership who would go along with us to certify the findings of the Jerusalem Council.

One of the men was Judas Barsabbas. The other was a Roman, Hellenist Jew like me by the name of Silas, sometimes called Silvanus.

Furthermore, they concluded it would be safer if they would go one step more by putting their decree into writing. This pretty much sums up the contents of the policy statement they had adopted:

"The apostles, elders, and friends send their greetings to all of our Gentile brothers and sisters in Antioch, Syria, and Cilicia."

"It has been brought to our attention you were somewhat upset over commands given by some gentlemen who claimed to be our ambassadors. We understand they told you that you must be circumcised, and that you must keep the law in order to be saved. We'd like you to know we did not issue such a command. They were not acting on our behalf!"

"The appropriate course of action when we heard this discouraging news was to assemble ourselves together and come to an agreement to resolve this dispute. In order to make sure you accept our recommendations as legitimate, we are sending two of our own appointed leaders with our beloved Barnabas and Paul. You are fortunate to have these two dedicated men serving you. Barnabas and Paul have put their lives in great danger on numerous occasions for the sake of the gospel message."

"We value them immensely for they are a source of inspiration and encouragement to all of us. We're sending Judas and Silas with them and these two will acknowledge verbally what we have put in writing."

"It's a good thing to the Holy Spirit of Jesus in us to lay upon you no greater burden than these necessary things:
1. That you abstain from eating meat previously offered to idols.
2. That you abstain from eating meat from strangled animals that haven't been properly drained of blood.
3. That you refrain from the impurities of sexual immorality."

"If you are able to follow these guidelines we are convinced that you will be able to guard yourselves from causing disunity, disharmony, and controversy amongst yourselves, and your Jewish brothers and sisters in Jesus."

"Best regards. All the best to you and yours."

Now, don't get too excited just yet. Hold your horses. Don't think for one minute this was perfectly acceptable to me. I suppose Barney and I had to bite our tongues a little and let them come to a consensus among themselves before we waded in with our arguments against such a policy. They had their own internal problems without too much input from us. However, when they wrapped all of that up, we put our foot down.

We not only disagreed with this plan, we hated it. We made it very clear to them we were very much committed to a ministry to the Gentiles, to those of the "uncircumcision." As a matter of fact, it had been the leadership of the Jerusalem believers who were the very ones who sent us out for that very purpose. We were no less valid than the ministry of Peter to the Jews, to those of the "circumcision."

I made it crystal clear to the group of leadership the same mighty God who had accomplished absolutely everything on behalf of the Jews had done the exact same thing for the Gentiles. No amount of good works could accomplish what God had already accomplished. He needed no accomplishment or belief from anybody on this earth to make it happen.

James, Peter, and John finally got the message. These pillars of the Jerusalem fellowship finally got it through their thick skulls nothing was going to change our minds about this fact.

What changed their mind?

The way I figure it, they looked at me and recognized how much grace it must have taken for God to make me righteous. If this was the case, then God must have enough grace for the rest of the world! Ha.

Recognizing the truth of the all-sufficient and all-inclusive love and grace of God were the keys in helping these "great" leaders to see my point. You can't put any kind of restrictions upon anyone. God set all mankind free of the bondage of "do" and "don't." He set the whole world free from the slavery of laws, rules, and regulations.

So, what happened?

They stretched out their right hands to shake on it. Let's just say we agreed to disagree about certain matters. They suggested we continue to do "our" thing, and they would do "their" thing. We could continue in our work among the Gentiles and they would continue to work among the Jewish community.

Well, that suits us just fine!

Oh, there was maybe one more thing. They wanted us to at least remember the poor. In other words, they wanted our "money." I informed them they had already benefited from the generosity of the Gentiles in the past out of the goodness of their hearts. They could count on the sweet spirit of generosity in the future. This would be one point of intention we had no intention of altering.

With all the hoopla over, we did what?

Riigggghhhht.

On the road, again...

Yes, Judas and Silas did come with us anyway. We were very happy to have them come along back to Antioch. Our dear friends had been anxiously awaiting our return with news of the important decisions of the Jerusalem leadership. When we got the multitude together the excitement had built to a fever pitch.

Without going into details, we introduced Judas and Silas to the group who had assembled. We asked them to read the letter the Jerusalem Council had come up with. After they had read it, Barney and I took the letter and ripped it up into shreds, right in front of everybody!

I can only tell you that the crowd went wildly bonkers!

We had to quiet the room down from the howl of laughter and rejoicing. We figured they were owed an explanation. So we told them about all of the proceedings at the Jerusalem Council.

They went ballistic when they realized they were totally free of any and all laws, rules, and regulations concerning their relationship to God.

Now, Judas and Silas were no slouches either. Both of them were accomplished speakers in their own right. They wanted to have their turns at exhorting and encouraging the believers to press on in their understanding of the wisdom of God. They confirmed what we had been teaching to them. Judas and Silas continued to minister with us for some time.

At a certain point in time the fellowship figured they perhaps were desirous to return to be of assistance once again in Jerusalem. Judas accepted the opportunity with a tinge of happiness and sorrow. Silas, on the other hand, wanted to stay with us in Antioch. Perhaps his "Roman-ness" was enjoying the liberty of working with the likes of a kindred spirit.

So Barney, Silas, and I continued to preach and teach the word of God with many others too. We enjoyed a tremendous time of fellowship and growth! Man, we really had the best jobs in the whole world.

31. FIGHT WITH PETER
(Galatians 2:11-21)

I've painted a pretty rosy picture of life in Antioch. Yes, we did have an exciting time for the most part other than two incidents that I look back upon as being quite unfortunate. O.K. They were downright nasty at the time.

The first incident involved Peter. "Peter?" you ask. "I thought he was in Jerusalem?"

Yes, I am talking about "the" Peter, the "Rock" of Jerusalem. If I could pick a nickname for him it would be Rocky, although I'd never call him that to his face. Anyway, Pete showed up in Antioch for a visit. He must have heard about the letter ripping incident and thought he'd better check this thing out personally.

There is no other way to say it. Pete and I had a real down home face staring contest. It wasn't a pretty sight. Hey, he was dead wrong for what he did!

What'd he do? Well, things were going pretty well at first. Pete was blending in just fine for the first few days. He thought nothing of sharing with Jews and Gentiles alike including eating together.

Now, legalistic Jews had a real problem with something as simple as eating take out together, let alone fine dining. As far as some folks were concerned Pete was out on a dangerous limb as he sat around the supper table chompin' on some mighty fine eats hot off the bar-b with a whole group of believers including both Jews and Gentiles.

Well, it just so happened another delegation from Jerusalem showed up in Antioch, sent by our buddy Jim (James). This group must have included a number of prominent Pharisee believers. Remember what I told you earlier about the segregationist tendencies of this mind set.

To put it mildly, Pete got chicken, and I don't mean the bird we were having for supper either. All of a sudden he found convenient excuses to avoid any contact with the Gentiles whom he previously had no problem being around. He was obviously scared spitless Jim's spies would rat him out for his indiscretion.

We were just getting ready to eat when Pete must have received word these reps from Jerusalem were on their way over to the home we had gathered in to see what was happening.

FIGHT WITH PETER   TRIP # 10

Since Pete was a respected leader his actions had a very noticeable affect on the other Jews in the fellowship. It was bad enough when Pete got up to excuse himself from the table. But I got choked up when a bunch of other Jewish brothers got up to leave because of his lead. What really took the cake was when Barney actually got up to leave as well!

"Hey, what the heck is going on here you chumps!"

I yelled out to them as they proceeded to leave the table. The sight of their abandonment of everything they'd come to believe in was very unsettling to me. I wasn't going to take this sittin' down. I jumped to my feet, ran over, and blocked any possibility of Pete walking out unchallenged. He was going to have to withstand my verbal tongue lashing before he could pass me.

"You two-faced hypocrite! If you, being a Jew, have no personal problems with associating with your Gentile brothers and sisters, quite unlike many of your Jewish compatriots I might add, why is it all of a sudden you're placing our Gentile friends in the awkward position of having to suffer from the same legalistic crap Jews love so much?

"Peter, don't you see? You and I both know we, who are Jews, have a nature that is a by-product of our heritage, our destiny, and our way of life. We have a lot of spiritual baggage because of it. The Gentiles aren't like us at all. They never were bound up in the legalistic pursuit of self-righteousness quite like us. Why are you trying to put them under it now?"

"We both know a man isn't justified by the works of the law! We're justified by one thing, and by "only" one thing. We're justified by the faith of Jesus. Yes, Jesus had faith in God, and in us. Now we have the absolutely fantastic privilege of believing in Him."

"Why? Our belief allows us to accept the reality God has vindicated us. God has acquitted us, pardoned us, accepted us, and has removed us from the liability of sin. God has done all of this without any help from mankind. The futility of human effort, however strenuous to get 'right' with God, is thwarted by our natural weakness to accomplish the obedience to the works of the law. Nobody has ever attained, nobody is now attaining, and nobody will ever attain the righteousness of God based on their performance of laws, rules, and regulations."

"N O B O D Y !"

FIGHT WITH PETER   TRIP # 10

"Track with me on this one Pete. If we go back under the law seeking the justification of Jesus, don't we only place ourselves back under slavery and bondage of a religious system that merely points out the condition of man rather than a remedy for it? If we have to go back under the leaking covering of the law, then what becomes of the work of Jesus?"

"Would this mean Jesus would become a mere perpetuator of an inadequate system? Wouldn't this actually make Jesus not a savior from sin, **but** rather responsible for supervising our obedience to laws, rules, and regulations?"

"GOD FORBID!"

"Listen, if I try to rebuild what I've torn down, then I make myself a transgressor. Did you hear that? When I step across the line of God's love, when I step across the border of the grace God has freely given to me, when I deliberately violate the liberty purchased by the blood of Jesus, then I'm the one who has made myself a loser."

"Placing myself back under the bondage and slavery of performance is my problem, not God's! Hey, I finally got rid of the belief I had to "do" something to gain the favor of God. Why in the world would I want to go back? I'd be nothing short of stupid!"

"I know the law wasn't all bad. Hey, it had its place. I tried as hard as anyone to keep it. My life was devoted to obeying every single tidbit of the law. What I found was all my attempts to put myself within the favor of God produced nothing other than a deeper and deeper sense that effort will never be enough. The law was good to show me how helpless I was. That's all it could do, and is all it was ever meant to do."

"And nothing more!"

"And now, I'm dead to the law because God has superseded the law with His grace. God sent Jesus to replace the law with His mercy and grace. The life I live now is in God because He has initiated His peace."

"I'm no longer at war with God, for I'm no longer liable for my effort or achievements."

"Yes, I've been crucified with Jesus!"

"I am participating in all the benefits of Jesus' death, including the freedom from the bondage to laws, rules, and regulations. Look at me! I'm still here aren't I?"

"Of course I am. You can touch me, see me, and hear me. I'm alive just like you are. What makes the difference to me now is that I live in the knowledge and the understanding of what God has accomplished for me with His grace."

"I now live by the faith of the Son of God. I'm keenly aware my life has purpose because Jesus has put His faith in me."

"How do I know that?"

"Because He loved me so much He gave Himself for me! Can it get any better than that?"

"Pete, I don't frustrate the grace of God! If righteousness would come by virtue of our keeping the law, then Jesus died for nothing at all!"

I'd have to say everyone knew exactly where I stood concerning all this legalism stuff, as if they didn't know it before. Been there, done that. It just don't work. Why is it folks have so much trouble with this concept?

Pete should have known better too. After my little tongue-lashing I didn't think he'd ever question my understanding of God's grace again.

32. HIGH ROAD
(Acts 15:36-39)

Yes, this little incident with Pete left a lasting, nasty taste in my mouth concerning folks who just can't escape the slavery of traditions, laws, rules, and regulations. Anyway, I mentioned there were two kinds of ugly incidents while we were in Antioch. This first involved Peter.

The second confrontation was with none other than my best buddy Barney. Ya, that's right. Barnabas. Can you believe it?

Barney and I never lost the itchy feet syndrome. Free spirits like to roam I guess. We both were feeling the same call of the wild and would discuss the possibilities from time to time. We contemplated the pros and cons of retracing the steps of our first journey to Cyprus and to the mainland cities to the northwest where we had previously preached the word of God. It certainly would be great to see how the believers in Jesus were doing, especially since we had such little contact from them.

One of discussions had to do with personnel. Who'd go on this trip? Would it be just Barney and I? Would anyone else even have the guts to come along? Did we even want anyone else to come along? I was taken back a bit when Barney came up with his surprise recommendation.

"I think we should take John Mark with us again."

"Are you serious? Do you not remember we sent him back home from Pamphylia the last time out? We didn't want to put him in danger then, and I don't think it would be the best idea to try to do it all over again. Look at what happened to us the last time!"

We spent a great deal of time going back and forth over this one, that's for sure. We agonized over this decision. I thought we'd just agree to disagree, but it went much further than this. Our initial difference of opinion graduated into a full-blown argument. It became all too obvious neither of us were going to change our mind over whether John Mark should come along or not.

There was only one solution. Barney took the high road and I took the low road. Barney preferred to team up with JM, and the two of them sailed off into the sunset. That's true. They left one gorgeous evening for their home island of Cyprus. We all wished them the very best. Yes, I did too.

You know, it wasn't an easy thing. Barney and I had been through a ton together. He was truly a great friend. JM was also lucky to have such a great man as a companion and teacher. Hey, JM was a good kid. I just didn't want to go through the hassle again. Sometimes in life you'd like to do things differently if you had the chance to do it again. This is probably one situation I'd pick to do over.

But, milk does spill! When it does you wipe it up and you move on.

That's just what we did.

33. SILAS
(Acts 15:40)

It was only logical Barney and John Mark should set their sights first of all on Cyprus. This was their homeland and they were anxious to once again set their feet on familiar soil.

Since it was our mutual intent to revisit the believers where we'd previously traveled it made natural sense for me to head in the opposite direction, returning to the mainland of Cilicia to complete my portion of this task. I looked forward with great anticipation to this trip however I knew I couldn't possibly carry out such an assignment on my own. Who could possibly want to accompany me?

"Hey, Silas, are you up for a little holiday? How 'bout going on a trip with me?"

I'm not exactly sure what his first reaction was. Perhaps he was down right scared out of his wits. I doubt he regarded my idea of a challenge as a "holiday." In the time we had ministered together in Antioch we had become good friends. We shared a common belief in addition to a common understanding of the need to inform others of the incredibly good news of the gospel of Jesus.

Indeed, Silas also had great credentials. He was a leading believer from the fellowship in Jerusalem. Yes, this would carry a certain amount of weight when we approached the Jewish synagogues wherever we went. Silas was a gifted orator, skilled in the art of communication. When Silas spoke, people listened.

One other critical piece of the puzzle was that he was a Roman citizen like myself. I quite often referred to him by his Roman name Silvanus when it was appropriate. You know what this meant, right? He could certainly relate to the pervasive Roman culture we would travel in.

The other believers in Antioch recognized the amalgamation of our talents and abilities. They blessed us with their encouragement and support. They recommended us to share the grace of God with all those we came in contact with.

"Hey Si, get out your sleeping bag, a warm coat, an extra pair of walking sandals, your tooth brush, and pack your pup tent into your back pack. We're out o' here!"

You guessed it.

On the road again...

Trip # 11
ANTIOCH TO CORINTH

34. TIMOTHY
(Acts 15:41-16:8)

The first time Barney and I traveled into the regions of Pamphylia, Pisidia, and Lyconia we arrived by boat. This time Silas and I decided we'd go over land via the major highway running north from Antioch through Cilicia.

Why?

Perhaps the best reason I could give you was that, like Barney, I was homesick. Yes, the highway ran right through Tarsus. The stop over in Tarsus would be a great chance for me to see my family and friends once again. There were many believers in this area as well. So we had a wonderful time of getting acquainted once again, sharing moments of laughter, great fellowship, and best of all, some of mom's home cooked meals.

At this time of the year the road between Tarsus and Derbe wouldn't be quite as treacherous. You may recall Barney and I had turned back from Derbe rather than continuing via the land route through Tarsus to Antioch. We had a super time with the believers in Derbe. They were very surprised to see us and welcomed us with open arms. They had lots of questions for us and we shared every ounce of understanding we had, and then some!

"I already told you more than I know!" That's what I almost felt like replying sometimes when they lambasted us with their intensive, curious, and hungry hearts.

The same can be said of the believers we encountered in Lystra. Oh, I just have to tell you the highlight of our trip to Lystra. It was here we came to meet a super young guy by the name of Timotheus. Sounds official, doesn't it?

Now, Timotheus came from some solid stock. His dad was a big, solid, rugged Greek character. He was a hoot. His mom? Eunice was a sweet thing, as Jewish as you can get, a real go-getter too. She just radiated life. Pessimism and negativity never darkened the door of her heart. She probably got her optimism from her mom, Lois, who was the consummate mother and grandmother. Lois was gentle yet strong, quiet yet forceful, flexible and yet persistent.

TIMOTHY   TRIP # 11

Tim seemed to possess a measure of each of these positive elements of his immediate family. This was a tremendous family who were able to bring together two backgrounds, Greek and Jewish, melding the differences into a harmonious home. Eunice and Lois had become believers in the work of Jesus and they had done their best to raise Tim in the knowledge of God's love. Everywhere we went, Lystra, Derbe, or Iconium, folks spoke very highly of the family.

Tim was a very nice young man. I liked him from the get-go. Often, as I watched him, I saw him do things like I did when I was a youngster. My, that seems like such a long time ago. I saw a lot of myself in him.

I got together with Silas to suggest we consider taking Tim along with us on our trip. We discussed the positives and negatives and concluded it would be a great plan. Silas had no objections whatsoever 'cause He had also seen and heard excellent reports about Tim's character and ambition.

There would be one stipulation that would need to be taken care of before Tim could join our expedition. It would be necessary he go through the Jewish tradition of circumcision.

Silas went ballistic!

"Are you crazy Paul? You're serious, aren't you? You are going around telling folks they don't have to obey laws, rules, and regulations, and here you go making Tim go through one of the Jewish hoops too. What's going on? Why do you want Tim to get circumcised?"

Good questions, eh? Silas probably asked the very questions you'd ask. Well, good questions deserve answers.

First of all, I never said Jews shouldn't be circumcised. I said Gentiles didn't have to follow the Jewish custom as a qualification to be included in God's grace. I have no problem with folks maintaining the cultures and traditions of their race. Many traditions, laws, rules, and regulations have merit because they're good and wholesome. The fact they bear no consequence whatsoever to one's eternal destiny doesn't mean they have no earthly application or benefit.

Secondly, the fact I accepted Tim as a Jew just goes to prove how liberated in my thinking I was. Tim came from a mixed marriage. A strict Jew would not even accept this to be a marriage. Furthermore, if a Jewish boy was to marry a Gentile girl, or if a Jewish girl was to marry a Gentile boy, they would be considered, by a strict Jew, as to be no longer alive.

Dead. None existent. Toast. Persona-non-grata. If you can believe it, on occasion, a funeral was even held by the Jewish family to declare their opposition to such a union.

I just wanted to show how much I accepted Tim as a brother Jew and as a brother in Jesus. We'd no doubt be meeting with many Jews along the way. Some of them would become aware of the fact Tim was from a questionable marriage. The fact he had been circumcised would enhance his acceptability by the Jews along our missionary journey.

When all was settled on the home front concerning Tim and his parents, off we went through the valleys and mountains of Lycaonia, Galatia and Phrygia. As we had in Derbe and Lystra, we spread the news of the Jerusalem Council as we met with believers in Iconium and Antioch. We shared with them the exciting news that the gospel message of God's grace in Jesus was not bound by the wisdom of mankind. Jesus was to be the example of our commitment to serve the needs of others with an open and gracious heart. With thanksgiving they received this good news as they reported their growth in understanding and numbers to us.

The roads throughout the regions of Phrygia and portions of Galatia were fraught with danger. Bandits were famous, or perhaps I should say "infamous." Some of the fear I experienced on my first trip returned and it spread to both Silas and Tim. I have to say there was something very different about this portion of the trip. All of us felt a distinct sense in our spirits we should get the lead out as we passed through these foreign lands. We decided any attempts to spread the gospel message might just hinder our progress to get to wherever it was that we were going.

How does that sound?

"I don't know where we're going, but let's get there as fast as we can!"

Ha. Most of the regions of Galatia and Asia we passed through were unpopulated simply because of the difficult terrain.

We did, however, pass through a couple of cities, namely Sardis and Pergamos. Eventually, we arrived in the city of Adramyttium in Mysia. While there we contemplated traveling north over land to the city of Chalcedon in Bithynia, across the water from the great city of Byzantium. I don't know, maybe it was because we were sick and tired of walking such mountainous terrain we all nixed the idea.

We agreed it would be best to finish our trip in Asia by heading to the port city of Troas. Once there we still could make up our minds if we wanted to head towards Byzantium by boat. The alternative would be to consider a trip by boat over to Macedonia, or even to Greece. Man, even Rome sounded like a potential destination!

I'm not sure if you could ever find three happier guys to see the sight of water again. After traveling with all the temperamental elements one can encounter on any land excursion the thought of getting somewhere without having to walk was a very pleasant thought indeed.

Well, now some tough decisions would have to be made. Where do we go from here?

35. DR. LUKE
(Acts 16:9,10)

Troas was located on the shores of the Aegean Sea, opposite the island of Tenedos. It lay about ten miles south of the ancient city of Troy (Ilium). The city, built on an ancient site named Sigia, was founded by Antigonus, one of the successors of Alexander the Great. He named the city "Antigonia Troas." It was renamed "Alexandria Troas" by the Lysimachus king of Thrace around 300 B.C. where Seleucid kings even took up residence there for a time. For a while it was a free city and in 133 B.C it came under the control of Rome. It was so large and important even Julius Caesar had thoughts of moving his capital to Troas. It became one of the renowned cities of the world when Augustus made Troas a Roman colony.

Two rather significant events happened to us while we were in Troas. The first involved a dream that helped to decide our next destination. The second saw our little group add another member to the cast of vagabonds.

Let me describe the first event a bit.

One night I had one of those dreams so real it was hard to believe it wasn't. I was sleeping like a baby. The next thing I know I could see this dude standing right in front of me. We engaged in a brief conversation concerning the weather, politics, economics, and our health among other general topics. I told him where I was from and he told me he was from Macedonia. The other thing I remember is his begging and pleading with me to come over to Macedonia. Apparently many folks over there needed some help.

Perhaps the part I remembered the most was the urgency. He made it sound like there was some kind of emergency. I can't really tell you a whole lot more about the dream, but, when I woke up, this urgent plea was deeply embedded in my mind. Of course, I shared my dream with the Silas and Tim. We decided if we needed an excuse to go across to Macedonia instead of north to Bithynia, we could always blame it on the dream.

Why not? Maybe there's someone there who could use our help. Surely we had the message of God's love everyone needed to hear. We might just as well go there and start spreading the good news around!

The second event also proved extremely valuable to me. It was in Troas we came to meet a wonderful, compassionate man. After our difficult journey across the hinterland of Asia we thought it would be a good idea to get ourselves a medical checkup. The physician we went to see was none other than Doctor Luke. This gentle man had a heart of gold. He graciously tended to our aches and pains with tender assistance.

Naturally we talked. We told him what we were up to, including our commitment to share the gospel message of God's love with the whole world. He suggested we had an ambitious goal and wondered whether we could use a hand.

Are you kidding, man?

And this was only the beginning of a beautiful friendship!

TRIP # 11

36. BOAT TRIP TO MACEDONIA
(Acts 16:11)

Alexander the Great had accomplished incredible feats in his time. The remembrances of this great leader were everywhere. The complete name for Troas as I have mentioned was actually "Alexandrian Troas." Philippi, where we were now headed, was named after the father of Alexander. Thessalonica was named after the half-sister of Alexander. He once said his aim in life was "to marry the east to the west." Man, did he ever come close to fulfilling his dream!

Just think. Alexander in his lifetime succeeded in uniting an incredibly diversified range of peoples and geography into a single, dominant force in the known world. What power! What authority!

As we sat on the boat heading out of Troas I couldn't help but think of another man who altered the entire course of humanity. He accomplished this not only by his life, **but**, by his death.

Of course, I'm thinking of none other than Jesus! What absolute power! What incredible authority! Alexander, in all of his glory, didn't even come close to the matchless glory of the very Son of our awesome God!

If only we could help the world to understand what Jesus had done for the whole world what an incredible change could be realized in the hearts and lives of everyone. The alteration has already happened. People just needed to hear about it then they really could start living!

We had a great job ahead of us. When we left Troas the sky was a glorious blue and the wind was brisk. There's just something special about sitting out on the deck of a boat in open water, letting the wind blow through your hair. Every once in a while the water splashed up over the bow refreshing not only the body but the spirit.

Four islands dot the Aegean Sea between Troas and Neapolis. The first large island to the left was called Limnos. The first one on the right was the smaller island of Gokceada. Just northwest was another small island known as Samothraki, or Samothrace. The fourth, just before Neapolis was called Thasos.

Well, I want to talk about the little island of Samothrace because that's where we spent the first night out. We'd traveled past Gokceada on the right side and then moved in a northwest direction toward Samothrace. We pulled into the port of Samothrace on the north coast.

BOAT TRIP TO MACEDONIA — TRIP # 11

This was the kind of place you'd love to spend a vacation at. Beautiful. Just beautiful. Not only was the scenery beautiful, the people were gentle and peaceful too.

Because it was on a sea-lane between Greece and Pontus Euxinus (Black Sea), it became a very important center for travelers and traders alike. Four mountain summits hovered over the island. Mount Phengari, the tallest, reaching a height of 5,250 feet served as a beacon for the sailors who plied their trade on the Aegean Sea.

Poseidon, of Greek mythology fame, was supposed to have watched the battle for Troy from the lofty heights of Mount Phengar. The island at one point also held a very special importance as an international religious center, home to a famous mystery cult.

We didn't get to stay very long on the island. One brief night and that was it. The rest of the trip from Samothrace to the mainland port of Neapolis was very pleasant. All of us were filled with nervous anticipation of what lay before us.

Neapolis, since renamed Kavalla, was actually the seaport for the city of Philippi. Located about ten miles from Philippi, Neapolis was the eastern terminus of the Via Egnatia. A bedroom community, it was economically dependent upon Philippi. Many of the rich folks of Philippi had residences in this quaint coastal spot.

Doc Luke seemed to know lots of folks in Philippi. He was very anxious for Silas, Tim, and myself to meet all of his friends. He was confident we'd have no trouble finding a place to stay for as long as we wanted to.

37. LYDIA OF PHILIPPI
(Acts 16:12-15)

One of the great benefits of traveling is that one's scope of the world is enlarged. I found it fascinating to find out about the history and culture of each of the areas we journeyed into. Philippi proved to be another fascinating place.

Philippi was located in East Macedonia (Greece) between the Strymon River on the west and the Nestos River on the east. The city lay on a plain enclosed by a series of mountains, the coastal range of Symbolon on the south, the Balkan Highlands on the north, the Pangaion on the west, and on the east, the Orbelos. The acropolis of Philippi was on a spur of the Orbelos massif, with the city at its feet. The Via Egnatia, the ancient military and commercial highway, ran directly through the valley as well as the heart of the city.

The ancient name of the city was Krenides, which means "the Springs," no doubt a reflection of the many natural hot springs in the area. However, the father of Alexander, Philip of Macedon, renamed the town after himself when he fortified it as a barrier against the Thracians. Although long silent from over work, the gold mines of the area had gained a great deal of fame.

You might be interested to know a very famous battle took place near Philippi. In 42 B.C. Octavian and Anthony defeated Brutus and Cassius in the famous Battle of Philippi. The battle was fought just west of the city near the River Gangites. Eventually, Octavian was designated "Augustus" by the order of the Senate in 27 B.C. He had the name of the city officially changed to "Colonia Augusta Julia Philippensis." What a handle!

Philippi was just one of the cities populated largely with retired soldiers. As a payoff for serving their country veterans were allowed to settle in various cities throughout the land. Roman colonies were proud places. Philippi was filled with folks who wore the Roman dress, spoke the Roman language, and used Roman law to govern themselves.

Interestingly enough there was no synagogue for the Jewish people. They had an interesting solution for this problem. There was a Roman arch along the Via Egnatia about one mile west of Philippi. Just beyond the arch, symbolizing the dignity and privileges of the city, was the River Gangites. It also marked the "Pomerium," a line enclosing an empty space outside the city wall. In this space no buildings were allowed, burials were prohibited, and strange cults were banished.

Consequently, if the Jews insisted on gathering, they had no choice **but** to leave the city, pass through this colonial archway, and head off along the river.

"Shall we gather at the river?"

Come Sabbath, that's exactly where we found some of Luke's friends. What can I say? This group consisted of only women folk! They were seriously involved in their prayer meeting when we approached them. We sat down and began to engage them in some serious dialogue about God and their beliefs.

One of the women stood out among the small group. It was actually quite obvious she was unique. The way she dressed was enough to set her apart. But you know, it didn't seem to matter, not to her, nor to the other women. They had obviously come to worship and not to compare wardrobes. Lydia just opened up her heart to us. She drank in everything we shared with her. She accepted the word of God like wool sucked in dye.

Speaking of dye, Lydia knew everything there was to know about wool and dyes. She was a professional, sharp businesswoman if you ever could meet one. Lydia was originally from the city of Thyatira (Akhisar, Turkey). She was a seller of "purple" goods made in Thyatira. This purple dye came from a variety of sources. Once source was gathered drop by drop from a particular shellfish. Obviously, to color a pound of wool was very, very expensive. The guild of dyers in Thyatira were also well known for a color known as "Turkey red," made from a special madder root. To deal in these commodities required an immense amount of resources. I mean capital. Money. Cool hard cash. Well, Lydia was loaded.

It hadn't gone to her head though. She wasn't afraid of meeting with this small band of worshipers from Philippi. Although she worked among the elite she found the simple source of joy from meeting with these Jewish friends. She had been drawn to Judaism from her contacts back home in Thyatira. In the midst of the moral and spiritual drought she faced in her business life, she found a peace and tranquility in the pursuit of God beside this quiet river.

Luke, Silas, Tim and I met with Lydia and her family on numerous occasions to share of the great love of God. We held our first baptismal service in Macedonia by the banks of the river to commemorate the new life her whole family came to believe in. She was so grateful to us for introducing the message of God's grace and peace to her and her family.

With a generous heart of thanksgiving and a true spirit of hospitality she extended an invitation impossible for us to resist.

"Look fellows, I've been more than blessed. You've shown me I am absolutely accepted in the eyes of God. This is a most incredible truth. I'd love it if you'd come and stay in our home as our guests. You can stay as long as you like. I won't take 'no' as an answer!"

Well, that was the way Lydia was. She got hold of the realization God, in Jesus, had gotten a hold of her life and wouldn't let go. She wouldn't either. Lydia was not only to become our source of sustenance while we were in Philippi, she would be the greatest supporter of my ministry throughout the following years.

38. DAMSEL IN DISTRESS
(Acts 16:16-23)

Black and white. Day and night. Love and hate. Joy and sorrow. Sweet and sour. Complete opposites, right?

We encountered two absolutely contrasting figures in Philippi. I've already told you about Lydia. She was rich, mature and personable. She was attractive, caring, and hospitable. She was eager to hear about the love of God.

Then there was the damsel in distress. She was poor and irritating, ugly as a mud fence. This young lady had no interest whatsoever in God. If she found anyone who displayed any inkling toward the worship of God she'd do anything and everything to disrupt the occasion.

We met her for the first time as we were on our way out of the city to a prayer meeting. My initial impression was that she was a few sandwiches short of a picnic, if you know what I mean. I could tell, however, she was being exploited like so many other young, unfortunate women. She was very obviously under the control of some terribly unscrupulous men who were making lots of money off the fortune telling ability of this young lady.

It may sound odd but there was a strange attractiveness or respect for the mentally handicapped in society. You see, half-wits weren't all that bad for it was believed the gods were somehow responsible for their problems. It was the gods who removed half of the smarts department so they could take over the other half. Therefore, any fortune telling skills were taken very seriously since the forecast was apparently from a god.

Sounds like a good title for a movie.

Hey, perhaps the gods must not be crazy!

Now, this young lady was also very clever in how she spoke. You couldn't even see her lips move, tricking folks into thinking the voice was coming from somewhere else, like a ventriloquist.

They called her a "python."

This name was first applied to the priestess of Apollo at Delphi and later to soothsayers in general. Because the symbol of Apollo was the python snake ventriloquists were known as pythons. Perhaps this is why when you see a python snake it sends shivers of fear up your spine.

Now, this poor little thing must have recognized something very special about us. She picked us out of the crowds and decided we were worth her attention. For several days she'd hang out wherever we went. We weren't sure if she was spying on us or just very curious about what we were up to. For several days she tried to annoy and taunt us. She attempted to get the dander up of those around us by yelling out in a loud voice the following proclamation.

"These men are the servants of the most high God. They'd like to show you the way of salvation!"

I have to admit most publicity is a good thing. Yes, sometimes even the kind you don't request can be used to your advantage. The sad thing about this little python was not that she was telling the truth, but she didn't know how accurate she was. Those who had no knowledge or concept of the one true God usually referred to the God of Israel as "the most high God." Moreover, "the way of salvation" was also a very commonly used expression of the Hellenistic religious systems.

I felt grieved to set her straight. You know, I hadn't felt quite the same way since Barney and I met the crippled man way back in Lystra. Sometimes the heart becomes so heavy with compassion you just have to follow the impulse to act. She was oppressed and she definitely needed to be set free. Instead of ignoring her by walking right by her, I turned directly to confront her. I looked her right in the eye and without a flinch in my voice I spoke with boldness right to the core of her spirit of understanding.

"I command you, in the name of Jesus, get over it! You have perceived the truth, now I think it's high time you actually understand what you're talking about!"

Her jaw dropped to the ground. Well, not literally, but her faced was a portrayal of her bewilderment. She was utterly stunned to hear me speak with such authority and honesty to her and she took off like she'd just seen a snake.

I'd never see her again. It did come to our attention, however, that what I said to her impacted her greatly. We were informed she had been a prostitute of sorts, her earnings from her fortune telling business turned over to a serious conglomerate of mindless pimps. Within an hour of my challenge to her she came to the conclusion her life was in for a dramatic change. Her view of herself had changed to the point she understood she was going to have to look for another job.

DAMSEL IN DISTRESS   TRIP # 11

Unfortunately, I did happen to meet her "old" employers. They were ticked! They were very unhappy campers let me tell you. We found ourselves in some serious hot water and I don't mean we were caught skinny-dippin' in the hot springs either. These hustlers went to some trouble to search us out. They had a plan too. Silas and I had the misfortune to be in the wrong place at the wrong time.

All of a sudden they wrestled Silas and I to the ground and tied us up like we were poor little calves in a rodeo or something. We were hoisted off on their shoulders to the very center of the city square. They seemed to be insistent on settling the issue right NOW! We wished they'd have told us what their problem was without putting us through all this discomfort. They dropped us off right in front of the rulers of the court, who, with great pomp and circumstance, were conveniently in session conducting hearings on that particular day.

"What's your problem?" quizzed one of the judges of our mennappers.

"Hey, that was my question?" I was about to say when I realized I had better shut up and pay attention. I wasn't exactly in a position to command first crack at the proceedings.

The response wasn't long in the making.

"Your honor, these guys, they're Jews by the way, are doing nothing less than creating a major disturbance in the whole city. They are teaching customs which are neither lawful for Roman citizens to receive or observe."

I have to give these guys credit, if not guts. They were choked because we had obviously caused them some financial discomfort, taking out one of their star performers. How could they get back at us? By playing the race card. Racial prejudice is insidious. They were well aware they could extract revenge by appealing to the anti-Jewish sentiment of the crowds, and more importantly, of the judges. The pro-Roman crowds went wild.

Their enthusiastic scorn became the lightning rod that catapulted the judges into action. They started railing on their regal robes. I couldn't believe it. They charged the crowd to start beatin' on us!

Trust me, you don't ever want to experience a whippin' like we had put on us that day.

Guess what?

On the road again...

Oh my. Oh my. This was a much different road than I was expecting. The signs were completely different.

"Go DIRECTLY to jail!"

"Do not pass go!"

"Do not collect..."

39. JAILBIRDS
(Acts 16:24-40)

The jailer was given strict instructions to guard us carefully. He was charged to put us one step beyond prison! Inner prison! Now prison is undoubtedly bad enough. Having your freedom robbed is one thing. Treating you worse than an animal is another. We were literally thrown down into the dungeon, the underground facility far below the main prison area.

Lights? What lights? What's to see anyway? As if we were going somewhere important they shackled our feet into an oxen-like yoke of bondage.

So picture this.

Silas and I sittin' in a pitch-black dungeon with our feet shackled. What'd they figure anyway? You'd think we're some kind of escape artists. Give your head a shake!

Finally, we had some peace and quiet as the soldiers left us alone in the dark. It was so musty and damp in there that either we both fell fast asleep from the stench, or because we were so exhausted from the beating we had just incurred. Hey, at least we were still alive!

It was so pitch dark in there I couldn't tell whether my skin and clothes were so wet from the dungeon, or from the blood that had escaped my body during the ruckus. Silas and I tried to engage in a conversation about the extent of our injuries. I suppose we were still too much in shock to be too coherent. I'm not sure who fell asleep first.

Without any kind of light to give us a clue we had no idea what time it was when we awoke. What to do? Can't go anywhere. Might as well start prayin' and singin.' Now you have to know I can't hold a tune much on my own. Silas? Man, he's no vocal technician himself. So the sound of our incredible duet surely must have woken up many of the other prisoners within hearing distance of the terrible waves of sound emanating from us.

Oh well, at least it was a way to break through the deafening silence and eerie darkness. What a joke if it were actually midnight when everyone else was trying to get some semblance of a night's sleep. Ha.

The next thing we realized the prison walls were getting in on the action too. Perhaps they were trying to harmonize with our beat. Everything started shaking like crazy.

Earthquakes in this mountainous region are not all that uncommon so we figured that must be what was going on. The prison shook so violently all the shackles, stocks, and doors were broken open.

Confusion and fear had gripped the entire group of prisoners. We seemed to be scrambling around, but we weren't really going anywhere because we couldn't see where we were heading. Groping is probably more descriptive.

It didn't take all that long for someone to recognize the cell doors were actually wide open. Then the shouting and screaming started and all too soon we were all startled by the torch lights coming down the stairs. Obviously, the guard had been awakened too. As if anybody could have slept through the shake, rattle, and roll. His torch would allow him to survey the damage as the shaking subsided. He knew full well his life was in jeopardy if anything would happen to the prisoners. If anyone got loose he would no doubt pay a hefty price for his failure to keep law and order. The hefty price would be his life! I suppose the justice system thought fair is fair.

In his panic the first thing he could see was the wide open doors of every cell. He instantly presumed all his prisoners had escaped and pulled his sword from his belt so he could save himself the embarrassment and anguish at the hands of his superiors. Suicide was his preferred way out of this catastrophe.

The flicker of light from his torch gave me an indication of his utter disbelief and horror.

"NO! NO! NO! Don't do it!" I cried out. "Stop! Stop! We're all still here!"

How do you spell relief?

He yelled back up the stairs for more light. He plunged into our little cell and trembled to the floor in front of Silas and I. He was shaking like a leaf and crying like a baby.

"Come with me. Let's go up out of this dungeon to where it's a whole lot safer. Help me out here guys. How can we save ourselves from this terrible situation?"

Now this poor jailer thought he was just asking us to give him some advice on how to save his life from the potential catastrophe of his superior officers in getting us all out of there safely.

I sensed that's what he had on his mind, however, I thought I'd give him a better piece of advice concerning his eternal destiny.

"Sir, you've already been saved! Just believe it. Grasp hold of the reality that Jesus has saved you, and then you and your family can get on with living an abundant life you never thought possible before!"

Right there in the prison Silas and I had the great opportunity to tell this guard and all of the other prisoners the wonderful liberating message of God's grace and peace. It was incredible. Here we were in the devastation of an earthquake and we were sharing the good news of peace and happiness beyond compare!

Go figure.

The tremor of the earth had stopped and the turmoil of the moment within the prison walls had subsided. More guards had come to assist in settling the prisoners into safer quarters. Recognizing how much Silas and I had helped him just moments before, we came under the personal protection of the top dog himself.

In the middle of the night we made our way to his very own house! After making sure all his family were safe from the quake he turned his attention to care for us. He and his wife made sure all of our wounds received medical attention with soothing warm water and bandages.

While they ministered to our earthly pain we assisted them with their understanding of their eternal plight. Our jailer wanted his whole family to be told the message of good news. Then they wanted to be baptized! They had heard about this Jesus character, but never quite understood it before. Now it all made sense. Why not?

Breakfast! My, how time flies when you're having fun. Daybreak was upon us sooner than we realized. Now our stomachs were growling from hunger. This kind family took care of that. We had a great breakfast together sharing in the exciting understanding of God's love. We also celebrated in the miraculous way in which we were saved from the earthquake, not to mention from the slavery to our own self-righteousness.

I should really put a name to the face shouldn't I? The head jailers' name was Stephanas. Big and burly on the outside, yet with a soft heart on the inside.

Come morning we heard this racket outside and a rapping on the wooden door. It was a number of military personal who came with instructions for Stephanas at the order of the chief magistrates. Stephanas was instructed to let Silas and I go free. He came back to the kitchen to us to give us the good news.

"I've been instructed to set you and Silas free. They don't want you hanging around the city though. Just go. And quietly. 'Please.' That's what they said."

Now, I'm not sure if they just didn't have any room for us in the damaged prison or if this was a convenient way of getting us out of town without causing a major uproar with the general public who had incited our problems in the first place. Well, stickler for principle me, I had no intention of letting them off that easy.

I told Stephanas what I had in mind. Having a descent sort of humor he kind of chuckled as he called in the sergeants to hear what I had to say.

"Look, your magistrates have had us beaten without a proper trial in the first place. Are you aware we're Roman citizens? You threw us into prison without the courtesy of hearing us out. Now they want us to leave without a hassle? I don't think so. It doesn't work that easily I'm afraid. **But,** you tell them to come here and tell us to our faces we can go!"

Boy, if you want to scare up some heap of trouble for these judges just inform them of what they've done to one of their own. They could get away with if another race were involved, but certainly not if it were a Roman. They were in the very real danger of serious punishment themselves for what they did to us.

The sergeants ran off with my instructions like scarred jackrabbits. When they heard we were Roman citizens the judges started shaking in their sandals. Even they were not immune from prosecution and the likely punishment of death. The next rap on the door was from a scared bunch of political magistrates. I took a moment to relish the possibilities.

This sad collection of rulers began their song and dance with obvious discomfort. In all sincerity they made their plea for us to accept their apologies. They begged and begged us to leave the city for the good of everyone concerned. It was their desire to see no further harm come to us and expressed their disappointment things had progressed way too far already.

Well, what do you say? I figured we'd all been through enough. Perhaps discretion is the better part of valor. We informed them we would not soon forget their action, but we would agree to leave quietly after we had said our farewells to our friends. I'm quite sure they didn't see the smirk on either Silas' face or mine. They hustled away rubbing their hands knowing they had dodged a big one.

Thus our liberty from prison was accomplished. I can assure you being incarcerated for those few hours in the home of Stephanas was a whole lot more comfortable than the dungeon of the public prison! We were extremely grateful for Stephanas and his entire family for their assistance.

We left his home and went directly to Lydia's place. We were reunited with Luke and Tim and many others who had been shocked to learn of our arrest and torment. In spite of all our injuries they were excited to see us up walking around. We stayed in the safe confines of this wonderful family until we were healed well enough to make our way out of Philippi. They all took such great care of us.

Yep, on the road again...

40. THESSALONICA
(Acts 17:1-10a)

Okay. Add this up.
33 miles from Philippi to Amphipolis
30 miles from Amphipolis to Apollonia
37 miles from Apollonia to Thessalonica
---
100 miles Philippi to Thessalonica

Just a pleasant stroll don't you think? Let me tell you a little bit of history of these interesting places.

Amphipolis was actually the capital city of the first district of Macedonia. This beautiful city lay three miles inland from the Aegean Sea. The River Strymon curved around the city on the north, west, and the south. It got its name from Hagnon, son of Nikias, in 437 B.C., and it means "around city," referring of course to the way the river surrounds the city. In order to further protect his little dynasty Hagnon built a wall across the unprotected eastern side.

War played an important part in the history of Amphipolis. The place was known as "Nine Ways" when Xerxes crossed the river in his invasion around 480 B.C. Several Greek colonies were short lived in the area. In 497 B.C. a military leader from Miletus named Aristagoras tried to settle there as he was fleeing from King Darius. Unfortunately for him, he was not only driven out, he also lost his life. Some thirty years later ten thousand Athenian settlers arrived only to be dispersed by the Thracians.

The Romans divided Macedonia into four districts in 167 B.C. Amphipolis was chosen to become the capital of the entire area from the Strymon River to the Nestos River. Furthermore, it became a pit stop along the Via Egnatia.

Apollonia was a much quieter place to pass through. It had a wonderful view of the scenic Lake Bolbe just to the south.

Cassander named the city of Thessalonica (Salonika) after his wife way back around 315 B.C. It just so happens she was the daughter of Philip, not to mention the sister of Alexander the Great. Thessalonica was located on the Thermaic Gulf (Gulf of Salonika), and its natural port insured she would be the premiere port of Macedonia. Just as Amphipolis had been made a capital of the first district, Thessalonica became the capital of the second district.

THESSALONICA — TRIP # 11

The Romans allowed Thessalonica to remain a "free city," conferring on it the special status of ruling itself with a democratic constitution, complete with its own set of laws administered by its own magistrates known as "politarchs."

Upon our arrival in Thessalonica we searched for the nearest Jewish synagogue where we could begin to spread the gospel message. I made it a priority to go into the synagogue to try to reason with these fine folks by using scripture passages they were familiar with to show the intent of God's love for all mankind. I explained to the Jews it was absolutely essential Jesus had to endure the inhuman suffering He faced. I also shared with them the incredible reality of the resurrection of Jesus, stressing the good news gospel we were preaching to them was based solely upon the one and only Jesus.

I know I shouldn't show a great deal of surprise, but some of the Jews actually believed us! Unfortunately, so many of them are so enslaved by the laws, rules, and regulations which govern their every activity it's quite hard for them to understand the liberty of the abundant life in Jesus.

To top it off, quite a number of these believers started to hang out with Silas, Tim, Luke, and myself. They just couldn't seem to get enough of hearing such a wonderful gospel message. I must add we had a great deal of success preaching the good news to many of the Gentiles in the city as well. There was an obvious hunger out there for hearing something that actually made some sense. A great multitude of very devout Greek folks also came to believe in the grace and peace of God, including many of the most prominent women of the city.

Amidst all of the positive happenings in Thessalonica turmoil was setting in amongst those Jews who chose not to believe in the gospel message. They became terribly annoyed we were attracting so much attention. Envy and rage hooked up together to create a dangerous recipe for disaster. It was bad enough when just the Jewish unbelievers got ticked off. What made matters worse was that they went out and scooped up some other rifraf to add to the mix. These were a sorry lot of skumbags to boot.

Together they made for a heavy-duty concoction of civil disobedience. They were very successful in stirring up virtually the entire city against us. Some spies figured we were hiding out in the home of Jason, one of the believers who so graciously shared his hospitality and home with us.

THESSALONICA — TRIP # 11

A large mob was enticed to descend upon Jason's place in order to extricate us to be charged with public mischief or something.

Too bad, so sad. We weren't there! Unfortunately, Jason and a few of his friends and family were at home. The crowd clamored, ranted, and raved until Jason came out of his house. They dragged him and some of his friends in front of the politarchs of the city, accusing them of harboring fugitives among other things.

"Your honors, there are a group of men who are traveling around turning the whole world upside down. Now they've come to Thessalonica. This dufus Jason has even taken them into his own home. What they are preaching and teaching is completely contrary to the decrees of Caesar. They're saying there's another king, namely, one Jesus."

Well, if the crowds weren't riled up before, they sure were now. More importantly, the politarchs were choked. When they heard these accusations the rulers were incensed into action. They had Jason brought right in front of them. Since the evidence (us) weren't there, the best they could do was place a bond upon Jason. He'd have to guarantee there'd be no more trouble. He was forced to promise his guests would take their traveling circus somewhere else. When Jason posted bond the rulers let him and his friends go.

Needless to say, Jason and his friends were somewhat intimidated by these proceedings. They certainly didn't need the hassle. They were finally able to track us down at the home of another of their friends and advised us of the situation. We all agreed it would be best we simply get out of town. We had been in this situation before and there was no point in putting the lives of folks in danger. We were terribly saddened we had to leave, heartened to know many believers had come to understand the possibilities existing in the freedom of God's grace and peace.

Under the cover of darkness our little band of troubadours did what we were getting all too familiar with, running from trouble. Literally! On the road again...

41. BEREA
(Acts 17:10b-15)

Berea would be our next target. This quaint city was about fifty miles to the southwest of Thessalonica. The Via Egnatia went right through Berea, situated at the base of Mount Bermios.

News of the unrest in Thessalonica had not reached the Jews in Berea by the time we got there. We at once began to teach in the synagogue as we were given the opportunity. At least these folks gave us the courtesy of listening attentively to the gospel message. They were very astute, sharp, and perceptive in their understanding of what we were telling them.

For once we found people who wouldn't just take hook, line, and sinker what we were teaching. They actually questioned not only us, but, the scriptures upon which we based our teachings. This was great!

Many of the Jews came to believe the reality of God's grace and peace. Once again, as in Thessalonica, many of the more prominent, honorable Greek women came to believe. Men? Lots of men came to understand the work of Jesus too.

News may not travel fast, but it does travel. Yep. Word did get back to the Jewish community in Thessalonica that we were doing God's thing in Berea. Man, you'd think they would have enough to do in their own backyard without trying to disturb the peace in other places.

Nope. Couldn't do it. They had to stick their noses where they weren't needed. The disgruntled Jews from Thessalonica sent a committee to Berea to straighten things out. They caused no shortage of disruption there.

We changed our plans a bit this time around. It was decided I was the target of most of their anger. The best tactic would be for Silas and Tim to stay behind to be of guidance and assistance to the many new believers in Berea. There was just too much work to be done to help these folks on their way to liberty. It did not seem prudent to leave them to fend against a legalistic mentality that held such power.

Luke and I would head toward the coast and then travel to Athens by sea. This plan would allay some of the anger the Jewish nuisance factor would bring to the new believers.

Here we go, on the road, again...

42. ATHENS
(Acts 17:16-18)

Luke and I were accompanied to Athens by a number of believer friends from Berea. They had traveled the route on numerous occasions so it was good to have someone along to navigate for us. They also were able to introduce us to friends in the city of Athens we could stay with.

One of my first tasks when we got settled was to write a note to Silas and Tim telling them they should come to Athens as soon as possible. I gave this little note to our friends just before they left to go back to Berea.

The time in Athens while Silas and Tim weren't with me was very trying. Walking around the city of Athens stirred me to the bone. I just couldn't believe how much the citizens were given to idolatry. Idols here, idols there, idols everywhere.

Here's just a short list of various idols I saw:

- Zeus: the father of gods and men, (this is what they called Barnabas in Lystra)
- Hermes: the messenger of the gods, (this is what they called me in Lystra)
- Artemis: a virgin huntress and patroness of chastity,
- Aeolus: ruler of the winds,
- Dionysus: god of wine, inspiration, and ecstasy,
- Helios: god of the sun, and
- Poseidon: god of earthquakes, and of water.

Athens was a remarkable city. It derived its name in all likelihood from the goddess Athena. Another name for Athena was "Pallas." According to the legend, she sprang fully-grown and armed from the head of Zeus, who had swallowed her mother, "Metis" (wise counsel). Athena personified wisdom.

Strange isn't it? Here she was the namesake for a city that had very little wisdom concerning the love of God.

You could consider Athens to be an ancient city since pottery found in the area was said to date back to the late Stone Age, prior to 3000 B.C. Now, that's old! Remains of fortified walls indicate the Acropolis was a remarkable citadel of defense dating somewhere between 1600 and 1100 B.C., during the late Bronze Age.

The famous Parthenon was rebuilt during the administration of Pericles (461-429 B.C.) following the driving out of the Persians, who had plundered and destroyed much of Athens, including an old Parthenon. It was also during the reign of Pericles that the Temple of Hephaestus and the Temple of Ares were constructed. Strangely enough it was the Syrian King Antiochus IV Epiphanes (175-164 B.C.) who rebuilt a fabulous Temple of Olympian Zeus during the Hellenistic period.

Augustus (27 B.C.-14 A.D.) is largely responsible for the addition of many buildings around Athens. The people erected a small, circular Temple of Rome and Augustus on the Acropolis. The center of the Agora became the home of the concert hall named the Odeum, or Agrippeum. The most famous builder of the day was a man by the name of M. Vipsanius Agrippa. It didn't hurt his credentials any to be the son-in-law of the big guy, Caesar Augustus.

The great and massive columns of the buildings were incredible to look at. The construction of these facilities was absolutely amazing. While the facades were impressive, the spirit of the buildings was as cold as the stone and marble they were built with. Hey, I know people like that!

Speaking of cold stones, I deliberated with the Jews in the synagogues. There were also a number of very interested people who just loved to get into discussions about life and all its mysteries. I even spent quite a bit of time just talking to people in the market places who had nothing better to do but sit and yak. A few of the folks I encountered were philosopher types. Now there are all kinds of folks who exercise their mental muscles. Two of the more recognizable of the many groups of philosophy clubs were the Epicureans and the Stoics.

Let me tell you a bit about the Epicurean school first. This particular branch of philosophical thinking was founded by a man named Epicurus. No way! Yes way. This chap lived way back around 300 B.C. If you want to pick a word to describe these wishful thinkers it would be "happiness."

Here's a brief, simplistic synopsis of what these philosophers believed keeping in mind there's so much more I'm leaving out:
- Everything happens by chance.
- Death is the end of everything.
- The gods were uncaring and remote from the world.
- Pleasure was the chief goal of mankind.

Groovy, eh? Be careful now! Pleasure to an Epicurean didn't mean a physical, lustful, fleshly, or materialistic kind of pleasure. The highest and deepest pleasure was a happiness that left no pain in its wake.

The second school of philosophical debate I want to mention originated around the same time as the Epicureans, with the ideas of a deep thinker named Zeno. His main claim to fame is his contention that "nature" commands all conduct. Once again, let me give you a few of the tenants of this philosophy:

- Everything is God.
- God is a fiery spirit.
- Even though the spirit is in everything, it grows dull when it inhabits matter.
- What gives men life is the little spark of the spirit. However, when man dies, the spirit returns to God.
- Everything that happens is the will of God.
- Consequently, accept whatever happens to you as the will of God without resentment, and without reservation.
- Every once in a while the world simply gets worn out, disintegrates, and starts all over again in a similar cycle of events.

Now, even though these two philosophical mindsets appear to be quite different, the practical ethics of both schools are actually quite similar. "Happiness" and "nature" seem to combine elements of:
- "Whatever will be will be."
- "So what? Just let it happen."
- "No problem."
- "Eat, drink, and be merry, for tomorrow we..."

As I explained the gospel of God's grace and peace to folks in the marketplace I could see the inquisitive expressions on the faces of a few of these deep thinking philosopher types as they entered into hearing range of our little discussion group.

"So, what's this seed-picker got to say?"

Never heard that one before. Interesting choice of word to describe me, if I say do so myself. Another term closely related to seed-picker is "gutter-sparrow."

Do you know what that is? They were accusing me of being a "babbler!"

Of course this term originally referred to a scavenger bird, but in this case, they implied I was just a useless animal picking up odds and ends of a variety of philosophies and using them to suit my own ends. You could refer to someone who steals the ideas of another as a plagiarist.

Not only did they question my technique and my style, they questioned my content. Sticks and stones may break my bones, but names will never hurt me. What they cannot harm is the truth of God's love for the whole world. The message is true whether they like it or not, and whether they believe it or not!

"He seems to be the heralder of strange divinities!" someone blurted out after they heard me preach to them about Jesus and the resurrection.

Now, you might be able to take this kind of statement with a grain of salt. I didn't. Do you remember a man called Socrates? Let me explain it this way.

- The charge: "Corrupting the young men, and not recognizing the gods whom the city recognized, but other novel deities."
- The place: Athens, the court of the Areopagus.
- The time: 450 years ago.
- The accused: Socrates.
- His fate: DEATH!

Get the picture?

This was a pretty serious accusation I certainly didn't take sitting down. To these philosophers I had been extolling the virtues of Jesus, and the "Anastasis," the resurrection. For all they knew, I was preaching about another god and goddess.

Man, let me tell you, this discussion was just getting warmed up. We were going to go to the top with this one! They wanted to hear me out around a few wobbly pops and munchies on Mars Hill.

43. MARS HILL
(Acts 17:19-34)

It was known by several names. Some called it the "Areopagus hill." Some referred to it as "Mars hill." Others preferred the name "hill of Ares."

In fact, the name of the hill may have come from the name of the goddesses of revenge and destruction, "Arai," whose shrine was in a cave at the northeast foot of the hill. Rugged and jagged looking, the dominating structure of rock reached its peak at about 370 feet. Traveling from the northwest towards the south along the Panathenaic Way you'd pass the Agora first on your right. As you moved further along this major highway you'd pass the Acropolis on the left and the Areopagus on the right. The Phyx would be further on past the Areopagus.

It was an interesting walk towards this ominous rock. It grew larger and larger as one approached it. I had heard all kinds of stories of this famous hill. It was said at one time there were two stones on the hill. One was called the "stone of Outrage," and the other the "stone of Ruthlessness." The accused was placed on the stone of Outrage, and the accuser on the stone of Ruthlessness.

As we walked up the fifteen steps cut out of the southeast side of the hill I wondered which stone I might be placed upon if they were still there. The expression "between a rock and a hard place," came to mind as we came to the top. The chairs were rock-hewn benches. The important people seemed to get the best seats.

Now, it's important to note the Areopagus was not just the name of the stone hill. It also became the name for the group of special people who met there. They became known as the "Areopagites," or the "council in the Areopagus." They had met there over the centuries to disperse justice. At some times the council was given authority to hear cases involving murder. At other times it had the power to deal with more menial cases of legal, political, educational, religious, and public morality. Whatever the case, its power was never disputed.

One of the responsibilities of the current Areopagites was to examine the credentials of traveling philosopher types. They were the board of acceptability. They made it their task to protect the innocent public from the possible misleading of over zealous, self-seeking, aggressive, silver-tongued orators.

Almost sounds like a good idea!

As a Roman citizen, I must admit I did feel pretty secure in my position. Although a Jew, I professed a religion recognized by law. I would not be liable to any formal trial. At first, I felt threatened by the crowds and by all the commotion they stirred up. I realized I had been given a special honor to be among this council. They were actually giving me a tremendous opportunity to share the very same message of the grace and peace of God with the Council as I had with all the folks down in the marketplace.

The chairman of the Council stood up. Like a well rehearsed choir the crowd of witnesses came to an obedient silence. The voice of the Areopagite was strong and commanding as he posed his first question to me.

"May we know what this new doctrine you are preaching and teaching is all about? I understand you've brought a certain new twist we haven't heard in these parts before. I think I speak for all the others when I say we'd love to hear how you can enlighten us concerning your message."

You have to understand almost every Athenian spent the greatest part of their time either listening to or talking about the latest new thing to come along. They couldn't have known it would be a dangerous thing to give me the opportunity to speak. Give me an inch and I'll be able to stretch it quite significantly.

How do you win friends and influence people? Start with some good old fashion flattery. Ha. As I stood in the midst of an august assembly on the hallowed Mars Hill I began my assault of their philosophical questions about the true meaning of life.

"Friends and Romans, lend me your ears."

How's that for a start? No, this is more like how it went.

"You men of Athens, you give me great honor to hear what I have to say. In walking about your fair city I've noticed you are a very religious and superstitious society. In fact, you are probably even overdoing it. As I've observed all of the idols that seem to be the object of your affections I've found one in particular that caught my eye. I came across an altar with this inscription on it. 'To the unknown God.'"

I'd heard this story and I have no reason to disbelieve it to be true. About six hundred years ago a very bad pestilence came upon the city of Athens. People were dying by the thousands as a grave sickness passed over the people. Nothing seemed to be able to put the brakes on the death and pain the disease was causing.

They say Epimenides, a poet from Crete, was one who came up with a novel idea. His plan was that one flock of black sheep and one flock of white sheep were to be let loose from the Areopagus to disperse into the city. Wherever a sheep would lie down it was to be sacrificed to the nearest god. Cover all the possible angles I guess. However, if one of the sheep were to lie down near a shrine of no known god it was to be offered at that spot to the "unknown god." Interesting, eh?

"I find it incredible you don't even know who it is you devote so much of your time and energy in worshiping. Well, I know who it is. Let me tell you something about a loving, gracious, caring, and wise God. He's actually much closer to you than you may think."

"God is not some construction project of mankind. God is the One who has made the whole world as well as everything in it! You say your gods live in temples, altars, and idols. Well, God is the Lord of heaven and of earth, and doesn't need to dwell in any kind of structure mankind could build. God doesn't even require the worship of mankind's works as though He actually needed something from us. What a joke! Look, it is God who breathed life into every human being, into every living creature, and into all things. Who are we to think we could give generate something to supply His need?"

"I know you Stoics have a fundamental belief in the unity of human nature. Indeed, God created all the races and nations of mankind from one man. And since you believe each nation has its allotted era of prosperity and predominance, I think you'll find this interesting as well. God not only established the nations, He fixed the appointed times and the boundaries of their habitations here on earth."

"Why?"

"So they should seek after and find the gracious peace of God. He's actually a lot closer to each and every person than we realize!"

"Wasn't it your famous poet Epimenides who is quoted as saying 'For in him we live, and move, and have our being?' Another of your poets, Aratus, wrote in his Phaenomena, 'we are also His offspring.' Hey, by the way, Aratus grew up around Soli in Cilicia, my home turf."

"Why don't you pay attention to your very own philosophers? They've told you God is the author and finisher of faith. Forasmuch then as we are the offspring of God, why is it we think God is entombed in some golden, silver, or stone structure created by the artistic, creative imaginations of mankind? By creating mere images of mortal men and animals to represent the very nature of an almighty God mankind has traded away the wisdom of God for the foolishness of their own understanding."

"God has shown an incredible amount of patience with the whole world. He basically winked at the foolishness of mankind for a long time, **but** then God concluded He'd have to rectify a good situation gone sour. He knew the time had come to have mankind turn completely around to a new eternal destiny. You see, God had appointed, in His will, a time when He would judge the entire world. His righteousness would be declared for the whole world by the accomplishments of the only man, Jesus, who could fulfill His great plan."

"How do we know God succeeded?"

"God has given His absolute assurance to every being of His great love in that He raised this man Jesus from the dead!"

I've come to the conclusion there are usually three different reactions when folks hear something.
- Some folks simply disagree with the information, some even to the point of downright mockery and insult.
- Secondly, some people don't care. They procrastinate any kind of reaction thinking time is on their side.
- The third reaction is agreement, or at least recognition of merit in the possibilities of the new information.

My analysis of my declarations on the hill of the Areopagus left me with the conclusion I must have hit more than a nail on the head. I must have stepped on a few toes, perhaps even fingers. Yes, when some of the audience heard me talk about the resurrection of Jesus they could do nothing more than mock. When I was finished others came and told me this was a very novel idea and they surely wanted to hear more about it some time in the future.

As I departed the awesome site I found myself surrounded by some who recognized the truth in this teaching. Of the many who came to understand the true and "known" God of grace and peace I remember well the names of two in particular.

One was Dionysius. Believe it or not, I found out he was actually one of the Areopagites. Although the Council was comprised of perhaps thirty members at any given time, to have this intellectual aristocrat come to believe in the message of Jesus was marvelous.

The other was a woman by the name of Damaris. We spent quite some time teaching these fine folks the reality of living in the abundant liberty of knowing a God who truly loved and accepted them because He wanted to.

Athens surely was an interesting place. It was really too bad so many folks were looking for something to believe in, albeit, in all the wrong places. At least a few people got a new glimpse of reality.

Yes, indeed, on the road again...

1 ½ YEARS IN CORINTH

43. CORINTH
(Acts 18:1)

It was originally known as "Ephyra," a name that means "lookout" or "guard." Very appropriate indeed. The city was situated about two miles inland from the Gulf of Corinth on an elevated terrace at the foot of Acrocorinth, rising 1,886 rocky feet above sea level. Ancient Corinth reached great power and prosperity during the seventh century B.C., when Cypelus and his famous son Periander (625-583 B.C.) ruled. Pottery and bronze work monopolized the trade activity.

Rome wasn't only a destroyer of this city but also its restorer. In 146 B.C. the Roman consul Mummius captured, burned, razed, and plundered the city, however, a decree of Julius Caesar in 44 B.C. shortly before his death issued in the reestablishment of Corinth. Its new name was given to honor the new founder.

"Colonia Laus Julia Corinthiensis.

Impressive, eh! For the sake of brevity let's simply prefer to call it Corinth.

Location. Location. Location.

Just because of its location Corinth became a very key city of the area. The sea virtually cuts the great country of Greece in two, the Saronic Gulf with its port of Cenchrea on one side, and on the other side the Corinthian Gulf with its port of Lechaeum. In between the two ports is a neck of land less than five miles across. Corinth stands on that little isthmus. Any traffic that flowed from one end of Greece to the other had to pass through its gates. Corinth grew in strength to the time when she was called the "Bridge of Greece."

Corinth was not only known for its north-south trade route. It was also known for its commercial activity of east-west trade. There was a saying well known to all traveling salesmen and merchants: "Let him who thinks of sailing around Malea make his will."

Yes, sailing around the water at the southernmost tip of Cape Malea was very dangerous. Treacherous probably is a better description. The trip through Corinth therefore became the route of choice and necessity.

Many things stand out in my mind about Corinth. The main drag was the Lechaion Road running from the northern port right into the heart of the city.

As it approached the main agora the street grew dramatically in size. It was about twenty-five feet wide, with raised sidewalks flanking each side, and stores lining the walkways. Above the shops of the west side of the road was a large basilica, a great rectangular hall divided by two rows of columns with rooms at each end. To the west beyond the basilica stood the great Temple of Apollo. It had been built in the sixth century B.C. with thirty-eight columns that were about six feet in diameter, and nearly twenty-four feet tall.

Simply amazing!

A large open court was located behind the shops on the eastern side of the Lechaion Road. The famous Fountain of Peirene, a natural spring, was enclosed in this area. Many of the shops in the entire area were supplied with water from the deep wells connected with the Peirene water system. Many of the shops were drinking taverns in honor of the various gods.

On the south end of the main shopping district, the Agora, was the main theater. It consisted mainly of a semi-circle of seats facing a large stage building. From here the road carried on towards Cenchrea.

Other famous landmarks include the Spring of Lerna, the sanctuary of Asclepius, the god of healing. On the summit of Acrocorinth was the Temple of Aphrodite. In its hay-day the temple had over one thousand priestesses! It would be more accurate to say they were sacred prostitutes, and in the evening they came down to the city streets to entice folks to "worship."

"Not every man can afford a journey to Corinth."

This was a proverb with profound truth. Getting "religious" could be a very expensive proposition. If any actor played the part of a Corinthian in a play he played the part of a drunk. The people of Greece had a saying "to play the Corinthian," which meant to live a life of lustful debauchery.

Corinth was certainly a great commercial city. It was also a great sports city. She hosted the Isthmian Games, great games of skill and competition second in prominence and stature only to the Olympic Games. Like any great event these games brought into the city of Corinth many people of different opinions and aspirations. It seemed to bring out the best and worst of people.

Yes indeed, Corinth would prove to be a very interesting place.

45. WORK IN CORINTH
(Acts 18:2-17)

"Friends in your life are like the pillars on your porch. Sometimes they hold you up, sometimes you lean on them. Sometimes it's just enough to know they're standing by."

Fairly wise insight I'd say. Friends were very important to me. I met two of my very best friends in Corinth. Their names? Aquila and his beautiful wife Priscilla. One unique and precious couple for sure.

I suppose one of the things that unite friends very quickly is the realization they have something in common. We soon discovered what brought us so quickly together for we had more in common than we could imagine. For one thing we were Jewish. Both of our families had been tremendous examples of love and kindness. We also shared a love of traveling, they as business people, and I as a traveling exponent of the gospel of God's grace and peace.

We also shared the turmoil of being refugees. Aquila and Priscilla had been driven from their home in Rome by the Emperor Claudius who frantically attempted to rid Rome of all Jewish people. I, of course, had been kicked out of more places than I care to remember. Pilgrims for sure, but citizens of a everlasting Kingdom and brothers and sisters in an amazing family of God.

Our occupations also drew us together. Aquila and I were excellently skilled in the art of tent making. You may remember I grew up in Tarsus of Cilicia, well known for its famous goats with their special kind of fleece. A cloth called cilicium was produced from this fleece and was used extensively in the making of tents and curtains. My father had apprenticed me well in the art of working with this beautiful cloth, as well as leather, to make the best tents around.

No foolin.'

Aquila was also a master craftsman. I could see in his work a mastery of technique both unique and special. He really poured himself into everything he produced. He was an astute businessman to boot. Priscilla was quite a businesswoman and saleswoman in her own right. Hospitality was definitely a true part of their charm. They made us more than welcome in their own home. We lived together and we worked together. We had a great time. On weekends we'd try to reason with the Jews in the synagogue and through the week we'd interact with Jews and Greeks alike.

WORK IN CORINTH   TRIP # 11

I'd have to say a turning point in our time in Corinth came when Silas and Tim finally came to rejoin us from their stint in Berea. Perhaps their presence gave me the support to really get bold about the message of liberty from the bondage of laws, rules, and regulations that enslaved the Jewish people. I started to declare unequivocally that Jesus was the Anointed One they had been looking for through the centuries. My goodness, they couldn't even agree with themselves about what they actually believed. They not only started to badmouth the message of Jesus, they began to get nasty towards me as well, with language you'd considered to be quite, well let's say, colorful.

There comes a point when a person realizes they're just beating their head upon a brick wall. The harder you beat, the more it hurts. Sooner or later you have to either stop beating or you'll become black and blue beyond recognition.

I hit the brick wall one too many times! I ripped off my coat and started shaking it like I was trying to rid it of a batch of useless dust.

"It's high time you start taking responsibility for your own understanding of the message of God's grace and peace. If you prefer to live in bondage, so be it. I've tried to explain to you that Jesus has freed you from your tradition of laws, rules, and regulations. I prefer to live in His abundant liberty. At least I've tried to help you understand. Now it's up to you. I'm out o' here! I'm toast. From now on, I'll preach to the Gentiles who are a whole lot more receptive to the gospel message!"

Needless to say, quite a few of the Jewish folks were thrilled to see me go. At least they thought they were finally rid of me. I say "Nay, Nay!" Little did they know we'd set up shop right next door to them. In fact, the house actually touched the walls of the synagogue!

And they say I didn't have a sense of humor!

You got it. Titus Justus lived right next door to the synagogue! He was devout in his worship and praise of God for the fact Jesus had liberated him and his family. They welcomed us with open arms to carry on preaching and teaching using their home as a place of meeting.

To make matters worse for the Jews was the fact their leader, Crispus, the chief ruler of the synagogue no less, left with us! No kidding! The top dog of the synagogue himself flew the coop. Crispus and his whole family had come to believe in the work of Jesus and they wanted to worship with us.

WORK IN CORINTH   TRIP # 11

People all around Corinth were starting to believe the great gospel message of God's grace and peace. As they believed they wanted to be baptized to declare to the world the fantastic transformation that had taken place in their lives because of Jesus.

Oh, I have to tell you about another vision I had. I don't know why, but it seems dreams have had a dramatic influence on my life. You will no doubt recall this wasn't the first vision I've had. In my dream Jesus came and spoke directly to me.

"Don't be afraid to speak out. Go ahead and be bold. Don't hold in all I have placed within you to share. Never forget I'm always with you. Nobody can take this away from you. This city is full of people who belong to me!"

If I needed any encouragement, this little session did the trick. It strengthened my resolve to tell everyone we could the great news everyone was a part of the family of God.

My. My. How time flies when you're having fun. A year and a half of it! That's right. We taught and we taught some more. We proclaimed the word of God's promise to the people of Corinth at every opportunity. The time was not without its moments of opposition from the Jewish community. Let me tell you about one of them.

It came during the time Gallio was just assuming his role as the proconsul of Achaia. I guess the Jews figured they could influence him before he really got settled into his position. Gallio was to be appreciated because his kindness was legendary. His brother Seneca probably summed it up best.

"Even those who love my brother Gallio to the utmost of their power do not love him enough."

Not bad, especially coming from a brother! And he wasn't finished.

"No man was ever as sweet to one as Gallio is to all."
Wow!

The Jews formed a united front against me in particular. I must have a great big target planted on my back where I can't see it. My goodness. Perhaps the effectiveness of the liberty of Jesus was affecting their precious grip of control just a little more than they appreciated. Their malicious plot was prepared to bring me into disrepute. The Jews had me arrested and taken before the proconsul Gallio himself.

The charge?

"This fellow is persuading and seducing people to worship God, contrary to the law."

I was just about to open my mouth to refute this ridiculous charge when I was politely interrupted by the judge, Gallio. I was already starting to like him.

"If this were a matter of some crime or of some wicked misbehavior I might be inclined to listen to you. However, since it seems like you merely have a question relating to words, talk, and a law that is observed only by you, fix the problem yourselves. I don't have any intention whatsoever of getting sucked into solving your problems. I will not become a judge to settle your internal disputes. Now, if you will excuse me, I have other more important matters to deal with."

I was immediately released and the courtroom was completely cleared out by the armor bearing soldiers who guarded the court. Gallio wasn't one to be intimidated.

Sweet poetic justice ensued. It was the Greeks turn to seek some revenge on the Jews. They grabbed Sosthenes, now the chief ruler of the synagogue, and beat the crap out of him, right outside the very courtroom they had brought me to. Gallio probably didn't even know what was going on. I secretly hoped he didn't even care!

TRIP # 11

1st LETTER TO THE THESSALONIANS

46. HAPPY CAMPER
(1 Thessalonians 1:1-10)

When Silas and Timothy rejoined us in Corinth they brought with them, of course, news from the folks in Thessalonica. They greatly encouraged us with the good news many of the believers were continuing to grow in their understanding of the wisdom of God. Unfortunately there was also a bit of not-so-good news.

    The debriefing I received from Silas and Tim indicated a number of problem areas. Some of our teaching was being reinterpreted, causing a certain amount of confusion. Some of the fine folks understood their new liberty to imply they had a license to do whatever they pleased. They were right as far as their relationship to God is concerned. However, the necessity to work if you want to eat, the duty to obey the laws of the land, and the beneficial constraints in the moral realm place certain limitations on the freedoms we enjoy in the affairs of this world.

    Other folks were having trouble dealing with the fact they were free from their Jewish heritage of self-righteousness. They were dogged with the dangerous notion to slip back into the do's and don'ts of legalism. Misguided charlatans insisted the requirement to "do" something to be blessed of God was still in existence.

    Another unfortunate circumstance was developing among these believers that, by its very nature, was divisive. When people start following other people instead of Jesus they are headed for problems. It also appeared some people thought I was in the ministry for what I could personally get out of it.

    Ha! If they only knew. The last thing I wanted was for people to follow after me.

    Well, what to do? I really would have liked to have gone back to Thessalonica and set them straight again. I only managed to stay there for three weeks the first time and barely made it out with my own life. A return visit seemed completely out of the question.

    Basically, my first letter to the believers in Thessalonica came about as I decided the best way to respond to these issues was to confront them head-on with my thoughts. So, here's the letter I wrote to the believers in Thessalonica.

HAPPY CAMPER   1ST THES

From:
Paul, Silvanus, Timothy

To:
the called out ones in Thessalonica who are in God the Father, and in the Lord Jesus.

Blessing:
God has granted, by His great love, His grace. He has blessed you with something which you never could have attained or deserved on your own, His righteousness. In addition, He has blessed you with his peace. You no longer need to live in fear of His wrath or punishment. Jesus has taken care of everything for you.

    We want you to know we think about you often. We're always mindful to give thanks to God for all of you in our prayers. We'll never forget how you set your minds to work without regard to the reward of your effort.
    We're inspired by your constant desire to demonstrate the love of Jesus in everything you do and say. We understand you've shown incredible patience as you come to grips with the understanding all our hope rests in our Lord Jesus. This is what God our Father planned all along.
    Isn't it great we know, my dear friends, God elected to have Jesus do everything necessary for the whole world to receive His gift of grace and peace! This phenomenal message didn't just come to the world in the form of some words of promise, BUT, the word of God was backed up and reinforced with the powerful statement of the life, death, and resurrection of Jesus. And now, the Spirit of Jesus assures us all of the reality of God's great love.
    I believe I can safely state you were able to discern the kind of men we were as we came to Thessalonica. I'm sure you could tell we came to bring you this most exciting news for your benefit, not for what we could get out of it. I'm most pleased you made the decision to follow our example of believing in this wonderful message of God's grace and peace. Jesus is indeed the One whose footprints established the path to the very heart of God for all.

There's no doubt your decision to accept the grace and peace of God has been met with a great deal of resistance from many of those around you. Persecution and tribulation should not be unexpected. In spite of the opposition, you joyfully accepted God's free gift of the Spirit of Jesus within you, for He has liberated you from the slavery of self-righteousness!

Surely you are shining examples to all of those who have come to believe in this message throughout Macedonia and Achaia. You've done a tremendous job in sounding out the word of God not only in Macedonia and Achaia, BUT, also in every place your acceptance of God's love is spoken of. Your testimony has shone the beacon of God's light upon many. So many, in fact, we don't even have to tell people about you. It seems they already know about you!

Yes, for they themselves tell us of the incredible impact the message we brought to you has had in your lives. They describe to us the way in which you have turned to trust in God's provision for your lives, and how you've completely turned away from the idolatry of self-righteousness, from the idolatry of laws, rules, and regulations, and from the idolatry of trying by your own effort to gain the favor of God. We are so pleased to hear how you are now serving the living and only true God worthy of your honor and praise.

I'm also happy to hear you are no longer waiting in fear for Jesus to come back to judge us all. There can be no denying God raised His Son back to heaven, yes Jesus, the very same One who has delivered us from the wrath of God we all so rightly deserved. The coming of Jesus again in the future will only be a time of great rejoicing and reunion!

47. REAL DECEIVERS
(1 Thessalonians 2:1-16)

I want to assure you, dear friends, we don't consider our entrance into your lives to be in vain. BUT, it's not like we haven't gone through suffering and persecution before. What we faced in Thessalonica wasn't altogether unexpected. We were treated quite shamefully in Philippi by the authorities before we arrived to meet you. None of these things deter us from speaking as boldly as we know how about God's wonderful grace and peace.

I'm not embarrassed to admit the message of the gospel of God we preach causes a great deal of contention for those who hear it. No, our exhortation isn't meant to deceive anyone. There's no hidden agenda to promote impurity or irresponsibility. We didn't set out on this missionary journey to trick folks into believing in something that is untrue solely for our own benefit. What a waste of time and energy that would have been.

BUT, God has blessed us with the awesome privilege of sharing His gospel message with others. That's all we're doing. We have no ambition to please people, telling them only what they like to hear. BUT, we do have every intention of pleasing God for He's the One who has purified our hearts in Jesus.

I'm sure you can attest to the fact we never used, at any time, flattering words to entice you. Our witness was not cloaked in a covetous spirit craving to gain something from you, or from God. God knows the intent of our heart. The acceptance and glory of men and women aren't objects of our affection. We certainly didn't seek any glory from you, did we? Well, we haven't from anybody else either.

Sure, we could have anticipated and expected you to honor us in some way. Other apostles of Jesus may have been burdensome to you, yet this is simply not our style. BUT, we were very gentle with you, perhaps as gentle as a mother with her new born child. We poured ourselves out for you because we truly had a deep affection for you. We were extremely honored to be able not only to share the gospel of God with you, BUT to also share something of our very own heart with you just because you were very dear to us.

Surely you remember, dear friends, our work and travail. Yes, we worked day and night so we wouldn't place a burden upon any of you to take care of us. We gladly preached to you the gospel of God's grace and peace without charge. You are witnesses, as well as God, of how we behaved in your presence. I believe we acted above reproach, fairly, and without blame to all of you who came to believe in the love of God for the whole world. You know we exhorted, brought comfort, and challenged everyone of you in the same way a father would to assist the children of his love.

We challenged and encouraged you to walk worthy of God. My goodness, He's done absolutely everything for you. Why wouldn't you want to honor Him with your love and devotion? God is the one who has called everyone to enjoy His kingdom and all of the glory He has placed in them!

What an exciting message!

This is the reason we're so thankful to God. We can never cease to be grateful for He has accomplished what we could never have accomplished on our own merit, or by our own accomplishments.

Hey, you have every reason to be thankful too. When we preached this word of God to you it was received not as some goofy kind of creation of the wisdom, I mean the foolishness, of mankind. BUT, you received the word of God as the truth that it is. The wisdom of God is the only thing you have going for you. His word of promise has effectively worked to engineer the righteousness of God for all mankind. It's especially beneficial to those who believe what God has done, for they truly are the ones who can enjoy the abundance of the life of liberty in Jesus for the rest of their lives!

Hey, you're not alone either. What you're experiencing is no different than other groups of believers of God in Judea. All of you are in Jesus, and He is in you. You suffer the same indignities your fellow countrymen are enduring. The Jews continue to harass and injure those who have crossed the line of acceptability and control they've developed. Don't forget it was the Jews who had the audacity to not only kill Jesus, BUT who have had a habit of killing off many of the very prophets God has given them to reveal His truth.

Unfortunately, there are many Jews who want to continue this tradition by persecuting us as well. I'm sure God isn't too pleased with their ignorance. I'll bet there are a lot of folks here who aren't all that pleased with their stupidity either.

Me for one!

They take some particular exception to the fact we're sharing the wonderful gospel message with the Gentiles. They don't like it that we confirm God has saved Gentiles every bit as much as He did the Jews. God has done away with sin completely!

It doesn't matter who did it. It's gone!

THE WRATH OF GOD HAS ALREADY BEEN EXECUTED IN JESUS!

48. CROWN OF REJOICING
(1 Thessalonians 2:17-3:12)

BUT,
dear friends, being separated from you is the pits. We may be separated in body, BUT we certainly aren't separated in spirit. Although we've been away from you for a relatively short period of time, there's still a great desire and eagerness within our hearts to see you face to face again. All of us would already have come to visit you, including me, BUT it always seems something deceitful comes up to interrupt our plans.

What is our hope, joy, or crown of rejoicing? Surely it's the presence of Jesus within us. When Jesus came He came so the whole world would become participants and partakers of His presence in this world. I can only tell you that just knowing you believe and understand you're a part of the family of God, that you're our brothers and sisters in Jesus is almost all the glory and joy I can handle! The thought just blows my mind.

It was unfortunate we weren't able to remain either in Thessalonica, or in Berea for that matter. We decided it would be best if Luke and I travel on to Athens ahead of the others. When we left we instructed our brother Tim, a great ambassador of God and our co-worker in spreading the gospel message of Jesus, to go to you to establish and comfort you concerning your new found understanding of the wisdom of God.

Let there be no mistake. When we were with you we told you in advance we'd suffer the indifference and oppression of those who don't take too kindly to the free gift of God. Hey, we were right, weren't we? You know very well we ended up having our share of problems.

I was concerned the fact we had to undergo these tribulations would demoralize and depress you. I just wanted to make sure you were doing all right. That's why I sent Tim to you. It was my desire to make sure those deceiving dirtbags would leave you alone. I certainly don't want to see some stupid legalists manipulate and tempt you to return to the life where they control you by their laws, rules, and regulations. There's no way I want to see scum like this destroy the liberating message of God's grace and peace we labored so hard to inform you of.

BUT, we're thrilled to have Tim back with us. He was finally able to track us down, and yes, He made it back safely. He, of course, brought us the good news about how you're standing firm in your understanding and how you're pursuing a life devoted to showing love and friendship to others.

That's just great! He told us you still have fond memories of us, and you truly would like to see us come back for a visit.

So, amidst all of our concern and anxiety for your well being, Tim has come to alleviate affliction and distress by giving us such a great report. We take great comfort in what Tim has shared with us concerning your stability.

You know, the only way to live is to stand fast in the Lord Jesus!

What could we possibly be more thankful to God for? We're more than tickled pink God has included you in His incredible plan for the world. I want you to know that day and night we pray exceedingly that we might have the chance to see your smiling faces again.

It would be so fantastic to be with you again to share more of God's wisdom with you and to help you come to a more complete understanding of His grace and peace for all.

Could you dig it?

We can only ask God, Himself our Father, and Jesus to direct our paths to cross again in the future. We also ask the Spirit of Jesus within you to inspire you to **INCREASE AND ABOUND IN LOVE ONE TOWARD ANOTHER,** yes indeed, toward all men and women. Perhaps we've been an inspiring example to you also of tolerance and acceptance of all.

49. PERFECTLY HOLY
(1 Thessalonians 3:13-4:11)

I'd like to remind you of the great news that we taught you. God, in Jesus, has established your righteousness. You're now UNBLAMEABLE IN HOLINESS before God our Father.

And you always will be. Forever!

When did all this happen? Why, it happened when Jesus returned in triumph to God's presence with the righteousness of all He loved secured in His resurrection!

Is that good news, or what?

Furthermore, yes there's more, so much more we'd like to encourage and exhort you in the Spirit of Jesus to continue on in your walk with God. We've been privileged to get you started. The hammer is now in your hands to keep building upon what you already know. Nothing could please God more than if His children would abound more and more in the assurance of His love and unconditional acceptance.

I'm sure you remember well the teachings we gave to you concerning Jesus. The will of God purchased your liberty and freedom from the oppressive slavery of self-righteousness. Therefore, honor Him in return with lives revealing your sense of awe and gratitude.

Abstain from sexual impropriety. Sex outside the sanctity of marriage is a dangerous trip. Self-gratification is grossly over rated. Every one of you should know how to live in a sensible and honorable way, not in the lust of selfish, greedy, and pervasive attractions of sexual desires. Many folks, including the Gentiles who don't know anything about God, are prime examples of wasted priorities.

Be careful to treat your brothers and sisters with respect. There ought to be no reason whatsoever to go beyond the natural course of acceptance and decency to defraud someone else in any matter.

Look, Jesus is already the avenger of all. We've already told you about this. We've confirmed to you God has already acted out His vengeance towards the whole world upon Jesus. There's no longer a valid excuse for you to take out any vindictiveness you may harbor upon your neighbor.

God has not called us out to be loose and filthy. BUT, God has called us out to be holy like He has made us!

Take out your frustrations upon others if you must. BUT, you'll find the damage you cause has far more serious implications than you realize. The intolerance and disrespect of those who believe in the work of Jesus toward those who do not believe brings more disrepute and repulsiveness concerning God than you can imagine.

Why would anyone want to believe in a God you proclaim to worship if you can't even be a proper example of unconditional acceptance yourself?

God has indeed given all the Spirit of Jesus. Those of us who believe this to be true ought to strive to be the very best examples of God's love, His grace, His peace, and His mercy so others might come to understand and believe in the mighty God we serve!

BUT, as far as brotherly love is concerned, I don't think I need to write a whole lot more to inspire you. You seem to already understand the teachings of God that encourage and stimulate you to love others. Indeed, you're already putting a loving attitude into practice throughout all Macedonia.

All I can say is "keep it up!"

BUT, my dear brothers and sisters, don't become complacent and satisfied with your accomplishments. There's always more you can learn. Don't be surprised to find out even though you're holy and perfect in the eyes of God you probably have lots more to learn about just "being" perfect and holy towards others.

Aspire to live a quieter, more peaceful life. Slow down! Smell the flowers! Taste your food! Take a deep breath of air! Make it your ambition to pursue activities in your life at a sensible pace. We've always recommended folks should have fun getting their hands dirty. Work with discipline, sincerity, and a deep sense of contentment.

1ST THESSALONIANS

50. DEATH
(1 Thessalonians 4:12-5:11)

"There is hope for those who are alive, but those who have died are without hope." (Theocritus)

"Once a man dies, there is no resurrection." (Aeschylus)

Kind of a bleak outlook on the prospect of death, wouldn't you say? Perhaps this attitude is shaped by the total ignorance that exists about the goings-on after this life is over. Life is very tangible. Everyone can relate to life while death, and the beyond, are intangible. Nobody in this life can relate to death, at least none I've met.

The Thessalonian believers had concerns about the "after-this-life" too. Certainly we all can be buoyed by the resurrection of Jesus and the prospect this offers to all human beings. But is there any kind of instruction, any word of encouragement that can be offered for those with legitimate questions about this topic?

Absolutely! There's exciting news! There's great hope! There's great comfort!

Back to the letter...

I'd like to exhort you to walk comfortably and respectfully in the footsteps of those who've gone before you. I don't want you to lack of anything concerning those who have already died. BUT, I don't want you to be ignorant, dear brothers and sisters, concerning those who passed out of this life.

There's no reason whatsoever for you to sorrow or despair like those who believe they haven't a hope in Arabia of making it to the "promised " land.

Listen to this!

We believe Jesus died and rose again, right? Of course right! Well, everyone who died up to that point in time when Jesus rose again were raised to new life with Jesus by God!

So, what does this mean for all of us who are still alive until we get to meet Jesus when our turn comes up?

There's absolutely nothing we can do to affect those who have died, or will die. It is completely out of hands. There's nothing we can do to control it.

What I can tell you, however, is that you'd better be pretty happy about that. Why? Because God has determined and accomplished what mankind had no power to bring about. You see, God Himself descended from heaven with a mighty shout heard throughout the universe. The voice of the archangel accompanied the trumpet of God to proclaim the triumph over sin and death as Jesus rose from the grave.

Everyone who was dead had the incredible privilege and honor of being the first to rise to their new life with God and Jesus!

Wait! It gets better if you can believe it!

The same thing will happen to us when we die! Sure, when we die we'll be caught up into the clouds to meet together with all of them in the very presence of God and Jesus. Forever we'll be united with God. This wonderful news should bring releasing joy to each and every one of you. In fact, I encourage you to comfort one another with this incredible truth.

BUT, if you think I can predict the order and timing of everything you're grossly mistaken. I can't predict the time of anyone's death any more than I can predict the weather. There's no reason for me to write to you proclaiming something to you that I have no control over. There is one thing I can reassure you about. It's something that you already perfectly know and understand in your heart.

The day of God has already occurred!

It came like a thief in the night. It caught everyone by surprise! Some folks probably had concluded in the incompetence of their own minds they were at peace, safe in their own self-righteous accomplishments. Then, in one mighty act of God, the destruction of the work of mankind's obedience and adherence to laws, rules, and regulations rectified our total inability to gain the favor of God by our belief or merit. The miracle of God's intervention is not unlike the miracle of birth every mother experiences. A mother has the joy of birthing a miracle of life.

Well, God birthed the miracle of new life into every human being! Nobody has escaped the miracle of God's touch!

BUT, this shouldn't come as a surprise to you. You no longer live in the darkness of ignorance.

The idea God has wiped out any notion you have to "work" for your righteousness, holiness, and perfection should not, at this point in your understanding, catch you off guard.

You are the children of light now! You are the children of a brand new day!

No longer do you need to stumble and fall in the darkness of the night. The darkness that robs folks of their sense of security no longer applies to you.

So, don't keep on living like you've lost touch with the reality of what Jesus has accomplished on behalf of the whole world. Get on with it! It's too bad there are so many folks out there who still are asleep in ignorance unaware the light of Jesus has come upon all.

BUT, let's keep on our toes to refrain from any perversion and deception that would lull us into the darkness of legalism and self-righteousness. Don't get drunk on the perversions of laws, rules, and regulations. Stay sober with the assurance of God's provision in Jesus!

Those who don't believe because of ignorance, or because of stupidity, continue to sleep away their lives in the darkness and futility of their own foolish attempts to "do" something to get closer to God. Those who are drunk are drunk in the darkness of their own vanity.

BUT, let us, who live in the bright lightness of God's new day, remain sober to the truth of God's love, grace, mercy, and peace. Arm and protect yourself with the assurance of the breastplate of the faith and love Jesus has put on.

For a helmet of protection for your mind, put your solid belief in the hope of salvation God has given to you in Jesus.

Don't loose sight of this amazing fact:

GOD HAS NOT APPOINTED US TO WRATH!

He's over it. He decided not to go ahead and punish us with what we so abundantly deserved.

BUT, He did ordain us to attain the salvation of His righteousness by the birth, life, death, and resurrection of Jesus! It was Jesus who died for us so whether we're alive or dead, we'll live together in His presence, forever.

If this doesn't cause you to comfort one another I don't know what will.

Remind each other of this wonderful, wonderful good news gospel message of God's loving grace and peace. Edify one another. Build each other up.

I'm sure you're already doing this. That's great. Just don't stop.

1ST THESSALONIANS

51. LIVE IN HARMONY
(1 Thessalonians 5:12-28)

It's our ardent hope you will get to know those who labor among you, especially those who've been placed in leadership positions. Brothers and sisters, please give your attention to those who strive to help you understand the wisdom of God. Esteem them highly in love for the work they are trying to do. Do what you can to live in harmony with one another.

Dear friends, we challenge you to warn those who get out of hand in their efforts to bring confusion and disorder. Comfort those who are having difficulty understanding the concept they are free from the slavery of laws, rules, and regulations. Be a pillar of support to those who need a strong shoulder to rest upon as they oppose tradition bent out of whack. And for goodness sake, be patient with other folks. Everyone doesn't necessarily have the same capability of grasping the wonderful message of God's grace and peace and applying it as you might.

Don't waste your time trying to repay one bad deed with another. BUT, do your utmost to always seek the ultimate best for others, not only for your fellow believers, BUT, also for those who don't believe in God's love just yet.

Rejoice. You can never do this enough.

Pray without ceasing.

In every thing, just give thanks.

The will of God concerning you is that you wouldn't quench the Spirit of Jesus within you. Don't attempt to negate what He has done for you by persisting to attain to His favor by your belief, or by your performance of the laws, rules, and regulations of mankind. Don't turn your back on all the promise of God all the prophets told us of.

If you find this gospel message hard to understand, then good on you. There's nothing unnatural about this. Search out the scriptures. Examine the promise of God for yourself, and you'll discover we haven't been leading you down some delightful, mythical garden path we've made up.

Then hold fast.

There it is again.

Hold fast to the phenomenally good truth of God's grace and peace.

Abstain from all appearance of evil.

What is evil?

Evil is thinking your belief, or your good works, will get you anywhere with God. Legalism is evil. Falling under the control of religious perverts who want to control you with their systems of laws, controls, and regulations is what evil is.

Run from it! Flee from this perversion for there's nothing you can do to gain what God has freely given to you!

Why?

You already have it! You're already as close to God as you will ever get.

YOU'RE AS RIGHTEOUS AND HOLY AS YOU WILL EVER BE!

Let me say it again. The very God of peace has made you totally righteous, completely pure, absolutely holy, and wholly sanctified!

I pray you'd never lose the understanding God has purified your spirit, your soul, and your body. Because of the coming of Jesus you're blamelessness before God is permanently preserved.

Look, God was faithful to call you, wasn't He? Well, He'll also be faithful to His carry out His promise. You can count on Him!

My dear friends, remember us in your prayers. Greet all of our brothers and sister with a great big hug and a good, old fashion holy kiss. In the authority of God, I charge you to read this letter to all of our holy and righteous brothers and sisters.

Remember, you've been blessed with the grace of God and Jesus.

That's just the way it is!

Talk to you soon again.

2ND LETTER TO THE THESSALONIANS

52. GOD'S VIEWPOINT
(2 Thessalonians 1:1-12)

One of the problems with mail is that it's a one-way method of communication. In spite of noble efforts to express concepts, ideas, and information in a clear, concise manner, the printed medium lacks the depth achieved in a face-to-face conversation. At least that's the way I felt about my first letter I sent off to my Thessalonian friends. All I could do was hope they got my drift. I'm sure it provided welcome relief and encouragement to some. For others it perhaps brought some additional pause for questioning.

I'd have preferred to simply go to Thessalonica in person only it was just not possible. However, some folks had occasion to come to Corinth from Thessalonica and they provided us with some additional information on the status of the fellowship in Thessalonica, just as Silas and Tim had done some time before. It became obvious I'd have to respond to a number of inquiries once again in the form of a letter.

Thus the second letter to the Thessalonians came about. I trust you'll enjoy these insights into the immense love of God towards the whole world too.

From:
Paul, Silvanus, Timothy

To:
the called out ones in Thessalonica who are in God the Father and in Jesus.

Blessing:
God has granted, by His great love, His grace. He has blessed you with something you never could have attained or deserved on your own, righteousness. In addition, He has blessed you with His peace. You no longer need to live in fear of His wrath or punishment. Jesus has taken care of everything for you!

There's just something about you that binds us to thank God for you all the time. Dear friends, it's only natural for us to be grateful because it appears your understanding of the wisdom of God continues to grow day by day. We also are aware of the noble efforts of charity and kindness you're demonstrating to many others all around you. We brag to other fellowships that believe in God about your patience and trust in the faithfulness of God as you endure persecution and oppression for what you believe.

Your stability confirms the righteous assessment of God's love for all mankind. God knew His grace and peace were accurately placed in His creation. His love saw the whole world as being worthy of being included in the family of God. Coming to belief in this profound wisdom of God has no doubt caused frustration and anxiety in others and they are, unfortunately, taking their anger out on you.

Never forget God has already vented His frustration and justice out upon entire world, yes, even to those who seek to do you harm. Look, I want those of you who are perplexed and troubled over the hardships you are enduring to come to the same sense of contentment and assurance we have come to.

GOD KNEW WHAT HE WAS DOING.

He recognized the inability of mankind to attain to His righteousness on their own. He knew it would take the revelation of Jesus from heaven to get the job done. God realized He would have to send His mighty angels in flaming fire to avenge His justice upon those who didn't know Him, and even upon those who wouldn't believe in the gospel message of Jesus. There would be no other hope for them.

What mankind really deserved was a punishment of everlasting destruction from the presence of God and from the glory of His power!

BUT, because of what God has done through Jesus, He came to be glorified in everyone who was made righteous saints in Him, and especially admired by those who actually believe what He has done. I'm so happy we were able to tell you about the incredible day when God changed the eternal destiny of humanity in that incredible day of the cross. I'm thankful you believed our testimony about the gift of grace and peace of God that He has distributed to all.

This is the very reason we pray always for you. We find it incredible God would count all of us worthy of His calling. We can't help being overwhelmed with the knowledge God fulfilled all the good pleasure of His goodness towards mankind. He concluded His work of faith with power beyond description.

Why?

So the name of Jesus would be glorified in all.

And that's only the half of it. The other half is that the name of the whole world would be glorified in Jesus!

It works both ways. All of this is according to the grace of our God and Jesus!

2ND THESSALONIANS

53. DAY OF THE LORD
(2 Thessalonians 2:1-17)

Now, we plead with you, dear friends, in the knowledge and understanding of the surety Jesus has come already and by the very fact the whole world has been united with Him, stand fast in what you believe.

Don't be so soon shaken in your minds to accept the deceptions of others. Don't be troubled by the controlling attitudes of others, or by the deceitful words of charlatans, or by copycat type letters which purport to originate from us.

What will they try to convince you of? They will attempt to deceive you into thinking the day of Jesus is yet to come in the future.

That's right. There are some people who'll use every means possible to convince you the day of Jesus will not come until certain conditions have been met.

What conditions?

- There's going to have to be a falling away of mankind from the pursuit of a relationship with God.
- A man of sin would have to be revealed. This "son of perdition" would ultimately have to be exposed for the evil he represents. He will be one who opposes everything God represents. He will try to exalt himself above even God Himself, or anything that is worshipped by anyone. He will attempt to suck people into thinking he is actually God who sits in the temple of his own creation. Yes, he will really actually think he is God!

Well, don't buy into this deception. Don't you remember when I was still with you I told you about these things? Now you know the truth about the wisdom of God's plan. Now you have an understanding of why God patiently waited for the right time to introduce Himself to the world in a completely new way in Jesus.

You see, the mystery of iniquity had plenty of time to show its ugly head. God showed incredible patience with the self-righteousness attitude and perversions of mankind's wisdom, a wisdom that should actually be called foolishness.

It became very evident the performance based systems of laws, rules, and regulations would never be successful in actually achieving the acceptance of God. God stepped into the picture to reveal His original plan.

Jesus was God's way of taking the belief and performance of mankind out the way completely. Jesus exposed the wickedness of mankind's attempts at self-righteousness. God consumed the spirit of legalism as well as the vanity of human achievement.

How?

With the fulfillment of the word of promise He uttered with His mouth to our forefathers. In one glorious stroke the brilliance of the coming of Jesus destroyed the darkness of the perverted notions of human aspirations.

Jesus!

Yes, Jesus. Even Him.

His coming came at the conclusion of the reign of deception and fraud of the wisdom of mankind. The power of mankind took its toll. So did all of the mighty works humans thought would get them somewhere with God. Even all the wonderful accomplishments of mankind were nothing more than lies. People actually went to their graves deceived into thinking righteousness was something worth striving for, even though unattainable.

Unfortunately, they'd been fed a miserable lie all their lives. They never were told the love of God was the only truth out there. They've never been told they had been redeemed by the love of God all along!

God permitted this strong delusion to go along for some time. He allowed mankind to continue to believe in and perpetuate the lie of self-righteousness.

Why?

So folks would come to the conclusion they couldn't get the favor of God by their accomplishments. God hoped mankind would come to the realization they could never be good enough on their own, and ultimately accept the gift of God's grace and peace on His terms. Mankind couldn't even understand getting something for free from God was in their best interest.

Go figure!

BUT, folks stooped so low they actually took pleasure in their unrighteousness.

BUT, we are bound to give thanks always to God for all of you. Everyone is our beloved brother and sister in God.

Why?

Because God has from the very beginning chosen all mankind to receive His righteousness through the complete transformation of their spirit into the Spirit of Jesus. You can believe in this wonderful truth whereby He has called all by the gospel message of His grace and peace so all would obtain the glory of Jesus!

Therefore, dear friends, stand fast. There it is again. STAND FAST!

Remain utterly committed to this heritage of truth we've taught you, whether from our own lips, or from the letters we've written to you.

Now, our Lord Jesus Himself, and God, even our Father, who has loved us beyond compare, and has given all an everlasting consolation and good hope through His grace, comfort your hearts and establish you to continue in every good word and deed for the right reasons. Say and do everything, not to gain something from God. You already have everything you could get from Him.

Say and do everything to show your gratitude and abundant pleasure of your liberty He has given to you.

54. LIVE IN PEACE
(2 Thessalonians 3:1-18)

Finally, my dear friends, please pray for us that the word of God may be received and accepted to the honor and glory of God, even as it has been with you. Pray also that we may be delivered from intolerant, unreasonable, and deceitful men.

Let's face it, there are many folks out there who just haven't heard about God and many others who truly want nothing to do with Him, for just as many reasons.

BUT, there's one undeniable, unchangeable fact: GOD IS FAITHFUL!

Yes, God has established righteousness for all. It's God who abolished the need for the whole world to pursue the evil of legalism and self-righteousness with its controls of laws, rules, and regulations. We have absolute confidence God has also engineered this remarkable miracle for you as well.

We're sure you're already enjoying the benefits of this liberty and will continue to do so. It's imperative you continue to progress in your understanding of the wisdom of God by adhering to the things we've taught you. God has directed your hearts into the very love of God and into the patient Spirit of Jesus within you.

Brothers and sisters, I'd like to charge you, in the name of Jesus, to withdraw yourselves from those who persist in walking in the disorderly pursuit of legalism. These folks are the ones who simply do not want to step into the liberty of God's grace and peace we've proclaimed to you. Look, you know what we've told you about laws, rules, and regulations, and what we've told you to do with them.

Did we come to you preaching anarchy and disorder?
Of course not.

You know very well we didn't accept free food from anyone. BUT, we worked day and night so we wouldn't become a hardship to any of you. We probably had every right to expect some kind of remuneration from you for what we did for you. Instead, we tried to show you liberty doesn't imply irresponsibility, carelessness, insensitivity, or injustice. BUT, hopefully we gave you an example to be grateful, diligent, and caring, open and tolerantly acceptable of others.

For even when we were with you we taught a very basic principle of life: "No work, No eat!"

It's come to our attention some of you have become somewhat, let's say disruptive, because you've come to the conclusion God has blessed you with grace and peace and now there's nothing left for you to do BUT to become busy-bodies and nuisances.

Well, get over it!

Once again, to those who are indulging in the disorderly conduct of legalism, as well as in the disgusting misrepresentation of liberty, we command and exhort you, in the authority of Jesus, "Smarten up!"

Life is full of responsibilities. You have the joy to fulfill your share. Don't waste all your time waiting for someone else to fill your face. Life isn't some big handout line, dispensing your every want or need. Do your part to make your own way.

BUT, my dear, dear friends, don't ever get tired of doing well.

If by chance there are those who don't heed the exhortations of this letter, make a note of them. Don't go out of your way to spend a whole lot of time with them. Hopefully the disgrace will cause them to be ashamed of themselves. Be careful now, I didn't say you should make them your enemy.

BUT, perhaps I should have said treat them like you would a brother or sister! I know this may be a scary thought for some of you. Maybe just think of the fact you are part of the same family, and in spite of differences that exist, love still is the motivating factor to instill and preserve harmony and unity.

Please remember the God of peace Himself has given you His everlasting and all pervasive peace in every way you could ever think of. God is with you always.

This salutation is written in my own handwriting so you can accept this whole letter as authentic. It's something I like to do in every letter. You better be glad you don't have to read the whole letter in my handwriting. I'm blessed to have someone else who can write better than I can. Anyway, hope you can read this.

The grace of Jesus is with you all.

Folks, that's just the way it is.

Trip # 12
CORINTH TO ANTIOCH VIA JERUSALEM

55. BALD
(Acts 18:18-22)

Our stay in Corinth was definitely a memorable one. We ended up staying there quite a bit longer than even I had expected to. We met many dear folks there and it was once again a sad occasion when it was time to bid our farewells. It was high time we went back to Antioch so all preparations were attended to with a touch of excitement at the prospect of going coupled with a touch of disappointment at the thought of leaving wonderful friends.

You got it. On the road again…

Our first pit stop was in Cenchrea. This seaport town was located about seven miles to the east of Corinth. It was the eastern port used by the Corinthians for trade from Asia as well as its eastern naval outpost. It was named centuries ago in honor of Cenchreas, son of Poseidon and Peirene. It was from this harbor we'd set sail for Syria.

I just had to mention Cenchrea. Perhaps you recall the scripture referring to a Nazirite vow taken by Jewish people when a special thanksgiving was given to God for a blessing He had bestowed. (Numbers 6:1-21) For a period of thirty days no meat or wine was to be consumed. Furthermore, you weren't allowed to get a haircut. At the conclusion of the vow certain offerings were to be made at the Temple, and then you got a haircut! The hair was to be burnt on the altar and offered up to God.

Sounds hairy, eh? HA! I just crack myself up sometimes!

Well, I had lots to be thankful for. Yes, I had taken the vow! Before we boarded the boat I had the big H C. I never realized I could still grow that much hair. You're probably trying to imagine me bald, aren't you? Not a pretty sight I assure you. At least all of my traveling companions had a good laugh, at my expense, of course!

Oh, Aquila and Priscilla came along with us. We were going to have to make a stop in Ephesus so they decided to accompany us on the boat trip.

Surprise. Surprise. I actually came under considerable pressure to stay in Ephesus.

From who?

The Jews!

Go figure.

Yes, the Jews. I had gone to the synagogue to try and reason with them. They were so intrigued and interested in what I was telling them they really wished I would stay a longer time with them to discuss the message of God's grace and peace. I wasn't used to being treated like this.

Unfortunately, I just felt I was running out of time. I informed them of my intention to try to get back to Jerusalem in time for the Passover feast. Even this was becoming a questionable goal. However, I did promise them I'd come back if everything worked out down the road.

Back on board the ship we set sail for the port of Caesarea. From there we made our way up to Jerusalem to visit with all our brothers and sisters there. After we spent some time in Jerusalem sharing our experiences with the believers we knew the time had come for us to make the final leg of our tour back to our home city of Antioch.

O.K., one more time for the record, on the road again...

We had been on, and off, the road for almost four years. It felt like it too. We had faced adversity of every imaginable scope and proportion. We'd seen people welcome us with open arms and others reject us with clenched fists. We witnessed people choose slavery over liberty. We also witnessed the liberating effect of the wonderful message of God's loving grace and peace upon many folks.

Man, what a trip!

Trip # 13
ANTIOCH TO EPHESUS

56. APOLLOS
(Acts 18:23-19:1)

"The happiest people in the world are those who discover that what they should be doing and what they are doing are the very same thing!"

If the wise observer of life who said this is correct then I'm one of the happiest people in the world. You know, we got back to Antioch with a great sense of fulfillment and accomplishment. We bathed in the comfort and fellowship of our home core of believing friends. They encouraged and strengthened us with their unselfish support of our endeavors.

One thing about friends is that they get to know the heart. The dear folks in Antioch knew my heart was bent towards spreading the gospel message of God's grace and peace, albeit, in some other place. So after spending some time in Antioch they told me to get lost!

No, it wasn't quite like that. They simply confirmed my desire to once again hit the road. Just can't seem to stay put.

Yep, on the road again...

Had a great visit once again with my folks and friends back home in Tarsus. It's incredible to me they put up with my wandering spirit. I suppose they wish I could just settle down somewhere and get a life! Then again, deep down they probably knew this is the only life I could imagine.

From Tarsus I made my way through the countryside of Galatia and Phrygia, strengthening and encouraging the many believers I'd come to know during my first two trips through the area. It was great to see all the folks in Derbe, Lystra, Iconium, and Antioch again. I was tremendously blessed to see how well they were doing.

Oh, I have to tell you about a chap by the name of Apollos. He happened to have been born way over in Alexandria, Egypt. It's important for you to know his parents were Jewish! Why? Well, I'm introducing you to a Jewish lad who came from the former land of captivity who was excelling in introducing others to the love of God for those who believe. I want to let you know I wasn't the only guy out there with something to say about God, even if their understanding of God's intentions were different from mine.

APOLLOS TRIP # 13

Apollos was developing quite a reputation for himself. He was not only eloquent he was very well versed in the scriptures. He knew them inside and out, unfortunately accepting the conventional wisdom of mankind's interpretation of God's will for mankind.

In other words, he blindly accepted the status quo of legalistic slavery to laws, rules, and regulations. Hey, he believed this with all his heart. He was utterly convinced this was the only way to go.

Been there, done that!

His speaking engagements were eloquent and inspiring. He taught with diligence of the traditional persuasions of the Jewish systems of controls and tradition.

The closest his understanding came to the message of Jesus was the pronouncements of John concerning the baptism of repentance and the anticipation of One who was to follow. In all sincerity and devotion Apollos spoke in the synagogue in Ephesus about his understanding of man's relationship with God.

That is until Aquila and Priscilla got a hold of him. You remember them don't you? This is the couple I worked together with in Corinth making tents between our forays into the work of spreading the gospel message of God's grace and peace.

Aquila and Priscilla accompanied us on the boat trip from Cenchrea over to Ephesus. They had remained there to open a new business in addition to speaking out about God's love for the whole world.

Anyway, Aquila and Priscilla happened to hear this young Apollos fellow. He certainly impressed them with his understanding of scriptures, but they just happened to have a different understanding of God's plan. So they took it upon themselves to take him aside and channel his understanding to a new level. They challenged him to renew his mind of God's wisdom in a totally new light. He had no trouble picking it up real quick.

Aquila and Priscilla saw something special in Apollos. They perceived him to be someone who could shine in the debating circles of Achaia and Corinth in particular. Along with many other of the believers in the work of Jesus they formulated a letter of recommendation to send with him to their friends in Corinth.

The letter exhorted the believers there to receive Apollos with their customary hospitable spirit and put him to work. Apparently, Apollos became a tremendous help to the believers in Corinth.

APOLLOS   TRIP # 13

He was able to share with many folks the wonderful message of God's grace. He became unwavering in his understanding of God's love for the whole world and wasn't embarrassed or timid in sharing about it with Jews and Gentiles alike. He took part in public debates whenever he was given the opportunity with great success. He had no qualms whatsoever in publicly showing to anyone who would listen his extensive knowledge of the scriptures and how they declared Jesus to be the One they'd all been seeking for.

Apollos was already in Corinth when I arrived on the scene in Ephesus after having first passed through the upper coasts. One of the first things I did when I got into town was to look up my dear friends Aquila and Priscilla. They took great joy in sharing with me all about their time in Ephesus, including what I've just related to you about Apollos. I also had the opportunity to tell them all about my trip to Jerusalem, Antioch, Tarsus, and all of the other cities on the way to Ephesus. We had a super time catching up on old times.

Boy, it was good to see them again!

TRIP# 13

3 YEARS IN EPHESUS

57. EPHESUS
(Acts 19:2-7)

- The "light of Asia."
- The "treasure house of Asia."
- The "vanity fair of Asia minor."

These are just a few of the nicknames for Ephesus. Her status as one of the premier seaports of Asia no doubt led to the importance of Ephesus through the centuries. Its busy port enabled it to become the western terminus of the major trade routes to the Euphrates River.

Ephesus was the seat of the Roman proconsul and also for the confederation of cities known as the "Asiarchate." The city definitely knew the pomp and ceremony of Roman power and justice. The imperial spirit was nurtured by the worship of the emperor. The Asiarch was the provincial high priest of the imperial cult. One of the jobs of the Asiarch was to oversee the Pan-Ionian Games. The whole country came to Ephesus during these Olympic style competitions so the president of these games held a very prestigious position.

Amongst all of the good of Ephesus was the ever-present element of corruption. Ephesus became a magnet attracting the criminal element of Asia.

One of the magnets was the Temple of Diana. This temple possessed the "right of asylum."

"What is asylum?" you ask.

If you've ever played tag or kick the can you'd probably be able to understand what an "asylum" is. If you could reach a certain area, whether it was a circle drawn in the playground or the trunk of a tree, you'd be safe from getting caught or having "it" stamped on your forehead. Well, that's what the asylum of the Temple of Diana meant for the criminal. If only they could get to the Temple they'd be safe. And safe they were until they left the confines of the hallowed site.

Pagan superstitions thrived. The "Ephesian Letters" were famous writings of special charms and spells. These magical documents were said to guarantee safety on a journey, children to the childless, and success in business and in love. A "rabbit's foot" if ever there was one.

People would come from all over the world to purchase these little pieces of magical parchment and place them in little bracelets worn around their necks and wrists. Maybe they got the idea from the scriptures of old!

Surely the Temple of Diana was the crowning jewel of the Ephesians. I should mention it was also called the Temple of Artemis. You see, Artemis is the Greek name, and Diana is the Latin name. The Temple was known as one of the Seven Wonders of the World. It was huge by anyone's standards, standing approximately 425 feet long, 220 feet wide, and towering 60 feet high. It was lined with 127 pillars, each donated by a king. Thirty-six of these shining marble pillars were inlaid and gilt with gold. Praxiteles, the greatest of all Greek sculptors, carved the great altar.

Unfortunately, the beauty of the Temple was not really enhanced by the image of Artemis. Most believe this image had just fallen out of heaven. It was a black, squatty figure with many breasts symbolizing great fertility.

It amazes me people can be so incredibly misled into believing in something so powerless. The challenge to spread the loving gospel of God to the folks of Ephesus was immense.

When I first met a group of folks who professed to believe in God I sensed a profound lack in their understanding of what God had done for the whole world. I tried to ask some specific questions to determine for myself what they perceived to be the truth.

"Have you received the Spirit of Jesus in your lives since you first came to believe in God?"

"Hey, Paul, we haven't even heard anything about theSpirit of Jesus."

"When you were baptized, what did you think you were being baptized into?"

"Into the baptism of John."

"Look, my friends, I better explain a few things to you. John accurately baptized folks into a baptism of expectation and repentance. He told folks they should believe in someone who was going to come after him. The one who came after John was Jesus."

I, of course, had to do a bit of explaining. I pointed out John stimulated folks to put the focus of their attention towards Jesus, the One who would bring about the salvation of the whole world from the slavery of self-righteousness.

It would be Jesus who would make it possible for the righteousness of God to be imparted into every human being for all eternity.

The life of every individual would be impregnated with the Spirit of Jesus. The expression of baptism was the symbolic gesture of understanding. It declared to all how our "old" nature was crucified with Jesus and our "new" nature was resurrected together with Jesus!

Well, these folks had been only been taught the legalistic approach to God. They had been deceived into thinking "what" they believed and how well they "performed" all of the laws, rules, and regulations would determine the state of their relationship with God. When I told them that God's gift of righteousness didn't depend on how effectively or sincerely they believed, and that it had nothing to do with their performance or merit, they were flabbergasted.

What did they do?

"Shall we gather at the river?" Heard that one before?

Well, they asked me to baptize them all over again. So, that's just what we did. We had a baptismal service down at the Cayster River. I put my hands on them one by one and dipped them completely under the water so they could fully understand the great truth of the miraculous change God had accomplished in their lives. Each one in turn confessed in their own words how much this revelation of the fact Jesus had literally joined Himself with their own spirit had revolutionized their understanding of the great love of God. They just couldn't get over how this change in perspective altered their own sense of awe and worship of God. They shared an amazing desire to upset the whole world with this new understanding.

I think there were about twelve men or so that day alone who demonstrated in parable form the transformation of their lives from a spirit of self-righteousness to the union of their spirit with the Spirit of Jesus.

Let me tell you, it was quite a sight to witness!

58. DIVERS
(Acts 19:8-20)

Now that incident was just one of many which occurred during the first days of my time in Ephesus. I made a point of it to go into the synagogue as often as I could. I'd get into some serious debates and disputations with the Jews, making every attempt to reason with them and to persuade them to give serious thought to a new understanding of the kingdom of God.

This went on for about three months after I had arrived in Ephesus. Don't be misinformed. There was also a core group of folks bent on perpetuating their own diversions and dissensions of the truth of God's promise. I guess this is why I decided to nickname them the "divers."

Ha! Their hearts were hardened in their own ignorance. They refused to listen to the best news to ever reach their ears. Realizing the gospel of God's grace and peace I was preaching and teaching posed a very real threat to their systems of control they began a concentrated attack on this glorious message, as well as a spirited character assassination of one its most ardent exponents, me!

You need to know it eventually came to the point where I decided I didn't have to put up with their crap anymore. So, what did I do? I stopped going to the synagogue! Yep, I quit going. I wasn't the only one either. I found I was surrounded by a great group of believers who decided liberty sounded much more appealing than bondage.

Go figure!

It was quite a common practice for most businesses to be open from early in the morning until around eleven o'clock. They'd break for lunch and perhaps even take an afternoon siesta in the extreme heat of the day. Somewhere around four o'clock in the afternoon the hustle and bustle would start all over again until the cool of the evening set in.

Not to upset the milk carts, we started to meet almost daily in the time between 11:00 a.m. and 4:00 p.m. in the assembly hall of a man named Tyrannus. The hall had a large meeting room with tables and chairs perfect for our needs. We'd work before and after our exciting daily mental exercise of discussing, reasoning, and debating all about the promise of God to gift the whole world with His righteousness through the faith of Jesus.

DIVERS   TRIP # 13

    Let me tell you, we had some interesting discussions! When everyone else was sleeping to get away from the heat, we were getting scorched in the perspiring heat of the mental exercise of renewing the minds of many who were previously bound and gagged by tradition and legalism.

    This went on for a period of about two years. That's right. Two years! No kidding! Folks all over Asia heard about the true word concerning Jesus. We made absolutely no changes to the message in respect to our audience. It didn't matter if we were talking to Jews or Gentiles. The message of God's love for all remained the same. If God doesn't see a difference in the ones He chose to love, then why should we?

    Right? Of course, right!

    I have to tell you some pretty incredible things happened during this time in Ephesus. We were blessed to witness many wonderful folks come to understand the miraculous touch of God in their lives.

    I've even heard there were some sick people who claim to have been healed of their diseases merely because they had touched some article of my clothing like a sweatband or apron which had been brought to them.

    I'm not exactly sure what to make of their claims, but I can assure you it had nothing to do with me! It's amazing what kind of things folks will lose when they come to understand and believe the amazing power of God to liberate and release from bondage of all kinds.

    Speaking of incredible stories I've just got to tell you about a particular batch of vagabond, Jewish crackpot exorcists. Common belief attributed most illnesses to the presence of evil spirits, and exorcism was the preferred prescription or remedy to cure the illness. Apparently, if you just happened to know the name of the evil spirit the chances were all the better of getting it out of the system of the afflicted.

    Well these divers guys were full of themselves enough to think they could, at the very least, con some folks into exalting their works of healing power. They happened upon someone who was sick and proceeded to start taking command of the "evil spirits" within them.

        "We adjure you, we command you, by the name of Jesus who Paul is preaching about!"

DIVERS   TRIP # 13

Well, how do you like that? They don't know me from Adam! I don't know them from Cain. And here they are trying to invoke the name of Jesus who I was preaching about.

Some nerve! Wonder where they came up with that idea?

I should tell you there were seven of these characters involved in this particular episode. They claimed to be sons of one "Sceva," a Jew no less. More far-fetched was the claim their father was a chief priest. It was obviously a pretty good try, except for the fact nobody had ever heard of a chief priest named "Sceva."

The way the story goes the evil spirit had a plan of attack too!

"Look, you pack of rug rats, I know this Jesus character. Hey, I even know who Paul is! Who the heck are you?"

I guess it was like a scene right out of a great comedy. It was as if these seven turkeys suddenly were overtaken by a spirit themselves, so much so, they took off out of the house faster than a mouse trying to escape being a meal for some mangy alley cat.

In their massive commotion to clear out they tripped all over themselves to the point their clothes were torn and ripped to shreds. These poor, ignorant deceivers scrambled almost buck naked with black and blue bruises all over them down the street to safety.

That must have been quite the sight!

I don't know who exactly started this story, but it sure got around. Almost everyone in Ephesus heard various repetitions of the tale. It probably even got juicier with each telling. Hey, don't kid yourselves 'cause it scared a lot of people. A great fear fell over the whole city.

To the positive it certainly did get folks talking about Jesus! The story had the effect of causing the name of Jesus to be glorified to incredible proportions. Many folks came searching for us to find out more about Jesus and left believing and understanding the great love of God and in His great grace and peace.

Many folks confessed how much they'd been taken in by the seductive power of self-righteousness and legalism. Over and over we listened to testimonies of folks who had been enslaved by the enticing grip of "good works."

Many of these same folks had idolized all kinds of trinkets, jewelry, and curious pieces of artwork. Many depended upon books containing the wisdom (foolishness) of mankind to give them guidance over their every step in life.

When they came to understand all of these things had absolutely no control or power as far as God's view and opinion of them was concerned, they decided the best way to rid themselves of these things was to get rid of them. That's how the burning ceremony got started. Folks brought all their crap and started a massive bonfire everyone could see. Someone calculated the value of all the stuff burned up that day was somewhere in the neighborhood of fifty thousand pieces of silver.

Hey, that's no chunk change!

Talk about being purified by the fire. These folks got seriously liberated from a lot of useless baggage.

To say the understanding of the word of God's promise to the whole world came into focus for many, many people would be a gross understatement. It was great to see how the good news message of God's grace and peace had such a lasting effect upon the lives of so many folks.

59. DEMETRIUS
(Acts 19:21-41)

It wasn't long after the "torching" incident when it became clear to me the work in Ephesus was well on its way and my time to press on was near at hand. We had heard about some of the terrible problems our believing friends in Jerusalem were enduring. We felt in our spirits the desire to do something to alleviate at least some of their pain and suffering. We thought it would be a great idea to take up a collection of money from the believers in this neck of the woods and take it to Jerusalem.

    I would pass through Macedonia and Achaia then proceed to Jerusalem. I promised myself the next trip would be to see the great city of Rome. Because there was still a bit of work for me to do in Ephesus I decided I would send two of my most trusted friends on ahead to get the collection started anyway. I chose Tim and Erastus to represent me by relaying the purpose of a collection to benefit our brothers and sisters in Jerusalem. I assured them I would catch up with them sooner or later.

    Another interesting episode occurred during this period I stayed in Ephesus on my own. You may recall the "buck naked" incident I mentioned a while ago. I'm, of course, referring to the story of the seven exorcist sons of Sceva who got the scare of their lives. Well, the whole city was all in a tizzy about the incident in spite of the truth, falsehood, or inaccuracy of the reports concerning this little episode.

    What probably upset some folks even more than this rather amusing tale was the big bonfire incident. A certain group of suits got pretty ticked off. This whole thing about the way of God was particularly upsetting to the businessmen whose economic viability depended upon the sale of trinkets, jewelry, and other symbols of idolatry to the masses. Isn't it just the craziest thing it happens to be "MONEY" which makes the world appear to go round and round!

    The ringleader was a chap named "Demetrius," a silversmith by trade. He buttered his bread with the exorbitant profit he made from selling his silver shrines for the worship of Diana. He recognized a threat to his livelihood when he heard of the tremendous amount of booty wiped out in the liberating fire of new believers. He felt forced into action and called for a union meeting of his fellow artisans.

"Look, guys, we've got to nip this thing in the bud, or we're going to be toast. Each and every one of us knows we make our living creating beautiful silver trinkets and idols. I'm sure all of you have heard about what is going on not only in Ephesus, but almost everywhere else in Asia. We've got to do something about this Paul character. He seems to be single handedly causing all the damage to our very existence. Paul has persuaded and turned so many people away from needing our products it isn't even funny anymore."

"What'd he say?"

"'These things aren't gods,' says Paul, 'and nothing made of human hands has any capacity to be a god!'"

"Well, not only our profession is in danger, everything the temple of the great goddess Diana represents is also at peril. He'd like to see the magnificence of something which most of the world worships utterly destroyed! Paul's teaching of the grace and peace of God is in direct opposition of our ability to our control and manipulate the public."

Talk about inciting a riot! If these guys weren't upset and angry before, the protestations of Demetrius did the trick. They were choked.

"Great is Diana of the Ephesians! Great is Diana of the Ephesians!

Over and over the chant rang out through their assembly. It spilled out onto the streets. Soon the whole city was filled with confusion. I found out some unruly crowd had seized two of my traveling companions, Gaius and Aristarchus. Both of them were from Thessalonica. They were literally kidnapped and rushed into the main theater to be made a spectacle of.

Well, when I heard about it, my immediate gut reaction was to rush to their aid. I wanted to get down to the theater pronto. I was constrained by a number of my friends who forced me to realize how dangerous my intention could be. In addition, a number of the Asiarchs, who were personal friends of mine, sent messengers to me advising me to stay put as far away from the theater as possible. They simply implored me not to go in.

The chaos inside the theater was mounting in direct proportion to the number of people who started to crowd into the massive structure. Some people were shouting one thing while others were trying to drown them out with other taunts and jeers.

People didn't really even know why they were there let alone know which way to turn when they got into the theater. Mass confusion predominated the ugly scene.

Even the Jews were getting scared. They thought they'd have to take the heat for the message I was preaching. Ha! Now that's funny! The Jews yanked Alexander out of the crowd to be their spokesperson to defend the Jewish leaders against the implication of complicity with me. They didn't want to have anything to do with me.

Well, Alexander raised his hands as high as he could to try to quell the noisy, voluminous crowd so he could speak. As soon as the crowd found out he was a Jew, Alexander couldn't get a word in edge wise. The crowd went ballistic. The theater seated some twenty four thousand people or so and it was filling up pretty fast as people got wind of where the action was.

The wave got started. Up and down. Round and round it went. Man, it must have been something to see. All over town you could hear the mob yelling in noisy harmony.

"Great is Diana of the Ephesians! Great is Diana of the Ephesians! Great is Diana of the Ephesians!"

You know what? They kept it up for almost two hours! Two hours! Can you believe it? Two hours! Man, the cheerleaders must have been something. Maybe they were trying for a record or something!

Finally, a sense of civility broke out as the mayor of the city showed up. This town clerk was the secretary for the city, responsible for sending and receiving important communication between Ephesus and Rome.

Important? No fooling.

I dare say he was a tad more interesting in his own welfare than he was of mine, or of anyone else for that matter. Rome didn't take too kindly to the news of rioting. Heads could roll. Literally! At long last he was able to restore a modicum of order and began to appease the moody audience.

"Calm down! Calm down! Listen to me. Give me a break!"

"Surely, everyone of you Ephesians doesn't need to be told people throughout the world know the city of Ephesus worships the great goddess Diana. Ephesus, like Thessalonica and Berea, are temple keepers. This is an honorific title Rome has conferred upon us because we possess a temple of the imperial religion. We take our religion seriously here."

"We guard the temple and the sacred image which has fallen to our city from Jupiter way up in the sky very seriously."

"Nobody can argue about these things. So what's your problem? You ought to be quiet. You have nothing to get all excited about. These men you have brought in here, Gaius and Aristarchus, are neither temple robbers, nor are they blasphemers against your goddess Diana."

"Now, if Demetrius or any other of his silversmith union members has anything against anyone they ought to bring up the matter in court. There is a forum for bringing legal action against another party. It's fair and it's open to all. Let the lawyers handle your disputes. There's no need for this mass confusion. Furthermore, if you have any other problems bring them up in a lawfully conducted assembly. That's how we deal with our problems in a civilized way!"

"We're in danger of being hauled up on the carpet for this uproar today! I won't stand for it! There's no reason for it because there's no explanation for the disturbance."

"So, go home! Get lost!"

With that the thousands of exhausted citizens mumbled their way out the many exits of the theater. The mayor dodged a big slice with his diplomatic, tactful, and authoritarian order.

Good thing!

TRIP # 13

1ˢᵗ LETTER TO THE CORINTHIANS

60. THE PREVIOUS LETTER
(II Corinthians 6:13-7:2)

It shouldn't come as a surprise to you that news actually traveled quite quickly. Information is quite mobile. We not only received news reports from Jerusalem, but from many other cities in the world. It almost seemed like the world came together in Ephesus because of its economic importance.

We, of course, were always interested in hearing the reports concerning our fellow believers from the various places we had visited on our many trips. Occasionally, the news wasn't all that comforting. We were very aware of the dangers lurking about causing folks to return to their former ways of depending on their legalistic heritage to control their lives. Deceivers hovered like vultures to divide and conquer to satisfy their own lust for power and control. Hey, the leaders of the religious systems were no different!

The dear folks in Corinth were no more, or no less, susceptible than anyone else. The melting pot of ideas took its toll. Old habits are truly hard to break. Only a proper understanding of God's great, compassionate grace and peace can bring stability. I felt compelled to send the Corinthian believers a letter of exhortation when I learned of the particularly hard time they were facing leaving their bondage to laws, rules, and regulations. These wonderful folks were very special to me, and I really hated to see them loose sight of God's only desire for them.

The following is a brief excerpt of that particular letter.

There's something very important I need to talk to you dear folks about. I'm going to speak to you as if you were my very own children, so please, accept this exhortation with all my love and good intentions for you. I want to speak to you in complete candor.

Don't allow yourselves to be placed into the same yoke with those who don't share in your understanding of God's faith in you. How is it possible a partnership could exist between those who are striving to become righteous with those who believe righteousness is a free gift of God through Jesus?

Is it possible for those who have seen the light of liberty and those who'd rather live in the darkness of bondage to be at peace and unity with one another? Furthermore, what kind of agreement exists between the abundant life enjoyed in the temple of God and the life sucking deprivation of the worship of self-righteousness? How can you even compare the two?

Listen up.

YOU ARE THE TEMPLE OF THE LIVING GOD!

If there is one thing you remember from this letter don't let this one truth slip through the crack. You, yes, you, you are the very temple of the living God!

What did God say?

"I will dwell in them, and walk in them; and I will be their God, and they will be my people." (Leviticus 26:11,12; Ezekiel 37:27)

"So, come out from among them, and be separate," said the Lord, "and don't touch the uncleanness of self-righteousness, and I will receive you. I will be a Father to you, and you will be my sons and daughters." (Isaiah 52:11; Ezekiel 20:34)

That's what God Almighty said!

My dear, dear friends, since we have these promises from God Himself, cleanse and purify yourselves from every kind of pollution of self-righteousness. Rid your lives of the crap you've been taught all your lives. Any attempt to win the favor of God through what you can do in your own flesh, or by anything you can try to get your spirit to figure out, will not get you one step closer to God than He has already made you!

God has already made you perfect in His sight!

Your reverence and awe of God's gracious love will only become more perfectly meaningful and intense as your understanding of what He has accomplished in Jesus increases day by day.

I sincerely want you to believe what I'm trying to tell you. I'm not trying to deceive you in the least. It has never been our intention to mislead anyone, at any time. We have not tried to trick or corrupt anybody into believing something different than what we have always understood. What we have taught you definitely will not defraud you of anything. Taking away from you the agony and defeat of self-righteous behavior can hardly be understood as fraudulent.

61. GOD IS FAITHFUL
(1 Corinthians 1:1-17)

The time in Ephesus seemed to go by so fast. Each new day brought new opportunities to share the wonderful gospel message of God's love, grace, and peace. We spoke often of God's faithfulness to His promises to all mankind.

Ever since I dispatched that first letter off to Corinth my mind often drifted back to the dear folks I had met there. Finally, we started to receive reports concerning how they were faring and how they had received my exhortations. Some of the relatives of Chloe showed up to visit. Then Stephanas, Fortunatus, and Achaicus arrived from Corinth with news. Their first hand accounts proved invaluable. We certainly appreciated their input.

In spite of my deep association with problems I must confess I'm not all that fond of them. You can relate, can't you? Well, it appeared the believers over in Corinth were still having their share of struggles, internal and external. More teaching and instruction was obviously in order and a personal trip was simply out of the question for the time being. My intention was to get to Corinth, but not until I had caught up with Tim and Erastus over in Macedonia.

For now, another letter would have to suffice. This then, is the second letter I wrote to my dear brothers and sisters in the city of Corinth. You'll notice right away I employ the term "all" to include literally the whole world, for indeed, these things have happened to "all" of mankind.

From:
Paul, called to be an ambassador of Jesus through the will of God; and Sosthenes, our dear brother.

To:
- All the believers in the promise of God who are in Corinth;
- all who have received the righteousness of God in Jesus;
- all who have been called to be the sons and daughters of God;
- all, wherever you are, who recognize Jesus our Lord is responsible for making us all righteous in the sight of God

GOD IS FAITHFUL 2ND COR

Blessing:
God our Father has amazingly blessed all with His glorious grace which nobody could ever have deserved, instituted His peace, and removed every mortal liability of sin, all of this accomplished through Jesus.

I always give thanks to my God, on your behalf as well, for His marvelous grace He has given to all as a free gift by the birth, life, death, burial, and resurrection of Jesus.

Why'd He do it?

So in everything you might be enriched in Him. He did it so you'd come to understand everything He has always been trying to tell the world. He did it so we'd come to accept the wisdom of God over the wisdom (foolishness) of mankind.

You should have absolutely no doubt about the reality of the work of Jesus. There ought to be no doubt concerning God's view and opinion of you. Jesus is the confirmation of God to the world He has not withheld even one single gift!

Jesus is going to come again. Make no mistake about it. You needn't be scared about it.

Jesus has confirmed you are a child of God. The very day Jesus died on the cross was the day your confirmation as a spotless, blameless member of the family of God was signed, sealed, and delivered!

That's all folks! It's already happened!

How can I possibly have the nerve to proclaim this so boldly? Well, 'cause God is faithful. You may be unfaithful, and faithless, from time to time, BUT, God is always faithful. Never will He be unfaithful concerning His promises to the whole world. Don't you see? It was God who called all to be a part of the family of God in the fellowship of His Son, Jesus our Lord!

How in the world do you think He could now go back on His word? Won't happen!

Now, there are some things I need to seriously share with you which are entirely consistent with the gospel message relating to Jesus.

GET ON THE SAME PAGE!

It's high time you get it into your thinking cap there is only one message you ought to understand. There's no need for disunity or differences of opinion in this regard.

I'm sure you are constantly being challenged to return to the old order of religious bondage, to the slavery of laws, rules, and regulations. Don't go there. There's no need whatsoever. There's no discrepancy or failings in the message of Jesus.

BUT, let's face it, Jesus has perfectly joined everyone together in the very same mind set of God and in the very same timetable of His judgment. Now, when God looks at anyone He sees only the blameless, holy, and righteousness of Jesus.

That's all He sees!

So, what's all the fuss about? It's come to my attention, my dear friends, by information provided by some of Chloe's relatives that you folks are arguing amongst yourselves. It appears some of you prefer to believe what I've told you, while others prefer the teachings of Apollos, Peter, or of Jesus Himself.

Are you mental or what? What's up with that?

Is it possible to divide up what Jesus has done for the whole world? Could it be within the realm of possibility there is more to be added to the work of Jesus?

Give your head a shake!

Was I crucified for you? Did you get baptized in the name of Paul? Of course not! Don't even think it.

In a way, right now I'm kind of glad I didn't have the honor of baptizing any of you BUT Crispus and Gaius of course. I think if I had done this it would have only added more fuel to the fire of your disputations. The last thing I'd want anyone to feel is that folks were baptized in my own name. The very thought is repugnant to me.

Oh, I now also remember I baptized Stephanas and his family. Besides them I don't think I baptized anyone else.

You see, Jesus didn't send me out to baptize the world. BUT, He sent me out to preach the good news of God's gospel of grace and peace. I believe I'm doing this without mincing words, refraining from extolling the wisdom (foolishness) of mankind and what we've screwed up over the years. It's never been my intention to exercise the manipulation of words to confuse and confound the true meaning of the gospel.

Why?

The wisdom (foolishness) of mankind propagates the notion the cross of Jesus didn't affect this world one iota.

62. WISDOM OF GOD
(1 Corinthians 1:18-31)

Let me give you a little background so you'll understand the next part of my letter. When I preached about the cross it always brought a reaction from the crowd. It didn't really matter who my audience was.

When I preached about the cross to the Jews the response was almost always predictable. For me, the cross was the ultimate proof Jesus was indeed the true, and only, Son of God. To the Jews, however, the fact Jesus died on the cross was ultimately the conclusive proof Jesus could not have been the Son of God. They used the text from Deuteronomy 21:23 stating, "He that is hanged is accursed by God." Even though Isaiah prophesied about the suffering Messiah the concept eluded them. The cross became a barrier to their belief in a Messiah who would save them from the Roman oppressors and lead them on to be a mighty nation.

The Jews wanted and searched for something spectacular. False messiahs were a drachma a dozen. Some guy by the name of Theudas managed to persuade thousands of people to leave their homes and follow him to the Jordan River. It was there he claimed he could divide the river at his simple command and they could walk through to the other side on dry ground, similar to what Moses had done. Another man who came from Egypt no less was able to convince about 30,000 people to follow him up the Mount of Olives. He claimed he could command the walls of Jerusalem to fall down. I didn't say just one or two people followed him. I didn't just say ten or twenty, or even a hundred people. I said "thirty thousand!" He must have been one smooth talker.

The point I'm trying to make is that the Jews were looking for some kind of dramatic savior. Jesus just didn't cut it for them. A dead messiah isn't something that accomplishes the plan of national supremacy. It's pretty hard to have a great nation if the leader chooses to die like a common criminal on a cross in disgrace.

Don't be mistaken for the Jews weren't the only ones with problems. The Greeks didn't think too much about the idea of a cross-dying god either. To the Greeks, a god who suffered is a contradiction of terms. One of the characteristics of their gods was apathy. Their gods had absolutely no ability to feel.

If God could feel that feeling was caused by someone else, and therefore if only even for a moment, that someone else was greater than the god. The result was an impotent god.

Plutarch had even carried this rationale much further. It would be an insult for a god to even be involved in human affairs. To the Greek mind the very notion of a god becoming a man was incomprehensible. It just didn't make any kind of sense at all. It was utter foolishness.

Yes, the Greeks thought themselves to be great seekers of wisdom. At one time it was really a good thing to be a wise person, ultimately receiving the noble distinction of being called a "sophist." Unfortunately over time, the meaning really got watered down. Certain people started to think they were wise, not because they were wise, but because they had a sharp and witty tongue, not to mention a clever imagination. Flowery language and useless rhetoric could charm many people for many hours of any day. A man who thinks he is wise is usually more miserable simply because he's the only one who think he is wise. How you say something becomes more important than what you say.

Many Jews and many Greeks had one thing in common. They didn't really like me all that much. They not only disapproved of the way I said things, they actually disapproved of the things I said! The gospel of Jesus, His birth, His life, His death, His burial, and His resurrection, were too distant from their belief systems. A God who cares and interacts with humans was out of the realm of possibility for the Greek mind set. A Messiah who could actually accomplish more through His death than through His life was totally foreign to the Jew.

Did I have a challenge ahead of me, or what?

Well, enough of that. Let's get back to the letter. Where were we? Oh yes...

Don't you get it?
The preaching of the message of the cross of Jesus is pure nonsense for those folks who have never been told how it applies to them. They'll die in their own foolishness and ignorance. BUT, to those of us who do understand the message of grace it's truly the power of God that has given us an abundant life of liberty and confidence.

Surely it is written, "I will destroy the wisdom of the wise, and will thwart the cleverness of the clever!" (Isaiah 29:14; 33:18)

Tell me, where are the wise philosophers to debate the ways of God? Where are all these wise scribes, the great men who record their words for all to read? Who would challenge with lofty notions the power and might of God's wisdom? Where are all the critics who think they have all the answers to the questions of life?

Isn't it plain enough to see the wisdom of God just messes with all the wisdom mankind professes to have attained. The wisdom of mankind is complete foolishness when compared to the wisdom of God! With all its wisdom the world still couldn't figure out the ways of God. Mankind tried to use their wisdom and built up for themselves ways to attain the favor and righteousness of God. God knew how foolish these attempts were. They were doomed to failure.

God wisely chose to accomplish on His own what mankind couldn't ever accomplish. Now God is using our simple preaching of His gospel of grace and peace to tell people of His great love. Those who believe this message are finding out how great His redemption truly is and have started to enjoy their liberty from the slavery of legalism.

Yes, it brought great pleasure to God to know He already made everyone to be righteous and to see this message preached to spread the good news.

The Jews are still wasting their time looking for some kind of special sign. The Greeks continue their search for some kind of wisdom that always seems to allude them. We don't have a problem because we see Jesus as a special sign of the wisdom of God that far surpasses human understanding. BUT, when we preach about the crucified and risen Jesus it poses an incredible stumbling block to the Jews. Jesus literally gets in the way of their own pursuit for something they already have!

To the Greeks, the crucified and risen Jesus is merely seen as foolishness. If they only knew!

BUT, to those of us who have come to believe and understand the wisdom of God, Jesus represents the very power of God. Even if you could conceive of God as being ignorant, His foolishness would still far exceed the wisdom of all mankind. Even if you could conceive of God as being impotent, His weakness would still far exceed the strength of all mankind.

Just take a look around. How many wise men have been able to get past their own smarts to comprehend God could actually love the whole world? How many mighty and strong men do you know who've come to realize there's a far greater force at work in the affairs of this world than they could ever develop in their own strength? Do you think it's kind of strange those with fame and fortune tend to place greater dependence on their own effort and accomplishment than on the grace of God? All it does is show how stupid folks are when they rely on their own wisdom and strength instead of accepting a free gift of God.

BUT, God has chosen to confound the wise with the simplest and best plan that makes the very best mankind has attempted look utterly foolish! Don't you just dig it?

God chose to send Jesus into this world in a way the foolishness of mankind would consider to be weak and powerless, being born as a baby, dying like a common criminal. Doesn't seem too almighty, eh? That's what the world thinks. No wonder they can't see a good thing when it's placed right in front of them! God's apparent weakness sure puts the effort of mankind in its place.

Talk about weak!

God has chosen a way that almost seems too logical and practical for mankind to comprehend. God, in His wisdom, decided to make a reality out of something that was an impossibility for humankind. He saved everyone who had absolutely no power to save themselves. God, in His wisdom, chose to nullify a system that existed for too long in utter failure.

Laws, rules, and regulations have been done away with! They've been superseded by God's love, His grace, His mercy, and His peace.

Why?

So no flesh could ever take credit or glory that their own belief or ability had gained them the righteousness of God!

Allow me to paraphrase what Jeremiah said. "No man has the right to glorify himself when he positions himself in the presence of God Almighty." (Jeremiah 9:23)

BUT, because of God, everyone has been united in Jesus! God is the only reason you could even consider yourselves to be in Jesus. God made Jesus to be the wisdom, the righteousness, the new life, and the deliverance.

Guess what?

GOD HAS GIVEN TO THE WHOLE WORLD THE VERY SAME THING!

No foolin'!

Let me paraphrase Jeremiah again. "If you want to boast in anything, boast in the Lord." (Jeremiah 9:24)

63. MIND OF JESUS
(1 Corinthians 2:1-16)

Surely you remember how I sounded when I first came to you. Dear friends, I didn't declare to you the testimony of God with flowery language, with craftiness of words, nor with some kind of supernatural wisdom. It would be impossible for me to give away something I do not possess or know.

However, I did share with you the only thing that makes any sense at all to me. The most important thing I know and the possession I cherish most is the understanding and knowledge of Jesus and the glorious revelation He was crucified for the benefit of the whole world!

I admit I was full of goose bumps when I came to share this glorious news with you. In contrast to the incredible power of God, I came to you in great weakness. In reverence and awe of His mighty works, I came to share the love of Jesus with you in fear and trembling. When I preached and taught you it wasn't with enticing and persuasive words of wisdom I had dreamed up on my own. BUT, all I could do was demonstrate the power of the Spirit of Jesus within me.

Why?

I'd never want you to put your confidence in the wisdom (foolishness) of mankind. The only thing you could put your complete trust and assurance in is the ability of God's mighty power to make you righteous, holy, and pure in His sight, all on His own.

How is it possible any other kind of wisdom other than God's wisdom could make sense to those whom He has already made perfect? The wisdom (foolishness) of mankind surely has never made anyone perfect, has it? The power of the mighty rulers of this world has never been enough to accomplish what God has accomplished in what the world considers to be the "weakness" of Jesus!

BUT, I speak the wisdom of God that seems to have been mysteriously misunderstood throughout the history of mankind. Even though we haven't been able to figure God out, He purposed, in His great wisdom, to glorify us even before the world was created!

Look, don't be troubled about the mystery. Even the great rulers of this world were unable to comprehend the wisdom of God. You've got to know that if the super-intelligent religious leaders would have understood the matchless love of God they'd never have crucified the very Jesus of all glory.

BUT, it is written,

"Eye has not seen, nor ear heard, neither has it ever dawned on the hearts of those that eagerly seek Him that God would have prepared so much for all." (Isaiah 64:4)

BUT, God has revealed His wise plan for the whole world to us by the very Spirit of Jesus. You see, Jesus was able to search out the plan of God, yes, even the heart of God's compassion for "all " of His creation.

Let me put it to you this way.

How does mankind understand the complexities of humanness? It's because the spirit of mankind is something we can relate to.

Right?

BUT, the Spirit of Jesus is capable of understanding the complexities of God because He is God. It's only reasonable to deduce mankind doesn't understand the wisdom of God. Well, at least that was true until Jesus came to earth! Things are different now.

Now, in Jesus, we have not received the spirit of this world. BUT, we have received the Spirit that is of God, the Spirit of Jesus!

Why?

So we might know the things freely given to everyone by God! Hey, this is what I'm talking about. This is exactly what I've been trying to teach you. These truths aren't something the wisdom (foolishness) of mankind could conjure up. BUT, these are truths the Spirit of Jesus reveals in us. It is in the Spirit of Jesus we are able to discern spiritual things with spiritual things.

BUT, the natural spirit of mankind could never receive or accept things relating to the Spirit of God. It only stands to reason God's wisdom is way beyond the capacity of natural mankind to comprehend the scope of God's heart for His creation. It was actually impossible for mankind to know the intention of His will for the whole world because it's out of the realm of mankind's natural capability.

BUT, those who are spiritual in nature can now know and understand the wisdom of God.

Who's that?

All!

There is absolutely no reason for anyone to judge another person's acceptability before God.

Why?

Because we should know and understand God has already accepted everyone into His family and into His kingdom!

What right has anyone who knows and understands this incredible truth about the mind of Jesus to tell God what He can, or can't, do?

BUT, WE HAVE THE MIND OF JESUS!

64. MILK AND MEAT
(1 Corinthians 3:1-23)

My dear friends, sometimes I think I can't seem to get through to the spiritual nature of Jesus within you. BUT, for some reason, it seems I still have to address your child-like, carnal nature because you're still acting like little babies, part of the family, and yet, without any comprehension of how good you already have it!

I always thought I'd been feeding you an understanding of God's wisdom. Perhaps this assessment is a little off base. Maybe I was feeding you something I thought you could handle. Perhaps you really can't handle the whole truth!

I thought I was weaning you away from the nourishment of the wisdom (foolishness) of mankind that perpetuates self-righteousness with the milk of laws, rules, and regulations. I'm not sure if you're even ready now to receive the meat of God's wisdom which nourishes and strengthens with a righteousness unconditionally and freely given as a gift of God's grace and peace.

You're still wrapped up in the swaddling clothes of your childish, immature nature that subscribes to the legalistic systems of this world.

How did I come to this conclusion?

Just take a look at how you think and how you treat one another. You still think what you "do" is important to God. Apparently, there's plenty of jealousy and envy to go around. Strife and divisions seem to plague your fellowship. If you're evaluating either your own or someone else's closeness to God based on the performance of laws, rules, and regulations you so religiously adhere to, then I'm afraid you're still suckling on milk, acting out your immaturity, living as slaves to the wisdom (foolishness) of mankind. I'd rather see you start living like the people of God you truly are!

What do you think?

One of you says, "I am of Paul." Another one says, "I am of Apollos."

What's that? Isn't that kind of childish behavior based on a set of outdated formulations?

Look, who in the world is Paul, who is Apollos, BUT simply two men who happen to spread the gospel message of Jesus? We had the great joy to bring to you an understanding of the wisdom of God to make righteous the whole world through Jesus.

We've only one claim to fame. We are members of the family and kingdom of God, saved and redeemed through the blood of Jesus!

Oh sure, I planted a few seeds of understanding. Apollos has done his share of watering our understanding with some more good teaching.

BUT, we had nothing to do with getting you a taste of the righteousness God has given to every person in Jesus! So don't knock yourselves out trying to give Apollos or myself any credit for either planting or watering. Never forget you are righteous, pure, holy, redeemed and all that other great stuff because of only one thing.

What's that?

It's the gracious love of God who changed His view and opinion of everyone through Jesus, totally without our assistance, permission, belief, or accomplishment!

You see, seed throwers like myself and hosers like Apollos are actually functioning as one, united in Jesus. The best reward of all is oneness with God.

How come?

Because God decided to reward everyone, yes everyone, according the great action of His own work in Jesus. For indeed, now are we also workers together with God because of the Spirit of Jesus within us.

Look, we "all" are the creation of God's handiwork! We "all" are the building that God in His great creative wisdom has created for His good pleasure!

Now, this is important.

Don't misunderstand this.

God is the wise master builder who has dispensed His righteousness to "all" according to His great grace. I'm doing my best to tell everyone about this truth. Others surely will add to the words of teaching and encouragement I've given. Good on 'em.

BUT, if anyone wants to go out and about sharing the way to righteousness and acceptance of God, just be careful what you say. Take heed on what message you proclaim. There's only one foundational truth out there.

What is it?

God, in His wisdom, chose to lay out Jesus as the only provision for the righteousness of the whole world! Jesus laid aside any and all other ways and means of working towards gaining the acceptance of God.

Beware of anyone who tries to tell you there is one iota of something you need to "do" beyond what Jesus has already accomplished!

There will be those who say your money can get you into the good graces of God. "Hey, gold, silver, and precious stones should be able to be of value to you beyond this world, don't you think?" "Perhaps, worshiping idols of wood could help?" "Maybe the hay and stubble of your good works will impact how God will accept you!"

BUT, let me tell you the work of every human being was made manifest on one glorious day, the day of the cross of Jesus.

On "that" day:
- the works of the whole world were declared to be null and void;
- God revealed His all consuming judgment of fire upon the failure of man's foolish attempts at self-righteousness;
- and the simply incredible truth was revealed that God rewarded "all" of mankind with His righteousness, in spite of their good effort, and not because of their good works!

The only thing that will happen to those who give up their bondage to laws, rules, and regulations to claim favor with God is that they will lose their dependence on any of it.

Now, that's what I call a good loss!

What do you gain?

The liberty of living in the peaceful awareness you've been saved apart from yourselves. The shame, guilt, despair, pain, and agony of your effort has already been destroyed in the fire of God's judgment on the glorious day of Jesus!

DON'T YOU KNOW YOU ARE THE TEMPLE OF GOD?

Don't you know the Spirit of God actually lives in you?

God has destroyed every need for mankind to defile themselves with acts of self-righteousness. Look, the temple of God is already holy. And what are you?

The temple of God are you.

Nothing, nothing, nothing could make you any closer to being what you already are! Don't be deceived. Don't kid yourself. You think you're smart? Get stupid. Then you'll be wise.

Go figure.

I've said it before and I'll say it again. The wisdom of this world is foolishness as far as God is concerned.

Do you remember what Eliphaz told Job? "God would take the wise in their own craftiness." (Job 5:13)

And again, what did David write? "The Lord knows the thoughts of the wise, that they are vain." (Psalms 94:11)

So, don't waste your time seeking the approval of men in gauging your spiritual performance. Man's view and opinion of you has no bearing on God's view and opinion of you.

What does God think about you?

Everything that belongs to Him belongs to you!

You know something? It doesn't make one bit of difference if you could be me or not. It doesn't matter whether you could be Apollos or Peter. It matters not one bit who in the world you are. In fact, it doesn't even matter whether you're alive right now, or whether you've died. Well, if you are dead, I'm not sure how you could be reading this right now. Ha.

Anyway, it doesn't even matter how you relate to things in the present or how you will relate to them in the future. Everything you ever needed or will ever need in your relationship to God is already yours!

You belong to Jesus and to God!

Everything that belongs to Jesus is God's!

65. FOLLOW ME
(1 Corinthians 4:1-20)

Let me repeat that.
    You belong to Jesus!
    Everything that belongs to Jesus is God's!
    That would include you!
    Hey, don't think it is any different for any Apollos, Peter, or myself. All of us are paddlers in the same boat. All of us have been given the great privilege of taking care of the great mysteries of the wisdom of God.

In the affairs of this world it's assumed if you want to rise up the corporate ladder you'd better be found faithful to tow the party line. BUT, as far as I am concerned, it's a very small thing I should be judged of you. My relationship with God is not something anybody has any right to judge. Hey, I don't even have the right to question God's view and opinion of me!

Look, I had nothing to do with the fact God loved even me. I did nothing to deserve His grace and peace, BUT, I had absolutely nothing to do with the fact God has justified me in His sight without my approval or merit! God is the only One who determined how He would treat me. He's the One who blessed me with His righteousness.

Don't be so quick to judge anything apart from the cross of Jesus. When Jesus came He brought light to the hidden darkness of the wisdom (foolishness) of mankind. Mankind has followed the counsel of their hearts to think that what they do, or don't do, influences God's opinion of them.

Utter nonsense!

The counsel of the hearts of mankind to trust in self-righteousness has been exposed by the mission of Jesus to inform the whole world of God's unending love and acceptance. When folks come to understand the grace and peace of God for all mankind they will turn their hearts to the praise of God.

With these things in mind, my dear friends, I offer Apollos and myself again to you as an illustration of what I'm writing to you about. Look, Apollos and I don't argue about who is the greater between the two of us. That's just plain stupid!

Scriptures plainly reveal God doesn't see any differences between us, so why should we? Hey, why should you?

There's absolutely no need for anyone to get a puffed up head thinking because of what they do or don't do they're any better in the eyes of God than the next person. Arrogance just doesn't cut it. Neither do superiority complexes.

Who makes anybody different from the next person? What have you got that you didn't receive yourself? So, if you possess something that was actually given to you, why are you gloating about it like you had it all the time as a result of your own merit or effort?

Let me put it another way.

If you received the righteousness of God because of His action in Jesus, why are you trying to claim some kind of glory, praise, and recognition from mankind as if you had something to do with getting His righteousness by your belief or activity?

You are as full as you are ever going to get! You are as rich as you could ever possibly become! You reign as kings because of what Jesus has done for you!

There's nothing that Apollos, I, or anybody else for that matter, could have done to gain it for you. My true desire is that you'd come to fully understand this truth. Apollos and I are already enjoying our reign in the Kingdom of God. We'd also love to see you start living like the kings you are!

Sometimes I think you're acting like those generals who ride with pomp and circumstance to show off your own accomplishments. We, some of us who happen to spread the message of God's grace and peace, just seem to be trophies you assume God has given to you to possess and treasure for your own purposes. Perhaps you even think we should die for you.

Perhaps your image in the eyes of this world would be enhanced if you could proclaim we are "yours." Maybe you think it somehow makes you look even better in the eyes of the angels. As if that would make any difference. Certainly you could take a great degree of pride in the knowledge other men hold you in esteem because you "possess" a few ambassadors of Jesus in your back pocket.

Well, give your head a shake!

We may look like nothing other than a bunch of fools in the family of God, BUT, the truth of the matter is you don't have to make us look like fools in order for you to be wise in the eyes of God.

BUT, you are wise in Jesus!

Consider us weak if you want to, BUT, you are strong because you are in Jesus and not because you hold some kind of power over us.

YOU ARE HONORABLE IN JESUS!

BUT, you will gain no honor from the world by holding us in contempt or by despising us with an attitude of superiority.

Our present circumstances?

Hey, they aren't all that noteworthy to write home about I must confess. We've often gone without food and drink. Sometimes it seems like we put on the same clothes day in and day out. Often we're confronted by situations that frustrate the heck out of us. Quite often we don't even know where we're going to spend the night.

Work?

My, we have to work with our hands just like the next guy.

When we're reviled we find it in our hearts to bless. We suffer when we're persecuted. We keep bottled up inside of ourselves the frustrations of being defamed without justification. Some folks seem to think we're the scum of the earth!

Go figure.

We are the dumping grounds for every kind of abuse imaginable even to this present time.

Now, why am I writing these things to you?

Certainly not to shame you, no, BUT, I want you to know I care for you dearly, surely like you were my very own children. However, I want to exhort you to a different attitude and understanding.

You may sit under the instruction of ten thousand teachers who will attempt to tell you their version of the message of Jesus. However, I can't imagine you could have so many fathers who truly care for you like God does.

Because of Jesus I've had the extreme joy of sharing with you the exciting gospel message of God's loving grace and peace for the whole world!

Therefore, I plead with you to give honor and recognition where it's due.

Follow my example in acknowledging the Father of all!

I have such a deep concern you return to this teaching I'm sending Timothy to you.

He's like a son to me and I trust him implicitly. Jesus found Tim was worth putting His faith in as well. Tim is going to remind you of the truths I've told you concerning the work of Jesus. I assure you this is the same message of the grace and peace of God that I share with everyone wherever I go.

Some of you have apparently grown conceited in your own accomplishments. Perhaps you've come to the conclusion I'm unconcerned about you and that I don't have any intention of ever showing my face in Corinth again. BUT, I will come to you very soon in the timing of God.

And when I do show up I'll soon be able to recognize not only the load of crap being spread by those arrogantly puffed up in self-righteous behavior, BUT, more importantly, the authoritative power manifested by the liberty and power in Jesus.

For the kingdom of God isn't dependent on the words of the wisdom (foolishness) of mankind, BUT only on the power of Jesus!

66. LEAVEN
(1 Corinthians 4:21-5:13)

I plan on introducing you to a concept of a corrupting influence in this next section. I thought it best to give you a touch of information concerning the Jewish viewpoint of the introduction of leaven into something designed to be unleavened. Perhaps you never knew anything about bread making so let me just give you a brief explanation.

Technically, leaven is a piece of fermented dough. It's any substance or liquid added to dough to produce fermentation. Usually it refers to a portion of fermenting dough reserved from a previous batch to be used for this purpose.

The bread Jewish folks used to commemorate the Passover with was to be unleavened (Exodus 12:34ff; 23:18). The Passover, of course, was the Jewish celebration of God's deliverance of the Israelites from the slavery and oppression of the Egyptians. Applying this event to the new reality, Jesus is the great deliverer from the slavery and bondage of the laws, rules, and regulations mankind has used to propagate the foolishness of self-righteousness.

Suppose the woman of the house planned to bake some unleavened bread but she made too much dough. She decides to set it aside so she could make some fresh bread in a day or two. In the keeping the dough ferments causing a putrefying odor hard to ignore. Now, if the lady took this fermented dough (leavened) and mixed it in with some new dough (unleavened), what do you think she would get? Right. She'd end up feeding her family with a stinky, rank tasting loaf of bread. The fermented leaven had a definite negative influence upon the purity of the unleavened loaf. It didn't just remain impure on its own, but its impurity wreaked havoc on the rest of what it came into contact with.

Ever heard of spring-cleaning? What you may not know is this practice may have originated with our dear Jewish friends. Why do I say that? Well, Jewish law set forth the regulation that on the day before the Passover feast every Jew was to light a candle and search their house in a ceremonial search for leaven. Every last bit of uncleanness would have to be eradicated.

Here's an interesting side bar. Even Zephaniah spoke about God doing a spring-cleaning with candles (Zephaniah 1:12).

Let me tell you, did God clean house!

LEAVEN 2ND COR

In rabbinical literature leaven symbolizes evil desires, and in Jewish theology it represents the inherited corruption of human nature.

Anyway, the point I was trying to make with this object lesson is the nuisance of a corrupting influence.

With this in mind, let me take you back to the letter…

Hey, the choice is yours! Do you want me to come over there and smack some sense into you? I don't want you to be following after the teachings of all the deceivers who are trying to convince you your salvation is dependent on your own accomplishments and merit.

Wouldn't you rather I came to you with loving concern and in the in the spirit of humble authority to encourage and exhort you to enjoy the glorious liberty the loving grace and peace of God has already given to you in Jesus?

It's unfortunate rumors are circulating concerning immoral behavior within your fellowship. This immoral conduct is so abhorrent it isn't even tolerated in the unbelieving world, let alone subject to death in the tradition of the Jews (Deuteronomy 27:20). **You know what I'm talking about. I'm speaking about the practice of a man engaging in an illicit sexual association with the wife of his father.**

If it's true, you should be ashamed of yourselves! Don't accept this practice with such apathy and self-complacency like it's really no big deal. You should be reacting with the kind of sorrow you'd feel to a death in your own family. Shame the violator from your fellowship!

I may not be physically present with you right now, BUT, I certainly am in spirit. This is my assessment of the actions of any who engage in this despicable deed.

When you're gathered together in the name of Jesus, with the assurance of the feelings of my heart in the authority of Jesus, loose this individual to the deceptive callousness of his own slanderous lifestyle. The choice this person has made will impale and harass his life. The only good thing I can say for this person is he's pretty fortunate his righteousness was secured the day Jesus died on that glorious day of the cross!

Don't take any pleasure in the misguided struggles of others.

There's nothing uplifting about someone who chooses a path of pain and suffering over liberty and peace. Don't you know that a little leaven leavens the whole lump of dough?

So, purge yourselves of impurity!

Why?

So you may live as pure as Jesus has made you!

God created you to be a brand new loaf in Jesus. You are an unblemished and unspoiled part of the bread of life in Jesus.

Look at it this way.

For even Jesus was sacrificed for us! Yes, Jesus is truly our Passover. It's because of Him the plight of eternal death and punishment has passed over the whole world!

KEEP THE FEAST!

Enjoy the liberty God's grace has made possible. Don't waste your time on the laws, rules, and regulations of self-righteousness that corrupt, contaminate, and pervert the truth of God's love. Don't let the fermenting influence of self-centered anger and wickedness ruin your liberty.

BUT, enjoy the freedom of your purity in the bread of life in Jesus. Be exemplified in your sincere understanding of the truth of God's grace and peace for all mankind.

I've already written to you once concerning your association with those who insist on living a life based on immorality and decadence. Unfortunately, this world is full of folks who seem to be devoid of conscience and morality. Many are creatures of mischievous greed and cunning extortion. Not only that, there are a whole lot of folks given to worshiping any old "god of the day."

I fully recognize the reality you can't escape from the world we live in. However, you don't have to participate in all these perversions, nor associate with those who do.

BUT, now, I'm writing to you, in no uncertain terms, refrain from keeping company with those who:
- participate in immoral sexual activity;
- covet what others have;
- worship the idols of the creative imaginations of mankind;
- who slander the reputation of others;
- are given to drunkenness; and
- with those who believe in extortion and thievery to get what they want.

Don't even waste your time to sit down and eat with them. This might shock you. It's not up to me to put standards of conduct upon those who still don't believe in God or in His work on behalf of the whole world in Jesus. Neither you nor I have any right to judge even those who do believe.

BUT, God has already decided the eternal destiny of the whole world!

This reality should not interfere with our responsibility to maintain a sense of purity and decency that reflects the life of liberty we enjoy in Jesus. If this means disassociating yourselves from those who'd rather take their liberty in Jesus to the wrong conclusion, so be it.

67. SHAME ON YOU
(1 Corinthians 6:1-8)

We sure do live in a strange world, don't we? Sometimes I wonder why we never seem to learn the lessons that would make the world a better place for everyone. Plato, I think, was right about many things when it came to human nature. He proposed a good and honorable man would always choose to suffer a wrong from another person than to do a wrong to another person.

How is it possible we still have not learned this valuable lesson about settling problems? We seem to live in a very legal society. We all have our "rights." Too many cry foul because someone is "violating their rights."

How absurd!

Some people go to sporting events for recreation. Other folks go to the courts for entertainment. In fact, taking legal action against other people is often considered a sport all on its own.

Take the legal society of Athenia for an example. Talk about overkill. These folks took their "sport" seriously. Almost every man could be a lawyer, prosecutor, defender, judge, or jurist at one time or another in his life. Let me explain.

Let's assume you have a beef with your neighbor. No, I'm not talking about having a nice eye of rib on the bar-b either.

First of all, you could try to solve the dispute by hiring a private arbitrator. You could each chose an arbitrator of your choice then you'd have to agree on a third impartial judge to mediate. You may or may not like his decision. If you don't there's no need to give up. Move to step number two.

Secondly, you could take the matter to the court known as "the Forty." In this court you could present your argument before a publicly appointed arbitrator. Who was this arbitrator? Any man who was at least sixty years of age. Did you have a choice about whether you wanted to be an arbitrator or not? Well, if you wanted to give up all your privileges as a citizen you could. Not much of a way out, eh? With any luck at all the decision may well be very poorly received anyway by at least one of the parties.

Thirdly, it's starting to get really serious now, you could take your dispute to a court where a jury of people would make a decision for you. Your chances of getting a fair shake out of any raw deal are pretty remote.

If your case involved a minor sum of money there'd only be two hundred and one people on the jury. If you were talking about a larger amount of money then you better be prepared for a jury of four hundred and one. Perhaps the amount was substantial. The jury could hit six hundred and one. There are cases recorded where the juries were anywhere from one thousand to six thousand citizens.

Perhaps this is why some legal battles made it all the way to the super bowl! If you were over thirty years of age you were a candidate to be a jurist. You even got a small appearance fee to make it worth your while. Where else could you receive entertainment and get paid for it? "Might as well line up for jury duty!"

The fourth option was to take matters into your own hands. This probably had its own set of complications. The Gentiles certainly liked the challenge of legal action.

The Jews, on the other hand, were a little more discreet. Airing their dirty laundry in public wasn't that cool. Discipline often remained in-house.

If you had a problem you'd take it before either three Jewish judges, the elders of the synagogue, or the elders of the village. To take a legal matter before a non-Jewish court was blasphemy against the "law" (Exodus 21:1).

Unfortunately, the fellowship of believers in Corinth weren't immune from problems. We heard reports some believing folks were taking legal actions against other fellow believers. Keep in mind I'm talking about civil matters as opposed to criminal cases. In the midst of a litigious society the believers in a new and dynamic way of living were in dire need of guidance and direction. You could even use the word exhortation.

It was my contention believers in the justice of God for the whole world should be commended for an attitude of living above the letter of the law. Folks who've been judged by the fairest of all judges should be concerned more with their responsibility to treat others in the same way rather than insist upon their rights.

So, let me take you back to the letter so you can read what I told them...

Aren't you ashamed in the slightest to see disputes arising between any of you end up in the civil courts? Why are you having so much difficulty in solving your problems with one another employing the common sense you all have?

Don't you realize believers have the role of judging this world in the same manner as God has judged it? And if you could see this world the way God sees it, then why in the world can't you make wise decisions concerning even the simplest and smallest matters you face on a day to day basis?

Hey, even the angelic host were subjected to the same kind of judgment. If you participated in the same out of this world assessment of God, then why in this world can't you judge and discern accurately things pertaining to this life?

If you truly understand the concept of God's impartation of His justice and wrath for the whole world upon Jesus, and if you realize your great opportunity to show the same attitude of grace and mercy, why is it necessary for you to submit your problems to the binding legal decisions of those who don't know, believe, or understand the same things concerning God's system of justice as you do?

SHAME ON YOU!

I find it hard to believe there isn't at least one wise person among you, not even one who can make decisions when disputes do arise among you. BUT, I just can't imagine you'd prefer to settle your differences in front of a civil court that doesn't believe in the mercy of God. Actually, the mere fact you take one another to court shows how bankrupt you are in your own understanding of how God has treated the whole world, including you!

Is making sure you are right the most important thing in life? Is proving a point that necessary? Is making sure your rights are preserved that imperative?

Why don't you try accepting sometimes you might be wrong, or perhaps deserved what you got?

I don't even think it would damage you all that much if you even had to suffer a loss than to prove a point or argue a right. No, there is nobody who gains from legal action. All parties are losers.

As far as I'm concerned both sides in a dispute get cheated of getting a glimpse of God's loving justice through His grace, mercy, and peace towards all mankind.

68. TEMPLE OF GOD
(1 Corinthians 6:9-20)

Don't you know it is impossible for any unrighteous person to inherit the kingdom of God? Don't be deceived!

Let me give you a partial list to help make my point.
- male prostitutes,
- idol worshipers,
- adulterers,
- homosexuals,
- perverts,
- thieves,
- coveters,
- alcoholics,
- foul mouthed folks, and
- swindlers.

Let's not kid ourselves. We all would have to agree that none of these kinds of individuals will inherit the kingdom of God. Hey, some of you probably fit somewhere in that list.

BUT, guess what? You are washed!
BUT, guess what? You are sanctified!
BUT, guess what? You are justified!

Was there something you did to deserve to get cleaned up like that? Did you earn it by your good works? Did you get washed, sanctified, and justified because you believed? Of course not! Then how did you get these blessed gifts?

You received it as a gift in the name of Jesus and by the Spirit of our God!

Because Jesus has released me from the bondage of laws, rules, and regulations I no longer fall under the restraints of legalism. In this sense, there's nothing at all preventing me from doing whatever I want to. BUT, in the same breath, I want to assure you I don't think all things are expedient or beneficial for me to do or to get involved with.

Yes, I have the liberty to do anything, BUT I will not be brought under the power and control of anything that might enslave me in the lust of its design.

Take food for an example. Food was meant to be eaten. Our stomachs were created so our bodies could be nourished by the consumption of food. Makes sense, eh?

BUT, I'm convinced God has planned it that someday we won't need either food or our stomachs to consume it.

What about our bodies? Our bodies weren't created to be enslaved in the bondage of sexual improprieties. BUT, our bodies were created to be the habitation of Jesus just as surely as God planned that the Spirit of Jesus was designed to inhabit our bodies!

Yes indeed. God has raised up both Jesus as well as all mankind through His own power to a new and abundant way of life. Don't you know your bodies are intricately united with Jesus?

Recognizing this incredible truth, why would I want to abuse my body needlessly and carelessly? It just doesn't make any sense. Why would I take the chance of destroying my physical health let alone the pain of mental stress by engaging in sexual impurity? That's just plain stupid! God forbid we disrespect the liberty He has given to us!

What? Surely you must realize when a person engages in a physical relationship with a prostitute they are engaging in something a lot more than just sex. There is a union that takes place we don't even understand.

"Two," God said, "shall be one flesh" (Genesis 2:24).

BUT, anyone who is joined with Jesus is united with Him in one Spirit! So, flee from sexual immorality!

Don't forget, there's absolutely nothing that will affect your relationship with God. Sin has been done away with as it relates to God. BUT, those who exercise their bodies and minds in sexual misconduct wreak havoc upon their own bodies and minds!

What?

You still don't know **YOUR TEMPLE IS THE BODY OF THE SPIRIT OF JESUS** in you?

Listen, you've received the Spirit of Jesus within you because God has given Him to you, and not because you deserved it, earned it, or believed it. You've been bought with an incredible price, the precious blood of Jesus!

So, glorify God with your body. Glorify God in your spirit.

69. MARRIAGE
(1 Corinthians 7:1-17)

Now, you wrote to me asking some very good questions. Let me try to answer some of them for you. First of all, let me respond to your enquiries concerning marriage.

The best thing for a man would be to never even touch a woman! Ha! Ha!

No, seriously now, give your head a shake. I think the very best situation is for every man to be content and fulfilled to live in happiness with his own wife, and for every woman to be completed and praised by her own husband. This is the best way to avoid the pitfalls of sexual impropriety. Let husbands and wives honor and cherish one another.

Marriage is supposed to be a blessed union in which sex isn't used as a bargaining chip.

The wife has no power over her own body BUT that which is shared with her husband. The same is true for the husband. Don't deprive each other of pleasure unless you agree together to abstain for a specific purpose, such as a time of prayer and fasting. Don't neglect enjoying the love and tenderness of sex for too long or else the fire of passion may be fanned into flame for someone else.

I hope you understand I'm speaking frankly to you about this delicate subject because I feel it's important. BUT, I don't want to give you the impression I'm speaking some commandments from God. I'm giving you my personal advice I believe represents the reality of God's presence as we live in a world of indifference, irreverence, injustice, brutality, and sexual immorality.

I wish everybody would be as content as I am! BUT, we all have the same gifting of God's grace and peace. No doubt, how we understand it and apply it to our lives may be different.

To those who are either unmarried or widowed perhaps you may find your happiness in living on your own, even as I have. BUT, if you can't keep your sexual impulses under control then you're probably better off getting married so you won't get scathed by the shallow emptiness and coldness of sex without love.

I have a heart's desire for those of you who are married. It's more than my desire, BUT, I believe it's actually the heart of God's desire. Wives, don't leave your husbands for the arms of another, BUT, if you have to leave, stay unmarried if you can. If nothing else it may give you the time and opportunity to be reconciled with your husband.

Husbands, don't give your wife a reason to pack her bags. Don't go kicking her out of the house for no reason either!

BUT, here's a bit of practical advice I want to share with you from my own way of thinking. This isn't to be taken as if it comes directly from God.

I can foresee a situation in which a brother in Jesus has a wife who doesn't believe, accept, or understand the tremendous love of God for herself. If she is perfectly willing to stay in the relationship there's absolutely no reason for her husband to kick her out of the house.

Again, for any sister in Jesus who may have a husband who doesn't believe in God's grace and peace, his unbelief is no excuse for her to leave him if he finds joy and contentment in their marriage.

Why do I say this?

Don't you realize the tremendous influence your lives have upon one another? An unbelieving husband receives a beautiful testimony of God's love from his accepting wife. An unbelieving wife is blessed by the loving care and attention of a faithful husband.

Hey, the kids are affected by your relationship too. The way you treat each other will impact your children more than you'll ever know. BUT, they'll grow up knowing they are accepted and loved if they see their parents showing affection and acceptance towards one another.

BUT, if the one who doesn't choose to believe in God's limitless love wants to get out of the marriage relationship, what can you do? You got to let them move on. And move on you must as well. The mate of the one who chooses to leave, whether it be a male or female, should not feel they are under any bondage to refrain from entering a new relationship if the opportunity arises again.

BUT, BUT GOD HAS CALLED US TO LIVE IN PEACE!

Wife, can you tell me in all honesty whether or not you'll be able to influence your husband to come to the same kind of appreciation of God's loving grace and peace you enjoy? Husband, what about your wife? Can you be certain she will come to believe in God's provision for the whole world?

BUT, know this: God has distributed His grace and peace to everyone, whether they believe it or not! God has called everyone to enjoy the abundant liberty of His life in Jesus. You might as well enjoy the trip!

This is the same message I've been ordained to preach wherever I travel and to whoever will listen.

70. CIRCUMCISION
(1 Corinthians 7:18-19)

If God has called everyone to be in His family, could there be a difference in His eyes whether a man has been circumcised or not? If you've been circumcised, would it make any difference to God if you could become "un-circumcised?" If you are uncircumcised, would it make any difference to God if you were to be circumcised?

Absolutely not!

Circumcision doesn't mean anything at all to God!

Hey, uncircumcision doesn't mean anything at all to God either! BUT, there was a time the practice had a measure of importance. That was during the time keeping of the commandments of God held were a measure of God's acceptance.

Since Jesus has obliterated the laws, rules, and regulations, there's no longer any need to consider these things as having any impact of God's view and opinion of any man!

71. CALLED OF GOD
(1 Corinthians 7:20-24)

Concerning your lot in life?

Be who you are!

Let everyone enjoy the fact God chose to love you whether or not you believe it, whether or not if you deserve it, or whether or not you could earn it!

Do you happen to be a servant who has discovered the tremendous revelation God called you to be a full-fledged member of His family? Hey, good on you.

DON'T WORRY, BE HAPPY!

BUT, if you happen to be set free of your obligations, hey, go for it. Enjoy your new possibilities every bit as much as you did your opportunities to serve. Everyone who happens to be a server is every bit as much called of God as those who are served. In Jesus, the servant is free just as the free are servants!

Yes, all have been bought with a price. Jesus paid the price with His blood. Don't be so shallow to think you owe anything to anyone else to gain God's acceptance. You have no obligation whatever to buck up to the laws, rules, and regulations the systems of religion have created for you to measure up to!

Dear brothers and sisters, I will say it again, be who you are!

Abide in the never ending reality God has called you to be His children. The ramifications of this are enormous. Enjoy them all. Live it up!

Perhaps I should mention something concerning slaves. You may have the impression it was impossible for a slave to become free. Nay, nay. A slave could, in fact, purchase freedom. It would undoubtedly require a lot of effort and extra-curricular earning prowess, but it could be done. Moonlighting could bring in some extra cash. Although a commission would have to be paid to an owner a slave could give the extra money over to the temple of some god.

When enough money had been saved apart the slave could bring the master before the priest of the Temple. The priest would ceremonially hand over the money to the master and the slave would then become free.

Well, not actually completely free. The slave would now become the property of the god although free of any obligation to another human.

Now, isn't that interesting?

Jesus paid the price on your behalf. He has liberated you from any and all encumbrances binding you to any performance of self-righteousness mankind can come up with, then set you up as a permanent participant in a brand new family!

Could hardly get any better, eh?

Talk about freedom!

72. VIRGINS
(1 Corinthians 7:25-40)

Before I continue with my letter I must explain to you about a very difficult custom you might have trouble comprehending. It certainly caused its share of concern in the fellowship in Corinth. This was the core of the problem.

Most couples would enter into marriage in the customary way. However, there were some who wouldn't exactly do everything most couples did. They'd live together, eat together, go on holidays together or perhaps even share the same bed. Well, by "sharing" the same bed I mean they slept on the same bales of hay and yet stayed on their own side of the bed.

Ya, they did everything most married couples did with one major exception.

NO SEX!!!

Ya sure. Hard to imagine. I told you this wasn't going to be an easy one. I thought it would be important for me to explain this to you since I will be talking in this next section about a the situation in which a wife is also a "virgin." For real. I'm serious.

Now, don't get your nose all out of joint. Before you're too quick to criticize and condemn a couple for this kind of relationship you must pause for a moment to consider why they'd even think of entering into such an agreement. The religious and spiritual zeal of these folks needs almost to be commended, if only it had a glimmer of merit in the eyes of God.

Couples actually bought into the idea they could share a wonderful life of spiritual intimacy without having the physical intimacy get in the way. If they could keep themselves pure physically they could dwell on the spiritual more completely. Placing themselves in this delicate, not to mention challenging situation, night after night, must have been a terrible burden and strain.

With this introduction, read on...

Now, concerning "virgins."

Folks, I wish I could give you some kind of perspective of the wisdom of God concerning this one. You're just going to have to accept my opinion and perspective as one who has been mercifully granted of Jesus the ability to remain faithful to his convictions. So, I suppose my practical advice for any who would enter into such a restrictive bond of marriage would be this:

Hang in there! It's a good thing to remain faithful to your convictions!

Have you entered into a marriage relationship with your wife with the understanding you wouldn't have sex? Then don't try to get out of it.

Have you agreed to terminate this unique "marriage" relationship with your wife? Then, think twice about it before you try it again!

BUT, and if, you choose to get married again, you won't be held responsible for getting on with your life. Likewise, if the virgin wife chooses to remarry, the same thing applies as far as God is concerned.

Hey, don't kid yourselves. While you certainly don't need to fear the consequences of God's disappointment or sorrow, you most certainly will not be spared some of the pain, guilt, and anxiety as a consequence of some of your decisions here in your little corner of the world.

BUT, I'd rather spare you from having to suffer the shame and embarrassment with this practical bit of advice.

BUT, my dear friends, because there is only so much of it to go around, enjoy the time you have at your disposal!

Perhaps most folks would be better off never getting married at all. Maybe those who cried would be better off not to have wept at all. Say, happiness may not even be all it's cracked up to be.

Possessions? We'd all probably be better off with half the junk we collect! How about everybody quitting their use and abuse of this old world? There's a point to which all these things will become of no importance anyway. Sooner or later this old earth as we know it might well have served its purpose and pass out of fashion too.

BUT, that's a pretty pessimistic outlook, don't you think? I wouldn't want you to think of this life with such carelessness. Rather, give serious thought to what you do.

It only stands to reason those who choose not to consummate their marriage vows by refraining from having sex may have more time to devote to serving God and discover ways of showing their gratitude for His faithfulness.

BUT, those who are married have a practical responsibility to devote more time and effort to care for the needs of their spouse and family.

Similarly, there is a difference between a wife and a "virgin" wife. The virgin wife has chosen to consecrate the bulk of her life to set her body and spirit towards a special search for the holiness of God. BUT, the one who is totally married gives her attention to the needs of her family and to the pursuit of happiness for her husband.

Look, I hope what I'm saying will be of benefit to you. I certainly don't want you to think I'm putting some kind of law, rule, or regulation to govern your lives. BUT, I do want you to know you'll find your greatest contentment in life by faithfully following your convictions! Do well what you choose to do! Attend to the calling of God in your life with diligence. Don't be distracted from recognizing His faithfulness towards you.

BUT, if a man feels he isn't being fair to his virgin wife by not giving her the opportunity of having children while she is physically able to, then for heaven's sake, he should get to it. If they decide together children would add a special blessing to their lives, then they should finally consummate the marriage.

Have sex with your spouse!

How can there be something wrong with that?

On the other hand, if a man has enough conviction in his heart to maintain this unique relationship with a partner who is in total agreement with the arrangement, good on 'em both! If both parties can maintain their sanity and control their passions for the sake of spiritual goals, all power to them.

So, those who enjoy the physical pleasures of sex within their marriage have a good thing going. BUT, those who choose not to make sex an integral part of their relationship have a pretty good thing going too, perhaps even better for them!

A virgin wife is bound, by the law of the land, to her husband as long as he's alive. BUT, if her husband dies, she of course enjoys her perfect liberty in God to become married to whomever she wants to. BUT, know this, she will be the happiest when she follows the desires of her heart. Whether she marries or not is up to her.

Well, that's what I think anyway! At least I know I also share this sense of liberty of **ENJOYING THE LIFE** of the Spirit of Jesus within me.

73. YOU ARE NOT WHAT YOU EAT
(1 Corinthians 8:1-13)

The believers in Corinth faced many interesting challenges, not unlike you I'm sure. Confusion, anxiety, and fear aren't limited to any particular generation. Some of the difficult decisions in life hit pretty close to home. In fact, they can be downright stomach turners.

My dear friends in Corinth often faced the difficult problem of determining what to eat, and perhaps more importantly for them, what "not" to eat! The larger picture must be seen in light of the religious practices surrounding their daily lives. Yes, contrary to what you might think, society was immersed in religion. The gods played a very important role in the lives of most of the population. There was little room for apathy in the religious realm. The gods might be crazy, but you dare not take the chance to upset them. Sacrifices were the made to appease and keep on the good side of the gods who controlled virtually every aspect of life and death. Almost everyone participated in one way or another.

Now there were two kinds of sacrifice that stood out among many. A sacrifice could be made either in public or in private. You might think when an animal was sacrificed it was placed upon some altar and completely burned up. On the contrary, rarely was the entire animal ever sacrificed. More often than not it was merely a very small part of the animal, possibly even just a few strands of hair.

So what happened to the rest of a "sacrificed" animal? Let me first explain what took place in the public ceremonies.

Public sacrifices were conducted on behalf of the state and were therefore conducted with some degree of regularity. The state would provide the necessary number of animals. The priests would take the animals and prepare the required amount to appease the gods.

What was left of the animals was divided up. The priests received a certain portion of the animal meat. Another portion of the meat was given to the magistrates and other public officials. What was left over would be available for others, much of it making its way to the local butcher shops and marketplaces.

Private sacrifices were somewhat less frequent, but still had a great deal of significance. Perhaps the required blessing of a wedding or a new child would require the sacrificing of an animal to bring good fortune, the sacrifice provided by those who wanted to receive the blessing.

The sacrifice was split up into three portions. The first portion obviously was dedicated to the god with the appropriate portion burnt on the altar to take care of business. Secondly, the priest received his portion. Call it his commission or gratuity if you like. The remainder, the third portion, belonged to the worshiper for their own consumption.

In spite of all these common practices the believers in Corinth had a bit of a problem of what do with all the leftovers from these various sacrifices. For them Jesus had become the ultimate sacrifice, reducing all other sacrifices to the value of zippo.

"So, what's the problem?" you ask.

I'm not exactly sure how vegetarians handled this problem however those who could snarf down a great chunk of marbled rib-eye steak or barbecued ribs would inevitably experience a dilemma. It would be virtually impossible to tell whether the meat on the table had been offered as a sacrifice or not. I doubt very much a butcher would advertise his meat as part of some burnt offering promotion.

Even the fine dining establishments wouldn't be so presumptuous as to divulge the historical life cycle of the food it served on its menu. It is also doubtful a person would be so callous to ask their host where the burger meat came from.

What to do? The thought of eating something offered to a pagan god seemed so repulsive to many folks. "Eat out?" "Eat in?" "Can I trust my own butcher?"

As if this problem wasn't enough for the Corinthian believers, they also had to face another common belief of the day. Most folks believed completely and fearfully in the presence of devils and demons. In their minds the spirit world was very much alive with demons and evil spirits looming everywhere. An evil spirit in your body could wreak havoc within your body, spirit, and mind. The spirits loved to get into your body through the best open hole you've got.

Right! Your mouth! All they'd have to do was to attach themselves to some food and wine and then, pop, pop, fizz, fizz, into the body they is!

This eating thing could be really dangerous. The common way around it, of course, would be to dedicate the meat to a "good" god before it was slaughtered. The "good" spirit would counteract any "evil" spirit. As a result, most meat was at least dedicated, if not sacrificed.

Another solution was also available. If the meat hadn't been dedicated to a "good" god before it was slaughtered, there was one other way to make sure it was o.k. to eat. You might be surprised by this. You could always "pray" before you ate!

What a novel idea. Pray before you eat! A sure defense indeed to ensure a great dining experience. Get it blessed by a "good" god!

Yep, the Corinthian believers were a tad confused concerning what they should and shouldn't eat. Watching their diet meant more than just shedding a few of those extra pounds. Those who'd been liberated from the dominating forces of their legalistic traditions faced a trying time deliberating how they should reconcile what they did want to eat and what they felt obliged not to because of its legacy.

How could they eat something with some kind of connection to a idolatrous experience? Since they had the privilege of sitting at the table of Jesus how could they think of sitting at the feasting table of unbelievers? Were they bound to give up the rights and liberty they possessed in Jesus at the expense of being enslaved to the expectations of others? Did an understanding of the wisdom of God make them immune from the infection of thinking they were "doing" something wrong by consuming food used in a sacrificial ceremony? Are there things they could get away with in private they couldn't in public?

They asked me for some advice.

So I gave them some "food for thought!" Sometimes I just crack myself up! I just did it again.

Read on...

Well, let me respond to your questions concerning eating food offered to idols.

Look, you already know everything you need to know. However, don't let it go to your heads! Live like you know it all and soon you'll find out your old friends will tire of your puffed head.

BUT, live with your heart and you'll discover love edifies and builds up everyone you come in contact with.

When you finally think you know it all you'll discover how much you really don't know. BUT, your love of God will lead you to the incredible, invaluable discovery God loves you abundantly too! Your view and opinion of God will be greatly overshadowed by your understanding God's view and opinion of you will never change!

Sorry, perhaps this isn't exactly the way you thought I'd answer your questions concerning food. Perhaps you'll come to see I actually make some sense by telling you that you are not what you eat!

Concerning the eating of things offered in some sacrificial ceremony to some idols, we know idols have absolutely no value in this world. Don't be misguided. There is no other God. There is BUT one God!

I will grant you many folks have made gods out of a variety of things from the celestial to the earthly. I don't care how many they think there are. They can think there are as many gods and lords as they want to think.

BUT, to those of us who believe there is BUT one God. He is the Father of all. God initiated everything and everyone.

Everyone and everything is in HIM!

There's only one Jesus. By Him are all things! We owe our very eternal existence to HIM! Why everybody hasn't picked up on this incredible good news of God's habitation within us is beyond me!

Some folks, still wrapped up in the delusion of some other gods and lords to this very day, think eating food offered as a sacrifice to these idols will somehow defile themselves. BUT, that's sheer nonsense!

WE AREN'T ACCEPTED BY GOD BECAUSE OF WHAT WE EAT!

Look, God didn't extend His grace and peace to us based upon what we do or don't eat! Food, in and of itself, is morally and spiritually indifferent.

BUT, don't let your head overrule your heart. Take heed, by any means, that this understanding of the inexhaustible liberty you possess in Jesus doesn't cause too much grief and friction for those who may not have come to the same conclusion as you have.

Suppose someone who hasn't arrived at your level of understanding of God's limitless grace and peace observes you sitting in the temple of idols having a fantastic feast of hopefully not too burnt offerings. Is it possible you'd be encouraging them to do the same thing without understanding the reason why they had the same liberty to do so?

Or could it be this person might get so upset at the sight of you enjoying yourself so much they could even revert back to the strangulation of the laws, rules, and regulations they were a part of for so long? Don't incite them to go back to systems of judgment and control.

Look, Jesus died for them to set them free!

BUT, when we act without regard to the ultimate best of others by ignoring their level of understanding of the wisdom of God, then I'm afraid we show our lack of respect for the attitude Jesus has for all mankind.

So, I would rather go without meat for the rest of my life if eating meat would cause a brother or sister to slip back into the bondage of laws, rules, and regulations!

74. WHY I DO WHAT I DO
(1 Corinthians 9:1-23)

Am I not an ambassador of Jesus? Am I not liberated from the bondage of laws, rules, and regulations? Have I not witnessed the incredible work of Jesus? Aren't you believers in God's grace and peace because I've shared this wonderful news with you?

I can't claim to have been the ambassador of the love of God to everyone however I can accept the honor of having shared the good news with you. Jesus has been sealed in my life by God and I've had the great joy of informing you He has done the same for you.

There are obviously some folks who are questioning my intention and motivation in spreading such a glorious gospel. Let me pose a few questions to them.

Don't you think I, as an ambassador of the message of hope in Jesus have the right to expect a measure of support from those I teach and preach so I could eat and drink like the rest of you?

Am I any less worthy of accepting the benefit of support for a sister or wife like any of the other fine ambassadors of God like James or Peter? Or do you think only Barnabas and I should have to support ourselves by working for our sustenance?

What soldier goes out to battle after paying for his own weapons and supplies?

What farmer plants a crop in his garden or vineyard and then doesn't reap some joy by eating and drinking the fruit of his hard work?

What rancher would tend to his herd of cattle or his flock of sheep without experiencing the pleasure of eating and drinking of the products they produce?

How absurd!

Do you think I'm just saying this to justify my point of view?

Hey, even the traditions of the law recognized the honor of enjoying the rewards of hard work. Surely it is written in the Law of Moses, "You should not put a muzzle on the mouth of the ox that treads out the corn" (Deuteronomy 25:4).

Does God take care for even the welfare of oxen?

Or could it be God gave this message to declare how much He cares for us? I'm sure God meant for us to put our shoulder to the plow in the hope we could receive a blessing from our hard work.

So, if I've worked tirelessly to bring you the most precious good news you could possibly hear, is it too much to ask you to share with me even a portion of good hospitality including food, drink, clothing, and shelter which you enjoy as a result of your hard work?

You've blessed others with your support. Is it too much to think you might bless me with your assistance?

Look, I'm not complaining. It's never been my intention to expect or demand your support. BUT, I continue to endure the hardships of life on my own so I wouldn't place a burden upon you, causing you to put up barriers in the way I spread the gospel message of Jesus.

Don't you see those who minister in the religious ceremonies live off of the abundance of the temple coffers? Don't those who serve at the altar tables of the land also enjoy the leftovers of the sacrificial ceremonies? Well, I don't think it should be any different for those who preach the gospel. I believe God has ordained it that those who minister the gospel message have a right to expect support from those to whom they preach.

BUT, I've never exercised this right. Neither have I made it a motive in any of my writings. I've never made the issue of compensation a condition of my service to anyone. I would frankly rather die than to allow any person to take credit for giving me the unspeakable joy of sharing the gift of God!

Look here. Though I preach the gospel message I've nothing to boast about in my own accomplishments. I do it because I want to do it. I feel a compulsion to spread the wonderful message of God's loving grace and peace. I'd do it regardless of the cost. Yes, I would be a miserable, nasty person if I didn't preach about what I know to be the true reason for living!

I could do nothing else! I have all the reward I need when I preach of God's great love for all mankind. BUT, if I received support against my will for preaching the gospel message committed to me then what could I consider my reward?

Truthfully, I just want you to know I'll continue to preach the good news message whether I get paid or not. I'll never abuse the rights that I could demand for the sake of the gospel.

I don't owe anybody anything! And yet, I owe everything to everybody!

Get the picture? I'm the one who is rich beyond compare.

For the Jewish folks, I'd become just like a Jew so I might share the message of God with them in a way they would understand God loves them all. They live in the bondage of the law as if it really had some kind of authority.

To those who are bound up in the stranglehold of laws, rules, and regulations, I'd try to explain their bondage in a way they could understand they'd been liberated from that slavery because of Jesus. They know they aren't bound by systems of performance BUT they can live in the liberty of the Spirit of Jesus.

To those who are weak I'd love to show them how weak I am to gain the righteousness of God on my own too. Perhaps this would reveal to them how they could come to grips with the grace and peace of God as well.

I'll go to any length or depth to help anyone see God has accomplished what mankind could never do on in its own power or accomplishment. I'm not doing this to advance my own cause. No, I do this for the sake of the good news which I have the honor of preaching and teaching. I'm just as much a **PARTAKER IN GOD'S GLORIOUS PLAN** as anyone, and this is what I want everyone to know.

75. RUN LIKE STINK
(1 Corinthians 9:24-10:15)

Are you not aware, in spite of the many who actually run in a race, there is BUT only one who will be victorious to win the prize?

Well, don't settle for second place. RUN LIKE THE WIND to be the best at what you do. Be assured those who aim high don't accept apathy, indifference, or ineptitude. They remain focused on their objective.

Now an athlete runs merely to win the ivy or pine wreath placed on the victor's head after the finish line has been crossed before any of the other racers. BUT, we don't run to gain an incorruptible crown. All have been granted the incorruptible crown of God's unconditional acceptance apart from our performance!

Therefore, I don't have to run scared spitless because I might lose! I don't have to live my life with uncertainty concerning my eternal fate if I fall short of my very best. I'm not fighting on in the blind pursuit of a reward I could never achieve. A shadow boxer may fight some imaginary battle as he flings his arms at an unseen target in the air around him.

BUT, I keep myself from this ambiguous approach to life. I bring this stupid notion of working for the righteousness of God in the proper subjection to the wisdom of God's grace and peace.

Why do I say this?

Because I don't ever want to be accused of preaching a message of self-righteousness to others that I could never achieve success at myself. If I would preach a message of self-righteousness through belief, obedience to laws, rules, and regulations, or by any other measurement or standard I'd be the first person to be considered a castaway of God's favor.

Moreover, my dear friends, I don't want you to be ignorant either. Look, history is a great teacher, yet, why is it we can't learn its lessons?

Consider our forefathers, for many of them were guided by a cloud in the desert, and eventually crossed through the great sea on dry land. Surely they were immersed into the laws of Moses through their experiences of being under the cloud and the sea.

All came under the same accountability the law proclaimed. All drank from the same cup of punishment which disobedience to the law would incur. This spiritual bondage to the law would follow them wherever they went.

We now know, of course, the spiritual rock (the law) from which they drank was actually the preview of the wonderful grace of Jesus. He got to drink of the cup of punishment that we all deserved to drink.

We also know our forefathers displayed their ignorant inability to measure up to the impossible standards of the law. BUT, how could God take any pleasure in their constant failure at self-righteousness? Surely their experiences in the wilderness proved the ineptness of their own works.

Why am I bringing all this history stuff up?

To show you these things were recorded for us as an example of God's great wisdom. I'm reminding you of the history of those who've gone before demonstrating over and over again we should not lust after the same evil things.

What evil things?

They include the evil pursuit of self-righteousness through the hopeless, tireless struggle to measure up to the impossible standards of laws, rules, and regulations. Yes, they lusted after things that they thought would gain them the acceptance and favor of God!

Don't become idolaters like many of them who chose to worship the false gods of human accomplishment. The scriptures even record the pitfalls of believing one thing and doing another. After presenting their early morning burnt and peace offerings, "The people sat down to eat and to drink, and rose up to play" (Exodus 32:6).

Just as surely as you avoid the pitfalls of bondage to laws, rules, and regulations, avoid the trap of thinking your new found liberty and license removes all the consequences of sexual immorality. Just ask some of the twenty three thousand folks who paid the price for messing around with the daughters of the Midianites and the Moabites (Numbers 25:1-9).

Don't become snake-bitten by the idea bondage to laws, rules, and regulations is better for you than the liberty of living in the abundance of God's grace and peace.

Many of our ancestors were obsessed with the feeling they were better off in the bondage of the Egyptians than in the promise of the land of liberty, falling prey to the fangs of an auspicious enemy, snakes (Numbers 21:5-9).

Don't murmur either. Grumbling and complaining about your lot in life just doesn't cut it with me and certainly not with God. The unfortunate consequence of singing the blues is that you will be robbed of your joy. The destruction of your peace will surely come as you walk the path of guilt and shame with self-righteousness as your companion.

Look, all these many examples the scriptures record happened for a purpose. Don't kid yourself. They should be for us an exhortation and admonition to get with the program of God rather than the agenda of mankind.

Who was it recorded for?

ALL.

Yes, it was recorded as an example and admonition to all of those for whom the ends of the world has already come.

So, I have two words for those of you who think you are standing on some pretty solid ground to justify your own belief and performance oriented pursuit.

WATCH OUT!

Let the person who thinks they can gain the favor of God based upon belief, favor, or accomplishment take heed their ignorance isn't revealed too dramatically before their very eyes. Put your trust in your own ability and you're headed for a big let down. You'll meet up with disappointment, frustration, guilt, shame, desperation, and hopelessness at every turn. It just can't work.

BUT, the temptation to trust in the belief and works of mankind is nothing new. Mankind has been wrapped up in the idolatry of this evil pursuit for a long time now.

Don't think you've come upon an amazing truth that you have to get closer to God by what you do or don't do, by how much you give, by how much you pray, by how much you meet together with others to worship, by how well you obey some religious commandments, or by how successful you are at fulfilling the laws, rules, and regulations of any religious system.

BUT, GOD IS FAITHFUL!!!!

Did you get that?

God isn't anxious to see you suffer! Nor does He get some kind of whacked out, perverted joy in seeing His children struggle and struggle to get something they could never achieve.

Give your head a shake!

He has no intention whatsoever to tempt you with this kind of nonsense. BUT, God will show you a better way!

In the midst of your temptation to trust in your own belief and works God has made a way for you to escape the perversion of your idolatry of pursuing the evil things of self-righteousness! He has provided, in Jesus, a way of escape you can handle! Tell me you can't bear to hear a good news message like this!

Let me say it again.

Flee from this idolatry of self-righteousness and these evil things. I'm convinced I am speaking to folks who can appreciate a good thing when you see it. How could you be so stupid as to ignore such a good deal like God's grace and peace because of His great, great love for all mankind?

Mark my words.

Consider carefully what I'm telling you.

76. EXPEDIENT
(1 Corinthians 10:16-11:1)

Is not the cup of blessing, the very blood of Jesus that we are so thankful to God for, the only reason we all can participate in His wonderful plan for the whole world? Is not the bread, the very body of Jesus who was broken apart on our behalf, the only reason we all are a part of the exciting body of Jesus?

Of course!

For we, being many, are part of one bread, of one body. Surely this means we are all partakers of everything one bread embodies. Hey, if you need a practical illustration of what I am saying just think about the nation of Israel. What united them together? Was it not the fact they participated in a system of sacrifices and laws, rules, and regulations?

So, what do you want me to say?

Do you want me to say an idol is somehow important? Do you expect me to tell you what is offered as a sacrifice to an idol has some significance? BUT, I say, give your head a shake!

Any thing offered as a sacrifice by those who don't believe to any idol of their own creative imaginations is nothing more than a sorry excuse to celebrate human achievement rather than a celebration of the wisdom of God. I would rather you didn't participate in this redundant excuse to exalt the wisdom (foolishness) of mankind.

You can't enjoy the life of liberty God has provided for you in Jesus and at the same time devote yourself to the attainment of God's favor by offering the sacrifices of your own belief and accomplishments in religious systems propagating laws, rules, and regulations. It just doesn't make sense. How can you say you are pigging out in the abundance of God's smorgasbord of grace and peace while at the same time you continue to nibble at the banquet table of self-righteous behavior?

Go figure!

Do you honestly think you can provoke God to get jealous of the self-righteous crap you seem so keen to pursue? Get real! Do you seriously believe the wisdom (foolishness) of mankind can hold a candle to the wisdom of God?

I don't think so! The notion is laughable, not to mention ignorant.

I have absolute license and liberty to enjoy the abundance of everything God has placed into this world! BUT, all things are not apt or suitable given the awareness of the mind of Jesus within me.

Yes, I still have absolute license and liberty to enjoy the abundance of everything God has placed into this world! BUT, all things aren't profitable in building up or exalting the image of Jesus in me.

Look, there's little point in trying to be totally self-centered in life. BUT, I can assure you there is great pleasure and satisfaction in seeking after the ultimate best of another person.

If you happen to be walking through the market place and see a nice chunk of steak in the butcher shop, go for it. Why put yourself through the mental hassles of trying to decide whether you should buy it or not? Why agonize over whether it's been used in some sacrificial ceremony? Hey, it doesn't matter one iota!

Absolutely everything in this fantastic world has been given to us all to enjoy as much as we can at the pleasure of our bountiful and generous God!

If you get invited out for supper by one of your unbelieving friends some night, hop to it. Eat whatever is set before you. Don't get hung up on silly speculation to ease your conscience.

BUT, if someone comes up to you and makes a big deal about the fact the meat had been offered in some sacrificial ceremony and you can tell he will undoubtedly be adversely affected by your choice of dining fare then, for his sake, you'd do well to show him the courtesy and respect of his conscience.

I know, I know. Everything in the earth is God's. And I mean everything! BUT, the welfare of your friend's conscience, not yours, is a worthy standard of the attitude of Jesus.

Why should my liberty take a second seat to the conscience of another person? If God's great grace has given to me the license to partake in all of His abundance, then why I do I bear any responsibility in accepting blame for enjoying what has been set in front of me?

Well, regardless of what you're eating and drinking, regardless of what you're doing, do it to the glory of God. Don't disrespect others. I don't care who they are.

They may be Jews or Gentiles. They may be members of your own fellowship of believers. It makes no difference.

I've made it a priority to SEEK THE ULTIMATE BEST for everyone I meet. I'll try to please them in every way I possibly can. I prefer to seek the profit of others over my own. BUT, perhaps the very best way to show them all the only way they've profited of God is to explain they've been saved from the slavery of self-righteousness.

Need an example?

Then follow my example of sacrificial love even as I also am of Jesus!

77. BATTLE OF THE SEXES
(1 Corinthians 11:2-16)

The battle of the sexes is not a new conflict by any stretch of the imagination. Folks in Corinth were caught in the struggle too. Fully cognizant of the fact all are equal in the sight of God, including men and women, they remained puzzled how to apply this knowledge to the on-going function of the fellowship of the believers steeped in a heritage of separation.

Before I share with you my response to a question I thought this might be an appropriate place to inform you about a symbol that crystallizes the separation between men and women. I'm referring to the veil worn by many women-folk of the eastern culture.

The "yashmak" was a long veil that left the forehead and the eyes of a woman uncovered, yet reached down almost to the feet. Some of the veils were even more concealing with merely an opening for the eyes, reaching down to cover even the feet. If a woman had any hope of being respected she never dreamt of appearing in public without it, for without the veil a woman was in danger of being misjudged.

What was the veil for?

On one hand, it was a sign of inferiority. Women were considered to be inferior to men in the sense men were to be the head of the affairs of the home. On the other hand, it was also a truly a source of great protection for women! The authority of a woman wasn't diminished by the wearing of a veil, it was enhanced by it. She carried her authority on her head, for she could go anywhere in security and profound respect when covered with the veil.

It was a mark of tasteless, bad manners to observe a veiled woman on the street. With the veil as protection she was completely alone, supreme amongst a crowd. To the people around her she was as completely non-existent to them as she was to them. Without the veil she was wide open for insult and abuse. The veil didn't mark the inferior status of a woman rather it was the inviolable protection of her modesty and chastity.

The status of women from the Jewish perspective wasn't as kind, if you can believe it. Under Jewish law women were far inferior to men because of the order of their creation. Check out this piece of Rabbinical gobbley-gook...

"God didn't form woman out of the head lest she should become proud; nor out of the eye lest she should lust; nor out of the ear lest she should be curious; nor out of the mouth lest she should be talkative; nor out of the heart lest she should be jealous; nor out of the hand lest she should be covetous; nor out of the foot lest she should be a wandering busybody; but, out of a rib, which was always covered, therefore, modesty should be her primary quality."

Women were objects. Sad, but true, in the eye of Jewish law. Wives were simply a part of her husband's property and could be disposed of virtually at will. Even in the synagogue men ruled supreme. Women were segregated and isolated in another part of the building altogether. Equality with men was a prospect Jewish women couldn't ever even dream of becoming a reality.

Men and women are equal in the eyes of God. Each have been crowned by God with great honor in His creative genius. How could one do without the other? Sure they have different roles! Let's not kid ourselves.

However, laws, rules, and regulations concerning who can do this and who can do that in their relationship to God have no place in the family of God! The difference between what I taught them and the baggage they had been raised with was immense.

Scared to read on? Aw, come on, don't wimp out on me now. Let's go…

I'd like to commend you, my dear friends, for maintaining a fond remembrance of me. I'm happy to hear you still remember all of the teachings I gave to you when I was with you.

BUT, I must take this opportunity to refresh your memory.

JESUS IS THE HEAD OF EVERY HUMAN BEING!

Surely you've grown up with the notion the head of the woman is the man, just as the head of Jesus is God. You've been sold a bill of goods that every man who prays or teaches having his head covered with a veil brings dishonor to himself because he's really superior to women.

BUT, on the other hand, any woman who prays or teaches without wearing a veil somehow brings dishonor to herself. Hey, it would be so disgraceful she might as well be bald! If she doesn't want to wear a veil, then let's cut her hair off!

BUT, with this logic the only alternative for robbing a woman of her beauty by cutting her hair off would be for her to have to wear some kind of veil to protect her.

Hey, the logical conclusion of this unrealistic thinking would assume it would be stupid for a man to wear a veil of protection forasmuch it is a man only who is the image and glory of God, BUT, a woman is merely the glory of the man. Man wasn't created from the woman, BUT the woman was created for the man.

Rubbish!

Old Rabbinic traditions say the beauty of a women's long hair tempts even the angels (Genesis 6:1,2). Women indeed carry tremendous influence over the desires of men. Nevertheless, let me remind you of the wisdom of God contrary to this foolishness of mankind's wisdom.

Men and women need each other. Men can't live without women. Women can't exist without men. Hey, that's the way God, in His wisdom, planned it. God knew from the beginning men couldn't handle having babies. However, He also knew a woman couldn't give birth if it were not for her male partner. BUT, the wisdom of God provided it would take the creative activity of both male and female to introduce new life into this world.

Is God good or what?

Just ponder about it for a minute. Do you really think it matters one bit to God whether or not a woman is wearing a veil when she prays? BUT, it seems only natural that beautiful long hair does a whole lot more on a woman than it does on a man. Why in the world do we think a veil would somehow be required to enhance the beauty God has already adorned women with? BUT, if this upsets some of you men, too bad!

There are no such customs and traditions that operate in the family of God.

End of story!

78. PIGGIES
(1 Corinthians 11:17-34)

Now, I've a bone to pick with you! Seriously!

It's apparent you come together not for the better, BUT, for the worse. First of all, when you gather for worship there seems to be a spirit of disunity among you. I actually can understand how this could happen. It doesn't surprise me in the least there'd be heresies making their way into your fellowship. Otherwise, you wouldn't be so supportive of a variety of leaders who've caused your selfish behavior.

When you come together to worship don't waste your time and effort trying to eat a meal to commemorate what God has done for you. For it appears this only turns into a big pig-out for some and a empty plate for others. Others just get drunk!

What gives?

Haven't you got your own houses where you can eat and drink?

Do you despise the rest of the family of God so much you bring to shame those who aren't as quick to hit the potluck line up?

What do you expect me to say to you?

Do you seriously think I'd praise you for this selfish, inconsiderate behavior?

Think again!

Listen, I'm not telling you anything different than what I've received of God in Jesus. The very same night Jesus was betrayed He took some bread and gave thanks for it. Then He broke it apart and said to those who were with Him, "Take and eat this. This is my body that is broken for you. Eat in remembrance of me."

After the same manner Jesus took a cup and took a drink. Then He said,

"This cup is the new covenant which is established in my blood. Drink, and as often as you drink, drink in remembrance of me."

As often as you eat and drink until Jesus chooses to return, demonstrate the fact He unselfishly died on behalf of the whole world.

So, all who participate in the blessing of the bread of life God has provided in Jesus and all who enjoy the refreshing liberty of an abundant life from the cup of God's grace and peace, without due consideration of the selfless love which accompanied the gift, really don't understand the true meaning of what it means to be a part of the family of God!

BUT, take a look at your own heart. Enjoy the feast of God's provision in the body and blood of Jesus. If you don't participate in the feast with a healthy understanding of what God has so completely and unselfishly done for all mankind, you are really missing out. You not only mess with your own life, you mess with the lives of your brothers and sisters in Jesus! I wouldn't be surprised this is the reason why many of you are weak and sick, and some of you have driven yourselves to an early or untimely death.

For I'm convinced if we got to judge ourselves we wouldn't even be judged at all! BUT, and listen carefully now, when we were judged of God, all the chastening God was going to punish us with, was harvested in the arms of Jesus!

Why would God do that?

So we should not be condemned with anyone else in the whole world!

So, my dear friends, if you're going to continue a practice of gathering together for the specific purpose of sharing a meal to commemorate God's blessings in Jesus, then do it up right.

Honor one another.

RESPECT ONE ANOTHER.

Prefer one another.

Look, if any one is that hungry let them eat at home before they come to the gathering. In this way perhaps the piggies won't upset everyone else's time of remembrance and celebration.

If anyone has a problem with this, I'll deal with them when I get there.

79. GIFT OF GOD
(1 Corinthians 12:1-31)

Now, concerning spiritual gifts.

My dear friends, I don't want you to be ignorant of the truth. You were all at one time unbelievers led and carried away by controlling, manipulative leaders into the fallacies of dumb idolatry, deceiving you into thinking laws, rules, and regulations could somehow gain for you the righteousness you were striving to achieve on your own, with their help of course.

I want you to know it is impossible for someone who truly understands and accepts the Spirit of God within them to curse the work of Jesus! BUT, it is just as impossible for a person to declare Jesus is the Lord of "all" unless their heart has come to recognize the reality of the Spirit of Jesus is in "all!"

Now, God has at His disposal a whole variety of gifts to use to demonstrate His great loving grace and peace. BUT, all of His gifts operate out of the same Spirit of Jesus. And God surely administers His gifts in many different ways. BUT, they all are administered with the very same Spirit of Jesus.

Most assuredly, there are diversities in the way God operates, BUT, never forget it is the very same God who has worked to bring everything in conformation to His wise plan for "all!"

BUT, the manifestation of the Spirit of Jesus is given to every human being so everyone, yes absolutely everyone, would profit from the righteousness His great work achieved!

The Spirit of Jesus has used His word of wisdom to bless some folks. He has blessed others with His word of knowledge. To others it was His faith that convinced them while others were healed with the same Spirit of Jesus. Others have witnessed the working of His miracles, while others have profited from His prophetic uttering. Some indeed have been blessed as He has helped them discern a variety of influences in their lives. The Spirit of Jesus isn't limited to one language so He can help folks relate to the message of God in a way they can understand it.

BUT, remember all of these gifts are at the disposal of the one and self same Spirit of Jesus. In spite of what we may think it is He who rightly disposes, administers, and operates His gifts as He so chooses.

You do the math. The one body of Jesus is comprised of everybody. Everybody is a member of a singular family of God.

Everybody=one.

Jesus is no different. He has many gifts, many ways of using them, and yet, He is one. For it is by the one and only Spirit of Jesus we are "all" baptized into the one body!

It doesn't matter if we are Jews or Gentiles. It makes no difference to Him whether we know we are free from the struggles of self-righteousness, or whether we're still bound up in the slavery to laws, rules, and regulations trying to gain the favor of God.

Absolutely everyone has been gifted with the same great privilege of dining together in one family at the table of the Spirit of Jesus!

Remember, the body is not comprised of just one member, BUT, "all!"

If the foot could say, "Because I'm not the hand, then I'm not a part of the body," does it make the foot any less a part of the body?

If the ear could say, "Because I'm not the eye, then I'm not a part of the body," does it make the ear any less a part of the body?

If the whole body were an eye, which part of the body would do the hearing? If the whole body was doing the hearing, which part of the body would do the smelling?

BUT, now God has placed the entirety of the Spirit of Jesus into every part of His body, precisely as it pleased Him! If there was only one aspect to the Spirit of Jesus would this make any difference to the body of Jesus?

BUT, of course not.

The Spirit of Jesus isn't limited to only one sphere of gifting. Indeed He possesses all of the wonders of God, BUT, in one body!

The eye can't say to the hand, "I don't need you!" Nor again could the head say to the feet, "I don't need you either."

No, the most unlikely attributes or functions are every bit as important to the body as the ones which seem more important. For some reason we like to attribute more honor to certain of the gifts of the Spirit of Jesus than we should.

To other attributes that we value less we actually ought to honor even more. The wisdom (foolishness) of mankind has come to think there are parts we can certainly do without.

BUT, God, in His great wisdom, has seen fit to merge the entire strength of the Spirit of Jesus together so no part lacks any honor that it is due. Why? So there'd be absolutely no schism in the body of Jesus!

BUT, every part of the body of Jesus should have the same care and affect upon each and every part! When one part of the body suffers, all of the parts of the body suffer. When one part of the body is honored, every part of the body rejoices in honor.

What am I driving at?

Now you are "all" a part of the body of Jesus! In fact, "all" of you are valued members of His body!

To top it all off, God has seen fit to set in place some of the gifts of the Holy Spirit of Jesus to bless the fellowship of His family. To demonstrate and relate His great, loving grace and peace God has sent delegations of folks like apostles, prophets and teachers to this world. He declared His intentions with miracles, healings, and other means of assistance. He has set in place governing bodies and a host of different languages to get out His message.

Now, does the Holy Spirit of Jesus operate in the sphere of apostles only? Does He only use prophets to get the message out? Do you think He only uses teachers to spread the gospel? Do you think He only will use a miracle to convince folks? Do you really think healings would be the only way He could show folks how much He loves them? Or would you suspect all He'd have to do is speak in the multitude of languages in this world?

Perhaps all He'd have to do is interpret the message in a way everybody could understand it?

BUT, GET WITH THE PROGRAM!

Covet to earnestly understand the wholeness of the Spirit of Jesus has been unleashed into this world to conform it to the image of God's holy righteousness!

You want me to draw a more excellent picture than this? Well, I can't!

80. KNOWN OF GOD
(1 Corinthians 13:1-12)

- Even if I could speak in the languages of either men or angels, and didn't possess the love of God, I'd be nothing more than a noise making blast from a trumpet or the tinkling of a cymbal!
- Even if I could have the ability or gifting to see into the future.
- Even if I could understand all the mysteries of life.
- Even if I had all the knowledge I could handle.
- Even if I had all the faith I could muster in my own ability.
- Even if I had the strength to move a mountain of any size, and didn't possess the love of God, I'd be absolutely nothing!
- Even if I was wealthy enough to feed all of the poorer people in the world.
- Even if I could become a martyr for what I believe in, and didn't possess the love of God.

Even if whatever...all of these things would profit me absolutely nothing!
So what is God's love like? Well,
- it is patient,
- it is kind,
- it sure isn't jealous,
- it is sufficient on its own merit,
- it isn't needing to be puffed up,
- it is impossible for Him to behave in an improper manner,
- it isn't selfish,
- it has no need to pursue self-righteousness,
- it rejoices not in the fallacies of foolishness,
  BUT,
- it rejoices in His wise truth,
- it bears up all things,
- it believes all things,
- it has hope in all things,
- it will endure all things, and
- it will never fail,

BUT, prophetic uttering will cease, languages will cease, and knowledge will vanish! Look, we know so little it isn't even funny. We think we can predict the future with the best of them. Hey, this idea alone shows how ignorant we truly are!

BUT, when the One who is perfect is come, then that which is in part shall be wiped out!

You know, when I was a child I spoke just like a child. When I was a child I had the level of understanding of a child. BUT, since I've become a man I've put away childish things.

At this moment right now we simply enjoy a glimpse of what the heavenly perspective might actually be like. BUT, soon we'll get to gaze and peer in pure amazement at the completeness of God's love.

Right now I feel like I only know a tiny, itzy-bitzy part of the whole scope of God's love.

BUT, and this is the best part, there's a day a comin' when I'LL FINALLY COME TO KNOW GOD THE SAME WAY HE KNOWS ME!

Whoa!

81. TONGUE TIED
(1 Corinthians 13:13-14:40)

And now, there are basically three things we ought to praise God for.
1. His undying faith in His Son Jesus and His entire family.
2. The hope that He has established for the whole world.
3. His great love.

BUT, THE GREATEST OF THESE IS HIS GREAT, GREAT LOVE for all of mankind!

Earnestly seek to accept the love of God and desire to appreciate His spiritual gifts. Why? So you may be able to proclaim it to the whole world!

Go spoutin' off stuff nobody can understand. What good could come of that? God is probably the only One who could understand you.

It may be true a lot of folks don't really understand the love of God. Just let the Holy Spirit of Jesus help reveal the mysteries of God. Continue to proclaim the gospel message of God's grace and peace so you might edify, exhort, and comfort those who hear you.

If you start yackin' in a language only you understand I can guarantee the only person to benefit from it will be you, and even that's questionable. Now others who hear you babble along may think you're pretty "spiritual."

BUT, those who can communicate the love of God in a way others can understand it are the ones who truly edify those around them.

Don't get me wrong. I wish all of you could speak in all kinds of different languages so you could communicate to a whole lot more people. BUT, I would just as soon have you proclaim the good news to those around you who speak your language. You'll be a whole lot more effective if you just spoke in a language folks could understand. Everyone would be built up with a message that actually made some sense!

Makes sense to you?

Look, my dear friends, if I had come to you speaking some strange dialect, do you think I'd get more than just a few of you to understand the drift of anything I said?

Hardly. However, if I spoke in a language you all could understand I'd be quite successful in giving you some wonderful new insights, some fascinating new understandings, some phenomenal proclamations, or even some new special doctrines.

It's no different in the inanimate world. The only way you could tell the unique sounds of a flute or a harp is to hear the distinctiveness of the musical sounds produced on them by the musicians. Hey, if the trumpet player made the thing sound nothing like a trumpet blast, how would the soldiers know when to prepare for battle?

Likewise, the only way people will comprehend what you are speaking is if you speak in an understandable language. If you aren't talking their language then you may just as well be wasting your breath. It may be true there are lots of different languages in this world, each of them with their own special characteristics. If I can't make heads or tails of what someone is trying to tell me in their language, then I'm just another foreigner to them as they would be to me.

Apply this lesson to your own lives as you earnestly seek to learn more about the special ways God is showing the whole world His loving grace and peace. Learn as much as you can so you too can communicate with those you come in contact with.

Therefore, encourage those who are attempting to communicate with you to seek out an interpreter who can let you in on what they understand of God's love. You can be sure if I start speaking or praying in a language I don't even know my understanding of it will be totally unfruitful even though I may sound like I know what I am saying.

What's my point?

Well, if I can communicate the love of God with the Spirit of Jesus within me, then at least I'll be able to understand what the world I'm talking about. When I sing of the glorious grace of God with the Spirit of Jesus within me, then at least I will sing the song within my heart with full understanding too.

How do you expect those in the room to echo a hearty "AMEN!" to what you've just said or sung if they can't even understand a word you spoke or note you sang? You may have just given your best speech or sung your lungs out, BUT, nobody else will share in the work of edification you were pursuing.

I'm grateful to God I can probably speak a number of languages, perhaps more than many of you. Yet, if I had my choice I'd much rather speak five words both you and I could understand than speak ten thousand words in a language that is nothing more than gibberish to all of you.

Look, my dear friends, don't rely on the childish understanding of how you could gain the righteousness of God through your own belief or accomplishment. This childish behavior leads to nothing more than guilt, shame, frustration, and anger towards God. BUT, proceed in the understanding of men and women who've been gifted with God's acceptance, without conditions.

This is what the scriptures say:

"I will speak to this people in the foreign languages of other men, and with the lips of strangers; and not even this will make them understand what the world I am saying to them" (Isaiah 28:9-12).

Yes, God even uses different languages to proclaim His love, not for those who already believe in Him, BUT for those who still don't believe in Him. BUT, the proclamation of the unconditional acceptance of God is needed more in the circle of believers than it is in the society of unbelievers!

Suppose in your mind all the believers in the world could come together in one spot to build one another up. Each one would try to do so in their own tongue. Suppose by chance a group of folks who haven't been exposed to the good news of God's love or perhaps some non-believers showed up. What do you think they would conclude? No doubt they'd think all those believers were a bit looped, if not totally off their rockers.

BUT, if everyone is proclaiming in the adult understanding of the universal language of God's favor and acceptance, what do you think the one who hasn't been exposed to such a message or one who doesn't believe will likely conclude? They'd be convinced they were judged of God in Jesus just like everybody else in the world was!

Listen, in God's sight there are no more secrets of the heart. Everything, including all the frailties and shortcomings of the human endeavor, has been made right in Jesus.

Response?

When folks are confronted with such overwhelming news of God's grace and peace, how can they not fall down on their faces and worship God? They'll go out and tell all their friends what they've heard. They will report God is in everyone and this is the only truth that matters!

So, my dear friends, what's it like when you get together? Do each of you want to take a turn in building up the others? Do you make room for some to share a song, to share a thought of doctrine, to speak in their own language, to share some revelation, or perhaps to share a special insight or interpretation of the scriptures?

I can only hope you'll let all things be done in an orderly manner so everyone will be built up and encouraged in the good news message of Jesus.

Now, if someone would like to communicate in their own language, then perhaps for times sake, it would be better for only two or three folks to speak through an interpreter. If nobody is there to interpret it would only make sense to encourage them to stay and continue to worship God in silence. Allow everyone to discern whether the two or three who proclaim the gospel message have a clue themselves as to what it's all about.

BUT, if there seems to be some disagreement, then let the one who disagrees make their point while the original speaker considers their understanding. The best way for all of you to learn and grow is to communicate your opinions and understanding of God's love with each other so you all may learn and be comforted by God's goodness to all.

Those who wish to tell everyone what the prophets of old have declared about God better teach the very same thing the prophets of old did. God, you see, isn't the author of confusion, **BUT, HE IS THE AUTHOR OF PEACE.** He introduced His peace and grace to the entire family of God.

"Women must shut up in church."

"Women are not permitted to speak in church."

"BUT women are commanded to be obedient, at least that's what the law says."

"Women, if you want to know something, ask your husbands at home later."

"Women, it's shameful for you to speak in church."

Where does this pile of crap come from? Did you get this nonsense from God? Or did you come by this incredibly ignorant point of view all on your own?

Well, give your head a shake!

If any man thinks he has some special corner on the blessing of God let him think again! If anyone thinks they are so prophetic or spiritual, then they'd better take another look at all the things I've taught and written to you concerning God's unlimited acceptance and inclusion of all, men and women alike.

BUT, if any man wants to remain in the shallowness of his ignorance, that's unfortunate. Let 'im stay stupid!

Let me repeat my opinion my dear friends.

Yearn to hear the proclamation of the wisdom of God.

Don't forbid those who may speak a different language than you to contribute to your education in the understanding of God's universal love. Just see to it that you do things in a proper order and climate for your mutual benefit and growth in your understanding of the great gospel message of God's grace and peace.

82. **STING OF DEATH**
(1 Corinthians 15:1-58)

My dear friends, since I've just shared with you again some thoughts regarding your attitude towards others this might be as good a place as any to remind you once again of the gospel message of God's loving grace and peace I preached to you when I was with you. You accepted the glorious good news and I'm confident God hasn't changed His mind concerning your eternal destiny! That's the only way you had any chance of standing in the righteousness of God. It was because of God's wise plan you were saved in the first place through the work of Jesus.

If you don't remember what I preached to you I'm afraid you'll continue to place your hope in the vain attempts of self-righteousness. For I delivered to you the very same good news I've received.

What do I know?

According to the scriptures Jesus died for the sins of the entire world!

He was buried then rose again on the third day, once again according to the scriptures. A number of folks like Peter and other disciples saw Him. Jesus was also seen by more than five hundred folks at one time, some are alive today to tell about it although unfortunately some of the witnesses of His appearance have passed away by now. He appeared to James as well as to many of the other leaders of the fellowship of believers.

To my knowledge I was the last one who saw the resurrected Jesus. I'm glad for the experience although it may seem to be out of timing with the earlier appearances to the leaders of the fellowship of believers. I feel like a child who didn't make his appearance on the anticipated due date, glad for the experience of birth in spite of the unexpected arrival.

In a way, I consider myself the very least of the directors of the band of believers. I hardly even qualify to be a leader because I persecuted the believers in the family of God so vehemently.

BUT, it is only by the grace of God I am who I am!

I'm confidant God is pleased His grace towards the whole world, and towards me in particular, was not placed in vain.

BUT, I've worked harder to spread the gospel of God's grace and peace more than anyone else. Maybe I shouldn't have said it that way because I certainly don't wish to imply I'm doing it to gain something from God. BUT, I want to assure you all the only reason why I work so hard is because I feel so overwhelmed God would impose His grace upon my life, and now I have the great honor and privilege of serving Him.

It doesn't matter one speck to me who gets the good news out. I'm more than happy to do it. I'm also pleased other leaders are sharing the gospel message. As we preach folks like you start to believe in God's great love for "all."

If the truth concerning the resurrection of Jesus is being preached by us, how come some of you are saying there is no resurrection of the dead?

BUT, if there is no resurrection of the dead, then Jesus hasn't risen either!

And if Jesus isn't risen, then we might as well toss all of our preaching and teaching out the window!

Any faith and hope you've placed in God's will and ability to carry out His wise plan would also be in vain. Yes, I'll even go so far as to say we could justifiably be accused of being false witnesses of the promises of God.

Why?

Because we've testified God did raise Jesus up from death. If God didn't raise up Jesus it's definite everyone else who dies doesn't have a prayer to see a life beyond this one.

Let me say it again in a different way.

If all those who die (and isn't that everybody?) will not rise up to a new life in Jesus, then Jesus wasn't raised from the dead either!

And if Jesus wasn't raised from the dead, your faith in His ability to give you the righteousness of God is useless, making it necessary for you to return to the pathetic struggle of self-righteousness, and making it absolutely essential for you to suffer the agony and defeat of living in the bondage of laws, rules, and regulations to help you work to attain the favor of God.

You know what?

Even those who've died believing Jesus died and was raised again for the whole world are dead in the water too. They are just as lost as if they had never believed.

Now, you may be blown over by this next statement.

If, in this life, we only have "hope" in Jesus, we are of all people most miserable!

BUT, now is Jesus risen from the dead!

Signed, sealed, and delivered! Done deal! Fact! Undeniable truth!

Jesus has become the very first of all those who have died or will die, raised to a new life in the abundance of God's life and liberty. You see, it was man who introduced death into this world. In this same way, it was man who introduced the resurrection of the dead!

Why do I say this?

Think of it this way. Like Adam, every person on this world is going to die. Even so, like Jesus, every person who's ever walked this earth will be made alive!

BUT, every person will go through the process of birth, of death, and of a resurrection to eternal life with God, the Father and Jesus the Son!

Jesus was the first to demonstrate the reality of this new order. Jesus was born a human being. Jesus died a human being. Then Jesus was raised to His eternal union with God in the fullness of His glorious nature in God!

The purpose for Jesus coming to this world was to make "all" a part of His family. Therefore, since every person, past, present, and future was made to be one with Jesus, the same incredible process and order will happen to everybody!

The final victory was won when Jesus delivered up His kingdom to God, even the Father of us all. With the birth, death, and resurrection of Jesus God put to rest any and all rule, all authority, and all power opposed to His reign.

You see, God must reign, and He reigned even before He'd put all His enemies under His feet. The death of Jesus took care of all enemies and opposition to God with one exception. There was still remained one last enemy God needed to deal with.

Death itself!

Yes, God took care of that one too!

With the resurrection of Jesus "all" things were put into subjection to God.

BUT, when the psalmist said "all things are put under Him" (Psalms 8:6), he basically meant everything would be put under God's subjection, with one notable exception, Jesus, the One by whom this subjection would be accomplished.

Then something incredible took place! After the birth, death, and resurrection of Jesus everything, including death, were subdued to God. Then the Son, Jesus, subjected Himself to the One who made it all possible!

Why would He do that?

So God would be all in "all!"

Explain this to me. If the dead aren't even going to rise from their deadness, why do their living kinfolk go and get baptized for those who are already dead? Why would someone even think they could affect the eternal destiny of some else who has already passed out of this life? Why does anyone waste their time worrying about what's happened to their loved one at their death?

I protest!

Just as sure as we rejoice Jesus has us in the palm of His hand, I face death literally everyday. I've fought in battles as fierce as those mighty men in the wild animal pits of the sports stadiums of Ephesus.

My question to you is this. If there isn't going to be a life with God in the life after this one, then what's the point of exposing my life to these stupid dangers?

If the dead won't rise again we might as well adopt the "live it up" mentality many have adopted. What do they say? It goes something like, "let's eat, drink, and be merry, for tomorrow we die!"

Well, be not deceived!

Stupid in, ignorance out.

Those who spout out the crap of contradiction to the grace and peace of God are only deceiving folks into falling under the control of their systems, Godly and ungodly alike!

WAKE UP!

Wake up to the righteousness God has already placed within "all" in Jesus!

Stop pursuing the nonsense of self-righteous notions belief or effort have any influence upon the eternal destiny of anyone.

Unfortunately, there are still those out there who don't understand or know about the wisdom of God's loving grace and peace for the entire world. If you still haven't got it after all you know, hey, shame on you!

BUT, I just know someone's going to stand up and ask, "How are the dead going to get raised up?" And, "What kind of body are we going to get when we do arise from the dead?"

What ignorant questions. Just think about it for a minute.

When a seed gets planted, what does the end product look like? Doesn't the seed die, and in a sense, get translated or reborn into a fruit, a grain, or a plant? You may plant some seeds of bare grain and end up with some wheat, barley, rye, or some other grain harvest.

BUT, God can jolly well do what He wants to do. God has seen to it everybody has a body in this life and surely He will see to it everyone has a body suitable for them in the next life. Hey, everybody down here looks different to me. Sure, humans looks like humans, animals looks like animals, fish look like fish, and birds look like birds.

Go figure! There are also heavenly bodies as surely as there are earthly bodies. BUT, the glory of the celestial body is one thing and the glory of the earthly body is quite another. There's one kind of glory the sun enjoys, a different glory the moon enjoys, and another glory the stars enjoy. For even one star is different from another star in the glory they share.

So also is the resurrection of those who are dead in their earthly body. There are some major differences between the earthly and the celestial body. Let me give you a short list of the differences:

The earthly body is:
- Corruptible.
- Dishonorable,
- Weak.
- Natural.

The celestial body is:
- Incorruptible
- Glorious.
- Powerful.
- Spiritual.

Yes, certainly there's a natural body all humans occupy while they're here on this earthly home. There's also a spiritual body all humans will occupy when they step into their eternal home.

The scriptures bear me up on this when it says "the first man Adam was made a living soul" (Genesis 3:7). Well, the last Adam (Jesus) was made a "life giving" soul.

Why do you think mankind was not first given a celestial body? BUT, God in His wisdom chose to give all an earthly body to enjoy while here on earth, and then afterward, He'll clothe us anew in celestial bodies. The first body of mankind was created out of the earth, therefore bears all the characteristics of the earthy nature. The second we'll inhabit is in the body of Jesus in our celestial home.

So, while we're here on this earth we'll continue to occupy these physical, earthly bodies. When these corruptible bodies deteriorate or cease to exist we'll receive from God the same kind of celestial body Jesus occupies! Just as surely as we've born the image of the earthy nature in our bodies we'll bear the image of the celestial nature when we die.

Pay attention my dear friends.

Mortal flesh and blood cannot inherit the kingdom of God! Neither does corruption inherit incorruption.

Listen up! I'll describe the mystery of God's wisdom to you again.

When we die, we don't just nod off into some great sleeping, slumber party in the sky. BUT, we'll "all" be changed!

In a moment, in the twinkling of an eye, when the last trumpet sounded to announce the death and resurrection of Jesus, "all" those who'd previously died were raised to incorruptibility and "all" those who follow in the footsteps of an earthly death had their eternal destiny completely reshaped!

You see, the corrupted, dead earthly body needed a celestial make over. The corruptible needed to be made incorruptible. Mortality was altered into immortality. So, when your corruptible earthly body passes away and is reborn in its incorruptible form and when your mortal body is exchanged for your immortal body, then the scriptures will truly be fulfilled.

"Death is swallowed up in victory" (Isaiah 25:8)!

"O death, where is your sting? O grave, where is your victory" (Hosea 13:14)?

What was the sting of death?

The sting of death was God's punishment for the self-righteous attitude of mankind. What was the strength of this selfish attachment to pursue our own way to God's acceptance? Laws, rules, and regulations!

BUT, thanks be to God.

Why?

He's given the entire world the victory over death through Jesus our Lord!

Therefore, my dear, dear friends, be steadfast and unmovable in your confidence of God's wisdom, always abounding in joy at the work of Jesus on your behalf!

Now you know you don't have to continue to labor in vain to gain the righteousness of God.

He's already given it to you in Jesus!

83. CONCLUSION OF 2ND CORINTHIANS
(1 Corinthians 16:1-24)

Now, here are a few words concerning the collection of gifts for the believers in Jerusalem who are suffering in very difficult times. I've put out a special request to all of the fellowships throughout Galatia and I'm making the same plea to you. I'd like to see each of you, at the very beginning of each week, set apart a sacrificial portion of the income you've worked so hard for. I'm confident in this way a great gift will already be established so I won't have to go around begging for a huge collection when I arrive at your doorstep.

When I do get to Corinth I'd like to send those whom you chose to represent you with your great and generous gifts to the fine folks in Jerusalem. If it works out I can make the trip to Jerusalem too I'd be delighted to have them join me. I plan on coming to you after I pass through Macedonia since I'd like to go that way anyway. There's a good possibility I'll stay with you for a while, perhaps even right through the winter months. Then you can give me a good send-off to wherever I have the opportunity to travel to next.

I don't plan on coming to see you now because if I did it would only be a quick pit stop visit. BUT, I'd rather spend a lot more time with you as I anticipate the timing of God. BUT, at the moment, I intend on staying here in Ephesus at least until the feast of the Passover, for a great door of opportunity has been opened up for me to do a significant amount of work in this area. The gospel of God's grace and peace has many adversaries and I find the challenge of sharing God's great love in these circumstances very stimulating.

Now, if Timothy happens to come to you please don't scare the poor kid out of his wits. Cut him a little slack. He's working as hard as he can to share the message of great news wherever he goes just as I do. In spite of the fact Tim might be a bit younger than many of you I encourage you to treat him with the respect he deserves. Let him work together with you in peace and harmony until he has the opportunity to come to me. Yes, I'm actually anticipating Tim will show up quite unexpectedly with some of you who may be traveling this way on business or pleasure.

CONCLUSION OF 2ND CORINTHIANS

Concerning our brother Apollos, let me just set the record straight. I really wanted him to accompany those who have brought you this letter from me. BUT, he just didn't feel this was the right time for him to leave me alone here in Ephesus. BUT, he definitely will come to you when he feels the timing is more convenient for all concerned.

Watch out for deceivers!
STAND FIRM!

Do not rely on anything else than the faith of Jesus that has accomplished your righteousness and liberty. Quit being like other folks who continue to live under the bondage of laws, rules, and regulations in the enslaving performance mode of pursuing self-righteousness.

Be strong to refute those who'd stand against the wisdom of God to extend His grace to "all."

Let the example of the unselfish, "all" encompassing love of God be the motivating factor in everything you do and say.

You're all very well acquainted with Stephanas and his whole family. They were the very first ones to believe in all of Achaia. You know they've become addicted with serving others. Well, I challenge every one of you to follow in their example. Submit yourselves to their guidance and to all those other wonderful folk who are laboring as tirelessly as we are to help others see the greatness of God's love for the whole world.

I'm tickled pink Stephanas, Fortunatus, and Achaicus have arrived here in Ephesus to see me. Seeing them makes up at least in part I can't see all of you at this particular time. I know they've refreshed my spirit in the same way they've been a blessing to you. Acknowledge their great contribution when they return.

I'd like to take this final opportunity to pass on greeting to you from all of the believers here in Asia. Aquila and Priscilla in particular, in addition to all of the other believers who meet together in their house, would like me to send along their best regards. Everyone wants to say "Hi!

In fact, why not just give each other a good old-fashioned bear hug and kiss as if we were there to do it ourselves!

Lucky for you I haven't written this whole letter in my own handwriting.

However, I'd like to write these final salutations just to prove I can still write, even though my penmanship leaves much to be desired.

Listen carefully!

If anybody would willingly be so stupid as to choose to ignore or disbelieve the incredible love of God in Jesus for the whole world, well, just let them continue to live in the guilt, shame, and fear. These are depressing symptoms and constant companions of those who seek the righteousness of God through their own systems of belief and accomplishment.

Jesus is already at hand! He has accomplished for "everyone" what "nobody" could accomplish on their own!

In Jesus, "all" have already received the righteousness of God!

The grace and peace of God in Jesus is with you!

I'm sending you all the love Jesus has flooded into my heart for you.

Take care. See you soon.

Trip # 14
QUICK TRIP TO CORINTH THEN BACK TO EPHESUS

3rd LETTER TO THE CORINTHIANS

84. INTRODUCTION OF THE "SEVERE" LETTER

"No news is good news."

Who said that anyway? Wonder if they knew what they were talking about. No news ever brought much comfort to me. Hey, bad news would be almost as good as no news.

What I'm referring to, of course, is a response to this second letter that I had dispatched to the believers in Corinth. I'm sure the letter would have been read to everyone in the fellowship. I waited and waited for a response. Things were tough enough in Ephesus however, I waged an emotional struggle waiting for news from Corinth.

What to do?

I couldn't stand it anymore. I decided the best way to get the information was probably to just go there and get it first-hand. The three-day boat trip to Corinth would have to be an obstacle I'd have to get over.

What I found when I arrived almost broke my heart. The believers were embroiled in petty squabbles and misunderstandings. Selfishness persisted to the point they just couldn't seem to get their act together. The great news message of liberty in the grace and peace of God was being distorted and misrepresented by any number of deceiving, smooth-talking scumbags bent on power and greed.

I did my best to restore a sense of calm and order by exhorting and inspiring them to stand firm in the message of God's great loving grace and peace. I said my piece and went back to Ephesus on the next available boat.

You know, sometimes you just have to put in your two shekels and let it be. Other times, two just isn't enough! This was one of those times.

Try as I might, I just couldn't get the Corinthians off my mind. I had this feeling another letter was in order. Perhaps another letter would just reinforce what I'd just told them in person. Some folks who've read the letter have accused me of being a tad severe with this one.

I'll let you judge for yourselves...

85. WEAPONS OF OUR WARFARE
(2 Corinthians 10:1-18)

Now I, Paul, am once again going to plead with you, with all the humility and gentleness of Jesus in me. Perhaps I should even start off by apologizing for being so timid when I'm with you, and yet, so bold in my letters.

BUT, I'm begging you, don't provoke me to the point I'll have to be so bold when I come to see you the next time. Some of you are really ticking me off. It's incredible to me folks think we, as believers in the gospel message of God's grace and peace, are the ones who are all mixed up, following after the wisdom of our own imaginations.

HUMBUG!

We may still walk around on this earth like everyone else does, however, I can assure you we no longer do battle in the warfare for God's righteousness like those trapped and bound in the pursuit of self-righteousness!

Why?

Because we don't need any weapons! The war has already been won far beyond the scope of human interaction. BUT, mighty is God, for He has already won the war for His righteousness on behalf of "all." Yes, it was God who pulled down the entire host of strongholds that bound and enslaved mankind to "do" something to gain His favor. God smote asunder all of the weird and wacky imaginations of mankind's wisdom.

Oh, did I say wisdom? I meant to say "foolishness!"

Let me say it again. God did away with every notion of every thing that tried to exalt itself against the wisdom of God. He brought into captivity every thought of human endeavor and put it where it belongs at the feet of Jesus. The obedience of Jesus to the will of God was all it took.

And that's all it took!

You see, God was fully prepared to give everyone what they deserved for their inability to master all of the laws, rules, and regulations mankind devised to gain God's righteousness. You bet. We all blew it. It was impossible to keep the standard. Good thing Jesus entered the picture to fulfill every jot and tittle of obedience required of the entire world!

Why is it you're still bound and determined to let the outward appearances of man's belief and accomplishments be the standard you think is key to gaining the righteousness of God?

Anyone has the confidence to know they're a part of the family of God in Jesus should give their head a shake and realize just as they've been adopted into the family of God in Jesus so has absolutely everyone else!

Look, if anyone has bragging rights it's me.

The authority I have in Jesus to build you up instead of ripping you apart is surely not something that I'm ashamed of. I'm not afraid of telling you these same things right to your face. Don't think I'm speaking so harshly just because I'm writing these words to you.

"Paul's letters," some say, "are pretty heavy duty and powerful, BUT, he sure does look goofy. Not only that, he talks funny too!"

Go ahead. Make fun. Let those who think like this have their little bit of fun with me. Let me assure them the next time I come I'll really demonstrate to them I can talk as hard and long as I can write!

It's not my intention to compare myself to anyone else. Others may enjoy boasting of their own accomplishments, BUT those who measure themselves according to their own accomplishments as well as the accomplishments of others are pretty stupid to say the least.

BUT, those of us who believe in what God has done for the entire world in Jesus know we don't have to boast in something we did. Why? Because what we have already is way beyond our capacity or ability to accomplish!

BUT, what we can boast of is the measure of the grace and peace God in His great love has given to each and every soul in the whole wide world, including you and I!

For it is impossible for any of us to gain the righteousness of God by whatever system of belief or achievement we might aspire to. We can compare ourselves to each other as much as we want. This just won't cut it.

The only thing worth doing is preaching the gospel message of Jesus.

There's no sense in boasting about things way beyond our control. There's nothing at all in the accomplishments of humankind worthwhile bragging about. BUT, we have the confidence as we continue to learn and grow in the knowledge the wisdom and work of God in Jesus on our behalf for we are abundantly enlarged by the spirit of grace and peace of Jesus at work in our lives.

It's our ambition to preach the great gospel message in the regions far beyond Corinth. Please know it isn't my intention to reap what other folks have sown. I'm not a seed picker! BUT, if anyone wants to take the credit for something let them rather accept all of the honor, glory, and praise Jesus has placed in them by what He has accomplished!

Why do I say that?

Because it not the ones who've commended themselves to God who are approved, BUT, only those whom Jesus has commended who are indeed acceptable to God!

86. BRAGGING RIGHTS
(2 Corinthians 11:1-12:10)

Humor me for a bit. Stick with me while I get a few more things off my chest.

I make no apology for being highly protective of you. Why? Because I introduced you to the One who loves and cares for you far beyond your wildest dreams. You are to Jesus the purest, most beautiful bride He could ever have asked for!

BUT, I'm scared by means as simple as the subtle way in which Eve was beguiled by a slithering serpent that you too will allow your minds to be deceived and corrupted away from the simplicity of God's loving grace and peace in Jesus.

I fear some bottom dwelling scumbags might come along preaching about another great savior of mankind, other than the One and only Jesus whom we have preached to you. I'm afraid you might get sucked into thinking there is some other kind of spirit that could work its way into your system other than the Spirit of Jesus who is already within you.

DON'T BUY INTO THE LOAD OF CRAP some "religious" farmers are spreading, exhorting you to fall in line with their system of beliefs, laws, rules, and regulations in order to gain the best results with God.

This pile of hooey is completely contrary to the one and only good news gospel message of God's unconditional gift of His loving grace and peace!

I suppose I may not hold a candle to some of the super preachers who've come along. BUT, though I may not be the most eloquent as far as public speaking is concerned, I certainly don't have to take a back seat to anyone as far as knowing and understanding the wisdom of God. BUT, I'm confident I've communicated to you the entirety of truth concerning God's manifestation of His love in Jesus for the whole world in all things.

Have I committed some kind of offense because I chose not to charge you a fee for the good news I've brought you, choosing rather to support myself while I continue to preach this glorious gospel?

Well I say, "Nay, Nay!"

On the contrary, I feel like I've robbed other groups of believers who've continued to support me financially even during the time I ministered in your neck of the woods. Hey, I need food, clothing, and shelter just like anyone else does. And yet, when I found myself wanting in your midst, I didn't come begging to you for handouts. In fact, it was our brothers and sisters in Macedonia who supplied what I was lacking. Yes, in all things I've kept myself from being a burden to any of you. That's the way I wanted it. That's the way I will continue to operate.

I know the truth of God's love in Jesus is within me and nobody will stop me from sharing and boasting of the reality of this message with anyone in the regions all around Achaia.

Does this mean you aren't important to me? Don't be ridiculous! Do you honestly think I don't love you anymore? Give your head a shake! God knows I care about you passionately.

BUT, I can promise you I'll continue to do what I'm doing right now. I'll carry on preaching the good news in Jesus so I can cause as much trouble as I can for those who try to spread a different message.

If I can eliminate any opportunity for these religious rapists to molest and plunder the unsuspecting, then I'll do it. They can claim whatever they want to about their way of belief or achievement. The only glory they have is in Jesus and He represents the only claim to eternal fame I can claim!

Believe me, these witchcraft artists are preaching a false message of hope in the self-righteous behavior of mankind. They are full of deceit, masquerading as true evangelists of Jesus. We shouldn't be so surprised by their tactics, however, don't marvel at even their fate. Hey, Satan himself has been transformed into an angel of light by God's love! Look, it's no big deal for God to transform all of those who've bought into the deceptive message of Satan's former strategy of linking the eternal destiny of folks with their works into ministers of God's message of righteousness for all!

Let me say it again.

Don't base the degree of my stupidity or ignorance on my looks alone. Ha! However, if you must regard me a fool, then at least accept me for a fool who isn't afraid to boast about what God has done for me in Jesus.

BUT, if I could leave Jesus out of the discussion for a moment, I could confidently boast as much as any other foolish folks about accomplishment. Many others glory in their grandiose achievements. Well, I can brag with the best of them. Apparently you seem to have no difficulty in tolerating foolish preachers and their ideas since you consider yourselves so wise in knowledge and understanding.

Well, you're a bunch of losers to trust in the wisdom (foolishness) of mankind. You're big losers if another person or system places you into the bondage of their laws, rules, and regulations to gain the favor of God. You're losers if you get devoured by those who prey upon the frailties of human understanding. You're losers if you place your eternal destiny in the palms of other humanoids. You're losers if you choose to exalt your own beliefs and abilities over the limitless gift of God. You're losers if you allow the speculations and opinions of others to govern the path of your liberty in Jesus.

I know it's an exercise in foolishness, however, let me offer some reasons I could boast if we were to leave Jesus out of the picture completely and only talk about the weak and fruitless venture of our performance based passion for self-righteousness. While you're so willing to accept the bold professions of fools who reveal confidence in their own ability, then please allow me the luxury of so proudly and boldly defending my own heritage and accomplishments, as if this actually accounted for anything in God's eyes.

Are these quacks Hebrews? Well, so am I!

Are these fools Israelites? Hey, so am I!

Are these deceivers descendants of Abraham? Right again, so am I!

Are they ministers of Jesus? Remember, I'm speaking as a total fool right now. I'm even more of a minister of Jesus than they are! I've labored more diligently and tirelessly than anybody else. I've been beaten more times than I care to remember. I've seen more prison cells than most career criminals. I've been left for dead on more than one occasion. The Jews themselves whipped on me at least five separate beatings with 39 lashes each time. Sure, I can count too!

Thirty nine lashes!

No more! No less!

Let me assure you the beater was counting ever fling of the whip with meticulous attention. Did you know if the person doing the scourging miscounted there were serious consequences to pay? The master of the whip himself would be beaten if he dished out 40 lashes. Yes, one small mistake could cost him his life, or he could find himself doing some hard time in some forsaken land of exile.

Getting a whipping isn't one of those experiences I'd highly recommend for anyone. The party would get started when the offensive, I should say "offending," person would be placed between two large pillars of stone, each hand tied to one of the pillars. The leader of the synagogue would grab hold of the garments of the prisoner and rip them apart, laying bare the chest for the whipping to be most effective. A stone step would be placed behind the "whooppee" so the "whoopper" could have a better vantage point.

The whip was made of calf hide, double wrapped around the wrist with two long straps dangling down. The hand-piece completely covered the large paw of the handler while the tail of the whip stretched all the way down to the scourger's navel.

Picture this. The whip, as it strikes the prisoner, hits on the shoulder with one end. However, it actually has its effectiveness stretched to the max as the rest of the whip strikes all the way down to the belly button. Ouch!

Thirteen of the stripes were to be administered to the front of the body. Twenty-six would be struck to the backside. It was permissible to hit the prisoner only when he was bending down, never when he was standing or sitting. The blows were applied with full force. It's little wonder death was more than a potential outcome!

Even the Romans beat me on 3 different occasions with the rods of birch wood, despite the illegalities of beating a Roman citizen. I was stoned so bad in Lystra, and they used real stones, they actually left me for dead! Traveling by boat wasn't exactly a cakewalk for me either because we were forced to abandon ship 3 different times. One time I spent a night and a day perilously treading water to stay alive. My constant traveling has put me in dangerous situations beyond description. I've had my share of problems on the waterways, with hoodlums and robbers, with my own kindred countrymen, with folks of other nationalities, in the cities, in the countryside, and on the ocean.

I've also faced the wrath of many who showed themselves to be my friends yet turning out to be gathered against me. I've agonized in weariness and pain, in sleepless nights, in hunger, in thirst, without food quite often, left alone in the cold without adequate shelter or clothing.

If these daily external things weren't enough to endure, I've also had to bear the responsibility of caring for all of the fellowships of believers I've helped to establish. Who is weak that I wouldn't give of my strength to make them strong? Who out there has been offended that I wouldn't gladly accept the burning pain of rejection and anguish so they may be spared?

If it's necessary I continue to boast there's only one thing to boast about. What's that? I'll only brag of my own inabilities and frailties in my quest to achieve the righteousness of God and to glory in the ability and wisdom of God to gift me with the glory of Jesus! The God and Father of Jesus, who is blessed forevermore, knows I'm telling you the truth.

Yes, I could regale you with stories like events that occurred in Damascus. The governor, under Aretas the King, kept an entire garrison of soldiers prepared to arrest me. Only because some friends lowered me down the outer walls of the city in a basket was I able to escape the cruel intentions of the governor.

However, it's not expedient for me to get carried away in tooting my own horn. Some folks get all excited about sharing their mysterious visions and revelations they've had of Jesus. I knew a fellow believer who claims to have had an extra ordinary experience more than fourteen years ago. Whether this experience was an actual physical event or an out of body experience of some kind I don't really know. God probably knows what happened. He believes he was literally caught up into what he called the "third" heaven!

I also know of another believer, again whether the experience was something he actually encountered or whether it was just a dream God only knows. Now he tells of how he was caught up into a paradise-like garden for an intimate walk with God. He confessed it wouldn't be right for him to even talk about their conversation!

Well, if someone else wants to brag about incredible experiences like these I can only say "good on ya."

I prefer not to boast about my personal experiences other than to use them to show how inadequate and unworthy I am to receive the righteousness of God based on my performance. Yes, I may have every reason to receive the applause of others for all I've done, BUT, I'd be a fool to think God loves me any more, or any less, because of what I believe or what I've accomplish! I'm telling the truth.

BUT, I'd like to make it abundantly clear, lest anybody thing more highly of me by what I appear to be, or by what my reputation has made me out to be, and lest I should be praised and exalted way out of proportion because of the many stories probably floating around out there concerning me, I bear a constant reminder in my physical body of my human limitation of achieving self-righteousness. I've actually even asked God three times to remove some agonizing thorn in my flesh.

You know what He said to me?

"My grace is all you need. It was sufficient for me to gift you with my righteousness. You see, my strength is made perfect to overcome the weakness of your inabilities."

So, most happily will I therefore rather glory in my inability and insufficiency to gain the righteousness of God.

Why? Why not? I'd much rather acknowledge the incredible power of Jesus resting upon my life.

Hit me. Bring it on. Sickness. Criticism. Rejection. Necessities of life. Persecution. Distress.

You name it. I don't care. Bring it on. I can handle it.

For the incredible joy of telling others of the most incredible message of God's loving aspirations for all of mankind I will glad bear any amount of stuff coming my way. I'm the absolute strongest when I know and understand completely I didn't have a hope of ever attaining the favor of God in my own strength or ability!

87. CONCLUSION of 3rd CORINTHIANS
(2 Corinthians 12:11-13:14)

You've compelled me to explain why it is I brag on God so much. Well, He's the only One who deserves any glory and praise! Oh sure, I'm more than happy to accept the fact you like me too. I'm thrilled you accept me as playing second fiddle to no one else, even though this doesn't prove anything to God. I'm positive the signs of my ministry were demonstrated to you in all patience, in demonstrations, in marvelous power, and in mighty works and deeds.

Is there something causing you to think you're inferior to any of the other fellowships? Is it because I didn't place a burden upon you to supply my physical needs? If you get that impression from me, please forgive me this indiscretion.

Look, I'm ready to come and visit you a third time if necessary. I'll tell you right now I won't place any burden on you even then. I bear no intention of seeking what's yours.

BUT, what I do want is you! It isn't the responsibility of the children to care for their parents, BUT it's the parent's responsibility to see their children mature in life and wisdom. Well, you're like children to me, so, to that end, I'll very gladly spend and be spent for you!

It seems, however, the more I love you the less you seem to love me. BUT, be that as it may, I still can say I didn't become a burden to any of you. Oh, you may think I'm clever enough to get something from you when you weren't looking.

Did I make a profit off any of you when I sent other workers to work on your behalf? I sent Titus and with him I sent another brother.

Did Titus make some gains from you? Didn't Titus and I walk in the same spirit of devotion? Didn't Titus and I walk in the same steps of integrity?"

Do you think we need to offer to you some sort of excuse for the way we conducted ourselves or because I need to justify my actions to you?

Not on your life!

We speak only to spread the good news of God' love demonstrated in Jesus for the whole world.

BUT, don't get me wrong. We do all things, my dear friends, so you might be built up and encouraged in the wisdom of God. For I'm afraid when I come to see you again I won't be happy to find you as mature as I'd like to. It wouldn't surprise me if you weren't too tickled to see me given all of the debates, envying, anger, fights, backbiting, gossiping, swelled heads, and tumultuous hostilities you're embroiling yourselves in.

Is it possible when I show up in Corinth again I'll be humbled and perplexed to find many of you continuing in your pursuit for self-righteousness, remaining unrepentant at your subservience to laws, rules, and regulations, and carrying on in your abuse of your liberty in Jesus in a life-style of sexual impurity and impropriety?

Well, this will be the third time I'm coming to you.

The scriptures say, "in the mouth of two or three witnesses shall every word be established" (Deuteronomy 19:15).

Let me assure you the exhortations I gave to you on my second visit are as valid as if I was still with you. Even though I'm absent from you right now, please understand the encouragements I'm writing to you now are just as important as they will be when I see you again this next time. I will not hesitate to speak my mind to all those who fail to understand the impact of God's grace upon all mankind!

You seem to want some kind of proof what I've told you is the truth.

Well, listen up. What Jesus has done for you isn't just some weak-hearted attempt to get you to change your life around.

I say "Nay! Nay!"

What Jesus did for you, and for the entire world, is nothing short of miraculously incredible! What He did for the whole world was absolutely mighty! Jesus may have been crucified as a result of the weak and cowardly foolishness of mankind, yet He lives as a result of the power and mighty wisdom of God!

We also may suffer the agonies and pain of death on the human level just as Jesus did, BUT, we also shall live with Jesus in eternal glory by the very same power and mighty wisdom of God He has showered upon "all."

Examine yourselves.

Are you living in the comforting awareness of the faith Jesus has in you? Your own attempts at self-righteousness should surely be telling you it's impossible for you to please God by what you believe or by what you do. Don't you know you can stop trying so hard to gain the favor of God? Have you still not come to the knowledge Jesus is already in you? If you don't, you're nothing more than reprobates, doomed to suffer the agony of guilt, shame, and fear every time you fail to meet the impossible standards laws, rules, and regulations demand of you.

BUT, I trust you'll know for a certainty in the sight of God there's no such thing as a reprobate. "All" have been made righteous, pure, and holy through the cleansing blood of Jesus on the cross.

Now, lest you think I've totally fallen off my rocker, I must add I pray to God you don't think this liberty in Jesus is given to authorize you to do as many wicked things as you can think of. You may have the license, however, you certainly don't have to use it! BUT, we should prefer to carry on life in an honest, wholesome fashion as though we still seeking to please God to garner His favor.

No matter what we do we can't overthrow the truth of what God has already done for us. BUT, the truth of God's loving grace and peace is still His truth, no matter what we believe, do, don't do, say, or don't say!

Even in the times of our weakness we're overjoyed at the reality you're strong in Jesus whether you know it or not. Our strongest wish is that you'd come to gain the full understanding and acknowledgement of the perfection God has gifted you with in Jesus!

These words of encouragement and exhortation may have been a bit heavy handed. However, I think I'd have used even stronger words if I'd be there right now to confront you face to face. I trust you'll understand I will exercise every aspect of the power God has placed within me to build you up rather than to tear you down.

Finally, my dear friends, so long for now.
Be as perfect as you are!
Be of good comfort!
Be of one mind!
LIVE IN PEACE!

The God of love and peace is with you!

Please demonstrate your affection for one another with a big hug and a holy kiss for extra measure. All of your fellow believers here send their best regards.

The grace of Jesus, the love of God, and the fellowship of the Spirit of Jesus within each of you is all part of the everlasting portion of "all!"

That's just the way it is folks!

Trip # 15
EPHESUS TO PHILIPPI

4TH LETTER TO THE CORINTHIANS

88. INTRODUCTION OF THE 4th LETTER TO CORINTH

I'm not sure if you're keeping track, but you've now read at least parts of three different letters I wrote to my dear believing friends in the city of Corinth. What I'm about to share with you is a part of the fourth letter I dispatched to them.

If you've been paying attention you would have noticed there's a common thread to all of the letters. It was apparent to me, in spite of the simplicity of the good news of Jesus, the danger of negating such a wonderful gospel by performance based self-righteousness is overwhelming.

Why anyone would want to return to the burden and slavery of works is beyond me. The fact of the matter is that religious leaders wanted to control the believers and the only way they could do this was to propagate the laws, rules, and regulations allowing them to retain their power over the people.

In some major way I had hoped my letters would contradict false teachings, adding additional strength to all of the instruction I had given them first hand. A deceiving batch of itinerant dung slingers were causing their share of problems and I had a hard time keeping my mouth shut warning folks their message wasn't only full of holes, it stunk big time!

I chose Titus to take the third letter to the Corinthians. I instructed him to make sure they'd read it and to add any explanations necessary so they once again would come to deeper appreciation of the greatness of the grace and peace God has given in Jesus to all mankind. I trusted implicitly the integrity and diplomacy Titus could bring to the situation.

Titus and I agreed we'd meet somewhere in Macedonia after he spent some time in Corinth. We both felt there was a definite need to turn things around there. They would also need some time to get together a wonderful collection of gifts that we wanted to take back to Jerusalem. The plan then was for me to go to Troas, across to Macedonia, then down towards Corinth.

INTRODUCTION TO 4ᴿᴰ CORINTHIANS   TRIP # 15

Titus was to go to Corinth and then head northward to meet me somewhere in Macedonia or perhaps come across to meet me in Troas.

The plight of our dear believing friends in the city of Jerusalem was still a hot topic of discussion wherever we traveled. I was confident all the fellowships would be anxious to bring together a sizable collection to aid their brothers and sisters. Letters had been sent out with a request for donations to be harvested to assist the many who were suffering very difficult times, in large part as a result of their stand in the work of God in Jesus.

The uproar with Demetrius and the silversmiths had died down a bit. I was feeling more and more comfortable with the idea of leaving the work of the spreading of the gospel message in some very capable hands. While I called Ephesus home during this time I was hardly ever there. I was out and about the countryside talking to as many folks as I could about the wonderful message of God's love.

All the while Tim had been doing a super job after he arrived giving me a hand in Ephesus.

I'd given him a special charge to see the good news message of God's love in Jesus be the only one which was to be preached, while any other doctrines were put in their place.

On the road again...

Troas would be the first stop. Had a blast there. The believers were flourishing. Of course, they tried to talk me into staying there with them however my intense agony over the folks in Corinth was still very fresh in my mind. My eagerness to catch up with Titus to hear his news was intense. I waited as patiently as I could.

I had no word from Titus. What to do? Take the next boat out for Phillippi!

On the water again...

We set out across the beautiful Aegean Sea just like we had some time ago. Samothrace beckoned us like it had before. It was great to see some of the folks I'd met before on this wonderful little island. Neapolis was the next harbor port where we disembarked. The ten-mile trek inland to Philippi was just a hop, skip, and a jump with incredible anticipation built in.

You can just about imagine the welcome I received from Lydia and all her wonderful friends. She was just as bright and energetic as the last time I saw her. What a joy to be among such terrific friends.

INTRODUCTION TO 4ᴿᴰ CORINTHIANS   TRIP # 15

    I had the great privilege of bringing them all up to date with all the different challenges I'd faced in all my travels. These dear friends had been so supportive of me, and my ministry. I have a hard time describing just how magnificent it was to be in their presence once again. If I was going to have to wait for Titus to show up Philippi was the best place I could think of to put up my feet up and relax a while.

    When Titus did show up I couldn't get the words out of his mouth quick enough. I was so anxious to hear his report that for the most part was very positive. Apparently the Corinthians took my ranting and raving to heart, determining to forge ahead with their understanding of the wisdom of God.

    I made up my mind very quickly to write a letter to them again. It was imperative they knew I was glad to hear of their response to my exhortations and essential they understood how much I cared for them.

    Oh, by the way, I should also mention Tim showed up in Philippi too. He was confident things were going well enough in Ephesus he could join me as Titus and I would make our way through Macedonia.

    And so, from the city of Philippi, on the sun deck of the charming home of Lydia, originated this fourth letter to the believers in Corinth.

    Read on...

4ᵀᴴ CORINTHIANS

89. COMFORT BEYOND MEASURE
(2 Corinthians 1:1-2:13)

From:
Paul, an ambassador of Jesus by the will of God, and Timothy, our brother

To:
The believers of God who live in Corinth, and indeed, throughout Achaia.

Blessing:
God our Father and Jesus have showered you with grace and peace. Blessed be God, even the Father of Jesus! God is the Father of mercies and the God of all comfort!

    Yes, it is God who brings comfort to us in all the struggles we put ourselves through to gain His favor. We have the great honor and privilege of sharing this incredibly great news of God's gift of grace and peace for all mankind with those who are still bound and enslaved by the pursuit of self-righteousness. We've found such great comfort in this matchless, merciful God we can do nothing less than share it with others!
    Why? Because the very sufferings of Jesus on the cross have abounded in us to make us righteous and holy in God's sight already! Don't you get it? The only assuring comfort and consolation in this life is a result of the abundance of the love of Jesus for "all."
    Some folks don't take too kindly to this message. We want you to know we gladly accept their indignation so you can come to terms with this incredible gospel message and apply it to your lives more effectively. You're going to have to go through the same kinds of harassment we endure.
    Hey, the same truth applies when folks treat us kindly. Makes no difference. Our mission to encourage and uplift you to persevere in the knowledge and understanding of the wisdom of God is stimulated. When you fully come to grasp the impact of Jesus' suffering on behalf of the whole world you'll truly understand the full impact of the consolation you have in Jesus!

COMFORT BEYOND MEASURE

Look dear friends, we don't want you to be ignorant concerning the degree of trouble we have come across in Asia. We were pressed way more than we could tolerate and beyond our strength to overcome it. Sometimes, we were actually in danger of losing our very lives.

BUT, that doesn't matter! The sentence of death hung over every human being at one time. Too many of us have had to learn the hard way we shouldn't trust in our own systems of belief or in our own myriad systems of laws, rules, and regulations governing our performance.

BUT, we can trust in God who reversed the entire course of history by raising Jesus from the dead! It is God who delivered us up from so great a sentence of death! You bet. He delivered on every promise He made! It is God whom we trust to deliver us as well!

We appreciate the prayers of thanksgiving you offer to God for the mighty gift He bestowed upon us. We are encouraged more and more folks will join you in this celebration of liberty God gifted us with.

What do we have to be thankful for?

We're thankful for the testimony of our hearts and minds, that, in simplicity and reverent sincerity, devoid of the wisdom (foolishness) of mankind. BUT, solely by the grace of God we have the immense joy of sharing the love of God with the whole world, including advancing our wonderful relationship with you! For we won't write you any other message than what you're now reading or acknowledge anything other than what we have told you in the past. I trust you will not be deterred from this understanding throughout your lives.

We take great joy in knowing you are as happy for us as we are for you because of the righteousness Jesus gained for us on the glorious day of the cross! In this confidence I had it in my mind to come to see you before. I actually planned to come and see you two more times. I thought I'd pass through Corinth on my way to Macedonia and then stop in and see you again as I returned from Macedonia on my way back toward Judea.

Do you think I'm just teasing you or just kidding around with you by sharing these thoughts with you?

Or do you think I'm just kind of wishy-washy, unable to make up my own mind or plan my schedule properly?

Perhaps you can't figure out whether my yes means yes or my no truly means no.

BUT, just as sure as everything I've said about God is true, the intent of our hearts towards you is certainly not to confuse you with a whole series of instructions about what you can do and what you can't do.

Listen, Jesus, the Son of God, who was preached to all of you by all of us, by me, by Silvanus, and by Timothy, is not about what you can do or what you can't do!

BUT, in Jesus, everything is about the abundant liberty and life you can enjoy! For all of the promises of God in Jesus liberate the whole world from the perilous journey of "yes" and "no." That's just the way it is in the family and fellowship of Jesus.

Why?

So the unending glory of God would be exalted in the whole world! Now the One who has established us into the family of Jesus with you, and the One who has anointed us with the magnificent majesty of Jesus is none other than GOD!

What else did He do?

God sealed us by giving to us the Spirit of Jesus to indwell us as an earnest, a down payment so to speak, of the incredible future we have in the eternal blessing of His presence.

As God is my witness, I must confess the real reason I changed my plans and didn't go through with my original strategy is because I was pretty ticked off with all of you. I haven't come to Corinth yet because I wanted to spare you the whiplashing I had prepared for you.

Make no mistake. We don't have any power or dominion over the way you live, BUT we are definitely positioned to help your joy in Jesus. You're able to **STAND IN COMFORT AND ASSURANCE** you already possess the righteous favor of God because of the faith of Jesus.

BUT, I made up my mind I wouldn't come again to you with the spirit of heaviness. What would be the point for me to depress the very folks who bring me a tremendous amount of happiness?

The reason I wrote you the last letter of exhortation was so when I did come to you I wouldn't be disappointed by those who I'd rather rejoice for.

I do have confidence you're participating completely in the same joy in the abundant liberty of Jesus as I am.

I want you to know I wrote the last letter with a heavy heart full of anguish and turmoil, with eyes filled with tears. I'm certainly not saying this to make you depressed, BUT only to let you know the abundance of love I have for you.

BUT, if any of you have caused grief it hasn't affected me.

BUT, in a way, the exhortation I give is to spare you all from the grief these few are enslaved to. The pain associated with bondage to systems of laws, rules, and regulations is a significant torment inflicting many folks who've been deceived away from the wisdom of God.

Your reaction to their plight is not to ostracize, banish, or add to their plight by dispensing your disapproval of them. Contrariwise, you ought rather to accept and comfort them, lest perhaps they'd become overwhelmed by the compilation of sorrow. I beg you to confirm your love to those enslaved by the folly of human wisdom (foolishness) in the pursuit of self-righteousness.

This is one of the reasons I wrote the last letter to you. I wanted to be assured you actually practice what you preach. I wanted to know whether you could actually carry through to put into practice the loving spirit of acceptance God displayed to the whole world, indeed even in you.

I have no problem accepting whomever you accept no matter what they've done. For if I accept everyone in spite of their actions or activities I'm just displaying for your understanding the great loving acceptance of the Spirit of Jesus within me.

Since we're not ignorant of how the deceivers of the gospel message operate let's make it our mission to demonstrate how the liberty of God's righteousness is infinitely and eternally better than dangling in the despair of self-righteousness through performance driven agendas of religious leaders.

Furthermore, a great door of opportunity opened for me when I arrived in Troas to preach the great gospel message of Jesus. However, my spirit was restless because I wasn't able to find my good friend Titus. BUT, I made the decision to forgo opportunities and proceed to look for him over in Macedonia.

90. TRIUMPH
(2 Corinthians 2:14-17)

Ever heard of an event known as the Roman "Triumph?"

First of all, the Triumph was a symbol of achievement reserved for the "creme de la creme." Only the best of the best could ever hope to achieve it. This great honor was reserved for a celebrated Roman general who brought great honor to his country through a mighty and glorious victory on the battle front.

What did he have to achieve? Let me give you a short list:

- A mighty campaign had to be completely finished.
- The targeted territory had to be completely subjugated under Roman power.
- All of the battle troops had to be returned to their homeland.
- At least 5000 of the enemy must have been killed during one battle.
- The victory had to come at the expense of a foreign power, not as a result of a suppression of a civil conflict.

It was hard to out match Rome when it came to pomp and ceremony. The honoring of a conquering general with this highest achievement award ranked right up there for glitz and pizzazz. Even the procession of the Triumph through the streets of Rome to the steps of the capital buildings was choreographed in magnificence.

- Out front were the state officials and the senators.
- Trumpeters led the processions of spoils from the conquered nation.
- Grand pictures of territories, and models of captured battle ships, and overtaken building, were displayed to the great enjoyment of the crowds lining the streets.
- A sacrificial white bull was led along in front of the prisoners of war.
- Humbled princes, leaders, and generals were led in chains to await their fate in execution chambers or prison.
- The lectors, bearing their rods of torture, were followed by more musicians with their instruments.
- Of course, what parade would be complete without the priests swinging their incense burning censers?

- The great general then appeared dressed to the max. He was robed in a purple tunic embroidered with golden palm leaves and covered by a purple tunic marked with golden stars. In his hands a Roman eagle topped an ivory scepter and over his head a slave held a crown of Jupiter. He was followed with appropriate pride by all of his family.
- Like all great parades it ended with the victorious army basking in all of the splendor and glamor of their triumphant leader, walking among the throngs of cheering spectators.
- Then it was "parties on!"

Well, God declared Jesus to be the "Triumph," and the entire world was declared fit to share in His great celebratory party and parade!

No foolin.'

Obviously, parallelism can be stretched only to a point and the idea of the complete victory of an earthly general can hardly compare to the victory accomplished by Jesus! What makes this great honor for Jesus so magnificent for us? Hey, God planned for us to share in this great "triumph" with Jesus!

Let me get you back to the letter...

Now, thanks be to God who has made it possible for the entire world to share in the "Triumph" of Jesus!

Yes, it's the great fragrance of God's wisdom that has made it possible for us to enjoy the parade of His grace and love throughout the world. For indeed, we all bear to God the unmistakable sweet aroma of Jesus!

Do you understand what I'm saying?

God has included, in His wisdom, all those who "think" they're saved, as well as those who "think" they're doomed!

Unfortunately, those of us who believe in the all-sufficiency of God's grace doesn't smell too good to those still bound up in a performance-based mentality. To them we must smell like the dead leading others to a certain death.

To others we're like a breath of fresh air, for in the message of God's grace and peace they'll be refreshed with the freedom of the guilt and shame symptomatic the pursuit of self-righteousness.

Who is sufficient to love us "all?"

Talk about a rhetorical question.

There are still far too many out there perverting the wisdom of God's promise and deceivers corrupting the message of God's grace and peace for the entire world.

BUT, in all sincerity,

BUT, as messengers of God in plain view of His sight; we speak of nothing less than the **MIRACULOUS GIFT OF JESUS TO THE WHOLE WORLD!**

91. IMAGE OF GOD
(2 Corinthians 3:1-18)

Is it necessary for us to start telling you who we are all over again? Do we have to give you letters of recommendations like some others have? Do you think you have to give letters of recommendation to us?

Well, you're already important to us for you're like letters written in our hearts. Others can read and know about you because we're proud to tell others about you.

Why?

Because God has manifestly declared you to be the testimony of Jesus' love to this world.

We've merely had the great privilege of sharing this information with you. God didn't declared this just with the ink of our pens, BUT with the living Spirit of God in Jesus. Neither was it confirmed on the stone tablets of laws, rules, and regulations, BUT in the fleshy temples of the hearts of all mankind!

This is the trust we have in God through Jesus!

Look, we shouldn't be so presumptuous to think we could ever believe strong enough or have the kind of faith to move mountains, or be able to accomplish enough to gain the favor of God.

BUT, the sufficiency of the whole world rests in God!

It is God who has made it possible for us to go out and share this wonderful new declaration of God's wise plan for His creation. The new covenant of God has nothing to do with the hoops of laws, rules, and regulations we need to pass through to gain God's acceptance.

BUT, it does have everything to do with the Spirit of Jesus placed within all!

You see, the letter of the law has no power other than to kill the will and break the heart of those who try to live by it. BUT, in reality, the Spirit of Jesus within all has exposed everyone to a wonderful life of liberty and contentment in His great love!

BUT, if the administration of spiritual death, written and engraved in the stones, was so glorious even the children of Israel couldn't bear to look steadfastly into the face of Moses.

WHY?

Because of the glorious countenance after he received the commandments, a glory I might add has long past away.

Then how much more is the glory of the administration of the Spirit of Jesus into everyone?

Did I confuse you?

Let me say it again a different way.

If, to administer a system of performance which only proved mankind had no capability or power to achieve and maintain the favor of God was such a glorious endeavor, then how much more incredibly marvelous is God's gifting of the entire world with His righteousness in Jesus? For even the glory of laws, rules, and regulations had no capability of bringing mankind the righteousness it so vigorously pursued.

Why?

Because only the wisdom of God's grace and peace would be adequate, glorious and excellent enough to supersede it.

Do I need to say it again?

For if the system of laws, rules, and regulations was so glorious to declare the righteousness of God, how much more glorious is the liberty of God's gift in Jesus for the whole world, which remains forevermore the standard of excellence?

Seeing we have such a phenomenal hope in the simplicity of the gospel message of Jesus, is it any wonder why we are using such common, ordinary, everyday language to spread the good news?

Hey, Moses had to cover up his face with a veil so the children of Israel couldn't even get a glimpse of him as he told them about the covenant God had established with them. Look what happened. The system of laws, rules, and regulations proved their purpose, establishing once and for all the incapability of mankind to attain to the favor of God through belief or effort.

In Jesus this system has been abolished forever!

BUT, folks still have their blinders on. For to this very day some remain blinded by the veils of perverted misunderstanding and misguided devotion whenever they read the obvious intent of the recordings of God's love for the entire world in the scriptures.

In Jesus there is no veil hiding the truth of God's love for "all."

The veil of secrecy and misunderstanding is done away in Jesus!

BUT, even to this day, when the laws Moses brought to the children of Israel are read this veil of misunderstanding of their purpose is cast like a blanket over the eyes of understanding of folks by those who wish to perpetuate this deception, and by those wishing to maintain a measure of control. Nevertheless, when the understanding and knowledge of God's gift to the world in Jesus is preached accurately this blinding veil of deceit will be cast away.

And now, the administration of the Spirit of God's glorious new declaration of love for the whole world in none other than Jesus in us!

And, where the Spirit of God is, there is liberty!

BUT, everyone, unveiled, standing completely exposed to the glorious majesty of God, is changed into the very same image of God!

Yes, we "ALL" HAVE BEEN CHANGED from the glory of bondage to the glory of liberty!

What did it take?

It took the wisdom of the Spirit of God in Jesus!

92. A DIFFERENT PERSPECTIVE
(2 Corinthians 4:1-5:7)

Therefore, since we have a job to let people know the wonderful grace of God in Jesus, knowing we've all received the mercy of God, we press on without giving up or losing our determination.

BUT, we've renounced the pressures to walk the thin line of creative craftiness or to communicate the gospel message of God's love deceitfully just so it will fit in with the wisdom (foolishness) of men.

BUT, what we'll continue to do is preach the truth. We'll let our message speak for itself, for it will reveal to the mind of all who will listen to the message God's view and opinion of all mankind.

BUT, if the great message of the gospel of God's love for all in Jesus is misunderstood it's probably misunderstood most by those stuck in the bondage of self-righteousness!

These poor folks who either won't believe or don't want to believe in the wisdom of God to gift the whole world with His righteousness have been following the wisdom (foolishness) of mankind promoting the perversion and deception everyone must somehow believe or work hard enough to gain the acceptance of God. Perhaps they are too afraid to recognize the light of the glorious gospel of Jesus, who truly is the image of God, has in fact actually touched them!

Listen, we're not preaching some kind of goofy message about what we can do for you. We can't do a thing for you! Hey, even you can't do a thing for you!

BUT, we do preach the good news message of Jesus. Sure, I'll gladly admit I'm humbly at your service on His behalf. For it was God who commanded the light to appear out of sheer darkness who obliterated any darkness occupying our hearts, replacing it with His light. He's given to all the light of the knowledge of the glory of God on the face of Jesus.

BUT, we have this very treasure too!
Yes indeed.
The glory of God is in our earthen vessels as well!
Why?
So the excellency of God's power would be exalted. We have no power in ourselves to attain to this kind of glory.

Now, we may run into problems every which way we turn, and yet, there's no need to become distressed. Surely we don't have the answers to all the questions of life. Life is perplexing and complicated to be sure.

BUT, there's no need to despair.

Persecuted perhaps, BUT, never forsaken!

Cast down perhaps, BUT, never destroyed!

Our earthly bodies bear the tremendous honor of being touched by the effects of the death of Jesus.

Why do I say this? Because the resurrected life of Jesus has been made manifest even in our bodies. For Jesus accepted the eternal fate of each and every person, including everyone still alive, so His life would have a dramatic affect on the mortality of our own flesh. Yes, we're all going to die. BUT, we have the great confidence we all will live forever in Jesus!

We, having the same spirit of confidence and trust in God's ability to gift the whole world with His righteousness as those who have written so extensively about His wisdom, have no trouble speaking about what we believe to be true.

The psalmist wrote, "I believed, and therefore have I spoken" (Psalms 116:10).

Well, I believe in God's wisdom and power and I'm not ashamed to admit it either. I have every confidence if God could raise Jesus then He can do the very same to us through Jesus. It is He who presented both you and I, as well as everyone else in this world, to God. Look, everything God has done is for the whole world! Yes, He has done everything for you.

Why?

So everyone would offer their praise and thanksgiving to God for His unspeakable, unquenchable, unchanging, unalterable, and abundant grace!

Good news or what?

Let me tell you this is the very reason I don't get too upset and worried about what life has got to dish out to me. BUT, though I know my body is taking a pretty good beating and the effects of age are taking their toll, yet, on the inside, in my heart, and in my mind I'm going through a daily renewal of my understanding of the incredible goodness of God's loving grace and peace.

I fully recognize the problems I encounter here in this life are undeniable, BUT they're a fleeting reality. They can hardly compare to the exceeding and eternal weight of the glory of God we share in Jesus. It's only possible to come to this peace of mind when you learn to look not at the things that are recognizable, BUT at those things which are still beyond our comprehension. Truly, the things we can touch and see for the moment are merely temporal. BUT, the things that we have trouble sinking our teeth into are eternal in nature.

Surely we need to understand when this earthly tabernacle of ours has served its time in this place we'll simply change habitations and locations. We've a house waiting for us that certainly wasn't built with human hands. No, this eternal home is somewhere beyond the realm of our comprehension.

I wouldn't doubt many folks are anxiously waiting the day they get their new wardrobe! It's going to be out of this world! Well, if this is true we can know we're going to clothed with such honor, surely we won't be found naked in the sight of God.

For those of us in these temporal bodies still are anxious, not that God isn't going to dress us up, BUT, over the hopeful thought even if God does clothe us anew He'll also swallow up our mortality with His immortality!

Well, I've got good news for you.

Don't worry! Be happy!

It's a done deal! The one who has already accomplished this great provision for the whole world is none other than God Himself!

Of course! He has already made it a certainty.

How?

God has guaranteed our new clothing as well as our new eternal existence in His presence, by giving to all the Spirit of Jesus!

Therefore, we can have absolute confidence knowing the only separation between us and God is merely the difference in the vessel and space we're inhabiting at the moment.

Don't put all your eggs in the basket of your ability to understand this great truth. YOU DIDN'T CARVE OUT THE PATH YOU'RE WALKING ON. You didn't establish your walk. It's been established by the faith of Jesus in God's wisdom and ability!

93. RECONCILED TO GOD
(2 Corinthians 5:8-21)

We would be most sanctimoniously confident, employing the wisdom (foolishness) of men, to proclaim our willingness to die so we could be with God. So, we'd labor with great diligence so we could gain a sense God actually might accept us. It really wouldn't matter whether it's in this life or the next. We just think we need to "do" something so God will love us.

Look, we all must appear sometime before the judgment seat of God. Right?

Every one of us is going to reap what we sow. Right?

Everyone is going to receive what is coming to them according to what they've done. Good or bad. Right?

Knowing therefore the terror of a vindictive and angry God we feel it's our noble role to persuade men and women to smarten up!

BUT! We're made manifest to God!

We've been seized by the hand of God! He sees us for who we are, His children!

I can only trust you'll get this message through your thick skulls. I've told you before and I'll tell you again. We've nothing to offer you to make you acceptable in the sight of God. Nothing we commend to you can take the place of God's gift of His grace and peace for the whole world. We offer only this great and wonderful news of God's love for all mankind so you might share with us in our great rejoicing.

This glorious gospel message you've heard from us is the only truth you'll need to confront those who refuse to accept what God has done to the heart of every person. Use this message to answer those who refuse to lay down the chains of bondage to the self-righteous pursuits through systems of laws, rules, and regulations.

Appearances are very deceiving. What you are on the inside is far more important than what others can see on the outside. If, because of what we preach you think we've had just a few too much too drink at happy hour, well then, I guess I'd just have to say I enjoy being a bit tipsy at the goodness of God's wisdom! Then again, if you think we're actually making a whole lot of sense to you, well then, good on ya!

You see, the love of Jesus constrains us. The only thing captivating us is the unrestrained, limitless love of God for the whole world!

Why?

This is the way I've come to understand it.

If Jesus died for "all," then "all" must have been as good as dead before! Furthermore, the reason Jesus died for "all" was so folks wouldn't have to live under the bondage of trying to gain the acceptance and favor of God by what they believe or by how they perform.

BUT, Jesus did die so folks could live in the abundant life and liberty of the very One who died for them and who rose again so all might enjoy the trip! This is the very reason we don't bother to waste our time judging whether others meet "our" criteria for being acceptable to God.

Sure, at one time, I spent a whole lot of time trying to figure out whether even Jesus Himself had what it took to be a Son of God. Well, we don't have to worry about this anymore either.

Listen, if any person is in Jesus (and who isn't?) they are a completely new creature!

Old things aren't going to pass away. No! They already have passed away!

All things aren't going to become new. Behold, all things "are" already new!

And all things are of God!

God has reconciled "all" to Himself by Jesus!

To "all" God has given the great privilege of letting others know of this great reconciliation God, in His wisdom, already dispatched to this world in Jesus.

What's the scoop?

God was in Jesus. That's how He did it! God simply reconciled the whole world to Himself.

GOD CHOSE NOT TO GIVE US ALL WHAT WE DID DESERVE, PREFERRING INSTEAD TO GIVE US ALL WHAT WE DID NOT DESERVE!

To top it all off, God chose not to impute everything we did, are doing, or will do against us. The liability of sin will never be held against anyone ever again!

God has given us His word of honor! His reconciliation is a once and for all deal! The full meal deal!

This is the reason we do what we do. We're simply ambassadors to tell others the good news of Jesus. God is merely using us to relay the message in a way you can understand it. We pray you wouldn't lose sight of this wonderful news of God's reconciling love for the whole world.

For God made Jesus, who knew no sin, to be sin for us! Why?

So we all might be made the righteousness of God in Jesus!

94. DAY OF SALVATION
(2 Corinthians 6:1-12; 7:3-16)

We then, as co-workers with Jesus, plead with you not to turn your backs on the incredible gift of God's grace and return once again to wasting away your days pursuing in your own foolish effort what God has already given to you.

For this is what God said, "I have heard you in an acceptable time, and in one day of salvation have I helped you" (Isaiah 49:8).

Well, now "is" the accepted time!
Now "is" the day of salvation!
You're living in it!

Don't bring shame upon the ministry of God's grace by attempting to prove to someone, especially to God, that your life is worthy of His acceptance. God can't be blamed for your stupidity if you continue to pursue self-righteousness in the bondage of systems of belief and performance.

BUT, in "all" things recognize you are as approved of God as you'll ever get! You are an ambassador of God's love all the time.

You are His child when:
- you're patiently doing what you do everyday;
- you suffer distressing periods of affliction;
- you endure the crumbling pang of need;
- you're swamped by distressing misfortune;
- you get physically beaten up;
- you're imprisoned;
- you find yourself in the middle of tumultuous riot-like scenes;
- you're pressed to carry on the stressful tasks of hard work leading to repeated vigils of sleeplessness and fatigue which undoubtedly affect even your eating habits.

You are approved of God by His:
- purity;
- knowledge;
- long suffering;
- kindness;
- Spirit in Jesus;
- genuine love;

- word of truth;
- power of God;
- armor of righteousness He has place on your right hand as well as on your left hand!

You are approved of God in spite of the honor or dishonor you gain from others. Yes, indeed, even if you attract negative or positive reports. Some may brand you as deceivers when this is the farthest thing from what we know to be true.

You may think you are unknown by God. I say, "Nay! Nay!" You are yet well known by God!

You may think you're as good as dead and gone. I say, "Nay! Nay!" Behold, you are more alive now than you've ever been!

You may think you don't have a thing to be happy about. I say, "Nay! Nay!" Now you have every reason to rejoice all the time!

You may think of yourselves as the poorest folks in the world. I say, "Nay! Nay!" Now you have the great opportunity and privilege of helping many others to see they are every bit as rich as you are in God!

You may think you have nothing to show for all you've done in this life. Well, I say, "Nay! Nay!" In God you possess absolutely "all" things!

Oh, my dear Corinthians friends, there's so much more I want to tell you. I love you all so much. I only want the very best for you. Just remember there's nothing I can do for you to straighten you out.

BUT, never forget you've been straightened out to the very core of your being by the grace and peace of a God who loves the whole world far beyond the scope of our understanding.

(7:3-16)

Please understand I'm not telling you all these things in order to condemn you for what you're doing. For I've said it before and I'll say it again, you're very much in our thoughts.
We've died to the pursuit of self-righteousness and are excited to enjoy the abundant, refreshing life in the liberty of Jesus. The very same thing has happened to you.

I don't mind saying I've taken great freedom to be a bit bold in speaking to you. I'm given to bragging about you as I talk of you with others. I'm filled with comfort knowing what God has done for the whole world. Even in the middle of some very difficult circumstances I'm overcome and overfilled with joy at the thought of His great love for "all."

Indeed, when we came to Macedonia it seemed we just couldn't get a break. We were completely exhausted, BUT we still faced trouble each and every way we turned. When we weren't struggling against external forces, we battled the insidious, complex internal anxieties of fear and insecurity.

Nevertheless God, who has brought comfort to all those who think they're cast down, has also brought comfort to us with the coming of our dear friend Titus. It wasn't only Titus who brought relief to us, BUT it was his message of how well you treated him. You must have spoiled him pretty descent. I was touched when he told us of your sincere desire, your deep concern, and your fervent thoughts for our wellbeing.

All I can say is "thank you from the bottom of my heart." I'm tickled pink at hearing his tender report.

I'm so excited I can hardly stand it. You've made my day. I know I may have touched a few raw nerves in the last letter I sent with Titus. However, I'm not sorry for writing it now even though I probably had second thoughts after I sent it. I can understand completely how the letter may have left you a little perturbed at me, BUT I just knew you'd get over it pretty quick.

Now I'm a happy camper, not that you were ticked off at me, BUT that you took my exhortation to heart, did some evaluation and started to move again in a positive direction.

I truly intended for you to get upset in a good way, in a way you'd understand what I was telling you was actually intended for your own benefit rather than just another letter to rip you apart.

There's no reason for you to confess or repent!

You view yourself as unworthy of God's great, loving grace and peace, BUT this idiotic, self-righteous attitude is exactly what's killing too many folks who've soaked up the wisdom (foolishness) of mankind.

Look, this is the best the wisdom (foolishness) of mankind has to offer in its pursuit of the approval and acceptance of God:
- Yes, you must sorrow in a "godly" sort of way.
- Yes, you'd better be careful about everything you do and say.
- Yes, you best clear your mind of every evil thought.
- Yes, you must be indignant of the misguided beliefs and actions of others.
- Yes, you'd better be scared spitless at what God is going to do to you.
- Yes, get a vehement grip and desire to set others straight.
- Yes, jolt your zeal to convert and inspire others to get with the program.
- Yes, what revenge God will pay to those who today heed the call to repentance!

I'm so happy you've come to realize and understand that all of this is nothing more than a pile of crap! You need to understand I didn't write the letter specifically to those who are trying to deceive you, nor to bring more attention to the heresies causing so much pain and distraction for you.

BUT, I did write the letter so you'd come to the realization we really do care for you and we really want you to grab hold of the wonderfully true message God loves and accepts the whole world because He wanted to!

Therefore, we were comforted to know this message brought you the assurance you needed in your own minds. Yes, and we were even happier when we saw first hand how happy Titus was. You really blessed and refreshed him. I've bragged a lot about you to him and I'm not ashamed of anything I've said.

BUT, whatever I've spoken to you, it was spoken truthfully. Well, our boasting of you is just as truthful and everything I've told to Titus about you has proven to be true as well. I think Titus loves you more now than ever. He still remembers how obedient you were and how well you received him in spite of the fact you seemed to be scared of him at first, shaking in your sandals at the prospect of what he might say to you.

All of these things have given me a great deal to be happy about. I have every confidence you'll continue to **LIVE IN THE ABUNDANT LIBERTY** of God's love in "all" things.

95. CHALLENGE TO GIVE
(2 Corinthians 8:1-9: 15)

Moreover, my dear friends, I'd like you to know how the grace of God has affected the lives of the believers in the fellowships of Macedonia. You can literally see how happy they are even in the middle of some very trying circumstances. They exist in virtual poverty, and yet, they abound in the richness of their knowledge they live in the abundant wealth of liberty in Jesus.

I bear witness to their own gracious spirit for they seemed so anxious to give way beyond their capacity to give. They actually entreated and begged us to accept their gifts for those who they knew were suffering even more than they were. I must confess we had certain expectations, BUT they went far beyond our wildest dreams by pledging themselves, first of all to accept the grace and peace of God, and then by offering their assistance to us just because they wanted to. Talk about the attitude of God!

One of the reasons why we sent Titus to you was so he could wrap up the assignment he'd been given some time ago. We know you possess the same great spirit of grace and generosity as your Macedonian brothers and sisters. So, since you abound in everything, in faith, in the ability to share God's love with others, in your knowledge and understanding of the grace of God, in your determination to live in liberty, and even in the love you show towards us, see to it you also abound in the gracious spirit of sharing what you can with those who are suffering so much over in Jerusalem.

This isn't some order I'm issuing for you to obey, BUT, I'd like to think you've been inspired by the generous heart and spirit of others. The sincerity of your love for others is demonstrated when you put your money where your mouth is.

We know Jesus is the ultimate example of a gracious spirit. He was rich beyond comprehension in the lap of God's luxury, and yet, He gave it all up for the whole world.
Why?
So "all" could become rich through His poverty.

However, I'd like to give you a bit of advice, expedient for you to heed. You started out with such great enthusiasm in this project of raising funds for the believers in Jerusalem. BUT, that was almost a year ago. Get on with it already!

There was such determination when you were first presented with this challenging opportunity. Well, employ the same grit and energy to get the package of what you've already got wrapped up and ready to go.

Look, the first step is a willing mind and spirit. If you've got that then the second step is easier. Give out of your ability to give. You can't give what you haven't got. I'm not suggesting you ought to relieve the need of others to the extent you place yourself into a similar state of distress.

BUT, I'd like to suggest a more balanced approach. At this time your abundance might be a source of supply and comfort when others have a need. Perhaps a time will come when their abundance will be needed to supply a similar need in your life. Sounds only fair, don't you think?

The scriptures give sage advice about the spirit of sharing.

"He that had gathered much had nothing left over; and he that had gathered little didn't lack for anything" (Exodus 16:18).

BUT, thanks be to God for placing into the heart of Titus this same spirit of sharing towards you. Indeed he accepted the challenge of taking up this collection for the believers in Jerusalem and ran with it.

BUT, he even took the project a step farther by coming in person to share this project with you. We also sent with him our good brother (Luke) who speaks only of his praise for the gospel of God's grace in all of the fellowships he visits.

He's not only the one who we recommend highly, BUT he's one who was chosen by all the fellowships to travel with us as we preach the gospel message. It's an exciting message of God's love for the whole world and we have the great joy of sharing with others so the glory of this same God would be magnified in all the earth. This gospel message declares the fact God has made you acceptable in His sight!

We want to avoid any appearance of mishandling the distribution of all these wonderful gifts everyone has collected. Our desire is to provide an accurate and honest accounting of all your gifts. Our intention is to be absolutely above board, not only in the sight of God, BUT also in the sight of anyone who might have a concern.

Along with Titus and Luke, we've sent another brother who has proved diligent in many things, BUT now he'll be even more diligent knowing I've given my assurances to you all of the gifts will be kept safe until they reach their intended destination and purpose.

If there's any question about Titus let me assure you he is my partner and assistant in everything concerning you. If there is any questions concerning Luke and this other brother let me recommend their integrity to you, for they are ambassadors of all the fellowships with no hesitation in ministering the great glory of Jesus. So, show to them, as well as all of the other fellowships, the genuine proof of your love and the fact all our boasting of you has not been in vain.

I don't think it's necessary to overkill the subject of this fund raising campaign. I've spoken to you about it very clearly and any more I say would be carrying it to excess. I'm confident of your eagerness and sincerity towards this project. I brag to the people in the north about all of you down south. I've told all of the fellowships in Macedonia the believers who gather throughout Achaia were ready to dig into their pockets a year ago. You've certainly provoked and challenged others to get involved in this worthy cause.

The reason I've sent these brothers to you now is we expect you're ready to fulfill your response to this financial appeal. We've bragged a lot about you so please don't embarrass us. Don't let our boasting be in vain. If I show up on your doorsteps with some of our Macedonian friends and you aren't prepared with your gifts we'll have a little more than egg on our face.

Hey, you will too!

With this in mind, I thought it necessary to send these brothers on ahead to assist you in the collection. I'd much rather you give generously out of your abundance with a good spirit rather than out of haste with an improper motivation of "what can I get out of it?"

BUT, I want to leave you with this thought. Nobody is ever a loser because he gives generously. A farmer who scatters only a few seed can hardly expect to harvest a very large crop. On the other hand, a farmer who plants seeds like crazy will also be able to reap a bountiful harvest.

CHALLENGE TO GIVE — 4ᵀᴴ COR

Motivation and attitude toward giving is key. Purpose in your heart to give, not grudgingly because you have to, or even because you think you'll get something in return. I'm sure God just loves it when we give out of the same gracious, generous, and cheerful spirit characteristic of Jesus in us.

Indeed, was not God able to make "all" of His grace abound towards you? Of course He was able to! God did it so you'd have "all" sufficiency in "all" things. Yes, He did it so you too could have a willing heart to share "all" of His liberty and "all" of His abundance with others.

We've an example of God's gracious giving in the scriptures. "He has dispersed His enemies abroad; He has given to the poor His righteousness which will last forever." (Psalms 112:9).

Now, it's this very same God who has provided the very necessities of your life who magnifies and multiplies the honor and glory of your righteousness in Jesus! You've been enriched in "all" things to enjoy and share the bountifulness of God's loving grace and peace. If this doesn't just make you thankful to the max I don't know what will. God has administered His love to supply not only our wants, BUT, even what we truly need!

Phenomenal!

It ought to result in our abundant gratitude towards God.

One result of our great thanksgiving ought to be a willing and generous spirit to share with others. We may experiment with our own ways of sharing the grace of God with others yet, I'm confidant it will produce positive results. Those you help will glorify God as well. They'll also be thankful to God for your demonstration of the love of Jesus in you. They'll really appreciate your liberal and generous support for them and indeed for the whole world. There's no doubt in my mind they'll be praying for you too. The example of the exceeding grace of God in you is not unnoticed!

THANKS BE TO GOD FOR HIS UNSPEAKABLE GIFT!

Trip # 16
PHILIPPI TO CORINTH

96. INTRODUCTION OF THE LETTER TO THE GALATIANS
(Acts 20:2,3a)

On the road again...

I had announced to the Corinthian believers we were about to come to conclude the collection of gifts for the saints in Jerusalem. So, it was time to say farewell to all of our good friends in Philippi. We traveled through Thessalonica, Berea, and other cities in Macedonia greeting our brothers and sisters, continually finding believers eager to hear the word of God. We taught, encouraged, and exhorted them to press on. It was a tremendous thing to see folks so eager to learn of the grace and peace God has so lovingly issued to all.

We finally arrived in Corinth after traveling south by boat and then over land through the city of Athens. That trip sure brought back a lot of memories. It was good to be back in Corinth among fellow believers. We sure had some catching up to do. It was such a blessing to be there and see their progress of understanding God's love. At the same time there was so much more the Corinthians needed to be taught.

We stayed in Corinth for approximately three months. What'd we do? In addition to exhorting and encouraging those who already believed in the sufficiency of God's grace, we were continually at odds with the religious community. I'm not only referring to the Jewish establishment. I'm also referring more specifically to a group of Jews we called the "Judaizers." They were a real pain in the you-know-what.

Who were the Judaizers? They were actually Jewish believers in what God had done in Jesus. So what could be so wrong with that?

Well, the unfortunate conclusion they'd come to was that Jesus had come to save the world all right, however, only the Jewish world! As far as they were concerned Gentiles were merely created to become fuel for the fires of hell.

Did you know it was illegal for a Jew to assist a Gentile woman during childbirth because it would be lending a helping hand to bring one more Gentile heathen into this world? Perhaps now you get a glimpse of why I love these Judaizers so much.

Look, you just have to love those who need help so desperately. I spent gobs of time with these folks attempting to teach them of God's grace for "all!"

This Judaizer mentality wasn't limited to any specific area. It was as pervasive in Corinth as it was in Macedonia, Galatia, or Judea. Precious believers in cities like Lystra, Derbe, Iconium, Antioch, and other cities were under constant susceptibility to being deceived into thinking the grace of God wasn't as sufficient as we had been telling folks it was. They also continued to spread the nonsense that laws, rules, and regulations were also required to maintain the favor of God.

I considered it one of my many duties to contradict such erroneous deceptions. Now, I can handle if it people want to question my credentials or my performance. What I can't handle is when ignorant people question the purpose and validity of the life, death, and resurrection of Jesus and the impact God's mercy and grace has had upon the whole world.

The concept of Gentile believers was pretty far fetched for many Jewish believers. If they did stretch to accept this reality, then surely it was necessary for the new Gentile believers to become Jews first.

How could one become a Jew? One of the requirements was circumcision. And then there was the Law of Moses. That had to be obeyed in every respect too, right?

Well, I don't want to spoil the next letter by giving you my responses to some of these fallacies right now. Suffice it to say I'll answer in a way you may even benefit. If you have a tendency to agree with notions of limitations upon God's wisdom, desire, and ability to gift the whole world with His grace and peace, perhaps you'll find in these words a challenging thought or two.

I actually wrote a couple of letters during my time in Corinth. If I can say so myself, I think both of them are outstanding treatises of God's love for all mankind. First of all, let me share with you a letter penned to all of the believers in Galatia.

Secondly, I'll share a letter I wrote to the believers in the great city of Rome.

So, here goes...

GALATIANS

LETTER TO THE GALATIANS

97. GOSPEL OF GRACE AND PEACE
(Galatians 1:1-16a)

From:
Paul, an ambassador, not of the wisdom of mankind, nor by the appointment of some human ordination, BUT, an ambassador of Jesus and of God the Father who raised Jesus from the dead. And from all the other brothers with me.

To:
All the fellowships of believers who meet together in Galatia.

Blessing:
Grace and peace are your everlasting portion from God the Father and from Jesus who gave Himself for the sins of the whole world so He might deliver "all" from the evil deceptions of the wisdom (foolishness) of mankind, in accordance to the will of God and our Father. To Him be glory for ever and ever. Amen.

You know, I'm just flabberghasted! I'm so amazed I can hardly believe it! I simply marvel you could be so easily persuaded to turn your backs on God, the very One who has called you into the grace of Jesus. Why in the world would you even think about walking away from the absolute liberty God has given to you so you could return to the stupid slavery of another gospel?

Well, I've got a news flash for you! What you've turned to, put your trust in, isn't a good news message in the least! BUT, these jerks who pretend to preach the truth are nothing more than manure spreading deceivers and perverts of the good news gospel of Jesus. And that's the stinking bottom line!

BUT, and let me state it so emphatically you couldn't possibly misunderstand me, if I, if we, or if an angel from heaven for that matter, preaches any other gospel message than the gospel of God's loving grace and peace we've preached to you, then I'd advise you to run them out of town at the first possible opportunity!

Strong enough?

I've said it once already. Perhaps if I say it again you'll get an idea of how strongly I feel about this. If you hear anyone preach any other gospel to you than you've already received show the quacks the door, lock the door behind you and throw away the keys.

Do you honestly think I need to persuade either men and women or even God there must be a better way to righteousness than God's grace?

Don't be ridiculous!

Perhaps you think I preach about the simplicity of the FREE AND "ALL" INCLUSIVE GRACE of God so I might gain the respect and favor of people.

Come on!

Do you seriously believe I'd go through everything I've gone through just so I could build up a fabulous reputation, with the applause of folks thrown in for good measure? Not! If you think this you sure don't know me very well. Man, if I wanted the accolades of people I sure wouldn't have gladly become an absolutely liberated slave of Jesus!

BUT, I tell you the honest truth, my dear friends, the gospel message of God's grace and peace in Jesus I preach certainly hasn't come from the wisdom (foolishness) of mankind. I didn't receive this good news from anybody else, nor was I taught it by Gamaliel, nor any other great teacher of the Jews I've studied under. BUT, I did get it from God's revelation of His love in Jesus.

I'm well aware my reputation has preceded me. No doubt you've heard of my past stature as one of the top dogs in the Jewish kennel of religious zealot hounds. You must know how I persecuted the believers in God beyond any measure of human courtesy and discretion, simply wasting believers to climb the corporate ladder.

Where did it get me?

Hey, I got instant recognition.

Reputation? You bet! Fame? I achieved the ultimate profits of the Jewish religious system, unequaled by many of my contemporaries.

Why?

Because I was exceedingly more zealous than anybody to uphold the tradition of laws, rules, and regulations our forefathers had established. BUT, in the perfect timing of God, the very same One responsible for the incredible miracle of my physical birth from the womb of my mother was responsible by His grace for the incredible miracle of birthing in me His Son, Jesus.

Why?

So I might preach the gospel message of God's love for the whole world to all who haven't had the privilege of hearing it!

98. FRUSTRATE THE GRACE
(Galatians 1:16b-2:21)

Now, when the almost unbelievable revelation God actually loved the whole world and not just a select few finally made its way through my thick skin and hard-boiled noggin, I knew I'd find myself in some pretty hot water with my Jewish peers if I started sharing with them my "new" understanding.

I know I may look a little goofy, however, I'm not stupid. The thought of going up to Jerusalem to meet those who were leaders of the believers in Jesus before me was an equally unwise notion. They would have been scared spitless of me. The incredible message of the abundant liberty in Jesus hit me like the rocks I'd used to beat upon those who believed in Him already.

BUT, I did go off into Arabia on my own before returning again to Damascus. I was three years before I stirred up enough courage to go up to Jerusalem to meet with Peter. I stayed with him for fifteen days. BUT, I didn't see any of the other leaders except for James, the brother of Jesus. I want you to know the things that I'm writing to you. I'm very serious now, as God is my witness, I'm not lying to you.

After I left Jerusalem I went into the countryside of Syria and Cilicia. None of the believers in Jesus in all of Judaea would have known who I was if they'd have passed me on the street. BUT, apparently the message was spreading "the one (me) who had persecuted the believers so vehemently in the past was now preaching the faith of Jesus he (me) once sought to destroy."

Even though they didn't know me from Adam, they still gave thanks to God for what He had done in me. Then, fourteen years later I went back to Jerusalem.

This time Barnabas took me with him as well as Titus. I went up to Jerusalem by shear determination so I could communicate with the believers there the very same message I was preaching among the Gentile community.

BUT, since I wasn't exactly a poster boy for either the Jews or the believers I thought it best we have a private meeting with those in leadership, not wanting to publicly offend or embarrass them by exposing the "all inclusive" message of God's love I was preaching.

BUT, for some strange reason Titus who was there with me, being a Greek wasn't compelled to be circumcised.

"Strange?" you ask.

Yes, because of a suspicious number of men looking somewhat out of place who showed up at the meeting. Somehow they managed to sneak into the meeting like clandestine spies attempting to discover the secret of the liberty we had found in Jesus. I'm sure their subversive mission was to catch us in their deceptive trap and return us captive to the bondage of their laws, rules, and regulations.

Fat chance!

Out of courtesy and respect we, being their guests after all, listened patiently for almost an hour to their babbling. You have to realize if we caved in on this point the very strength and security of the liberty you now enjoy would have been in jeopardy.

BUT, some of these leaders who were a little bent out of shape (I don't really care if they were leaders or not 'cause it really made no difference to me who they were and surely God isn't impressed with man-given credentials) really tried to score some points with their arguments.

I have to tell you I'd heard it all before and they didn't convince me of any truth in their folly.

BUT, I was a tough nut to crack myself.

After hearing my two shekels they realized I was unshakably committed to preaching the gospel of God's grace to those outside the Jewish faith just as Peter was to preaching it to the Jews. (God was using Peter to effectively lead the new Jewish believers just as He was using me to mightily educate the Gentile folk) when James, Peter, and John, apparently the pillars of the Jerusalem believers, perceived God had truly blessed me with His grace they decided it was in everyone's best interest to recognize the focus of our ministry. So they stretched out their right hands to Barney and I and we shook on it.

"You go your way! And we'll go ours!"

We were given their blessing to go out to share God's love with the Gentiles and they were given our blessing to continue sharing God's love with the Jews.

Suits me just fine.

Oh, there was one condition. The one thing we were asked to do was to remember to think of those who were less fortunate than others. Hey, I had no problem with this 'cause we were already doing that.

BUT, when Peter came to Antioch to check out how Barney and I were doing up in our neck of the woods I had a face-to-face confrontation with him. Peter was clearly in the wrong because he was trying to live in the land of political correctness, instead of in the land of liberty. He really showed how two-faced he was. He had no problem eating with us and our Gentile friends (something strict Jews would never even think of doing).

BUT, when he was told a certain group of emissaries obviously sent from Jerusalem by James were not only in town, they were on their way over to see what was happening, things changed drastically.

All of a sudden we weren't good enough for him. Fearing the reaction and repercussions of what these Jewish spies might report back to Jerusalem Peter figured he'd better high tail it out of there right in the middle of our meal!

Well, I'd be jiggered if he didn't just set off a chain reaction. A bunch of other supposedly "liberated" Jews took Peter's signal and figured the best course of action was to follow his lead.

Now, it was bad enough these little chickens were leaving. The last straw for me came when Barney even got up to leave with Peter and the rest of the coop. To say it got my dander up would be an understatement. BUT, when I saw they were clearly trying to walk a treacherous line between the liberating truth of the gospel of grace and peace and the enslaving deception of performance based self-righteousness, I rose up from my seat at the table and just yelled out at Peter so everybody in the room could hear me.

"Hey Peter! What's up?"

"If you, being a Jew, are enjoying this wonderful meal and fellowship with these fine folk like you were a Gentile like them, even though it's in direct conflict with the practices of the Jews, why do you now want to compel these Gentiles to abide by the same laws binding and enslaving the Jews?"

"What's with that?"

"You and I are Jews by birth, familiar with all the laws, rules, and regulations we've formulated to gain the approval of God, quite unlike our Gentile friends. Yet, we know nobody is justified, vindicated, acquitted, or pardoned in the sight of God by successfully performing the works of the law, BUT, only by the faith of Jesus!"

"That's right! Even we believe in Jesus and that we are justified by the faith Jesus had in God's wisdom and ability to gift all of mankind with His righteousness and not by the works of laws, rules, and regulations. For the keeping of laws, rules, and regulations could never ever gain for anyone the righteousness God has freely given to all!"

"BUT, if we go back under the law seeking the justification of Jesus don't we only place ourselves back under the slavery and bondage to a religious system that simply points out the condition of mankind's inability as opposed to a remedy for it? Wouldn't it actually make Jesus merely responsible for supervising mankind's obedience to laws, rules, and regulations rather than liberating us all from that bondage?"

"All I can say to this notion is, GOD FORBID!"

"Listen Pete, if I try to rebuild the process of trying to live up to the expectations of others and their laws, rules, and regulations after I've finally accepted I'd been liberated from them, then I'm the one with the big problem!"

"Hey, the law helped to show me I was totally incapable of gaining God's acceptance on my own. God superseded the law with His grace and peace through Jesus!"

"Why?"

"So I might live in the abundant liberty of God!"

"I am crucified with Jesus!

I'm participating right now in all of the benefits, privileges, and opportunities of Jesus' death and resurrection, including the freedom from the stranglehold of laws, rules, and regulations."

"Look at me. I'm still here, aren't I? And yet it isn't really me, BUT it's Jesus who lives in me!

And the life I now live here in this world I live in the luxurious liberty of the faith of Jesus, the Son of God.

He's the One who loved me and He's the One who gave Himself for me!"

"Pete, I'm not frustrating the grace of God!"

"You are!"

"**FOR IF THE RIGHTEOUSNESS OF GOD WERE TO BE OBTAINED BY THE ADHERENCE AND PERFORMANCE OF LAWS, RULES, AND REGULATIONS, THEN JESUS SURELY DIED IN VAIN!**"

99. YOU FOOLS
(Galatians 3:1-18)

What in the world have you Galatians been thinking? How can you be so foolish? Who is bewitching and deceiving you into believing you still need to obey and trust in the legalistic standards of the law? Why do you even crave the idiotic thoughts or dare to look into the evil eye of those who preach a false perspective of God's grace and peace?

We, who are preaching the truth, have paraded a great big news bulletin of the cross of Jesus for all to see. I need you to discover what you really think. Did you receive the Spirit of Jesus into your lives because you were so successful in performing all the works of the myriad number of laws, rules, and regulations God simply couldn't turn His back on you?

Or, did you come to understand and believe God has already placed the Spirit of Jesus in you because of His faith?

Can you be so stupid to not see the difference? You started out in the freedom of grace and now you want to return to the bondage of legalism thinking this will bring you God's righteousness? Is the liberty from the oppression of adhering to laws, rules, and regulations so painful? How can you even consider God's free and unconditionally awesome sense of freedom from guilt and anxiety to be a pain in the butt?

Get real!

If anything is painful it's the immense pressure of having to measure up to the standards of others.

God is the One who has ministered to you by placing the Spirit of Jesus within you, not to mention many other miraculous things He has accomplished in this world. Has He done all of these things because of your ability to keep laws, rules, and regulations that simply pointed out your hopelessness? Do you honestly think God would give His righteousness to mankind based upon the level or strength of our faith and trust in Him?

Preposterous!

None of us would have it if that's what it took!

Let me use Abraham to illustrate. Abe didn't go around trying to please God in order to be righteous. No. God had accorded His righteousness to Abe and he just put his trust in what God had told him He had done.

If you can wrap your brain around the concept of what God has done then you're no different than good old Abe. You're part of the same family of understanding.

The scriptures verify this. Understanding God would justify "all," Jew and Gentile alike through the faith of Jesus, scripture proclaimed the gospel message to Abe long before it actually happened! "All nations will be blessed of God in the same way as you have been blessed"(Genesis 12:3; 18:18).

So then, since God blessed everyone with His righteousness based on the faith of Jesus we all get to enjoy the same life of liberty Abe got to enjoy. For absolutely everyone who thinks they will receive the righteousness of God based on the works of the law have placed themselves under the power, control, and authority of self-righteousness.

What do the scriptures say? "Cursed is everyone who fails to comply with, abide by, or continue to accomplish all things which are written in the book of the law" (Deuteronomy 27:26).

BUT, absolutely nobody is justified by the keeping of the law in the sight of God. There should be no mistaking this incredible truth!

Why?

Read the scripture. "The justified, the righteous shall live because of God's faith and faithfulness" (Habakkuk 2:4).

Look, the keeping of the law has nothing to do with God's faith and faithfulness towards all mankind. BUT, the person who wants to remain under the bondage and slavery of the legalism of any religious system is bound to be cursed in the guilt and shame the inability to keep every law would produce.

Hang on!

Jesus has saved us from the curse of the law!

How'd He do that?

By being made a curse for us!

Again, what do the scriptures say? "Cursed is every one that is hung on a tree" (Deuteronomy 21:23).

How does this apply?

The blessing of God's righteousness given to Abe would also become applicable to Gentiles (non Jews) through Jesus when He died on the wooden cross!

Why?

So that "all" might receive the promise of the Spirit of Jesus.

Jesus' faith in the faithfulness of God was undaunted and unwavering.

My dear friends, I'd like you to understand what I'm going to tell you, so, I'll try to make it as simple as possible. Say two parties enter into a legal contract, an agreement, or perhaps even draw up a will. Say they even sign on the dotted line. BUT remember, I'm only talking about a covenant of sorts between two ordinary humans. Well, the contract is binding upon both parties. Once enacted neither party can just ignore one part of it nor could they add something else to the arrangement.

Here's my point. If the promises mere mortal men enter into have such a binding element to them, how much more is the agreement God entered into with Jesus?

Now to Abraham and his seed were the promises made. God didn't say "and to seeds," as if He was referring to all Abe's descendants. BUT, God spoke of "one seed."

Who's the "one" seed?

None other than Jesus!

Do the math.

Consider the logic.

Abe received the covenant agreement from God that He'd grant to all mankind His promise of righteousness based upon the faith of Jesus.

Then along came the "law of Moses." When did this agreement come into effect? Some four hundred and thirty years later!

Oh my goodness!

This law can't nullify, cancel, add to, or even modify the original covenant God had entered into with Jesus. There's no way it could ever make this incredible promise God made of no effect. For if the inheritance of righteousness already given in the promise of God to Abe were to instead come from the adherence of laws, rules, and regulations, then it wouldn't come from the promise of God, would it?

BUT, God gave a promise to Abe. **RIGHTEOUSNESS WOULD BE THE INHERITANCE OF GOD IN JESUS FOR "ALL!"**

100. SCHOOL MASTER
(Galatians 3:19-4:11)

In many families there was a very trusted servant, usually older and wiser, who was given the responsibility of guarding over the physical development and moral character of the children. One of the duties of this custodian, this "school-master," was to prepare the children, making sure they were safe until they were presented to the care and keeping of their parents. The servant wasn't the parent, just a pretty good assistant.

What's the difference between the "law" and the "promise?" Here are a couple of quickies before we continue with the letter.

The covenant agreement called the "law" had a number of deficiencies.
- The law was added. Why? Because of sin!
- The law required the mediation of more than one mediator.
- The law governed over the actions of two parties, a giver and an acceptor.
- The acceptor (mankind) had problems keeping their end of the bargain while the giver (God) had no problems at all.
- The law had no power to make anyone righteous.
- The law was merely a "school-master" to bring mankind to the great Parent.

The "promise" of God to gift the world with His righteousness through Jesus on the other hand was the ultimate from the get-go.
- The promise was eternal!
- The promise required the mediation of only one mediator (Jesus)!
- The promise depended on only one party, God!
- The giver (God) had no problem with being faithful!
- The giver (God) had absolute love to make whoever He wanted to righteous!
- The giver (God) was the great Father of all mankind!

What's your problem anyway?
Why do you hold the performing of laws, rules, and regulations in such high esteem?

The law was only added to point out the sinfulness and inability of mankind until the "seed" would come to those to whom the promise of God was actually made.

Furthermore, the law was mediated through the mediation of angels and of Moses.

You do need a mediator if two parties are involved in an agreement. BUT, there's no need for a mediator if a promise is made by one party.

Who's the only party who could possibly make such an irrevocable, all-inclusive, and everlasting promise?

GOD!

And, God is a party of one!

Did the law stand in opposition to the promises of God? God forbid! For if there had been even one law, rule, or regulation with the ability to give life, surely, even the righteousness of God would be granted to all who had the ability to keep every jot and tittle of every law.

BUT, even scriptures have led us to the conclusion the whole world could do nothing more than break the agreement between God and man. This is the precise reason God promised, by the faith of Jesus, to gift the whole world with His righteousness.

And those who understand and believe it will indeed find themselves liberated from the oppressive slavery of their self-righteous pursuits.

BUT, before the faith of Jesus was awesomely displayed on the cross, mankind was kept under the control of laws, rules, and regulations that governed their activity, shut out of the freedom the faith of Jesus would introduce.

Think of it this way.

Laws, rules, and regulations were simply like a "schoolmaster," entrusted to bring us like little children to Jesus, who would by His faith, introduce us to a life of righteousness. BUT, since the faith of Jesus became effective in the lives of all humanity, nobody remains under the tutelage of the schoolmastery of laws, rules, and regulations.

For "all" of us are the children of God by the faith which resides in Jesus!

For as many as have been immersed into Jesus, the very same number have been clothed with His character!

How many? As many as! In other words, "ALL!"

In the sight of God there's absolutely no distinction made between Jew or Greek; between someone still bound up in the slavery of laws, rules, and regulations or someone who's currently enjoying the liberty of Jesus; or between male and female.

Why?

We are "all" one in Jesus! He leveled the playing field.

And if everyone now belongs to the family of Jesus then surely everyone is the recipient of the righteousness promised to Abraham as well!

A child, even though an heir of a vast financial empire, has no legal right to control any of it. For all intents and purposes this child has no more authority than a hired servant would have in spite of being an eventual master of the family fortune. BUT, the child remains under the tutelage of a guardian, tutor, "school master" until such a time appointed by the father.

Using this analogy we, being children of God, remained under the governance and guidance of a "school master," the elementary systems of laws, rules, and regulations. The limitations upon our freedom to enjoy the vast riches of our inheritance were significant.

BUT!

In God's perfect timing He sent His Son, Jesus, birthed of a woman born herself during the time when the law was still in effect.

Why?

To redeem those ("all") under the management of the systems of laws, rules, and regulations.

Why?

So those folks ("all") could receive the full meal deal!

The deal was signed, sealed, and delivered as Jesus introduced the whole world to receive the totality of the benefits of full child-ship in the family of God!

And, because everyone is now a full-fledged child of God, He has sent into the heart of everyone the Spirit of His Son Jesus. Since we have the character of Jesus living in us we've no need to hold back from addressing our gracious, loving God with the name he truly deserves, "Abba," or "Father."

What does this mean?

Well, you're no longer a servant to systems of laws, rules, and regulations, that's for sure. BUT, you are a fully entitled, fully empowered, liberated child of God! And if you're a child of God, then indeed you're an heir of the righteousness of God through Jesus!

It's undoubtedly true when you didn't even know about God, or realize what He had actually done on your behalf you were enslaved by the powers and controls that didn't have any right to claim any authority over you. You paid homage to those who by their very nature weren't even close to being any kind of god.

BUT now, after you've come to know and appreciate what God has done for you, or rather and more importantly, since you're fully convinced of God's view and opinion of you, how in the world could you turn once again to the weak, the beggarly, the childish, and the elementary systems of laws, rules, and regulations enslaving and entangling you in the chains of bondage to legalistic, self-righteous pursuits of performance?

Apparently some of you folks still persist in observing rituals performed on certain days, months, and even years, as if they had some role in your lives.

You scare me! Sometimes I wonder whether all my hard work to set your minds and hearts at ease has actually accomplished anything at all in you.

101. CHILDREN OF THE PROMISE
(Galatians 4:12-31)

My dear, dear friends, I'm begging you to be like me. Hey, in God's eyes, I'm no different from you. I'm very well aware you've never tried to injure me in any way. You're very well acquainted with the physical problems I encountered when I came to preach the good news to you for the first time. You didn't despise me because of my disability, nor did you reject me, BUT, you did accept me as if I were an angel of God, or perhaps, as if I were Jesus Himself.

Where has this great spirit of acceptance gone? You can't pull the wool over my eyes. I know some of you would have gladly plucked out your very own eyes and given them to me if you thought it would've help me out. So, what's up? Have I become your enemy simply because I tell you the truth?

Listen up!

Zealous, deceitful preachers are obviously spreading a message that is having a significant impact upon you. BUT, the impact is a negative one.

Yes. Can't you see it? Their message is one of exclusivity. Your inability to keep up with their laws, rules, and regulations only makes them look good, meanwhile, keeping you guarded under their controls.

BUT, it's a good thing to be zealously affected by the good news of liberty in Jesus. You can enjoy the benefits of this glorious news even when I'm not with you!

Seeing you pursued by those who continue to pervert the good news of Jesus makes me as sick as a mother experiencing the pangs of childbirth. I'll probably never get over this nauseating feeling until I'm confident you've completely accepted the reality God birthed in you the Spirit of Jesus. I just wish I could be with you right now. Perhaps I'd say some things differently, or maybe I'd say the same things in a different tone of voice. I'm betwixt and between because I just can't figure out which way you're heading.

Tell me please, those of you who have such a burning desire to return to the slavery of legalism, haven't you learned anything at all? Don't you even hear what the law is saying to you?

Let me remind you what the scriptures (Genesis 16-17) record.

Abraham had two sons. One was born of a servant maid Hagar and the other son was born of his free-woman wife Sarah. BUT, Ishmael, Abraham's son by Hagar, is representative of those born under the bondage of the law. BUT, Isaac, Abraham's son with his wife Sarah, is representative of those born of the promise of God's righteousness.

Accept this example as an allegory of the two kinds of covenants. One covenant, its roots in the giving of the Mosaic Law on Mount Sinai, placed folks in the bondage of legalism. This is what Hagar represents. She symbolizes the destitute nature of the law given on Mount Sinai. And now, the authority for administering the slavery of laws, rules, and regulations rests in none other than the religious powers who rule over Jerusalem. These rulers have saddled themselves and all those who follow them with the baggage of legalism.

BUT, the other covenant, the covenant of the "heavenly" Jerusalem has no strings attached. It's absolutely free! This covenant is the promise of God to birth in "all" the righteousness of God.

For it's written, "Rejoice, you childless woman (Sarah). Break out of your misery and weep for joy. Even though you haven't experienced the wonderful pain of childbirth yet, you will actually have many more descendants than the woman (Hagar) who has given birth to a son with your husband" (Isaiah 54:11).

Now we, my dear friends, just as Isaac was, are the children of that promise of God! BUT, don't be surprised! The descendants of Ishmael, born of legalism, have been a thorn in the side of the descendants of Isaac, born of the Spirit of Jesus. Things haven't changed at all. The same battle is raging to this very day.

Nevertheless, what do the scriptures say?

"Cast out the servant maid (Hagar) and her son (Ishmael). For the son of the servant maid (Ishmael) will not be an heir with the son of the free-woman wife (Isaac)" (Genesis 21:10).

So then, my dear, dear friends, we are not descendants of the servant maid Hagar, BUT we are descendants of the free-woman wife Sarah.

Legalism, represented by Hagar and Ishmael, is fraught with problems. It's bondage. It represents a past of temporary gratification, no more than a tool to satisfy man's own selfish wisdom (foolishness). It represents a present filled with agony, disappointment, and rejection. It represents a future clouded with uncertainty, forever searching for a measure of comfort, a place it can call home.

On the other hand, liberty, represented by Sarah and Isaac, is limited only by the excessive, loving grace of God! It's past is built upon a promise. It's present is to be enjoyed with sheer excitement. And it's future is crystal clear in scope.

God now views the whole world as **CHILDREN OF THE PROMISE!** No longer are we children of the covenant of legalism. We all have been set free in Jesus.

God has cast out the old covenant, and with it, the notion mankind can achieve the acceptance of God through laws, rules, and regulations. It shouldn't be hard to accept. For some reason there are still folks who can't accept the reality of the promise of God.

What a shame!

102. JUST A LITTLE SNIP
(Galatians 5:1-12)

STAND FAST, therefore, IN THE LIBERTY wherewith Jesus has made us free!

Don't get entangled again with the yoke of bondage!

Listen up! I, Paul, want to tell you something very important.

If you go out and get yourself circumcised thinking it'll get you closer to God then you're only fooling yourself! You might as well conclude the death of Jesus did absolutely nothing to benefit you. Once again, any man who thinks circumcision is the only law required to gain the righteousness of God is ignorant of the facts. Such a one becomes a debtor to do the "whole" law.

Adopt this kind of thinking and Jesus is become of no effect whatsoever to you!

Add one law, rule, or regulation to the grace of God and you effectively remove Jesus from the picture.

Anybody who thinks they are justified by laws, rules, and regulations are fallen from grace! For we, through the Spirit of Jesus within us, remain in the assurance our righteousness has been gained by the faith of Jesus in the faithfulness of God to fulfill His promise to the whole world.

Indeed, since we're already in Jesus, hey, neither circumcision nor uncircumcision play any role at all anymore.

BUT!

Our righteousness was made possible only by the faith of Jesus through the love of God!

You were doing so well.

Who came along and ripped the rug of assurance out from under your feet?

Who deceived you so craftily by throwing roadblocks in your path causing you not obey the truth?

This perversion and persuasion certainly didn't come from the very One and only God who called you to be His very own without any consideration of your belief or performance! My goodness, a snippet of infectious leaven certainly will take its toll on a whole lump of dough.

I have the fullest confidence in Jesus that He has done for "all" what He said He'd do, and am equally confident you'll continue to enjoy the great liberty which comes as a result of accepting this truth. I'm sure you'll resist the perverted wisdom (foolishness) of mankind suggesting belief and performance will affect the will of God to gift the world with His righteousness.

BUT, the goofs, whoever they might be, who perpetuate the entrapment to laws, rules, and regulations will get to suffer the consequences of their own stupidity by spending their lives suffering the agony, guilt, and shame accompanying the intolerant anxiety bondage delivers.

What a shame! They'll get theirs. Their own judgment I mean. Not God's. Their own!

As for me, my dear friends, if I still preached the need to accept circumcision as a condition for righteousness, why in the world am I still getting persecuted so much by the legalistic control freaks who pursue me with such reckless abandon?

If I still preached the requirement of even just one law, rule, or regulation like circumcision, then the very reason for the cross of Jesus would be nullified!

I wish those who are deceiving you would be forced to endure a more serious snipping!

I know! I know! Sounds a little cruel. However, if I had my way I'd have anybody who preaches the need for a little snip of circumcision suffer the indignation and pain of being totally snipped. This would certainly make them think twice about preaching what they preach!

My goodness, if they think just a minor snip could help in the pursuit of righteousness, then they ought to consider what could happen if they had a major snip. I'm certain you won't hear them preach the value in that. Well, this is just how stupid they are! At the very least their foolishness reveals how ignorant their rationale is. The logic just leaves something to be desired.

Do you know what is offensive to the cross of Jesus?

The law!

God took offensive action to free the whole world from the illusion the performance of laws, rules, and regulations could gain for them the righteousness of God.

The offensive action?

The cross of Jesus!

On it He destroyed the law along with all of its inability. He replaced the burden of slavery with the freedom of liberty in Jesus!

Stand therefore in the liberty wherewith Jesus has made us free!

103. WALK IN THE SPIRIT
(Galatians 5:13-6:10)

My dear friends, you've been called of God to live in the land of liberty! Just don't waste this liberty by taking every opportunity to revert back to the systems of laws, rules, and regulations to determine the measure of your acceptability to God. BUT, let the love of God within you be the inspiration to serve other folks around you.

For even the law finds fulfillment in this one command, "You shall love your neighbor as yourself" (Leviticus 19:18).

BUT, if you persist in chewing up one another in a judgmental, negative, and accusatory atmosphere, devouring the spirit of loving and gracious acceptance, you'd best watch out you just don't wipe each other out altogether.

Want my advice?

Live in the liberty of the Spirit of Jesus within you and you'll have no need to lust after the pursuit of self-righteousness through your performance!

Why do I say that?

Because the bondage engendered in the pursuit of self-righteousness is diametrically opposed to the gift of liberty in the Spirit of Jesus in you. The liberty you've received in the Spirit of Jesus has nothing in common whatsoever with the legalistic lifestyle many seem to aspire to. They are as opposite as you can possibly get. Listen, the slavery to laws, rules, and regulations is so prohibitively restrictive it's literally impossible for anyone to actually do what they set out to do.

Self-righteousness is an impossibility!

BUT, if God actually did what He said He'd do, if you are led of the Spirit of Jesus within you, then you're no longer under the legalistic power and control of laws, rules, and regulations.

Now, what kind of activities do laws, rules, and regulations govern?

They govern sexual misconduct like adultery, prostitution, unfaithfulness, and other sexual vices. They rule over religious activities such as idolatry, witchcraft, and sorcery. They even rule over conduct of behavior like strife, jealousy, selfishness, dissension, sectarianism, envy, murder, drunkenness, carousing, and other such tendencies.

I've told you of all these kinds of laws, rules, and regulations before. Well, in times past, as a pharisaical zealot bent on defending the laws and traditions of my religious heritage, I was the loudest to proclaim folks who perform any of these anti-social activities would never inherit the kingdom of God.

BUT, I was wrong! You see, the fruit of the Spirit of God is:
- His love.
- His joy.
- His peace.
- His long-suffering.
- His gentleness.
- His goodness.
- His faith.
- His meekness.
- His temperance.

Measured against the standard of total acceptance of God, there isn't one single law that could bring anybody into the righteousness of God through merit or performance!

Furthermore, all those Jesus died for have been freed from the bondage of laws, rules, and regulations. Even though the aspiration of self-righteousness through legalism is very attractive and addictive, its power was crucified with Jesus on the cross!

My recommendation?

If everyone now lives in the Spirit of Jesus, why shouldn't all of us start living like we actually "are" in the Spirit of Jesus!

Let's not be desirous of pursuing the vanity of self-righteousness, provoking one other with intolerance, conceit, and bigotry, and jealously envying the strength of belief, faith, and performance in one another.

My dear friends, I'd sincerely encourage those living in the spirit of liberty in Jesus to restore in a spirit of meekness those who've been overtaken by this fault of self-righteous deception in legalism. Be careful they don't turn the tables on you and persuade you to join in their dissimilation.

Bear up those folks who are struggling with the anguish and pain of performance based religious systems. Life under the law of Jesus is based on freedom, not on captivity, so live like it!

For if a person thinks they've what it takes to be approved in the sight of God, when in reality there's absolutely nothing they can do to impress God, they're merely deceiving themselves.

BUT, everyone will ultimately figure out the incredible instability of self-righteous performances. What will it gain? The only place success or failure will be recognized is in one's own eyes. The insidious slavery to laws, rules, and regulations will not leave any time to consider the plight of others. The burdens of indignation, guilt, embarrassment, anxiety, fear, and loneliness will have to be carried alone.

A student should share in the knowledge of the teacher and a listener ought to participate in the knowledge of the speaker. Well, be not deceived by those who teach a perverted message of the good news of God's grace and peace. God is not mocked nor affected by the foolishness of man's wisdom, for everyone will reap what they sow.

What do I mean by that?

Well, those who sow the seeds of self-righteousness will reap the corruption of the never-ending bondage to laws, rules, and regulations, which, in this life, will produce nothing other than guilt, shame, and fear. BUT, those who sow the seeds of liberty in the Spirit of Jesus will reap nothing less than the everlasting, exciting freedom in the Spirit of Jesus who made it all possible!

Hey, let's not get tired of God's unconditional acceptance and along with it, the great opportunities we have to share His grace and peace with others. Don't wimp out thinking God's gift isn't for real. The benefits and privileges of being the children of God are applicable in every season of our lives as long as we don't lose consciousness by the deception our performance or lack thereof will deter God's intention and will for the whole world.

Therefore, as we have opportunity, let's determine to SEEK THE ULTIMATE BEST for our fellow human-beings, and in particular, for those already aware the faith of Jesus has purchased the righteousness of God for "all."

104. CONCLUSION OF GALATIANS
(Galatians 6:11-18)

If I could write my desire for you in any bigger letters to drive home the gospel message of the grace and peace of God I would. There are those who want to manipulate and control you as a means of making themselves look important in the eyes of others. One of the laws exalting their authority and defining your subjection to a religious system is the requirement of circumcision.

The truth of the matter is they're afraid to stand up for the true application of the cross of Jesus. Declaring the grace, peace, mercy, and righteousness of God for the whole world, without the belief or accomplishments of anyone, is a dangerous task for those who travel in religious circles!

Listen, even those who are circumcised haven't the ability to keep the very laws, rules, and regulations they espouse! BUT, this sure doesn't stop them from wanting to gain fame and glory for their domination over you.

BUT!

God forbid I should glory or boast in anything other than the cross of Jesus!

What did He do?

It's because of the death of Jesus that all the laws, rules, and regulations religious systems practice for the sake of righteousness have absolutely no affect upon me at all.

Likewise, it's because of the cross of Jesus that I am totally absolved of having to depend on the strength of my belief and faith or on the resolve of my performance and accomplishments to gain the righteousness of God!

In Jesus circumcision won't change the character of anybody one iota. Hey, even un-circumcision will not alter God's view and opinion of anyone.

BUT, in Jesus all have become new creatures!

Those who live and walk in this understanding, who accept without reservation God's wise plan for all mankind, will truly be able to enjoy the incredible peace and mercy God has blessed the whole world with, indeed, the chosen people of God.

I hope this letter will put a plug in the notion I'm preaching a man made gospel designed to tickle the ears of those who wish to live without constraints, or, at the opposite end of the spectrum, that I'm simply pussy footing around difficult issues, sucking up to the dictates of a select few. I'm not afraid of the stand I've taken. I'll bear the scars of persecution proudly for I'll gladly choose liberty over bondage any day.

My dear, dear friends, **THE GRACE OF JESUS IS ALREADY CONFIRMED IN YOU!**

That's just the way it is folks!

LETTER TO THE ROMANS

105. INTRODUCTION OF THE LETTER TO THE ROMANS

So, how'd you like the letter to my Galatian friends? Think they got the message? I'm not sure I could explain it any clearer. The dangers of returning to a life where laws, rules, and regulations do nothing except bring anguish, shame, fear, and the constant torment of guilt and inadequacy is hard to overemphasize. Why anyone would have even the slightest desire to exchange complete liberty for absolute bondage is way beyond me.

Well, it's on to some more good stuff. At this point it would be my extreme pleasure to introduce you to another one of the letters I dispatched from Corinth. Our gracious host, Gaius, was so hospitable to provide for our every need. His generosity allowed us to pursue many different opportunities of spreading the gospel message, including writing. In the case of this next letter you may be more inclined to think of it as a major theological treatise!

You may recognize it as my letter to the Romans. Even though I hadn't yet actually set foot in the city of Rome at the time of its writing I sure had heard plenty of stories about it. It fascinated and captivated my curiosity. Friends like Aquilla and Priscilla, among others, kept me awake many a night recounting the splendor of this magnificent city. I truly couldn't wait for any opportunity to get there. It was, in fact, on my agenda.

However, the first task at hand was to complete the collection of gifts for the suffering folks back in Jerusalem. All that remained was to make a few more pit stops and then get the considerable collection of gifts to their intended recipients. I was quite certain they wouldn't be expecting such generous assistance from those they'd never met, Gentiles to boot. Without a doubt the Jerusalem believers would be overwhelmed to the max.

Even though I wasn't really familiar with the message the believers in Rome had been given, I thought it would be beneficial for them to have a rather detailed perspective of the love of God toward humanity. No doubt, since Rome played a pivotal role in the political, sociological, economic, and religious life of virtually the entire civilized world, it would be a good thing for the believers there to possess a substantive declaration of God's wise plan for the whole world.

INTRO TO ROMANS   TRIP # 16

    The certainty this letter would be circulated far beyond the confines of the considerable walls of Rome was a no brainer. This fact was not lost in my consideration of what I'd write. I won't belabor my excitement. This is a tremendously important letter, if I do say so myself. I'm sure you'll enjoy it too. I'm also convinced you'll come across some very interesting perspectives many of you may never have even considered before.

    Scary? Keep your mind open.

    Let's get on with it...

106. I AM NOT ASHAMED
(Romans 1:1-32)

From:
Paul, a servant of Jesus, called to be an ambassador, separated out to preach the gospel of God, that, I might add, He promised a long time ago through His prophets in the holy scriptures concerning His Son Jesus who arrived on this earth as a human, born a descendant of the great king David. God, according to the spirit of His holiness, didn't withhold His power when He declared to the world Jesus was indeed His glorious Son. For God is the One responsible for raising Jesus from the dead, providing the only way the whole world could received the grace and blessing of adoption into His family. The obedience of Jesus to the faithfulness of God has been declared among all nations to the honor and glory of God's name, among who you are also called of Jesus!

To:
Everyone in Rome, the beloved of God, called to be His children.

Blessing:
Grace and peace have been issued to you from God our Father, and Jesus.

First of all, I want you to know I thank my God through Jesus for each and every one of you. It blesses my heart to know your understanding and acceptance of the gospel of God's grace and peace is an encouragement to others throughout the whole world. As God is my witness, whom I serve with all my energy preaching and teaching the gospel of the Spirit of Jesus within me, I want to assure you I unceasingly make mention of you always in my prayers.

One of the things I ask of God is that this long journey, which we have undertaken to deliver the gifts of assistance to Jerusalem, will proceed according to plan, not taking any longer than absolutely necessary. I just can't wait to see you. I have so much I want to share with you.

I'd like to assist you to fully comprehend the majesty of the gifts God has blessed you with in Jesus, thus entrenching in your hearts and minds who it is you believe in.

Perhaps I should rephrase that. I really want us to be comforted in the fact we believe and understand the same things, being positively inspired of each other.

Now, I don't want you to ignorantly think, my dear friends, the only reason I've planned to come to you, BUT, obviously unsuccessful as yet, is that I want to gain the acclamation and reputation for having great success among you as I've had among other folks.

Well, think again! I'm the one who is indebted to others. I've benefited immensely from the cultured Greeks to the less cultured folks of many different nationalities. I owe a lot to those who have great wisdom to contemplate the things of God, as well as to those who haven't even been exposed to the good news of God's grace and peace.

Therefore, with all the love of the Spirit of Jesus within me, I'm fully prepared to preach the gospel message to those of you who are in Rome too!

Listen! I'M NOT ASHAMED OF THE GOSPEL OF JESUS!

Why?

Because the gospel message of Jesus is the power of God bringing liberation to those trapped in the slavery to the pursuit of self-righteousness through laws, rules, and regulations. Those who believe in the message of God's great compassion for this whole world are saved from this great tyranny of legalism. Some Jewish folks have been among the first to understand the scope of God's will and power, and now, many Gentile folks are coming to understand what God has done applies every bit as much to them!

This is simply the bottom line: In the gospel message of Jesus is the revelation of the righteousness of God. He has faithfully revealed Himself to the whole world in the faithfulness of Jesus.

Surely it is written, "Those who are righteous have been justified by the faithfulness of God, and now live in His abundance and liberty" (Habakkuk 2:4).

For the wrath of God has been revealed from heaven against all the ungodliness and unrighteousness of mankind, against all those who hold on to the pursuit of self-righteousness as if it were a truth to respect and honor. You see, what there is to be known about God is already manifest in everyone and everything. Yes, God has revealed Himself to the whole world in Jesus!

For the invisible things of God from the very beginning of the creation of the world are very clearly seen, understandable by everything created, yes, even His eternal power and Godhead. There is nobody, nor anything, without excuse for not recognizing the sovereignty and wisdom of God. The folly of mankind is that even when people recognized the reality of a supreme God, they refused to give Him the honor and glory He deserved.

A thankless lot to be sure. BUT, instead of doing the right thing, the wisdom (foolishness) of mankind kicked in, exalting our own vanity through goofy, wild imaginations, which only served to darken foolish hearts. Professing and proclaiming ourselves to be so smart we actually displayed the immense scope of our stupidity!

How'd we do that?

We changed the glory of the incorruptible God into an image that had as much stability as the corruptibility of human life, of birds, of four footed beasts, and even creeping, crawling creatures.

What did God do about that?

Well, God decided to let mankind fend for themselves for a while. He chose to let mankind wallow in the muck of our own making. The lust of our hearts produced nothing other than the sickening filth and stench of bondage to self-righteousness, given over completely to the complexities of selfishness and immorality due to our inability to gain the favor of God through our performance based legalistic systems.

The superiority complex of mankind allowed us to change the truth of God's loving intention for all His creation into a lie, leading to the downward spiral of worshiping and serving the created over the Creator, who is blessed for ever and ever whether we like it or not.

That's just the way it is!

This is why God could only hope mankind would eventually recognize the folly of our vile affections and misdirected passion. My goodness, women abandoned their instinctive, natural passion for unnatural and demeaning things. Alas, men haven't done any better. They've degraded themselves by leaving the natural desire for women and scorched themselves on the fires of desire for other men. There's just something unnatural and unseemly about men and women having sexual relations with members of their own sex. The implications and consequences of sexual perversity can't be understated.

Even as folks were making a conscious decision to leave God out of the picture all together, God didn't interfere. He simply let us wander off with our reprobate minds and all, allowing us to do whatever we wanted to do in spite of the fact most of the activities were fraught with peril, disdainful and unpleasant to ourselves as individuals with no positive benefit to society as a whole.

Here is a partial list of activities that reveal an incredible lack of respect for God, as well as the deep depravity of human character:

- Injustice: self-centered motivation at the expense of God and others;
- Destructive badness: active, deliberate will to inflict injury and harm;
- Covetousness: love of "having" without regard to the rights of others;
- Maliciousness: devoid and destitute of positive characteristics;
- Envy: grudging resentment;
- Murder: not only the deed, indeed the very spirit of hatred and anger;
- Strife: contention born of selfish ambition, jealousy, and pride;
- Deceit: cunning, plotting attempts to gain with ulterior motivation;
- Evil-natured: malignity, supposing only the worst in everything;
- Whispering: character assassination, the tongue being the weapon of choice;
- Slandering: openly accusatory and demeaning;

- Anti-God: defying God with the objective of license over liberty;
- Insolence: sadistically cruel and insulting for the sheer pleasure of it;
- Arrogance: contempt for others in the attempt to look good over them;
- Boasting: pretentious spirit exalting oneself beyond reality;
- Inventing evil: search for new thrills due to discontentment and boredom;
- Disobedience to parents: loosening the bonds of family ties;
- Senselessness: inability to use the mind, heart, and experience for good;
- Breaking of agreements: loss of integrity;
- Love-less-ness: devoid of human affection and familial love;
- Implacability: action without pity or empathy;
- Mercilessness: empty of emotion or caring.

Mankind chose a path of destruction knowing full well the judgment of God upon those who practice these things. Those who commit these horrific injustices to themselves and others were worthy of the ultimate punishment from God, namely: DEATH!

Not only did folks keep on doing them anyway, BUT they seemed to take pleasure in doing them, condoning others who participated in these kinds of activities as well.

Go figure!

107. INEXCUSABLE
(Romans 2:1-16)

Therefore, anyone who sets themselves up as a judge of the beliefs and performances of others better be careful for they're just as inexcusable as the next person. When you judge somebody else you might just as well condemn yourself in the same breath.

Why?

Because even as you sit in judgment you'd be indicted by the same charges you'd press against another. BUT, we can be sure the judgment of God against those who live in the gutters of ignorance is measured according to the truth in Jesus!

Do you really think, and I'm talking to those of you committed to finding fault with others even though you have plenty of faults all on your own, that you have some kind of special connection with God allowing you to escape the wrath of God while others won't? Or do you actually despise the glorious riches of His goodness along with His great patience and tender, compassionate heart of faithfulness?

Are you not aware the goodness of God's grace and mercy should lead you to change your mind about the folly of mankind's perception regarding the magnitude and scope of God's great love?

BUT, it is true the hard and unrepentant heart of mankind did nothing more than store up a treasure house of wrath in the heart of God. And then He unleashed His anger upon all on the wonderful day of wrath.

Day of wrath? When was that?

Well, it occurred on the day of the cross when the righteous judgment of God upon the whole world was deposited upon Jesus! On "that" day He rendered His judgment against every person according to what they had a comin.'

Who did He pronounce His judgment upon?

Upon those who patiently continue the pursuit of doing good to get good from God. Upon those who persist in self-righteous well doing, seeking for glory, honor, immortality, and yes, for eternal life!

BUT, He also pronounced His judgment upon those who are downright contentious.

Even to those who don't or won't heed the truth of the gospel of Jesus, BUT rather obey the folly of self-righteousness, believing God is still filled with indignation and wrath, set to rain down a tribulation and anguish upon every living soul who does something wrong.

These folks believe God's punishment will someday off in the future surely be realized upon Jews first and foremost, and then naturally include the Gentile folks as well. BUT, they maintain glory, honor, and peace will undoubtedly flow to those who do good, of course to the Jew first, and then also to the Gentiles.

My goodness, I'm sure glad God doesn't view all of us with this kind of prejudice, indiscretion and insensitivity! There's nobody who deserved any better or any less than anyone else in the eyes of God.

Get a load of this.

All those who weren't even enslaved by laws governing their relationship to God were due to receive the punishment of eternal death completely apart from any standard of measurement. In addition, all those trapped in the bondage of living up to the standards of laws, rules, and regulations were also destined to be judged according to how well they did or didn't do in measuring up to these standards.

(For you see, it wouldn't be only those who've simply heard of laws, rules, and regulations of religious systems, without getting enslaved to keep them to gain the favor of God, who are now justified before God, BUT, those who've tried to live up to the conditions of laws, rules, and regulations will also find themselves justified regardless of their success or failure. You see, Gentile folks, who don't live under the same laws, rules, and regulations as the Jewish folks, still by nature try to be descent folks as if they were actually under the Jewish system. They actually find themselves to be every bit under a systems of laws, rules, and regulations of their own creation. Their very actions show they're just as bound to perform up to a standards of conduct measured against the dictates of their own hearts. They are similarly captive to their conscience as anybody else. Inherent patterns of thought confirm the spirit of judgment, intolerance, and self-righteousness that accuse or excuse the beliefs and activities of others.)

Well, when will all this judging of God take place? **MISSION ACCOMPLISHED!**

It was done the day God judged the secrets of all mankind by Jesus!

This certainly is in accordance with the very good gospel message of God's loving grace and peace through Jesus that I preach.

108. CIRCUMCISION OF THE HEART
(Romans 2:17-29)

Look, they don't call you a Jew for nothing!

You put all your trust into systems of laws, rules, and regulations. You aren't ashamed to brag and boast about "your" God. Of course, you know His will, approve and appreciate the excellence of the strong moral values and principles you've been taught from a religious system of laws, rules, and regulations.

Moreover, you're confident you were placed here on this world to act as a guide to the blind, to be a light for those floundering in the darkness of another way. Indeed, even to be a wise instructor of the foolishly immature, oh yes, a teacher of babes.

By what authority?

Of course, it's because of the superb form of your knowledge and of the great truths you perceive in these laws, rules, and regulations.

Well, if this is accurate then why don't those of you so committed to teaching others try teaching yourselves a thing or two? Is it possible those of you who so strenuously preach that stealing is wrong could actually be guilty yourselves of the very same thing?

Have any of you bitterly opposed to adultery been caught with your own hands in the cookie jar, so to speak?

Could it be those of you who get their dander up over the idolatrous behavior of others are just as guilty of committing the sacrilege of abusing the grace and peace of God?

How come it's those who make such a big deal about adhering to laws, rules, and regulations are the most apt to break them, shattering by their visible contradiction their own testimony as well as being a dishonor to the God they profess?

Don't kid yourselves.

The name of God is mocked and blasphemed among the Gentiles as a result of your beliefs and actions. They mock God because of what you are doing, not because of what He has done. Hey, don't take my word for it. Read it for yourselves. Because of the hypocrisy and contempt the Jews display, "the name of God is blasphemed among the Gentiles" (Isaiah 52:5).

Now, obeying the laws concerning circumcision would have some value if it were possible for anyone to keep every last jot and tittle of each and every law, rule, and regulation. BUT, if the law is broken, any law, in any way, degree, or point, then circumcision has no merit whatsoever. You might as well put the skin back on, or at least as a more reasonable alternative, regard the ceremony as totally irrelevant.

Now, track with me.

If those who haven't been circumcised would be so good as to keep every law, rule, and regulation, wouldn't you agree they should actually be treated by God in the very same way He would treat those who have been circumcised and who have gained the righteousness of God through their obedient performance?

Furthermore, doesn't it only make sense those who are just naturally good in spite of their un-circumcision would be the ones who have more right to judge you, who, in spite of your circumcision, have trouble maintaining your purity because you can't even keep one itsy-bitsy letter of the law?

Being a Jew has nothing to do with whether your wings have been clipped or not! What's on the outside doesn't make any difference to God! Circumcision, an external parable of flesh and blood, is not what makes a person a child of God!

BUT, true Jews, the children of God, have been CUT AND SEPARATED out in the very image of the heart of God Himself. We're all children of God in the Spirit of Jesus and not as a result of any belief or performance based systems of self-righteousness dependent upon the letter of laws, rules, and regulations!

The children of God don't receive the glory, honor, and praise of mankind. BUT, they do receive the praise of God!

109. FALLING SHORT
(Romans 3:1-29)

Then, what advantage is there in being a member of the Jewish race? What profit is there in the rite of circumcision? Oh, I'd say there's a great advantage and benefit. Mainly because it was to them God committed His oracles and promises.

Think about this for a moment. Just what would happen if some of the Jewish folks didn't believe what God told them He was going to do? Should their unbelief make the faith and faithfulness of God ineffective?

God forbid!

Yes, one thing you can count on to be true is the faith and faithfulness of God, BUT just the opposite can be said about the commitment behind the words of any human. God's fidelity to His promises isn't denied by mankind's failure to keep their promises.

Surely the Psalmist wrote, "God would certainly be justified in His punishment of my sin, and that there would be no mistake when He came to judge me" (Psalms 51:4).

BUT, I know what you're thinking. "Why should we be condemned for what ultimately commends the righteousness of God?" "Wouldn't God be kind of unjust to punish what abounds to His glory?" Oh, isn't this just the wisdom (foolishness) of mankind!

God forbid!

The proposition that evil is actually good is preposterous to say the least. How in the world would God even judge if this were the case?

Perhaps you're thinking, "If I lie, doesn't this simply make God's truthfulness look even better? Why not do whatever, whenever, and to whomever I want to so God would be glorified even more? Why I should I be judged a sinner if God's going to come up smelling like honey-suckle anyway?"

Some folks have slanderously accused me (because I preach the liberty of Jesus) of affirming we might as well do as much evil as we can so more good can accrue to God. Hey, if I actually preached this then my accusers would be right on in pointing their finger at me. However, this is not what I've preached. The idea is ridiculous!

So what then? Are we who live in the liberty of choosing to do what we know to be right because we want to any better off than those who literally live in the liberty of doing whatever they want for all the wrong reasons?

Absolutely not!

Look, I think I've already proven to you both Jews and Gentiles alike were all found to be floundering in the same misdirected, unstable ship on an uncharted course to destruction. Up a creek without a paddle so to speak.

As it is written:

"There are none righteous. No, not even one! There are none who understand, nor are there any who seek after God. Everyone has turned to go their own way and each and every one has become enslaved to filth. Nobody has ever accomplished, nor will accomplish enough good to satisfy the wrath of God" (Psalms 13:1-3; 53:1-3).

"Their throat is an open grave which entombs fraud, and deception is all they know what to utter with their lips" (Psalms 5:9).

"They have sharpened their tongues like a snake and the poison of the venomous adder snake is ready to strike under their lips" (Psalms 140:3).

"Their mouths are full of cursing, deceit and fraud, under their tongues is mischief and vanity" (Psalms 10:7).

"Their feet run to evil and they make haste to shed innocent blood, their thoughts are thoughts of iniquity, wasting and destruction are in their paths. The way of peace they don't know" (Isaiah 59:7,8).

"The transgression of the wicked says within my heart there is no fear of God before His eyes" (Psalms 36:1).

Now, you and I both know the dictates of laws, rules, and regulations apply equally to those who fall under their bondage. Nobody can use any excuse, such as ignorance or insanity, as a defense strategy. Laws, rules, and regulations helped identify the reality the whole world was playing on the same field in the eyes of God. One person was just as guilty as the next!

Therefore, it's impossible for anybody to be justified in the sight of God by measuring their performance according to the standards of laws, rules, and regulations!

Laws, rules, and regulations were never intended to provide righteousness for anyone, however, they certainly were beneficial to give all mankind the knowledge and understanding of the difference between right and wrong.

BUT, the righteousness of God, completely apart from laws, rules, and regulations, has been manifested upon the whole world!

Hey, did you know laws, rules, and regulations actually knew this to be the case? Well, so did the prophets.

Yes, even the very righteousness of God, achieved by the faith of Jesus, has been applied to the whole world, just as it has been upon those who believe already in what God has done. You see, there's no difference between the two because "all" sinned, and "all" have come up way short of the standards of the glory of God based on belief and performance.

How has this righteousness been applied to the whole world?

"All" have been justified by the free gift of God's grace through the redemption in Jesus! God put His faith in the blood of Jesus, and "PASSED OVER" the sins of the whole world when He saw the sacrifice that satisfied His wrath and the demands of His justice. Thus God declared His righteousness with the complete obliteration of sin. Sin is a thing of the past thanks to the great forbearance of God who declares at this time His righteousness upon all.

Why'd He do it?

So the whole world would know He in fact is just, recognizing God as the great justifier of "all," including those who believe in Jesus. So, is there any point in bragging about how well you believe or how well you perform?

I say "Nay, Nay!" Bragging rights are excluded.

Are there some laws, rules, and regulations I could thank for getting me the righteousness of God?

Don't be ridiculous!

Can I brag about my great performances and super work ethic?

Again I say, "Nay. Nay!"

BUT, righteousness has been attained by nothing less than the law of God's faith.

Therefore, we conclude mankind is justified by the faith of God completely without regard to the performance of laws, rules, and regulations.

Let me ask you, "Is God the God of the Jews only? Is He not also God of the Gentiles?"

The answer is an unequivocal, "YES!"

God is God of the Gentiles also!

110. LESSONS FROM ABRAHAM
(Romans 3:30-4:25)

It's pretty plain to see there's only one God who could faithfully carry out His promise to justify both the circumcised and uncircumcised alike. So what's our reaction? Knowing this do we set about to recognize the fact laws, rules, and regulations have been canceled out and nullified because of the faith and faithfulness of God?

My, my! God forbid we'd be this intelligent!

Yes, we've done just the opposite by making laws, rules, and regulations the be all and end all of everything.

What should we say then about what Abraham our ancestral father figured out? For if good ol' Abe thought he was justified by his performance he certainly would have had a lot to brag about to his peers, BUT, he definitely couldn't accept one shred of glory before God.

What do the scriptures record?

"Abraham believed in the faithfulness of God to credit him with the righteousness he not paid for himself or worked to get" (Genesis 15:6).

So, those who think they work for the reward of righteousness would not receive it because of the grace of God, BUT of a debt God would owe to them.

BUT, those who know they don't have to work for their justification, BUT simply accept and understand it's God, and God alone who has justified the whole ungodly lot of humanity can put their implicit trust and confidence in the faithfulness of God to impart His righteousness to the whole world.

Hey, even King David described the blessedness of a person whom God has imputed His righteousness to without regard to accomplishments.

"Blessed are those whose iniquities are forgiven and whose sins are covered. Blessed is the one who will not be held liable by God for the sins they commit" (Psalms 32:1,2).

Does this incredible blessing apply only to those who've been circumcised? Or has God also covered the sins of those who haven't been circumcised? We seem to have no trouble in agreeing God was faithful to count Abe as one of His righteous ones merely because He "wanted" to.

When did Abe get the righteousness of God? After he was circumcised or before he was circumcised?

Well, not after he was circumcised, BUT before he was circumcised! Abe was cut out and deemed to be a child of God long before he was circumcised, a ceremony that only sealed the truth of the righteousness he had received by the faith and faithfulness of God.

You see, this fleshly parable is a declaration God indeed is the Father of all and everyone can believe they've been justified and made righteous even though they may not have been circumcised.

Yes, God's not only the Father of "all" who haven't been circumcised, BUT, He's also the Father of "all" who walk in the steps of righteousness our forefather Abe walked in even before He was circumcised.

For the promise of an inheritance of righteousness for everybody based upon the performance to any system of laws, rules, and regulations wasn't made to Abraham or even to any of his descendants for that matter!

BUT, the blessing of righteousness for "all" was always conditional upon the faith and faithfulness of God Himself!

Look, if those who successfully completed the tests of laws, rules, and regulations would be the only ones to inherit the righteousness of God, then God's faith and faithfulness would have had nothing to do with it! Obviously, if performance had anything to do with the gaining of His righteousness, then any promises God made concerning our inheritance would be made completely useless, not worth the breath He wasted to utter them!

Why?

Because the only thing systems of laws, rules, and regulations can bring to the table is wrath.

The other reason is there aren't any laws, rules, and regulations to break in system where there aren't any laws, rules, or regulations! Therefore, the inheritance of righteousness is only possible because of the faith and faithfulness of God.

Why?

So it might be as a result of the grace of God, and nothing else! This is the only way God could make sure His promise of righteousness would be applicable to the whole world.

His promise applies not only to those who participate and struggle in systems of laws, rules, and regulations, BUT, also to those who apply their liberty in a confident trust of God's will and ability in the same way Abe did.

God is surely the Father of us "all." God put His belief and admiration in Abe and made a promise to him, face to face. The promise was written down. "I've made you the father of many nations" (Genesis 17:5).

That's right, the very same God who gave this promise to Abe is the same God who raised Jesus from death. It's the very same awesome God who has brought into existence things which never existed before and who has created this world out of nothing. And it was this very same God of faithfulness who gave Abe the reason to believe and hope for something he never could have achieved through his own ability.

What was the promise to Abraham again?

God spoke a word of promise He'd be the God of Abraham and He'd also be the God of "all of your descendants who will follow you" (Genesis 17:7).

Staggering as this promise was Abe maintained the strongest confidence in God's intention. The fact he was way beyond the age of being a suitable donor of sperm in the child bearing department, being at least a hundred years old or so, didn't seem to faze ol' Abe. The fact his wife Sarah wasn't exactly a spring chicken didn't have much impact on him either. He didn't compromise on His confidence in God's will and ability, BUT, he remained steadfast in his understanding God was worthy of all the glory and honor.

Why?

Because **GOD WAS SIMPLY GOD!**

Abe was fully persuaded God had the absolute power and ability to perform what He'd promised. No ifs, ands, or buts about it!

And God did it!

He did what He promised to do. Abe was given the righteousness of God as a gift. And the promise of righteousness wasn't only recorded for the sake of this old patriarch named Abraham, BUT, for "all" of us too!

Yes, indeed. The righteousness of God was imputed upon "all."

Oh, if only we could all come to the great understanding and acceptance of what God has done for the whole world! If only we could put our simple trust in the faith and faithfulness of the God who raised up Jesus from the dead.

It was Jesus who was delivered up for the offenses of the whole world.

It was Jesus who was raised again to His glorified nature, making it possible for God to issue His righteousness and justification to "all!"

111. MUCH MORE
(Romans 5:1-19)

Therefore, being justified by the faith and faithfulness of God, we have peace with God through Jesus! We've been granted access into the realm of God's grace in which we now reside through the faith of Jesus, rejoicing in the certainty of the glory of God within us.

And not only can we glory in the knowledge we are no longer at odds with God, BUT, we can also glory in the midst of difficulties we experience on the human level. We know problems develop within us a sense of patience, and through an attitude of patience we gain a measure of experience, which births in us a sense of certainty and assurance that will never let us down.

Why?

Because of the certainty the Spirit of Jesus, whom God has placed within us, has completely wrapped our hearts in the love of God.

There was a time when mankind didn't have an adequate supply of strength to believe or perform to gain the favor and acceptance of God. And then, in the perfect timing of God, along came Jesus to die for the ungodly, for all those inadequately struggling in the bondage of self-righteousness.

Now I seriously doubt there are too many folks who'd gladly give their life to save the life of someone so full of themselves, so heavenly minded they're no earthly good. Then again, there may be the odd duck who'd be willing to sacrifice their own life to save a genuinely a good person.

BUT, God wasn't afraid to demonstrate His undying love for the whole world, for while all of us were still miserable sinners, incredibly short of the standard of righteousness, He sent Jesus to die for us!

MUCH MORE then, since we've "all" been justified by the blood of Jesus, will we come to understand we've been saved from the wrath of God because of Jesus!

For if, when we were actually enemies of God through our rebellion, we were reconciled, made to be at complete peace with God by the death of His Son Jesus,

MUCH MORE then, being placed into the realm of total absence of enmity or liability, will we come to discover ourselves to be completely saved by His life!

And not only so, BUT, we also get to share in the joy and contentment of God through Jesus, who took upon Himself the punishment we deserved, securing for us "all" the peace of God!

You see, one man, namely Adam, became the first to sin by thinking what he "did" affected God's view and opinion of him. Adam clearly disobeyed a command of God, assumed the worst, and set about to "do" something to get back into God's good book.

The result of Adam's self-centered approach to life cost him dearly, both physically and spiritually. In fact, everyone who has lived since Adam has pursued a similar tragedy of self-righteousness, suffering the agony and pain of its inevitable consequences too.

(Hey, it didn't take systems of laws, rules, and regulations to show people how to be self-righteous, for sin was an ever present reality even before laws, rules, and regulations entered the picture to stir things up even more.

BUT, please don't forget, sin is not imputed when there is no law!

Nevertheless, it's a fact of life folks from Adam to Moses have died. Yes, there were even some folks who died who hadn't sinned in a similar fashion to Adam's sin. Adam, of course, is a great type and shadow of Him who was to come.

BUT, there's no comparison between Adam and Jesus as far as the offense is concerned. Neither is there any way to compare Adam to the priceless yet absolute free gift of God to this world in Jesus!

Surely if the whole world could suffer the same agony of death as a result of following in the steps of one such as Adam,

MUCH MORE then, the grace of God, and the gift that He gave to the whole world.

This grace, declared to His creation by another human being, namely Jesus, has had an incredible affect upon "all!"

Although the scope of affect is the same, the gift of God's grace through Jesus can't even be compared to the results of Adam's self-righteous behavior, not to mention all those who've followed him.

The bondage of death was a consequence of disobedience that Adam initiated, BUT, the free gift of God's grace had the contrary affect of liberating "all" from the consequences of those offenses, replacing it with the unmerited favor of God!

If we like to attribute poor old Adam for getting us "all" started down the offensive path of self-righteousness, leading ultimately to the certainty of eternal death,

MUCH MORE,
MUCH MORE,
MUCH MORE then,

has the abundant grace of God established the eternal reign of life with the gift of righteousness He had for the whole world in One, namely Jesus!)

Because one person was just as guilty as the next person of walking in the dangerous footprints of self-righteousness, the judgment and wrath of God to condemn "all" was completely justified. At the opposite end of the spectrum, and yet, with the exact same magnitude and scope, the free gift of the grace of God became the inheritance of "all" as we walk in the footprints of righteousness of One, Jesus!

Adam just happened to be the first who disobediently tried going it on his own. Everyone else simply followed him down the garden path, so to speak.

Jesus, on the other hand, just happened to be the first to walk obediently down the path of righteousness, opening the gate and clearing the way for everyone in the process.

112. A GIFT OF GOD
(Romans 5:20-6:23)

Ah yes, let's get back to the law, introduced for the purpose of revealing just how futile mankind's efforts would be to achieve the righteousness of God by virtue of merit or accomplishment.

BUT, wherever this offensive behavior of self-righteousness abounded, the grace of God did what?

The grace of God did MUCH MORE abound!

Why?

So, just as the terror of self-righteousness reigned, the subjects of its empire being "all" of mankind, making us "all" as good as dead in every eternal sense of the word, EVEN SO, does the grace of God reign, the subjects of His kingdom being "all" of mankind, liberating and making us "all" good, pure, and righteous, through Jesus!

Fantastic, eh? Well, what should we conclude from this incredible truth?

One possible idea batted around is that we might just as well continue in our pursuit of self-righteousness and in our own stupid paths of destruction. Why? So it would serve to make the grace of God abound all the more!

God forbid!

This conclusion is mute, irresponsible, stupid, utter nonsense, and completely contrary to the intention of God's love. How in the world can we, now dead to laws, rules, and regulations continue to live in the pursuit of self-righteousness by strengthening our resolve to believe or by disciplining ourselves to the point of breaking down in trying to accomplish something sufficient enough to gain the favor and acceptance of God?

Don't you know as many of us as were baptized into Jesus, the very same number were also baptized into His death? Therefore, we "all" are buried with Him by baptism into death.

Why?

So, like Jesus Himself was raised up from the dead to the glory of the Father, EVEN SO, we're "all" supposed to walk together with Him in the newness of life!

For, if we "all" have been planted together in the likeness of His death, it logically follows we "all" have also been planted in the likeness of His resurrection!

Knowing our need to gain the righteousness of God by what we believe or by what we accomplish was crucified once and for all with Jesus, never again should we feel compelled and enslaved by systems of laws, rules, and regulations to strive for what we already have been given in Him.

Accept it for the gift it is!

Stop trying to get what you already have!

Listen, if you're dead to self-righteousness you're freed from its bondage! You don't have to go on living like you need to believe harder, increase your faith, or do something spectacular to get God's attention.

Once again, if we can agree Jesus was crucified for us "all," and we "all" were just as dead as He was, then we must also agree we "all" are every bit as alive as He is! We must realize the very fact Jesus has been raised from the dead implies He isn't going to have to die again.

Only makes sense death doesn't hold any dominion over Him whatsoever. For, in that He died, He died to liberate us from the enslavement of self-righteousness through laws, rules, and regulations, once for "all," and once for "all" time!

BUT, in the fact He is alive, He lives to the honor and glory of God!

Likewise, consider it to be an undeniable truth you're just as dead to the pursuit of God's righteousness as Jesus is, BUT, don't forget you're every bit as much alive to share in the very same liberty of righteousness and glory as Jesus in the eyes of God!

Don't get trapped into enticing, lustful doctrines instructing you to believe stronger, scold you to improve the strength of your faith, cheat you into sacrificing your creativity, your business acumen, your beauty, your intelligence, or shame you into increasing your commitment to serve others. Don't allow yourselves to be played as instruments in the symphony of self-righteousness, the music of which produces only the guilt and ridicule of personal achievement.

BUT, get in tune with the great Conductor, and with all of the others who've been brought back to a new life by God from the self-righteous pit of death. Play the wonderful instrument God has given to you in harmony and pleasure with the righteous band of God, to His honor and to His glory!

Look, systems of laws, rules, and regulations no longer have jurisdiction or authority over you concerning your relationship to God. God's view and opinion of you is not dependent upon the success or failure of laws, rules, and regulations.

BUT, you are covered by the grace of God!

What then?

Should we continue to pursue self-centered desires knowing laws, rules, and regulations don't have the power to condemn us anymore, BUT that our insufficiencies and indiscretions are covered under the grace of God?

God forbid!

Once again, the very question is ridiculous. Let me put it to you another way.

Don't you know you're the servants of whatever or whoever it is you yield your allegiance to obey? You may be enslaved to the sin of self-righteousness through performance that led everyone down the slippery path to eternal destruction. The only other alternative is to live in the liberty and obedience of the good news of God's grace that led to the only righteousness that counts in the eyes of God.

BUT, I'm so thankful to God! You were formerly the servants of laws, rules, and regulations, BUT now you have come to believe the wonderful message we've had the great privilege of preaching to you of God's grace and peace, and of the incredible work of Jesus on your behalf. Set free and delivered from the tyranny of your own effort you've become servants of an entirely new way of life, the way of righteousness!

I make no apologies for trying to speak so plainly to you. The whole concept of God's faithful love, grace, mercy, and peace is way out of our league as far as fully understanding it is concerned, however, I've tried to put it into the simplest words I know how so even the simplest among you can grasp on to it.

We'd all have to agree at one time you were enslaved to the attempt of gaining the righteousness of God by what you did or didn't do. One law perpetuated the need for another law. One rule illuminated a different rule. One regulation invoked another regulation.

Well, all this is unnecessary now.

You've got the great opportunity and privilege of yielding your lives to the freedom of righteous holiness. When your lives were overcome with the habits of performing good works you were truly as far removed from the life of righteousness God desired for you as you could possibly be.

So, where did all of your accomplishment get you? What kind of fruit did all your effort produce? It's almost embarrassing isn't it? Zippo! Nada! Zilch! The end of all good work is nothing less than the death of our spirit because it produced nothing more than guilt, shame, emptiness, fragility, desperation, etc., etc., etc.

BUT now, being liberated from the curse of self-righteousness;

BUT now, becoming covered and blessed in servant hood to God;

everything, absolutely everything we produce is a reflection of the holiness we've been given in Jesus, and there's no end to the liberty and freedom we can enjoy in His presence!

For the sin of being addicted to the performance of systems of laws, rules, and regulations had only one way of paying its servants (victims), **ETERNAL DEATH**.

BUT,

the gift of God, (not merely a payment) the gift of God is a gift of an eternal life, righteous and holy, precious and pure, through Jesus!

113. A NEW SPIRIT
(Romans 7:1-6)

I don't think I have to remind you, for I'm quite certain you're familiar with legal terminology, of the fact laws only have power over a person while they're alive. It almost sounds stupid to suggest otherwise, doesn't it?

A married woman is bound by law to her husband for as long as the husband is alive. BUT, if her husband dies she's freed from those laws that kept her in the state of matrimony. However, if, while her husband is still alive, she up and marries another man, she would no doubt be a two-timing adulteress. BUT, if her husband is dead we'd all agree she'd be free of any laws preventing her from marrying another man. In this scenario, she definitely wouldn't be considered an adulteress.

Your first husband is dead is the spiritual application of this natural analogy. Listen dear friends, your relationship to laws, rules, and regulations is dead thanks to the birth, death, burial, and resurrection of Jesus! He went through all He did to free you to enter a brand new relationship with another husband, namely God.

Indeed, it was Jesus who was raised from the dead so "all" of us can now start enjoying the liberty and freedom of the fruitfulness of God.

Yes, our former "marriage" merely allowed us to go through the motions of adhering to and performing to a standard of obligations which kept us under the control of our master, whether we liked it or not. Any effort we put forward in the task of performance driven duties were successful only to the extent it produced fruit which counted for nothing other than death as far as God was concerned.

BUT now, we've been delivered from those old systems of laws, rules, and regulations. Our "old" husband is dead and along with it our "marriage of inconvenience." The systems that held us captive are null and void.

Why?

So we can now serve in a completely renewed spirit of excitement, joy, and liberty. We are FOREVER FREE of the tyranny, emptiness, guilt, and shame of the old letter of the law!

114. WAR IS OVER
(Romans 7:7-25a)

Here we go again. All of this begs the question. "Are laws, rules, and regulations sin?"

God forbid!

I say, "Nay! Nay!"

I'd never have come to the understanding all of my belief and all of my accomplishments were totally insufficient to gain the righteousness of God BUT for all of the laws, rules, and regulations that made my inability so glaringly apparent.

Let's use "lust" as an example. I'd never have known what lust was had the law specifically not stated "you shall not covet" (Exodus 20:17).

BUT, the commandment simply enhanced within me the ardent desire to experience the spirit of coveting what others have. Without the commandment I wouldn't even have known what "lust" was.

If I think back to my childhood days I can state, without any hesitation, I lived a wonderful, joyful existence during this time when laws, rules, and regulations had no impact on my life. BUT, when I grew up and the expectations of laws, rules, and regulations were influenced upon my, the sin of performing for God's approval had the effect of killing the liberty I previously thrived on.

The commandments and indictments of laws, rules, and regulations given to be a guide and directive in life suddenly became to me the pale, stifling burden and stench of death! The sin of thinking being "good" could gain me the favor of God, and being "bad" would put my butt in dangerous proximity to the wrath of God's almighty hand was deceptive to the core. The deceit ruined me because I could never quite measure up to standards impossible to reach. Try as I might I was fighting a loosing battle that not only threatened to slay my spirit, it succeeded.

We ought not go around blaming laws, rules, and regulations for our problems. Laws, rules, and regulations have had their place. The commandments of God are holy and just, for surely God revealed in them His good intention for all mankind.

So, were laws, rules, and regulations, supposedly good for me, meant to kill me in the process of trying to live up to them?

God forbid!

BUT, don't you see, our attempts at self-righteousness had to be exposed for the sin it really was? Our inability to attain God's favor through our belief or performance constantly brings us to the point of desperation, despair, frustration, guilt, and shame. It's almost funny, if not at least ironic, that something actually so good could be used to point out how hopeless and dead we are on our own merit. Yes, laws, rules, and regulations really did point out how exceedingly sinful we were in our attempts to obey and follow after them, for all the wrong reasons.

I'm sure we could all agree laws, rules, and regulations have a spiritual affect upon all of us because it was indeed God who permitted them for our own benefit.

BUT, I want to assure all of you I'm not above the struggles of this temporal existence either. I'm not immune from the battle often raging within the minds of those who've been sold a bill of goods by those who want to control us with the wisdom (foolishness) of mankind. The wisdom (foolishness) of mankind allows me to rationalize away anything I want to do, and yet, it permits me to rise up in righteous indignation when others think they can do the very same thing. It condones my behavior when I don't practice what I preach.

BUT then again, I hate it when others put the pressure on me to live up to their standards and then I go and study, analyze, and criticize them right back. The trouble is if I measure my standing in God's eyes with the weigh scale of human achievement then I'm actually admitting laws, rules, and regulations actually do have a measure of importance in God's evaluation of me.

I've come to the conclusion IT'S NO LONGER MY RESPONSIBILITY TO ALTER GOD'S VIEW AND OPINION OF ME.

BUT, I confess the battle does rage on from time to time what I "do" still must count for something.

Not!

For I do know in me, I mean in my own fleshly processes of thought and action, there isn't one decent or honorable thing that qualifies me for the righteousness of God!

Oh sure, I want to "be" and "do" whatever it would take. Unfortunately, I succeed in failing more than I do in succeeding! I really have every good intention of doing the right stuff and yet I fall so short of even my own expectations, BUT man, it sure is easy to do what I know in my heart I ought not do. Oh sure, I can always use the good old standby response, "I didn't really want to do it, BUT, the devil made me do it!"

This is why I take great delight in the law of God that looks far beyond the capacity and intention of a human heart.

BUT, I'm constantly reminded of the laws, rules, and regulations of the wisdom (foolishness) of mankind which war against what I know to true of God's grace and peace, ever battling to bring me into the captivity of self-righteousness.

Oh my. What a goof I am!

Who could possibly deliver me from the systems of laws, rules, and regulations that pave the road of life with grief, shame, guilt, embarrassment, not to mention the hopelessness of eternal death?

Thank God He did!

Yes indeed, God has already liberated me from the agony of defeat through Jesus!

115. NO CONDEMNATION
(Romans 7:25b-8:13)

So then, with the renewed mind of Jesus within me, I'm honored to obey the law of God's grace and peace.

BUT, in the perverted mind set of the wisdom (foolishness) of mankind, I was compelled to obey the self-righteous, performance driven systems of laws, rules, and regulations.

There is now, therefore, no need to fear the certainty of condemnation and punishment of God for those who've come to understand and accept the reality they've been covered by the blood of Jesus! Condemnation is a thing of the past for those who aren't hung up on trying to gain their own way into the favor of God, BUT, who are living in the life and liberty of the Spirit of Jesus!

Look, what laws, rules, and regulations couldn't accomplish, because the success or failure of them depended on the weakness of human inability, God was able to accomplish all on His own, without our approval, assistance, or merit!

How? By sending His own Son, Jesus, in the very likeness of human flesh.

Why?

Jesus came to solve our inadequacies in achieving the acceptance and favor of God through our own systems of belief and merit. He condemned the very sin of trusting in human achievement, and along with it, the very notion the successful obedience to laws, rules, and regulations could gain us the righteousness of God.

Who'd He do it for?

He did it for the whole world!

Those who stop walking in the foolishness of their own self-righteousness, BUT, with a RENEWED MIND to start walking in the Spirit of Jesus within them are the ones enjoying the unbelievable liberty this understanding delivers!

For those who are enslaved to systems of laws, rules, and regulations get so wrapped up in themselves and their achievement they're simply captivated and bound by the tyranny of success and failure. All they can think about is how "they" believe and what "they" do.

BUT, those who have renewed their minds to accept the liberty of God's grace and peace can simply live in the luxurious liberty to the honor and glory of God which the Spirit of Jesus has exemplified!

Living under the constant pressure of performance will kill the spirit for it can only pay its victims with guilt, shame, anxiety, and fear. BUT, on the other hand, the inheritance of those who live in the Spirit of Jesus is nothing less than everlasting life and peace!

Why is this so?

Because the mind set of self-righteous behavior is at complete odds with the love of God. Those who stupidly depend on their own systems of belief and accomplishment have little time to accept the entire scope of God's grace and peace.

How indeed could they accept God's grace for what it is when they insist on placing conditions on "how" folks can gain it? So then, it's impossible for those trapped in self-righteousness to please God. BUT, you aren't living any longer under the control and authority of laws, rules, and regulations to gain you the righteousness of God!

BUT, you are living in the realm of God's grace and peace if (and of course it is) it's really true the Spirit of God actually dwells in you.

Now, if anybody doesn't have the Spirit of Jesus they aren't children of God! And if the Spirit of Jesus is in you the entire body of your sin of self-righteous performances to gain God's approval is dead.

BUT, the fact the Spirit of Jesus is within you confirms the abundant life you enjoy as a result of knowing the righteousness of God has already been imparted to you!

BUT, if the Spirit of God, who raised up Jesus from the dead, does indeed dwell in you, then God, who raised Jesus from the dead, will also see to it the care and keeping of your mortal physical body is entrusted to the Spirit of Jesus who dwells in you.

Therefore, my dear friends, we're indebted alright, not to the wisdom (foolishness) of mankind, not in legalistic self-righteousness, nor to live in the treadmill of desperate attempts to succeed in the accomplishment of laws, rules, and regulations.

For if you insist on placing your eternal destiny in your own hands you'll surely die in the vain struggle.

BUT, if you, by joyfully understanding and accepting the reality God has placed the Spirit of Jesus within you, will kill off any thoughts the strength of your belief or merit can alter in the slightest degree God's view and opinion of you, then you'll start living life the way it was meant to be lived!

116. ADOPTION

Ever heard of "Patria Potestas?"

Absolute power. Complete control. Unequivocal authority. Total ownership.

These might be a few choice descriptions of the power a father held over his family. His rule over his family was unchallenged. Many stories have been told of ruthless domination.

Patria Potestas gave the father power over the life and death of his children, even at childbirth. As long as the father was alive, it was impossible for a child to escape his authority. Respect, honor, and obedience were always in season.

Being a biological child was one thing. Being "adopted" was quite another!

The reasons for adoption were as varied as the kinds of children. Love, infertility, and inheritance come to mind. Oh, of course, I better not neglect to mention it was the politically correct thing to do for some.

Nero was adopted by the Emperor Claudius so he could have a successor to the throne. In fact, although not a blood son, Nero wanted to marry Octavia.

What's so unusual about that?

Octavia was the daughter of Claudius for real!

In law, Nero and Octavia were brother and sister in spite of the fact Nero was adopted. In order for them to be married, the senate was called into special session to give their approval!

How did adoption take place?

Several things were required for an adoption to take place.

First of all, there had to be witnesses, seven, in fact. In case of a dispute of any kind, whether over property rights, legal rights, or inheritance privileges, any of these seven witnesses could be called to testify as to the validity of the adoption process. In the case of an adoption inquiry, a witness would have to swear an oath the adoption was done correctly and completely.

If the adoption process was done right, the adopted person was no longer just a visitor or guest in the home, they became a full-fledged member of the adopting family. They became a son or daughter just like any other member of that family. Even if children were born into the family after them, their rights of rank, seniority, and inheritance were the same as if they had actually been born in that order.

"Mancipatio."

This was the first step of the adoption process. A sale had to be conducted to symbolically indicate a transfer of possession. A scale was set up and copper was used as a form of currency. The sales transaction was performed a total of three times.

The selling parent (the father) would put the child up for auction. Before someone would offer to make a purchase the father would buy the child back. He did this then a second time.

The third time he wouldn't repurchase the child. It was just as if he had three chances to change his mind.

It was at this point his rule over the child was over. His "Patria Potestas" over the child was no longer in force. His power and control was forever broken.

"Vindicatio."

At this stage in the adoption process the adopting father would make his appearance before one of the Roman magistrates, a "praetor." The legal papers would be filed. Then the praetor would make sure everything was in order before granting legal custody to the adoptive parents.

Once the stamp of approval was applied to the papers the adoption was complete and legally binding. The new father assumed his "Patria Potestas" over his new child.

But what about the "adoptee?"

What were the legal consequences as far as he or she was concerned? Perhaps after you finish reading this little list of items you probably wish you could be adopted!

- All rights, privileges, and responsibilities to the "old" family were completely wiped out! Any inheritance due from the "old" family could never be passed on.
- Any, and all, "old" family ties were broken. Sisters were no longer sisters. Brothers were no longer brothers. No cousins. No "old" mom. No "old" man. How many of you have told your parents you'd like to go and move in with Samuel or Ruthie down the street? Well, this was serious. No joking matter in the adoption process. Come to think of it, living with people who really don't want you could be kind of tough anyway.

- Here's a real kicker! Any debts were canceled. I told you there was something good about this whole thing, especially if you weren't exactly a financial whiz-kid. All the records about you were wiped out. You weren't "you" anymore. It was like someone came in and blanked out your entire file! Your slate was wiped clean!
- All rights, privileges, and responsibilities to your "new" family were now completely initiated and established. Any inheritance eventually to be yours was guaranteed as if you were naturally born into your "new" family.
- New mom and dad. New brothers and sisters. New friends. Probably even a new school! Certainly, a new place to put your feet up to call "home."
- You start your life all over again with a "new" file. Old things are passed away and you begin to fill up all the blank pages with wonderful challenges and possibilities!

Interesting, eh?

The possibilities of being given up by a father who has absolute no regard for you whatsoever to a father who longed to have you take up the full scope of his love in a new family is mind-boggling. The prospect of wiping out any past, and starting out with a clean new slate is more than just a bit refreshing. The reality of going from a state of bankruptcy to enjoying life and liberty as an heir with all the rights and privileges that follow is almost miraculous.

Don't even these few thoughts get you thinking about the miracle of your adoption by God?

Well, hang in there. We'll pursue this a bit further as we continue.

Back to the letter...

117. SPIRIT OF ADOPTION
(Romans 8:14-39)

For the same number of folks who've been led out of the captivity of self-righteousness by the Spirit of God is exactly the same number as those who are now the children of God!

Listen, God has not initiated some goofy plan to place folks once again in the tremendous anxiety and fear they formerly "enjoyed" in the spirit of bondage to performance-based systems of self-righteousness.

BUT, what everyone has received from the Spirit of Jesus within them is the confirmation of their adoption into the family of God! Now everyone can cry out to God in excited honor, respect, and joy by calling out "Daddy! Daddy!"

The Spirit of Jesus within us bears witness in our spirit that we truly are the children of God. Hey, if we are children, then we're also heirs!

Wow! Wait! It gets better.

We're actually JOINT HEIRS with Jesus!

If Jesus actually did what God sent Him to do by taking all of our deserved punishment and suffering upon Himself, then simple logic would lead us to conclude we also get to participate in the glory He's enjoying right now!

We may want to conclude the sufferings we seem to endure here in this life somehow clouds the reality of the glory that we now enjoy in the Spirit of Jesus. I don't think we've seen anything yet, because, in our limited vision of eternity, I earnestly expect there's a whole lot more to this "children of God" thing in store for us.

It's sad to come to the not-so-revolutionary concept all humanity have become creatures of their own vanity. We've been led down the garden path of self-righteous and legalistic behavior, not necessarily willingly, BUT by virtue of following after the wisdom (foolishness) of mankind. We persist in believing we have what it takes to gain the favor and acceptance of God. So we dig in our heels, put all our trust and hope in "our" systems of belief, and in "our" measurements of "our" accomplishments.

Why am I a happy camper?

Because all of God's creation has been delivered from the bondage of the corruptible authority, domination, and control of self-righteousness into the glorious liberty we can enjoy as full-fledged children of the family of God! There can be no denying all mankind has groaned and struggled in pain and agony with the pressure of the despicable notion of vanity and self-righteous behavior.

Until now that is!

Those dead and gone aren't the only ones who have it made in the shade now because of what God has done in Jesus, BUT we get to start enjoying our initial taste of the great feast prepared for us in the Spirit of Jesus.

No doubt the thought of leaving this old world with all of its headaches, fully anticipating the full understanding of our adoption into the family of God when even our physical bodies are liberated from the struggle, is a pleasant thought to ponder.

For we are saved from the perilous task of achieving God's favor with the strength of our belief or the sum total of our accomplishments by the hope of Jesus.

BUT, the hope mankind has put in the visible, tangible expressions of self-righteousness isn't hope at all.

Look, if you can assess the dedication and discipline of your belief, and if you can tally the balance sheet of your performance, then why in the world would you go to the trouble of putting your eternal destiny into the hands of Jesus?

BUT, if we accept the awesome truth our eternal inheritance has been established without our permission, certainly without our merit, and definitely beyond our capacity to fully visualize or comprehend it, then we have everything to live for right now, and even more to look forward to after we're done with this part of the journey.

The attitude of hope the Spirit of Jesus had in the faithfulness of God for our eternal destiny is the same loving faith He placed in "all" mankind, in spite of the severity of our calamity and infirmity. We didn't even have a clue how to approach God. BUT, the Spirit of Jesus Himself approached God with His intercession on behalf of all humanity.

Now I don't know what Jesus said to God, however, whatever He said, surely touched the heart of God!

And God, who searches out the secrets of the heart knew exactly what was in the heart of the Spirit of Jesus, because He made such a great case on behalf of "all" His chosen ones according to the very will of God Himself!

And we know all things work together for good for all those who love God with all their heart and for all those who are called according to God's purpose.

Let there be no confusion. God knew what He was doing! He planned it all along that everyone would be conformed to the very image of His Son Jesus whom God knew would be the first to be resurrected of many, many folks to a glorious new life!

The news just keeps getting better and better.

He purposefully planned to give His righteousness to "all" His creation, to "all" mankind.

Then, He called us all!

And then, He justified everyone He called!

To top it off, God glorified everyone He justified!

My goodness, what's left to be said?

If God is on our side, then who in the world could possibly stand against us?

God didn't even spare the only precious Son He had for us, BUT He delivered Him up for us "all!"

Can you possibly imagine a scenario in which God, along with Jesus, would want to withhold a single blessing from all of us? Who possibly could have the right to say, "You don't deserve to be one of God's chosen because you don't measure up?"

It's God's prerogative to justify whoever He wants to! Who's the only one who had the authority and power to condemn?

Jesus!

And why would He condemn us?

It is Jesus who died, yes rather, who is risen again, who is even now at the right hand of God, who broke through to eliminate the lines of communication and to bridge the gulf that had for too long separated God and His creation.

WHO SHALL SEPARATE US from the love of Jesus?

Shall tribulation, distress, persecution, famine, nakedness, or peril? What about a sword?

Surely it is written, "For Your sake are we killed all day long; and we are counted like sheep awaiting their turn at the slaughter house" (Psalms 44:22).

I say "NAY! NAY!"

In all of these things we are more than conquerors!

Because of our belief or accomplishment?

Oh no! Only through Him who loved us, Jesus!

I'm absolutely persuaded and utterly convinced neither your absence from this life, nor your participation in it, could separate you from the love of God!

Perhaps you may think, like some of my Rabbi friends, that the angels were ticked off at God when He created us mere "mortals," and that they might hatch a plan to spoil our relationship with Him.

Don't think so!

There aren't any kinds of principalities, powers, or any laws, rules, and regulations that could come even remotely close to preventing you from enjoying the benefits of God's grace and peace! Nothing in this present age, or anything in any age to come could prevail to diminish the love of God for His creation. Don't even think any kind of astrological force could ever affect the relationship between the Creator and His creation either. It doesn't make one hill of beans difference how high or low the stars are in the skies. The rising and the setting of the suns and moons will never affect your status in the family of God!

There remains one indisputable fact.

There is not one single, solitary created object, animate or inanimate, that could separate us from the love of God that He demonstrated to "all" in Jesus!

118. TRIED, TESTED, & TRUE
(Romans 9:1-33)

I tell the truth in Jesus, without a lie, for my conscience also confirms the witness of the Spirit of Jesus within me that I'm deeply saddened and continually troubled in my heart. I would even go so far as to wish Jesus would cut me out of the picture all together if it would help any of my Israelite brothers and sisters come to understand and accept God's view and opinion of them.

God's plan of adoption and the distribution of His glory and righteousness pertains to the Israelites as much as it does to anyone, even though the Jews have been blessed with:
- the opportunity of sharing in a covenant relationship with God;
- the challenges associated with the giving of the law;
- the visitation of God's interaction on their behalf;
- the great privilege of hearing the promises of God;
- the heritage of forefathers worthy of respect; and
- the great honor of having come from its lineage the birth of none other than Jesus, who is over "all" blessed of God for ever and ever.

That's just the way it is!

Don't assume the promise of God hasn't had an affect upon the whole world. Don't think for a moment only the people of Israel have been chosen by God to be His children. The adopted children of God include even those who aren't Israelites. The fact some may claim to be descendants of Abraham doesn't give anyone of them a special status with God.

BUT, God also made the promise to others as well.

"For in Isaac will your seed be called, and also of the son of the bond woman will I make a nation, because he is also your seed" (Genesis 21:12,13).

Here's my point.

The children of the flesh, those who insist their self-righteous belief and accomplishment will gain them the acceptance of God, are not children of God because of those things at all. BUT, the only factor identifying the children of God is the fact all of His children have been issued a promise.

Let me give you a few examples.

Abraham and Sarah received a word of promise. "At this time will I come, and Sarah will have a son" (Genesis 18:10,14).

And not only this, BUT Rebecca, Isaac's wife, was also given a promise before their baby was even born. I'm sure you'd agree an unborn baby hasn't even had a chance to demonstrate either "goodness" or "badness." Doesn't this just prove the purpose of God's choosing of everyone is just, without bias, completely void of something as arbitrary as works, and is rightly based solely on the One who has done the calling and has made the promise!

BUT, for those who don't remember, the promises God made to Rebecca was first of all that she was going to have twins, and secondly, that "the eldest (first-born) would serve the youngest (second-born)" (Genesis 25:23).

And the rest of the story?

"Jacob have I loved, BUT, Esau have I hated" (Malachi 1:2,3)!

Oh my, what does this do to my theology? Am I all screwed up, or what? Maybe it's God who is messed up!

God forbid!

Listen, this is what God said to Moses,

"I will have mercy on whomever I want to have mercy, and I will show compassion to whomever I want to show compassion" (Exodus 33:19).

So then the righteousness of God doesn't have anything to do with the person who believes, nor with anyone who runs up the ladder of accomplishment, BUT it depends solely upon the grace of God, who has displayed His mercy at His own discretion!

God instructed Moses to tell the Pharaoh of Egypt that,

"even for this very reason have I raised you up, that I might show my power in you, and that My name may be declared throughout all the earth" (Exodus 9:16).

Therefore it is the prerogative of God to show His mercy on whomever He chooses to have mercy, and let there be no mistaking, He holds exactly the same right and capability to withhold it if He would have wanted to do so.

I know what you're thinking.

"Why does He still seem to find fault in the things we do and say?" Or, "How can God find fault with mankind when we are predestined to obedience or disobedience by God Himself?"

I say, "Nay! Nay!"

BUT, who the heck do we think we are to question the will and motivation of God? Shall the created say to its creator, "Why have you made me like this?" Doesn't the potter have the creative power and authority over the lump of clay as it rotates on the spinning wheel, choosing to make one lump into a beautiful masterpiece and another lump into something less functional?

Here are a few more good questions for you.

What if God, on one hand eager to show how ticked off He was at mankind, and on the other hand, lovingly predisposed to demonstrate His power, hung in there with unbelievable patience with "all" of us who so richly deserved all the punishment we "all" had coming to us?

What if God fully intended to make the boundless riches of His glory evident upon "all" those He choose to show mercy upon, to "all" whom He had prepared beforehand to be the recipients of that great honor and glory?

And what if this include even us, whom He has also called, and I don't only mean those of us who are Jews only, BUT, those of us who are also Gentiles?

Hear what God spoke to Hosea:

"I will say to those who were not my people, 'You are my people!' And I will have mercy upon those who had not obtained mercy" (Hosea 2:23)!

"And it shall come to pass, that in the place where it was said to them, 'You aren't my people,' there it shall be said to them,

'You ARE the sons of the living God'" (Hosea 1:10)!

Hear how Isaiah cried out concerning his beloved people of Israel:

"Though the number of the children of Israel be as the sand of the sea, a remnant shall be saved (from the bondage of laws, rules, and regulations). For God will finish the requirements of works, and cut it short in righteousness, because a short work (the cross) will the Lord make upon the earth" (Isaiah 10:22,23)!

Isaiah said this a long, long time ago:

"Except the Lord of Saboaoth had left us a seed (Jesus), we would have been no different than Sodom, and our fate would have been the same as Gomorrah" (Isaiah 1:9)!

What am I trying to say?

The Gentiles have been given the gift of God's righteousness in spite of the fact they weren't looking for it, or without thinking they even needed it.

Why?

Because God was faithful to apply His grace, mercy, and peace across the board!

BUT the children of Israel, I'm afraid, because of the enslaving baggage of self-righteousness have a hard time understanding and accepting the fact God's righteousness was applied through the law of His grace alone.

Why?

Because they searched for it, not based upon the faith and faithfulness of God, BUT as if it was something they could accomplish by virtue of their own belief and performance, based upon a set of laws, rules, and regulations. They simply stumbled over a stumbling stone that got in the way of a precious gift!

As it is written:

"Behold I lay in Zion preparing for a foundation a stone, a tried stone, a precious corner stone, A SURE FOUNDATION, and he that believes it shall not be put to shame" (Isaiah 28:16).

"And He (Jesus) shall be for a sanctuary, except for a stone of stumbling, and for a rock of offense, to both the houses of Israel, for a trap and a snare to the inhabitants of Jerusalem" (Isaiah 8:14,15).

119. END OF THE LAW
(Romans 10:1-11:11)

My dear friends, my heart's desire and prayer to God for the people of Israel is that they might be saved from their perilous journey of self-righteousness. For I can appreciate, yes even applaud, their zeal and dedication towards God, BUT without proper knowledge and understanding. For they, being ignorant of the reality of God's gifting of the whole world with His righteousness, going about like chickens with their heads cut off trying to establish their own righteousness, have still not submitted themselves to the righteousness which God has already applied to them!

For Jesus "is" the end of every system of laws, rules, and regulations, and everyone who believes this knows and understands the great liberty this fact illuminates. Permit me to paraphrase our good buddy Moses as he described the kind of performance that would be required if the righteousness of God were dependent on the "works" of laws, rules, and regulations.

"If you are going to be justified by the law, then you'd better practice it to the very letter of the law" (Leviticus 18:5).

BUT, the righteousness that is the result of the faith and faithfulness of God is also spoken of in the scriptures:

"Don't question in your own heart, 'Who can ascend into heaven'" (Deuteronomy 30:12)?

(The point being, just whom do we think we are that we could somehow accomplish something good enough to get Jesus to come down out of His heavenly home to make things right for us because of our accomplishments?)

or,

"Who will descend down into the depths" (Deuteronomy 30:13).

(The point being, just whom do we think we are that we could do something of our own merit to entice Jesus to rise from the dead because of it?)

BUT, what do the scriptures say?

"The promise of God is very close to you. It's in your mouth, and it's in your heart" (Deuteronomy 30:14).

What is? It's the promise of God's faith and faithfulness to impart His righteousness to the whole world by His grace!

This is exactly what we're preaching!

If you confess with your mouth your righteousness has been given to you as a direct response of the activity of Jesus, and if you believe in your heart God's the One who raised Jesus from the dead in miraculous victory, you'll be saved from the plague of thinking you had something to do with it and saved from the bondage and slavery of trying to become good enough by living up to the unattainable standards of laws, rules, and regulations.

Listen, you must let the reality of God's righteousness sink deep within your heart, and then confess to others you've been saved from the desperate need to perform up to the standards of the wisdom (foolishness) of mankind which lead only to guilt and embarrassment. Remember the scripture I referred to earlier?

"Whoever believes on Him (Jesus) will not be ashamed" (Isaiah 28:16).

I remind you also there's absolutely no difference between the Jew and the Gentile. God has, through Jesus, demonstrated the richness and completeness of His loving grace, mercy, and peace to "all" those who would recognize His sovereignty.

"For whoever will call upon the name of God will be saved" (Joel 2:23).

Now, how is it possible for someone to put their trust in God if they've never even believed in Him?

How should they believe in God if they've never even heard of Him?

How in the world are they going to hear the truth of His marvelous grace and peace if they don't have someone to tell them

And how will the proclamation take place if nobody is sent out to spread the good news?

Oh, what wonderful truth as it is written:

"How beautiful are the feet of them who proclaim the gospel of peace, and bring the glad tidings of good that publish salvation" (Isaiah 52:7).

BUT, not everybody has even obeyed the gospel message after they had received it! Even Isaiah questioned God about this:

"Who has believed our report" (Isaiah 53:1)?

The revelation of God's faith and faithfulness comes when folks hear the good news and the way they will hear it best is to listen and pay attention to the promises of God. BUT, haven't folks heard the promises?

Absolutely, without question!

The spectacular sounds of God's promises have gone out into all the earth and the declaration of His will have been spread to the very ends of the world!

BUT, didn't the people of Israel know about the faith and faithfulness of God to honor His promises?

Of course they did. Listen first of all as Moses describes God's actions to their stubborn rejection of His intention for them:

"I will provoke you to jealousy by those who, in your eyes, aren't even considered to be a people, and by a foolish nation I will anger you" (Deuteronomy 32:21).

BUT, Isaiah was just as bold in declaring how God told him that He was known by the rest of the world:

"I was found by those who weren't even looking for me. I have shown myself to those who didn't even ask about me" (Isaiah 65:1).

BUT, God also spoke through Isaiah to rebuke the Israelites who weren't paying attention to Him:

"All day long I've stretched forth my hands towards a disobedient and rebellious people" (Isaiah 65:2).

So, did God cast away the very people He loved so much in spite of the fact they weren't looking for Him, they weren't asking about Him, or because they were disobedient and rebellious towards Him?

GOD FORBID!

How could I possibly believe this? Hey, I'm an Israelite myself, a descendant of Abraham no less, and in particular, from the tribe of Benjamin. I'm very familiar with the bleak history of the Jewish responses to the faith and faithfulness of God.

My own life story proves my point there's no way God could even think of casting away any of His people He loves so much to call His own!

Consider the pleading of Elijah the prophet as he interceded to God on behalf of the people of Israel:

"Oh Lord, they've killed Your prophets, and trashed Your altars, and I'm left alone, and now they're searching for me so they can kill me" (I Kings 19:14).

BUT, what did God tell Elijah?

"There are still seven thousand men whom I have reserved for myself, and they have not bowed their knees to pay homage to the image of Baal" (I Kings 19:18).

Even so then, at this very moment in time, there's still a remnant according to the election of God's grace who unquestioningly accept His promises for who they are! And if the righteousness of God is applied by His grace, then it is no more of the works of any system of laws, rules, and regulations!

Otherwise, God's grace wouldn't be God's grace!

BUT, if self-righteousness were a reality, then it surely has nothing to do with the grace of God, otherwise, effort and performance aren't just work, they take on a whole new strategy of survival. Perfection would be the target and that would spell big trouble for us all!

What am I trying to say?

The people of Israel never attained to the gift of God's righteousness because they worked for it or because they manifestly fulfilled the letter of every law, rule, or regulation, BUT, they did receive it because God elected everyone to receive it by His grace! The sad reality is some folks still don't get it, blinded and impaled by their own stupidity and stubbornness.

(Moses was pretty ticked off as he was accosted by this awareness. He said, "God must have put you to sleep, closed your eyes, and plugged your ears, because you haven't paid any attention to what He has done for you until this very day" (Deuteronomy 29:4).)

And the voice of a pretty frightened King Dave as he begged God to intervene against those who had no use for him, or for God:

"Let their table become a snare before them, and that which should have been for their welfare, let it become a trap and a stumbling block that they might be repaid for what they are doing to me. Let their eyes be darkened so they can't even see where they are going, and then they will have to get down on their knees and crawl to escape" (Psalms 69:22,23).

I'd like to ask you, "Do you think the Israelites have stumbled so bad they should be destroyed?"

GOD FORBID!

BUT, rather, the fact people have fallen on their face in their own effort is the very reason God was gracious enough to give His righteousness to everyone, including folks who many thought should, and would, never get it!

The message of God's grace for "all," regardless of their belief, or their performance, surely must provoke to jealousy those who expect everyone to be obliged to struggle on their own to attain to it.

120. **OLIVE TREE**
(Romans 11:12-36)

Now,
    if the failure of the Israelites to achieve the righteousness of God by their own merit has ultimately led God to bless the entire world with the immense riches of His grace,
    and if the strength of self-righteous systems of belief and performance has been diminished and nullified, leading to the inclusion of the "godless" Gentile world in the richness of the family of God,
    then how MUCH MORE is even the fullness of liberty now for the people of Israel?
    In as much as I count it a great honor and privilege to be a messenger of the good news gospel to those outside the Jewish culture I speak boldly and clearly to all Gentiles who may also be paralyzed in the deception somehow God hasn't called you out to be something special.
    I'll gladly employ any means I can to provoke the members of my own race into a jealousy of the wonderful news they are forever free from the bondage, guilt, and shame which the systems of self-righteous performance have trapped them, thereby saving them from the miscalculated, dangerous journey they've traveled for so long.
    For if God's reconciling of the whole world has resulted in the casting away of all the systems of laws, rules, and regulations formulated to assist mankind in the gaining of God's favor, what will it do for everyone when they finally get it through their thick skulls?
    Nothing BUT the liberation from the shackles and death of works to an exciting life with endless possibilities!
    How did I come up with this?
    Well, if the first fruit (Jesus) is holy, then surely the whole lump (the whole world) is also holy!
    And if the root of the tree (Jesus) is holy, then surely the branches (the whole world) are too!
    Some folks refuse to accept the fact they're already branches in the tree of God by His grace alone and have chosen instead to wander needlessly on the paths of self-righteousness.

On the other hand, you, being like branches of a wild olive tree, with little appeal to anyone, were grafted and adopted into the family tree of God by His grace too, making you equal participants in the life, death, and resurrection of the root (Jesus) and of the richness and abundance of God's tree of blessing!

Don't let this reality go to your head to the point you become conceited or disdainful towards those who remain mired in their own performance driven misery. BUT, if you plan on boasting about something, boast you aren't the one who supports the root (Jesus), BUT the root (Jesus) is your source of support!

You may well be inclined to brag "these 'self-righteous' branches were cut off by God so I might be grafted in!"

Well, because folks insisted self-righteousness was the row to plow instead of accepting the unmerited and unconditional love of God, He was totally justified to exercise the wrath of His judgment against the whole world. And now, as a result of God's faith and faithfulness of Jesus, the whole world gets to stand completely immersed in His glory and righteousness.

Don't get cocky! You had nothing to do with it! BUT, stand in awe and reverence of the great grace of God! For if God saw fit to withhold His acceptance from those who valiantly struggled to gain His approval by their faith and performance, take note He could also have withheld His grace from even you! Stand in amazement at the magnificent goodness of God, as well as the justified severity of the wrath He exercised on all mankind upon Jesus.

BUT, towards you He has exercised His goodness and grace and you will experience this incredible liberating expression of His love if you continue to live with this understanding. If you insist on returning to the bondage of laws, rules, and regulations you'll find yourself cut off from the life of freedom in Jesus!

And what about those self-righteous "spiritual" zealots of the systems of belief and accomplishment? If folks like this would finally decide to get out of the pit of their own ignorance, misunderstanding, and selfishness and accept God's gracious provision of His righteousness through Jesus, they too would come to discover God's prerogative and ability to graft folks into His tree of life is not compromised by the actions of mankind.

You, in your "un-Godli-ness," were removed from a naturally wild olive tree and were grafted, contrary to sound horticultural practice I might add, into the naturally good olive tree of God's grace where you thrive in liberty. How MUCH MORE have those, who insist they have everything going for them to declare their own "Godli-ness," cut themselves off, being grafted into their own olive tree of belief and performance?

Look, my dear friends, I don't want you to be ignorant of this mystery of mankind's foolishness or else you may yourself become conceited in the abundance of your wisdom (foolishness). This kind of blindness is exactly what has happened to the people of Israel!

Well, the blinders are off now!

"All" Gentiles have been grafted into the tree of God. And so have "all" the people of Israel been saved from the liability of their own performance! As it is written,

"There will come, on account of my decision in Zion, a Redeemer, who will deliver all mankind from the ungodliness of human achievement that has plagued humankind since the time of Jacob. This is a promise I've made to them all" (Isaiah 59:20,21).

"I will purge and take away "all" their unrighteousness" (Isaiah 27:9).

Concerning this liberating gospel message, those steeped in the seductive power and control of systems of belief and performance are your enemies because of what you have come to enjoy! BUT, do not be mistaken, as touching the election of God they are loved of Him every bit as much as you are, to His honor and glory. For the gifting of "all" with His righteousness and the calling of God of "all" into His family is irrevocable!

God will not change His mind, nor will He alter His activity towards those He has chosen of His own free will!

In times past you may not have accepted, believed, or understood what God has done for you in Jesus.

And yet, you've obtained the mercy of God because of the continued unbelief of those who thought they had it made in the shade because of their own goodness. Even so, there are still folks out there who do not have an understanding or appreciation of what God has done for them.

Perhaps the gracious and merciful spirit you show to them will inspire them to consider God's merciful gift applies to them as well.

For God concluded that "all" were doomed in their self-righteousness or in their ignorance.

Why?

So He might have mercy upon "all!"

Oh, the depth of the riches both of the wisdom and the knowledge of God! How unsearchable are His judgments and His ways far beyond our capacity to figure out!

For who truly has been able to discern the complexity of the mind of God? Or, who has been an advisor to God? Or, who has first given something to God or done something so special for God so they could gain His righteousness because of it?

Get this:
- "of" Him,
- "through" Him, and
- "to" Him,
- ARE
- "ALL" things!

To God be glory for ever and ever! Amen!

121. **TRANSFORMED**
(Romans 12:1-21)

Therefore, since your righteousness is based solely upon the will and activity of God and not upon the resolve of your belief, nor upon the successful adherence to laws, rules, and regulations, I plead with you, my dear friends, accept the mercies of God for what they are.

You "are" living examples of the sacrifice of Jesus, not skillful players in the game of offering sacrifices of works that are as dead as doorposts.

LIVE LIKE YOU "ARE" HOLY!

Live knowing you "are" acceptable to God the way you are!

This is a very reasonable way to live!

Don't be conformed to the wisdom (foolishness) of this world that would have you sucked into the downward spiral of performance based guilt and shame. BUT, be transformed.

How?

By the renewing of your mind!

WHY?

So you may prove what is the good, acceptable, perfect will of God!

For I say, through the grace of God given to me to each and every one of you, don't think of yourselves any more highly than you ought to think, BUT, to think soberly, according as God has dealt to every human being the measure of His faith and faithfulness, aware there is no room for the superiority/inferiority complexes that plague the way of mankind's wisdom (foolishness).

For as our physical bodies are made up of the cumulative total of many different faculties functioning in a variety of ways, so we, being many people, are actually one body in Jesus and every one of us are brothers and sisters in the family of God!

The grace of God has been applied to "all" and we "all" have the great privilege and responsibility to share and demonstrate the love of God which has taken up residence in us, in many different ways.

Here are some thoughts for you to consider:
- If you have the nerve to get out there and proclaim the good news gospel message, then get out there and let everyone know the full extent of the faith and faithfulness of God.
- Do you have the patience to minister to the needs of others? Wait for the opportunities that surely will come and then pitch in.
- Teachers ought to teach.
- Exhortations are needed from those who know how to exhort.
- Let those with the heart of generosity give without strings attached.
- Those who have the honor and challenge of authority should exercise their rule with due diligence.
- The demonstration of mercy ought to be accompanied by a measure of good cheer.
- Genuine love is without dishonor and distraction.
- Abhor the putrid stench of self-righteousness.
- Hang on tight to the reality of the goodness of God's righteousness.
- Treat each other with the kind affection of brothers and sisters.
- In honor, seek the ultimate best for others, preferring to build up others before you consider the opportunity to exalt yourself.
- Laziness and apathy have no place in the business world. Get on with it!
- Develop a positive, adventurous spirit.
- Serve God.
- Base your happiness in the hope of God within you.
- Be patient in the midst of trouble and turmoil.
- Maintain a constant attitude of praise and thanksgiving to God.
- Be a part of the distribution of assistance to those who need it.
- Make the spirit of hospitality a way of life.
- Find a way to bless those who delight in making your life miserable.

- Raise the standards of others rather than lowering your own.
- Have a great time with those who are having a blast and share the sorrow of those in mourning.
- Seek to show respect for one another.
- Don't be so heavenly minded you aren't any earthly good, BUT think like an ordinary, average person.
- Don't get trapped into thinking what you think or do makes you any better than someone else. Just because others may judge you based on your "works," refute the inclination to judge them by the same standards of performance.
- The compensatory attitude of "An eye for an eye, and a tooth for a tooth," just doesn't cut it. We'd all end up blind and toothless.
- Live with transparent integrity.
- As much as possible, seek the way of peace with everyone.
- My dear friends, there's no need for you to justify your thoughts and actions to anyone else, BUT rather, put the responsibility for judging on the One who had the right to judge all. For surely it is written, "'Vengeance is mine; I will repay,' God said" (Deuteronomy 32:35). Since this is the case, and the vengeance of God has already been dealt with on the cross of Jesus, any responsibility you may presume to have to judge and punish anybody doesn't exist.
- If you come to find out someone who is making your life miserable is hungry then give them something to eat. If this thorn in your flesh is thirsty, give them something to drink. Your generosity and kindness will be recognized in the same way as if you gave them a bucket of hot, red coals of fire from your own fireplace to rekindle the fire that has gone out in their home on a cold evening.
- Don't be overcome with the evil of self-righteousness, BUT overcome the lust of self-righteousness by renewing your mind to the reality of the righteousness of Jesus within you.

122. HIGHER POWER
(Romans 13:1-7)

Need I remind you every single soul is subject only to the heart, will, faith, faithfulness, and power of the Most High God? There's no power you might gain the righteousness of God from BUT from Jesus, for His authority alone is ordained of God!

Whoever, therefore, thinks they can accomplish on their own what only God has the power to accomplish are not only fooling themselves, and perhaps others as well, they are also resisting the promise of God!

Those who continue to walk in opposition to the liberty of God's grace shall surely walk in the perilous slavery of the pursuit of self-righteousness.

Understand the rulers, manipulators, and controllers of the wisdom (foolishness) of mankind are not a terror to the grace of God, BUT they are a terror to the evils of the "good works" doctrines.

Why in the world would you need to be afraid of the power of God's grace?

Live in the liberty of the grace of God and you'll bask in all the warmth, peace, and praise of God's power in Jesus you could ever hope to stand. For surely Jesus is the minister of God to you for everything good.

BUT, if you remain mired in the evil muck of obeying laws, rules, and regulations to gain the favor of God you are no doubt living scared spitless of what you consider to be an impending administration of the wrath and justice of God.

Listen folks, God's wrath has already been dealt with! Jesus did not die in vain!

Let me say it again.

Jesus is the minister of God.

God chose to execute His justified wrath against the stupidity and ignorance of the whole world, however, Jesus became the recipient of that execution on behalf of "all" enslaved in the evil of self-righteousness. Jesus is the reason you are subject only to the grace of God for His righteousness as opposed to your dependence on your own belief or accomplishment.

Not only has God satisfied His wrath, BUT, He has liberated each and every person from the evil mind set of guilt and shame which comes as a result of the endless, unsatisfying struggles of performance based systems of belief and accomplishment. If there is any need for a reason to pay tribute to God this should do it.

Surely the peace of God and the abundant liberty of life in Jesus are two of the greatest things ministering to your spirit. These realities continue to affect your lives.

Give credit where credit is due! Pay tribute to whomever tribute is due! Pattern your life after the One who is the pattern of life! **STAND IN AWE** of the One who is worthy of your reverence! Honor only the One who is truly worthy of your honor!

123. WAKE UP
(Romans 13:8-14)

Do not be misguided or deceived into thinking you owe something to any other person BUT the benefit and warmth of your love. For surely the one who loves is the one who has fulfilled every law ever given.
- You shall not commit adultery.
- You shall not kill.
- You shall not steal.
- You shall not lie.
- You shall not covet.

If there is any way to sum up these and any other of the myriad laws, rules, and regulations it could be accomplished in this brief saying:

"You shall love your neighbor as yourself."

You see, if you love it's impossible for you to cause harm to your neighbor. The fullness of the law, therefore, is love!

Understanding this great truth, in addition to the fact we know the time of God's ultimate display of His great love has already been displayed in Jesus, it's high time we wake up out of our deep sleep!

Listen, the understanding and awareness of the miracle of God's loving, gracious acceptance of the whole world is much greater right now than the first moments when we came to understand He really did it.

The nighttime of self-righteousness is over! A new day has dawned for all mankind!

Let us therefore throw off the terrorizing works of the systems of beliefs and accomplishments that have cast a spell of darkness over the whole world. Let us rather wrap ourselves in the protective armor of warmth and comfort of the light of God's love. Let's walk about in the light of a new day with integrity and confidence. There's no need:
- to spread mischief,
- to find comfort in alcohol,
- to seek pleasure in the acts of sexual misconduct or public exhibitionism, or
- to engage in terrorist acts of jealousy, envy, and greed,

BUT, activate and mobilize the mind of Jesus within you.

EMBRACE THE GARMENT OF PRAISE Jesus has blessed you with. Shed the garments of heaviness weighing heavily against you. Pay no attention to the deception how you believe or how you act can deter God's love for you. Your attempts at self-righteousness are spoiled in darkness.

Do not continue to lust after the alluring, enticing words of the wisdom (foolishness) of mankind that endeavor to impress upon you the importance of your struggle to gain the favor of God.

124. CLEAN vs UNCLEAN
(Romans 14:1-15:7)

Assume the very real possibility there'll be folks out there who may not share your understanding of the faith and faithfulness of God. Accept them with all the courtesy and friendship you can muster, BUT don't waste your time disputing all of their doubts concerning God's view and opinion of all mankind!

Those who have a strong understanding of the message of God's grace and peace enjoy the liberty of eating whatever they like. And there are those still struggling in the bondage of laws, rules, and regulations whose diet is based upon the restrictions of these systems.

There's no point for those who live in liberty to despise those who struggle in slavery. Equally, there's no point for those bound to systems of laws, rules, and regulations to judge those who enjoy life in the liberty of God's grace.

Why?

Because God has accepted everybody!

Who the heck do you actually think you are to judge the will and activity of the servant of all, namely, Jesus? Look, Jesus either succeeded or He failed to accomplish what God asked him to do. Yes, well Jesus has been lifted up, for God is certainly capable of having His Son rise in triumph!

Now one person may place a higher value on one day of the week over another, while another person may think any given day is just as important as the next. Whatever! Just be fully persuaded you know why. Good on those who set aside a particular day to show honor and respect to God. And good on those who regard every day as a good day and don't give God any more credit for one day above another.

Good on those who eat whatever they enjoy and are grateful to God for every mouthful. And good on those who refrain from eating certain foods based on legalistic, religious principles with similar expressions of gratitude to God.

None of us live simply to benefit ourselves. How we live won't change God's view and opinion of us and how we ultimately die cannot alter our eternal destiny. Our lives are testimony to the glorious love and grace of God, and when we die, our death will declare the glory of God's triumph over death!

So, whether we are alive or whether we are dead we are expressions of God's love and of His grace to all.

Do you see the big picture now?

Jesus died, rose again, and was reestablished in the fullness of glory and honor so God would be the God of "all," including those who've already died, and indeed, of those who are still alive!

BUT, why do you continue to waste your time judging other folks? Or why do you find it so easy to write other folks off?

Look, everyone's in the same boat. We're all on the same page. For we "all" stand in the righteousness of God as a result of the judgment of God executed upon Jesus on the cross.

For scriptures have recorded,

"God said, 'As I live, every knee will bow to me, and every tongue will confess to God.' Surely will one say, 'in God have I righteousness and strength'" (Isaiah 45:23,24).

So then, every one of us will rise up and give our thanks to God for the covering sacrifice of Jesus. Let's not, therefore, waste our time judging things we have absolutely no control over. BUT, if you feel the compulsion to judge, be critical of your own thoughts and actions towards others, refusing to give in to the temptation of placing stumbling blocks on the paths of others as they come to grips with what God has done for them.

I know and am personally persuaded by the gospel message of Jesus that there's nothing at all unclean of itself, BUT, to the person who doesn't quite see it this way there are probably things which are quite dirty indeed. BUT, if there are others who take offense with your liberty you're treading on shaky ground by not taking into consideration their point of view. Don't use your liberty as an excuse to depreciate another who doesn't share your understanding.

Keep in mind Jesus died for everyone.

Let not then your liberty be spoken evil of either for the kingdom of God is not about what you eat or about what you drink, BUT, the kingdom of God is all about righteousness, about peace, and about joy in the Spirit of Jesus!

For only those who live in the righteousness, peace, and joy of Jesus are acceptable to God! And those who live like they are righteous, peaceful, and joyful, will also find the true acceptance and approval of those around them!

What to do?

Let us, therefore, follow after things that make for peace and search for ways of seeking the ultimate best for one another, exploring creative ways of building one another up.

Listen, laws, rules, and regulations will never destroy the work of God! All things indeed are pure to God. BUT, to those who are bound in the slavery to systems of laws, rules, and regulations, everything is certainly not pure. To them it's highly offensive if you eat the wrong thing, it's offensive if you drink alcohol, and it's certainly a nasty to do anything that would cause someone else to backslide, to fall off the wagon, or to miss the mother ship altogether.

Where do you put your trust for your acceptance before God? Be happy to leave God in charge of your righteousness or you would never get it!

Boy, the ones who figure out they've been liberated from the struggle of analyzing and condemning themselves for every little thing they do or don't do are happy campers indeed. Those who doubt the absolute, unequivocal, and irreversible grace of God will continue to live in the unhappy pursuit of self-righteousness, thinking they'll be damned if they do something and damned if they don't.

Why?

Because they're trying to gain the favor of God by depending on laws, rules, and regulations.

For any kind of righteousness not a result of the faith and faithfulness of God is nothing less than falling way short of the mark!

Those of us who have come to know and understand even a glimpse of the grace and peace of God have a responsibility to support those still struggling with the lust of doing for themselves what Jesus has already accomplished. And certainly not with the motivation of making ourselves look good! Let every one of us edify and encourage our neighbors for their benefit, not ours.

For even Jesus sought no honor or pleasure for Himself, BUT as it is recorded,

"The reproaches of those who reproached You fell on me" (Psalms 69:9).

Let's remember whatever has been written down before has been recorded for our education so we might patiently and comfortably come to an awareness and understanding of the hope we solely have in Jesus. I can only ask the same God who has shown to all His incredible patience and grace to also grant you the same ability to exercise the patient and gracious spirit towards one another in accordance to the Spirit of Jesus within you.

In addition, may you with one mind and with one mouth glorify God, even the Father of Jesus!

So, **ACCEPT ONE ANOTHER** as Jesus also has received all of us into the glory of God!

125. ROOT OF JESSE
(Romans 15:8-33)

Now I want to reaffirm that Jesus was sent into this world:
- to sever humanity from the tyranny of self-righteousness,
- to introduce "all" to the truth of God's grace and peace,
- to confirm the promises God made to our Jewish forefathers, and
- to reveal the great privilege the Gentiles also now have of glorifying God for His mercy!

As it is written,

"For this very reason will I give thanks to you, O Lord, among the Gentiles, and sing praises to your name" (Psalms 18:49).

"Rejoice, you Gentiles, with the Israelites" (Deuteronomy 32:43).

"Praise the Lord, all you nations, and praise Him, all you people" (Psalms 117:1).

"And in that day there shall be a root of Jesse, and He who will rise to reign over the Gentiles, and in Him will the Gentiles put their trust" (Isaiah 11:10).

May the God of hope fill you with joy and peace as you come to this wonderful understanding of His love.

Why? So you may ABOUND IN THE HOPE of God introduced through the power of the Spirit of Jesus.

As for me, I'm persuaded all of you, my dear friends, are also full of goodness, filled with all the information you need to know and are completely capable of encouraging and stimulating one another to press on in the liberty with which Jesus has cut you free to enjoy.

Nevertheless, my dear friends, I'm very aware I've written some pretty heavy stuff to you, using from time to time some very strong words with the intent of getting you to start the process of renewing your minds. Because of the grace that God has given to me I consider it an honor to be an ambassador of Jesus to the Gentile folk, ministering to them a message that should be totally acceptable to them declaring Jesus was offered up as a sacrifice on their behalf, making them every bit as acceptable as everybody else, blessed as well with the impartation of the Spirit of Jesus.

The only glory I might claim pertaining to God has been made possible through Jesus. For I will not even dare to waste my time bragging of any accomplishments that Jesus has not been a part of.

Why?

To help those who never thought they had a chance with God to become obedient, in word and in deed, to the grace and peace that was accomplished on their behalf through the mighty signs and wonders displayed by the power of the Spirit of God.

That's the good news and I've preached this gospel message of Jesus from Jerusalem to the Roman province of Illyricum on the Adriatic Sea. Yes, it's been my ambition to preach the gospel to folks who've never heard the wonderful news before. I have no intention of interfering with the ministry of others.

BUT, as it is written,

"For that which had not been told them will they see, and that which they had not heard will they consider" (Isaiah 52:15).

This mission is the very reason I've been unable to come and visit you sooner. BUT, now I find it difficult to find a place where the gospel message hasn't been preached. I've had a great desire for many years now to come to you so whenever I take my trip to Spain I'll definitely stop in to see you. Before I continue on my journey I'd love to be somewhat filled up with your fellowship and hospitality.

BUT, for the moment my plans are to go to Jerusalem with the collected blessings of support we've gathered for those suffering there. It's been great to witness the concern and generosity of many in Macedonia and Achaia toward those poor folks in Jerusalem who are struggling to cope with a variety of hardships. They're delighted to be able to help, for they recognize the debt of gratitude they owe to their Jewish brothers and sisters. They understand they've been made partakers of the same inheritance of God as far as "eternal" things are concerned, so they feel a sincere sense of responsibility to lighten the load of those suffering as far as "earthly" things are concerned.

So, when I've completed this task and have securely placed these generous gifts into the hands of those who desperately need it I'll come through Rome on my way to Spain.

I'm confident when I finally get there I'll have a lot to share with you about the abundant blessing of the gospel message of Jesus.

For now, I plead with you, my dear friends, for the sake of Jesus, and for the love of the Spirit of Jesus within each of us, diligently continue to pray with me to God on my behalf. Let me give you three specific things that you can pray for.

- Pray that I may be able to escape the attention and wrath of those who don't exactly take too kindly to the message of God's loving grace and peace for the "whole" world.
- Pray that those to receive these special gifts of love will do so with the same gracious spirit of appreciation with which they were given.
- Finally, pray that when I come to you with the great joy I've received by the will of God we will take great pleasure in refreshing each other with our friendship.

Until then, know and understand the God of peace is with you all.

May it be so.

126. CONCLUSION OF ROMANS
(Romans 16:1-27)

I'd like to commend to you our sister Phoebe, a faithful patron in the fellowship at Cenchreae, the port city of Corinth. Please accept her as a sister in the Lord and lend her your support and assistance if there is anything she might require, for she has been a tremendous source of supply to many folks, including myself.

Greet Priscilla and Acquila, my helpers in the ministry of the gospel message of Jesus who've willingly stuck their necks out to save my skin. I'm not the only one who is grateful to them, BUT all of the Gentile fellowships are also very thankful for them. Likewise, greet all the others who meet together in fellowship at their home.

Furthermore, please greet and extend my very best wishes to the following folks:

- my beloved friend Epaenetus, one of the first in Achaia to accept and understand the gospel message of Jesus;
- Mary, who has tirelessly labored on our behalf;
- Andronicus and Junia, my kinsmen and fellow prisoners who are well known by the other leaders who were aware of the work of Jesus before I was;
- Amplias, my dear friend in the family of God;
- Urbanus, our helper in Jesus;
- Stachys, my good buddy;
- Apelles, approved for sure in Jesus;
- the whole family of Aristobulus;
- the whole family of Narcissus, who are also proud members of the family of God;
- Tryphena ("Dainty") and Tryphosa ("Delicate"), co-laborers in the spreading of God's work;
- the much loved Persis, another who labors tirelessly telling others of God's love;
- Rufus, chosen of God, and his mom who has truly been like a mother to me as well;
- Asyncritus, Phlegon, Hermas, Patrobas, Hermes and all of the brothers and sisters who fellowship together with them;
- Philologus, Julia, Nereus and his sister, and

- Olympas and all of those who fellowship together with them.

Show your warm affection and recognition of one another with a kiss of honor and respect. The fellowships of Jesus send to all of you their warmest regards.

And now I'd like to plead with you, my dear friends, to keep your eyes wide open to recognize those who consider it to be their mandate to bring division and confusion to the understanding of God's grace and peace which you've come to know and appreciate. Avoid them like a plague. For they're the kind of people who are definitely not serving Jesus BUT, who are motivated only by their own insatiable need for power, control, and self-gratification.

Count on them to employ eloquent words and lofty speeches to deceive the hearts of those who may have a difficult time recognizing how slick they promote the lust of self-righteousness. The strength and maturity of your understanding of God's love is well known far and wide.

I'm tickled pink for you, BUT I'd still like to make sure you remain wise to the liberty of God's grace and peace and competently aware of the empty, hollow perversions of the pursuit of self-righteousness. Plant yourselves in the wisdom of God for He has laid asunder the wisdom (foolishness) of mankind and its domination over you when He did a short work on the cross of Jesus!

The grace of our Lord Jesus remains with you.

May it be so.

P.S.

There are a whole lot of people here who would like me to pass along their best regards:
- Tim, my co-worker;
- Lucius;
- Jason;
- Sosipater, my fellow countryman;
- Tertius, who has so diligently penned this letter on my behalf;
- Gaius, my host, and all the fine folks who fellowship in his home;
- Erastus, the city treasurer; and
- Quartus, a dear brother.

The grace of Jesus be with you all. May it be so.

And now, to the only One who has the power to establish you in the everlasting light and liberty of His love and acceptance according:
- to the truth of the only good news worth talking about,
- to the preaching of Jesus, and
- to the revelation of the mystery of God's love for all mankind.

The declaration of God's love was a virtual secret since the world began, **BUT** it's now **PLAIN AND CLEAR** for all to see. It's been revealed in the scriptures of the prophets who recorded the promises of the everlasting God. The promise of God's grace and peace has also been made known to each and every nation in accordance and obedience to the faith and faithfulness of God's love.

To this only wise God be glory through Jesus for ever!
Folks, that's the way it is!

Trip # 17
CORINTH TO JERUSALEM

127. **REVIEW TIME**
(Acts 20:3b-6)

Well, how'd you like the letter to my Roman friends? Were you able to see I was very concerned these precious believers were under intense pressure to succumb to the deception of those still convinced the favor of God was dependent on the strength of a person's system of beliefs and accomplishments? I sure hope you picked it up.

In fact, I surely trust you'll come to recognize you face no less of this danger. Your entire perspective of God, how He relates to you, and how you relate to Him will be altered dramatically when you renew your mind to what God has graciously done for all mankind. It will make you fall in love with God ways you never thought possible!

However, there will be MUCH MORE for you to sink your teeth into the following pages!

I think now would be a good time to review a bit. It's very important for you to remember it's impossible to tell you absolutely everything that happened to my friends and I throughout the years. Time has a way of going by so fast it's hard to believe. So it is in my recollection and recording of our activities. Sometimes a year went by and one couldn't help but wonder where it went. So, let me see if I can bring you up to date.

Remember, I was on my thirteenth trip. Let's start off from the riot in Ephesus.

- Demetrius and the silversmith riot in Ephesus is quelled by the town clerk.
- From Ephesus I wrote my first letter to the Corinthians because of the sad report we had received concerning them.
- The arrival of Stephanas, Fortunatus, and Achaicus brought an update of the problems in Corinth, prompting a second letter to my dear friends over there.
- I made a quick trip (my 14th) to Corinth to restore their confidence then returned to Ephesus.
- I wrote a "severe" letter (3rd) to the Corinthians, sending it with my associate Titus.

REVIEW TIME   TRIP # 17

- I traveled from Ephesus to Troas, then on to Philippi, (trip # 15) where I stayed with Lydia until Titus arrived from Corinth bringing good news.
- I wrote my fourth letter to the Corinthians from Philippi.
- We traveled through the cities of Macdonia (Thessalonica, Berea, etc.) eventually arriving in Corinth (trip # 16).
- From Corinth I wrote the letter to my Galatian friends and also to those fine folks in Rome whom I was so anxious to see.
- Undoubtedly you'll recall the most pressing thing on my agenda at this point was the collection of gifts for our dear brothers and sisters in Jerusalem who were facing some very difficult times. Wherever we went we encouraged our fellow believers to lend their support to this cause.
- We spent the three winter months in Corinth preparing for the trip (# 17) to take the gifts to Jerusalem and were very anxious to get on with it. It had been my intention to board one of the Jewish pilgrim ships traveling to Syria in time for Passover.

There's one thing about boats that frighten me. They make great targets for those who prefer to make a vocation out of taking from others what doesn't rightly belong to them. "Man overboard!" is a phrase you probably wouldn't hear in the darkness of night by someone intent on destroying any incriminating evidence.

There was no doubt I'd be an obvious target for attack. I was a poster boy for the Jewish community all right, although the poster was one of the "most wanted" variety. In addition, I'd be in possession of a significant amount of money I had every intention of getting to those who needed it very desperately.

It came to our attention a plot to thwart my plans was being hatched by a groups of Jewish thugs, so alternative plans of getting to Jerusalem definitely became a high priority. We felt it would be best to travel back through Macedonia. This would also give us the opportunity to visit one more time with many of the folks we had come to appreciate so much. Perhaps, we could even collect some more gifts for the collections along the way!

One more change. I would definitely not be going alone!

Representatives of the various fellowships would be traveling with me. All of these dear brothers had come to meet us in Corinth in order to accompany me all the way to Jerusalem. Finally, we were all set to go, albeit in a different direction.

REVIEW TIME   TRIP # 17

So we said our goodbyes to Corinth and traveled up the familiar roadway through Athens, Berea, Thessalonica, Apollonia, Amphipolis, and on to Philippi.

The clan who joined me on the trip included:

From Achaia:
- Corinth: Titus

From Macedonia:
- Berea: Sopatros, the son of Pyrrhus
- Thessalonica: Aristarchus and Secundus
- Philippi: Luke

From Galatia:
- Derbe: Gaius
- Lystra: Timothy

From Asia:
- Colossae: Tychicus
- Ephesus: Trophimus

Luke, Titus and I wanted to stay in Philippi for the days of unleavened bread. This began with the day of the Passover and lasted for one week. You may recall this is the period of time during which the Jews remembered the deliverance of their forefathers from Egypt by eating unleavened bread. However, the rest of our compatriots decided to go on to Troas where we'd catch up with them after a week or so.

To say the least, we had a wonderful time in Philippi. The same can't be said for our boat ride from Neapolis to Troas. It took us five miserable days! It only took us two days when we traveled from Troas to Neapolis on our previous trip. The winds were something else. It actually seemed like we were going backwards much of the time.

The sight of Troas off the bow of the boat was a welcome sight indeed! Just to set foot on solid ground again would be enough to make anybody happy. We, however, had a double dose of joy. We were once again to meet up with Tim and all of our other traveling companions! We spent one eventful week in Troas.

128. **EUTYCHUS**
(Acts 20:7-12)

To say this trip through Troas sticks out as one of those unforgettable deposits in my memory bank would certainly have to be an understatement. It's quite funny whenever we talk about it and yet when it happened it was somewhat frightening. Let me tell you about it.

On the first day of the week the believers of Troas had come together in a very nice home to fellowship with one another. Knowing it was our intention of leaving the next day they invited me to speak to them. They should have known giving me an opportunity to preach about the gospel message of Jesus would mean a long, long evening for everyone.

Well, we all had just a fantastic meal together. Can these people put on a spread! Following the meal we adjourned to a large room upstairs where we could seat ourselves more comfortably to enjoy some good fellowship and to hear what I was to tell them. Candles and oil lamps were lit as the evening progressed, adding immeasurably to the warmth of the beautiful evening air.

I know it was getting a little late. What can I say? I get cranked up a bit too tight sometimes. Many of you who've fallen asleep hopelessly enduring the droning sound of a long winded speaker will be able to relate very well with what happened to a very nice young man who valiantly attempted to survive my pronouncements. The young chap's name was Eutychus.

Well, Eutychus thought he had the best possible solution to endure the warmth of the evening as well as the length of my sermonizing. He spotted what appeared to be the best viewing spot closest to some fresh air, a vacant ledge of an open window. He was confident he was blessed to have the best of both worlds.

You know what's coming, don't you?

Perhaps it was the full stomach. Maybe it was the warmth of all the candles. Hey, it could have been the fresh air. Doubtful it was my speaking. Whatever the case, the eyelids of poor Eutychus simply could not retain the strength to remain in the open position.

Yep, you got the picture. He fell asleep, completely oblivious to his surroundings. He was paying as little attention to us as any of us were paying to him. "Dead to the world" you might say.

There are certain things that happen when you fall asleep. In the beginning your body tries to fight it, then it dips into some involuntary, sporadic twitching exercises. Gradually, the mind becomes numb to things happening around you. Finally, you become intoxicated with the sense of a rapturous peace. Lights go out. Literally!

Now, falling asleep is one thing. Falling asleep in a rather precarious position is quite another. The fact the precarious position is three stories off the roadway below is still another incredible thing!

It must have been a somewhat freaky moment for the person who spotted Eutychus disappear from his window perch. A shriek interrupted the sound of my voice. The heads of others spun as they heard the unusually loud thud! All of a sudden people were scrambling for the stairs, unable to get to the bottom fast enough.

Concern and astonishment were emotions felt by everyone as they arrived at the side of the motionless young lad. By the time I got there some of the folks were convinced Eutychus was a goner.

I bent over placing my head over his heart, and reached my arms around his head and shoulders. With great relief I said, "Don't worry folks, he's still alive."

Good thing we had Luke along. We all backed up in order to give Doc a chance to have a better look as well as to give Eutychus some breathing room.

Young people! What was on his mind when he finally came to? Food! Hey, why not. We all needed a break anyway, although this wouldn't have been the way I'd have picked to interrupt a rather inspirational dissertation.

Just kidding! Anyhow, it didn't really end. We kept the party going until the light of day. Time flies when you're having fun. Sleeping people, however, shouldn't fly. If you don't believe me, just ask Eutychus!

Let me tell you, we were a mighty happy lot to see him up and around.

129. **FAREWELL AT EPHESUS**
(Acts 20:13-38)

I don't know. I just wasn't all that excited about stepping onto another boat after our rough trip from Neapolis over to Troas. I'd just as soon take a hike. Of course, all of the other fellows wanted to go by boat around the Gulf of Adramyttium. So I told them to go ahead and I'd meet up with them at Assos. I figured the twenty miles I'd have to walk would take me less time than the thirty mile boat trip around Cape Lectum, especially given the boat would have to face strong north easterly winds.

    The city of Assos had a beautiful view from its terraces of a steep volcanic cone. Although about a half a mile from the sea, its harbor formed by a large artificial mole, was still adequate for coastal shipping. A mighty city wall two miles long and sixty-five feet high added to the natural defenses of its physical location. I really enjoyed the walk because of the great natural agricultural scenery. The quality of wheat that came from this area was well known.

    Sure enough, I got to Assos first. I met up Luke and all the rest of my compatriots down at the dock. Unfortunately, I had to go by boat for the next leg of our journey. We set off for the island of Lesbos, arriving in the chief city of Mitylene, a wonderful port city with unique charm. It was very easy to see why it was a favorite residence for many influential Romans. The Romans had at one time destroyed the walls and acropolis (80 B.C.) because the people of Lesbos revolted over taxation issues. Pompey, while finding asylum there from Julius Caesar, had restored its freedom. We had a very pleasant stay overnight in Mitylene.

    The next day we set sail for the island of Chios. This rocky, mountainous island is located in the east central region of the Aegean Sea. From top to bottom the island measured about thirty-two miles. From side to side it measured anywhere from eight to eighteen miles at various spots. It was separated from the mainland of Asia Minor by a strait about five miles wide, dotted with many small islands. It just so happens the main city on the island was also called Chios. We anchored overnight opposite Chios under the protection of the mainland.

    Our next day was spent sailing for the island of Samos. This island had been a very important naval base throughout its history.

The island measured about twenty-seven miles from east to west and about fifteen miles at its greatest width. Samos was the chief city of this Ionian island.

We didn't stay there overnight even though we passed right by it. Instead, we put anchor just off the nose of Trogllium, a promontory formed by the western part of Mount Mycale on the western shore of Asia Minor. I find it kind of interesting an anchorage just east of the western tip of Trogyllium is to this day still called "St. Paul's Bay." Who'd have thunk it?

The next day we traveled as far as Miletus. Did you know the city of Miletus was one of the first places to mint coins for use as a currency? The port city had four harbors to handle its commercial activities along the coast of Asia Minor. Miletus was situated on the southern shore of the Latmian Gulf that served as the estuary of the Maeander River.

You may be wondering why we went all the way to Miletus when we could easily have stopped in Ephesus. Well, the first reason is 'cause I was in a hurry to get to Jerusalem before the day of Pentecost. I'm just not the kind of person who likes to eat and run. Man, we had so many friends in Ephesus we'd never be able to get away.

Secondly, I was not particularly looking forward to getting into any more trouble with the likes of Demetrius and all his silversmith union. I figured if anyone wanted to see my buddies and I they could take the twenty-eight mile hike from Ephesus to Miletus to see us.

I sent a message off to the leadership of the fellowship in Ephesus that we had reached Miletus. I'm happy to report they were so anxious to see us they came almost immediately. I knew we wouldn't have a whole lot of time to sit around and gab so I seized this most precious occasion to give them my words of counsel one last time. We were all very distinctly aware of the reasonable possibility we might never get to see one another again.

Here's basically some of what I told them:

"Since I first arrived in Asia you've become intimately acquainted with the way I've treated you in every situation. I've served God with all humility of mind. I've shed more than a few tears. Beyond all this, I was subjected to the temptations of going back under the spell of legalism by the cunning and deceitful ambitions of the Jews.

FAREWELL AT EPHESUS   TRIP # 17

You know I didn't hold anything back profitable for you to know, BUT, I demonstrated and taught you publicly from one house meeting to the next."

"Indeed, I proclaimed the gospel of God's grace and peace both to the Jews and also to the Greeks. I didn't shy away from inciting you to renew your mind toward the grace of God and to place your trust in the work of Jesus on your behalf instead of in your own self-righteousness."

"And now, just think of it, I find myself compelled in the Spirit of Jesus within me to get to Jerusalem even though I'm not really sure what's going to happen when we get there. One thing we do know, however, is there seems to be mounting evidence confirmed by past experience I'm bound to meet up with some stiff opposition and persecution wherever I go. I must have a target stamped on my forehead, because I seem to be a marked man."

"BUT, none of these factors deter me from this mission. Neither does the price of the contract we've heard has been put out for me. I hardly think my life is worth what they seem to be willing to pay for my capture. I simply want to get on with my life with the happy contentment of knowing I did my very best to proclaim the message given to me by Jesus of the gospel of the grace and peace of God!"

"And now, pay attention."

"I'm quite well aware all of you as well as all of those I've had the great privilege of exalting the kingdom of God to will probably never see my face again. I want you to remember this day I'm declaring one final time to you I bear absolutely no responsibility for anybody's righteousness! For I've not shunned one iota from declaring to you all the counsel and wisdom of God to cover the punishment to be exercised upon the whole world!"

"Watch out! For yourselves and for those whom you lead."

"The Spirit of Jesus has blessed you with the privilege of overseeing others and of teaching and leading along the children of God whom Jesus purchased with His very own blood! For I know one thing for sure, after I've left there are going to be deceivers who will come into your fellowships like grievous wolves who sneak up to devour a flock of defenseless sheep."

"Don't even be surprised if some of you will become like those wolves yourselves, speaking perverse things to draw folks away from the grace of God back to systems of laws, rules, and regulations in the painful struggle to gain self-righteousness. Therefore, beware. Watch out! Remember I've spent almost three years warning you every chance I had, night and day, with many tears of the dangers of going back into the darkness of legalism."

"And now, my dear friends, I simply commend you to God and to the true word of His grace which is the only thing able to restore you and to give you an equal share of the inheritance He has blessed the whole world with."

"I've had no desire for anybody's silver or gold or possessions. Yes, you should know for yourselves I've labored to provide for my own needs and for the needs of all those who ministered with me. I've been a demonstration of God's love. I hope I've been an inspiration to you of the challenges you have to support those who've not reached this maturity in the process of renewing their minds. Remember the words of Jesus, and how He said, 'It's more blessed to give than to receive.'"

I had to stop before I started crying. I was overwhelmed by the significance of our time together. I knelt down on my knees and prayed with all of my dear friends who were gathered around me. There wasn't a dry eye around. We hugged one another, patted each other on the back, and even threw a few farewell kisses.

I think when you realize it's a final goodbye it's always harder. Don't you? I hate saying goodbye. It was pretty quiet as they accompanied us down to the ship waiting for our next segment of the trip to Jerusalem.

It was tough time for everyone!

TRIP # 17

130. **DON'T CRY**
(Acts 21:1-17)

It's a good thing the shipping vessel companies had to keep some kind of schedule or else we'd never have gotten away from Miletus. It was such a sad thing to leave all our precious friends.

    The boat set sail directly for the island of Cos. Incidentally, there's also a city named Cos. The beautiful island just off the coast of Caria in the Aegean Sea was known not only for its magnificent wines and wonderful silks, but as an important banking center for the Jews. People referred to it as one of the "Isles of the Blessed." We made the port in plenty of time to anchor in a great spot for the night.

    Continuing on our journey we spent the next day cruising the coastline from Cos to the island of Rhodes. This island is second in size only to Crete in the Aegean Sea. It was about forty two miles in length and about seventeen miles in width, separated from Asia minor by a channel about ten miles wide. In spite of its convenient position along the shipping lanes the city of Rhodes was known more for its cultural heritage than for its commercial status. We spent one night in the harbor of the city of Rhodes, located at the northern tip of the island.

    Patara is the city where we had to get off our small coastal boat and board a larger ship for the next leg of the journey. Patara was a large, prosperous city with commercial ties to Egypt. The favorable westerly winds of the Mediterranean made the trip from Egypt to the fertile Xanthus Valley region of Lycia and the territories beyond very convenient. Patara was also very well known for its temple dedicated to the worship of Apollo Patareus because, according to legend, it was Patarus, the son of Apollo, who founded the city. Well anyway, it was an interesting city to visit.

    We managed to get ourselves on a very nice ship for the trip across the Mediterranean to Phoenicia. Boy, did we ever make good time. The three hundred and fifty miles sailed past quickly as we moved south of the island of Cyprus passing the city of Paphos.

    The harbor at Tyre was a welcome site. It was easy to see why this southern city of Phoenicia was well known for its navigators and merchant traders. Location. Location. Location. These are perhaps the three most important ingredients in the success of a business. Well, Tyre had location, becoming a melting pot for commerce and culture.

And you know who else were there? Followers of Jesus! What a welcome we received. Since it was going to take about seven days for them to unload and reload the ship we took full advantage of the time to fellowship with our new found friends. They took care to warn me about continuing to Jerusalem because they sensed danger lurked in wait for me. However, we were so close to our final destination now and the mission was paramount in my mind. What happened to me was inconsequential to the desire of my heart.

Entire families gathered to walk us all down to the harbor where the ship was waiting to depart. It reminded me of our time not too long ago in Miletus. Well, we stopped beside the road just outside town and enjoyed a time of prayer together. We said our tearful goodbyes and best wishes to each other and then each group went their own ways, our friends back to Tyre to carry on with their lives and our little troupe to board the ship for the last boat ride on our way to Jerusalem.

It didn't take us all that long to go the twenty miles from Tyre to Ptolemais by boat. We spent an entire day with a great group of believers in Jesus here at this pit stop. Then it was on to Caesarea, forty miles to the south.

Augustus had given the city to Herod the Great. So what did he do? He named it Caesarea in honor of Caesar Augustus and he named its seaport Sebastos (Augustus). It took him twelve years of extensive, ambitious building to turn Caesarea into the capital city of Palestine. A theater, aqueducts, an amphitheater, colonnaded streets, an impressive temple dedicated to the Caesar, and a man-made harbor are but a few of the rebuilding projects that made Caesarea a real Roman piece of work.

A safe haven for all of us would naturally be the home of the great evangelist Philip. Let me remind you who Philip was. He was one of the seven Hellenistic officers appointed in the early days of the Jerusalem church to supervise the food bank. Philip had been involved for some twenty years now in missionary activity in Samaria and along the coastal plains of Palestine. Not only was he blessed with a tremendous outreach ministry, he was also very blessed with a lovely wife and four wonder daughters! Very single each and every one, very able in proclaiming the wonders of the love of God to boot!

During our stay in Caesarea we had a visitor who had come to see us from another part of Judaea. His name was Agabus, well known for his prophetic teachings.

He employed an object lesson very reminiscent of the way the prophets of old revealed their messages from God.

Agabus came to me and asked me for my belt. He then took it, tied up his feet and then continued to use the belt to wrap up his wrists as well. It was very obvious he was trying to give us the idea of being shackled and handcuffed like a prisoner.

And then he spoke,

"This is what the Spirit of Jesus within me has to say to you. 'This is the way the Jews at Jerusalem will bind the one who owns this belt and will deliver him into the hands of the Gentiles.'"

Needless to say his proclamation had a very dampening effect on the excitement that had reached its peak as we were ever so near to our destination. All of the folks gathered at Phil's place, as well as the entire group of men who had traveled all this way with me, started in on me. They begged me not to go the rest of the way to Jerusalem.

I would have none of it.

"Why do you all have to go and cry now? Why are you trying to break my heart? Listen, I have a job to do and am fully prepared to accept the consequences of my actions. Furthermore, I not only am ready to be bound and imprisoned if that is what is before me, BUT, I'm also ready to die in Jerusalem for the name of Jesus!"

It became abundantly clear to my dear friends I was not about to be dissuaded. I finally convinced them the will of God has already been done and anything that could happen to me wouldn't affect His will one bit.

After spending quite a few days in Caesarea the time finally come for us to make the sixty-five mile trek to Jerusalem. We packed our bags and loaded them onto the carriages. A number of the believers from Caesarea wanted to go along with us, including a fellow by the name of Mnason, an older believer from the island of Cyprus. Wisely thinking we could maintain a relatively low profile at an inconspicuous location he graciously invited us to stay at his home in Jerusalem.

Seeing Jerusalem once again brought back so many memories. Just walking through the city gates was a pleasure I had only dreamt about on many occasions during the many years of traveling abroad.

We finally made it!

Safe and sound no less. I was thrilled at the reception we received at the home of Mnason by the many folks gathered to welcome us. You'd almost think they'd been waiting for us for a long time. I'm sure the word was out concerning why we'd come!

TRIP # 17

IN JERUSALEM

131. AUDIENCE WITH JAMES
(Acts 21:18-25)

It sure was good to put our feet up and rest for at least a little while again. A nice warm bath, some freshly washed clothes, and a great food can certainly do wondrous things for one's body and spirit. We all knew the next day would be the beginning of a very hectic time in Jerusalem.

Our schedule the next day included a meeting with James. He was commonly known as "James the Just" and for good reason I'm sure. He must have been doing a great job as the chairman of the board of the elder statesmen of the rather large fellowship of believers in Jerusalem. He had gathered together all of the elders for this special occasion. I don't even know the exact number present. I'd heard the number of believers in Jerusalem numbered in the thousands so I would expect there must have been at least sixty or seventy elders in the room.

What a sight!

And into this august assembly came little old me, my small band of living testimonies of the grace of God among the Gentiles, bringing with us the sacrificial gifts from the wonderful folks throughout Asia, Macedonia, and Achaia.

I took great pride in introducing my co-workers to them and brought greetings from all the fellow believers whom we represented. It was my pleasure to remind them of the incredible work God had accomplished for even the Gentiles, and of course, to inform them of how we had been spreading the message of God's grace and peace wherever we traveled.

James led the cheers of gratitude towards God. When things settled down a bit it became obvious James had something to say. He raised his arms to calm the boisterous crowd and then proceeded with his little speech.

> "Dear brother Paul, we're delighted with your reports. I think it's pretty clear to you and to your mates the numbers of Jews who believe now number in the thousands. And they're all more than zealous to maintain the customs and traditions of the law.

A rumor has been spreading among the people you've been teaching and encouraging the Jews who meet together with the Gentile believers it's all right if they abandon the laws of Moses, and there's no need for them to have their children circumcised, nor even for them to maintain their traditions and customs of their ancestral heritage."

"Although I'm confident there's nothing to substantiate these rumors, something must be done to bring peace to the confusion surrounding your ministry. Word has already spread about the fact you've arrived and the matter surely will come up when everyone gets together. I think there's a way for us to clearly show once and for all you have not violated your commitment to the edicts of the Jerusalem Council a number of years ago."

"Allow me to share this idea."

Now, before I continue telling you about this "idea" James had, I want to give you a little background to the whole idea of a "Nazarite vow." A vow was a very serious thing to be observed, not to mention fairly expensive.

It was undertaken either in gratitude for some kind of special blessing received from the hand of God or as a purification rite as a result of a particular ceremonial defilement.

Whatever the reason the time of the vow lasted about thirty days. One had to abstain from eating meat and drinking wine for the whole time. You were also not allowed to cut your hair or even shave. The last seven days were to be spent secluded in the Temple.

A number of offerings were expected:
- a male and a female lamb for a sin-offering,
- a ram for a peace offering,
- a basket of unleavened bread, with cakes of fine flour mingled with oil,
- a meat offering, and
- a drink offering.

At the conclusion of the seven days the hair was to be cut off and burned on the altar with all of the other sacrifices. Now, the cost of this vow would have to be substantial. You couldn't go to work and earn your normal wages and you had to pay a healthy sum for the required offerings.

AUDIENCE WITH JAMES   TRIP # 17

Since the cost was a big factor it was considered to be an act of charity and some piety for a wealthier person to help defray the expenses of the person taking the vow.

And, I guess, this was where I was to come into the plan because James continued with "his" way for me to demonstrate I truly was an observer of the law.

"There are four men currently involved in fulfilling a vow. I'm going to suggest you participate in their purification rite by being at their sacrificial service when their hair is shaved and offered with the other offerings. Furthermore, I think it would be a fine testimony for you to financially assist them in their endeavors. I'm confident your participation in these rituals will let folks know the rumors are just rumors, BUT, that you're walking appropriately, following after all of the laws, rules, and regulations of your heritage."

"In regards to the Gentiles who've become believers, we want to assure you it's not our intention to revisit the decisions of the Jerusalem Council. The decisions reached at the time have been sent out long ago and there's no reason to conclude they're not being followed. We asked the Gentile believers to continue to observe only these things:
1. Refrain from eating things offered to idols;
2. Abstain from eating the meat of animals killed in such a way the blood hasn't been properly drained; and
3. Stop illicit sexual intercourse outside marriage."

132. **TEMPLE RIOT**
(Acts 21:26-40a)

I want you to know this whole idea was not all that palatable to me. In fact, the whole suggestion to me was quite distasteful. I never thought what I was doing needed anyone's approval. At certain times, however, the act of compromise should not be viewed as a sign of weakness or capitulation, but as a sign of strength and wisdom. This would be one of those times. Little did I think going along with James' little plan would almost get me killed!

The next day began somewhat ceremoniously as I accompanied the men who were about to complete their "Nazarite vow." We entered into the Temple to begin the final week of the purification and sacrificial ceremonies for each one of them.

It would be well for you to know the time of Pentecost was a very significant date on the Jewish calendar. Folks literally came from around the world to Jerusalem for the celebrations and the Temple was jam packed with people every day. I thought things were actually not going too badly as I was able to maintain a rather inconspicuous presence in the masses.

Towards the end of the week all you know what broke loose!

I didn't recognize them but they sure did recognize me. I'm talking about a batch of Asian Jews. They spotted me in the Temple and caused a fuss you wouldn't believe. They stirred up the crowd into a frenzy faster than you can say "Noah's ark!"

All of a sudden I was overtaken by the unruly mob and I was grabbed on both sides by some very strong young men who roughed me up quite a bit in the process. They hoisted me up onto some steps so everyone could have a good view of the goings-on. It wasn't long before some young buck started shouting to get even more attention than he already had.

"Men of Israel. HELP! HELP! This is the guy! He's the one who's been teaching to all men everywhere they should despise the Jewish people. He teaches against the law and against the Temple! On top of this we've seen him bring Greeks with him into the Temple and has thereby defiled and polluted our holy place!"

What the world are these guys talking about? I've never said anything like that! And whom did I bring into the Temple? Oh, they must be thinking about Trophimus, my Ephesian friend.

Perhaps he had been seen in the temple area, but I certainly didn't bring him in where he wasn't allowed to be. As far as I knew he was still in the outer courtyard.

Let me explain a bit about the Temple so you can appreciate the problem I was facing. Gentile folks were permitted only in an outer courtyard area of the Temple facilities. Between this "Court of the Gentiles" and the "Court of the Women" was a barrier set up to prevent any Gentile from proceeding past it. Just so no one would mistakenly get by warnings were posted in both Greek and in Latin to the barrier at the foot of the steps leading up to the inner precincts.

The inscriptions read something like this:

"No foreigner may enter within the barricade which surrounds the Temple and enclosure. Anyone caught doing so will have only himself to blame for his ensuing, untimely death!"

The seriousness of any infraction was supported by the permission the Romans had given to the Jews to carry out a death penalty for any such violation. Obviously, I was being accused of aiding and abetting a criminal activity, punishable with the exact same sentence as the perpetrator, death!

Scared out of my wits or what? No kidding. People started to crush in from every direction. Like a giant funnel a stampede of wild creatures were getting sucked right into a stream of anger appearing hopeless to stop. I was moved amidst the turmoil to a position just outside the Temple doors and then I could hear the doors slam shut behind us. Obviously, it would be a crying shame for my death to defile the sacred proceedings of the inner sanctum! People were punching me, kicking me, spitting on me, and calling me names even I hadn't heard before.

Fortunately for me word had gotten out to the commander of the security forces that trouble was brewing in lotus land and the religious world of Jerusalem was throwing an execution party. The commander was no dummy. He knew full well the dangers he faced if a riot broke out.

The Roman military establishment was very well prepared and equipped to handle any emergencies, especially during holidays and special events such as Pentecost. Herod the Great had the fortress of Antonia built on the north west corner of the Temple area to house a mighty garrison of Roman troops under the command of a garrison commander and a military tribunal.

Two flights of steps connected the fortress to the outer court of the Temple so it wouldn't take very long at all for the military police to quell any kind of disturbance.

Without getting into any gory, sordid details I was pretty close to being a goner when everyone hesitated as the drumlike, staccato, precision sounds of two hundred marching soldiers, led by the superior officers, raced onto the scene. The commander approached the center of mess to find me coherent, yet in rather serious physical shape. He grabbed me away from the monstrous crowd and handed me over to be handcuffed to some pretty muscular soldiers on each side of me. Funny as it might sound, I felt a little more secure than I had a few minutes before.

The commander demanded to know who I was and what I had done. I really didn't expect to get a word in edge wise. Well, everyone else sure did!

The crowd just roared, everyone wanting to talk at once. They all started wailing and yelling at the top of their vocal capacities. Babbling is the only thing discernible. Unable to understand a word the commander ordered me to be taken into the safety of the military bastion where he could get to the bottom of the matter. They literally had to pick me up and carry me through the monstrous crowd in order to get to the steps leading up into the fortress.

A chant rose up throughout the multitude,
"KILL HIM!
KILL HIM!
KILL HIM!"

Talk about role reversal. Some years ago it would have been me leading the uprising. I was the one who enacted swift justice upon those who violated the laws, rules, and regulations of my heritage. Now I was the target!

As we proceeded into the fortress I was able to secure the attention of the commander.

"Sir, what's your name?"

"I'm Claudius, Claudius Lysias, if it makes any difference to you."

"Commander Lysias, I'd like to have a word with you, if I may."

I spoke to him in fluent Greek so he'd be impressed enough to pay attention to my plea.

"What? Can you speak Greek?" responded the commander. "Aren't you the Egyptian who started a major riot and led some four thousand mercenaries into the desert not too long ago?"

Obviously my lingo caused some consternation for the commander. He'd pegged me for someone else. Apparently, there had been a major uprising led by some Egyptian character about three years earlier. He commanded an unruly batch of some four thousand desperate men out to the Mount of Olives with the promise he could make the walls of the city fall down before them all. At his command, when the walls crumbled he would order them to march in, overthrow the Roman garrison, and take possession of the city and all its inhabitants.

The Roman military, however, hearing of the plan were dispatched rather quickly to quell the uprising. Most of the followers were scattered like dust in a windstorm, only to survive in another format. The gang had been given the name of "dagger bearers," because these violent nationalists became ruthless assassins, concealing their knives and daggers under their cloaks. They blended in with any crowd, struck their targets with deadly accuracy then easily escaped amidst the confusion of the moment. Unfortunately for the Romans the eloquent, crafty leader of the gang had escaped. Claud obviously figured I could be the spineless leader of these "dagger bearers."

I was in no mood to be the fall guy!

"No way! My name is Paul. I'm a Jew from the great city of Tarsus in Cilicia and I believe I can remedy the situation if you'd just give me the chance to speak to all these people."

Coming to grips with the fact he'd mistaken my identity he compromised enough to at least give me a chance to help him out of an ugly situation. He stopped the procession and attempted to quiet the crowds, leading me out in plain view where I could raise my arms as well as the arms of the two soldiers attached to me to gain some attention.

133. **APPEAL TO THE MOB**
(Acts 21:40b-22:29)

The intimidating presence of the army of soldiers had the crowd silent before too long. Then commander Claudius Lysias gave me his permission to address the crowd. With the double intention of letting Claud and the audience know they had nothing to fear, I began my appeal in my mother tongue, Hebrew.

"Men, brothers, and fathers, please be kind enough to hear me out. I'd like to defend myself from the accusations you've leveled against me."

When they heard me speak to them in Hebrew it seemed to silence the hum of the stirring crowd even more.

"Hey, I'm very much a Jew, born in the city of Tarsus, a city in Cilicia and yet I received my education in this great city of Jerusalem under the tutelage of the great Rabbi Gamaliel. No doubt you're all aware of his credentials for he taught according to the strictest standards of the observance of the law of our forefathers and was equally zealous in his reverence toward God. I'm sure you all must share his passion by virtue of your presence here in the Temple today."

"I was probably even more zealous than any one of you for I persecuted the believers in Jesus with such severity many, both men and women, who followed after the teachings of 'the way' ended up either bound in prison, or dead.

The High Priest, as well as all the members of the Sanhedrin, can testify on my behalf I carried out their instructions with their blessing to search out the city of Damascus for the renegades of 'our' way. I was charged with the responsibility of finding them, and bringing any "believers" back to Jerusalem for trial and punishment."

"And then something happened on the way to the forum. It was high noon as I approached the city of Damascus. Suddenly a phenomenal light from heaven surrounded me. I literally fell to the ground and covered my eyes 'cause the light was so bright. And then I heard a voice talking to me."

"'Saul. Saul. Why are you persecuting me?' the voice called out."

"'Who said that?' I replied. 'Who are you Lord?'"

"'I am Jesus of Nazareth, the one you're persecuting.'"

"All of my traveling companions were scared out of their wits because they could see the light, hear me talking, yet they couldn't see or hear who I was talking to. I continued my conversation with Jesus."

"What do you want me to do, Lord?"

"'Get up, and go into Damascus. When you get there you will be told what you are supposed to do. I have a job for you.'"

"I was so blinded by the glorious light surrounding us I had to be led into the city like a blind man. I was taken to the home of Ananias, a devout and well-respected man among the Jews. Ananias walked up to me like he knew I was coming."

"'Brother Saul, receive back your sight!'"

"Sure enough, within minutes I could see clearly again. And then Ananias continued."

"'The God of our fathers has chosen you for a purpose. He wants you to know His will for the whole world. He wants you to see the Just One who has made it all possible. He wants you to hear the words He's speaking to you. You are now to be a witness to everyone of what you've seen and heard. What are you waiting for? Get up, go and be baptized. Call on the name of Jesus who has washed away your sins and be baptized as a symbolic demonstration of this cleansing.'"

"Some time later when I eventually had the nerve to come to Jerusalem again I was praying in the Temple when I actually saw Jesus in a vision speaking to me."

"'Hurry up, you'd better get out of town quickly for there are many different folks in Jerusalem who simply will not accept your testimony concerning what I've done for all mankind.'"

"I didn't understand the significance of what I was hearing."

"Lord, everyone knows I imprisoned and beat those who believe in You in every synagogue possible. They know when the blood of Your martyr Stephen was spilt it was I who stood by in agreement by giving my blessing to his slaughter. Hey, I even held the coats of those who rocked him to death."

"'Get out of town,' He replied, 'for I'm sending you to share my love with the Gentiles.'"

I guess if they were a bit ticked off with me before, I just incited them even more with my impassioned appeal.

APPEAL TO THE MOB — TRIP # 17

I should have known saying the word "Gentile" in a crowd just outside the Temple doors to a mob of angry Jews wasn't the smartest thing to do. Now, they were really cheezed off at me. They had patiently listened to what I had said for long enough and the crowd erupted in defiance.

"Kill him!"

"Away with him! Why should we have to put up with someone like this scum on this earth any more!"

"He doesn't deserve to live!"

With that many started ripping off their outer coats and throwing dirt up into air to show their contempt for me. What resulted was a pretty nasty dust storm of mob proportions.

Well, this was enough for commander Lysias. It was more than evident to him my speech hadn't exactly endeared me to the crowd. He gave the command and I was hustled out of there into the safe confines of the fortress. I would think even the soldiers were relieved to get inside.

Concluding I was out of a forest of trouble just because I was on the inside of the garrison was not a luxury I would enjoy very long. Claud embarked on his plan of exacting the truth out of me. He desperately wanted to find out who I was and how come the Jews were so ticked off at me. I was taken down to a special interrogation room in the basement where I was bound and shackled to a new set of pillars. I wasn't particularly fond of what was happening to me. I could see a scourging about to happen.

Perhaps you may have the wrong idea of what scouring is all about. It was often used as a tool of interrogation as much as it was an exacting of a punishment. Now don't get me wrong. Knowing this wasn't very comforting to me. Pain isn't exactly a feeling I crave all that much.

The scourge, or "flagellum" as it was called, was an instrument of torture certainly not meant to be a thing of beauty. It consisted of leather thongs, weighted at the ends with rough pieces of metal or bone attached to a heavy wooden handle. I've heard if you didn't actually die from the scourging you probably would be crippled in some way for life. Now this kind of torture may have been applied to slaves quite often. It wasn't supposed to happen to a nice guy like me. I've been beaten up a few times in my life so far, yet I certainly wasn't looking forward to this particular occasion.

As they started to make me lean forward to receive the lashes of the whip I just thought I'd ask the senior office a rather simple question.

"Say, tell me sir, is it lawful for you to scourge a free 'Roman' citizen who hasn't been convicted of any crime?"

This put a kibosh on the whole proceeding in a hurry. Knowing full well the trouble he'd get into if he were to continue with the inquisition he made the very wise choice to go over his own head to get some good advice. The whip was withdrawn as he fled off to see my good buddy, Claudius Lysias.

"Sir, I humbly suggest you'd better reconsider your course of action against this guy. He claims to be a Roman citizen."

I'm not too sure if he didn't believe his own soldier or if he just wanted to hear it for himself. Claud was down in the interrogation room within minutes.

"What's this I hear? Are you trying to pull a fast one over on us or what? Are you truly a Roman citizen?"

"You got that right!" I confessed.

"How is it possible?" barked the commander. "I'm very well aware of how much it can cost to become a citizen of Rome because I had to pay a pretty penny to become one myself. They must be really getting cheap if they're letting a dirt bag like you to become a citizen. I know you're a Jew, so how the heck did you manage to pull this off?"

With a touch of arrogant pride I proclaimed,

"Hey, you may have had to buy your citizenship. I didn't pay anything for mine. I was born a Roman citizen!"

The commander had to swallow the taste of a rather large slice of humble pie. He was wiping the egg off his face as he quickly left the dungeon suite of terror. The sporting event was over for all the other soldiers too. The consequences of scourging one of their own, without cause on top of it, was too dire to continue with the fun. Protecting their own backs from the whip now became their first concern!

Very quickly I was left hanging in the dark. Pain started to kick in as I was left alone to ponder my own future. I'd taken quite a bit of abuse from the soldiers, not to mention all the crap I had to endure from the angry mob. To tell you the truth, I don't even recall falling uncomfortably to sleep.

134. **BEFORE THE SANHEDRIN**
(Acts 22:30-23:10)

I was awakened the next morning by the noise of stomping feet and the banging of swords against the prison cell bars. It's not too hard to miss the sounds of soldiers when you're locked up in a dungeon.

Claudius Lysias wanted to find out from the Jews what they had against me. He was bound and determined to get to the bottom of the matter to prevent any more disturbances. Hey, it would be more accurate to say I was bound and he was determined! Claud sent a message to the high priest to get his act together by gathering the rest of the chief priests and all the members of the Sanhedrin to appear before him at a designated time.

They finally removed my wrists from the handcuffs and released my ankles from the shackles of chain. How do you spell relief? I wouldn't want to say it was a great breakfast, however, they at least let me eat a bit of grub. They were generous to allow me to clean myself up enough to be presentable for an audience of some significance. Nobody would tell me what was in store for me.

When the appointed time came I was hustled out of my cell and led down the stone cold halls by a full armored detail of soldiers as if I was an important political figure worthy of protection. It would have felt a whole lot more gratifying if I didn't know I was actually a prisoner. The procession ended in the largest meeting room of the Roman garrison where I was ordered to sit in the witness box with armed guards surrounding me.

The sight of the high priest with the horde of pious, religious hypocrites who made up the Sanhedrin watching me like vultures got my dander up the moment I figured out what was going on. With pomp and ceremony the emcee of the meeting was introduced to the assembled collection of officials. Commander Claudius Lysias made sure everyone knew who was in charge.

First of all, the commander told me to say what I wanted to say to my Jewish accusers. Perhaps it would be a good thing to have a bit of fear once in a while. The truth is all these guys, from the high priest down, didn't scare me one iota. I got off to a great start.

The proper, or respectable, way to begin an address to the Sanhedrin would be with honey-coated phrase like, "Honorable high priest, rulers of the people, and elders of Israel."

Well, I didn't have that much respect for them. To let them know in no uncertain terms they were no better in God's eyes than I, nor anyone else for that matter, I began with an introduction laced with a stinging amount of contempt.

"My fellow men and brothers, I want to tell you right from the start I've lived my entire life at peace with myself and am at peace with God."

Right out of the shoot this certainly didn't go over very well! Ananias, the high priest, was the first to react to my indiscretion. He barked out a command to those around me to give me a good smack on the mouth. I glared right back at him with such intensity 'til we were virtually locked in an extra ordinary visual battle. He obviously didn't know whom he was dealing with.

"Listen you white washed wall, God has already dealt with the likes of you! You sit here and think you can judge me according to all of your laws, rules, and regulations, and yet you're breaking those very same laws by ordering them to smack me around. How dare you?"

Let me give you some information about this "high priest." I've already told you his name was Ananias. His dad was Nedebaeus if that helps any. Ananias became the high priest as an appointment from Herod of Chalcis who was himself a brother of Herod Agrippa I. Of all the people who have served in this prestigious position Ananias had to be the worst of all.

He had even been recalled to Rome because the governor of Syria suspected he had something to do with an outbreak between the Jews and the Samaritans. Unfortunately for all, he was cleared of any wrong doing by Emperor Claudius thanks probably in large part to the advocacy of the younger Agrippa. The wealth Ananias amassed largely by unscrupulous, illegitimate methods of course made him a man to be feared. He was definitely not against using violence as a means to an end. Contract hits were certainly within his capability. Because he was so pro-Roman, Ananias did manage to make some major enemies within the Jewish community at large.

Unfortunately, you rarely get to find out what happens to some of these jerks so I might as well tell you what did eventually become of him. When war did break out against Rome, Ananias was captured from an aqueduct in which he had been trying to hide and put to death along with his nasty brother Hezekiah.

Poetic justice?

Anyway, back to the story. I wanted to tell you about the law I referred to. According to their law, "he who strikes the cheek of an Israelite, strikes, as it were, the glory of God." The rights of any Jewish defendant were carefully safeguarded in the Jewish law books. A man is to be innocent until proven guilty. I was very well aware of the fact I hadn't even been charged with anything yet, let alone been tried and convicted. Ananias knew exactly what I was saying!

Oh, about the "white washed wall" comment. This was pretty rough I must admit. Things considered contaminated to the Jews were washed with white paint so nobody would miss seeing them and be able to avoid them. This is why the sepulchers (grave sites) were always white washed. Who would want to touch something so unclean as a grave? Basically, I was telling Ananias to his face I had an unlimited amount of contempt for him as a high priest.

Talk about ticking someone else off! I was abruptly interrupted by a bunch of elders who were almost within striking range of me.

"Hey, watch your mouth! Don't you even know whom you are talking to? He's the "High Priest!" How dare you talk to him like this?"

I had to think quick. Discretion is a better part of valor.

"I'm sorry brothers," I stumbled, "I didn't realize a man who spoke like that could possibly be the high priest. Had I known, I certainly would have contained myself because I'm well acquainted the law is very clear, 'you ought not speak evil of a ruler of God's people.'"

Hey, I've been around the bush a few times myself. I'd spent enough time to survey my audience and peg them into their respective corners. I figured the best way to challenge them was to divide and conquer. You see, the assembled group of political, religious leaders were a mixture of Pharisees and Sadducees. You may find it a touch humorous to note when I began my next verbal assault I didn't bother to change my introduction.

"My fellow men and brothers, I'm a Pharisee, in fact, the son of a Pharisee. I'm a true champion of the best traditions of Judaism. If you're accusing me of preaching the ancestral hope of Israel is based on the resurrection of the dead, hey, then I am guilty."

I wish I had the nerve to show on my face how much I was laughing on the inside. Talk about causing a disturbance and confusion in my audience. I really opened up a jar of worms this time.

Let me tell you, when I said I believed the hope of all the people of God is dependent upon the resurrection of the dead, the place erupted in confusion. The gulf separating the two groups seemed to grow by the minute.

Pharisees and Sadducees were Jews. Make no mistake for they shared the same heritage. However, it would be a big mistake to think they operated on the same page. Major differences of belief and practice existed. Let me give you a few points to illustrate.

PHARISEES
- adhered to the minutest bits of
- followed written & oral laws, rules, and regulations
- believed in predestination
- believed in angels and spirits
- believed in the resurrection of the dead

SADDUCEES
- adhered only to the minutest bits of the written laws, rules, and regulations
- believed in free will
- didn't believe in angels nor a spirit world
- didn't believe in the resurrection of the dead

Look at the last one. Now do you see why I had aggravated a very sore spot between the two major factions of the audience?

The noise was almost deafening. At some point a group of high ranking Pharisees managed to get the upper hand perhaps simply because they were a larger group. At the top of their lungs they managed to get their point across.

"Look, this guy's 'NOT GUILTY' of anything. We find no evil or fault in this man. Maybe he has heard from an angel. Perhaps it was a spirit of some kind. Who are we to argue with God?"

The impasse was insurmountable. The Sanhedrin wasn't going to come to any conclusive decision that's for sure. I'm sorry. I just had to chuckle inside.

Claud probably was chuckling too. Anyway, he decided enough was enough. He probably thought I was going to be pulled to shreds in the melee. So he ordered the soldiers to intervene with force to separate the combatants and save me from harms' way. I was quickly hustled away back to the safe confines of the fortress prison.

Who ever thought a prison was a "safe" place to be?

Trip # 18
JERUSALEM TO CAESAREA

135. PLOT THICKENS
(Acts 23:11-32)

Restless is the best way to describe my sleep that night. All the commotion of the day brought an uneasy sense of security. However, I was convinced I'd be all right, remaining resolute to accept whatever happened to me. Perhaps the dream I had during the night reinforced this conclusion. It seemed so real. I recall vividly God walking beside me trying to cheer me up. I remember Him saying to me,

"Hey Paul, don't worry! Be happy! Look, you've been doing a great job telling everybody here in Jerusalem about my love for the whole world and now I need you to carry the same message all the way to Rome as well."

Well, the morning introduced a whole new set of activities. I guess I wasn't the only one who didn't get a whole lot of sleep! A large number of Jews must have laid awake in their sleeping bags scheming of a way to get rid of me. Ideas were hatched before the roosters got out of bed to do their thing. More than forty conspirators bound themselves together with the common purpose of undertaking a pledge to fast until I was done away with.

The vow was called a "cherem." Basically, if you took this vow you were saying, "May God curse me if I fail to do this!"

Yes, they meant business. A hastily arranged meeting with the chief priests and the elder statesmen of the politburo was convened to hear these determined folks.

The spokesman summed up their plan.

"Look, we've bound ourselves under this great vow we will not eat a thing until we've killed Paul, well aware of the curse we fall under if we fail. So, we implore the Sanhedrin to get in Commander Lysias' face to make sure Paul is brought before our court tomorrow. We think it's important you examine him more thoroughly to determine exactly what he's up to. You do your part and we'll do the rest. If he comes close enough we're as prepared as we are determined to kill him."

Well, I'm thankful these guys couldn't keep a secret of that magnitude. Obviously the details of the assassination attempt were leaked and word spread like wild fire.

PLOT THICKENS   TRIP # 18

Fortunately for me, one of the people who heard of the plot was my nephew, my sister's son. He had the smarts to know I was in deep doo-doo if he didn't get word to me as fast as he could. He headed straight for the Roman fortress and begged the guards for permission to speak to me. As soon as he told me what was up I called one of the military guards to come over.

"Listen, my nephew has something real important he has to tell Commander Claudius Lysias. Can you please take the young fellow to him so he can tell him the very important news."

The soldier was kind enough to consider my plea and took my nephew to the Commander right away. He delivered the introduction.

"Sir, Paul, you know, our prisoner, called me over and begged me to bring this young man to you because he has something very important you should know about."

The commander was definitely curious. He took my nephew by the arm, slowly guiding him to a more private area where they could talk in confidence.

"So, I hear you have something to tell me."

"Yes I do," said my nephew with a hint of brave naivete. "The Jews have hatched a plan to trick you into bringing Paul to their council chambers tomorrow under the guise of wanting to interrogate my uncle on their own turf. But, don't get sucked in by their conniving plot, for there are more than forty men who are just waiting to get their hands on Paul. They have bound themselves in an oath to engage in a hunger strike until Paul has been killed. They are ready and waiting for you to cave into the pressure from the head honchos so they can complete their assassination plan."

Commander Lysias was very happy my nephew had the courage to come and relate this news to him. He advised this fine young man to make an inconspicuous exit and then gave him the following advice.

"Hey, I don't want you to tell anybody you were even in here or that you told me anything about this. Ya hear?"

Claudius Lysias was no fool and he had no intention of being made to look like one. He had already done his homework on me. He knew if something would happen to me more than just a riot could break out. He could be accused of accepting bribes from the Jews, thereby being an accomplice in my death.

To complicate things more for him, I was as Roman as they come. He knew he had to tread softly, very softly.

I was about to find out how softly! Get this:
- two personal body guards
- 200 heavily armed soldiers
- 200 light infantrymen (spearmen)
- 70 cavalry (horse mounted) troops
- mules and horses to carry me and my things (as if I had many)

Think that's enough security for a little old dufus like me?

He called in my two bodyguards and gave the order to prepare the security force. The plan was to sneak (like they could sneak!) out of town under the cover of darkness at 9:00 P.M. so the Sanhedrin wouldn't have a clue what was happening.

The commander then wrote a letter to send along with the bodyguards. It was addressed to Felix, the procurator of Judaea. It probably read something like this:

> To: Felix, Most Excellent Governor of Judaea.
>
> Hey, Felix, old buddy, old pal. How ya doin? Got a little problem out here. Thought perhaps you could help.
>
> Got this fellow here named Paul. The Jews don't seem to like him all that much in fact, they have in mind to kill the poor sucker. I found out he was a Roman citizen so I happened to step in just in the nick of time. It took a small army to save him from the vicious crowds. I had a lot of trouble trying to find out exactly what the problem was and what Paul was being accused of, so I had the Sanhedrin call an emergency meeting to bring specific charges against him.
>
> Obviously, they were trying to drum up some kind of religious charges against him but I couldn't determine why he should be executed, or even imprisoned for that matter. I was informed of a plot against the life of Paul. Well, I didn't want to take any chances of trouble so I have sent him to you to examine his case. I'll inform his accusers if they want to bring charges against Paul they'll have to bring them before your honor.
>
> Good luck and many thanks!
> Best Regards,
> Claudius Lysias
> Commander, Jerusalem Division

Impressive is all I have to say. Can you just imagine the scene of some four hundred marching soldiers with some seventy horse mounted troops storming down the highway through the middle of the night guarding little old me and my dufflebag? The light from the oil pitched torches and the noise of the syncopated marching sounds must have caused anyone near to get out of bed and take notice.

We traveled, with some speed I might add, all the way at night to the town of Antipatris. This town, built by Herod the Great and named after his father Antipater, lay at the foot of the Judaean hills in the well-watered, wooded plain of Kaphar Saba. The thirty-five miles between Jerusalem and Antipatris was inhabited by Jews for the most part, so, if an attack was going to be mounted to kill me, this section of the journey would have been the best place to make an assault on the processional.

The trip, however, due to the cunning plan of Claud, was uneventful other than the obvious commotion it caused along the way. Since the remaining twenty-five miles or so to Caesarea was fairly open country, occupied mostly by Gentiles, it didn't make too much sense for the whole army to go all the way.

So the next morning I was escorted from Antipatris to Caesarea by only seventy horsemen.

Bummer!

I thought the extra four hundred guys were enjoying the holiday out of Jerusalem and now they had to go back to their routine duties in Jerusalem. Ha! I guess seventy soldiers on the fastest horses in our territory would just have to do! A bodyguard duty of four hundred and seventy armed soldiers was a little much, even for my standards. I almost felt quite honored by the precaution Claudius had taken for my protection.

136. BEFORE FELIX
(Acts 23:33-24:27a)

The escort delivered the letter of Commander Claudius Lysias into the hands of one Antonius Felix. Then they presented me to him like I was some kind of unexpected present. Of course, it didn't take very long for him to read the letter from Claud.

"So Paul, tell me, where'd you come from anyway?"

This was a very normal question to ask, consistent with Roman rules of procedure. Roman law allowed the accused to be tried either in his own native country or wherever the alleged crime was said to have been committed. Felix would have jurisdiction over me because he was procurator of Judea (where the "crime" was committed), as well as my administrative superior because he was a deputy of the legate of Syria and Cilicia. When I informed him I was from Tarsus of Cilicia he seemed satisfied he held my fate in his hands on either count.

"O.K. then," Felix proclaimed, "I'll hear your case when your accusers show up to present some evidence against you. Guards, take him away, and keep him secure in the palace of Herod."

Five days passed before Ananias the high priest and a bunch of his cronies finally showed up in Caesarea. They also brought a real piece of work by the name of Tertullus with them. He gave me the shakes, being a pompous, arrogant lawyer and all! Apparently he had a gift for the gab. It was just like the Jews to employ a professional Roman "causidicus" (lawyer) to plead their case against me.

As the hearing got under way Tertullus was given first crack by Felix to present their case. He started off with the conciliatory "captatio benevolentiae." Some folks refer to it as "brown nosing," "sucking up," or, more politely as "buttering up" the audience. I could tell Tertullus was very well experienced in the practice.

"Felix, your honor, thank you for seeing us. We owe to you personally, your excellency, a debt of gratitude to you because we're enjoying this time of lasting peace during your term of office."

Oh, gag me!

"We appreciate due to your foresight and planning the reforms you've initiated are succeeding in giving us a high standard of living the envy of every nation."

"We're happy to accept your contributions to our society. Most noble Felix, please accept our genuine thanks."

Almost makes you nauseous, don't it? Tertullus was just warming up!

"Now I know I could go on heaping praise on you, however, I also recognize you're a very busy man. So please, accept our thanks for hearing our complaints with your customary kindness."

"Essentially, we have three major charges to lay against this turkey, I mean, against Paul."

"First of all, we've determined he's a pestilent fellow, a trouble maker to boot. Civil disobedience seems to be his main objective for he incites sedition among the Jews wherever he travels throughout the world. Paul has traveled extensively inflaming the populace to rebel against authority. We're confident you won't stand for this kind of insurrection."

"Secondly, we've determined Paul is a ringleader of the revolutionary sect known as the 'Nazarenes,' or the 'Salvationalists.'

He's been linked with other Messianic movements as well. I'm sure you know full well what these little false messiahs are doing to whip the crowds into hysterical uprisings."

"While the first two charges primarily affect you and your jurisdiction, our third charge against Paul is the most serious, from our perspective of course. We've found him to bring offense against our most sacred traditions and we believe we have jurisdictional rights over these matters. We've found him to be in contempt of our Temple laws and boundaries. While we've had trouble proving he actually profaned the Temple by bringing a Gentile into the sacred precincts, we do believe we were in the process of stopping him before he could carry out his plan."

"Liar! Liar!" I felt like screaming it out, however, I bit my tongue.

"It was during this time when were going to arrest him to conduct our own trial that the chief captain Lysias, with no right to interfere I might add, sent his army among us, and, with an unjust amount of violence and harshness, took our prisoner away from us. Unfortunately, Lysias didn't have the guts to decide the fate of Paul on his own."

"He conveniently passed the buck to you, placing upon us the unnecessary, not to mention inconvenient, task of pleading our case before you. We're very confident when you've examined Paul firsthand and after you've heard all of the facts in the case you'll see the merit in our accusations and turn him back over to us."

The articulate Tertullus had crafted a marvelous argument to be sure. His argument was short and concise, delivered with flair and pizzazz. It certainly drew a thunderous response from all the Jews who hired him as their spokesperson. Wild cheers and hand clapping erupted throughout the halls of justice.

Felix looked over at me as if to say, "Well, you little wimp, what have you got to say for yourself." He beckoned me to make my pitch.

"Governor Felix, I know you're no dummy. You've been in power for a number of years now, very familiar with the administration of Judaea, accomplished in governing the Jewish nation with all its quirks. I have no problem letting you judge my fate. I trust your judgment."

Tertullus was certainly not the only one who knew how to win friends and influence people. I can flatter too when flattery is required.

"Let me tell you, from my perspective of course, what's going on here. My goodness, I've been away from Jerusalem for several years now. In fact, I had been back in Jerusalem to join in the celebrations of Pentecost for only twelve days! Tertullus and his buddies give me far too much credit for being able to stir up the masses in such a short amount of time."

"I confess to being guilty of being a worshiper as they themselves were. However, I certainly do plead not guilty to their charge I was a troublemaker. I had no disputes with anyone, nor did I incite anyone to riotous behavior, either in the synagogues, the Temple, nor anywhere else in Jerusalem."

"They can't prove any of these charges. In fact, they can't substantiate a single claim against me. They didn't bring any evidence to the Sanhedrin, to Commander Claudius Lysias, or to your honor. Where are those individuals who had a dispute with me? Where are the people who rioted? Get serious!"

I always figured the best defense is a good offense. I decided to go for the jugular.

"BUT, Felix I confess I am guilty of a number of things. Let me enumerate."

I could see the jaws of my Jewish accusers drop. They couldn't believe what I was doing.

"First, I confess to being a believer in the way of Jesus. The Jews may call this heresy. Let them. I worship the very One who established the family of God."

"Secondly, I believe as my accusers do in the God of my forefathers. I believe in everything recorded in the books of the law and in the books of the prophets."

"And third, and perhaps the most importantly, I confess to have hope in the future with God because of a resurrection of the dead in Jesus. Many of these fine fellows even believe this. Well, most of them do. The resurrection from the dead of the just and unjust alike is consistent with Jewish eschatalogical teaching, even if the Saducees have trouble with it."

"I'm confident I've done nothing, by word or by deed, to give me a bad conscious of offense towards God or my fellow man. In fact, my desire is for the good of all. I've just spent a significant amount of time traveling around raising donations of money and goods to alleviate the suffering of my own people in Jerusalem. Upon my arrival in Jerusalem for the Pentecost celebrations I was in the Temple worshiping like everyone else, participating in a ceremonial purification rite. I was neither causing a ruckus nor participating in a disturbance."

"It wasn't until a group of Jews from far a way Asia recognized who I was. Shoot, they weren't even from Jerusalem. They were outsiders, for Pete's sake. If they have something against me, why aren't they here to accuse me? They could have brought charges against me in front of the Sanhedrin in fact. Hey, were they even there? No! Perhaps they were offended by the fact I boldly declared I believe in the resurrection of the dead."

"If that's the only reason why I'm standing before you today they have a pretty lame argument against me. In fact, I see the problem. We're not facing a political problem here. We have a doctrinal issue at the core of the dispute. They can't even agree amongst themselves about it. I appeal to your sense of fairness. Let's just forget the whole thing. Dismiss the case against me and let me go home."

Felix, as I had told him to his face, was indeed no dummy. He was intelligent enough to know what the Jews were up to. He was a lot more familiar with Jewish traditions and with the up and coming groups of believers in the way of Jesus than most gave him credit for. I think his Jewish wife Drusilla, sister of Herod Agrippa II and granddaughter of Antony and Cleopatra had given Felix a great deal of background information.

As an aside, Drusilla's first husband had been Aziz, king of Emesa. It took the assistance of a Cypriot magician named Atomus for Felix to seduce her away from Aziz. This Felix character was no slouch when it came to conniving and getting his way. A real fine, upstanding, moral person, at least in his own mind.

It didn't take a long time for Felix to make up his mind to hand down his decision. Sit on it! That's right. He tabled his ruling for another day.

"Look, I'd like to hear some more testimony before I render my decision. I will announce it after Commander Claudius Lysias comes down here to Caesarea to inform me further concerning the case against Paul."

Bummer. Here I thought I'd be let go. Instead, I was placed under military house arrest.

The Romans called it "custodia liberior."

I was safeguarded from my accusers until such time as the trial would be convened without being subjected to the discomfort of a public jail. I was able to receive friends and communicate with virtually whomever I wanted to. I actually had quite a bit of freedom of movement too. However, I did have a bodyguard who went with me wherever I went. To tell the truth, I actually felt a whole lot more secure having soldiers responsible for my safety.

On occasion, I was able to meet with Felix and his wife Drusilla. We had more than one occasion to chew the fat, so to speak. We discussed a number of issues including the faithfulness of Jesus to the plan of God. I had the privilege of talking to Felix about things he really didn't want to hear about. He wasn't too keen to discuss righteousness, self-control, nor the impending judgment of God that had been averted in Jesus. I'm sure I scared him a bit as I challenged his systems of beliefs and practices.

Refusing to face up to my challenging way of thinking Felix chose the path of procrastination by putting me off.

BEFORE FELIX   TRIP # 18

"Look Paul, I think we'd better agree to disagree. You go your way and I'll go my way for a while. I'll be in touch. We'll get together again another time perhaps."

Don't give too much credit to Felix. Remember he was a real sneaky character. I wouldn't put it past him to sweet talk me with the hope he could extract some kind of bribe out of me. Perhaps he had the misguided impression I could convince my supporters to come up with some hush money and do an under the table deal to secure my release.

So we got together quite often for these little chit0chats. I never bit the bait he was dangling in front of me.

This went on for about two years!

Can you believe it?

Two years!

137. FESTUS TAKES OVER
(Acts 24:27-25:12)

Unfortunately for Felix civil war broke out in Caesarea between the Jewish and Gentile inhabitants. At issue was the status of the city of Caesarea. Was it a Jewish city or was it a Greek city? Felix lost control of the situation as the Jewish faction seemed to gain the upper hand. Literally hundreds, perhaps thousands of innocent people, mostly Jews, lost their lives. To add insult to injury Felix gave his encouragement and consent for the troops to loot and sack the homes of some of the wealthiest people (Jews) in the city. The Jews retaliated by ratting on Felix. Yes, they reported his actions to the authorities in Rome.

Felix was recalled to Rome and given what could be best described as a court martial. Only because of the intervention of his brother Pallas was Felix saved from execution. His one last gesture of goodwill towards the Jews, and it was only so he could get at least a measure of sympathy, was to leave me entangled in the legal system instead of giving me my outright release. Perhaps it was because I didn't pay him off. I certainly have my suspicions, however, I don't really know for sure.

The new governor was left with the problem of sorting out the mess Felix had left for him. I just happened to be one of those problems.

Porcius Festus was his name.

My first impression of "Porky" was that he was a descent sort with the capacity to be somewhat honorable, in spite of the fact he was a little green under the collar. I think Porky was given a job a little above his head.

Oh well, I had no choice except to give him a chance.

Three days after he took power he was off on his first diplomatic mission. He knew he'd better see how things were going over in Jerusalem. It was appropriately obligatory he pay a visit to the chief priest and the Sanhedrin for it provided both sides with the opportunity of sizing each other up.

I became a major topic of discussion given the Jews were pretty much obsessed with my case. Up until now they'd been discouraged at every turn in their desire to see me handed back into their jurisprudence. With a greenhorn CEO they presumed they could rekindle their pet project, my demise.

FESTUS TAKES OVER   TRIP # 18

The religious leaders petitioned Porky to release me into their hands. They informed him the most serious charges against me were religious in nature rather than political so they were best suited to try me in their own court. No doubt another plot to kill me was probably in the works to keep me from ever seeing the sunrise on any scheduled trial date.

Thank goodness Porky had the Roman instinct for justice. His response to their petition? I would remain in custody in Caesarea, the capital city for the civil government. Porky told them he was going to return to Caesarea very soon and if any of them felt up to it they could return with him and lay charges against me in Caesarea.

So, after ten days or so Porky did return to Caesarea. In tow were the Jewish band with a legion of legal advisors. It certainly didn't take him long to get my case moved up the docket schedule. The day after they got back to town I was hustled into the courtroom under the watchful eyes of my guards, not to mention the glazed stares of my Jewish accusers.

All these buck-toothed buckaroos circled round about me like a pack of wolves ready to pounce on their prey. Porky allowed them time to make their accusations and lay their charges. Hey, half the stuff I know they just made up. I guess they figured the new guy wouldn't know all the facts anyway so why not just go for the gusto.

I knew they couldn't prove any of the charges they laid against me. In my own defense I informed Porky I had committed no crimes against the laws of the Jews, I had not violated the sanctity of the temple, nor had I stirred up the crowds by inciting an insurrection against Caesar nor the Roman people.

Porky apparently was shrewd enough to look for any possible way out of a jam he could find. The bottom line for him was to search for a way of putting himself in the best positive light to the Jewish delegation. I believe they call it "ingratiation." Porky put the question to me in rather simple question.

"Paul, would you be willing to travel up to Jerusalem to be judged in a trial proceeding in which I would be the judge?"

You must remember I had a great deal of time over the past number of years to consider a great number of possible scenarios. I had considered a wide variety of possibilities like it was a game just to pass the time. However, I didn't have a whole lot of time to waste as I prepared my response to Porky's question. I didn't exactly like the odds of this Jerusalem idea.

Porky was certainly a new player in the game, however, I was unsure I could trust his impartiality in front of the hostile environment which surely would envelope any proceeding in Jerusalem.

My hand was forced to play the only card that would give me a fighting chance of staying in the game. The likelihood of Porky abdicating his role of impartiality for the expedient opportunity of sucking up to the Jewish establishment was all too apparent for a seasoned veteran like me.

My last recourse was to appeal to Rome on the basis of my Roman citizenship. Hey, I always wanted to go to Rome anyway, right? Besides, the Jews would certainly have a much harder time mounting a campaign against me way over there.

"Thanks Festus, but no thanks!" I responded. "Look, I'd rather not go back to Jerusalem if you don't mind. I'm a Roman citizen and I have the right to be tried in a Roman court of law before Caesar himself. I haven't done anything wrong to the Jews as you well know, so I don't see any reason why I should have to be tried by them."

"If I've truly done something wrong to someone, or if I've committed a crime punishable by death, hey, I'm not afraid to accept the consequences of my actions, even if it means the death penalty."

"BUT, these clowns don't have a leg to stand on with these senseless accusations. They can't prove a thing. I refuse to give in their shenanigans. There's no way I want to be delivered into their jurisdiction."

"With all due respect, I prefer once again to appeal to Caesar."

I know this option didn't leave Porcius Festus anywhere to go. My appeal had serious implications in Roman law. The appeal to Caesar (Ad Caesarem Prouoco) was only invalid if you were a murderer, a pirate, or if you were a thief caught in the very act. Since I was none of the above, any litigation against me locally was to be stopped and I would have to be dispatched to Rome for the personal intervention of the top dog!

Porky let the entire assemblage know his hands were now tied. He could not have been more keenly aware I had just given him the break he was looking for. He couldn't have been so stupid as not to realize I had just made his job a whole lot easier.

FESTUS TAKES OVER   TRIP # 18

I had given him, on a silver platter, a way of escaping from a very difficult, disagreeable challenge to his authority. Relishing his new lease on life Porky didn't take long to spout out his legal determination.

"So, you want to appeal to Caesar do you?" he inquired of me with what he presumed to be a rhetorical question. "Well, O.K. then. To Caesar you shall go!"

Wow!

I almost thought I'd won the lottery or something. An all expenses paid trip to Rome! Who'd have thought this would be the way I'd finally get to see Rome?

Well, certainly not in my wildest dreams.

138. BEFORE HEROD AGRIPPA II
(Acts 25:13-26:1)

Let me tell you about my next important brush with royalty. I was about to have an opportunity of seeing nobility I hadn't counted on meeting. Agrippa the king, along with Bernice were coming to Caesarea to pay a visit to their comrade and neighbor, Porcius Festus.

His correct name was Herod Agrippa II. Don't forget the "II."

He was the son of, you guessed it, Herod Agrippa I. As a matter of fact, he was the great grandson of Herod the Great. His father (Agrippa I) had been the king of all Judaea and will go down in history as having been the first royal persecutor of those who believed in Jesus. When he died quite suddenly in the city of Caesarea his son Agrippa II was only seventeen years old. Unfortunately for him, the Emperor Claudius accepted the counsel of his staff not to appoint Agrippa II as the successor. Judaea was instead placed under the administration of a procurator, the office that Festus now held.

Agrippa II wasn't left empty handed though. Upon the death of his uncle Herod, the king of Chalcis, Agrippa II was granted the rule over the small kingdom. Some time later he gave up this territory in exchange for a larger one, including the former tetrarchies of Philip and Lysanias. Nero even enlarged it some more by adding to it a number of cities and towns around the Lake of Galilee. Agrippa II was so tickled he changed the name of his capital city Caesarea Philippi to "Neronias" in a classic case of political correctness. Others saw it as brown nosing.

One of the major cash cows of his rule resulted as he became entrusted with the custody of the Jewish Temple treasury. In addition, he assumed the role of appointing the rather influential post of "high priest." No doubt this gave him a very prominent role to play in the affairs of the Jews. So Agrippa II became a "suckee" as well as a "sucker."

Bernice mustn't be forgotten in the mix. She wasn't the wife of Agrippa II, however, she may have been the wife or mistress of just about any other important person you could find. Most recently, she had been the wife of the deceased Herod of Chalcis, younger brother of Herod Agrippa I. In reality, she was the daughter of Herod Agrippa I.

That's right.

This made her the sister of Agrippa II at the very same time she was his auntie. Although a year younger than him, Agrippa II could easily call her "sis," or "Auntie Bernice."

This falls into the "strange but true" file. Hey, that's not all.

In addition to being the sister of Agrippa II, Bernice was also the older sister of Drusilla. Who's Drusilla? How soon you forget. Drusilla was the wife of Porky Festus.

Get the picture?

What we were about to have was somewhat of a family reunion. Throw in some political protocol and you have a reason to write off the expenses of the trip as a legitimate business expenditure.

So, if Drusilla was a Jew, does this mean Agrippa II and Bernice were Jews too? Well, there must have been some Jewish blood mixed in there somewhere. Don't kid yourselves though, they were bred and raised in the inner circles of Roman society, fully prepared to gorge themselves in the pomp and ceremony of any circumstance!

It seems Agrippa II and Bernice planned to stay a little longer than they had intended. They must have been having a great time together. Obviously Porky couldn't resist the temptation to confer with his brother in law to give him some advice concerning the problem festering under his command, ME!

I can just imagine the conversation.

"Hey Grip, I'd like to talk to you about this character Felix sluffed off on me to deal with. I was up on business in Jerusalem when the chief priests and Jewish elders approached me to hand this character Paul over to them so they could judge him in their own courts. Of course, I advised them we weren't predisposed to comply with their every wish and whim. It just isn't like us Romans to simply hand someone over to a sure death sentence before they have at least a chance to defend themselves face to face with their accusers before the noose is ready to drop. So I told them they could come to Caesarea if they wanted to and I'd hear the case myself. Sure enough, they showed up the next day after I got back. I hastily arranged the courtroom and had Paul brought in to sit in the prisoner's box for the trial."

"Man, I thought they were going to accuse Paul of some heavy duty offenses. Ha, what a joke! Was I ever wrong. I don't think they could prove any of the ridiculous charges they brought against him."

"Their problems with this guy were obviously religious in nature because they claimed he had ridiculed their superstitious laws, rules, and regulations. They also took pot shots at some guy by the name of Jesus who was supposed to be dead, and yet, Paul claimed was actually alive. Go figure."

"The whole thing seemed a bit absurd to me. I really doubted the logic of the entire line of questioning by the Jewish legal team so I asked Paul if he wanted to go back to Jerusalem to be tried in the Jewish courts. I thought we might have a better chance of hearing from some credible witnesses back there. Paul didn't take too kindly to my offer. I can't say I was all that surprised. Instead, as a Roman citizen, he chose to reserve the right to appeal directly to the big guy (Caesar Augustus). I had no choice but to grant Paul his wish. Right now he's under my jurisdiction until I can get him sent off to Rome."

"My problem is if I send Paul off to Rome I'm going to have egg all over my face if I don't have a descent case against the guy. Hey, the big fellow is going to think I'm a bit whacked if I can't even explain why I went to the incredible trouble and expense of sending him to Rome in the first place. You understand the Jews better than I do. Can you at least talk to Paul and see what you think?"

"Pretty please?"

I'm sure Porky must have said "Pretty please?" It sounds just like him. Well, always the hero, Agrippa II must have been eager for the challenge.

"Sure Porky," (hey, that's my nickname for him) "set up a meeting. I'd be glad to give you my advice. Name the time and place as soon as you can 'cause Bernice and I can't stay here forever. How 'bout tomorrow?"

"No problem!"

Putting on the Ritz!

This King Agrippa II really knew how to throw a short conversation with a little itinerant preacher into a real media opportunity. The press corps was there in force. And what a scene they witnessed. I'll bet one needed some special security passes to get through the security laced gates of the courthouse. The rich, the famous, and the well connected no doubt received special invitations to the pomp and ceremony. Crack military leaders were lined up like fence posts in full regalia.

Political leaders like the mayor and city councillors were seated in order of importance. Of course the appropriate collection of religious leaders garbed in all the piety they could muster were also in attendance.

In came King Herod Agrippa II with his sister (auntie) Bernice at his side. Announced by trumpeters and heralded by banner wavers they made their pompous way to the front of the elegant room. In true regal fashion they were guided along to their thrones.

The meeting was called into order, by none other than Porcius Festus, as soon as the royal highnesses took their seats.

I had been allowed to watch the elegant procession from the side of the great hall and at the command of Porky I was brought into the prisoner's box before Agrippa II and Bernice.

Ask me if I felt a little out of place.

"Did you feel a little out of place?"

You bet, and thanks for asking!

Here I was, just a small, shriveled up little Jewish/Roman tent maker who sidelined as a spokesman for the gospel of the grace and peace of God, sitting in front of the king of the land. The least they could have done was dress me up a bit for the occasion. The standard issue prison garb wasn't exactly the get up I'd have picked for such an auspicious event.

None-the-less, I was not intimidated in the least by these circumstances. I remained steadfast in the confidence of my innocence and undeterred by all the fuss over my case. I knew the decision of my fate lay far beyond the determination of these little puppets of Rome.

Porky began his address to Agrippa II with sufficient dribble and posturing to make it impossible for the entire assemblage to leave complaining they didn't get their money's worth.

"King Herod Agrippa II, and all invited guests, I welcome you all. Let's get right to the point. We're gathered here today to undertake an examination of the man seated in the prisoner's box in front of us. His name, as you well know by now, is Paul. I've been petitioned by the Jewish leaders, both in Jerusalem as well as here in Caesarea, to have Paul executed."

"I've come to the conclusion, after hearing their case against him and his defense of their charges, that Paul has committed no crime and is guilty of no offense worthy of the death penalty."

"Paul has used his legal right and his prerogative to make application for his case to be taken up by the Emperor Augustus himself. I have no choice except to send him to Rome. Unfortunately, I really don't have anything to charge him with when I write to his majesty."

"With this problem in mind, I've requested my good Roman colleague and friend, Herod Agrippa II, hear for himself more about Paul and his case. I'm hoping that you, esteemed guest, will be able to assist me in formulating some kind of accusation against Paul.

It surely doesn't seem reasonable or prudent to send a prisoner to Rome without at least some kind of written documents outlining the charges laid against him."

Now, this little setup speech by Porky surely was not for the sake of good ol' Grip the II. He knew very well what was going down and he was not going to let a great opportunity like this to go by without milking it for everything he could get out of it. They don't call it politics for nothing!

It didn't take too long for the big Gripper to size me up. I'm positive he knew more about me than he let on. He was very well aware of who I was and what I'd been up to. He had to have enough snoops in the Jewish community to know of my background. He was equally aware of the rapid growth of this movement which professed belief in the life and works of Jesus, and no doubt, of my involvement in the spread of His message of God's love.

He appeared genuinely anxious to hear what I had to say. What he was unprepared for was my enthusiasm to tell Jesus' side of the story to whoever would listen to it, royalty included! King Herod Agrippa II looked over to me and proceeded to give me his blessing to speak.

"Paul, thanks for coming out."

As if I had a choice!

"I understand you're having a big problem with the authorities over here these days. Well, I'd like to hear you out."

With a composed gesture of regal importance he stretched out his arms towards me and continued,

"Please Paul, go ahead. Tell me whatever you want to say. I give you my permission to defend yourself at this time."

Finally I was given another great opportunity to tell my piece of God's peace. So I let him have it!

139. **TAKING THE STAND**
(Acts 26:2-29)

"I'm actually a happy camper, King Agrippa. You've granted me a great privilege and opportunity to appear before you today to answer any of your questions and to defend myself against all the ridiculous and scandalous charges the Jews have leveled against me."

I figured it never hurts to start out on a positive note. I was about to embark on one of the most important speeches I'd ever deliver, and since I'd been given the floor, not to mention a captive audience, (ain't that a switch!) I figured I might as well make the most of the opportunity. In my own grand, regal fashion I stretched out my arms to beckon the attention of everyone in the great hall.

"I truly appreciate the willingness of your highness to hear my defense. I'm very well aware of who you are and am especially pleased you've shown both wisdom and experience in dealing with the customs and disputes which exist among the Jewish people. Therefore, I'm honored you've agreed to patiently hear me out."

"It's not like almost every important Jew doesn't know who I am. On the contrary, they're very familiar with me and have been since I was a very young man. I literally grew up in Jerusalem, educated and trained at the very highest levels concerning the laws, traditions, and customs of Jewish culture. I'd even go so far as to say if you put almost any Jew worth his salt on the stand they'd have to testify to the fact I lived an exemplary life as a Pharisee, becoming as strict and obedient to the laws, rules, and regulations as they come. I talked the talk and I walked the walk."

This tactic of splitting hairs worked once before so I thought I might as well give it a shot again. Pharisees were adamant believers in the resurrection of the dead, recognizing the ancient hope of Israel was inseparable from the reality of a resurrection. My defense depended on arguing similarities over differences.

"I can hardly believe I now stand here before you being judged for declaring the great news of Jesus, the hope of the promise which God issued to our forefathers. The promise of a redeemer, by the way, was given of God to the all twelve tribes of our people, giving hope to generation after generation."

"Day and night the promise of God has given folks a sense of purpose and meaning to life."

"My goodness, King Agrippa, I'm now being accused by my Jewish peers of the religious equivalent of being a traitor, all because I unreservedly and unashamedly spread the great, good news of the very One God promised, for He has indeed come and is truly the only hope of the whole world."

"Go figure!"

"Why in the world should it be such a stretch for you to think it's within the capability of God to raise His promise, Jesus, from the dead?"

"Well, let me tell you, I didn't think it was possible myself for a long time. I actually thought it was my mission in life to do as many things as possible completely contrary to everything the name of Jesus of Nazareth stands for. I created most of my havoc within the city of Jerusalem itself. I sent lots of folks to prison with the authority and blessing of the chief priests themselves. Before they were persecuted to the point of execution for opposing our view of God's plan for mankind it was I who testified against them to seal their fate."

"I set about to punish anyone who acknowledged this Jesus of Nazareth as the promise of God as often as I could, in every synagogue where they dared to show up. I forced them to admit their blasphemy against the laws, rules, and regulations we held as a sacred trust for our people. These radicals really ticked me off! The more their numbers increased, the more angry and zealous I became to crush them wherever they could be found, even if it meant I had to track them down in cities I'd never been to before."

"As an emissary and ambassador, carrying with me the authority and commissioning of the chief priests of the Sanhedrin, I was approaching the city of Damascus. In the middle of the day, O King, when the light and heat of the day challenged our resolve to continue I saw on the road in front of me a light coming down from the sky. It was a light that seemed far brighter than even the brightness of the sun shining round about me and those traveling with me on this mission to eradicate some more traitors."

"All of us stumbled to the ground in amazement and fear."

"Suddenly I heard a voice speaking to me in my own Hebrew tongue, 'Saul, Saul, why are you persecuting me? It mustn't be easy for you to constantly kick against the spikes.'"

"Kick against the spikes."

What the heck! Where did that come from?

Well, let me explain.

Attempting to get a yoke onto a young ox wasn't exactly an easy chore. The ox would always try to kick himself out of the yoke until he got used to it. One of the methods to train the ox into submission was the use of a "goad." If you had an ox yoked to a one handed plough, the farmer would hold in his free hand a long stick with a sharpened end to hold close to the heel of the ox. Every time the ox would try to kick it was jabbed by the spike. If the ox was yoked to a cart or wagon, the front of the wagon was equipped with a bar studded with wooden spikes that poked the poor ox if it rebelliously kicked against it. The obvious application of this illustration was to question the stupidity of rebellion against a force far greater than one's own effort.

"Recognizing the incredible magnitude of what I had just heard I could only question, 'My God, who's that?' Well, I got the answer back pretty quick."

"'You're right! It's me. I am Jesus, the One you are persecuting. Get up, and stand on your own two feet for I have appeared to you for a very good reason. I want to make you an emissary and ambassador of mine, to be a witness and testimony both of what you've already come to understand of Me and also of the many things I will continue to show you. I've delivered you from the folly of the wisdom of mankind and from the hopelessness of the Gentiles to whom I'm now sending you. I want you to open eyes to the reality of God's love, to turn folks from the panic and futility of darkness to the light and warmth of the hope in the promise of God, and to turn them from the powerful deception and confusion of self-righteousness to the matchless grace and peace of God. Why you ask? So all may know and understand the reality their sins are forgiven and so all may appreciate the inheritance God has blessed them with because of the faith in Me.'"

"Since then, O King Agrippa, I haven't been disobedient to this heavenly vision."

"BUT, I've carried out this mission first of all to the Jews in Damascus, then in Jerusalem, later throughout all the coasts of Judaea, and ultimately also to the Gentiles. My challenge to all folks is simple: repent from the deceit of self-righteous, turn to accept the free gift of God's grace and peace, and then start living the kind of lives revealing the righteousness of God He has placed within all because of Jesus."

"This message of hope in Jesus is the very reason the Jews seized me in the temple and thereafter set in motion a plan to have me executed. Knowing and understanding I've received the gift of God's righteousness I continue to this day to witness to folks both great and small in the eyes of mankind saying nothing else than those very same things that the prophets and Moses foretold would happen."

"What did they say?"

"That Jesus, the 'Anointed One,' would suffer and die and that He'd also be the first who'd actually rise again from the dead. It would be Jesus who would be the light of the Jews, as well as the Gentiles."

I was just rolling merrily along in my defense when I was rather rudely interrupted by good old Porky barreling out in his unmistakable loud bark.

"Hey Paul, are you whacked, or what? You must have been hitting the books pretty hard to come up with some of this stuff. Me thinks you've gone mad!"

"Well most noble Festus, I'm not mad." I retorted in confidence. "BUT, I'm only proclaiming the logical words of truth and intelligence. Listen, the good King here knows of these things and I'm not ashamed to speak freely before him. I'm persuaded nothing of what I've said is new to him, for all of these things haven't happened in some kind of vacuum or in some corner where nobody would notice them."

I turned my attention back to King Agrippa.

"King Agrippa, do you believe what the prophets had to say? I know you believe at least this much."

The old Gripper knew I was painting him into a place where he was feeling a tad uncomfortable.

"Look Paul, you've almost persuaded me to become a follower of Jesus."

"Well," I replied, "I just wish to God not only you, BUT, everyone else who has heard me in this hall today would come to the same understanding of God's view and opinion of mankind as I have come to, and would realize God sees each and every person in exactly the same way as He does me."

I thought I'd throw in just a little humor to lighten the mood.

"Although I must admit I'd rather He didn't have to see me in these chains like this!"

Trip # 19
CAESAREA TO ROME

140. OFF TO ROME
(Acts 26:30-27:26)

My appearance before King Agrippa, Porcius Festus, Bernice, Drusilla, and the rest of the entourage came to an abrupt conclusion with my last remark. They all had a good chuckle. In spite of my quick wit, I was confident they had heard the good news of God's love for all mankind and were certainly left with something to think about.

As soon as the King bolted from his makeshift throne, Porky, Bernice, and all the other puppets rose to follow him. I'll just bet lunch was being served in some banquet facility in another corner of the palace. No doubt I was the topic of discussion around the bar-b.

Inside sources informed me of some of the gossip. Apparently someone echoed the common agreement when they were heard to say, "This guy hasn't done anything worthy of death, nor even of being incarcerated." Apparently Grip had even told Porky, "If I had kept my mouth shut and not appealed to Caesar he would have set me free."

Well, if I hadn't made the appeal to Caesar I'm convinced I'd have been a goner by now. The only way I survived the contract on my life was under the protection of the Roman military, therefore, being kept under house arrest was undoubtedly the best possible alternative for me. I'm sure the Jews were thoroughly ticked off with the knowledge I was allowed this option. Moreover, I was being sent on an all expenses paid trip to the center of the Roman universe far, far away from Jerusalem, the center of their little world.

Preparations were made to have me transferred to Rome posthaste. I don't think they could get me out of their any faster since my little chat with the Gripper was over. The decision was made to send me off with the next batch of prisoners on the very next floating jail. Along with a group of other lucky stiffs I was handed into the "care" and "keeping" of a Roman centurion by the name of "Julius."

He was really a nice sort and I felt instantly like we were going to get along. No, I didn't nickname him "Juli." I affectionately referred to him as "Julius Maximus," or "JM" for short. He was quite amused by my incredible sense of humor. At least somebody was!

OFF TO ROME   TRIP # 19

Julius came from a special corps of liaison officers known as the "Augustan Cohort," acting more like sheriffs than military personnel between the Emperor and the provinces.

The ship we boarded came from the city of Adramyttium, way over in the area of Troas, north of Ephesus. The island of Lesbos lies just off the mainland coast where Adramyttium is located. You may recall I passed by there before. The ship was scheduled to make a number of pit stops along the way until it arrived by in its home port.

I was especially blessed to be allowed to bring with me two of my best buddies. It goes almost without saying it was absolutely super to have Doc Luke with me. He tended to my spirit as much as to my physical well being. Aristarchus was also permitted to travel with us. Remember him?

He was from Thessalonica over in Macedonia and was with Gaius and me when we got turfed in Ephesus by Demetrius and his silversmith cronies. Ari was also one of the fellows who accompanied me as we brought the gifts and donations to Jerusalem. He hung in there with me through this whole sordid affair. I was extremely relieved to know Doc and Ari would be able to accompany me all the way to Rome.

On the second day of our trip we arrived in the port of Sidon, about sixty-nine miles north of Caesarea. The town was actually situated on a small hill projecting into the Mediterranean about twenty-five miles north of Tyre. Trade was still an important part of the economy of Sidon because folks from all over the world treasured the fabrics that the "purple" industry had created. The forest industry was sustained by the persistent demands for the diminishing supply of wood products from the fantastic cedar forests around Sidon.

Did you know Jesus preached in the area at one time?

JM was very good to us all, and especially lenient towards me. He was very sympathetic to my situation, taking quite a liking to me. Surely it must have been my great character and pleasant disposition. JM even caved into our request we be allowed to head off into town to grab a bite to eat and to hopefully meet with some friends of ours in the area. He was pretty confident we weren't about to miss the boat.

Literally!

We launched from Sidon heading north, northwest past the island of Cyprus. Since the summer winds were predominantly westerly or northwesterly it was easier to sail around the eastern side of the island.

Remember, when we were going back to Jerusalem we went on the west southern side. I hadn't been this way since I came home from a missionary journey eons ago. Eventually, we came to the coast of Cilicia and Pamphylia where we had to stay fairly close to land so the offshore breezes could help us westward.

Our port of call in Lycia was the city of Myra. Myra was one of the six largest, most influential cities in the Lycian confederation however it was made the capital city of the Roman province of Lycia. Myra was situated on the River Andracus about two and a half miles in from the sea. The good harbor port town of Andriaca was commonly considered to be a part of Myra. It was here we left the ship that would continue on up the coast to Adramyttium.

JM had arranged for us to board a larger governmental vessel carrying grain, corn, and other supplies to Italy from the supply depots in Egypt. I had this funny feeling it was going to be a long trip. It took us several days bucking the wind just to get as far as Cnidus. It's always easiest for the captains of the ships to navigate close to the mainland with enough areas to set anchor in secluded harbors, and because they could get points of reference from the various elevations of the mountains.

Cnidus was a port on the Carian promontory of Triopium. The captain had one of two choices to make at this point. First, he could either stay in the larger of the two ports that could easily handle a ship of this size to wait it out for a good wind to come so we could sail due west for the island of Cythera at the bottom tip of Achaia. The captain's second choice, if he didn't just want to sit around twiddling his thumbs, was to make a run for the eastern extremity of the island of Crete near Salome, then sail along the southern coast of the island.

The choice?

Door number two!

The captain must have had some kind of bonus clause in his contract because he was definitely in no mood to sit tight.

Coasting along the south of Crete (coasting, hey that's a good one) was very difficult with the wind blowing from the northwest. We finally made it to a tranquil little bay known as "Fair Havens." Quite appropriate name I thought. Quite a beautiful little stop if I do say so myself. It wasn't very far away from a city named Lasea. Just around the corner from Fair Havens the land proceeds sharply north where you could get the full blast of the northwesterly winds.

OFF TO ROME TRIP # 19

It was getting late in the year as even the Jews had now completed the fasting celebrations of the great Day of Atonement in early October. Shipping season normally ground to a halt between the time from say September 14 until about November 11. Anyone who dared sail during this time was really taking their chances. It was now time important decisions would have to be made.

"Go?" or "Not to go?" These are the two questions the captain faced.

Even though I wasn't asked, and even though my advice probably wouldn't count for much, I still figured it was worth chucking in my two shekels worth. Hey, I was a seasoned, veteran tourist and since my skin was on the line here too I owed it to myself, JM, Doc, and Ari to stand up for our safety concerns. I put on my travel agent badge and proceeded to offer the captain the benefit of my counsel.

"Gentlemen, gentlemen. It's my humble opinion we'd better stay put. If we continue on, even if we only go as far as the safe harbor of Phoenix some forty miles west of here, you'll not only be putting at risk your ship with its considerable cargo, you'll be endangering the lives of everyone on board."

Unfortunately, JM didn't see eye to eye with me on this one. Instead, he sided with the captain and owner of the ship. I don't know, maybe it was because I was just a natty old prisoner. What did I know anyway about sailing? I guess they figured Fair Havens wasn't exactly enough of a "haven" to spend an entire winter at. The decision was made to travel at least to Phoenix to comfortably sit out the nasty weather in a reasonable among of comfort.

A pleasant turn of events made their decision much easier for them. The south winds came up and they obviously thought they'd have no trouble lifting anchor and sailing along the coastline.

We didn't get very far when we hit headlong into an incredible wind from the northeast. Wicked is all I have to say. Technically it was called either an "euroclydon," or an "euraquilo." Whatever. It's a contemptuous mixture of winds from both the north and the east reeking havoc on the helpless waves of the sea. All you could see, if you were brave enough to look, was the symphonic billowing and whirling motion of the clouds and the sea the contrary currents of air were causing.

All, you know what, broke loose.

When we came around Cape Matala we lost the protection of the shoreline. You just knew we were in trouble.

No matter what the crew did it seemed like the ship was destined to let Mother Nature give the orders. They decided to let her fly, I mean sail, on her own.

You probably have no idea what a corn ship looks like. Well, it was usually about 140 feet long, 36 feet wide, with a draught of about 33 feet. Looking at it you couldn't tell the front from the rear of the vessel since both ends had the goose necked shape common to these cargo ship. Since there wasn't a functional rudder mechanism, two great paddles emanating from the stern, one on each side, had to handle the steering chores. It's no wonder a storm would put the vessel at a grave disadvantage. Sometimes, literally!

The other disadvantage of the ship was the sail. There was one large, square sail. Ours was made of linen. Others were made of stitched hides. It was tied to only one mast. Sailing into the wind was an impossibility. The worst thing about the single mast concept is that it places too much of a strain on the timber construction of the vessel. To stop it from floundering the ship had to be frapped by placing hawser cables under the ship, tightened up with winches like you would wrap a parcel to make sure everything stayed inside during postal delivery.

We ended up about twenty-three miles off course near the small island of Cauda. We finally ran into some calm waters on the leeward side of the island. This gave the crew some very much-needed time to get reorganized. Everybody pitched in by scurrying around trying to get the ship secure once again. Normally the ship's dingy life raft would just be towed behind the ship.

It was so full of water by this time we had a bummer of a time yanking on the rope to get her close enough to bail her out and bring it safely on board. Other members of the crew struggled to winch all the bracing cables as tight as possible.

The peril of this kind of gale was well known for the inability of a crew to gain control of any floundering vessel would surely result in the ship being blown inevitably upon the Syrtis Sands, the quick sands off the North Africa coast near Cyrene. This mariner gravesite has often been called the "Goodwin Sands of the Mediterranean." Just the thought of this possible destination scared the living daylights out of even the hardiest of sailors. The captain certainly didn't need to resort to giving any hostile threats to get his crew into action.

The sails were also prepared for the next round of storms sure to hit us once again as we passed the calming influence of the island.

They lowered the large main sail onto a lower deck. The storm sails were set into place with the hope they would help us claw our way back on coarse. The captain set the ship with her right side to the wind so the storm sails could assist her to drift slowly at a speed of about one and a half miles per hour in a direction about eight degrees north of west.

The calm didn't last very long. When we hit open water again the tempest tossed us from side to side. What a ride!

The next day the captain gave orders for the crew to start throwing unnecessary equipment overboard to lighten the ship. Anything on deck that seemed obstructive got the heave ho. By the third day the captain was giving orders to all of the passengers to give the crew a hand in throwing all the spare gear overboard. All we saw for days on end was cloud, wind, and rain. Sun, moon, and stars were distant memories. Without these natural lighthouses the captain didn't have a clue where we were. We simply drifted hopelessly through the furry of the storm.

Any hope of survival seemed to be fading away for many of the weary travelers. Most of the people were so sea sick the thought of food was repulsive. Folks were getting weaker and weaker by the day. Spirits were at an all time low with discouragement and strain written on exhausted faces. What they all needed was a pep talk. I started off with a word for the captain.

"What can I say? I know you don't want to hear me say I told you so, BUT I told you so! You should have listened to me. We should never have left Crete. The only gain achieved has been our misfortune and the loss of many supplies.Now, it's not my intention to point fingers and be negative. I simply want to encourage and exhort you to be of good cheer."

"In spite of your worst fears, nobody on the ship is going to die, BUT, the ship is going to be destroyed. I had a dream last night an angel of God, to whom I belong and serve, spoke to me saying, 'Don't worry Paul, be happy. You must be brought to stand before Caesar so God will continue to protect you and all those sailing with you on this journey.' So, once again gentlemen, cheer up. I have every confidence in God's faithfulness to honor His promise to save us all from the catastrophic event certain to occur. We may be shipwrecked, however, all of us will land safely on an island somewhere up ahead."

141. SHIPWRECKED
(Acts 27:27-44)

Encouraging news, eh?
    Bad news: we're gonna be shipwrecked!
    Good news: we're gonna land safe and sound on some island!
    Loony tunes!
    Boy, I suspected they all thought I was a bit looped. Hey, I didn't think so.
    Well, some fourteen nights after we'd left the calm of the island of Cauda, according to my best guesstimates, we were drifting merrily across the Adriatic Sea. Around midnight a bunch of the crew got to figuring we must be close to land. Even though it was so dark out they couldn't see a thing they thought they could hear the crashing of the waves onto a shore.
    So the crew took a depth sounding and figured we were in water of only about one hundred and twenty feet. After a short time the sounding announced approximately ninety feet. The excitement grew by leaps and bounds at this good news. Then, as suddenly as the excitement had billowed, a deep sense of terror gripped everyone as the realization the ship could come to a crashing halt at any moment hit the brain cells.
    The order was given to throw all four anchors off the stern of the ship. The commotion on deck was amazing. In the north wind the rear anchors would hopefully help keep the front of the ship pointing towards the beach if we indeed were going to run aground. Nobody could wait for the light of dawn to cast some light on the situation.
    A few ingenious members of the crew thought they had a better idea. They made it look like they were going to drop some anchors off the front of the ship as well. Actually, what they were doing was putting a lifeboat over the bow with the intent of escaping on their own. When I saw what was really happening I had to put a stop to it. I went and grabbed JM along with a group of soldiers who were with him at the time.
    "Look big guy, if those guys get off this ship you might as well kiss your life goodbye!"
    They had the good sense to listen to what I said this time. The soldiers ran to the front of the ship and cut the lines connecting the dinghy to the ship.
    Plop! Plop! Fizz! Fizz!

No more life raft! It dropped mercilessly into the water and set off on its own course. I'm not exactly sure how much one little boat could have done anyway to assist all the crew and passengers in any emergency. As dawn approached I knew time was becoming of the essence. Once again I found myself inclined to pass on some practical advice to anyone who'd listen.

"Look everybody, you've all got to eat something to give yourselves some strength. Hungry people aren't very efficient, or very productive. We've been out here at least fourteen days now and most of you have hardly eaten a thing. You'll need more than determination in order to survive what is before us. And you will survive! I've told you not one hair of your head will be damaged or lost from any of you. Now, let's get some food ready and dig in."

People scurried about trying to collect whatever food they could scrounge up. It was my honor to lead by example. I offered up some thanks to God for His bountiful blessings then started munching with all the gusto I could manage. It didn't take others very long to follow my lead. We even had a few good laughs as we watched each other eat our portion. Two hundred and seventy-six people can slam down a mean buffet in no time. I'm sure it's no secret folks are a lot more content with their situations when they have something in their belly.

The task of preparing the ship for landing became the top priority as the buffet came to a close. It was imperative the weight of the ship be lightened so the captain gave the order to heave everything unnecessary overboard. The crew even started to cast the heavy bags of wheat from the cargo hold over the sides of the ship.

Daylight finally started to peek through the darkness. As dawn progressed the outline of a nearby body of land became evident. It would have been nice to know where the heck we were, however, nobody had a clue as to what chunk of land we were close to. The captain finally spotted what looked like a creek or stream and figured he could drive his baby right into what he hoped would be a soft landing in the natural harbor formed by the funneling shores.

In order to beach the craft he ordered the crew to hoist all of the anchors. All of the tethering cables holding the rudder oars in place were loosened and the main sail was raised to snag the wind. The captain just let her rip for the shore. Its resting place was now completely in the arms of the winds and waves.

SHIPWRECKED

TRIP # 19

As we got closer to shore we could actually see the creek meeting up with the water from another channel created by a small island laying about a hundred yards off the mainland. We were headed straight for the spot where the two bodies of water collided. It wasn't long until we hit the landmass with a mighty force knocking most of us right off our feet. The sound of the incredible jolt was phenomenal. Due to the speed of the impact the nose of the ship hit the sand and embedded itself so solidly nothing was going to budge it.

However, the same couldn't be said for the rear end. The ship's stern was left to battle the pounding waves and wind on its own. The violence of the wind exacted its toll very quickly. The rear timbers started to crumble apart moments after the unanticipated, sudden jolt to its system. Bodies were strewn about like toothpicks. The struggle for survival was on big time. The first consideration was to get off the ship as fast as possible.

This reality posed big problems for the soldiers who were entrusted with the duty of guarding their allotted prisoners. Panic set in rapidly. The soldiers were well aware under Roman law the escape of a prisoner didn't go over too well with the justice department. The penalty or sentence due to the prisoner would often have to be executed upon the hapless guards.

Ouch!

Scared spitless, they decided their first duty was to kill all the prisoners before they could jump ship and make a swimming escape to freedom. Saving themselves from the imminent danger took second place to duty.

Good thing Julius Maximus had other plans! He had no intention of seeing me killed. Don't think for a moment his kindness didn't sit too well with me. I really would rather apply my energies to getting out alive like everyone else than to consider my untimely demise at the hands of some panicking soldiers. JM wisely commanded those soldiers who could swim to jump into the water and swim for their lives. He told those who didn't know how to swim to grab a hold of some chunks of broken timbers from the ship or anything else they could find to use as a float to make their way to the safety of the shore.

So it actually came to pass every single person from the ship made it to the shore. A little worse for wear perhaps.

What a sight it must have been for those on the island to see the ship come in for a crash landing!

Folks obviously had seen us coming and ran to the shore to pick us out as we reached the beach. I'll bet they weren't even expecting company!

142. FROM MALTA TO ROME
(Acts 28:1-15)

It didn't take all that long for someone to pop the question.

"Where the heck are we anyway?"

Word spread like wildfire we'd made our crash landing on the island of Malta. As opposed to the linguistic beauty of the Greek language, the island inhabitants spoke some kind of goofy dialect most curious indeed. I'd have to say seeing anybody at this point of our perilous journey was a welcome sight, regardless of whether we could communicate intelligently or not.

The folks really treated and cared for us with unexpected hospitality. They went completely overboard to help us out. Well, not literally. O.K. O.K. You know what I mean. It was us who literally went overboard to receive their assistance! After helping us all safely onto the shore our rescuers sent word to their village to hurry to the beach with blankets and towels.

Someone had the common sense to get a big bonfire going as we began to congregate to make sure each other was all right. We all huddled together like a herd of cattle trying to keep each other warm. It didn't seem to matter our clothes were soaking wet because it was pouring rain anyway.

Still a little numb with shock some of us started to help collect driftwood debris to help get a fire going. I had gathered a whole arm full and was starting to put some branches onto the growing fire when I was accosted by something that mistook me for a tasty snack. Man, I had just been through a couple weeks of the worst sailing nightmare I'd ever endured and had just survived relatively unscathed from a earth shattering ship wreck.

Now this! What could possibly be next?

All of a sudden this slimy snake slithered out from the branch as I dangled it towards the screaming heat of the fire. The snake must have been scared of its wits too! It slithered in sheer panic off of the wood latching itself directly around my arm and hand. I obviously hadn't noticed the camouflaged viper as I picked up the wood on the beach. The "coronella austiaka" has a pretty nasty bite even though it doesn't have any poison in its fangs.

Many of our Maltese hosts saw the snake with its fangs delicately clinging onto my hand. Man, they all freaked right out. They figured I was some kind of murderer or something.

FROM MALTA TO ROME — TRIP # 19

They assumed the viperous attack was punishment for crimes I must surely have committed. As if my unceremonious dip in the ocean wasn't reward enough!

Well, as the sudden pain of the fangs engaged my senses I gave my arm a violent shake. The viper jumped off to a search for a more cooperative target. Too bad it landed right in the fire.

"Felt like a snake bite! Looks like a snake bite! Must have been a snake bite!"

Funny. My hand wasn't beginning to swell up. I was still kicking. I hadn't fallen over dead or anything. Everyone who saw it happen came rushing over to me to check it out. When they realized I was o.k., they drastically changed their opinion of me. A moment ago I was a vicious murderer. Now I was a god or something!

"How could it possibly be I could survive this kind of attack from the viper?"

Go figure!

Anyway, we were very fortunate to be part of a group taken in by a man named Publius, a very kind man with a really nice family. It just so happens he was the head honcho of the island. He owned all the land around the area on which we had run aground with the ship. He provided us with lodging and surrounded us with his courteous hospitality for three days.

We found out the father of Publius was very sick with a high temperature and dysentery. I asked if I could go in to visit with him. He looked pretty pathetic when we first saw him. His condition just overwhelmed us to pray for him. Doc, Ari, and I all gathered around him and laid our hands on him as we prayed. It wasn't very long at all before he on the mend.

Word of Publius' dads' restoration to health spread as quickly as the word of our unfortunate arrival on the island. Soon we were besieged for our attention from sick folks who had come from all over the island. It was sure great to have Doc along to help diagnose and treat the folks too.

It was three months before shipping season was under way again. Another grain ship from Alexander had made it to Malta safely before the winter and was preparing to set sail from the port of Valletta. The ship was called "The Heavenly Twins."

Neat, eh?

The figureheads on the front of the boat gave the name away. The two patron deities of the sailors were Castor and Pollux.

The carved images of these two gods, whose zodiac sign was the Gemini, were thought to bring good luck from the dangers of the sea.

Whatever! Doesn't do anything for me. Not too sure why they think these carved images could do anything for them either.

It was very obvious our presence had touched their lives as they indeed had blessed us. They heaped upon us words and expressions of gratefulness. When it was time for us to finally leave their island the wonderful folks blessed us abundantly with anything they thought we might need for the remainder of our journey.

JM saw to it we had a place on the ship. After all the goodbyes were spoken we left on our one-day sailing trip to Syracuse at the southeastern corner of the island of Sicily. We were able to do a fair bit of sight seeing at Syracuse because we had to stay there for three days until the winds improved.

Syracuse was a fascinating and important city with a double harbor enhancing its booming economy. It became the home for the governor of the colony of Sicily. Part of the city was actually on an island connected to the mainland via bridges. The temples of Diana and Minerva, the palace of the governors, and the famous spring of Arethusa were on the island. The forum, town hall, senate house, and the temple of Olympian Jupiter were all located in the mainland quarter known as the "Achradina." We also got to see the phenomenal theater in Neapolis. Syracuse was famous for its fishing, shipbuilding, as well as its bronze works. We packed in a whole lot of sightseeing.

Before leaving Syracuse the captain of the ship was able to secure a compass to help him navigate a bit better. We tacked our way over to Rhegium at the southern most tip of Italy. Rhegium is on the Strait of Messina, separating the seven miles between the island of Sicily and the mainland of Italy. Apparently, old legend has it Sicily had been "rent" apart from the mainland by an earthquake, hence, the name of the city. Other people think Rhegium got its name from the Latin word for "royal." We happened to make only a pit stop there while we waited for the right winds to come along.

Two days after the south winds came along we found ourselves in the city of Puteoli, about 180 nautical miles from Rhegium. This principal port city of southern Italy was in the most sheltered part of the Bay of Naples. Puteoli was the main harbor for the city of Rome, even though it was some distance away. Just to the north was the port of Nisenum where the Roman navy fleets were stationed.

Nearby, were the crowded beaches of Baiae. Also anchored nearby were the yachts of the rich and famous, adorned with their bright, multi colored sails.

It must have been quite a sight to be on the shores watching the ships come in. To tell you the truth, it was great fun coming in on a ship. All the ships entering the bay were obliged to strike their topsails ("suppara"), with the exception of the great grain ships like ours. It was common practice to send the smaller, faster vessels ("tabellariae") to announce the speedy arrival of the naval fleets. So, when we sailed into Puteoli it was easy for anyone to tell us apart from the navy because we were the only topless ones in the procession.

What a rush!

We weren't surprised to find believers in Jesus in Puteoli. I assumed somehow word would get out we were on our way to Rome, however, I was quite surprised by the incredible, enthusiastic welcome we received as soon as we disembarked from the ship. They begged us to stay with them for at least a week before continuing on to Rome. JM kindly consented to this request. He figured seven more days wasn't really going to make much difference given the incredible length of time it had already taken us to get this far. We spent a super time with these fine folks.

The excitement of actually getting to Rome was building faster than I could stand. Rome was merely a hundred and thirty two miles away. The fact my fate at the hands of Caesar Augustus was uncertain didn't deter my enthusiasm for hitting the road once again.

We traveled about twenty miles to the city of Capua. It was here the road intersected with the great Appian Way. The highway had been built by the great censor, Appius Claudius, about three hundred years ago. The worn and well-known track of Appia was often called the "Queen of the Long Roads." We traveled along this main thorough fare until we came to the little junction town called the "Forum of Appius" (Appii Forum), about forty three miles from Rome.

It was at this junction we were met by another group of believers from Rome who'd heard we were getting close. They had come to greet us and to accompany us into Rome itself. Some of the folks couldn't make it as far as Appii Forum so they had stopped to wait for us about ten miles earlier at a place called the "Three Taverns." This motel mecca was great for travelers at this intersection of the Appian Way and the road to Antium.

It was certainly exciting to know all of these wonderful people were so anxious to finally meet us. I got quite choked up by it all.

My goodness, I was extremely grateful to God for all these tremendous folks who provided such encouragement and strength to me in this very exciting climax to a rugged trip.

IN ROME

143. ROME! FINALLY!
(Acts 28:16-31)

Even JM was pretty tickled to see Rome again. Our trip had been quite an adventure to be sure. His present job of escorting me to the authorities in Rome was about to come to an end. I'd have to say there was a touch of sadness for both of us as we approached the Caelian hill home ("stratopedarch") of the "praefectus praetorii," the commander of the Praetorian Guard.

You could say we had "bonded" together very nicely.

The commander accepted us with the usual pomp and ceremony designed to reinforce his authority and prestige. After looking at my "resume" he assigned me to one of his officers ("princepus peregrinorum") for safekeeping. Call it house arrest if you like. I came to think of it as having been issued a personal bodyguard. It was almost flattering in a way.

The whole idea of the bodyguard was to prevent me from causing any more disturbances, while at the same time, preventing any possibility of harm coming to me before I'd have the opportunity to have my day in court. There obviously didn't seem to be a timetable or schedule as to when that particular day would be. I was assigned a rotating corps of officers who guarded me twenty four hours a day, sometime literally chained to me when they thought it necessary.

Don't get the impression I was doing "hard time" or anything. I actually had a great deal of freedom. I was allowed to move about freely, accompanied by the bodyguard of course, and took every opportunity to take in the sights and sounds of the great city of Rome. Room and board was not a part of the deal unfortunately. I was required to fend for myself and I considered myself lucky to have learned the tent making trade when I was just a youngster.

If you're going to go into business it's always a wise decision to consider a number of things, not the least of which is public demand for a product. Tents were a pretty safe bet to remain on the top ten list of consumer necessities for a long time to come. Picking an item the military establishment required didn't hurt either. Thanks to JM and some of the bodyguards posted to me it wasn't long before I had a military contract sure to keep me busy for as long as I needed to be.

I got along quite well, thank you very much.

One of my first objectives whenever I arrived in a new location was to seek out the Jewish synagogue to meet with the Jewish leaders. It always seemed to be proper protocol and the right thing to do, being a Pharisee and all. I figured, in my case at least, the Jewish leaders of Rome might just as well hear all about me from the donkey's mouth himself. So, three days after I arrived in Rome I contacted the Jewish head honcho, together with his buddies, and requested a meeting to explain my situation to them. I wasn't really sure how much they actually knew about me or how many goofy stories they had heard. They were probably just as nervous as I was when we finally met each other.

Basically, this is what I told them.

"Friends and brothers, thank you very much for meeting with me. I'm not exactly sure why I'm here today, other than the fact I asked to come here under the protective custody of Rome. I haven't broken any Roman laws, nor have I committed any offenses against the laws, customs, or traditions of our Jewish ancestors."

"However, I was rescued from the Jewish authorities in Jerusalem who seemed preoccupied with the notion of assassinating me. The Roman authorities couldn't find a shred of evidence against me or my activities that could justify the death sentence laid against me. How could they possibly sentence me to death when there wasn't even enough evidence presented to bring me to trial?"

"BUT, these same leaders wouldn't accept the findings of the Roman magistrates. They continued with their deceptive plans to have me handed back under their control, where they could try, convict, and execute me in a court where all the cards would be stacked up against me. As a Roman citizen, I naturally decided to pursue my legal rights to appeal directly to Caesar."

"Please understand I've nothing against my Jewish heritage. This is the very reason I felt compelled to come to see you today and to speak directly to you. I've been shackled and bound in chains like these simply because I've been bold enough to proclaim the message of good news, the hope of all of God's people."

I thought I was off to a good start when I was not so rudely interrupted.

"Hold on! Hold on!" bellowed out one of the leaders. "We have neither received letters from Judaea concerning you, nor have we received a personal visit from anyone from back there to inform us of any difficulties they may have had with you. However, your initial comments intrigue us. We sure are anxious to hear of your ideas. With respect to some radical sect of believers in Jesus, we only know they haven't garnered very much respect or acceptance wherever they are to be found."

I guess I couldn't really argue with them. I was encouraged they hadn't been tipped off to me, and furthermore, that they wanted to hear more from me concerning the message I was preaching. We agreed on a time when it would be convenient for both parties to get together for another little chat over some milk and manna bread.

Lots of folks showed up at my quarters. Hey, given my situation, my place was a logical choice for a meeting spot. I took the liberty to expound and testify about what I understood of the kingdom of God. From dawn to dusk I continued to inform and persuade them Jesus was who He claimed to be and that He actually accomplished what God sent Him here to this earth to do!

I was careful not to rankle them with my own well-oiled vocabulary or my incredibly intimidating sense of logic. No, I figured the best thing to do was relate the message of God's grace and peace to something they would recognize. I taught them what the Law of Moses was all about. I used direct quotes from the prophets of old to explain to them the wise plan of God for the whole world.

Now, I'd like to tell you everyone understood or believed what I told them. Well, some did. And some didn't. Oh yes. Some folks took it all in and understood the message, and yes, some didn't understand. There was an obvious difference of opinion and consensus regarding what I told them. Before they all got up to leave I had one more chance to make absolutely sure there would be no mistaking what I understood about the plan of God.

"Well, if you won't take my word for it, give heed to the instructions of God to the prophet of Isaiah. Isaiah described God's instructions to our forefathers saying:

'Go to these people and tell them even though they've heard very plainly the message of my will they just don't seem to get it. Furthermore, I've demonstrated my love for everyone to see, and yet, they can't seem to see it for looking at it.'

ROME! FINALLY!   ROME

'For the hearts of these people have grown ice cold and their ears have become plugged with so much wax they can't even hear anymore. In addition, their eyelids have simply drooped closed.'

'These people need to open their eyes and start to see the reality of my faithfulness. They need to clean out their ears and pay attention to what I've declared. And they need to stop trying to figure me out with their minds by letting their hearts rule their understanding. A renewal of their minds is the only way they can be converted from the perversions of self-righteousness, and then they'll discover I've already healed them of their diseases' (Isaiah 6:9,10).

"Yes, it's an unfortunate reality the people of Israel are too blind, deaf, and dumb to recognize the grace and peace of God. However, the message of the salvation of God is being received by the Gentile folks, and they seem to have no trouble comprehending it!"

With this conclusion the Jewish leaders took their leave. It was visually apparent they'd be thinking long and hard about what I shared with them. The great debate was on! I must have rattled more than a few chains. Not just mine either.

Two years!

I spent two years in Rome in my little rented pad. It was my pleasure to welcome anyone and everyone who had the patience and stamina to come and visit with me. I'm sure I wore some folks out. I taught and preached about the kingdom of God to all who would take the time to listen.

In total confidence and boldness I shared with folks the wonderful news of Jesus and how He had accomplished the wise plan of God to bestow His righteousness upon the whole world. Nobody stopped me. Go figure. The Jewish leaders left me alone for the most part. They did their thing, and I did mine. The Romans didn't hassle me either. Good thing.

I even had plenty of time to write some letters too. Want to read some of my verbal diarrhea? It's a virtual theological smorgasbord!

Alllriiiiighty then! Let's get into it! There's a whole whack of good stuff comin' up now!

ROME

THE LETTER TO PHILEMON

144. INTRODUCTION OF PHILEMON

One of the many letters I wrote during my "tenure" in Rome was written to some wonderful folks living in the beautiful city of Laodicaea. Now, for those of you who've forgotten where Laodicaea is, let me give you a brief refresher in geography.

Laodicaea was one of the cities in the valley of the Lycus River, a tributary of the Maeander River in the southwest Phrygia. The city was spread out on an almost square plateau some hundred feet above the river valley. Actually two smaller rivers, the Baspinar and Gusmuscay, tributaries of the Lycus River, protected the flat hillside of the city. The high mountains of the Babadag and Akdag Ranges protected the southern side of the plateau.

The ancient highway leading up from Ephesus through the Maeander and Lycus valleys ultimately ended up in Syria. Ten miles to the east lay Colossae, while Hierapolis was located six miles to the north of Laodicaea.

A number of my good friends still lived there, including my buddy Philemon, his wife Apphia, and their son Archippus. I felt compelled to write to these fine folks concerning the future of one of my most valued assistants. His name was Onesimus. For all you word buffs out there, the name Onesimus means "profitable." This he was to me without question.

It was time for us to set the record straight and deal with a delicate, yet important, issue. The issue was slavery and the rights of ownership.

Who did Onesimus belong to?

According to the letter of the law Onesimus actually was the property of my friend Philemon and his family. I had introduced Philemon to the grace and peace of God in Jesus some years ago and now he was an instrumental figure in the fellowship of believers in the area around Laodicaea. In fact, they held their meeting in his home. Philemon was a very successful businessman, excelling in whatever he set his heart, mind, and energy to do.

Onesimus just happened to be one of the servants. There came a point in time when Onesimus decided to do something extra ordinarily dangerous.

The consequences of going AWOL were serious to say the least. Onesimus had obviously given careful consideration to all the factors before he decided to fly the coup.

Would you be surprised to know it's estimated that there were approximately 60,000,000 slaves in the Roman Empire? That's a six with seven zeros following it. Sixty million! Can you imagine the havoc if they would have banded together to form a union? Or, can you contemplate the chaos if they had a "Moses" to lead them out of captivity?

My goodness!

Let me assure you the Roman authorities did not take too kindly to the notion of independence for this captive work force.

Unfortunately, slaves weren't even considered to be real people. Rather, they were like tools, with a little life thrown in. The master had absolute control over every aspect of the life of his slaves. Beatings, whippings, and other forms of inhuman activity were common occurrences. I heard one story of a poor slave who dropped and broke a crystal glass on the floor of his master's courtyard.

He was summarily thrown into the fishpond out in the front courtyard where he became a spectacle of a grotesque public execution as he was savagely ripped to nothingness by a cast of pet lampreys. I also heard of slaves being branded with a hot iron for simply stealing some towels.

A rebellious and disobedient slave definitely failed any test of tolerance. Merciful punishment ran the gamut from tongue lashing to execution. At the very least a the slave would be branded by a hot iron on the forehead with the letter "F." The "F" was short for "fugitivus."

Get the picture?

Now you know where "fugitive" comes from.

It would be inaccurate for me to imply all masters were bloody tyrants. Many slaves were treated with at least a modicum of civility. The life of a slave was definitely not a weekend picnic, however, freedom wasn't one of the luxuries they were able to enjoy without risking a substantial portion of the remainder of their life on this planet.

Which brings me back to Onesimus.

With the intention of giving freedom a shot Onesimus ran away from his master. Rome seemed like a logical destination to hide. What are the chances of being spotted amidst the backdrop of an over populated metropolis like Rome?

At least, this is what he was thinking!

Onesimus never bargained on meeting me! Little did he know I actually knew Philemon, not to mention the rest of his family.

We hit it off from the get go. In a short time he became like a son to me. It didn't take me long to introduce him to the most glorious news he had ever been told. His understanding of the liberty of God's loving acceptance was almost too good to be true for Onesimus. My understanding of his slavery and dependence upon another human being also increased as he shared with me of his past.

Onesimus was not unaware of his responsibility to face the music, so to speak, for his actions towards his boss. He eventually asked me if I'd be willing to smooth things over a bit with Philemon and the clan if he went back. Adding in my two shekels worth on behalf of Onesimus is the primary reason for this particular letter.

The secondary reason, without being too blunt or obvious, is that I had a hidden agenda of my own. I really wanted Philemon and Archippus to release Onesimus so he could come back to be of assistance to me! I had to craft my letter in such a way that it would be impossible for them not to see the transparency of my intention too.

PHILEMON

145. PROFITABLE TO ALL
(Philemon 1:1-25)

FROM:
Paul, a prisoner, both figuratively and literally, of Jesus, and Timothy, our brother

TO:
- Philemon, our dear friend and co-worker,
- Apphia, your good wife and our dear sister,
- Archippus, your son and comrade to us,
- and all of the believers who meet together in your home

BLESSING:
Grace and peace are yours through God our Father and Jesus.

I'm so thankful to God for all He has accomplished in Jesus and I continually thank Him in my prayers for all He has done for you too. I've heard of your love, acceptance, and trust of what Jesus has accomplished on your behalf, as well as for all the children of God.

I pray the communication and demonstration of your faith and trust in God's gift of grace and peace will be a shining testimony to others of every good thing in you because of Jesus. I can proudly tell you we're overjoyed, taking great pleasure in how you show your love to other folks, keenly aware of how you've touched and refreshed the lives of many of God's children.

With this in mind, I believe I could, with a measure of boldness in Jesus, enlist you to do something I know is the right thing for you to do. However, I won't do it. Rather, I'll simply plead with you to follow the dictates of the love in your hearts. You know I'm not getting any younger, and on top of it, I'm a bit tied up at the moment, if you know what I mean. I'd come there to talk to you about the matter personally if I could however I'm resigned to let this letter make my plea to you on behalf of someone who has become like a son to me.

Of course, I'm writing to you about Onesimus. It's been my pleasure to befriend this remarkable young man during my incarceration. There may have been a time in the past when he wasn't worth his salt to you.

BUT now, my goodness, I'm confident Onesimus, like his very name suggests, is and can be not only "profitable" to you, he could again be very "profitable" to me.

Look, I've sent him back to you. Receive him back into your household in the very same way you would if he were my very own son. Indeed, to tell you the truth, I'd have preferred to keep him here with me. I really could have used him here to help minister to my needs while I'm under house arrest for my part in the spreading of the great gospel message.

BUT, it would have been unfair of me to take advantage of our friendship or to presume you'd give your permission to such an arrangement in light of the actions of Onesimus towards you in the past. I don't want to impose something on you that is not mine to impose.

I'd much rather see you demonstrate grace and peace to him willingly rather than out of a sense of obligation or necessity.

There can be no denying Onesimus went AWOL for a while. Perhaps you should receive him back into your home not just as a simple servant, BUT, as one who is valued much more than a servant. Welcome him as a brother, especially as he has been to me, BUT, more importantly, as he is to you all as well.

Is not Onesimus a brother in the sense he's a fellow human being as well as in the sense he's a brother of yours in Jesus?

If you consider me to be a close associate and friend then welcome and receive him like you would if it was I who was returning to you. If he has done something wrong to you or even if he owes you something, please, pretty please, put it on my tab. Look, you have my word on it. I'll pay you back!

I don't want to appear too much like I'm calling in a few chips here, even though we're all well aware of how much you are indebted to me for what I've done for you over the years. O.K. Maybe I am asking for a big favor!

Dear friends, please let me rejoice in the graciousness of the spirit of Jesus within you. Refresh my heart with the loving acceptance, kindness and peace of Jesus. I have absolute confidence in your desire and capacity to go even beyond what I've asked of you.

BUT, there is something else.

Please prepare a place for me to stay. I trust with your prayerful support it will be possible for me to come and visit with you.

I'd really appreciate it if you'd greet a few folks on my behalf. Please salute Epaphras, my fellow captivated servant in Jesus, and my co-workers John Mark, Aristarchus, Demas, Lucas.

Now remember, **YOUR SPIRIT IS ONE WITH THE GRACE OF JESUS!**

That's just the way it is.

THE LETTER TO THE COLOSSIANS

146. INTRODUCTION OF COLOSSIANS

So, there you have the letter I primarily wrote to Philemon and his family concerning my buddy Onesimus. I was a bit concerned about letting Onesimus make an unexpected reappearance to his master without at least a bit of support. This is why I decided to send Tychicus along with him. I trusted Ty to be a buffer of strength for Onesimus as he made this difficult attempt at reconciliation. The letter you've just read is one of the letters I sent along with Ty to deliver.

You're probably curious as to whatever became of Onesimus. Well, if he wrote a book about his experiences he probably could entitle it, "From slavery to captivity!"

Yes, Onesimus went from being a slave of an earthly master to being captivated by the grace and peace of God. He proclaimed the incredible news incessantly, eventually becoming a leading figure among the believers in Ephesus.

Ephesus!

Yes.

Ephesus.

Now if you take a look at your map you'll understand it isn't such a stretch to see why Onesimus would become so important in Ephesus of all places. Ephesus was, of course, the headquarters for over two years of challenging opportunities for me during my third missionary journey. It was from Ephesus we launched many campaigns to spread the great gospel message of God's great grace and peace. The Lycus valley was one of the territories we visited. I met Philemon, his dear family, and many other fine folks during my time in and about the city of Laodicaea.

And whom did Onesimus serve? I know you haven't forgotten. Of course, it was Philemon. Epaphras was another great friends who came from the Lycus Valley. Let me come back to him in a moment.

The Lycus valley was approximately 100 miles to the east of Ephesus in the Roman province of Asia. The River Lycus flowed through the valley separating the two cities of Hierapolis and Laodicaea, while Colossae straddled the river about 10 miles or so upstream.

Geographical influences played a major role in shaping the notorious history of the Lycus valley. Earthquakes destroyed Laodicaea more than once, however, the rich and independent inhabitants were determined to rebuild with little or no financial support offered by the Roman government. Fantastic grottoes, cascades, and archways of stone were formed through the ages by the build up of chalk that impregnated the Lycus River and its tributaries. The unusual, impressive scenery of the area made any trip there a virtual visual smorgasbord. The gleaming hillside glaciers of chalk could be seen from twenty miles away.

Whatever lands not covered by layers and incrustations of the chalk were as fertile as you could imagine. It is no secret volcanic ground is as fertile as ground comes. Perhaps the best wool industry in the entire world was supported by great flocks of sheep dining on the lush fields. The chalky waters of the river enabled artisans to create an astoundingly beautiful array of colors to dye the wool. A unique color even bore the name of the city of Colossae.

Politically and financially it was Laodicaea that eventually emerged as the leading center of activity. Hierapolis, although a great trading center in its own right, became famous for its tourism industry due to a multitude of hot springs and health spas. The medicinal quality of the springs together with the vapors pouring out from the chalky caverns and chasms were drawing cards for seekers of eternal youth from around the world.

Colossae?

Well, unfortunately, although once as important as its two sister cities, it really didn't have the staying power. Although very Roman in character, the entire valley wasn't without a Jewish influence. It's estimated as many as 50,000 Jewish folks were living in the area. The success of the financial climate of the area was largely due to the business acumen of the Jews.

Enough of history, sociology, and geography.

Let me get back to talking about my friend, Epaphras.

"Papy" to me, as I mentioned before, was another of my great friends who came from the Lycus Valley. During my stay in Ephesus it had been my honor to have a part in developing in Papy an understanding of the wealth of God's love for all mankind through Jesus. Papy had an outstanding career guiding and teaching believers over the years in the tri-cities region.

We stayed in touch over the years as best we could. When Papy heard I was "stuck" in Rome he took the time and extensive energy to get himself to Rome to visit me. He was convinced I should write a letter he could take back to Colossae to bless his fellow believers with. Apparently, something as tangible as a letter of encouragement and exhortation would mean a great deal to the folks who gathered together in this part of the world.

So, the next letter you're about to read is the second letter I penned from Rome to folks in the Lycus Valley region. The rambling thoughts and instructions of this letter was intended to be read in Colossae and also in the cities of Hierapolis and Laodicaea, just as the letter to Philemon and his family was to be read to the other believers in Laodicaea, Hierapolis, and Colossae. I took great pains to see Ty understood the importance of relating my best wishes and heart felt love and appreciation as he delivered these two letters to their intended recipients.

How is it possible to get everything you want to say in a letter? Impossible. I was forced to trust the tidbits of my experience and understanding would rub off on those who listened as my words were read to them.

OK. Here goes...

COLOSSIANS

147. **TRANSLATED!**
(Colossians 1:1-22)

FROM:
Paul, an ambassador of Jesus who brought to completion the will of God, and Timothy, our brother

TO:
all the children of God, faithful brothers and sisters in Jesus who live in and around Colossae

BLESSING:
God our Father and Jesus have blessed you with His grace and peace!

It's certainly our great privilege to give thanks to God and the Father of Jesus! We've been unceasing in our gratitude to God since we heard you've also come to an understanding of the accomplishments of Jesus on your behalf. We're so happy to hear you've chosen to demonstrate the loving spirit of Jesus within you towards everyone in the family of God.

    We thank God for the incredible hope He has laid up for you in heaven. You undoubtedly have heard all about this amazing truth when the words of the gospel message were first introduced to you. God's loving grace and peace was distributed to you in the very same way He introduced it to the whole world! The fruit of God's blessing has been manifested to all and it's been very evident in your lives since the day you came to understand what the incredible truth of God's grace and peace is all about.

    I know Epaphras, our dear co-worker, has been a great teacher and faithful servant of the message of Jesus. It is he who also has declared to us the way you practically demonstrate the tremendous loving spirit of Jesus within you. Surely, since the very first time we heard the reports we continue to thank God for His miraculous activity on your behalf.

    From the bottom of my heart here are a few tidbits I'd like to leave with you to ponder and explore.

1. Expand your understanding of the completeness of God's will. God knows what He did! He's not stupid. God's wisdom of everything, including His unsurpassable understanding of the condition of every aspect of the spiritual aspect of nature, is unquestionable.
2. Learn to walk worthy in the understanding Jesus has made everyone pleasing in the sight of God! Every good work Jesus accomplished was fruitful. He accomplished everything God sent Him to do here on this earth for all mankind!
3. Enlarge your knowledge of God's view and opinion of you!
4. Be strengthened with all might, according to His glorious power. What will this do for you? My goodness, you'll have more patience than you know what to do with. You might be surprised at the depth of compassion at your disposal to bless others. And you'll be happy about it to boot!
5. Be generous in your gratitude to God the Father. "Why?" Well, here are a few good reasons:
    - It was God who made it possible for us to be partakers in the inheritance He established and provided for all of His children!
    - It was God who translated mankind into the light of His glorious kingdom of his dear Son, delivering all from the tyranny, power, and darkness of the wisdom (stupidity, I would say) of our own self-righteous attempts to gain His favor!
    - It's through the blood of His dear Son Jesus we've all been made 100% righteous in the sight of God. Hey, we even have the forgiveness of sins through His blood!
    - Jesus is the very image of the invisible God!
    - Everything that exists owes its origin to Jesus! All things were created by Him. It doesn't matter whether you want to talk about, things in heaven; things in earth; things you can see; things you can't see; powers such as thrones, dominions, or principalities. Hey, "ALL" things were created "BY" him! And "ALL" things were created "FOR" Him!
    - Jesus is the preeminence of "all" things!
    - Jesus is the One who holds "everything" together!
    - Jesus is the head of the "whole" body, the family of God!
    - Jesus is the very beginning of everything!

- Jesus is merely the first to experience the glorious liberty of being raised from the clutches of death! "Why?" Well, because God wanted Jesus to have first place in absolutely every aspect of anyone and anything! We're talking about preeminence aren't we? Yes we are. For it pleased God the Father that in Jesus would dwell the total fullness of everything.

6. On top of that, as if that weren't enough, this is what God did:
   - He made peace with "all" mankind through the blood of the cross of Jesus!
   - God reconciled "all" things, animate and inanimate alike, to Himself by the work of Jesus!
   - God has, through Jesus for everything on this earth, for everything in heaven, for even you, yes you, you who were sometime alienated and enemies of God in your own mind by the wicked works of self-righteousness!
   - Yes, even yet has God reconciled "all" to Himself! How? In the body of His own flesh through the death of Jesus on the cross!

What did He accomplish? Look folks, Jesus died and rose again to present you HOLY, UNBLAMABLE, and UNREPROVEABLE!
Where?
In God eyes!

Allow me to mention a few thoughts about the fact Jesus is the "image" of God.

In the writings of the Proverbs (chapters 2 & 8) the word "wisdom" is the very same word as "image" employed to describe the goodness of God. Greek philosophers, such as Philo, used the word "image" to portray the invisible and divine "logos" ("word") of God that only the mind can perceive. Could it be these great authors knew more than we give them credit for? The wisdom and the word of God are both consummated in Jesus!

Is it not also true, "God created mankind in His own 'image,' in the 'image' of God He created them" (Genesis 1:26,27)? Could it really be true God all along intended for mankind to be nothing less than the very "image" of God too? Seems to me Jesus finally overcame all the obstacles preventing humanity from realizing the will of God!

Did you know the root word for "portrait" in the Greek language is the word "image?" In fact, when a legal document like a receipt or IOU was drawn up it always included a description of the chief characteristics or distinguishing marks of the parties who entered into the arrangement. Why? So there could be no mistaking who was involved.

When God and Jesus entered into an agreement to issue their grace and peace to all mankind they rubber-stamped it with their portraits. Jesus is the very "image" of God. There can be no mistaking as to who was involved!

Not only was Jesus the "image" of God, He was in reality the "fullness," or the "completeness" of God!

Nothing of God was left out in Jesus!

He is the full revelation of God. Nothing else was necessary to make more of God.

148. WHAT MYSTERY?
(Colossians 1:23-2:15)

Oh yes, there's something else I want to encourage you in.

Continue to put your confidence solely in the faith and faithfulness of God to accomplish what He set out to do in Jesus! The issue of the righteousness for God's creation is grounded in Jesus and has been settled once, and for "all!"

Don't be moved away from the hope of this glorious gospel of good news that you've heard and which was proclaimed to every creature under the dominion of heaven itself. I'm proud I've been entrusted with the great honor and privilege of spreading this gospel of grace and peace wherever I go.

Look, I'm not even depressed about my current state of affairs. I rejoice in the fact I'm suffering this imprisonment as a result of my convictions. Any persecution I'm forced to endure for the sake of the family of God merely affirms my understanding of the unbelievable impact of the suffering Jesus endured for those He loved, His entire body, the Kingdom of God. It's my great honor to share my understanding of God's will for all mankind.

Perhaps the heart of God has been somewhat of a mystery in ages and generations past BUT it certainly isn't a mystery any longer!

The revelation of God's love for his creation has been impressed upon all with the blood of Jesus. Now those of us who have gotten the picture ought to start declaring the riches of God's glory to those who still regard the whole thing as a bit of a mystery and to those who consider themselves outside of the provision of God's love.

What was the mystery?

Jesus is in us!

Jesus is the only hope of glory we'll ever have!

Jesus is whom we preach about. That's all. It's all about Jesus folks.

We challenge folks to consider the possibility God did a whole lot more than we give Him credit for doing. We continue to teach folks about the only wise God who made it possible for "all" to attain to His "image."

Why?

So every person who hears the message will come to the life altering understanding each and every person is 100% perfect in God's eyes through the blood of Jesus! Nobody will ever be more perfect than they already are!

Wow! Is that good news, or what?

Well, it's the reason I do what I do. I'm so grateful to God for the work He has mightily done in my life. I can't think of a better way to express my appreciation to God than to tell others about this wonderful, almost unbelievable, good news!

I wish I could tell you how much trouble I've gotten myself into because I have the nerve to preach this gospel message to you, the Laodiceans, and to others who haven't even seen me face to face yet. I won't stop preaching it either. My goal is to see hearts comforted from the agonizing pain and suffering of following after the wisdom (foolishness) of mankind's attempts at self-righteousness.

My objective is to see folks stitched together in a bond of love that can't be unraveled by the blades of competition for God's approval. I will not be satisfied until I help folks come to the full assurance of understanding the riches of God's provision for all, until they acknowledge the mystery God does indeed dwell in us, and understand all of the treasures of wisdom and knowledge are hid in God, the Father, and in Jesus.

Why am I exhorting you with these thoughts? Well, I don't want anyone to "bewitch" you with enticing words to the contrary of this good news. I may be absent from you in body, yet I want you to know I'm certainly with you in spirit. I'm so glad you're enjoying your liberty, maintaining a sense of order, and remaining steadfast in the faith and faithfulness of Jesus towards you.

You've received Jesus in your spirit. Well, live like it!

You're rooted in Him! You've been grounded and built up in Him! You've been established by His faith and faithfulness!

So, abound in those truths with thanksgiving!

BEWARE!

Don't let anyone spoil your confidence in the work of Jesus on your behalf. Crafty philosophies are nothing more than vain, hollow, and deceitful piles of crap. Their pursuit of control over you is perpetuated after the traditions and wisdom of mankind's creative genius (stupidity).

Their objective is to keep you running on an aimless treadmill of laws, rules, and regulations, accomplishing nothing more than wasted energy!

Adhering to the rudimentary wisdom (foolishness) of this world will get you nowhere with God. None of these things mankind asks you to perform has any basis whatsoever in Jesus!

Listen up!

In Jesus dwells "all" the fullness of the Godhead. Jesus is the complete embodiment of God.

If this isn't enough to make you jump for joy, get a load of this.

You've been made the completeness of God too!

That's right!

You "are" totally complete in Jesus! Jesus has overtaken any authority or power set up to organize and control your eternal destiny.

In Jesus you've received a circumcision that has absolutely nothing to do with cutting off a piece of earthly flesh. You've received a much greater circumcision.

You've been cut off from sin!

Did you get that?

Sin has been cut off!

Jesus has cut off any requirements you may have had to gain the righteousness of God. He has preempted your dependence upon laws, rules, and regulations, as well as any other standards that have enslaved you in measuring your status before God.

Furthermore, your former lifestyle of self-righteous activity has been buried with Jesus!

And just as He arose, so too have you risen with Him, through the faithful operation of God's will to raise Him, and you, from the dead.

What does this mean for you?

Let there be no mistake. You were as done as burnt manna bread. You didn't have a prayer of gaining God's favor on your own merit or accomplishment. You were as eternally dead as you can get in your sins and in your inability to keep up to the standards of the myriad levels of laws, rules, and regulations that abound in the religious economies of mankind.

And then what did God do when there was absolutely nothing you could do on your own to gain the righteousness of God? Well, here are just a few things that He did for you:

- God made you alive in Jesus!
- God forgave you of all your sins!
- God has blotted out the handwriting of charges and IOU's piling up as one huge indictment against you!
- God took everything interfering with the application of His grace and peace and chucked it. Yes, He took every law, rule, and regulation and threw them all on the cross, nailing them upon the back of Jesus!
- God spoiled the authority and rulership of the wisdom (foolishness) of mankind. He publicly exposed the sheer ignorance and inability of every effort of humanity to gain the righteousness of God through what they believe, through what they do or don't do, or because of some adherence to a set of terms and conditions established to keep track of progress towards the goal.
- God has triumphed over anything and everything you may have dreamt up to gain His acceptance. You already have it! You have it in Jesus!

I want to explain a bit more about that "blotting out" idea.

Documents, like my letters, were written either on papyrus, a kind of paper made of the pith of the bulrush, or else, they were written on vellum, a substance made of the skins of animals. In either case, the material was fairly expensive. Hucking paper in the garbage can was a no-no! We used acid free ink so the actual script would just lie on the surface without biting into it. Recycling was common practice of prudent and cash conscious secretaries. They would take a sponge and simply wipe off the previously written material. Because the ink had merely dried upon the papyrus or vellum it could be wiped off like it had never even been there. Not even a trace was left.

Are you starting to get the picture?

God didn't just take the blood colored ink pen and write something new over top of the previous charges that had been leveled. Nor did He take the blood of Jesus and smear it all over all our failings so He couldn't recognize the accusations any more.

I say "Nay! Nay!" God wiped the charges away completely. Totally. Gonzo. Toast. History. Bye-bye.

Then He wrote your name down, and beside it, He wrote the words: HOLY! UN-BLAMABLE! UN-REPROVABLE!

Is that good or what?

149. DON'T GO THERE
(Colossians 2:16-23)

Don't let anyone, therefore, judge you for what you do, or don't do. What you eat or drink doesn't affect God's view and opinion of you. Whether you participate in the celebration of religious ceremonies once a year, once a month or even once a week, it makes absolutely no difference to God's view and opinion of you. Anything surrounding the symbolisms and rituals of all these celebrations are no more than a shadow of the truth to come.

BUT, since the cross, true religion is the reality Jesus "is" in you!

So, LET NOBODY BEGUILE YOU or rob you of the liberty you've been gifted with by God to enjoy His great grace and peace. Others will attempt to entice you into a voluntary, false sense of pride in your own performance. They may even tempt you to seek the affirmation of angels and the like. Don't be surprised to come to a realization there are those who'd seek to persuade you to find hope in things that don't even make sense. Those who perpetuate laws, rules, and regulations can't even keep them themselves. They are nothing more than hypocrites, stumbling around with swelled heads puffed up by their own vain imaginations.

Another way to spot those you should beware of is to listen carefully to what they're presenting. There's usually little in their agenda magnifying the only One who has bound the entire family of God together. The entire body, with all its various joints and muscles, is nourished and held together in Jesus. The only reason for any increase it can experience is a result of an increase in the measure of God's grace and peace.

Now, let me ask you a question.

If you're dead with Jesus, liberated from all the rudimentary laws, rules, and regulations the wisdom (foolishness) of mankind has formulated to govern your beliefs and behavior, then why, as though you were still living under that regime, would you be so stupid to continue to subject yourself to their tests of God's acceptability?

"Don't touch that!"

"Hey, you can't taste that!"

"Handle that, and you're dead meat!"

What's with that? The moment you've swallowed what you're eating or drinking they cease to exist. They perish in the consumption. Why in the world would you want to fall victim to the laws, rules, regulations, and doctrines of mankind?

Oh, I grant you they may appear to have a measure of validity. Indeed, they may even show an aura of wisdom.

150. SEEK THOSE THINGS
(Colossians 3:1-15)

Alrighty then, if you've been given a new life in Jesus, put your trust in the things God has already settled on your behalf. Jesus is already sitting on the very right hand of God!

So, set your affections and security on the fact your redemption, your righteousness, your holiness, and your liberty have already been established!

What you do or don't do on this earth can't ever alter this truth. You're already dead to laws, rules, and regulations. You're no longer bound by belief and performance! Your eternal destiny, including your abundant life right now, is hidden in the closet of God's protection through Jesus.

The moment Jesus our very life-blood appeared God's view and opinion of us was secured forever! Henceforth, our glory in God's eye is based 100% upon the glory of Jesus.

Mortify the lifestyle the wisdom (foolishness) of mankind has perpetuated. Sexual immorality, in and out of marriage; dirty mindedness; uncontrolled passion and lust; and the idolatry of greed are by-products of mankind's inability to live up to the standards of laws, rules, and regulations.

God just couldn't take it any more. He got so ticked off His wrath was kindled against the disobedience and ignorance of mankind.

Let's not kid ourselves. You were probably trapped in this lifestyle yourself at one time or another BUT now, these are the kinds of things inconsistent with the Spirit of Jesus in you:
- long-lasting, slow burning, thoughts of anger,
- furious fits and explosions of wrath,
- malice, a vicious mind bent on all pervasive evil,
- blasphemous, slanderous, and insulting speech,
- foul and obscene language, and
- lying.

The clothes of your old life in the systems of this world have been stripped off and discarded at the cross. You've been clothed anew with the purified robes of your new life in Jesus.

You are in Jesus, and He is in you!
What's changed?
Has God changed?

No, it's your knowledge and understanding of what God has accomplished in Jesus. That's what! Your mind has been renewed to the reality you are the "image" of God because God has made Jesus to be the very "image" of God!

Everyone bears the "image" of God now.

In the system of God's grace and peace there is no longer a category called Greek or Jew. There's absolutely no difference between those who've been circumcised in the flesh and those who haven't been. God hasn't rejected anyone due to the barbaric nature of their language, or, as in the case of the Scythians, the rather infamous, wild, and goofy nature of their character. Likewise, free folks and slaves are identical in the eyes of God.

BUT,

Jesus is "ALL," and is "IN ALL!"

Get used to wearing the clothes of your new life in Jesus! You're chosen of God, elected to be His holy and beloved children!

The following are recognizable characteristics of the wardrobe of Jesus within you:

- mercy,
- kindness,
- humility,
- gentleness,
- patience,
- forbearance, and
- forgivingness.

Look, if you've got something against another person, get over it. Allow the forgiving attitude of Jesus towards you to be the guiding example of your treatment of others. And after you've dressed up in all of these clothes, put on the cloak of charity and love that binds it all together so perfectly well.

Furthermore, allow the peace of God to rule in your hearts! Remember, God isn't angry with anybody any more, for He has called everyone to be a part of the family of God!

This ought to make you giddy with gratefulness. This glorious understanding ought to make you triumph in thanksgiving!

151. WALK THE WALK
(Colossians 3:16-4:6)

I think it's important you allow the promise of God in Jesus to grab hold of your very being. His wisdom is so rich!

Teach and exhort one another with poems, hymns, and spiritual songs that extol and magnify God for the grace placed in your hearts through Jesus. Whatever you do in word or deed, do it all in the Spirit of Jesus within you, expressing your gratitude to God the Father through Him.

Practical application? Here are a few thoughts:
- Wives: commit yourself to love, honor, and cherish your own husband, for this attitude fits perfectly with the Spirit of Jesus;
- Husbands: love, honor, and cherish your own wife as well and don't let covetousness or bitterness spoil your marriage;
- Children: obey what your dad and mom advise you to do because obedience is a characteristic Jesus is very familiar with;
- Parents: don't provoke your children to the point where they get totally choked up or off by you, for all it will do is discourage and alienate them from you;
- Servants: I have a longer list for you:
    - in this life do what you're asked/told to do, not merely with the aspiration of reward or with the integrity of a total suck, BUT rather, with the single motivation of your awesome love of God;
    - if you're going to do something, then do it with all the gusto you can muster, and yes, with a happy heart, inspired by your dedication to God as opposed to possibilities of the rewards and accolades of others; be fully convinced the only reward worth getting is the inheritance you've already received of God in Jesus, whom you serve;
    - BUT, screw up for your earthly master and you'll surely find out where it gets you, for your master probably has little regard for your rights or your future;

- Masters: treat your servants with equality and justice remembering you also have a Master in heaven who has given you a pattern to follow.

Remain vigilant and persistent in your thanksgiving to God. Continue to pray God will open doors of opportunity for us to speak about the mystery of Jesus, the very reason I'm imprisoned right now. I don't intend to quit preaching this marvelous message of grace and peace and I will not make any apologies for speaking out the truth of God's will for all mankind as clearly as I possibly can.

I challenge you to walk in wisdom as you interact with those who don't yet believe what God has done for them. Don't waste your time bickering about who is right and who is wrong, or about things that are way beyond your control anyway.

CLOAK YOUR CONVERSATIONS WITH GRACE.

Season your words with the appetizing appeal and pleasantness of salt. Use intelligence and tack to answer with dignity and clarity the questions anyone may pose to you.

152. FINAL GREETINGS
(Colossians 4:7-18)

O.K. Allow me wrap this up real quick.
Tychicus will fill you in completely as to how I'm doing. He's not only a beloved friend of mine he's also a very faithful minister of the gospel and a great fellow servant in the kingdom of God. I've also have sent Ty with the purpose of determining for me how you're doing, as well as to bring comfort to your hearts concerning my situation.

I've sent Onesimus to accompany Ty. He has steadfastly stayed by my side like a true friend. I'm sure you already are familiar with him since he comes from your neck of the woods. Well, both of them will inform you of what's happening over here in our chunk of the world.

The following friends want to send their best wishes to you:

- Aristarchus: he too has been captivated by God's grace and peace;
- John Mark: Barney's nephew, who, if and when he makes his way to you, please receive him cordially and pass on to him the instructions you've received for him;
- Jesus: oh, perhaps you know him as Justus. These three great Jewish buddies of mine have overwhelmed me with their assistance and comfort during this difficult time.
- Epaphras: one of your very own, who slaves to present the gospel message of Jesus, greets you as he labors tirelessly, unceasingly in prayer that you'll steadfastly remain in the knowledge and understanding you are perfect and complete in all of the will of God, for I can unequivocally state Papy has a very special place in his heart for all of those of you in Colossae, as well as those who live in Laodicaea and in Hierapolis;
- Doc Luke;
- Demas.

Would you please greet all the believers in Laodicaea. We also send our best regards to Nymphas and to all who fellowship together in his home.

When you finish reading this letter in your fellowship make sure it's passed on so it can also be read to those in Laodicaea. Hopefully, they'll also share with you the letter I wrote to them.

Please give Archippus the following message: "You've been given a tremendous honor and opportunity to share the gospel message of God's grace and peace. You're doing a great job. Keep it up!"

I'll even sign the letter with my own sloppy signature.
P.S.
Continue to remember me while I'm stuck here under house arrest. And don't forget...GOD'S GRACE IS ALWAYS WITH YOU!
Folks, that's just the way it is!

ROME

153. SIGNED, SEALED, AND DELIVERED
(Ephesians 1:1-14)

No, circular letters weren't written on round paper! However, my letters were certainly written to get around. The gospel message of God's grace and peace through Jesus is intended for all people, and the more folks who read or hear about God's love, well, all the better.

The next letter you're about to read is the third in the installment of letters I wrote from Rome to some of my good friends and to all the believers in the gospel of God's grace and peace over in Asia. This letter was formally addressed to the believers in the city of Ephesus, and then it was to be passed on to the believers in Laodicaea, Hierapolis, and Colossae just as the letters I originally sent to those folks was to be passed back to the Ephesian believers.

I trusted Ty (Tychicus) to be my postal courier. I had full confidence in him to deliver and read these letters in the fellowships as my ambassador, gathering and disseminating information on my behalf as he traveled about.

You may recall I spent almost three years in Ephesus and the surrounding territory earlier in my career. I count it a privilege to have met so many wonderful folks in different cities and towns throughout the area. My objective in writing a letter at this point was to encourage those who came to believe in the message of God's grace and peace to continue enjoying the liberty in the abundance of God's love. I also wanted to challenge them to affirm their righteousness was a result of God's love and mercy, exhorting them to exhibit the wealth of God's wisdom within themselves before all folks.

So, here goes, the letter to the Ephesians...

FROM:
Paul, captivated by the will of God to be an ambassador of the good news of Jesus.

TO:
the believers in Ephesus and to all those who continue to accept the faith and faithfulness in Jesus.

BLESSING:
Grace is yours, and peace too, from God our Father and from Jesus. Blessed be the God and Father of our Lord Jesus.

You know, God has blessed us with "every" spiritual blessing existing in heavenly places. Can't get any better than "everything!"

How'd He do it?

In Jesus!

Look, God literally chose us to be "in" Him before He even created the world. According to His plan, mankind was created to be absolutely holy and without blame for Him, in His love.

How'd He do it?

He predetermined and predestinated our adoption as children into the family of God by the faith and faithfulness of Jesus according to the good pleasure of His will!

Why'd He do it?

To the praise of the glory of His grace!

This is the reason He has made us all acceptable and accepted in the family of His beloved, Jesus, in whom we've been ransomed and redeemed through His blood. It's through the blood of Jesus that we've the complete forgiveness of sins according to the riches of His grace!

In Jesus, God has displayed His absolute wisdom and insight into the total picture and scope of eternity, while at the same time, displaying His wonderful understanding of His incredible creation. Through Jesus, God has revealed to all of us what could only be described as a mystery, at least to those who don't understand it, of His will. And God did it according to his good pleasure, and in Jesus, He purposed to do all of this of His own volition.

Why?

As one who manages his household to run like a well-oiled machine God sustained His entire creation until He decided the time was right to pull everything together in one neat package. This is when "all" things were made one in Jesus!

That's "all" things folks!

Yes, everything in heaven and everything on the earth have been joined together, even in Jesus!

Incredible, eh?

In Jesus we also have **OBTAINED AN INHERITANCE!**

An inheritance was predetermined according to the perfect intention of God who has worked out all the details according to the counsel of His very own will.

Now, why'd He do that?

So we would be to the praise of His glory!

154. IN TIMES PAST
(Ephesians 1:15-2:10)

Let me tell you I'm so grateful to God for what He's done for all mankind. And since I've heard you now fully understand the work of Jesus on your behalf are demonstrating your trust in Him by showing love towards your brothers and sisters in the family of God I never stopped giving thanks to God for what He's done in your lives too.

I pray the God of Jesus, the very Father of glory, would continue to give you the spirit of wisdom, expanding the horizons of your understanding to discover the infinite knowledge He possesses concerning all. The eyes of your understanding have been enlightened from the darkness, fear and hopelessness of self-righteousness so you may know without a shadow of a doubt:
- what the hope of His calling is,
- what the riches of the glory of His inheritances are for all His children, and
- what the exceeding greatness of His power is to those of us who understand the incredible working of His mighty power.

It was God's power carried out in Jesus when He raised Jesus from the dead and set Him at His very own right hand. Jesus now reigns in glory far above any law, rule, or regulation, above any power, authority or government, and even far above every other thing you could think of which has been given a name, not only in this world, BUT, also that may ever come to be named in the future!

It stands to reason if there's nothing above Jesus then everything is under Him! Yes, "all" things have been put under His ownership and authority. God set Jesus to be the head of all things concerning the family of God, that in fact, is His body, the very fullness of God, who has completed every thing needing to be accomplished in order to make "all" completely "all" it could ever be!

And you? What did He do for you?

Ha! He's brought you back from the dead too!

Yes, you. You were dead in trespasses and sin. You were dead folks walking in the darkness of self-righteousness.

Well, not any more!

In times past, you walked according to the wisdom (foolishness) of the systems of mankind. You succumbed to the wild imaginations of goofy deceivers who misled you into thinking there was some mystical powers in the air to get you closer to God. Well, the very same spirit of self-righteous is a darkness still hanging over too many folks, impaling their liberty with an ignorance and disobedience of the truth in God's love.

Don't kid yourselves we've all been there.

When? In times past!

We too have engaged in conversations discussing how we can get closer to God, how we need to believe more, how we need to have just a little more faith, how we need to act more responsibly, and how we need to do this, or do that.

On and on the circle would go. More like a treadmill. All we did was work harder to fulfill the demands of our self-righteous systems. We tried to satisfy our own minds we were actually getting to be more righteous by lusting after everything we "thought" was right. We were, by our own stupidity, deserving of all God's wrath, and then some. What we were is actually no different than everyone else. We were all in the same boat.

BUT, God, who is rich in mercy, for He has shown all mankind the greatness of the love that He had for all, even when we all were dead as doornails in our sins, has quickened us! Yes, He raised us up from the dead at the very same moment He raised up Jesus from the dead!

It is by His grace and the faith Jesus had in God that you are saved!

IT IS THE GIFT OF GOD!

It is not of works, lest anyone should boast about what they have accomplished of their own belief or merit.

Listen, we are the products of God's workmanship. We have been created in Jesus, fully dependent on the good work He accomplished. That is what God had in mind all the time for He ordained we all would live in His acceptability only in the provision of the blood of Jesus.

155. HABITATION OF GOD
(Ephesians 2:11-22)

Wherefore!
Wherefore remember, you, in times past, were simply out of the loop as far as some folks thought. You were called Gentiles, uncircumcised scum-bags, at least by those who thought snipping a piece of flesh in a ritualistic ceremony gave them exclusive dibs on God's acceptance.

Once upon a time you actually had no idea who Jesus was or what He was prophesied to do. You were aliens from the common wealth of Israel, strangers to all of the covenants of promise, totally without hope, and absent of any awareness of God's activity in this world.

This was the way it may have been in times past, BUT now, in Jesus, you who sometimes were pretty far off the target are made nigh! Yes, you are as close as you are ever going to get to God.

Why?
Because of the blood of Jesus for He is our peace! He has made the uncircumcised and circumcised one!

No kidding! Jesus has broken down the middle wall of partition between these two diametrically opposed peoples. He literally abolished in His body all of the anger and wrath of God towards all mankind.

Hey! Not only that Jesus abolished every set of laws, rules, and regulations sustained and perpetuated by the systems of mankind's attempts at self-righteousness.

Why did Jesus have to break down the walls?
- So He could make in Himself one kind of people out of two. This was the only way God's peace could be made effective.
- So He could reconcile both to God in one body through the cross having also slain the anger and wrath by absorbing it on behalf of "all."
- Remember the words of Isaiah? "'Peace, peace to him who is afar off, and to him who is near,' God said, 'and I will heal them'" (Isaiah 57:19).

- So, through Him, everybody would have access to God through the one Spirit of Jesus who lives in each and every one of us.

Now, therefore, you are no more strangers or foreigners. BUT, what you are is a fellow citizen of everyone else in the kingdom of God and a full-fledged member of the family of God! You have been built upon the very same foundation as everyone else, including all of the other great leaders and prophets.

The foundation is none other than Jesus!

He is the chief corner stone of the whole building. Every part of the building has been fitly framed together in Jesus. The building has been built with one purpose in mind, to be a holy temple in God!

Yes, in Jesus you've been BUILT TOGETHER to become the habitation of God through the Spirit of Jesus in all!

Please allow me to give a few notes to assist you in understanding some of the dynamics.

First of all, what Isaiah said was pretty interesting to me. You see, when Rabbis spoke about accepting a convert into the Jewish religion they referred to such a person as having been "brought near." There's a story of a Gentile woman who approached a Rabbi Eliezer, confessed she was a sinner and asked to be admitted to the Jewish faith. She pleaded with him, "Rabbi, bring me near." Unfortunately, as the story goes, he refused and promptly shut the door in her face.

Well, I've got good news for that woman, or anyone else like her. The door is not in the control of any human being. Furthermore, God has opened the door for all to come in and nobody can do anything about it!

God "has brought everyone near!" He called us all, from near and far alike, and healed us with His peace!

Secondly, I want to go back to the fact God has broken down the "middle wall of partition." Judaism isn't the only culture to erect barriers differentiating people from each other, or that has established laws, rules, and regulations to govern the requirements of a relationship between people and their God. However, let me describe a bit about the Jewish temple to help you get my drift in the letter. Of course, most of the folks who originally read the letter knew exactly what I was driving at.

The temple courtyard consisted of a series of courts, each one raised a little higher than the one preceding it. From the outermost court to the temple building itself were a number of courts on the various levels as follows:
- Court of the Gentiles,
- Court of the Women,
- Court of the Israelites,
- Court of the Priests,
- Temple.

The only courtyard a Gentile (non-Jew) could enter was the first outer area and it was separated from the Courtyard of the Women by a wall beautifully constructed wall of marble. Tablets adorned the massive stone pillars at various intervals pronouncing in a variety of languages including Greek and Roman the penalty for any unauthorized foreigners who passed beyond a certain point.

Oh, the punishment? Merely the pain of instant death, that's all. "Let no one of any other nation come within the fence and barrier around the Holy Place. Whosoever will be taken doing so will himself be responsible for the fact his death will ensue."

This is what the warning was like. Cool, eh?

I doubt if I need to remind you the very reason I got into all this mess in the first place is because the grand pooh-bears accused me of aiding and abetting Trophimus, an Ephesian Gentile, to proceed beyond the point of no return. I was just as guilty as the offender and thus subject to getting my butt kicked as well. I have a rather different perspective on the events needless to say. Anyway, the cookie's crumbled.

The Jews thought they could rightly discern the will of God so they came up with the great idea it was the great honor of the Jewish people alone to enter into a relationship with God beyond a certain point. Erecting barriers was an impenetrable defense to keep the riff-raff out.

Need I remind you what transpired on the cross? The veil was rent in two, removing once, and for "all," every barrier which ever existed between mankind and God! The barriers between God and mankind were broken apart as dramatically and as equally as the barriers that have existed between Jew and Gentile, Greek and barbarian, poor and rich, free and slave, male or female, or old and young.

The peacemaker was Jesus!

156. FULL OF GOD
(Ephesians 3:1-19)

For this reason, I, Paul, captivated by Jesus, bring to those of you who thought you were beyond the scope of God's intention the very message of the grace of God shown to me. I'm sure you've all heard the story of how God revealed Himself to me and shed some "light" on me, so to speak.

(I've already described the mystery to you on the preceding pages, so, as you read it, I'm going to assume you've been able to figure out what I know and understand about the mystery of Jesus.)

Well, in times past, this mystery of God's grace and peace in Jesus was obviously unknown to mankind in the same way it is now understood by many of us who are instrumental in helping folks recognize the wonderful good news exists by virtue of the Spirit of Jesus.

The mystery has now been made manifest Gentiles are every bit as much fellow heirs of God's grace and peace as the Jews! Jews and Gentiles are equal members of the very same body of Jesus!

All mankind share and partake of the promise of God in Jesus.

Now this is what I call good news!

Fabulous news I'd say!

This is all I want to talk about I gladly minister to others about the gift of grace God has given to me by the faith and faithfulness of His power. Listen folks, God gave His gift to even little old me! Man, I'm less worthy of this precious gift than most of His children.

And yet, He gave His grace to me! It's incredible! And now I get to cast the "light" of the vast, measureless, and unsearchable riches of grace in Jesus to all those who once thought they had no hope of attaining the acceptability of God.

I have the glorious task of helping all mankind see the implications of this mystery for everyone. The union of God and mankind has been from the beginning of the world hid in the heart of God who created all things through Jesus.

Even all of God's creation in heavenly places is being shown the manifold wisdom of God for His kingdom according to the eternal purpose that He intended in Jesus.

In God we now have boldness and accessibility with complete confidence.

Why?

Because of the faith of Jesus!

Look, don't get your rope in a knot on my account. Don't lose any sleep over the difficulties I find myself in because I've brought you this wonderful good news extolling the glory of God in you.

I consider it a great honor to bow my knees in honor to praise the Father of Jesus, of whom the whole family in heaven and earth is named.

God has empowered Jesus to grant you according to the riches of His glory to be strengthened with might by the Spirit of Jesus within you. God made it possible for Jesus to dwell in your hearts by "His" faith!

Why?

So, being rooted and grounded in the love of God, you may:

- be able to comprehend along with everyone else the scope, the breadth, the length, the depth, and the height, of the family of God;
- know the love of Jesus that surpasses anything we could actually understand, and
- **BE FULLY AWARE OF THE FULLNESS OF GOD DWELLING IN YOU!**

157. CRAP SHOOTERS
(Ephesians 3:20-4:16)

And now, to God who is able to do MUCH MORE than we could possibly ask or think, according to the power working in us, to Him be glory in the family of God through Jesus throughout all the ages, forever and ever!

This is just the way it should be!

I, therefore, captivated by the incredible love of God, plead with you to carry on in the blessed assurance of the fantastic inheritance God has imparted to you. How? Well carry on:

- with all the humility you can muster,
- with all the gentleness and self control you can handle,
- with great patience, compassion, and understanding,
- with a sincere will to seek the ultimate best for others in love, and
- with a determination to maintain the unity of the Spirit of Jesus in the bond of peace.

Why? Because:

- There is only ONE body!
- There is only ONE Spirit of Jesus!
- There is only ONE hope you have been called into!
- There is only ONE God!
- There is only ONE faith!
- There is only ONE death and resurrection!
- There is only ONE God and Father of all, who is above all, through all, and in all!

BUT, each and every one of us has been given as much grace as Jesus had at His disposal to dole out. And to top it off, the full measure of it was His gift to us!

Just listen to what God said concerning His Son,

"You have ascended on high. You have led captivity captive. You have given gifts to mankind; yes, for the rebellious also, that the Lord God might dwell among them" (Psalms 68:18).

As an aside, since Jesus has "ascended" from earth, would it BUT not make logical sense He also had to "descend" to earth?

You see, Jesus, who "descended," is the very same One who "ascended" into the heavens so He could bring to completion the will of God for all things.

Some of the folks whom Jesus has blessed with His grace may now be your leaders, preachers, evangelists, pastors, and teachers. And why did Jesus give His grace? He offered grace:
- to perfect all the children of God,
- to complete the work God gave Him to do, and
- to build up and strengthen the entire body of Jesus!

How much grace did Jesus give?
- Enough until we were all unified in His faith!
- Enough until we could know that He truly was the Son of God!
- Enough to make us perfect!
- Enough to make us as complete in stature as He is in the eyes of God!

Why is this so important for you to know? I'm telling you these things so you'll stop acting like children, tossed to and fro in indecision, whipped about with every whiff of wind spreading the seeds of false doctrines and creeds invented and propagated by the shady, shallow wisdom (foolishness) of mankind. There are lots of "crap" shooters out there who make it their mission in life to manipulate the dice of clever argumentation to deceive and control the destiny of others.

BUT, I tell you the truth concerning the grace of Jesus in love so you may indeed mature to the point where you know and understand everything He's done for all mankind. You see, you are in God because you are in Jesus!

Hey, the whole family of God has been fitly joined together in Jesus. He has supplied every joint and muscle of it with all the nutrients it will ever need. The very reason for the eternal survival rate of all humanity is the incredible measure absolutely effective in carrying out the mandate of Jesus to ensure each and every part was included in the plan of God. It is the matchless gift of grace that made it possible for the entire body of Jesus to be built up to know and appreciate the immense love of God it took to make all of this possible!

EPHESIANS

158. RENEW YOUR MIND
(Ephesians 4:17-32)

I'd like to encourage you, therefore, as one who can testify to the work of God in me to stop walking from now on in the same steps as those who don't think there's any hope for them. Stop thinking like those who vainly pin all of their hopes for their attainment of God's acceptance and their eternal destiny upon their own beliefs and accomplishments.

Clouds of darkness hang over their knowledge and understanding of the grace and peace of God. They've alienated themselves from the incredible abundance and liberating freedom of their life in God because they're too stupid to comprehend a good thing when they hear it and because their hearts are so blind they can't see a good thing when its plunked down right smack in front of them.

Callous people without hope actually have petrified hearts. They're way beyond the scope of caring about what happens to themselves or others. Consequently, their insatiable, shameless lust to possess what doesn't belong to them has overtaken them. Coveting the apparent success of others leads to performances that are often less than wholesome, even by their own standards.

BUT, you haven't learned this goofed up, hopeless lifestyle from Jesus. If you've been paying even the least amount of attention to what you have heard from Him, and if you've learned anything at all from the teachings of Jesus concerning the truth in Him, then you'll know at least few things you're to do with your life:

1. Put off the old nature! Stop the ignorant conversations you used to engage in with others, comparing notes and exchanging bragging rights of self-righteous performances. The deceitful lusting of your former lifestyle which based your acceptance of God upon the acceptance and adherence of standards set up through systems of laws, rules, and regulations may have been enticing, however, it was completely ineffective, not to mention corruptive.

2. Give your head a shake! Shake out the cobwebs and alter your ego. In other words, "smarten up." Be renewed in the very spirit of your mind! Put on the new nature that God created in you. He has clothed you in His righteousness and His true holiness.
3. Stop telling lies to others concerning the fate ready to befall those who fail to tow the party line or to those who refuse to follow the status quo of the wisdom (foolishness) of mankind. Just tell the truth to those around you about the truth of God's love. Why? For we're simply just brothers and sisters in the great big family of God.
4. Go ahead and get ticked off when others try to entice and convince you to accept "what" you believe and "how" you perform will determine your eternal destiny. Don't give in to this crap! Just don't loose any sleep over what other folks think of your understanding of God's grace and peace.
5. Neither give any occasion to maliciously utter slanderous, false reports which will undoubtedly injure the reputation of another. There's absolutely no need for this kind of silly behavior any longer. Look, for those of you are hooked in the habit of taking from others what doesn't rightfully belong to you, **KNOCK IT OFF!** BUT, if you need something to keep yourselves occupied get busy doing something thoughtful and productive. Give other folks a hand when they need it.
6. Watch your mouth! Trashing others won't accomplish anything, 'cause it's just corruptive, harmful, and pointless. BUT, if you must open your mouth, then let words of encouragement and edification flow out in waves to minister the grace of God to any willing to listen to you.
7. Why would anyone desire to turn away from enjoying the Holy Spirit of Jesus within them? The day of our redemption was sealed when God place His Spirit within all of mankind! There's nothing in this world we should be bitter about. We certainly don't have anything to be angry about. Nor is there any reason someone would need to get into a war of words or fisticuffs with someone else. We have no justification to bad-mouth others either. Malicious behavior? What for?

8. On the other hand, there's every reason you could ever think of to be kind to one another. You have every reason to be tenderhearted and compassionate to others. And you certainly have the very best reason in the world to maintain a forgiving attitude when confronted by the ignorance or insensitivity of others. "What's that?" you ask. Just think for a moment about what God has done for you. God forgave you, not only for your sake. He forgave all of the ignorance and insensitivity of all mankind for the sake of Jesus!

159. GET A LIFE
(Ephesians 5:1-20)

Be, therefore, followers of God as His dear children in His wonderful family.

Make love your habitation.

Imitate the unselfish charity of Jesus who demonstrated His love by giving everything He had, including His very own life and His very own blood to purchase our life and liberty. Let me tell you God took as much pleasure in the faith and faithfulness of Jesus' offering as you would have enjoying the incredible smell of a beautiful, thick chunk of steak on the bar-b, or of sniffing the wonderful fragrance escaping a precious bottle of perfume.

BUT, engaging in sexual impropriety and misconduct is self-seeking and self-serving, not to mention unhealthy. The itch to get your hands on what doesn't belong to you runs contrary to the Spirit of Jesus within you. Don't plague your conversations with the insensitivity of filth, senseless rumor-mongering, or of flippant character assassinations. A tongue filled with disrespect is distasteful even before the words break past the lips. BUT, you'd be much better off with words of thanksgiving, praise, and encouragement.

It's absolutely true the wisdom (foolishness) of mankind has placed limitations on who would and who wouldn't get to enjoy any of the inheritance in the kingdom of God in Jesus. Most of us just knew those who were unfaithful to God wouldn't get anything from God. And then there are the scum of the earth who muck about in the filth of degradations of unmentionable proportions. We didn't give them a chance.

Hey, why should the greedy get what they don't deserve? Idolaters? Why should God bless them? They outright reject God!

Well, don't let anyone deceive you with words that so completely glorify the vanity of mankind. God dealt with all this on the cross of Jesus! All of those things demonstrating the selfishness of mankind are the very reasons God was so ticked off with the world. We were simply a batch of disobedient kids.

Don't be caught in the trap of mankind's total ignorance of God's marvelous grace and peace for all, or, too stupid to accept His gift!

There may have been a time when you participated in the mindset that reduces the loving grace of God to a blip on the horizon of this world, content to stumble and falter in the darkness of self-righteous systems of belief and accomplishment.

BUT, not any more!

Now you are LIT ABLAZE IN GOD. You aren't just "in" the light you "are" the light! So, illuminate the little corner of the world you inhabit. Shine like crazy!

The fruit, the by-product, of the Spirit of Jesus is the impartation of all His goodness and of all His righteousness to all those He loved. This is the truth of God's grace and peace.

Go for it! Prove it!

Demonstrating the selfless love of Jesus will assist you to understand just how much of everything is acceptable to God.

Don't hang out with folks still trapped in the bondage and slavery to the systems and controls of laws, rules, and regulations. The unfruitful, seductive darkness surrounding the tyranny of self-righteousness is inexplicably intoxicating. Stay as far away from it as you can!

BUT rather, tell them to give their head a shake. Better yet, tell them they've already got a life, so they might just as well start enjoying it. I'm so disgusted by the shame of self-righteousness I don't even like talking about the nonsense it perpetuates. The secretive judging going on behind the closed doors of people's hearts and in the cloistered, hallowed halls of the minds of self-seeking do-gooders is repulsive. It runs contrary to everything God has done for all mankind.

BUT, each and every thing the dark wisdom (foolishness) of mankind has placed into its systems of laws, rules, and regulations to gain the acceptance of God has been completely exposed by the light.

Who did that?

Jesus! Yes, He's the One who has obliterated the darkness of mankind's self-righteousness.

What did God say would happen?

"The people who walked in darkness have seen a great Light; those who live in the land of the shadow of death, upon them has the Light shined" (Isaiah 9:2).

"Arise, shine; for your Light is come, and the glory of God is risen upon you" (Isaiah 60:1).

So, stop stumbling around in the darkness of your own systems of belief and performance. Don't be stupid, BUT give your head a shake! Start living your lives to the fullest. Don't get caught in either the trap of reckless abandonment as those who think they have no hope or fall under the control of those who've become prey to the desperate struggles of legalism.

Don't waste your time and speculation trying to figure out how to gain the righteous acceptance of God, BUT understand the will of God for all mankind has already been signed, delivered, and sealed!

Alcohol may numb your sense from reality if you go overboard with it along with many other excesses, BUT if you'd just renew your mind to the reality the Spirit of Jesus is already in you then you'd understand how His light exposes the unreality and superficiality of the self-righteous attempts of belief and performance.

Meditate on the poems, hymns, and spiritual songs that magnify the loving goodness of God. If you're too embarrassed to sing out loud in public, make some melody in your heart. Heap your gratitude and praise all the time for all things to God the Father in the name of Jesus!

160. NOT EVEN A ZIT
(Ephesians 5:21-6:9)

Don't be afraid to put the interests of others above your own. "Self-less-ness" rather than "self-ish-ness" is the appropriate response in awe and reverence of God's grace and peace for all mankind.

Wives, show the same kind of love, honor, and respect to your husbands as you would if he were God Himself. You know, God's not stupid. He came up with the whole idea of husbands-for-wives and vise-versa in order to provide for them abundant life and liberty.

Look, isn't this what Jesus did for all the children of God? Jesus is salvation, He's righteousness, He's life, and yes, He's everything for the family of God!

Wife, this is what your husband is for you. Therefore, in the very same way all mankind has received of the goodness and greatness of God from Jesus, accept the challenge of dishing everything good in you onto your very own husband's plate.

Husband, L O V E your wife!

How?

Even as Jesus loved each and every child of God! You see, He not only loved everyone, He gave everything He had for us, even His very own life!

Why?

So He might separate all mankind out to be even more special than we already were, cleansing us all with the washing waters of the promise of God's word.

And why did Jesus place us all in the giant washtub of His blood?

So He might present all mankind to Himself as one glorious family of God, without a single spot, without a wrinkle, and without even a zit of unattractiveness! BUT, of course, He has made us all holy, totally without blemish!

Men, do you want to know how to love your wives?

Treat your wife with the same love, affection, and devotion you shower upon your very own body. Show me a man who loves his wife and I'll show you a man who loves himself!

There's never been a man yet who hates his own body, BUT men nourish and cherish their own bodies in the same way God cares for His children.

To quote God Himself:

"This is now bone of my bones, and flesh of my flesh...for this cause will a man leave his dad and mom, and will be joined to his wife, and the two shall be one flesh" (Genesis 2:23,24).

The thought of two people being joined together in a union of one is an outstanding mystery in its own right. BUT, the great mystery of the union of Jesus with all the children of God is something all together out of this world!

I challenge each of you husbands out there to honor and cherish your wife with the same gusto you do your very own body. And wives please honor and cherish your husband.

O.K. Kids, it's your turn.

Obey you parents! You have a God-given, innate instinct to do what is right and pleasing for your dad and mom.

"Honor your father and mother," says the very first commandment which carried a promise with it, "so the number of days the Lord your God will give to you on this earth will be numerous and fulfilling" (Exodus 20:12).

Dads? Don't provoke your children to anger! Don't tick them off with inconsistency and indifference. BUT, in tenderness and care, educate your children by embracing everything directed toward developing their mind and character in a positive way, setting a pattern for them to enjoy a healthy understanding of God's view and opinion of all mankind.

Servants, I urge you to be obedient to your masters in this world. You may be scared spitless, trembling often at your lot in life. Well, make it the primary purpose in your heart to perform each and every task as if you were doing it for Jesus. Sucking up with performances based on ulterior motives is more demeaning than you know. Don't serve constantly worrying about what other folks are going to think or with the objective of what you can get out of it. BUT, work with the dedication and servanthood of Jesus, for indeed, this is the will of God in your heart. With good will go about your jobs as a declaration of your love for God and not of your obligation to any master.

Don't forget God made no distinction between those who are slaves and those who are free when He blessed us all with the gifts of His grace and peace.

Yo masters! Return loyalty, respect, and servitude to those from whom you expect it. There can be no reason for issuing threats or abusing the power your may have. Keep in mind the example of your heavenly Master for He didn't make a distinction between those who qualified for good treatment and those who didn't. Fortunately for us, God didn't differentiate between those who deserved His grace and peace, and those who didn't!

EPHESIANS

161. ARMOR OF GOD
(Ephesians 6:10-24)

Finally, my dear friends, be confidently strong in God and in the power of His might! Clothe yourselves in the whole armor of God.

Why?

So you'll be able to stand against the crafty deceptions of those who slander God's gift of grace and peace for all mankind. Look, there's no need for us to wrestle against the flesh and blood Jesus sacrificially gave on our behalf. BUT, what we do wrestle against is the legalistic oppression of laws, rules, and regulations. We wrestle against powers that would rob us of the abundance and liberty of our life in Jesus. We wrestle against the leaders of the stagnating self-righteous wisdom (foolishness) of mankind. And yes, we wrestle against elitist doctrines, creeds, and systems of belief and accomplishment that administer control through guilt and fear.

So, arm yourselves completely in the whole armor of protection God has amassed to ensure your eternal destiny. You'll need to know and understand the unconquerable love of God to help you withstand the continuous onslaught of the deceivers and slanderers who perpetrate the seductive myth of self-righteousness. Getting a grip on God's view and opinion of all mankind will help you remain securely planted in His grace and peace.

STAND THEREFORE IN THE ARMOR OF GOD! Look:

- God has wrapped you in the liberating belt of His truth!
- He has protected your heart with the breastplate of His righteousness.
- Walk around in your sandals fully assured God has already cleared the way for all to freely abide in the glorious good news of His everlasting peace.
- Above all, defend yourself in the shield of God's faith and faithfulness in Jesus.
- Use His shield to extinguish all the dangerous, fiery darts of the self-righteous wisdom (foolishness) of mankind.
- Protect your mind with God's helmet of salvation.

ARMOR OF GOD — EPHESIANS

- Arm yourself with the sword of the Spirit of Jesus, who has proclaimed and demonstrated the will and promise of God to the whole world.
- Fill your prayers with the praise and adoration of the Spirit of Jesus within you.
- With all perseverance keep your eyes peeled wide open to be of assistance, encouragement, and comfort to all the children of God.

How can you help me?

Well, pray God would continue to open the doors of opportunity for me to open my big mouth and tell everyone about the incredible mystery of the gospel of God's grace and peace. I'm still an ambassador of God's incredible love even though I'm somewhat tied up at the moment. This won't stop me from telling like it is, as boldly as I know how.

BUT, if you want to know about my mission and how I am doing I'm afraid I'm going to have to leave it up to Ty, my beloved brother and fellow minister of the good news of God's love, to give you the latest scoop. Actually there are two reasons why I've sent Ty to see you. First, to inform you concerning my present condition, and secondly, so he might bring comfort and joy to your hearts.

In conclusion, for all of you who are standing fast in the armor of God, never forget the faithful love of God the Father and Jesus is the very reason you can confidently live in the abundance and liberty of peace and grace!

Take care.

ROME

162. INTRODUCTION OF THE PHILIPPIAN LETTERS

Ahhhh. Philippi.

Few of the cities I've visited on my travels bring back fond memories quite like Philippi. You may recall my first visit there came during my eleventh trip. I had received the challenge to come over to Macedonia while I was in Troas. We arrived at the seaport of Neapolis and then traveled the few miles inland to the city of Philippi.

I'll briefly bring to your remembrance a few of the memorable events of those first few days there. We were introduced to the beautiful businesswoman by the name of Lydia. This fairly well to do fashion designer and fabric merchant literally threw open her home to use as a base for our attempts to spread the gospel of good news in Jesus.

And then there was the "slave girl" incident! Boy, this one got us into a heap of trouble. The fact she became unproductive and consequently unprofitable to her masters enraged them to the point we were actually thrown into prison.

Therein lies another fabulous story. I'm talking about the rock concert we entertained at late one evening. Well, Silas and I aren't exactly song birds, however, the fact the earth started shaking during our little nighttime serenade was a bit unsettling for a whole lot of folks. When all the dust settled a door was opened for us to relate the wonderful news of God's loving grace and peace to more than just the jail warden and his family.

The chief magistrates of the city finally gave us a one-way ticket out of town for our troubles. The discovery of our Roman citizenship caught the authorities off guard, prompting them to forgo some unthinkable consequences they had contemplated for us to endure.

It was some five years or so, if my memory serves me correctly, before we would return to Philippi again. We were traveling from Ephesus to Athens and Corinth on our fifteenth excursion, precipitated by the collection of gifts for those who were suffering terribly back in Jerusalem. The spirit of the believers in Philippi to lend a helping hand to others in great need was definitely inspiring.

On more than one occasion these wonderful folks also blessed me with special gifts to help me get by so I'm indebted to them for the love they've shown me. I consider Epaphroditus to be one of their gifts. You should have seen faces take a jolt when folks heard me call him "Papy!"

The difference in our age proved rather convincingly my nickname for him was an obvious misrepresentation of the truth of a son-father relationship. Anyway, Papy proved over and over again to be a most valuable assistant and one whom I could trust implicitly.

Papy became my link to the fine folks in Philippi. He would bring me information from back home and then courier my letters of instruction and encouragement to them.

The very first letter I wrote to my friends in Philippi was written shortly after Papy initially arrived on the scene in Rome to assist me. He brought me some troubling news concerning a number of deceptions being promoted amongst the believers and I wanted to respond to them right away.

So, here's a part of one of the letters I wrote to the Philippians.

1ST PHILIPPIANS

163. **DIRTY DOGS**
(Philippians 3:1-4:1)

Finally, my dear friends, rejoice in the goodness of God. To write to you over and over again of the matchless grace and peace of God is certainly not something I'll ever tire of, BUT, for you, it's the only message offering the security of God's eternal acceptance.

Dirty dogs!

Watch out for them! BE ON GUARD for the mutts who scavenge for prey with noses trained to sniff out the ravages of deception and ignorance. Beware the religious hounds that chase after the wisdom (foolishness) of mankind's vision of self-righteousness. Beware of those who practice a ritualistic ceremony of circumcision thinking it confers a special status in the eyes of God. This mutilation is nothing more than a confession the mercy and graciousness of God is somehow inadequate to encompass all, or, they're conceited enough to think God would bless only them because of their adherence to ceremony and tradition.

Well, I have news for those dirty dogs.

We are "all" the circumcision of God!

"Who is?" you ask.

God has cut everyone out to worship God in the Spirit of Jesus! He has given to all a reason to rejoice in Jesus. God has initiated a way to be liberated from the pathetic need to put our confidence in any of the systems of belief and accomplishment of mankind.

Look, if there was ever a person able to brag about towing the party line it would be me. Let anybody else throw their name into the proverbial hat of self-righteous worthiness with mine in a contest for God's acceptance and I'm confident I'd win hands down.

Take a look at my pedigree!
- I was circumcised when I was just eight days old.

Now, as an aside, let me just interject a bit of history after some of each of these points so you'll understand what my intended readers would understand without any greater explanation.

The first point was to drive home the significance I was neither an Ishmaelite who circumcise their boys at the ripe old age of thirteen, nor was I a proselyte to the Jewish faith because a proselyte normally would be circumcised later on in life.

- **I come from good Israelite stock!**

I could trace my ancestors back to Jacob. It was God who called Jacob by the special name of "Israel" after His wrestling match with Jacob. Other people, like the Ishmaelites and the Edomites, could trace their roots back to Abraham and Isaac respectively, however, they couldn't claim the distinct bragging rights Jews could.

- **I come from the tribe of Benjamin!**

The tribe of Benjamin is the elite of the elite in the Jewish nation. You history buffs out there may remember Benji was the son of Jacob and his favorite wife Rachel, able to claim the distinction of being the only one of the twelve patriarchs to be born in the "promised" land. The first king of Israel came from the tribe of Benjamin. Yes, it was King Saul! When my mom went to the good book of names before I was born guess whom she named me after? Good on you if you made the connection.

My ancestors remained faithful with the tribe of Judah when all the tribes split up, playing a prominent role in rebuilding the nation. Don't forget it was Benji's tribe who held all the pivotal positions on the battlefields of Jewish history. (Judges 5:14; Hosea 5:8)

When I said I came from good stock I meant I came from "good" stock!

- **I am a Hebrew of the Hebrews!**

I could rightly brag about the fact I was born a Hebrew, the son of proud Jewish parents who lived far away from their Jewish homeland, and yet, who cherished and preserved their "Jewish-ness." It took a profound amount of discipline and effort to live in a Greek-speaking environment while retaining the Hebrew tongue. Indeed, I was truly blessed to have parents who recognized the need for me to be able to speak fluently in a number of languages.

- **As touching the law, a Pharisee!**

Not only could I claim special status because I was born right, I could brag of things I'd been able to accomplish. I knew the law inside and out. I had a doctorate degree in Phariseeship from one of the most prestigious schools of Jewishdom, studying at the feet of none less than the great Gamaliel. We weren't called the "separated ones" for nothing. Keeping even the smallest details of the good books was what we lived for. There were never more than six thousand of us at any one time however we certainly were the elite athletes of the spiritual world of Judaism.

- **Concerning zeal? Hey, I persecuted believers with a vengeance!**

I took first prize in zeal. There may not be a greater characteristic in life for a Jew than zeal. The passionate desire to know God, to obey His commandments, and to do the work of God (as if that's even possible!) was the motivation of every Pharisee. I was so good at it I moved up the corporate ladder rung after rung. I pursued opponents of our religious system with an obsessive zeal. I wanted to purge most anything interfering with our traditions. An annoying pest in the religious bottle of Jewish ink was none other than the little band of believers in a man called Jesus. I was placed in a prominent role to blot out the nasty imperfections in the ink.

- **As for righteousness obtained through the adherence to laws, rules, and regulations? Blameless!**

Yes, I thought I was this good! No, I considered myself to be better than good. I was the best! In my eyes at least, I was a top dog!

If someone were keeping score at the dog show I'd be the one with the most blue ribbons. If someone were grading achievement I'd have received the highest marks. I'd have collected the most golden stars. There wasn't anything I did wrong! Talk about arrogance, eh?

BUT each and every thing once so important to me has become entirely meaningless in light of the faith and faithfulness of Jesus!

Let me say it again so there can be no doubting what I just said.

I count all things BUT loss! Total nothingness! Absolutely useless!

Everything has been exchanged for the excellency of the knowledge and understanding of the work of Jesus. It's for Him I've gladly suffered the loss of any hope I had placed in everything, including my belief, my ability, and my accomplishments to gain me the righteous of God.

I count absolutely everything of my self-righteous human endeavor to be nothing more than a pile of *!#*!

Yes, you read it right.

Everything I've done to gain the acceptance of God is nothing BUT a pile of stinking crap!

Why is this such a good thing?

Ha!

Let me give you a few good reasons:

1. I've come to the awesome revelation I've already won the totality of God's favor through Jesus!
2. I've come to grips with the reality my eternal destiny has been established in Jesus alone. You see, I don't have a shred of righteousness in me because of my adherence to any systems of belief, laws, rules, or regulations. BUT, the only righteousness I have is a result of the faith of Jesus. This righteousness is nothing less than the righteousness of God through His faith and faithfulness!
3. God is clearly the only truth I need to know about! The awesome power of the resurrection of Jesus is what it took for me to be unconditionally adopted into the family of God. Because of His suffering I've been made conformable to Him in death, all for the specific purpose of attaining the resurrection to a new, eternal life.
4. Look, it's not like I'd already attained self-righteousness, nor had I attained even a measure of perfection. BUT, my goal now is to simply seek to apprehend the truth for which Jesus has already apprehended for me!

My dear, dear friends, I didn't do anything to get where I am right now in the eyes of God, BUT, there's one thing I've set my mind to do. I've decided to forget about all my vain self-righteous pursuits.

Why?

To gain what I could never gain so I might concentrate on reaching out to accept the matchless gifts of God's grace and peace He has set before me to enjoy!

My goal is now to press towards consciously accepting God's view and opinion of me as a holy, pure, and righteous child of His. This is solely based upon the faith and faithfulness He sees in Jesus!

So, let's get this straight. All of you who are perfect should start thinking like you're already perfect! And, if any of you can't quite wrap your brains around this concept, then God will surely let you see the picture sooner or later.

Nevertheless! In spite of what you may think, since we've already attained the righteousness of God, let's at least start living like we are perfect in the eyes of God! Let's be mindful of this very truth.

My dear friends, I've already shown you I'm a perfect (oh, that's good) example of how far a life dedicated to self-righteousness will get you. It couldn't get me anywhere in the eyes of God! It breaks my heart as it even brings tears to my eyes to tell you the folks who valiantly, yet ignorantly, strive to believe and act in a way to gain God's favor are nothing less than enemies of the cross of Jesus!

There are many folks who can conceive of no higher good than the satisfaction of their own bodily appetites. They seek for all of the right things in all of the wrong places. Those who place all of their hope in the wisdom (foolishness) of mankind will surely find the only glory they receive here on this earth will be shame, embarrassment, guilt, and fear.

What a waste of human effort!

There's nothing we've done on earth we can brag about as having an effect upon God's love. There's only one thing we can talk about which has accomplished anything and that's what was accomplished in heaven on behalf of the whole world.

The only place we could have found a Savior was in heaven. He's none other than Jesus.

Jesus has changed our vain imperfectness into the embodiment of His glorious body in accordance with the work He did to subject all things to Himself.

DIRTY DOGS — 1ˢᵀ PHIL

Therefore, my beloved brothers and sisters whom I long to see again, my pride and joy, my wreath of celebration, I exhort and encourage you to continue on in the abundance and liberty of God's grace and peace.
Stand fast in God, my dearly beloved!

In our Jewish tongue we have a great saying, "Yada! Yada! Yada!"

I'm sure you've probably heard the phrase. Do you know what it really means?

The term refers to the intimate knowledge of another. In some circles, the inclination to consider the sexual connotation of "Yada! Yada! Yada!" would be somewhat justified, however, it means a whole lot more. It encompasses a totality of knowingness.

Well, this is precisely the thought I was trying to drive home to my Philippian friends. My desire in life has shifted from knowing every trick in the book to sway God's view and opinion of me to simply accepting God's unchanging and unchangeable view and opinion of me.

You see, God sees me in the same light as He does Jesus. Hey, He's as perfect and righteous as you can get! The challenge of my existence is to renew my mind to accept this unalterable truth. Those who persist in thinking they have something to do with getting their salvation waste their lives in shame, guilt, and fear!

If God changes His mind and decides to come up with a better plan than the all-inclusive, free gift of His grace and peace then I have all the confidence in Him to let us in on it. He's already shown us the desire of His heart when He sent Jesus to alter our eternal destiny. How much better could it possibly get for us?

Here's a thought I've come across from someone wiser than I to wrap this up:

"You already are what God wanted! There's absolutely no reason for you to try to become something He needs!"

2ND PHILIPPIANS

164. FRUIT OF EXCELLENCE
(Philippians 1:1-11)

I'll bet that little letter probably raised more than a few hairs around Philippi!

I could only hope. Anyway, you're about to read another letter that I wrote to my dear friends over in Philippi. I trust you can see I felt very comfortable letting them know what I really thought!

Call it Second Philippians if you like. Here goes...

FROM:
Paul and Timothy, ambassadors of Jesus

TO:
all the believers in Jesus who live in Philippi, including those who lead and serve

BLESSING:
Grace and peace are yours from God our Father and from Jesus.

I'm so thankful to God for what He has done for you every time I think about you. No kidding. I never forget to joyfully express my gratitude to God for making it possible for you to enjoy the reality of the fellowship of His grace and peace from the very first day you came to know and understand it until now.

I maintain an unshakeable confidence in one very important truth: God started the whole ball rolling for you when He creating you and He fulfilled His promise to all mankind when He brought His entire creation to complete perfection on that momentous day of Jesus' intervention.

Don't be surprised I'm so happy for all of you because you occupy a very special place in my heart as well. I'm keenly aware of your continued support of me through my arrest, my incarceration, and during all of the trials scheduled to determine the guilt or innocence of my defense and confirmation of the great good news gospel of God's love for all mankind. I know all of you have become partakers of the very same grace accorded to me as a gift of God. I want to reassure you, as God is my witness, my love for you is inspired by the very love which Jesus has for the whole world.

I'm not afraid to let you know there are a number of things I pray about concerning you. Allow me to mention a few.

1. I pray your love for God, yourselves, and for others would only abound more and more as you grow in your knowledge and understanding of the wisdom of God.
2. I pray you'd approve of the excellency of God's grace and peace.
3. I pray you may be sincerely secure in the knowledge you've been liberated from the tyranny and oppression of self-righteousness since Jesus did His work on the cross.

Like a precious metal strained and burnt free of any impurity, and like a traveler who arrives at a destination unscathed by the journey, you've been brought to perfection with the fruits of God's righteousness.

Do not be mistaken to ignorantly think you've been filled with God's righteousness through the fruit of your own belief or accomplishment.

Oh no. You've been **FILLED WITH THE RIGHTEOUSNESS OF GOD** as a result of the faith and faithfulness of Jesus!

Now, why would Jesus do this for you?

To bring glory and praise to God!

165. I'M A WINNER
(Philippians 1:12-30)

BUT!

I'd like you to know most of the things that have happened to me lately have actually turned out rather well, all things considered. For it's resulted in the spreading of the great gospel message far beyond even I had envisioned.

The truth of my unjustified imprisonment for preaching the work of Jesus is well known among the entire praetorian guard who protect me, among all of the various ranks of the military and political establishment right up to the big guy himself, and even among many of the common folk in a whole lot of places.

I'm happy to acknowledge many of my fellow believers have taken some inspiration from the suffering I've endured. Lots of folks have cast off the fear that previously held them back and have begun to speak out boldly about what they have come to know and understand about the love of God.

There are, of course, some folks who don't take too kindly to the message I preach. They've taken it upon themselves to declare their own misguided versions of the message of Jesus. They waste more time trying to stir up envy and strife over who is right and who is wrong rather than concentrating their efforts on the simple truth.

Then there are those who just like to preach the gospel message because they know without a shadow of doubt what God has done for them.

Yes, I'm convinced there are some who preach the message of Jesus just to spite and discredit me. It's pretty obvious to recognize them for their insincerity is very apparent. They mustn't like what I preach all that much 'cause they seem to take pleasure in seeing me suffer all the more.

BUT, I know there are folks who preach the love of God the way I do. They know and understand I've had the courage and determination to stand up and be counted for the gospel message of God's grace and peace.

So, what then?

Notwithstanding the different motivations for informing others about Jesus, whether it be from an ignorant or incomplete portrayal of the work of God, or, on the other hand, the accurate declaration of the truth of the wisdom of God's all-inclusive love, I'm a happy camper. I can live with it. I'm just happy to hear people are talking about God.

I share the confidence of Job in God as he declared, "I know God will also be my deliverer, my salvation." (Job 13:16)

My positive outlook for the future is buoyed by your vigilant support and by my absolute recognition of the Spirit of Jesus within me. It's my earnest expectation and hope in Jesus that I'll never have to be ashamed for one single thing I've done. BUT, in similar fashion to the frankness I've had to speak my mind in times past, I now can boldly declare Jesus is magnified in my life. And He will continue to be magnified whether I am alive or dead!

Look, I don't see a difference between life and death. My life is **WRAPPED UP** in Jesus. And when I die, hey, I suspect my new life will be even better! BUT, if it be my portion to live a bit longer, then I'll continue to labor spreading the message of the fruit of God's blessing.

To tell you the truth, I've come to the stage in my life when it's getting a bit more difficult to decide whether I'd like to continue on in this life on earth, or just get on with discovering the limitless possibilities of my eternal life.

I admit I'm kind of stuck between a rock and a hard place. Both choices are very palatable. On one hand, I have a desire to loosen the tent ropes, take down the pegs and tent, and strike camp for the great campground in the sky to be eternally in the presence of Jesus. Perhaps I might untie the mooring ropes, hoist up the anchor, and set sail into the wild blue yonder on the good ol' gospel ship. Talk about an exciting trip!

On the other hand, sticking around down here to give you folks a hand, and to pump you up, sounds pretty good too. I feel very confident I'm still needed here. So, as long as I'm here, I'll continue to encourage and exhort you to live in the abundant life and liberty of the faith and faithfulness of God. I know when I get to see you again I'm going to be tickled pink to see how abundantly happy you are in Jesus.

Do me this one favor though. Let your conversations reflect the good news message of Jesus in you. Why? So, whether I actually come and see you or not I may hear you're standing fast in the kindred Spirit of Jesus, united with the common purpose of working together to share the faith and faithfulness of God with others.

Furthermore, don't get startled like panicking horses attempting to avoid a disastrous collision in some intimidating situation. Don't allow those who don't share your enthusiasm for the gospel message to scare, intimidate, or dissuade you with their deceptive attempts to control you with the wisdom (foolishness) of mankind's pursuit of self-righteousness. They may regard your confidence in the all-inclusive, all-sufficient work of Jesus to be nothing short of treason, heresy, or apostasy, BUT, to you, it's the only force to liberate all mankind to enjoy all the blessings of God's grace and peace.

Look, God, on behalf of Jesus, has made it possible for all to enjoy an incredible life free of the guilt, shame, and fear of having to perform. Everyone has the great and awesome privilege of just simply accepting His free gift. BUT, you also ought to expect you may have to suffer a bit for standing fast in your understanding of God's wisdom.

I'm a perfect example of this unfortunate reality. You've been witnesses of the suffering I've had to endure for my stand concerning the gospel message. Now I ask you to bear witness and to pay attention to what I am telling you!

166. CHUNK OF GODNESS
(Philippians 2:1-18)

So:
- if there is any support and encouragement whatsoever in Jesus;
- if there is any comfort you derive from His love;
- if there is any fellowship of the Spirit of Jesus within you;
- if there is any affection and sympathy you have received of Him;

then, complete my joy. I'd like all of you to get on the same page.

Why?

Let me give you a few good reasons.
- Because you all share the very same love of God.
- Because you all share the one accord of God's will.
- Because you all share the same place in the mind of God!

Look, don't go around doin' stuff just to cause trouble, or worse yet, with goofy, self-righteous motivations.

BUT rather, with a conscious awareness of who you are in Jesus, let each one of you seek the ultimate best for one another. Don't waste your time always thinking simply about yourselves BUT everyone ought to also give diligent care and attention to the needs of others.

I'd like to challenge you to have this mind in you.

"Which mind?" you ask.

The very same mind that is in Jesus!

Hey, Jesus knew who He was! He was, is, and will always be, GOD!

His very divine nature is as undeniable as it is unalterable. There was no need for Jesus to reach out to snatch and grab a "chunk of God-ness."

Why?

Because He already was completely God.

Nor did He have to somehow hang on to His "God-liness" as if He could be separated from it.

BUT, Jesus chose to abdicate His divine rank. He didn't merely disguise Himself as a servant, He actually became the substance of one, in the likeness of mankind.

In the shape and appearance of a human Jesus laid aside entirely the honor and privileges rightly His. He surrendered all personal ambition and all self-seeking impulses without reservation to the will of God.

How far did He humble Himself? Until His DEATH!

No, not just death. He died on the cross, the most despicable, ignominious of any mode of punishment. God, for one, was pretty impressed! What'd He do? God has highly exalted Jesus! He has given Him a name that is above every other name. Why?

So:
- "in" the name of Jesus each and every thing will bow!
- "in" the name of Jesus each and every thing in heaven will bow!
- "in" the name of Jesus each and every thing on earth will bow!
- "in" the name of Jesus each and every thing which was on earth will bow!
- each and every tongue will confess Jesus is in fact God. What for? To honor, glory, and praise God the Father!

Is this good news, or what?

Take a look at this archive. This is what prompted my encouragement to my Philippian friends.

"Look to Me, and you will know you've been saved, all you ends of the earth; for I am God, and there is none else. I've sworn by Myself, the word is gone out of My mouth in righteousness, and I won't take it back, that unto Me every knee will bow and every tongue will swear. Surely, will one say, 'In the Lord I have righteousness and strength, even to Him will all mankind come and even all those who are incensed against Him will be ashamed they didn't see it sooner.' For in the Lord will the whole world be justified, and will glory in it" (Isaiah 45:22-25).

So, my dear friends, just as you've always understood the work of God in Jesus on your behalf, not only when I have been kickin' around with you, BUT, perhaps even more so when I'm haven't been, I want to encourage you to keep on truckin' with the humble frame of mind which has been instilled in you in the Spirit of Jesus.

We all know we had nothing to do with God's view and opinion of us. For it is God, and God alone, who has done a work in us.

Why?

He has done so, both because He simply wanted to, and also, because it just made Him happy to do it! You have no excuse to mumble about, groaning and grexing at every turn like a bunch of wilderness orphans who missed out on the abundance of God's blessing because of their inability to simply accept Him at His word.

Why do I say this?

Look, I don't want you to give folks a reason to look at you like you're some kind of hypocrite or as some kind of threat to their health and happiness. My goodness, you're the sons and daughters of God!

You're without rebuke!

You're holy!

You're pure!

You're the righteousness of God!

In the midst of a crooked, mixed up, confused, and perversely ignorant world you're perhaps the only shining light some folks will ever have the good fortune to see! So, shine on! May your example hold out to folks who live in the darkness of the wisdom (foolishness) of mankind even just a glimpse of the incredible excitement possible in the abundance and liberty of life in Jesus!

Now, my dear friends, if you will do even this simple thing you'll make me a very happy camper!

Look, I've taken great joy in the day of Jesus when He died on the cross. Don't be mistaken. Everything I do now certainly is not in vain, nor has all of my effort in the past been worthless. Hey, I just do everything for an entirely different purpose. I've gladly taken on the role of being a servant to shed some light upon your path.

If it be my portion to sacrifice and suffer on your behalf, hey, bring it on. It's what I live for. It brings me great joy to see you live in the abundance and liberty of God.

Once again, take on the mind of Jesus too and you'll have all the motivation you need to live life to the fullest.

And then, you'll find out how happy I am!

Can I throw you another curve from the archive? Again it's from a favorite character of mine, Isaiah.

"And He said to me, 'You're my servant, my child, in whom I will show my glory.' But I replied, 'I've toiled in vain, I've spent my strength for nothing and vanity; yet surely the justice due to me is with the Lord, and my reward is with my God'" (Isaiah 46:3,4).

167. GOOD ON 'IM
(Philippians 2:19-30; 4:2-4a)

BUT, I trust in the Jesus!
    I plan on sending Timothy to you shortly. I'd also like to take good comfort in the knowledge you're doing o.k. I can't think of anyone other than Tim who cares as much for you as I do and I'm confident he'll employ his natural instinct to do everything he can to bring encouragement and comfort to you.
    This world is too full of folks who are contemptuously content to look only after their own self-righteous pursuits instead of living in the example of Jesus. BUT, you know this is not true of Tim. Indeed, you know very well he has served me like a son would serve his father as we spread the good news of God's love. Therefore, I hope to send Tim to you very soon, the sooner the better. I'll just have to wait and see how things go here, BUT, I've put my trust in Jesus for I'd really like to come to visit you myself asap.
    In the meantime, I feel compelled to send Epaphroditus along with Tim. As we've shared the gospel message Papy has been a dear brother, a companion in our labor, as well as a super trooper. BUT, I recognize he's been of assistance to me on your behalf. To be sure, he's done a fantastic job of taking care of me. Papy has been terribly homesick. He's been distraught, aware a rumor had spread concerning his health. Well, it's not just a rumor. The fact is Papy was so sick he just about bit the proverbial dust.
    BUT, we acknowledge God's mercy upon him. Hey, God didn't only have mercy on Papy, BUT He's been mighty merciful to me too. Having Papy die right now would be quite unbearable considering the multiple other problems I'm facing.
    I've sent Papy after careful consideration so when you see him again you'll be very excited once again. Knowing this will no doubt reduce the sorrow of my own loss. Therefore, in the Spirit of Jesus, receive him back into your fellowship with great joy. Honor him with your respect for he has earned a great reputation for his work as an ambassador of Jesus. He was so diligent and focused he almost completely forgot about his own health to the point of near exhaustion and death.

His ambition was to supply me with every assistance all of you would have rendered if you'd been here with me.

Good on 'im!

By the way, I'd like to earnestly plead with Eudoia and I beg of Syntyche, get on the same page! I invite you, dear friend, to assist these women who've labored together with me, Clement, and with all of our other co-workers.

Remember, everyone's name is registered in the book of God's abundant life.

Don't worry.

Be happy!

REJOICE IN GOD ALL THE TIME!

2ND PHILIPPIANS

168. WHATSOEVER THINGS
(Philippians 4:4b-23)

And again, I say, REJOICE!"

Allow the reality of a totally renewed mindset of servanthood and charity be visible by all those you come in contact with. God, indeed, is with you! Don't worry about anything, BUT, in every single situation that may arise to cause you a concern, in your prayer and petitions with thanksgiving, let God know what your problem is.

"What good will that do?" you ask.

The peace of God, which far surpasses all our ability to understand the all-inclusive complexities of His great love, will encompass your hearts and minds from the hopelessness, fear, guilt, shame, and disappointments associated with the darkness of self-righteousness ambitions.

"And how will God do that?" you ask.

He already has, through Jesus!

I'd better start to wrap this up pretty quick here. Finally, my dear friends, let me give you some things about God you ought to consider very seriously. Think about:
- things that are unequivocally true,
- things that are unabashedly honest,
- things that are unquestionably just,
- things that are totally pure,
- things that are divinely beautiful, and
- things that are absolutely worth talking about.

If there's any virtue, any virtue whatsoever in any of these things, and if there's any thing at all worthy of praise, any praise at all in any of these things, then give your head a shake!

Rattle your cage:
- around everything you've already learned about God,
- around everything you've already received as a promise of God,
- around everything you've heard concerning the all-inclusive love of God, and
- around everything you've observed in my life.

Then what?

You'll have no doubt whatsoever in your mind whether or not the peace of God has any place in your life!

BUT, I want you to know I abound in my rejoicing of God's blessing, especially since you've been once again able to so generously provide your assistance to me. I know you've always wanted to help me out, BUT the opportunity to do so wasn't always there.

Be careful now. I don't want you to misunderstand me. I'm not saying this to make you think I want your help, for I have learned how to get along. I've found out it's possible to reach a level of contentment that sustains me in whatever state I find myself. I know how to get along when I have very little and I'm equally equipped in the art of enjoying the luxuries of plenty. In every place I've been and in every situation I've found myself in I've always been taught there's little difference between being full and starving.

On the one hand, my stomach is stuffed to the max, and on the other hand, my stomach is anguished with pangs of hunger.

Big deal!

The thing that keeps me going in any situation is the knowledge Jesus has empowered me to live in the abundance and liberty of God!

Don't be mistaken. I take my beanie off to y'all. You've been most generous and kind to me. You've done a great job in helping me out over the years. You've been super! You Philippians surely know as well since the very beginning of our ministry to spread the gospel message after I departed from Macedonia no other fellowship has even entered into a discussion with me concerning the giving and receiving assistance, BUT, of course, you're the only exception. To be sure, even while I was in Thessalonica you sent once and then once again gifts to be used to minister to my every need.

I'm not braggin' on you to entice you to extend your kindness to me again. BUT, I'd like you to know the generosity of your heart accrues to your own account, not mine. Listen, you don't owe me a thing! BUT, I actually have everything I need right now. In fact, I have more than I need. I, of course, have already received from Papy the things that you sent with him to bring to me. Let me tell you, the smell of the meat from the bar-b was incredible! It drove the neighbors crazy.

The sacrifice was so acceptable and pleasing God Himself probably enjoyed it as much as we did!

BUT, be assured my **GOD SHALL SUPPLY EACH AND EVERY NEED** you will ever have.

How?

According to His riches in glory through Jesus!

Let me close with this affirmation: "Now, unto God and our Father, be glory for ever and ever. Amen."

P.S.

Please greet every child of God in Jesus for me. All of our brothers and sisters with me here want me to send you their best regards. In fact, all of the children of God salute you, especially those employed in the imperial service of Caesar. And don't forget: The grace of Jesus is with all of you. Take care!

ROME

169. INTRODUCTION OF 1ˢᵀ TIMOTHY

I've previously mentioned I was basically under what you could call "house arrest" in Rome for about two years. I was surrounded by all the amenities of home, and yet, I wasn't exactly free to go about as I pleased. I was under the constant surveillance of personal bodyguards, requiring special permission from the powers that be to leave the house on day trips.

It was during this period of being cooped up I resigned myself to pursuing a new career. My creative juices started flowing like never before. As I examined the alternatives concerning my ability to spread the great gospel message I started to feel more and more comfortable in the development of my writing career. If my penmanship weren't half bad I probably would have written even more than I had.

Let me tell you, it's a good thing some folks choose to be secretaries. I think they're highly under rated! I've had some great ones. Most of the letters you've read thus far have been written to various groups of people. Even the letter concerning Onesimus was actually written to Philemon, as well as it was to all of his family, and to all the folks who gathered together in his home.

The next letter, however, was written specifically to a very wonderful friend of mine by the name of Timothy. You're probably already familiar with him to a certain degree because his name has come up on several occasions in previous letters. Tim, as I called him to his face, was very special to me. He's one of those people who cross your path to make a profound impact upon your life.

I first met Tim way back on my first visit to the city of Lystra. He was living with his parents at the time. Interesting family. His grandmother Lois was a chip off the old block. She was awesome! Tim's dad was Greek while his mom, Eunice, was a Jew. According to Jewish law, this inter-racial marriage was illegal, making Tim an "illegitimate child" as far as Jewish laws, rules, and regulations were concerned. Tim became a unique protege, loyal to the core. I trusted him implicitly. Actually, he was more than just a friend. To me, Tim was a son!

Tim spent a fair bit of time with me during my "forced vacation" in Rome. It was sadly becoming evident my imminent release may not be as imminent as I would have preferred. Tim was too valuable to the cause of spreading the gospel message to be sittin' around watching me be bored out of my tree.

So, I decided to send him on ahead to Philippi as a courier of my letter and as an ambassador of mine to inform all of my dear friends the latest concerning the goings on in Rome. I knew full well he'd be a tremendous encouragement and comfort as he traveled about.

Ephesus was also on his itinerary. His mission there would be to establish, uplift, and strengthen the resolve of those who'd come to understand the grace and peace of God. I was not unaware of the difficulties to face my young compatriot as he moved forward in his role as a leader and as an example of the love of God. This particular letter was penned to give Tim another installment of sage advice he had already heard from me during the many times we spent together over the years. This refresher course was meant to be an encouragement to him.

1ST TIMOTHY

170. IMMORTAL, INVISIBLE
(I Timothy 1:1-17)

FROM:
Paul, an ambassador of Jesus because of the promise of God our Savior and of Jesus, who "is" our hope!

TO:
Timothy, like a son to me, definitely a true child of the faith and faithfulness of God!

BLESSING:
Grace, mercy, and peace are yours from God our Father and from Jesus.

Tim, disregard the purely speculative, imaginative, fictitious, and deceptive wisdom (foolishness) of mankind's pursuit of self-righteousness, along with the goofed up notions of the endless possibilities of genealogical prognostifications. All of these things do nothing other than raise more questions about life instead of providing answers.

I'd much rather see you concentrate your effort on expanding your knowledge and understanding of the edifying "God-li-ness" which you already have in you because of a promise of a faithful God!

Just do it!

The underlying foundation of the promise of God is His love, overflowing out of His pure heart, a result of His perfect will, and because of His unconquerable faith and faithfulness!

Unfortunately, everyone doesn't see the heart and activity of God in this way. Some folks have swerved off the path, choosing to follow the detour signs erected along the way by those who'd rather struggle along in the vanity and strangulation of self-righteousness. Some even have a very noble aspiration to become teachers of laws, rules, and regulations thinking they actually have a handle on the truth of God's grace and peace. The sad part is they don't have the foggiest idea of what they're talking about, much less understand what they ignorantly affirm.

BUT, we all know there's nothing wrong with laws, rules, and regulations provided one understands what they're for!

Get this straight. Laws, rules, and regulations were not created for those who were righteous BUT for a world of people who had more than one problem.

Here's a short list of folks who needed at least some laws, rules, and regulations to give them some direction:
- those who didn't even have a target to shoot at,
- those who couldn't handle the wisdom of God's truth right from the get go,
- those who decided they had no use for God,
- those who missed the target even when they attempted to shoot for one,
- those who were irreverently defiant,
- those who were profanely abusive to others,
- those filled with so much hate they felt no sense of shame to kill even their very own fathers and mothers,
- those who disrespected life so much they stole the life of others,
- those who found satisfaction in the traffic of people abuse,
- those who practiced the perversions of sexual immorality,
- those who thought nothing of kidnapping, and
- those who were liars, frauds, and cheaters.

There's no way I could give you a complete or exhaustive list. There's got to be a batch of other things folks did contrary to heart of God, contrary to the glorious good news of God in Jesus, a message made known to me. Boy, am I ever glad Jesus was faithful to do what God asked Him to do. I'm so thankful He enabled me to be a faithful communicator of the gospel message.

Hey, I know I wasn't exactly a model citizen. My goodness, I'd been an absolute critic of Jesus, rejecting Him outright. In fact, I persecuted those who believed in Him with a vengeance, punishing them mercilessly with self-righteous abandon.

BUT, I OBTAINED THE MERCY OF GOD!

Why?

Two reasons.

I was stupid! I did the things I did first of all in ignorance, and secondly, in unbelief! This was my problem.

The grace of God was the exceeding abundance of the faith and love in Jesus!

This was the heart of God!

Now, if there was ever a faithful saying, this is it:

"Jesus came into this world to save those who didn't have a hope of hitting the target of self-righteousness."

Well, I couldn't hit the barn door if it was right in front of me 'cause I was the worst shot of all!

Can you believe it? I actually obtained the mercy of God because Jesus had a heart of long suffering to see me accepted unconditionally, irrevocably, and eternally in the eyes of God. I figure if He could do this for a woos like me He could do it for everyone! I'm a perfect example of God's merciful grace and peace to anyone who may happen to come after me. I'm a pattern to all those who believe in this incredible good news of what an abundant, everlasting life can be like.

Now, praise is on my lips.

To the King eternal, immortal, invisible, the only wise God, be honor and glory, forever, and ever!

Folks, that's just the way it ought to be.

1ST TIMOTHY

171. ONE MEDIATOR
(I Timothy 1:18-2:7)

I challenge you Tim, my son, in accordance with all the revelations concerning God's love for the whole world we've been blessed to receive, war on! Look, it's not always going to be easy. Hold on to what you know and understand. You have a good conscience since you renewed your mind to the truth of God's wisdom.

Unfortunately, some folks just can't seem to let the gospel message keep them afloat. They get shipwrecked on the sea of life because they let the wind and waves of the guilt, fear, and oppression of self-righteous behavior swamp their vessel.

Hymenaeus and Alexander are two examples that come to mind who are drifting aimlessly trying to gain the acceptance of God like they used to. I don't know what else to do except let them chart their own foolish course. Hopefully some day they may learn that slandering the gift of God caused them to miss out on catching some pretty awesome rays on the calm surf of God's grace and on the peaceful, groovy beach of life.

I exhort therefore first of all, offer your praise, adoration, and thanksgiving to God for what He has done for all mankind. Don't even leave out kings and all the others folks in places of authority.

Why?

I suggest this is the first step in helping you understand God has made it possible for everyone to live a quiet, peaceful life in Him. It will heighten your awareness and understanding all are righteous and pure! For this is what God really wants! No foolin.' This is good and acceptable in the sight of God our Savior.

How do I know this?

The heart and will of God is that "all" mankind would be saved from themselves and that they "all" might come to the knowledge and understanding of the truth.

What truth?

There is one God and only one mediator between God and all mankind!

Who's that?

The man Jesus!

And He gave Himself a ransom for "all."
For who?
For "ALL!"
When did He do this?

Jesus testified to the will of God when He gave Himself in the perfect timing of God on the cross. Look, this is the only reason I do what I do. What other reason could there be to spend a life preaching and teaching? I can't help it. I want to be an ambassador of this incredible gospel message.

I'm telling the truth about Jesus. Why should I lie? I have the great honor and privilege of teaching those who thought they didn't have a hope they were wrong. I get to tell folks about the faith and faithfulness of God. I get to share with them the surety of God's love for all mankind!

172. GOOFY HAIRDOS
(I Timothy 2:8-15)

Tim, d'you know what I'd like to see?

I'd like to see men all over the world offering their praise and thanksgiving to God with their righteous hearts opened wide and with their holy hands lifted high. No longer is there a place for anger, argument, and conflict. The doubting of self-righteousness can be abandoned.

Women too! Encourage them to use their beauty, serenity, charm, and common sense as they offer their praise. There's no need to go overboard with fancy hairdos, expensive jewelry, and elaborate clothing as if they needed to impress someone BUT women should practice their godliness in very practical ways. Allow women to grow in their understanding of the heart wisdom of God in the intuitive, perceptive way men can only wish for.

BUT, I strongly recommend you instruct women to refrain from trying to teach men what they've figured out so instinctively. Nor should they interrupt men from coming to their own conclusions about the grace and peace of God in their own way and timing, BUT they should just patiently keep quiet.

Look, Adam was created before Eve. Perhaps Adam wasn't the first one to bite into the fruit of self-righteousness BUT it was Eve who had the smarts, however inaccurate, to think striking out on their own might be the best way of being like God. Ha! I'll bet the reason why God blessed women with the joy of childbirth is because women understand things of the heart. He must have known men didn't have the pulse, or shall I say, "stomach," for it!

Anyway, both men and women should CONTINUE TO LIVE IN THE FAITH, LOVE, AND HOLINESS OF GOD with due diligence and sensibility.

1ST TIMOTHY

173. LEADERSHIP
(I Timothy 3:1-13)

If a man aspires to hold a position of leadership and authority, good on'im! If they want to talk the talk, they'd better learn to walk the walk. Here's a short list of worthy characteristics for leaders:
- of blameless reputation, above and beyond criticism;
- the husband of one wife;
- vigilant;
- poised, well-balanced, and self-controlled;
- dignified, well-behaved, and unruffled;
- hospitable;
- apt to teach;
- not quarrelsome, violent, or given to drunkenness;
- free from bad tempered, assaulting speech or action, BUT, gentle, peaceable, refraining from violence and greed;
- governs well his own family with dignity and sincerity (For if a man can't even run his own family properly, how effective can he be as a leader of the children of God?);
- a mature veteran of life, so he won't get all puffed up with pride in his own accomplishments like those who slander and revile against the wisdom of God; and of good repute with those who still don't understand what God has done for them so he won't be an easy target for those who'd have a field day with a leader unsure of the truth of the amazing, great news of God's grace and peace.

Likewise, those who'd like to make it their goal to serve the needs of others have a responsibility to integrity and dignity. Here's another short list of worthy characteristics for those who wish to serve others:
- serious;
- not double-tongued, prone to say one thing to one person while another thing to someone else, and one whose word is his badge of honor;
- clear headed, not given to drunkenness;
- not soiled with greed and covetous intentions;
- possess an unquestioning, unwavering acceptance of the mystery of the faith and faithfulness of God;

- seasoned with experience in helping others;
- blameless and above reproach;
- have a wife of noble character, discreet with her tongue;
- sober in her deliberation, and consistent in all things;
- the husband of one wife; and
- a fair and consistent governor with his wife over the affairs of their children and home.

Those who pursue the task of serving others are well on their way to understanding the magnitude and scope of the attitude of Jesus and of His faith in God to **ACCOMPLISH THE ULTIMATE BEST** for all of mankind.

174. IT'S A GOOD THING
(I Timothy 3:14-4:16)

I'm writing these things to you right now in the expectation I'll be able to come and see you shortly. BUT, if I don't make it, at least these thoughts will help you understand and enjoy the great liberty there is in the household of God, indeed, in the family of God. God is the pillar.

Yes, He's the very foundation of all truth! There's no controversy concerning the greatness of the revealed truth of "god-li-ness" which God has imparted to all.

What was the mystery again? Here's a short list to remind you:
- God expressed Himself as a human being in Jesus.
- The Spirit of Jesus was declared to be righteous and pure in the sight of God.
- Jesus was placed in honor and authority over all things.
- The good news of Jesus has been preached to all those who thought they didn't have a chance.
- Many folks around the world have come to know and understand this miraculous gospel message.
- All mankind have been received in the Spirit of Jesus into the glorious righteousness of God's eternal acceptance.

We shouldn't be surprised for God told us it would happen, that, in the days before Jesus came, folks would turn their backs on the faith and faithfulness of God. For some goofy reason it seems people would rather put their eternal destiny in the seductive, illusive wisdom (foolishness) of mankind, and in the doctrines of the slandering deceivers who perpetuate self-righteousness through laws, rules, and regulations.

A pack of liars is what they are!

Hypocrites!

Like cattle identified with a searing hot iron, these manure spreaders can be easily spotted because they've been branded with the scars of the guilt, shame, and fear as a result of their self-righteous attitude and lifestyle.

Just think for a moment about how many laws, rules, and regulations have been established to govern things like marriage. And then there's a whole lot more concerning what you should and what you shouldn't eat and drink!

IT'S A GOOD THING — 1ST TIMOTHY

My goodness, all those of us who know and understand the truth of God are fully aware everything God has created is good. We should be thankful for things like marriage and food. God Himself blessed all things by proclaiming,

"It's a good thing!" (Genesis 1:31)

If you constantly remind your brothers and sisters about these truths you have nothing to be ashamed about in your ministry of spreading the truth of Jesus. You'll find nourishment as you feast on the words that proclaim the faith and faithfulness of God and in the good doctrine He has placed His righteousness in you.

BUT, don't waste your time getting entangled in the profanities and crap of laws, rules, and regulations, or, in the web of old wives' tales with their corresponding myths, as if either had anything at all to do with how you might attain to the righteousness of God.

Rather, train, exercise, and discipline your mind in the understanding of the liberating truth of God's loving grace and peace.

The discipline of your physical body in respect to food and exercise may be helpful for your overall health here on this earth BUT they have absolutely no impact on your relationship with God. The truth of God's view and opinion of "all" mankind is profitable for everyone, in every situation! God's promise of an abundant life was given to fulfill the life in which you now find yourself, as well as for the life that is yet to come.

The faith and faithfulness of God is unquestionable, worthy of being accepted for what it is! It just can't get any better than this!

The very reason both of us are working so hard, yes, even to the point of suffering reproach and indignation, is we've put our trust in the living God, Who is without a doubt, the Savior of "all" mankind.

I'll have to admit this truth has become so much more incredible to those of us who have come to know, accept, and understand the universal, unconditional scope of God's love! Don't let anyone despise the wisdom of your understanding simply because they don't expect it to come from someone as young as you. BUT, prefer to be an example of what believing in the grace and peace of God can do for a person.

IT'S A GOOD THING   1ST TIMOTHY

Allow the Spirit of Jesus within you to:
- encourage the words proceeding from your mouth to be genuine;
- channel your conversations to be encouraging and positive;
- activate your behavior based on seeking the ultimate best for others;
- stimulate your attitude with thanksgiving and joy;
- enlarge your consistent acceptance of the faith and faithfulness of God; and
- encourage a bountiful life of purity and wholesomeness.

Until I get there, give attendance to read as much as you can of the scriptures, to the exhortations and encouragements of the prophets of old, and to the doctrines and truths of Jesus. Don't neglect the precious gift of God's grace and peace in you. Treasure it because it was given to you by the promise of God and nothing else. Your progress in this liberty has been confirmed by others who've blessed you with their acceptance of God's calling on your life.

Meditate on these things.

BE DILIGENT TO PRACTICE THE LIBERTY YOU PREACH. Stick to it!

Don't give in to the nonsense flying all around you.

Remain securely planted in the truth of God's grace and peace.

Others need to be encouraged by your knowledge and understanding of the promise of God's righteousness for "all" in Jesus.

By persevering, you'll not only save yourself from a heap of problems, you'll also liberate a whole lot of other folks from the paralysis and bondage of the guilt, shame, and fear that accompany the self-righteous controls of laws, rules, and regulations.

175. WIDOWS
(I Timothy 5:1-16)

Don't go around harshly rebuking men who are older than you, BUT, appeal to their sense of integrity and dignity with respect as if you were talking to your very own father. Treat younger men than you like they were your brothers. Affectionately honor women who are older than you as you would any mother. In regards to younger women, well, be vigilant to guard their purity as if they were your sister.

BE GRACIOUS TO CARE for the needs of those who've lost a mate, forced to carry on without the support of family. BUT, if any widow has children or other close relatives who can assist them, let these relatives learn first of all to demonstrate a gracious, respectful attitude of thanksgiving to those who've given so much over the years to raise and help them along. Surely this good and acceptable behavior demonstrates the character of God's unconditional love for all mankind.

Now, a woman who has lost her mate and indeed has been left truly alone to scrounge for the necessities of life understands the concept of utter dependence upon the grace and peace of God. She often has plenty of time throughout the day and evening to offer prayers of thanksgiving and appeal.

BUT, a woman who seeks a destructive road to self-sufficiency will get lost in the tragedy of missing out on the generous support of others. Tim, make sure these folks, both the widow, and her family if she has one, fully understand the importance of doing the right thing.

BUT, if anyone doesn't accept the honor and responsibility of assisting their relative, especially those of their very own family, then they're showing a complete disregard for the example of the faithfulness of Jesus. In fact, if they don't lend their support, they display an attitude worse than someone who has never even heard of the heart of God.

Who should receive your assistance?
Women who:
- are at least 60;
- have been the wife of one man;
- have a good reputation of helping others;
- have raised children;

- have been hospitable to strangers;
- have the humility to attend to even the most menial of tasks of servitude;
- have brought relief to others afflicted with suffering; and
- have diligently devoted themselves to performing all kinds of good deeds.

BUT, widowed women under 60 should be able to look after their own needs. It's tough to be sure. On one hand, they may have had every intention after they lost their mate to dedicate the remainder of their lives to the service of Jesus. However, on the other hand, it's only natural they may still crave the understandable urge and instinct to remarry.

It would be cruel to put them into a period of guilt or embarrassment simply because they abandon a pledge of servitude to return to a blissful state of marriage. Moreover, idleness is a by-product of living without purpose.

Young women who are too dependent on others for support are more likely to find themselves roaming from home to home looking for something, or someone, to sink their teeth into! Idleness is one thing, BUT, it can easily degenerate into a vocation of delivering inaccurate information, otherwise known as spreading rumors, or develop into the nasty habit of sticking one's nose into places where it ought not to be!

Look, I'd just as soon see younger women get married, have kids, set themselves to guide the household, and avoid the temptations of allowing themselves to fall into situations which could bring them into disrepute. It's sad to know many young women have already decided to seek a path that undoubtedly will bring them into harms' way.

To repeat what I said earlier, it should go without saying the ones who should care and support the widowed, first of all, are members of their own families. The fellowship of believers has enough to care for without the extra burden of supporting those who can find assistance within their own family circle. These suggestions will free up the much needed resources of the group to assist those widows who are truly in need.

1ST TIMOTHY

176. GENERAL COUNSEL
(I Timothy 5:17-6:21)

The last portion of this letter to Tim was written to give some general advice as he became an influential leader among those he served. These rambling remarks exploded into the letter without a whole lot of thought of a logical or thematic approach. They just came out. Tim would take each one of these thoughts seriously knowing I meant every word of it.

Some of the elder men who assist in the administrative affairs of the fellowship are probably worth their weight in gold. In fact, those who also help out in the teaching and proclamation of the gospel message are probably worth double their weight. Even the scriptures teach workers ought to receive the honor and praise they deserve, not to mention a decent salary.
  "You shouldn't muzzle the ox that treads out the corn" (Deuteronomy 25:4).
  Jesus even added his two shekels when He wisely added, "a laborer is worthy of his wages" (Luke 10:7).

O.K. I can just hear you say, "What's up with that?" Why bring oxen into the letter?" Let me explain.
  Sheaves of corn were laid on the threshing floor of the barn so oxen, usually in pairs, could be repeatedly driven over the harvest. Sometimes they were tethered to a post in the middle and herded in a repetitious circle pounding the corn. Perhaps the oxen were harnessed onto a threshing sledge that would be dragged to and fro across the corn. Whatever method was employed, it was more than a common courtesy to the oxen to leave them unmuzzled so they could snarf down a bit of the corn for their hard work.
  For the Jews, it was a "LAW!"

Don't just accept any accusations against a respected person BUT make sure an accusation is well founded, supported by the witness of at least two or three witnesses. those who insist on returning to the bondage of the self-righteous strategies of the wisdom (foolishness) of mankind.

GENERAL COUNSEL — 1ST TIMOTHY

The insipid danger of folks going back to the controls of laws, rules, and regulations is worth the risk of rebuking them publicly to make an example of stupidity.

I charge you before God, before Jesus, and before all His creation, pay attention to what I am telling you. Any attempt to set down laws, rules, and regulations that set up a hierarchy of worthiness is against everything God has done for all mankind. Everyone should be treated with equal respect and consideration, nobody receiving preferential treatment.

Don't be too quick to jump on the bandwagon of success or failure of another. Neither become trapped or entangled in a web of perverted legalism some weave to control others. Just don't go there! Enjoy your liberty.

Some folks don't want you to touch alcohol. Well, stop drinking water 'cause this is probably what made you sick in the first place. BUT, a glass of wine once in a while could be just what the doctor ordered to calm your stomach and it might just sooth of few other aches and pains to boot!

There are some folks who blatantly demonstrate the fact they're still stuck in the muck of self-righteousness. They can't get out of the fear what they believe and what they do will rescue them from some perilous judgment that surely must be awaiting them. Go figure! What's worse, some folks think these people are having so much fun in the cesspool they jump in head first to join the party.

Then there are those who demonstrate the art of doing good things liberated from the cloak of self-righteousness and enthralled with the attitude of the Spirit of Jesus within them to seek the ultimate best for others. It's not impossible to see the difference between the two motivations.

Instruct those who serve under the yoke of slavery to count their earthly masters worthy of the honor and respect they are due.

Why?

So the name of God together with the truth of His matchless, loving grace and peace will not be mocked.

Furthermore, those who actually serve folks who believe in the grace and peace of God ought not despise their masters either. Hey, they're actually their brothers and sisters. BUT rather, they ought to serve them just as diligently because they are equally recipients of God's faith and love, heirs and participants of all His benefits.

Tim, I want you to give instruction and encourage folks concerning these things. If anyone teaches something else, disagreeing with these wholesome words, even the words of Jesus and the promise of God to gift His godliness into all mankind, they're nothing more than proud and arrogant. They actually know nothing BUT to dote over meaningless questions and trivial arguments concerning the technicalities and meanings of words. All this does is stir up a whole lot of needless envy and strife, provoke nasty, hostile exchanges of insults, and conjure up the mysterious suspicions of innuendo.

The more folks argue about and contest who has the inside track on the wisdom (foolishness) of mankind the more depraved and defrauded they become of the truth of the great gospel of God's grace and peace. They actually think they can believe and accomplish their way into God's good book!

Goofed up, or what?

Tim, just stay away from those kinds of people.

BUT, when you mix contentment with the "God-li-ness" so graciously and abundantly given to you, you'll understand you have the greatest gift in the whole wide world.

Look, we didn't bring anything into this world other than our squeaky-clean little bodies and I'm not the only one who'll tell you we won't leave here with anything more than our squeaky clean little bodies either.

Since we have something to eat and something to wear let's learn to be content. BUT, those who go overboard in the pursuit of fame and fortune put themselves into the precarious position of falling into the pools of self-righteousness and into the traps of over-abundance and over-indulgence. The foolish and harmful arrogance of self-sufficiency is a destructive force.

Look, the passionate, driving force to attain wealth is a major contributor to the evil of self-righteousness. The stench of greed pervades the aura of those who think they have what it takes to get ahead on their own. Self-righteous folks err when they fail to understand they are who they are only because of the love of God. Failing this, they're doomed to suffer needlessly in the pits of guilt, shame, disappointment, fear, etc., etc.

BUT, you, oh man of God, run like the wind from these tortuous frailties of the pursuit of self-righteousness!

WALK IN THE RIGHTEOUSNESS God has already imparted in you. God has placed His "God-li-ness" in you, so live like it. Enjoy the grandeur of His love, the comfort of His patience, and the warmth of His peaceableness. Be strengthened in the knowledge and understanding the good fight of faith has already been waged, and won I might add, by Jesus. Grab hold of the hope of the eternal, abundant life God has called you to participate in. You've already told many folks this is what you know and understand. So, hang in there. You're doing better than good!

Tim, I charge you, in the sight of God, who has breathed eternal life into each and every thing, and before Jesus, who before Pontius Pilate witnessed the good confession of God'sfaith and faithfulness in Him, never, ever lose sight of this incredible promise of God to you as well!

Listen Tim, you "are" without spot!

Listen Tim, you "are" unrebukeable!

For how long?

You'll be spotless and pure until the day you get to meet Jesus face to face.

On the great and glorious day when your life on this earth has passed, Jesus is going to introduce you to the One blessed and only Sovereign ruler, the King of kings, and the God of gods. God is the only One who could claim immortality. He dwells in a space of light nobody could ever hope to approach through self-righteous belief and accomplishment. Yes, Jesus will introduce you to the One whose majesty is beyond anything anyone could ever comprehend and whose holiness is unfathomable.

My goodness, to God be honor, glory, and power for all eternity. Is He worthy, or what?

Challenge those who have accumulated a fair bit of wealth in this world not to let it go to their heads. Being rich doesn't come with the right to think more highly of oneself, or more highly of one's accomplishments above anybody else.

Tell them not to put their trust in the uncertain frailties of earthly possessions and accomplishments, BUT trust instead in the living God who has given to all mankind the totality of the riches in His eternal storehouse to enjoy!

Encourage the rich to share the wealth! Let them exercise the opportunities to lend a helping hand to those who could use it, to distribute acts of kindness and generosity, and always be at the ready to communicate the greatness of God's grace and peace for all mankind.

What will this accomplish?

Well, it certainly will help them understand the principle of the servant attitude of Jesus towards all mankind when they see folks faced with difficult times. Surely it will help them to become more aware their eternal destiny has been secured as a result of the love of God to freely give it to a world who didn't deserve a morsel of it.

Oh, my dear Timothy, don't forget all of these things that I've told you. Don't get trapped in the ridiculous profanity and vanity of self-righteous babbling. Don't waste your time negotiating with those who perpetuate the confusions and contradictions of the wisdom (foolishness) of mankind.

The science of self-righteousness is totally whacked! Some folks seem to want to put all of their stock in how they believe and in what they accomplish. Well, don't go there! They've totally missed the boat concerning the faith and faithfulness of God!

P.S. Tim, the grace and peace of God is with you. That's just the way it is!

ROME

177. PACK OF LIARS
(Titus 1:1-14)

What a great guy! They don't come much better than Tim.

Well, I guess there's Titus. He's right up there in my books too. These young bucks were more like sons to me. I often thought I was probably just as enthusiastic and driven when I was their age.

Pioneers! Trailblazers!

I regret they don't get the credit they deserve for their great work. Let me get back to Titus.

You may recall when Barney and I went to Jerusalem for our little set-to with the leadership concerning our missionary activities among the Gentile folk, it was Titus who accompanied us. It was Titus who received the rather tough assignment of delivering a fairly heavy letter I had written to the believers in Corinth. No, I don't mean the letter was too heavy, rather, it was a touch on the serious side. Oh yes, it was Titus who spearheaded the collection of money from the many different fellowships on behalf of the suffering believers in Jerusalem.

Titus had a tremendous ability to organize and administer in very practical ways. This is one of the reasons why I sent him to the island of Crete to be a pattern to the believers there. This letter, like the one you just finished reading to Timothy, was intended to inspire and encourage.

FROM:
Paul, a servant of God, an ambassador of Jesus to spread the good news of God's faith and faithfulness towards all of His children, and to acknowledge the truth concerning the great gift of "God-li-ness" which He has imparted into mankind. In Jesus we have hope of eternal life which God, and we all know God cannot lie, promised to give before the world even began. BUT, God has in the PERFECTION OF HIS TIMING let word get out, and He's given me the great honor to declare the integrity and fulfillment of the promise of God our Savior.

TO:
Titus, like a son to me, joined together in the common faith and faithfulness of God.

BLESSING:
Grace, mercy, and peace are yours from God the Father and Jesus our Savior.

Titus, there are some pretty specific reasons why I've had you stay on the island of Crete. I'd like you to organize the believers there because it seems they aren't all exactly on the same page. Appoint some leaders to oversee the various fellowships in every city, just as I've appointed you to this task.

How do you pick leaders? Well, look for folks who:
- are solid in reputation, above and beyond criticism;
- are married to one person;
- have well-mannered and well-behaved children who respect their parents;
- are above reproach as administrators of God's truth;
- are not so conceited they think too highly of themselves, not so contemptuous they think so meanly of others;
- are not so arrogant to cause them to act indifferently towards others;
- are free of the kind of anger which one nurses to keep it warm, ready for use when an appropriate time occurs to vent it;
- aren't alcoholics;
- aren't prone to strike out against others in word or deed;
- aren't greedy, BUT, who love being hospitable;
- have an unselfish appreciation and respect of good people;
- are prudent and sober minded;
- are just and fair;
- are pious, reverencing the fundamental decencies of life; and
- are steadfastly grounded in the knowledge and understanding of the faith and faithfulness of God's word which they've been taught.

Why are all these things so important?

They need to be able to exhort and instruct those who seem bent on perpetuating and following the systems and dogmas of the wisdom (foolishness) of mankind.

You see, there are far too many folks out there who simply are too busy doing their own thing, thinking they have what it takes to please God. They're so full of themselves! Not only this, they persist in leading others to follow them in the ridiculous folly of self-righteousness.

The ones you have to especially watch out for are those who think they have it all together, considering themselves particularly cut out of the forest to greatness and acceptability. It is imperative to stop this nonsense! These subversives are ruining it for everyone. They teach systems of beliefs and works that are nothing less than total ignorance and deception.

Why do they do it?

Power! Control! Greed! Selfishness!

Hey, don't be surprised by this. One of their very own great poets has written,

> "The Cretans are chronic liars, cheats, gluttons, and traitors." (Epimenides)

No kidding! What a perfect description of those who put their trust in their self-righteousness. Look, tell them in no uncertain terms God's view and opinion of them is dependent on one thing, and only one thing, the faith and faithfulness God Himself.

Tell those who put all their stock in the adherence to systems of belief, laws, rules, and regulations they're wasting their time! Getting hooked in the teachings of the wisdom (foolishness) of mankind is very painful. Rebuke outright those who abandon and turn away from the singular truth of God's loving grace and peace!

178. A PECULIAR PEOPLE
(Titus 1:15-2:14)

Now, **TO THE PURE, ALL THINGS AR PURE!**

BUT, to those who are defiled in self-righteousness, to those who don't believe in the unmerited favor of God's grace and peace for all mankind, nothing is pure.

BUT, don't be so surprised 'cause even their minds and consciences are defiled with the debauchery of self-righteousness! What's so funny is these self-righteous misfits actually profess they know the will of God, BUT, they actually deny Him by what they believe and by what they do!

What an abomination! They're actually disobedient to the heart and soul of God. Reality? Those who live in the legalistic world of the wisdom (foolishness) of mankind can't even live up to the laws, rules, and regulations established to keep them in line. Every self-righteous good work they attempt to master is nothing more than a detestable, futile effort to alter the unchangeable will of God!

BUT, Titus, spend your time and energy speaking about things that make sense, about things that actually exalt the sound doctrine of God's grace and peace.

Encourage the older men to be sober minded and reasonable, serious and sensible, unwavering in their loyalty to the truth of the gospel message, healthy in compassion and love, and fortified with patience.

In like manner, enlist the older women to act out the purity and holiness of God within them so others might see some true beauty. Contrary to popular opinion, gossiping isn't the way to win friends and influence people. Having sipped a bit too much of the wine cellar stock isn't a charmer either. Older women have a wonderful opportunity to be excellent teachers and role models of the incredible number of good things in life.

It's the honorable duty of wise and experienced women to pass on to younger women the nobility:
- of being sensible;
- of loving their husbands and children;
- of being discreet;
- of being pure in design and expression;
- of being good domestic engineers;

- of kindness and gentleness; and
- of living in harmony with their husband.

Why?

So nobody can make fun of the promise of God to instill His purity and righteousness in his creation!

Young men?

Well, likewise, exhort them to keep their heads screwed on right. Stimulate the appetite of youth to soberly place their passion under the control of self-discipline.

Titus, in all things set yourself up as an example of doing good things with the proper motivation. When it comes to doctrine let others know you won't be fooled, deceived, intimidated, or corrupted by the wisdom (foolishness) of mankind. Don't put a price tag on the free gift of God.

Lining your own pockets, even for something as noble as the message of God's love, is contemptible.

When you talk make sure folks recognize the seriousness of your understanding, the sincerity of your tone, and the strength of your resolve to communicate the gospel message. Don't provide anyone with the opportunity or excuse to condemn you with your very own words. Those who blabber the self-righteous crap of mankind's wisdom (foolishness) will be confounded by your logical approach to the revelation of God's wisdom. They'll be so amazed by your knowledge and understanding they'll be ashamed to poke fun at you, or, at the very least, be embarrassed to argue with you.

Exhort servants to be obedient to their own masters, serving them with the very best of their ability and capability. Servants ought to ignore every impulse to talk back to their bosses with insults and complaints. Stealing is out of the question BUT a healthy dose of honor and respect in all things is surely a good thing.

Why?

Servants are to be the very living representation of the grace and peace of God our Savior in all things!

Why are all these things so important?

Well, this is why:
- The grace of God which carries with it salvation from the peril of self-righteousness has appeared to "all" mankind!

- God's grace teaches us that in denying the "un-God-ly" self-righteous pursuits of the wisdom (foolishness) of mankind we have the great honor and privilege of living in the security, luxury, and liberality of His righteousness and "God-li-ness" right now. Yes, right now! In this present world! That's right, now!
- In addition to all of this, the grace of God has made it possible for us to look forward with incredible assurance and hope to the glorious time when we'll get to meet face to face with the great God, and Jesus, Who, gave Himself for "all" of us!

Why'd Jesus do that?

So He could redeem us from each and every inadequacy of our own belief and achievement! He gave Himself so He could purify for Himself a peculiar people indeed, a sad lot of human folk hell-bent zealous, not to mention incapable, of performing good works to gain the righteousness of God all by themselves!

179. JUSTIFIED BY HIS GRACE
(Titus 2:15-3:11)

Talk about these things.
    Exhort folks.
    Rebuke them and if you have to, do it with authority.
    Don't let folks despise you for what you know and understand to be true of God's love, His grace, and His peace for all mankind!
    Challenge folks that's it's all right to be subject to the governments and leaders who rule over you. It's all right to obey the laws of the land. Being ready to do as many good things as possible is nothing to be embarrassed about. Caution folks to watch their mouths, for there's nothing to be gained from spitting on others. Fighting and arguing all the time accomplishes little, BUT, gentleness, well, there's a characteristic we see all too little of. Our world could use a little more humility mixed with mercy.
    Now, don't get me wrong. I'm not trying to paint a portrait of my life to illustrate I've acted like a little saint in the past. Hey, I didn't just look stupid. For years I was foolish enough to think what I believed and what I did counted for something with God. Dumb and dumber, or what?
    Disobedient?
    I know. I know. Rhetorical question.
    Deceived?
    I was not only led down the garden path of self-righteousness for a long time, I actually devoted a nasty part of my life deceiving others into following my footsteps through the stumbling blocks of legalism, all in the name of religion and the pursuit of God's favor of course.
    All this selfishness was bound to end up in the lust for power, fame, and fortune. Let the good times roll. Roll they did. My life was dominated with malice and envy towards anyone who shot the crap out of liberty better than I did. I practiced hatred against those who opposed my vision of piety and dedication to the cause of being a "chosen" one of God.
    BUT, then it happened!

The kindness and love of God our Savior appeared to all mankind, included me! And the real kicker is an absolutely amazing revelation.

It's not by the works of righteousness that we've done, BUT, according to God's mercy He has saved us from the hopeless peril our self-righteous pursuits!

How'd He do it?

Well, God gave us all a big bath!

He totally washed the filth of our systems of legalistic beliefs and works until the only thing left was purity and holiness. We were REGENERATED AND RENEWED with the righteousness of the Spirit of Jesus, re-clothed in garments washed spotlessly clean with the blood of Jesus our Savior shed on behalf of the whole world!

Why?

So that, being justified by the grace of God, we all could be made heirs of the eternal promise of God!

Look, what I am about to say is worth paying attention to. You'll be able to verify and affirm the truth concerning these things again and again. Those folks who know and understand we've been saved only by the mercy and gracious love of God and not by the works of righteousness that we have done should be vigilant to continue doing good works. Nobody has said doing good works was a bad thing. They benefit everyone.

BUT, avoid stupid questions that will undoubtedly be posed to determine which of the noble works will get you closer to God. Stop wasting your time trying to respond to every new fad of star gazing quacks and contention seeking deceivers. Most of all, stay clear of those pompous, arrogant, legalistic control freaks who persist in the self-righteous slavery to systems of laws, rules, and regulations. All of the wisdom (foolishness) of mankind is not only unprofitable, it's selfishly vain to the core.

I suggest you admonish the heretics who proclaim a self-righteous route to gain the acceptance of God. If they don't want to reconsider their position after a couple of rebukes, well, tell them to go fly a kite.

You see, too many folks are simply subverted to the deceptions of the wisdom (foolishness) of mankind.

They're bound in the self-righteous bondage of self-righteousness thinking they have or they can get what it will take to alter God's view and opinion of them.

Dumb, dumb, and dumber!

The goofs don't ever realize they're simply condemning themselves!

180. CONCLUSION OF TITUS
(Titus 3:12-15)

I'm going to send either Artemas or Tychicus to you. When either of them get to you please come to meet me in Nicopolis for it's my intention to spend the winter months there. I believe Zenas, one of my legal team, together with my buddy Apollos are coming your way. It would be great if you could make sure they have everything they need to continue on their journey. Learning to help others on their way will do wonders for the health and happiness of both the giver and the receiver.

Everyone here with me has asked me to send their best regards to you. Please greet all of our dear friends who love us as brothers and sisters in the family of God.

Remember what I told you at the beginning of this letter. **GOD'S GRACE IS WITH YOU ALL.**

Take care.

181. HEBREWS INTRODUCTION

Well, have you just about had enough of me and my writing?

Bear with me just a little longer. I'm convinced you'll enjoy this next letter. I almost don't want you to think of it as a letter. I'd prefer you think of this as a compilation of thoughts to convince those of you not yet sufficiently convinced God is who He is, or that the work of Jesus is insufficient or incomplete. I believe there are still folks out there who continue to question the relevance of God and His actions towards mankind.

I trust this treatise will challenge your minds. It's my hope these thoughts will revolutionize your knowledge and understanding of the intention of God towards the entire world, including you.

If you can't figure out whom this letter was written to don't lose any sleep over it. It should come as no surprise the contents of this letter are a bit more impersonal than many of my letters. In fact, you may be downright surprised at the abundance of Jewish culture and theology.

Hey, theology is important. Don't disregard it because it sounds heavy. Believe me, how you act is governed by what you know and understand too.

Lest you think I've tipped off my rocker let me give you a bit of contextual background so you may understand what you will be reading, and perhaps, why I wrote what I did.

I hope you've heard of a fellow by the name of Plato. He hobnobbed around these parts about 500 years before Jesus made His mark upon history. It would be pretty hard to sum up in a few words the full impact of what Plato brought to the table of knowledge, however, let me attempt a simplistic stab at it.

The Greek understanding and philosophy of life can be viewed as a continuous struggle between what's real and what's un-real. There are things we can see, and then, there are things that can't be seen. Doesn't sound too difficult so far. There are temporal things and there are things that will last forever. They tried to make sense of the whole meal deal by claiming in the great somewhere out there the real world actually existed. The world in which we exist and the things that surround us like creation, animals, buildings, etc., are merely shadows or copies of the real thing.

Plato shows up and explains his idea of things by suggesting perfection does indeed exist somewhere. What we experience is merely a copy of this perfection. In fact, this is what he's quoted as saying,

> "The Creator of the world had designed and carried out His work according to an unchangeable and eternal pattern of which the world is but a copy."

Let me suggest an object lesson to illustrate the point. Think of a common chair you'd sit on. Plato would have you believe there's a perfect chair somewhere, only it's not to found on this planet. What you get to sit on is just a copy of the "real" thing. It may be the most comfortable chair you've ever lounged in, it may be the best looking piece of furniture you've ever laid your eyes on, and it may even be perfectly functional for the practical side of you. However, it can't be, and never will be, the perfect chair!

Plato convinced the Gentile world our only hope in life is to grope, stumble, and guess our way through it. Somewhere out there, in a world impossible for us to see or comprehend, is perfection. Nobody will ever see it in this life and nobody will attain it in this lifetime. One can only hope reality may strike when we arrive at the time of departure from this copied, imperfect body. Death must be understood as a journey away from shadows and copies to a place where perfection and reality abide.

Too bad Plato wasn't able to put it all together. He actually wasn't too far off the mark about some things.

Don't think Jewish folks had a lid on things any more than the Gentiles did. They were a pretty screwed up lot as well.

You might be inclined to think the Hebrew-ites at least had a concept of God. Granted, however, it didn't really do them too much good. They knew about God, yet, they were scared spitless of Him for they figured it was a dangerous thing to get too close to him. Wasn't Jacob astonished by the fact he'd seen the face of God, and still, by some miracle, was still around to tell about it (Genesis 32:30)?

Into the Jewish scheme of things entered the idea of a special "covenant" relationship with God. God apparently approached the people of Israel and offered them a unique relationship, even though they certainly didn't deserve such profound access. A condition, however, was set up to rule over this friendship. The condition was the observance and adherence to the "law." You can read the dramatic scene in Exodus 24:3-8.

Breaking the "law" was sin. The consequence of sin had an incredible impact on God and the people of Israel. Time and time again sin became a barrier to the relationship.

What was the only thing that restored the relationship?

It took the entire system of the Levitical priesthood together with the rituals of sacrifices to break down the barrier. Once a year, now this is important, once a year "all" the built up sin of "all" the people of Israel was dealt with. On the greatest day of Jewish worship, the Day of Atonement, the High Priest would enter into the area of the Jewish Temple known as the "Holy of Holies."

This was no mean feat given the extremely dangerous nature of this event. Staying in the presence of God for too long was a sure death sentence as prescribed by the "law." In fact, a rope with bells attached to it was attached to the ankles of the High Priest before he entered the hallowed halls!

Now, why'd they go and do that?

Hey, if the bells stopped jingling the anxious attendants knew they'd better start yanking on the High Priest's chain! Since nobody else had the nerve to go in and fetch him, the last resort to retrieve the dead body would be to drag it out.

Fortunately, and I mean fortunately, the entire sacrificial system proved to be absolutely ineffective in bridging the relationship gap which existed between God and mankind. The Jews fought a never-ending, losing battle to remove barriers the "law" erected. An earthly High Priest proved inadequate to fulfill the mission of a mediator between the parties of the covenant.

We'll really get into this in a bit.

It'll become obvious that much of this letter would be readily understood by folks raised in the Jewish community. It seems only natural this letter has been adopted as a letter to Hebrew folks. While this may be so, don't be mistaken to ignore the obvious implications of the heart of God for all mankind. The need to stumble, grope, and guess our way through life has been eliminated for all time. The legalistic bondage to systems of belief and practice has been broken forever.

You see, it doesn't really matter whether you're a Jew or a Gentile. The hopeless search for meaning in life, along with a resolve to know and understand a God beyond the scope of our imaginations, isn't limited to a particular race, sex, or a special social, economic, or political stripe.

I guess this is why I'm so excited about this work of linguistic eloquence. The hopes and aspirations of "all" mankind are resolved in the faith and faithfulness of God! The loving kindness of God prompted the gifting of His grace and peace through Jesus, towards "all" people. The all-sufficient, eternal extent of God's view and opinion of mankind is more than just a bit breath taking.

For those of you who question the supremacy of Jesus in the plan of God, I've got great news for you.

There is no one who, and no thing that can compare to Jesus!

The prophets of old, angels, Moses, the high priests, the first covenant, the blood of bulls and goats, laws, rules, and regulations, and even human faith, are no match for Jesus in the wisdom and economy of God. Jesus is all the perfection we could ever need to gain the favor and acceptance of God.

Oh, we'll get into all of these things! Suffice it to say, I'm confident you're going to enjoy this one. This stuff is just rippin' fantastic!

Feast up!

HEBREWS

182. PURGED
(Hebrews 1:1-3)

Hey, I haven't even started the letter yet and I need to interrupt myself already. Pretty good start, eh?

It may help you to appreciate the wisdom of God all the more if you come to understand a bit about how the Jews viewed "time." The Jews managed to come up with a plan to divide "time" into two basic categories.

First of all, there's the present age. This time is altogether bad, a time of incompleteness, guessing, and groping. Almost sounds Platoistic, doesn't it?

Secondly, there's a time that is to come. You may think of it as the "last" days if you wish. This age to come will be the glorious, golden age of God's reign.

Now, somewhere in the middle of the present age and the age to come is a period of time referred to as "the day of the Lord." The experience of this time would be similar in nature to a pregnant woman enduring the months of agony and pain in enormous anticipation of the delivery of a joyful new creation, a child.

You know where I'm headed with this, don't you?

You bet, and I just love it. Fits right in there with the wisdom of God if you ask me.

The "day of the Lord" is a masterful way to describe the invasion of God in Jesus into the history of mankind on this world. Our framework of time has forever been altered on this momentous occasion. Nothing will ever be the same again. The present age, the time of aimlessness, desperation, and hopelessness is over. The "day of the Lord" has occurred, and now, the glorious end of the ages has actually started!

WOW!

What a way to start.

The pregnancy is over! The pain has been dealt with! A new creation has been borne out of the love of God! The family of God has been established for all eternity. The whole world became the sons and daughters of a Heavenly Father!

God at various times and in diverse ways revealed Himself to our forefathers through the fragmented understanding of the prophets.

However, in these "last days," it's His Son, Jesus, who has revealed the awesome fullness of the heart of God towards His creation.

Let me tell you a bit about His Son, Jesus.
- Jesus was appointed by God to be the heir of all things.
- It was actually Jesus who was God's agent in the creation of all things.
- Jesus is the radiance of the very glory of God.
- **JESUS IS THE EXACT CHARACTER AND IMAGE OF GOD.**
- **Jesus was not only the creator of all things, He also sustains the entirety of creation, by the promise of His power.**
- **After Jesus, and He did it all by Himself, purged the sin of all mankind He sat down at the right hand of God Almighty on high.**

Sorry, I have to come up for air for a moment. I just got the wind knocked out of me. This is so good. Unfortunately, it's all too easy to just read these truths, skipping over the immensity of what it actually means.

God and Jesus are an incredible team. God used His Son to communicate to the whole world the riches of His loving grace and peace. God set it up so His Son would be the heir of everything. Together, God and Jesus were the ones who created everything in the first place and the reason why it sticks together is Jesus. His power sustains everything, including the promise of God's love towards all of creation.

Everything! Not just an itsy-bitsy piece of it, not just one of the fields, not just some of the animals, and certainly not just a few individuals who might believe the right things well enough or perform the correct deeds throughout their lives.

No, Jesus is the heir of "all" things!

Please understand the prophets of old did their best to relate the nature of God to the rest of us. At best, their fragmentary understanding of the heart of God gave mankind nothing more than a glimpse.

Jesus, on the other hand, was perfectly able to be the revelation of God Himself because, in fact, He also "is" God.

You see, Jesus is both the radiance of God's light as well as the reflection of His light to the whole world. Furthermore, Jesus is the flawless expression of God. Perhaps a little object lesson may help you to understand this principle a bit more.

Think of a legal seal placed on a document to declare its authenticity or legitimacy. The seal is heated then burned into place in a wax formula, leaving the imprint of the seal on the document. The imprint would be "just like" the real thing. It is no less valid because it's merely an imprint. The value of the "real" seal is guaranteed by the wax impression.

This object lesson may not really do justice to the reality Jesus isn't merely an impression. He is the full meal deal! He is the genuine article. He's the ticket. He is, in fact, the real thing!

Jesus is the real character and image of God!

And one more thing. He's done something for all mankind they were unable to do for themselves. No amount of belief could make it happen. No amount of good work could achieve the same result.

What'd Jesus do?

All by Himself, no less, He obliterated sin from the world! It's gone. He purged it away!

How?

With His precious blood!

Now, if sin has been purged, how can you sin? If sin has been dealt with, why do folks spend so much time worrying about it?

Think about it for a moment.

If you still have to fear the consequences of sin then what Jesus accomplished on the cross is totally useless. If sin is still an ever present danger God's going to have to send Jesus once again to finish off the job He must surely have goofed up last time, or a job at which He merely achieved only minor success.

Well, this whole notion is just plain stupid! In no uncertain terms, sin was dealt with. Once is all it took, and for once for "all." When the job was done, where'd He go?

Jesus took the place of honor and authority right next to God Almighty Himself!

Can it get any better than this?

183. ANGELS

The next portion of my letter is going to be about how He relates to angels. However, before I continue with this I thought it might be informative for you to have some background to the Jewish doctrine of the angelic beings.

It's very interesting to me how the belief in angels has developed over time. Who are they? What do they do? How do angels impact our relationship with God? These may be only a few of the questions you may even have concerning angelic beings. Well, books could be written on the topic, nevertheless, let me attempt to give you a brief, simplistic response to a few questions, from a Jewish perspective.

What are they?

Mankind, in their superior wisdom (foolishness), determined there was a vast distance of time and space separating God from themselves. The introduction of intermediaries to somehow "bridge the gap" seemed almost natural.

So someone said, "Let's call them angels!"

I don't know, could have happened like that.

In fact, the more common name for these go-betweens is "messengers" because it came to be believed angels bridged the gulf between God and humans. God communicated to man through these messengers, who, reciprocated by carrying to God the prayers of mankind. At one time God did communicate directly with humankind, but over time mankind progressed into believing God decided to use the angels to carry His directions to mankind instead.

What do these messengers do?

God apparently lives surrounded by His angelic host (Isaiah 6:1; I Kings 22:19). Some of them (seraphim, cherubim, ofanim) are always around the throne of God. Many act as the army of God (Joshua 5:14). Some folks might even be inclined to call them the "familia" of God. Some believe angels act as the general counsel to God, performing the functions of His government, providing God with advice, dispelling the pros and cons to most decisions made concerning mankind.

Apparently, we can thank angels for objecting to the creation of humans in the first place. They objected to the giving of the "law," and can be credited with attacking Moses on his way up Mount Sinai.

Jealousy and the fear of having to share some of the attention of God with mere mortals no doubt was a contributing factor to their objections to God's heart and will towards a certain segment of creation, namely, humanity.

What do they do?

According to Jewish tradition angels do lots of things. Two hundred angels control the movements of the sun and stars, keeping them on their courses. They control the never-ending succession of the passing of days into months, and months into years. One mighty angel supervises the sea. Some angel manages frost, another the dew, and another the rain, hail storms, thunder, lightning and so on, and so on. There are angels who guard the fortress of hell, and others who torture the damned. Yes, don't forget the angel of death! Oh yeah, can't forget the guardian angels and the fact everybody has one, right? Surely babies do. Any rabbi could proclaim that "every blade of grass has its angel."

How many are there?

How high can you count? Millions and millions I'm sure, if you give credence to Jewish records. Some angels are lucky enough to have names assigned to them. There are seven angels who even have the special title of "arch angel."

Can you name them? I can remember a few, Raphael, Uriel, and Phanuel. Of course, we can't forget Gabriel who brought the messages of God to certain individuals at appropriate times. Michael, can't forget him either, for he had the role of presiding over the destiny of Israel.

How could I leave out the bad dude angel? Lucifer, otherwise known as Satan, got his start as a angel too. It's this prosecuting angel who, on every day, with the exception of the Day of Atonement, would continuously bring charges against mankind to God. The exception is very curious indeed!

What were they like?

Now this is an interesting topic for discussion. Some thought they're made of an ethereal, fiery substance like a blazing light. When God created them on either the second or the fifth day of creation, depending on your calendar of events, God must have created them with a certain splendor and majesty. It was thought angels aren't dependent upon food and drink to sustain themselves. Procreation seems to be out of the question. Some folks think they're immortal. Others think they aren't immune from being annihilated by God. Some even think angels only live for one day.

Don't laugh. Some rabbinical schools taught a new batch of angels are created each and every day to utter a song before God, then they disappear!

Don't believe me? Read this:

> "The angels are renewed every morning, and after they've praised God, they return to the stream of fire from whence they came."

In some rabbinical circles, it's believed God changed the angels hourly, sometime into fire, and then at other times, He'd change them into a mighty wind. In 4 Esdras 8:21 it speaks of God,

> "before whom the heavenly host stand in terror and at Thy word change to wind and fire."

Now, what place do they play in our relationship to God?

Who really knows for sure. Angels may be none of the above, all of the above, or perhaps, just some of the above. Some of the ideas get pretty kinky, while others sound half reasonable and acceptable. If you place some stature in the wisdom (foolishness) of mankind, the notion of a set of messengers who mediate between God and mankind may be somewhat attractive.

With even a casual understanding of the wisdom of God, however, the notion of a set of "messengers" like angels created for the purpose of mediating between God and mankind is more than just unpalatable, especially in light of the role of God's Son, Jesus!

For the purpose of this discussion and what's about to follow, let's assume, as do the Jews, angels do exist and have a function in the economy of God. Be careful to place them in a proper perspective. They're created beings as much as the rest of God's creation. They're no more and no less important to God than humans, birds, trees, water, air, time, etc., etc.

Perhaps as you continue to read you'll come to a new appreciation and understanding of the rightful place of honor and majesty that Jesus has been given by God.

Here's an offering of six or seven passages from the scriptures that illustrate the supremacy of the character and activity of Jesus over the angels.

184. BAD MISTAKE
(Hebrews 1:4-2:8)

- Jesus ranks way up there, heads and tails above the created angels!

My goodness, even the name He's inherited is especially unique to Him because He in fact is the one and only true Son of God! Look, when was the last time you ever heard God saying this about any of the angels?

"You are my Son. On this day, my purposes and intentions for mankind will be revealed through you" (Psalms 2:7).

Or how about this one:

"I will be to Him a Father, and He will be to me a Son" (II Samuel 7:14)!

And again, when God introduced Jesus to the whole world in a form folks could recognize, He said,

"And let all the angels of God worship Him" (Deuteronomy 32:43; Psalms 97:7).

And of the angels God asks the rhetorical questions:

"Who is it who makes His angels subject to His will in the same way He commands the wind to blow? Who is it who causes His messengers to act on His behalf, and can subject them to His will in the same way as He controls a flaming fire" (Psalms 104:4)?

BUT, to His Son, Jesus, God said,

"Your throne, O God, has been established to last forever and ever. In your hand is a scepter of righteousness that proclaims the authority of Your kingdom. You have loved righteousness, and you have hated iniquity. That's why I, your God, have anointed You with the oil of gladness above and beyond any of creation" (Psalms 45:6,7).

And God also said,

"You, O God, in the beginning have laid the foundation of the earth. The heavens are the work of your hands. Now, the heavens and earth have their limitations and will ultimately perish. BUT You, on the other hand, will remain for all eternity! The heavens and the earth will one fall apart from old age just like a tattered old garment will after a period of use and abuse."

"They are akin to a light overcoat you'd wrap up and place in a closet when its usefulness has been served."
BUT, You, on the other hand, are, and always will be, the same as you always have been! Your very nature transcends the boundaries and frailties of the ages" (Psalms 102:25-27).

BUT, have you ever heard God say this to any of the angels?

"Come and sit down right here beside me until the perfect time comes along for me to honor you with the dominion over everything which is in opposition to your reign" (Psalms 110:1).

What's my point?

Are not angels simply ministering servants in the service of their God, employed to reveal His love to those (mankind) who'd become heirs of the riches of God's eternal acceptance and blessing?

So, carry on! Pay attention to the greatest good news we've ever had the privilege of hearing, the supremacy of Jesus.

Don't drift away from the truth of God's wisdom to reveal Himself through Jesus, lest we slip back into the guilt, fear, and hopelessness of self-righteousness.

Ha, we could believe every word attributed to intermediary angels as legitimately true. We could even believe every legalistic system of belief and accomplishment defending the notion everyone will receive an appropriate set of rewards and punishments depending on whether they step across the boundary lines or turn a deaf ear to the voice of God. If we grab hold of either or both of these freaking, scary notions, my oh my, how in the world could we possibly believe we could ever escape the wrath of God?

NEGLECTING THE SALVATION GOD HAS SO LOVINGLY AND FREELY GIFTED TO ALL MANKIND IS A BAD, BAD MISTAKE!

Look, God told mankind right from the start how much He loved what He had created. This news shouldn't come as such a surprise to us, furthermore, God's heart and intention was confirmed to us by those who heard God tell them this right to their face! God didn't leave these folks hangin' out to dry on their own credibility.

No indeed. God backed the prophets and messengers up by revealing Himself with signs and wonders, not to mention all the incredible variety of miracles He performed. And then, He blessed us with the greatest gift of all, the Spirit of Jesus within us.

Why?

According to His very own will!

God certainly didn't put the future of the world in the hands of angels! I'm well aware this concept may be contrary to what some folks would have you believe! BUT, someone wise, in a certain place in his life, deliberated,

> "Who are humans that You are so mindful and considerate of us? Why would You take such a keen interest in mankind You'd visit Yourself upon us in such a glorious way? I know You created humankind to be just a little lower than Yourself, yet You crowned us with glory and honor and set us to rule over everything You've created. You've put all things in subjection to our power and authority. In fact, you put everything in subjection to us and You left nothing which hasn't been put under our control" (Psalms 8:4-6).

BUT, even now, we still don't have the foggiest clue what it really means that God would honor us with such a great blessing to freely enjoy all He has created for us.

HEBREWS

185. CAPTAIN OF SALVATION
(Hebrews 2:9-15)

BUT, now we see Jesus for who He truly is!
- God sent His Son, Jesus, crowned with glory and honor, into our world in the imperfect physical nature of humankind so He might be perfectly suited to suffer the indignity of death.

Why?

So Jesus, by the grace of God, could TASTE DEATH for each and every human being!

Isn't it just like God to achieve the goal of righteousness for everyone the way He wanted to! Hey, everyone and everything was created for His good pleasure in the first place. In addition, He's the One who sustains everyone and everything. Why should it surprise us to figure out He'd send Jesus among us to identify Himself with us so "all" humankind could participate in His glory?

It was entirely within the prerogative of God to make Jesus the pioneer of our glory, the captain of our salvation, fully adequate to qualify everyone to enjoy the peace and liberty of God's grace by blazing a trail through His suffering!

Listen, both God who issued the righteousness, and mankind who received His righteousness, are now joined inseparably together. Is it any wonder God is no longer ashamed to call us all the children of God?

Daaaaah! Stupid question, I know. Don't take it from me. Read the proclamations of Jesus in the scriptures.

"I'll declare Your name to all of my brothers and sisters and in the midst of their fellowship will I sing praise to You" (Psalm 22:2).

And again,

"I'll put my trust in the faith and faithfulness of God" (Isaiah 8:17).

And again,

"Look at me, together with all of the children whom God has blessed me with (Isaiah 8:18) .

It's a slam-dunk to realize the children of God are truly human, with all of the characteristics of flesh and blood.

Well, it's to this very same degree to which Jesus assumed all of the characteristics of humanity, joining in totality with the human experience.

Why'd He do it?

So, through death, He might forever destroy the devilish, deceptive power eternal death held over all mankind. The death of Jesus liberated all those who, because of their fear and trembling of the wrath of God, have spent their entire lifetime subjected to the bondage and slavery of the legalistic requirements of the self-righteous systems of the wisdom (foolishness) of mankind.

186. SET YOUR GAZE
(Hebrews 2:16-3:6)

- It's crucial you understand Jesus didn't take upon Himself the nature of angels BUT He took upon Himself the nature of the children of Abraham.

To accomplish the will of God there was no way around it. He didn't have a choice. He had to come to this world and identify in every way with His earthbound brothers and sisters.

Why?

- It was incumbent upon God to make Jesus just like His human brothers and sisters so Jesus might become a perfect, merciful, and faithful High Priest, in each and every thing pertaining to God, fully qualified to bring about a resolution between God and Himself for the sins of the whole world!

For in that Jesus Himself suffered the pressure and agony of being tempted with the plague of self-righteousness and of being exposed to the wrath and judgment of God, He is able to completely understand everything humans face.

So, my dear, precious brothers and sisters, partakers of the heavenly calling of God, please fix your eyes upon the great Ambassador of the will of God. Really sit up and take notice of the great bridge builder, Jesus, our great High Priest. Gaze in amazement at the very One whom we have come to know and understand to be our only hope, for it is Jesus who was truly faithful to God who appointed Him to this gracious, merciful task.

I don't think it would be a stretch for most folks to accept Moses was a pretty important guy. God Himself even told Aaron and Miriam,

"... My servant Moses isn't like the other prophets, for he is faithful in all of my house" (Numbers 12:5-7).

The point?

- The man, Jesus, was counted worthy by God of even more glory than the very honorable and highly respected Moses.

Look, it doesn't take a rock scientist to understand the one who builds a house would naturally receive and be able to accept more honor than an inanimate house itself would or could accept.

It may be correct every house is built with the creative ability and expertise of some human being BUT it's also absolutely true the One who has created everything is God!

No doubt, Moses faithfully attended to the affairs of all those who were under the scope of his leadership and as a servant to those he led. There may be none in all of the history books who could be his equal. The reputation of Moses is indisputable.

BUT, Jesus was even **MORE FAITHFUL** than Moses, for the simple reason, as the Son of God, He rules over the entire house of God, which was created by Him, and for Him!

Hey, we, as humans, are nothing less than members of the household of God and we'd do well, for as long as we have breath to do so, to hold fast with a confident rejoicing in this glorious hope in Jesus, established for us all.

187. REST UP
(Hebrews 3:7-4:13)

Heed this inspiring exhortation:
"Today, be careful to hear the voice of our great God."
"Don't harden your hearts, nor provoke Me like the wandering people did when they arrived in the wilderness at Massah and Meribah." (read the story in Exodus 17:1-7; Numbers 20:1-13)
"Your forefathers grew quite restless and were often found to be distrustful of My guidance and disobedient to My instructions. They were a constant pain in My neck for forty years or so. In fact, I grew to be quite annoyed and grieved with that whole generation. So I said to Myself, 'Self, these folks just can't get their act together. Their hearts have gone bonkers and they act like they don't even have a clue about how I've treated them.' I was pretty ticked off to say the least. In the midst of my anger I swore 'these folks will never get to enjoy a life of abundance and liberty in the land I've promised them'" (Psalms 95:7-11)!

Therefore, pay attention my dear friends, lest there be in any of you a deceitful heart of unbelief. Don't depart from your knowledge and understanding of the living God, BUT, exhort one another daily to get with the program. In fact, do it today while you still have a chance, just as the poet of old encouraged folks in his day.

Why?

So none of you will become hardened through the deceitfulness of self-righteousness! Look, it's entirely possible for us to mature in our understanding of the grace and peace of God, however, in order to do so we must maintain a trust and confidence in the truth of the free gift of all Jesus accomplished on our behalf, refusing to go back to the legalistic bondage of self-righteousness for the remainder of our lives.

"Today, be careful to hear the voice of our great God. Don't harden your hearts like the wandering people did when they arrived in the wilderness" (Psalms 95:7-11).

At the very same time this exhortation rang out some folks actually heard the message loud and clear and yet they chose to take matters into their own hands.

Go figure!

Allow me to pose some rhetorical questions.

- Weren't these rebels the very same folks who took their leave of the desperate slavery of Egypt under the very capable guidance of the greatest leader of all time, namely Moses, BUT, with whom God had nothing other than grief for some forty years?
- Were not those who chose the rebellious, deceptive path of self-sufficiency the very ones whose carcasses littered the land of their wilderness?
- And furthermore, to whom was it God swore He wouldn't permit to enter into the promised land of abundant tranquility BUT those who chose not to put their confidence and trust in the provision of God?
- How could it be possible for folks to enter into the peace of God's grace if they can't, or won't, even accept the incredible gift God has given to all in Jesus?

I want to warn you to fear the deceptive messages promoting the notion some folks could come out on the short end of the stick of entering into the never ending, abundant peace and rest God has promised to all.

Look, the good news of God's love has been revealed to us just as much as it had been to the folks way back in the time of Moses. BUT, it's certainly not surprising the wanderers didn't benefit very much from the blessing of God, if, for no other reason, they figured they could go it on their own.

Those of us who don't dispute the promise of God for all mankind have entered a wonderful space where the relaxing thrill of contentment, completeness, and acceptability rule our lives and where hopelessness, guilt, and fear no longer threaten us.

Remember what God said when He warned folks:

"As I have sworn in my wrath they will never get to enjoy the blessings of abundance and liberty" (Psalms 95:11).

Hey, the rest God established for folks to enjoy in the peace of the Promised Land didn't just all of a sudden disappear. No way. They just didn't get to enjoy it because they were stupid! The will of God and the subsequent promise of His heart was established from the very foundation of all creation.

An author, relating the events of the creation of the world, recorded for us in a certain portion of the scriptures what God did on the never ending seventh day.

"And God took a break after surveying all He had created and He's been resting ever since" (Genesis 2:2).

Let me repeat the portion of scripture I referred to earlier.

"They will never get to enjoy the blessings of abundance and liberty" (Psalms 95:11).

Look, the reality is the peace of God has been established, and furthermore, it still exists. Some folks have entered into it and will continue to enter into it, while those to whom the message of God's provision was first preached to didn't enter into it.

Why not?

Because they chose not to know and understand the only way they could was to put their confidence and trust in the faith and faithfulness of God to honor His promise!

Once again, hundreds of years after the wilderness fiasco where the frustration of God became obvious, David employed again the terminology of a particular moment in time, "today," to inspire folks to get with the program.

"Today, be careful to hear the voice of our great God. Don't harden your hearts like the wandering people did when they arrived in the wilderness" (Psalms 95:7-11).

Obviously, if Joshua would have been successful in leading all the children of God into the land of promise there would have been no subsequent necessity to bring up the whole subject again. The fact remains God's promise of peace for His children hasn't changed.

Those who gladly accept and enjoy the peace of God realize they've been liberated from the bondage of self-righteousness and have been freed from the strangulating pressures of legalistic systems of belief and accomplishment. Hey, God took a break to enjoy creation, why shouldn't we?

My goodness, if you must work at something work at enjoying the peace of God, otherwise you'll fall into the trap of unbelief that leads directly into the slavery of self-righteousness.

For the promise of God was enacted quickly and powerfully!

HIS PROMISE IS SHARPLY MORE EFFECTIVE than even any two edged sword, for it illuminated once and for all the physical and emotional struggle of mankind to gain the favor of God through systems of belief and merit.

His promise reached down as a discerner of the innermost thoughts and intentions of our hearts.

There isn't a single creature that He doesn't recognize as one of His! BUT, all things are naked, completely and inescapably exposed in the eyes of our God who has blessed us so abundantly with His peace!

HEBREWS

188. GREAT HIGH PRIEST
(Hebrews 4:14-5:9)

There are more concepts of God out there in this world than you can shake a stick at.

My Stoic Greek friends think of God as apathetic, unfeeling, and a most uncaring being, totally incapable of relating to the experiences of mankind. My other Greek friends of the Epicurean philosophy maintain that the gods live in perfect happiness and blessedness in the land of the "intermundia," the space between the worlds where they aren't even aware of the world in which we live. And then there are my Jewish friends who view God as being "different" from any other gods because He is holy, therefore, in no sense could He share any of our human experience, and is in fact, incapable of sharing in it because He is such a "different" God.

Well, I've got great news for everyone!

God is God! And God does have feelings for all of His creation! He does care!

He cared so much for humanity He sent His only precious Son, namely Jesus, to become one of us and to become for all a great High Priest. He wasn't conferred with this role by some human authority or election. No, when God made Jesus our High Priest, He was able to accomplish what no earthly priest was ever able to do, in spite of all the trappings of rituals, ceremonies, and sacrifices.

Seeing then WE HAVE SUCH A GREAT HIGH PRIEST, One whom the heavens of God's presence cannot contain, namely Jesus the Son of God, let's hold fast to this knowledge and understanding we so gladly profess.

Listen, we don't have a great High Priest who can't be touched with the feelings of our helplessness, BUT, He was in every way tempted as we are with the frustrating stranglehold of self-righteousness, and yet, He never succumbed to the pressure.

So, let's get on with it.

We have every right to boldly access the throne of God's grace where His mercy has been freely dispatched to all. In His presence we have the great honor and privilege of enjoying the matchless grace bringing assurance, comfort and hope to us at every turn.

It's true. Every human High Priest has been ordained, by other humans, to serve them concerning things pertaining to God. Their role included offering both gifts and sacrifices to God so He wouldn't be ticked off with the people any more, well, for at least another year anyway.

An earthly High Priest was also supposed to shower sensitivity and compassion on those totally ignorant of all the laws, rules, and regulations governing the attempts at self-righteousness. They were even supposed to demonstrate the spirit of acceptance and compassion on those who fell outside the parameters of the "faith," so to speak.

Any human High Priest wasn't immune from the human condition of self-righteous behavior.

Ha, it only stands to reason, just as they made intercession and offered sacrifice on behalf of all they serve, they also had to do the very same things on their own behalf too!

There's absolutely no one person who can take upon themselves the role of being our great High Priest.

BUT, God called upon Jesus to perform this specific task, just as Aaron was called upon to serve in a particular way.

Hey, Jesus didn't go looking for the job of being our great High Priest.

BUT, God said to Him,

"You are my Son, and today, (the day of the cross) I've made you become what I want you to be" (Psalms 2:7).

It's also recorded in another place where God said this about Jesus,

"You are a High Priest forever, following in the same great role after the order of Melchizedek" (Psalms 110:4).

Jesus, while He was here on this earth, offered up prayers and petitions to God crying mightily, eyes overcome with tears under the tremendous tension and searing agony.

Still, He recognized full well it was God who was able to save Him from suffering through the terrible ordeal of death before Him.

Those who were with Him and heard Him during this time were amazed a sense of fear and trepidation was conspicuously absent from His countenance.

Fully cognizant He was the Son of God, Jesus learned obedience, putting His full confidence and trust in the knowledge and understanding of the faith and faithfulness of God. Suffering was merely a stepping stone to honor and glory for those He came to give His life for.

Consequently, as a result of the confidence and trust God saw in Jesus, He made Jesus to be our perfect, great High Priest, precisely suited to author eternal salvation from the peril of self-righteousness for all those who place their confidence and trust in God's faith and faithfulness.

It's imperative you understand the supremacy of Jesus as our great High Priest, heads and tails over what any earthly High Priest could be. Here are some points to ponder:

- Any earthly high priest was usually designated through systems of patronage or lineage or else they were hand picked through a selective process of peers. No human honored Jesus with this title, or bestowed upon Him the role to be a servant of all. No, Jesus was made to be our great High Priest by God Himself.
- Any earthly High Priest was supposed to show compassion to both those who were out to lunch as far as laws, rules, and regulations were concerned, and also to those who weren't even considered to be part of the game. As if there's a fat chance this would ever happen. Well, our great High Priest didn't discriminate against anyone, exhibiting the same love and mercy to one and all alike.
- Any earthly High Priest would offer sacrifices and gift to God, once a year, for the waywardness of the people. Our great High Priest has made a one-time sacrifice that has covered the self-righteous infirmities of all humankind forever!
- Any earthly High Priest was bound to offer sacrifices for himself as much as for the people because they were just as prone to failure as anybody else. Our great High Priest may have been tempted with the deceptiveness of self-righteous, and yet, Jesus never did buy into the package. So when Jesus laid Himself up as the sacrifice He did it for everyone with one major exception, He didn't do it for Himself!

189. MELCHIZEDEK
(Hebrews 5:10-6:20)

Ever heard of this Melchizedek character?

No doubt his name isn't one of those names you'd be instantly familiar with. However, in Jewish tradition at least, Melchizedek stands pretty tall. Believe it or not, he probably ranks way up there with the likes of Abraham, Moses, and Aaron. His name means the "king of righteousness."

Coincidence I'd use this name to magnify Jesus over an earthly priest?

I say, "Nay! Nay!"

His name was actually "Adoni-zedek." He was a Canaanite king of pre-Israelite Jerusalem (Salem), and a priest of the Most High God. In the passage from the Psalms (Psalms 110:4) that I've just alluded to in the letter concerning Melchizedek, he's the representative priest in whose succession the Davidic King (Jesus) is ordained. Even Abraham submitted in authority to him. (Genesis 14:18-20) He must have had some clout to retain such a tradition.

There may have been many similarities between Melchizedek and Jesus, and yet, a major difference exists in that the reign of Jesus is forever! Melchizedek may have been top dog for a while, however, Jesus became our great High Priest for all time!

Called of God, a High Priest after the order of Melchizedek, there's so much to say about Jesus. In fact, it's impossible to say everything there is to say about Him. Unfortunately, I sometimes feel like I'm speaking to people whose eyes have been exposed to the truth, and yet, with minds clouded with the impregnable nature of a rock, with ears dulled to hear the fantastic good news.

By now you ought to be able to teach others about our great High Priest, however, you seem to need to be taught all over again about the very elementary principles concerning the will and promise of God. It's almost as if you feel compelled to return to the legalistic systems of the wisdom (foolishness) of mankind, the milk of self-righteous laws, rules, and regulations. It's like you can't handle the truth, the wisdom of God's gift of grace and peace for all mankind. Now this is the diet of strong meat you should be swallowing by now.

Look, everyone who thinks milk (systems of laws, rules, and regulations) is what it takes to survive doesn't have a clue about the promise of God to gift all with His righteousness!

BUT, a diet of strong meat (the understanding of the wisdom of God to impart His righteousness to all through Jesus) is the portion of those mature enough to enjoy it. Yes, it's these folks who follow the very logical course of reasoning to discern the difference between the free gift of God's loving grace and peace and the evil bondage of legalistic, self-righteous systems of belief and merit.

Therefore, let's make a move beyond just simply understanding the basic principles of what God sent Jesus to this world to do. Our great High Priest established within us the righteousness of God, perfection!

Let's start living like it!
- Stop wasting your time trying to re-establish the foolishness of repenting! What's the point of repenting from the breaking of laws, rules, and regulations that have no authority over you any longer? Any work you do thinking it will gain you the favor of God is a dead work!
- Stop wasting your time attempting to formulate a foundation of self-righteousness based upon the amount of faith or belief you have in God. God's view and opinion of you will never change, no matter how strong or weak your faith or belief is.
- Stop wasting your time getting hung up on the multitude doctrines of baptism, thinking a ceremonial washing could somehow have the effect of cleaning you up for God!
- Stop wasting your time on the doctrine of laying on of hands, for the transfer of your guilt to an animal accomplishes absolutely nothing in light of the work of our great High Priest.
- Stop wasting your time trying to come up with a model to decide who will and who won't participate in the resurrection of the dead.
- Stop wasting your time outlining the parameters for an eternal judgment for you're getting folks all worked up about a judgment that has already taken place.

We have the great joy and privilege of living as the righteous, perfect children of God only because He has chosen to make it possible for us to do so.

Don't you get it?

You see, it's impossible:
- for those who've been enlightened to the truth of the wisdom of God;
- for those who've experienced the heavenly gift of righteousness;
- for those who've been made participants of the Spirit of Jesus;
- for those who've known and understood the incredible promise of God; and
- for those who've hope for another life beyond the present one, even if they go back to a life of bondage to the legalistic systems of belief and merit, to be renewed once again to systems of repentance!

It just can't be done!

It's impossible for stupid, self-righteous folks to make Jesus die over and over again for their every indiscretion.

It's impossible to mock the work of our great High Priest!

Look, the very same earth that drinks in the rain which comes to it each time it falls from the sky, and the very same earth which yields its harvest of herbs and produce to those who farm the land, receive the same blessing from God.

BUT, in the wisdom (foolishness) of mankind, the earth that bears thorns and thistles is totally worthless. The only way to restore the tormented earth would be to curse it and burn the crap out of it!

BUT, my dear friends, we are persuaded God has a completely different view and opinion of His creation. He has an entirely different perspective concerning the salvation He has blessed all of us with.

Just because I've said you had nothing at all to do with the blessing of God's righteousness in your life don't think for a moment God is so unmoved not to recognize and remember all the good work you do and all the labor of love that you honor Him. You have ministered to the children of God in the past and you continue to do it even now.

Good on ya!

We'd all like to see every one of you continue to diligently demonstrate for the rest of your lives the full confidence of hope you have in our great High Priest. Don't become complacent and lazy, BUT, follow the example of those who through the faith and faithfulness of God have inherited all the riches He promised to all.

Look, when God made a promise to good ol' Abe, because there wasn't anyone greater than Himself, He actually spoke an oath that He personally backed up by saying,

"Surely I will bless you with My blessing, and will multiply even that blessing with more than you could possibly imagine" (Genesis 22:16-18).

Now it may not have been exactly in the way Abe could see it coming, however, he did obtain the promise of God's blessing.

When a human makes a promise they usually have to back it up with an authority greater than themselves. An argument or dispute can be resolved by having an oath substantiated with a bonafide guarantee.

Well, this is why God, abundantly willing to demonstrate to the heirs of His promise the immutability of His word, confirmed it with the honor of an oath, His oath.

There are two things that are absolutely unchangeable as far as God is concerned.
1. His promise.
2. The oath by which He backed up His promise.

Listen folks, God cannot lie! It's simply impossible for God to lie! My, that's good news!

Why? We can have the fullest confidence in the faith and faithfulness of God. Those of us who have fled for refuge in His promise can lay hold upon the Hope that He has set before us. **THIS HOPE IS AN ANCHOR FOR OUR SOUL**, providing stability and security forever.

Oh yes, this Hope has entered into the very holiest of holy places, the presence of God Himself, to pioneer, to prepare the way for all the children of God to follow.

Who is this Hope?

Jesus!

Jesus indeed, made to be our great High Priest for ever, after the order of Melchizedek.

HEBREWS

190. KING OF RIGHTEOUSNESS
(Hebrews 7:1-17)

Remember now, Melchizedek was the King of Salem as well as a priest of the most high God. Abraham was returning from doing battle with some other kings (Genesis 14:17-20) when Melchizedek showed up to bless him. However, it was Abe who honored Melchizedek with a tithe of one tenth of all the spoils of the battle he had just won.

First and foremost, Abe honored Melchizedek as a high priest, because, by interpretation, his name actually meant "king of righteousness."

Secondly, he paid honor to Melchizedek because he was royalty, the King of Salem, alternatively known by the title of "king of peace."

What makes Melchizedek quite unique is there's no record of his father or mother. He jumps onto the scene literally without a traceable genealogy and with no documents to substantiate when he was born or when he died. BUT, what we do know is he was given a role to be a high priest just as the Son of God was for the role of the priesthood has continuously been a part of people's lives throughout history.

Now, just consider how great this Melchizedek chap was, especially considering none other than the great patriarch Abraham honored him with a tenth of the spoils. It's not really so unusual for the priesthood to receive a tithe. The sons of Levi who were charged with the office of the priesthood had been given the right to receive tithes from the people according to the law. That's right, the priesthood could exact a tithe from their own brothers and sisters, given the fact they all, the priesthood and the people, were direct descendants of Abe.

BUT, this character Melchizedek, a high priest who can't really be counted as a descendant of Abraham, since there's no genealogy to trace, exacted a tithe from Abraham and then blessed the very one (Abe) who had received the very promise of God's blessing!

Go figure!

Well, in blessing circles, it goes without saying the one who receives a blessing is inferior to the one who issues the blessing.

However, the Levitical priests who received the tithes of the people died every bit as much as those who brought them the tithes. BUT, Melchizedek received the tithe from super Abe, yet, it isn't recorded anywhere concerning the death of Melchizedek.

And if I may add even one more curiosity to the mix, since an ancestor really represents all of his descendants, Abe in effect paid the tithe to Melchizedek when they met on behalf of Isaac. In turn, on behalf of Levi and all of the priest and people who followed after him.

I hope your tracking with me because this is really important.

Now, if perfection, the righteousness of God, were to come to the people as a result of the intervention of the Levitical bridge builders (priesthood), for they're the ones who administered the system of laws, rules, and regulations, then what in the world would mankind need another great High Priest who would rise high above even the stature of a Melchizedek? On top of that, a great High Priest who would not even come from the order of Aaron?

Go figure!

Hey, if the priesthood that couldn't get the job done had to change, then there of necessity must also have been a CHANGE OF THE SYSTEM of laws, rules, and regulations!

For Jesus, our great High Priest whom I'm speaking about, has literally come to us from a place out of this world, and is a descendant of a different tribe than the Levities all together, a tribe from which no one ever served at an altar of sacrifice. It's a well know fact Jesus was a descendant of the tribe of Judas and Moses certainly didn't leave any instructions about a High Priest who would arise out of that tribe!

There's something even more fantastic than this. After the unique ministry of the high priest Melchizedek, there has arisen another great High Priest, Who was made, not according to a mere human injunction based on a hereditary system of laws, rules, and regulations, BUT, according to the injunction of the indestructible and eternal power of God.

For it was God who testified,

"You, Jesus, are a great High Priest forever, after the order of Melchizedek" (Psalm 110:4).

My Jewish readers, especially any Jewish scholar, wouldn't have too much trouble with the license of interpretation I employed in my letter. Passages, such as the ones you read (Psalm 110:4, Genesis 14:17-20), were subjected on my part to the rationalities of one or more of the four part rabbinical interpretations:
1. The "peshat" was the literal and factual meaning.
2. The "remaz" was the suggested meaning.
3. The "derush" arrived after a tedious and arduous examination of the content.
4. The "sod" permitted an allegorical interpretation, or inner meaning.

Furthermore, it was common knowledge that which "isn't" said is almost as important as what "is" stated.

Case in point?

Melchizedek.

Without accurate historical documentation, it's easy to make certain conjectures concerning him and then extrapolate on them to exalt the High Priesthood of Jesus. Each of these little tidbits serve the purpose rather well I think.

- His name meant "King of Righteousness."
- He was the royal King of Salem, which means he was the king of "peace."
- He was a high priest based on his character, upon who he was, not upon his lineage.
- He doesn't have a specific birth date, or a specific date of death, hence eternal.
- He was worthy to receive the tithe from the greatest of the great, Abe.
- He was qualified to issue blessing.

I could go on. Are you starting to get the picture? Do any of those things give you an inkling of the greatness of Jesus?

KING OF RIGHTEOUSNESS?

Indeed!

KING OF PEACE?

No foolin'!

Oh, by the way, did you catch the rhetorical questions? Let me restate them for you in case you missed the obvious.

If the old priesthood, who administered the sacrificial system with the myriad of laws, rules, and regulations to govern it, were able to bring righteousness to the people, then why in the world would God need to send a new High Priest after the order of Melchizedek?

If the old priesthood was so good, why did it need to be replaced? Furthermore, if the old priesthood was abolished, what would be the point of keeping the entire system of laws, rules, and regulations?

Well, both the priesthood and the system of laws, rules, and regulations, would be redundant!

No kidding!

191. **PERFECT HIGH PRIEST**
(Hebrews 7:18-28)

Did you know there were 142 physical blemishes that could disqualify a priest? (Leviticus 21:16-23) An ordination ceremony (Leviticus 8) dictated a priest would have to take a bath before any ceremony so he might be made clean. He was clothed in the four priestly garments:
- linen knee breeches,
- long linen garment woven into one piece,
- the girdle around the breast area, and
- a turban, or bonnet.

He would be anointed with oil, then, with the blood of certain sacrifices that had been made, he would be touched on the tip of his right ear, his right thumb, and then on his right great toe. Every single item in the ceremony affected some part of the body of a priest.

And this was just for his ordination ceremony!

The physical implications for the entire life of a priest were mapped out in laws, rules, and regulations. Hair had to be cut in a certain way. Bathing was a ritual in itself. Personality, ability, or character actually had little to do with carrying out his functions.

Without going into a detailed, moment by moment account, here are a few significant activities of a high priest on his most special day of any year that should suffice for the purposes of this next section of my letter.

It was of course the high priest who was the officiating officer on the annual Day of Atonement celebrations. Once a year, before he could offer up sacrifices on behalf of the people it was his duty to remove the slivers out of his own eyes. Another one of those heavy-duty baths was prescribed to scrub off all the physical impurities. The gorgeous robes, very much a part of the rather elaborate, grandiose show, were removed. Spotless, white linen robes became one of the dramatic symbolic gestures.

An animal, which, by the way, was purchased with the high priest's own money, was brought before him. He would put both of his hands on the bullock's head to transfer his transgression onto the animal. Confession of his own sins and the sins of the people was eventually followed by the accompanying sacrifice of the animal.

Two things:
1. The previous systems of laws, rules, and regulations just had to go! Why? It had to be annulled because it was too weak to be effective. It was completely unprofitable for it never was able to achieve for mankind the righteousness of God through belief and effort. Any system of laws, rules, and regulations were absolute failures because they couldn't make anyone perfect.
2. BUT, with the entrance of a better hope, Jesus, everything changed! Why? Because He has now made it possible for all of us to have direct access to God!

Listen, Jesus was made our great High Priest by nothing less than the very oath of God!

The earthly priests gained office without the benefit of an oath, BUT, Jesus became our great High Priest by the will of God when He proclaimed this promise backed up with His own word of honor:

"I (God) make this solemn oath, and I'll never change my mind about it, You (Jesus) are a great High Priest after the order of Melchizedek" (Psalms 110:4).

Jesus, by the pronouncement of God, became the very guarantee of a much better idea God had for all mankind.

You've probably figured it out there have been a whole lot of earthly high priests through the years. Why? Well, they didn't have to suffer the agony of being in this very difficult position indefinitely because they had were susceptible to a major human flaw, namely, death!

BUT, Jesus, because even death couldn't conquer Him, will remain our great High Priest forever and will be the servant of all in an unchangeable priesthood! The honor of His priesthood can never be transferred to any other.

Look, this is the only reason Jesus is able to save to the max everyone who has come to God through His intervention upon this world. His eternal purpose was to be the great bridge builder between God and all His creation!

My goodness, we sure needed a great High Priest like Jesus! In fact, Jesus actually became one of us so He could faithfully accomplish on our behalf what God had sent Him to do. Jesus doesn't have the heart to hurt a soul. Talk about someone without a blemish!

One major difference between our great High Priest, Jesus, and all the other earthly high priests is He never gave in to the enticing, deceptive bondage of the self-righteous wisdom (foolishness) of mankind.

Furthermore, as our great High Priest, Jesus was given a position of honor and glory above everything else.

Jesus did not daily, as the earthly priests were bound to do, offer up sacrifices, first for their own shortcomings, and then for the people's. Jesus made only one sacrifice. And it wasn't a sacrifice of some animal substitute either.

JESUS WAS THE SACRIFICE!

Once, and for "all!"

What made the earthly high priests fallible? Laws, rules, and regulations!

BUT, the authentic guarantee of the promise of God Himself which He made after the systems of laws, rules, and regulations became the obsession of the wisdom (foolishness) of mankind made Jesus our great High Priest and consecrated Him as a servant of all for evermore!

192. WHAT SIN?
(Hebrews 8:1-12)

What have I said thus far? Let me summarize.

We have such an incredible great High Priest!

At this very moment Jesus sits on the right hand of the heavenly throne next to our majestic God. He serves as a minister of the sanctuary of God's creation as well as the great High Priest of the true tabernacle of God's dwelling place, people! Look, God Himself established the boundaries of His habitation, not mankind.

So, it's absolutely necessary our great High Priest had something to offer as well. For if Jesus were on earth right now He wouldn't have to be a high priest because there already are high priests who offer gifts and sacrifices according to the systems of laws, rules, and regulations of the wisdom (foolishness) of mankind.

Earthly high priests serve in a sketch, silhouette, or a shadowy outline of the true reality of the heavenly wisdom of God. Remember Mo, when he was about to construct the Tabernacle, was admonished by God.

> "See," said God, "that you make everything according to the pattern you've been shown on the mountain" (Exodus 25:40).

BUT now, Jesus has obtained a more excellent ministry! Hey, not only this, our great High Priest is now the mediating bridge builder of a brand new covenant God has established based upon a whole new perfect set of promises!

I'm telling you, if there weren't any problems with the first covenant then there wouldn't have been any need to establish a second! To put it bluntly, God was ticked off with mankind. Listen to how He puts it:

> "Look, the day will come," God said, "when I'll invoke my own will upon the children of God, and with the household of God. It won't be anything like the covenant I entered into with your forefathers as I took them by the hand and led them out of the land of slavery and bondage in Egypt. Why? Because they didn't hold up their end of the bargain and I was bitterly disappointed in their inability to measure up."

And God continued,

"For this is my will I'll initiate on my own with the children of God since they've blown it. I'll put my laws into their minds and I'll write my laws into their hearts, and I'll be to them a God and they'll be to me a people."

"And they won't have to go around teaching all their friends, neighbors, and family with the admonition, 'You'd better get with it and get to know God!' Listen, everybody will know me, from the very least to the greatest of all. For I'll be merciful to their unrighteousness! For **THEIR SINS,** (their frailties, their indiscretions, their ineptitude, their stupidity, and anything else you wish to throw in there), **WILL I REMEMBER NO MORE!**" (Jeremiah 31:31-34)!

193. EARTHLY TABERNACLE
(Hebrews 8:13-9:10)

The very fact God talked about "...a new agreement..." implies the truth He's made the first agreement null and void. It only stands to reason when something has become ineffective and redundant, it's better to just let 'er go.

Keep in mind the first covenant had some merit in the sense it was symbolic in nature, a type and shadow of God's will for all mankind. Hey, if the earthly sanctuary of God was so fantastic, can you just imagine the splendor of His eternal abiding place?

When the first tabernacle was built, the candlestick, the table, and the sacred loaves were placed inside the outer sanctuary courtyard. Inside, beyond the second veil, in an area called the "Holy of Holies," is where the golden incense altar and the golden overlaid Ark of the Covenant were. Inside the phenomenal Ark of the Covenant were stored a golden pot of manna, the walking stick of Aaron, as well as the tables of the covenant. Above the Ark of the Covenant were fixed representations of the cherubim of glory, casting their shadow over the ark's covering, known as the mercy seat.

Now, there's so much meaning to all of these things, however, I simply don't want to get into a detailed explanation at this point, BUT, the second area, the "Holy of Holies," was entered into only by a high priest, and by him alone. Significantly as well, he could enter only once every year!

The high priest didn't dare enter this second compartment without some blood. Some of the blood was to be first used as a sacrificial offering for the errors of his ways, and the remainder, for the errors of the rest of the people.

God's intention with this whole sanctuary thing was to signify it was impossible for mankind to have unlimited access into the presence of God as long as the first sanctuary was still in existence. This first sanctuary, together with all of the symbolism and ritual it stood for, was simply an object lesson.

While gifts and sacrifices were offered there all this ritual was incapable of cleansing the very heart, mind, or soul, of any of the worshipers who gathered there.

The ceremonies dealt with food and drink, together with rituals designed to symbolize washings and cleansing of the exterior of the human condition. The minutest details were contained in the systems of self-righteous laws, rules, and regulations. The wisdom (foolishness) of mankind imposed incredible bondage upon all the people until God, in His wisdom, decided to reform the whole mess!

What was the earthly tabernacle like?

Well, the wilderness tabernacle is described in great splendor for us in the scriptures (Exodus 25-31, 35-40). The people of Israel supported the project so overwhelmingly the freewill offerings had to be halted due to the lavish giving (Exodus 36:5-7).

Let me attempt to give you at least a glimpse of what it was like.

The Court of the Tabernacle

A 7½ feet high curtain-like fence surrounded the 150 by 75 feet outer courtyard. The beautiful white, fine-twined linen represented the wall of holiness surrounded the presence of God. Supporting the curtains were 20 great pillars on the north and south sides, with 10 pillars on the east and west sides. The base of each pillar was set into sockets of brass while the tops were covered in silver. The only gate was located on the east side, measuring 30 feet wide by 7½ feet high. Stunning stitching of blue, purple, and scarlet adorned the elegant curtain gate of white, fine-twined linen.

There were two objects in this outer courtyard.

1. The "brazen altar" was built of acacia wood, sheathed in brass. It was 7½ feet square and stood 4½ feet in height. The sacrifices would be laid on its top made of a brazen grating.

2. The "laver" was made of brass mirrors used by the women folk. The priests would bathe themselves with water in this sink before they carried out their official, sacred duties.

The Tabernacle

The tabernacle itself was constructed with 48 acacia beams that were 15 feet high, and 2 feet 3 inches in width. They were overlaid with pure gold and set in sockets of silver.

Connecting rods bound them together on the outside and by a wooden tie-beam that ran through the center. The first 2/3rds of the two-part tabernacle was known as the "Holy Place," while the second 2/3rds was a 15-feet cube called the "Holy of Holies."

The Holy Place

There were three objects in the "Holy Place.

1. The "golden candlestick" stood on the south side. Pure olive oil fed the ever-burning lamp stands crafted by artisans out of a talent (about 75 pounds) of pure gold.

2. The "table of the shewbread" stood on the north side. Also made of acacia wood covered in gold, it was 3 feet long, 1½ feet wide, and 2 feet 3 inches high. Every Sabbath twelve loaves, baked with the finest of flour, were laid on the table in two rows of six each. The bread that was leftover was to be consumed by the priests.

3. The "altar of incense" was 1½ feet square by 3 feet in height. Gold sheathing covered the acacia wood frame. Incense was burned on the altar every morning and every evening to symbolize the prayers of the people rising up to their God.

The Holy of Holies

The "Holy of Holies" was separated from the "Holy Place" by a spectacular veil of beautiful white, fine-twined linen embroidered with scarlet, purple, and blue thread. Five brass pillars, adorned by cherubim, supported the veil.

The "ark of the covenant" stood sanctimoniously in the Holy of Holies, containing three prized items:

1. The golden pot containing manna.
2. The rod that Aaron had used.
3. The table of the covenant was constructed of acacia wood sheathed on the inside and outside with gold. It measured 3 feet 9 inches in length, 2 feet 3 inches in width, and 2 feet 3 inches in height. The lid of the table was called the "mercy seat" on which sat two cherubim, made of solid gold with overarching wings. The presence of God rested on this seat (Exodus 25:22).

Beautiful to behold, or what? The sad reality is very few people ever got to see the inside. Ordinary folks could only come up to the gate of the tabernacle court. Only priests and Levites could enter into the "court of the tabernacle." Only priests could enter the "holy place," and nobody, and I mean nobody, dared enter the "holy of holies" with the exception of the high priest. And even then, once a year was all they could handle!

194. DAY OF ATONEMENT

Before I continue with the letter, I've just got to tell you about a very special day in the collective life of the people of Israel, namely, the "day of Atonement."

Keep in mind a covenant relationship existed between God and His people. The relationship broke down when the people decided they had a better way. In their ultimate wisdom (foolishness) a myriad system of laws, rules, and regulations were created to do something to restore some kind of significant relationship with God.

Unfortunately, the errors of their ways kept catching up with them. Provision had been established by God to help get them back on the right track. The comprehensive act of wiping out the errors of everyone occurred once a year, on the "day of Atonement" (Leviticus 16:33). This momentous day fell 10 days after the opening of the Jewish New Year.

The occasion was more like a fast than a feast. Everyone, including the kids, didn't get to eat for the whole day. Devout folks would even fast for at least 10 days prior to this special day. If it was special to the common folks, it was super special to the members of the priesthood. For the high priest, the highest-ranking religious official in the land, it was the greatest day of any calendar year.

And you thought you had a lot to do to make yourself pretty enough to face the music of the day. Read a bit of what a high priest had to put up with.

The day started early for a high priest as he rose to cleanse himself with a bath. He got dressed with clothes that came out of the closet only on this particular day each year. Talk about puttin' on the ritz!

The undergarments consisted of white linen breeches that reached right down to the feet. The "robe of the Ephod" was a long, dark blue robe. At the foot of the robe was a fringe of blue, purple, and scarlet tassels made in the form of pomegranates, interspersed with an equal number of small golden bells. The "Ephod" itself was placed over the robe. It was a linen tunic embroidered with scarlet, purple, and gold, accompanied by an elaborate girdle. Two onyx stones, each engraved with the names of six of the tribes, dangled from the shoulders of the tunic. A "breastplate," measuring a span (about 8 inches) square, also fit over the tunic.

The names of all twelve tribes were engraved on twelve precious stones that were attached to the breastplate.

Why?

The high priest approached God on behalf of all the people of Israel. He carried their representation both on his shoulders, as well as on his heart.

In the "breastplate" was the "Urim and the Thummim," meaning "lights and perfections" (Exodus 28:30). A precious diamond had the engravings of the consonants "I H W H," the consonants of Jahweh, the name of God.

And let's not forget the tall "mitre." This was the headdress made of a fine linen cloth with a gold plate bound by a band of blue ribbon. Inscribed on this plate were the words: "Holiness unto the Lord."

The activities of the special day started out much like most any day. The morning incense was burned, the morning sacrifice was offered, and the lamps on the seven-branched lamp stand were trimmed.

The unique ritual (once a year) started to kick into high gear from this point on. Dressed in all his glorious splendor, the high priest sacrificed a bullock, seven lambs, and one ram (Numbers 29:7). Off came the beautiful robe. He took a shower to get purified once again, then dressed down into a simpler outfit made also of white linen.

A bullock, one that the high priest himself had purchased, was then brought before him. He put his hands on the head of the animal, and in front of the masses in attendance he cried out his confession for himself and for all the people.

It went something like this:

"O God, I've committed iniquity, I've transgressed, and I've sinned. Surely not only I, but also my whole house has done this. God, I beg you, cover over (atone) my iniquity, my transgression, and my sin as well as the iniquity, transgression, and sin of my whole house. Surely Moses your servant has written, 'For in that day, He will cover over (atone) you to make you clean. From all of your iniquity, transgression, and sin will you be cleansed.'"

The bullock remained before the altar at this point. Off to the side, next to two goats standing by was an urn with two lots in it. One of the lots was marked with a label "for Jehovah," and the other lot with a label marked "for Azazel."

I'm sure you already know the name for God was "Jehovah." However, do you know what "Azazel" means? It literally means "scapegoat!"

Think on that one for a moment.

Well, the lots were drawn and placed accordingly on the head of each of the two goats. A tongue shaped piece of scarlet was tied to the horn of the "scapegoat."

The high priest turned his attention back to the bullock, slaughtering it by cutting its throat, the blood caught in a basin by a priestly assistant. It was important the basin be moved continuously so the blood wouldn't coagulate until it could be used later in another part of the pageantry.

The crowd was really into it by now. The high priest took some coals from the altar and placed them into a censer. Into a special dish he placed some incense, then proceeded delicately into the "Holy of Holies" to burn incense in the very presence of God. "Lest he put Israel in terror" it was stipulated he couldn't stay in there too long. They actually tied a rope with bells on it to his ankles so just in case it got too quiet his assistants could yank him out of there.

Anxiously, the folks waited. And waited. A gigantic, collective sigh of relief erupted as the high priest returned from his first visit with God. With pomp and ceremony he took the basin of the blood from the bullock, and ventured off on his second visit into the "Holy of Holies." Once inside, he sprinkled the blood upward seven times, and then downward seven times.

Once again, his reappearance brought great relief to the crowd. Next, the high priest turned his attention to the goat labeled with the sign "for Jehovah." It was this goat's turn to donate its life. With the carefully collected blood from this particular goat swirling in the basin, the high priest reentered the "Holy of Holies" for the third time. Yes, the blood was scattered again. Seven times up. Seven times down.

Great rejoicing rang out again with the reemergence of the head honcho. The ceremony continued with the collection of some of the blood from the bullock and some from the goat "for Jehovah." Portions of the blood were mixed together in a common basin then sprinkled onto the horns of the altar of the incense and on the altar itself.

Seven times!

The remaining blood was left at the foot of the altar of the burnt offering. Both the altar and the "Holy of Holies" were now cleansed by blood from any defilement that might be upon them.

Now came the really exciting part!

The "for Azazel" goat was brought before the high priest. He laid his hands on the "scapegoat," then confessed again his own sins, and also the sins of all the people once again. The "scapegoat" was then led out into a desolate place in the desert where the "scapegoat," bearing the sins of the high priest, as well as all the people, was slaughtered as a sacrifice for the sins of all.

The duties of the high priest were still not completed. He returned to the bullock and the goat that had been sacrificed earlier in the day. He read a passage from the sacred scriptures (Leviticus 16; 23:27-32), and from memory he recited another passage (Numbers 29:7-11). This was followed up with a prayer for the priesthood, as well as for all the people.

Off with the simple white linen clothes. Have another shower. Get dressed in the full splendor of the beautiful, religious uniform.

Talk about costume changes!

His next duty was to sacrifice a kid of the goats on behalf of the sins of himself and of all the people, followed up shortly after with the normal evening sacrifice. The already specially prepared parts of the bullock and the goat would comprise the ingredients for the last sacrifice of the day.

Oh, Oh.

Another costume change.

Yes, out of the beautiful, back into the simple stuff.

For the fourth time of the day, the high priest entered into the "Holy of Holies" to remove the censer of incense still burning inside.

Here we go again.

Off with the simple. Into the shower. On with the beautiful garments.

He proceeded at this point to burn the evening offering of incense, trimmed the lamps on the golden lamp stand, and ladies and gentlemen, this almost concludes the most important day of the year.

Ah, but then came what they all had been waiting for.

FOOD!

Perhaps it was because he had the good fortune of coming out of the four trips into the "Holy of Holies" alive the high priest threw one humungous party. It was a fabulous feast lacking for nothing.

For the creme de la creme of society an invitation to this monster ball was most coveted. Anyone who was anyone was sure to be there.

Party on!

I probably shouldn't be poking so much fun at this monumental day.

The "day of Atonement" surely was the highlight of any given year. The significance of all the ritual and ceremony cannot be understated, or even overstated for that matter. However, there was only one problem with this entire system.

Sorry, I take it back. There are tons of problems with it.

The major one, however, is it just didn't accomplish what it was set out to do. Oh sure, it may have been spectacular to witness, even more so to participate in it as a high priest. Everyone was off the hook so to speak. Well, at least for another year anyway!

Consider this question.

"How could the blood of bulls and goats, offered once a year, by someone who had to take so many showers in one day, possibly cover over (atone) the iniquities, transgressions, and sins of a people who persisted in breaking their commitment to love, honor, and serve their God?"

You've got to know I'm not through yet.

Let's get back to the letter...

195. ALL CLEANED UP
(Hebrews 9:11-26)

BUT, Jesus, on the other hand, has become our great High Priest of all the good things God actually intended for everyone.

How?

Through a greater and more perfect tabernacle of God's presence, not made with human hands, that is to say, not something which mankind could come up with on their own, and certainly not as a result of the blood sacrifice of a herd of goats or calves either!

BUT, Jesus accomplished the desire of God's heart with the sacrifice of His very own blood! Furthermore, it only took Jesus "ONE" time to get the job done!

You see, He entered into the true "Holy of Holies" of God's presence once with His own blood sacrifice.

What did it accomplish?

It accomplished for "all" the eternal redemption unattainable with systems of laws, rules, and regulations!

Look here, if the blood of bulls, of goats, and the ashes of an heifer sprinkled over the scars of the unrighteous had the effect of temporarily (at least for a year) cleaning the slate, then, how MUCH MORE has the blood of Jesus, who, through the eternal Spirit of God within Him, offered Himself to God, totally without spot, blemish, or wrinkle, purged your conscience from "dead works" to attain the eternal favor of the living God?

Don't you get it?

This is the very reason Jesus is the mediator of the new covenant of God. Jesus has the power and authority, based upon His sacrificial death, to right the wrongs of everyone bound under the first covenant of laws, rules, and regulations.

Why?

So "all" God has called to be His children could receive the promise of His eternal inheritance!

Look, for a will to come into effect it's necessary for the person who established the will to die. Let me say it another way. A will only has legal clout when the "will-er" is dead.

Let me say it another way. A will doesn't mean anything as long as the "will-er" is still alive.

You see, even the first will was effective.

Why?

Because it involved the shedding of blood, for after Moses presented the system of laws, rules, and regulations to all the people he took the blood of calves and of goats and mixed it with water. Mo then dipped in some wool and together with the scarlet wool, took a sprig of hyssop and sprinkled some of the blood over the book containing the covenant of God which all of the people had agreed to abide by, saying, "This is the blood of the covenant which God has enjoined you to."

And then he sprinkled blood on the tabernacle and upon all the vessels used in the ceremony (Exodus 24:1-8).

Almost everything governed under the system of laws, rules, and regulations is purged with the sacrifice of blood.

"For the life of the flesh is in the blood, and I've given it to you on the altar to make an atonement for your souls: for it's the blood which makes an atonement for the soul" (Leviticus 17:11).

This is why it was necessary for earthly things, types and shadows of the heavenlies, to be purified with the offerings and sacrifices of the blood of bulls and goats.

BUT, to have the everlasting effect God desired it would take a much greater sacrifice than the imperfect and ineffective offering of animals by an imperfect high priest.

Look, Jesus didn't enter in the "Holy of Holies" of God's presence created with the imaginative ability of human hands, a space merely a foreshadowing of the true presence of God, BUT, He entered into heaven itself as our great High Priest, now to eternally appear in the very presence of God on our behalf!

Nor did Jesus go to heaven with the notion He'd have to make a similar sacrificial trip down to earth every once in a while just like the earthly high priest would enter into the "Holy of Holies" every year with the blood of bulls and goats.

My goodness, can you just imagine how many times Jesus would have had to suffer the humiliation and agony of death on our behalf since the foundation of this old world?

BUT now, ONCE, and for ALL, IN THE END OF THE WORLD has Jesus appeared.

For what? To PUT AWAY SIN!

How?

By the sacrifice of His own blood!

HEBREWS

196. RE-DESTINATED
(Hebrews 9:27-10:18)

Can't avoid it.

Everybody, at one time or another, is going to die.

BUT, just as surely, it was the wise judgment of God that Jesus would be offered up to bear the sins of all. And those who look for Him to come a second time will be looking as people totally without sin, saved from all unrighteousness.

Why?

Because the system of laws, rules, and regulations, undoubtedly a shadow of all the good things to come, and yet, certainly not the exact picture of these exciting things I've been speaking about, could never, with all the sacrificial ceremonies they engendered continuously, year after year, make the people perfect!

Hey, if the sacrifices adhered to in accordance with all the laws, rules, and regulations actually did the trick of making people perfect at some point, wouldn't it be fair to assume the offerings could have ceased at some point? My goodness, if the people had been cleansed they should have had no more consciousness of sin and unrighteousness!

BUT, they kept coming back for more. The mere fact people went through all the elaborate ceremonies of sacrifice is testimony to the fact they remembered they'd goofed up again and again throughout the year.

Look, give your head a shake until your mind is renewed to this indisputable fact:

IT IS IMPOSSIBLE THAT THE BLOOD OF BULLS AND GOATS SHOULD TAKE AWAY SINS!

This is precisely what Jesus had to say about the whole situation after He came into the world:

> "You (God) realized the sacrifices and offerings of the blood of bulls and goats would never cut it as far as your demand for justice is concerned. BUT You (God) have prepared a way for Me (Jesus) to replace, with the single sacrifice of My own blood, the whole system of burnt offerings and sacrifices to take away the sins that You (God) couldn't tolerate."

"And then I said, 'Behold, I (Jesus) delight (and there's plenty of recorded evidence to back this up) to do Your will, O God'" (Psalms 40:6-8)!

In addition to the fact Jesus declared sacrifices, offerings, burnt offerings, and offerings for sin inspired and directed through a system of laws, rules, and regulations wouldn't have any lasting impact on God, and wouldn't give God any amount of pleasure, Jesus had the audacity to add these incredible words:

"Behold, I delight to do Your will, O God" (Psalms 40:8)!

The bottom line?

God took away the first, "imperfect" system so He could establish the second, "perfect" system.

It is by this "perfect" will of God that we are made "perfect" through the offering of the body of Jesus, ONCE, and, FOR ALL!

Every earthly priest has stood daily ministering to the people, offering oftentimes the very same sacrifices, none of which could never take away sins.

BUT, this man Jesus, after He had offered one sacrifice for sins for all eternity, sat down on the right hand of God as our great High Priest. From that moment on every enemy of God has been placed under the authority and subjection of Jesus.

How'd He do it?

With one offering of His own blood! So God, with the single sacrifice of Jesus, perfected for all eternity everyone covered by the sacrifice!

Don't believe me?

Just listen to what the Spirit of Jesus confirmed to us concerning the promise God had made to folks a long time ago.

"'This is the promise I'll make with everyone when the days of the systems of laws, rules, and regulations have come to an end,' God said. 'I will put my laws of my heart into their hearts. I will rewrite the book and renew their minds to understand my grace and peace'" (Jeremiah 31:33).

"'And their sins and iniquities will I remember no more'"(Jeremiah 31:34).

Now, since sin has been taken away there's no longer a necessity to make the offering of sacrifices to get sin taken away ever again!

At best, the old sacrificial system, built upon the myriad pronouncements of laws, rules, and regulations were nothing more than a silhouette of a better thing to come. Perhaps one should say it was a pale copy of the best to come. And the best thing to come was none other than Jesus.

The sacrificial system was nothing more than a reminder of failure. The blood of bulls and goats couldn't wipe out all the failure compounded throughout any given year.

Ha. How could it?

It ought to be impossible to think it could.

Perhaps I should describe briefly just a few of the various sacrifices made every morning and evening (Numbers 28:3-8).

1. Burnt offering: a one-year old male lamb, without spot or blemish.

2. Meat offering: $1/10^{th}$ of an ephah (approximately .05 of a bushel) of fine flour mixed with ¼ of a hin (approximately one quart) of pure oil.

3. Drink offering: ¼ of a hin (approximately one quart) of wine.

4. Meat offering of the high priest: similar to the meat offering, however this mixture was then baked in a flat pan, with ½ of it offered in the morning and ½ of it offered in the evening.

5. Incense: before and after each offering in the morning and evening.

Is it any wonder this treadmill of sacrifice left everyone incredibly conscious of sin and their subsequent alienation from God?

It's no wonder to me why God decided to rewrite the book and start from scratch on a whole new page. God was certainly faithful to His promise. Boy, did He ever do a number on the eternal destiny of all mankind.

We were destined for an eternal death, and with the death of Jesus, He "re-destinated" us for an eternal life of grace and peace.

He removed from our consciousness the torment of the consequences of sin. Hey, God promised us He'd never even remember sin again! He instituted a new and living way. Sin has been dealt with once, and for all!

HEBREWS

197. HANG IN THERE
(Hebrews 10:19-39)

My dear, dear friends,
    since we have the boldness to enter into the true "Holy of Holies" of God's presence as a result of the one time sacrifice of the blood of Jesus, by a new and living way He consecrated for us when He ripped the veil in two, yes, in fact, when His very own body was ripped apart on our behalf, and
    since we have a great High Priest who now rules over the household of God,
    let's **APPROACH GOD WITH A TRUE HEART** in full assurance of the faith and faithfulness of God, having our hearts sprinkled clean from an evil conscience, and having our bodies washed spotlessly clean with pure water.
    Furthermore, let's hold fast the profession of our trust and confidence in God's power, ability, and faithfulness to accomplish what He promised He would.
    Oh, and one more thing, let's consider it an honor to provoke one another to love and serve one another, rejecting the bigoted notion of some to disassociate themselves from those they perceive couldn't possibly fit into the family of God, BUT, exhort one another to renew their minds, all the more as you start to get a glimpse of the incredible accomplishment of "that" day when God adopted everyone into His family.
    Look, in spite of having received the incredible knowledge concerning the truth of the wisdom of God's eternal and universal love, if we deliberately persist in following after the wisdom (foolishness) of mankind as if systems of laws, rules, and regulations had an effect upon our relationship with God, it doesn't alter the fact there's no longer any kind of earthly sacrifice which could possibly wipe out sin!
    BUT, the only thing this kind of ignorance will perpetuate is an immense, fearful expectation of the judgment of God coupled with His fiery indignation that will devour the adversaries of God.
    Anyone who refused to buckle under to the Law of Moses, with appropriate evidence and the testimony of at least two or three witnesses, was summarily sentenced to be executed without the mercy of even an appeal (Deuteronomy 17:2-7).

Just think about this for a moment.

What kind of punishment do you think would be appropriate for those who simply reject the authority and power of the Son of God, who count the precious sacrifice of Jesus, the very blood that secured for all the righteousness of God according to His promise, totally insignificant, ineffective, and insufficient, or, who still live like they're under the old systems of laws, rules, and regulations despite the introduction of the Spirit of God's system of grace?

We all know God declared,

"Vengeance belongs to me, and I'll take care of the problem" (Deuteronomy 32:35)!

And the exhortation continued,

"It is God who will judge His people in whatever way He chooses to do so" (Deuteronomy 32:36).

Well, let me tell you this is the best thing that could have ever happened to mankind! It's absolutely awesome our eternal destiny falls into the hands of a loving, gracious, and merciful God!

BUT, just remember the journey you've been on since you've renewed your mind to the wisdom of God's grace and peace for all. You've had to put up with quite a bit of crap and abuse in the last little while. Part of your suffering is a result of the fact those who toe the party line have made you out to be a species worthy of ridicule and outright rejection.

Another reason for your affliction and persecution from the religious community is because you've made a conscious decision to become friends with those outside the "box," so to speak. Hey, you've even had the nerve to extend your compassion to someone as objectionable as me, a prisoner of some goofy cause, no less.

Well, you've taken great pleasure in sharing your resources with others, knowing full well your eternal abundance and liberty has been provided for in the heavenly wisdom of God!

Please don't ever chuck your confidence in God away! Your renewed understanding of the truth of God's love will yield more peace than you can handle.

Hang in there!

Enjoy the will of God, and in doing so, you'll be participating in the promise of God.

Take a load of this prophetic insight:

"There's going to be a time very soon when He (Jesus) who is to come will in fact come. And when He (Jesus) does come, it will be so all will live in righteousness, by His (Jesus') faith and faithfulness. BUT, if He (Jesus) doesn't do what He (Jesus) says He (Jesus) will do, then my soul has little to hope for, and I can take no pleasure in paying any attention to Him (Jesus) at all" (Habbakuk 2:2,4).

BUT, we're not like those who've returned to the bondage and slavery of systems of laws, rules, and regulations!

BUT, we are a part of the group of folks who've renewed their minds to the knowledge and understanding God has faithfully completed the full measure of His promise to distribute His righteousness to all mankind.

HEBREWS

198. FAITH OF GOD
(Hebrews 11:1-40)

Now, it's the faith and faithfulness of God that is the substantive assurance of everything we could ever hope for, and indeed, the evident, true reality of everything that we as humans can't even imagine or visualize. Hey, it was the faith and faithfulness of God that enabled our forefathers to gain the favorable acceptance of God as well.

Creation itself is testimony to God's faithfulness! Its incredible beauty and miraculous complexity speaks volumes of God's creative genius to frame such a home for mankind by the authority and power of His command. We can't even comprehend how God could create something we can enjoy so much out of something we'll never get to see.

It was the faith and faithfulness of God which Abel understood clearly enough to offer a more excellent offering than Cain did. The testimony of God's faithfulness was confirmed to Abel, for he knew he was righteous in God's eyes without attempting to do something to gain it. The first recorded murder cries out loud and clear about the folly of those who misunderstand the full extent of God's faith and faithfulness (Genesis 4:1-15).

It was the faith and faithfulness of God that transformed the life of the great fashion designer Enoch. God surely must have taken Enoch to be with Him 'cause one day he just didn't show up for work. However, before he left the scene unannounced, folks recognized God was well pleased with this classic character (Genesis 5:24).

BUT, APART FROM THE FAITH AND FAITHFULNESS OF GOD IT IS IMPOSSIBLE TO GAIN HIS FAVOR!

You want to understand God? Well, accept God is who He is! Furthermore, those who diligently seek to know God will come to understand He has rewarded them with more than they could possibly imagine, including the free gift of His grace and peace.

It was the faith and faithfulness of God to warn folks, including Noah, of things that were about to happen.

Despite evidence to the contrary and with reverent diligence Noah accepted the instructions of God to build an ark. What happened? His whole family was saved from the perilous flood that wiped out the rest of the world! What became of Noah? Well, he too became an heir of the righteousness of God as a result of the faith and faithfulness of God (Genesis 6 - 8)!

It was the faith and faithfulness of God that Abe recognized when he obeyed the call to go out into a place that would become his inheritance. Hey, he went even though he didn't have a clue as to where he was going (Genesis 12:1)!

It was in the shadow of God's faith and faithfulness Abe lived in the land of God's promise even though he was stranded in some strange, foreign territory, living there in tents with Isaac and Jake, heirs also of the very same promise of God. And yet, Abe never gave up on his dream of living in a city with real homes designed and built by God Himself (Genesis 12:2-10).

It was the faith and faithfulness of God that provided to Sara the strength to have sex with crochety ol' Abe.

Don't laugh!

My goodness, she gave birth to a child at an age when giving birth was more than out of the question.

Why'd she go for it?

Well, because Sara knew when God makes a promise He was faithful enough to keep it!

So, what happened?

Along came Isaac! And from this one man, not exactly a pillar of vitality himself came descendants as numerous as the stars of the skies. In fact, you couldn't even count that high, just like you can't count the number of grains of sand on a sea shore (Genesis 17:15-22; 18:9-15; 21:1-8).

Abe, Isaac, Jake, and Sara all died living in the faith and faithfulness of God too. Oh sure, they may not have received the promises of God in Jesus, BUT, they could see it coming and were persuaded of the absolute blessing of God. They embraced the promises of God, confessing all the while they were merely itinerant strange foreigners and transient pilgrims in a journey on this earth.

Now, anyone who talks like this is clearly saying they're still searching for a better place to call home.

Ha, if they had good memories of the place they left behind, they'd probably have had plenty of opportunities to go back to it.

BUT, their minds were set on finding a more desirable place to live, a heaven on earth so to speak. God wasn't ashamed to be called their God for He certainly prepared for them a city beyond their wildest dreams.

It was the faith and faithfulness of God that Abe clung to as he went through the difficult task of offering up Isaac. Having received the promises of God Abe was prepared to make a sacrifice of his only precious son. The promise of God to Abe was this:

"All your descendants will trace their heritage through the lineage of Isaac" (Genesis 21:12).

Hey, Abe figured if God said He was able to raise Isaac up to this kind of greatness then God could surely raise Isaac from the dead to accomplish this enormous challenge, even if he actually went through with the sacrifice. Isn't this just what transpired? In a manner of speaking, Abe actually did receive his son back from certain death (Genesis 22:1-18).

It was the faith and faithfulness of God that Isaac counted on when he blessed Jacob and Esau concerning the future (Genesis 27:28,29,39,40).

It was the faith and faithfulness of God that Jacob, in his final days of life, invoked to bless the sons of Joseph and the reason he worshipped God as he lay comfortably at peace on his deathbed (Genesis 48:9-22).

It was the faith and faithfulness of God that Joe, just before he died, made mention of as he spoke of the exodus of the children of Israel and of his instructions concerning what he wanted to happen to his bones after he died (Genesis 50:22-26).

It was the faith and faithfulness of God by which Moses, when he was born, was hidden away for three months by his parents because he was a really cute little kid, and because they refused to be intimidated by the cruel severity of the king's ruthless, royal edict (Exodus 2:1-10; 1:15-22).

It was the faith and faithfulness of God that inspired Mo, when he finally reached a level of maturity, to refuse to go along with the charade of being the son of the Pharoah's daughter.

Rather, Mo chose to suffer under the same affliction with the people of God than to enjoy the seasonal pleasures of self-righteousness. Yes, like Jesus in His situation, Mo recognized suffering for others would yield far greater riches than all the treasures in Egypt. For he truly knew earthly rewards are contemptible when compared to the ultimate rewards of God's promises (Exodus 2:11-14).

It was the faith and faithfulness of God that strengthened Mo as he courageously left Egypt in the dust, undeterred by the anger of the king. He survived the ordeal maintaining his focus on the promises of One who is invisible (Exodus 2:14-22).

It was the faith and faithfulness of God that Mo depended on as he made all the arrangements for the first Passover ceremonies, including all the instructions for the doorpost blood sprinkling caper, safe-guarding the first born children from certain destruction (Exodus 12:12-48).

It was the faith and faithfulness of God that provided a way for Mo to lead his people through the Red Sea as if it were a stretch of desert highway. This very same route became the drowning site for all the Egyptians who were relished the chase to obliterate the menacing people once and for all (Exodus 14).

It was the faith and faithfulness of God to do what was humanly impossible when the walls of Jericho crumbled after folks marched around the city for seven days or so (Joshua 6:1-20).

It was the faith and faithfulness of God that saw the prostitute Rahab and her family preserved from the fateful slaughter of those who acted in their own self interest after she had given refuge to the spies Joshua had sent to check out Jericho (Joshua 2:1-21; 6:25).

Do you need me to give you some more examples? My goodness, I don't think I have the time to tell you the wonderful stories of the likes of **Gideon** (Judges 6,7), **of Barak** (Judges 4,5), **of Samson** (Judges 13-16), **of Jephthah** (Judges 11,12), **of David too** (I Samuel 16:1-13), **and Samuel** (I Samuel 1), **and of some of the other prophets.**

The accomplishments of these folks, in the confident assurance of the faith and faithfulness of God are myriad. Some of these folks:
- subdued kingdoms;
- ruled over nations in righteousness (David-2 Samuel 8:15);

- received promises from God;
- shut the mouths of lions (Daniel-Daniel 6:18,23);
- quenched the furious violence of fire (Shadrach, Meshach, Abednego-Daniel 3:19-28);
- escaped the edge of the sword (Elijah-I Kings 19:1 ff; Elisha-2 Kings 6:31 ff);
- saw weakness turned into strength (Hezekiah-2 Kings 20:1-7);
- fought valiantly in battle;
- caused the armies of bitter enemies to retreat like scared chickens;
- were women who saw their loved ones return from the dead (1 Kings 17:17 ff; 2 Kings 4:8 ff);
- were tortured to death without giving up on their convictions, knowing full well they'd be heading off to a much better place,
- endured trials of cruel mockery and beatings, yes, including bondage and imprisonment,
- were stoned to death (Zechariah-2 Chronicles 24:20-22);
- were cut in two (Isaiah);
- were tricked into the promise of release only to be killed by the sword;
- were forced into slavery and refugee status with nothing other than the skins of sheep and goats to cover themselves with;
- had everything they possessed taken away from them;
- were spurned and ridiculed;
- were tormented by a world of folks who didn't recognize their worth; and
- wandered in the wilderness, in the mountains, and in the dens and caves of the earth like scavengers.

And every single one of these folks was totally acceptable in the sight of God through His faith and faithfulness, even though they never did get to see the revelation of God's promise in Jesus!

God certainly did provide some better thing for us, eh?

Doesn't it just make you feel grateful and thrilled God decided He wouldn't make all those incredible folks perfect without making a much better provision for our perfection as well?

HEBREWS

199. TALK ABOUT PERSECUTION

We don't have to read very far into the scriptures to begin reading account after account of incredible folks who lived and died holding fast to the faith and faithfulness of God. This characteristic is a common trait of those who've felt the impact of God's love in their lives.

There was a period of time between the last of the great prophetic voices and the arrival of Jesus upon the scene of history, known in certain circles as the Maccabean period, in which atrocities of unbelievable severity were enacted upon folks who certainly didn't deserve it.

Literature, predominantly from the pen of a great contemporary historian Josephus, is a fantastic source for amazing tales of fortitude and resolute trust in the faith and faithfulness of God in the face of immense opposition. Please allow me a few moments to share some pretty scary stuff which you've probably never ever even heard about before.

The enormous and brutal persecution of the Jewish people under Antiochus Epiphanes is a good place to start. He ruled over the kingdom of Syria around 170 B.C. For all intents and purposes, he wasn't all that bad as kings go, at least for a while. He had a major thing for anything that smacked of the Greek culture. He became an unofficial ambassador of sorts for the Greek way of life and attempted to bring this influence into Palestine, meeting with a certain amount of success. Greek drama, sporting competitions, and cuisine were just some of the culture he perpetuated.

Don't kid yourselves into thinking the religious community in Palestine was immune from this persuasion. While some of the Jewish priests went so far as to remove the marks of circumcision from their bodies, the vast majority of Jews remained unshakeable in their opposition to the "Hellenization" of their homeland.

Things took a change for the worse about 168 B.C. when Egypt became a target for an expansionist, ambitious, and aggressive Antiochus Epiphanes. Let's nickname him "Anti" for the sake of expedience. I can't handle these long names all the time. It almost suits him though, ya think? Anyway, Anti assembled an army and began the procession to invade Egypt at the very same time the head honchos in Rome got wind of his plan.

They decided to put a big ki-bosh on the plans of this zealous Anti dude. So they dispatched an ambassador by the name of Popilius Laena to tell Anti where "not" to go!

Here we go again. Let's nickname this guy "Pops." As you can imagine, Anti and Pops didn't exactly hit it off when they met. Anti certainly wasn't too impressed with this unsolicited interference in his affairs. He knew better than to tell Pops to stick it somewhere, so he told Pops he'd think it over and get back to him.

Well, Pops hadn't come all this way simply to soak up some rays in the desert. He knew he had the mighty power of Rome to back up his commission of authority. Pops took a stick, literally, and drew a circle in the sand around the spot on which Anti was standing.

Politely, and yet in no uncertain terms, Pops suggested to Anti he consider his alternatives very quickly. In fact, Pops expected a response before Anti left the circle. Humbled and embarrassed, Anti realized he had no choice but to return home, abandoning his takeover plans.

Guess who took the heat for this painful humiliation?

Riiiiiggghhhtttt!

The Jews!

They bore the full weight of Anti's wrath. On his return to Syria, he attacked and plundered the city of Jerusalem. It's said as many as 80,000 people were killed. Another 10,000 were captured and forced into slavery as a result of this one raid alone.

Wait. There's more.

The Temple was completely ransacked. The golden altars of the shewbread and of the incense, the golden candlestick, the golden vessels, the curtains, the veil, all were taken away. The treasury was left barren.

Could it get any worse than that?

Oh yeah.

Sacrifices of pigs were offered on the altar of the burnt offerings to the Greek God named Zeus. The chambers of the Temple were turned into brothels and no act of indecency was left uncommitted.

And more?

He outlawed the Jewish rite of circumcision. He banned the possession of the scriptures, not to mention the books of the law. Jews were ordered under strict supervision to eat meat unclean and forbidden under normal circumstances to be consumed.

If they were going to sacrifice to anyone it was to be done in honor of Greek gods. Anyone caught defying these new orders by government inspectors would undergo misery and torment beyond your wildest imaginations.

People were whipped with rods until their bodies were bruised beyond recognition.

Some were crucified alive.

Women who had their sons circumcised were strangled, and their infant sons were hung by their necks as if upon their crosses.

Anti may well have directed one of the most sadistic and deliberate attempts to wipe out a people this world has ever seen. The people of Israel seem to be a popular target because of their unwavering and steadfast confidence in a God they consider to be unwavering in His faith and faithfulness to them.

Here's another story for you.

Eleazer, an aged priest, was brought before Anti and ordered to eat some pig meat, with dire consequences of course, if he refused. Citing his dedication to the law of God the priest politely replied, "Thanks, but, no thanks."

The king's goons promptly had Eleazer mercilessly abused by stripping him, spitting on him, kicking him, and scourging him with whips. There were a few soldiers, exercising a bit of compassion and pity on the old guy, who even secretly proposed to bring him some non-pig meat so he could pretend he was eating pig so he might escape any further harm.

Once again, Eleazer refused to capitulate on the grounds it would be setting a bad example to the young, providing them with an excuse to bend the rules to save themselves a similar fate.

Tough nut to crack I'd say.

Well, Eleazer was in for a bit more. They assaulted him with cruelly contrived instruments and poured stinking liquids down into his nostrils. Eventually, he was chucked like a worn out old log onto a huge fire started just for him.

His last words?

"I am dying by fiery torments for the law's sake" (4 Maccabees 5-7)!

Can you stomach another one?

This one's the story of seven brothers (4 Maccabees 8-14). They were given a choice to make.

Would they choose to stand in the confident trust in the faith and faithfulness of God, or, would they willingly accept the consequences of wheels, racks, hooks, catapults, cauldrons, frying pans, finger racks, iron hands, wedges, and hot embers?

I don't think I need to tell you what their decision was. Here's what happened to each of the brothers.

Brother # 1:
- was whip lashed,
- was tied to a wheel that dislocated and they broke every bone in his body,
- was heaped with fuel oil and set on fire,
- covered with burnt flesh, blood, and gore he was stretched again on the wheel

Brother # 2
- was bound to catapults,
- was beaten with spiked iron gloves,
- like panthers they dragged all the flesh off his muscles and ripped the skin off his head

Brother # 3
- because he was bald they dislocated his hands and feet with racking engines wrenching them from their sockets,
- they fractured his fingers, arms, legs, and elbows,
- they tore what was left of him off the catapult and flayed him alive

Brother # 4
- they cut out his tongue,
- they submitted him to merciless tortures

Brother # 5
- they bound him to the wheel and bent his body around its edge,
- they fastened him with iron fetters to the catapult and tore him to pieces

Brother # 6
- they tied him to the wheel and lit a fire under it to roast him,
- they heated sharp spits and applied them to his back,
- they pierced his side as they burned away his bowels

Brother # 7
- they roasted him alive in a huge frying pan

And you think you're being persecuted!

Here's another story.

A town called Modin was the site of an altar that agents of Antiochus Epiphanes had set up in order for the residents to sacrifice to the Greek gods. An influential, outstanding Jewish man named Mattathias was brought forward to become an example. He was outraged another Jew had capitulated to the decrees of Anti. As he was set to make a sacrifice, Matt, in uncontrollable rage, grabbed a sword and killed his fellow Jew, as well as the king's commissioner.

Oh my!

If the plan was to tick off the king, this did it. Big time! Anti invoked a whole new standard of persecution, and a rebellion ensued. Matt and his whole family though it best to flee into the mountains, leaving absolute everything behind (1 Maccabees 2:28).

Judas Maccabaeus, along with friends, decided to join in the desperate chance for survival and escaped into the hills as well, living like scavenging animals nonetheless (2 Maccabees 5:27).

Others, wanting to secretly observe the Sabbath, secretly hid in caves nearby. Once the king's soldiers tracked them down they were burnt together as a group (2 Maccabees 6:11).

People, desiring to maintain the traditions of their heritage, wandered in the mountains and in dens and caves like beasts (2 Maccabees 10:6).

How'd it all end up?

Well, it wasn't until Judas Maccabaeus and his brothers led a successful revolution that freedom and peace were restored for a whole lot of people. The Temple was eventually reclaimed, cleansed, and restored.

These brief accounts of events which happened over many years are intended to let you know more folks than you will ever know have suffering bitterly for taking a stand and for following after their convictions.

Who said it was going to be easy?

What really makes it intriguing is that these folks lived and died way before God made His dramatic mark on history by sending Jesus to intervene. These folks could only hope in the faith and faithfulness of God to see them through.

They were not mistaken!

He did see all of them through. Every one of them received a good report. Jesus saw to it for them as well as He has for the whole world!

200. RACE IS ON
(Hebrews 12:1-3)

So, since we've been so blessed to be surrounded with such an amazing, immense cloud of witnesses to the faith and faithfulness of God, let us:
- lay aside every weight which diverts us from our course of confident trust in the faith and faithfulness of God, including the plague of self-righteous systems of laws, rules, and regulations which so easily gets in the way,

and, let us:
- patiently run the race of our lives in the abundance and liberty of God's grace and peace which have been set before us to enjoy.

How?
By looking to Jesus.
Why?
BECAUSE HE IS THE AUTHOR AND FINISHER OF FAITH AND FAITHFULNESS!

Jesus, knowing full well the joy set before Him of what His faith and faithfulness was to accomplish for all humanity, endured the agony and anguish of the cross. He despised the utter shame of the whole experience.

And now what?

And now Jesus is sitting down at the right hand of the throne of God in majesty and honor!

I want you to think about what Jesus did for a moment. Do you realize what an absolute contradiction it was for the majestic and glorious Jesus to accept the wrath of God's punishment on behalf of the whole world?

Give your head a shake! My goodness.

This knowledge and understanding of the faith and faithfulness of God and Jesus should be the only thing you need to stop your minds from getting sick and tired trying to figure out whether God will ever accept you or not!

201. FRUIT OF RIGHTEOUSNESS
(Hebrews 12:4-13)

You'll never need to shed a drop of blood in the war against the bondage and slavery of self-righteousness!

I'm glad you've forgotten the very dramatic exhortation held out over you as if you were still little kids:

"Now, now, my son, don't get all choked up when God gets ticked off at you. Don't go fainting when He rebukes you. Listen, God disciplines everyone He loves, and punishes every child He accepts. If you happen the go through a bit of suffering, then God's dealing with you like a child, for what child doesn't need a little pat on the bum once in a while" (Proverbs 3:11,12)?

BUT, if you'll never be chastised by God, in the same way all humanity will never be punished again, then you must really be something unique and someone a whole lot more special than just a child.

Furthermore, we've all had dads who at one time or another found it necessary to correct us when we crossed the line or got out of hand. Hey, we all must admit we gave our fathers the respect they deserved. Well, shouldn't we also give God the reverence and respect He, the Father of all, deserves? We ought to live in gratitude and appreciation.

Our earthly fathers tended to take it out on us convinced they were doing something to make their own lives more tolerable and pleasant.

BUT, God exercised His discipline upon His Son for the benefit of all of us!

HE BROUGHT THE FULL WRATH OF HIS CHATISEMENT UPON JESUS SO WE MIGHT BECOME PARTAKERS OF HIS HOLINESS AND HIS RIGHTEOUSNESS!

Now, it's got to be true no amount of chastening could ever be considered a happy event. BUT, more likely, we'd consider it to be downright nasty. Nevertheless, the exercising of God's wrath upon His only begotten Son yielded results beyond our highest expectations.

It resulted for all in the peaceable fruit of His righteousness!

You bet!

Jesus took the heat for everybody who had it coming to them!

So, if you're hands are dragging along beside you in depression and despair, lift 'em up! Get those feeble, knocking knees goin' again. Start truckin' down the pathway Jesus has straightened out for you.

What's the alternative? You'll be crippled and lame to fend for yourself in the pursuit of self-righteousness.

BUT, I'd rather you know and understand your bodies have been healed from all unrighteousness!

202. UNSHAKEABLE
(Hebrews 12:14-29)

PURSUE THE PATH OF PEACE with everyone.

Separate yourselves from the path of self-righteousness to pursue the path of holiness with everyone, since without God's gift of His righteousness, nobody would ever be able to gain the favorable acceptance of God.

Be diligent to praise and worship God for what He's done for all mankind.

Why?

- Lest any of you fail to keep up with the knowledge and understanding of the precious gift of God's grace.
- Lest any root of bitter, poisonous fruit grow up inside of you which would irritate you that someone else is performing better, racking up more brownie points with God, causing you to fall right back into the trap of the legalistic systems of self-righteous laws, rules, and regulations.
- Lest there be any tendency to revert to an irreverent, undisciplined, and apathetic character, devoid of any awareness of interest in God until it suits your purpose.

Look, learn a lesson from that bonehead Esau. Here's a guy who, for one stupid morsel of meat, sold away all the rights and privileges of his own birthright, as well as the corporate destiny of all his descendants. He passed up a sure thing for a taste of something that could never satisfy. We all know after he came to his senses he tried to get it back. Too bad, so sad! Nothing he did could get the blessing back, not even baby tears (Genesis 25:28-34; Genesis 27:1-39).

Well, you certainly are a whole lot better off than he was! You see, there's nothing for you to fear about losing something and never getting it back.

For you have not come upon a mountain which might be touched, nor do you have to climb a mountain being consumed with fire, nor do you have to stumble in the black darkness and cloudy gloom, nor crumble in the tempest of a storm, nor fear the sound of a trumpet, nor tremble hearing the words of a voice, a voice scaring spitless those who heard it, pleading they wouldn't have to listen to it anymore.

(For they couldn't handle what they had been commanded to do. And if so much as a beast would touch the mountain it would have to be stoned to death or killed with a spear, and so terrible was the sight Mo said,

"Man I'm scared. I'm shaking like a leaf, trembling like an earthquake" (Exodus 19:12-22; 20:18-21; Deuteronomy 4:11-12; 5:22-27; 9:19)!)

BUT, you've come to a better place, the mountain of Zion, and to the city of the living God, a heavenly Jerusalem so to speak.

You've come to a place that is home to:
- an incalculable, joyful company of angels,
- the general assembly and church of Jesus, whose names are recorded as citizens of the heavenly kingdom,
- God, the Judge of all,
- the spirits of all who've been justified and made perfect, and
- Jesus, the mediator of a brand new covenant, our great High Priest, whose blood was sacrificed to open the way of reconciliation with God, as opposed to the much inferior sacrifice of Abel which called for vengeance (Genesis 4:10).

Don't turn your backs on this incredible message God has revealed to all. Look what happened to folks who refused to pay attention to those who attempted to transmit the love of God to the whole world in the past. Well, I'm telling you it's more impossible for anyone to escape the impact of the very message of Jesus, the voice of God Himself, even if one does become indifferent or even if one outright rejects the gift of God's grace and peace!

There was a time when the voice of God was sheer terror to any who heard it. BUT now, God has promised saying,

"I'm only going to shake, rattle, and roll not only earth, BUT heaven as well, one more time, and that's it (Haggai 2:6)!"

This phrase, "one more time," refers to the removal of everything bound to fade away, and of those things created so the unshakeable, eternal truth of God's love will be the only thing left.

So, since we've already received a kingdom that cannot be moved, let's enjoy the grace of God!

Knowing and understanding the grace of God is the only way you'll be able to serve in the kingdom of God the way you ought to, with great, grateful reverence and awe.

"For our God is a consuming fire (Deuteronomy 4:24)!"

203. ESTABLISHED WITH GRACE
(Hebrews 13:1-16)

- Continue to seek the ultimate best for those around you.
- Don't forget to entertain strangers with your hospitality. Hey, folks like **Abe and Sara** (Genesis 18), **Lot** (Genesis 19), and **Manoah** (Judges 13) all entertained messengers of God without even knowing it.
- Consider the plight of those imprisoned by one thing or another in the same way you'd like someone else to be empathetic to you if it were you in a desperate situation.
- Engage compassion towards those suffering through adversity the same way you'd like to be treated.
- Honor and respect the sanctity of marriage. Be sure to safeguard and foster the purity and pleasure of your own bedroom, BUT leave the immoral and adulterous relationships of others in the hands of God.
- Remove any trace of covetousness from your conversations.
- Be content with what you've got, for God has said,
    - "I certainly won't fail you in any way, nor will I ever stop caring for you (Joshua 1:5)."
- Contentment is much more satisfying than pleasure, and it gives us the boldness to proclaim,
    - "God is my helper, and there's absolutely nothing that scares me. What could anybody possibly do to me that would remove this confidence I have in the faith and faithfulness of God (Psalms 118:6)?"
- Don't forget to honor and respect those who've brought you into the awareness of God's loving grace and peace.
- Study the confidence and trust of those who acknowledge, appreciate, and apply the faith and faithfulness of God.
- Imitate those who talk the talk of the gospel message of God's grace and peace as well as those who walk the walk of abundant liberty.

Jesus will never change. He was the same yesterday as He is today and He'll be the same on every tomorrow of eternity as He was yesterday, and as He is today.

So, don't go getting all carried away with all the goofy proclamations and strange doctrines that the wisdom (foolishness) of mankind have concocted to deceive and control.

Let me tell ya, it's a good thing the heart of mankind has been established in the grace of God! What a catastrophe it would have been to leave our eternal security up to the sacrifice of meat! This old system of laws, rules, and regulations certainly didn't cut it for those who lived under their controls, did it?

We have an altar all right! And nobody who worships in the tabernacle of self-righteousness can lay any claim or maintain a unique right to gain the favor of God other than through the sacrifice of Jesus on the altar of God's promise! For the bodies of those bulls and goats, whose blood was used in the sanctuary by the high priest as a sacrifice for sin, were completely burned up outside the city walls so nobody could benefit from the consumption of the left over meat.

Well, the blood of Jesus was sacrificed too and He suffered the agony of God's wrath on a cross outside the city gates.

Why?

SO GOD COULD MAKE RIGHTEOUS ALL THE PEOPLE WITH THE BLOOD OF JESUS!

What to do?

Let's venture out beyond the confines of our comfort zone, beyond the structured hallowed walls of our legalistic systems of self-righteousness, to acknowledge and appreciate what Jesus has done for the whole world!

Look, the sanctuary of self-righteousness has no future. BUT, we certainly can explore all the riches of our eternal home blessed abundantly in the righteousness of God!

Because of Jesus, therefore, let's continuously offer the sacrifice of our praise to God.

Look, God has freely given to us the peaceable fruit of His righteousness, so, we should consider it our great honor and privilege to worship His Holy name with our gratitude and praise.

BUT, we also should not forget to seek the ultimate best for others as well and to communicate the love of God with those around us. God is well pleased with our sacrifices of praise and servanthood too!

Did you know one of the popular names the Greeks had for their big guy?

It was "Zeus Xenios," which means "the god of strangers."

How much more is our God, the King of Kings, the true God of strangers! God gifted us with His spirit of grace and peace to put into practice.

Whereas the bodies of bulls and goats were banished outside the city gates so no one could benefit, Jesus confidently went beyond the city gates to bear His "dis-grace" so the whole world might benefit by being "graced" of God!

Good news or what?

HEBREWS

204. CONCLUSION OF HEBREWS
(Hebrews 13:17-25)

As I wrap this letter up I'd like to remind you once again to give heed to those who bear the responsibility of increasing your knowledge and understanding of God's faith and faithfulness to the whole world. Honor them with your attention and appreciation, for they bear a very difficult task of guarding over you, protecting you from the deceitful lusts of a former lifestyle committed to self-righteousness. They're accountable to you to tell you the truth of God's love and they should have no greater joy than fulfilling their responsibility. This role should not be a grievous one, and if it is, let me tell you, you'll certainly not profit from their toil.

I ask you to pray for us, for we trust we've presented to you a message we believe is absolutely true and accurate. It's been our ever-present desire in all things to willingly and honestly live in the grace and peace of God. BUT, I'd just as soon plead with you to live the same way. If you'd do this, I'm confident you'll readily open your heart to restore our relationship once again real soon.

And now, know and understand this:

THE GOD OF PEACE, who brought to life again from the dead Jesus, the great shepherd of the sheep, through the blood of the everlasting covenant, HAS MADE YOU PERFECT BY EVERY GOOD WORK HE HAS DONE TO FULFILL HIS WILL, AND HAS WORKED A WORK IN YOU WHICH IS WELL PLEASING IN HIS SIGHT, through Jesus, to whom be glory for ever and ever.

AMEN!

And finally, I beg of you, my dear friends, please graciously accept the burden of suffering through this rather long and painful letter of exhortations.

I'd like to inform you Timothy has freed up some space on his rather busy schedule, and if it can be arranged, I plan on traveling together with him to see you.

Please greet everyone in positions of leadership as well as all the other beloved members of the family of God. All of those around me here in Italy send their greetings to all of you.

The grace of God is with you all. Amen.

205. HOLY CALLING
(2 Timothy 1:1-14)

Well, after that deep theological book, a reprieve.

This is a final deposit of instruction and encouragement to my protege Timothy. This young man had so much energy and potential it was staggering. The influence upon all those Tim encountered was enormous. To say the least, I was extremely proud of him.

From:
Paul, an ambassador of Jesus according to the will of God, and according to the promise of life in Jesus.

To:
Timothy, my dearly beloved son.

Blessing:
Grace, mercy, and peace are yours from God the Father, and from Jesus.

I'm so thankful to God whom I've had the great honor and privilege of serving as did my forefathers. I can honestly say I never stop thinking about you as I pray throughout the day and into the evening. Man, I'd sure love to see you again! I shed my share of tears when we said our goodbyes the last time and now I anticipate weeping with joy when we finally get to meet again.

My goodness, I'm thrilled when I stop to think about the faithfulness of God towards you, which, I might add, was also placed in your grandmother Lois and in your dear Mom Eunice. I'm equally convinced His grace and peace are entrenched in your life as well.

With this confidence I challenge you to fan into flame the loving gift of God's grace and peace within you. I take great pleasure you've come to know and understand all about this great gospel as a result of my involvement in your life.

You see, God hasn't given us the spirit of fear, BUT, He has given to us:
- the spirit of His power,
- the spirit of His love, and
- the spirit of His sound, logical mind.

So, don't be ashamed of the promise of our God, nor of me, for I've been happily captivated by His love. BUT, be assured you've also benefited from the affliction of Jesus for this is surely the gospel message according to the power of God!

That's right!

FOR IT IS GOD WHO HAS SAVED US FROM THE BONDAGE OF SELF-RIGHTEOUSNESS!

HE HAS CALLED EACH AND EVERY ONE OF US TO BE ABSOLUTELY HOLY IN HIS SIGHT!

Oh no, it's not according to any of our works, BUT, according to God's own purpose and grace, the promise of which was given to the whole world in Jesus before the world even began.

BUT, this very promise has now been fulfilled with the appearance of the initiator of a new life of abundance and liberty for all mankind, none other than Jesus!

What'd He do?

Well, Jesus totally abolished the certainty of eternal death! Instead of exalting the darkness of this fate, He has brought to light the reality of an incredible life right now, together with the surety of an eternal existence, through the fulfillment of the gospel message of God's loving grace and peace.

This is the fantastic message I've the great honor to preach, to proclaim, and to teach to men and women everywhere, including the Gentile folks.

As a matter of fact, this message of God's unequivocal acceptance of all mankind is the very reason why I've been detained so unnecessarily right now.

Well, I don't care.

I'm not ashamed of this glorious gospel!

I know, without a shadow of doubt, what I know and understand is the truth and nothing other than the truth!

I'm equally persuaded God was faithful to keep His promise.

Everything I had coming to me was taken care of on the wonderful day when Jesus abolished death. With His resurrection, God initiated the reality of an eternal life of abundance and liberty!

Guard carefully the presentation of the sound, logical instructions you've heard me speak to you concerning the faith and love in Jesus. This is a good thing God has blessed us with. I want you to embrace the knowledge and understanding God has fulfilled His promise of blessing your life with the Spirit of Jesus.

206. BE STRONG IN GRACE
(2 Timothy 1:15-2:26)

You know many of the fine folks here in Asia have decided, for safety reasons, to avoid any contact with me given the hostile environment which exists between both the Roman and Jewish power brokers and myself. Phygellus and Hermogenes are two of those who've been encouraged to stay away from such a hot commodity like me.

God has given His mercy to the Onesiphorus clan as well. Onesiphorus has often been a breath of fresh air for me, never one bit ashamed I've been imprisoned for preaching the gospel message. BUT, whenever he came from Ephesus to Rome on business, Onesiphorus would diligently search until he found me. God has certainly granted to him the knowledge and understanding of the great mercy of God revealed to the whole world on the marvelous day Jesus died on the cross. You're very well acquainted with the many ways he ministered to me back when I was headquartered in Ephesus.

Let the confidence and courage of guys like Onesiphorus and myself be an example to you, my son.

BE STRONG IN THE GRACE THAT IS IN YOU BECAUSE OF JESUS!

Call to remembrance all the things you've heard me speak to everyone who'd listen to me.

Challenge folks to renew their minds with the very same gospel message, and those who believe it will become reliable and dedicated to teach it to others too.

Hang in there!

Jesus was the ultimate soldier and He's already won the battle on our behalf. You see, no soldier who goes to war allows things outside the scope of the military operation to become a distraction so the commanding officer will be satisfied with the effort.

And no person who struggles to become the very best in their field of endeavor, whether it be sports, academia, economics, politics, etc., will ever get to enjoy the sweet fragrance of success by cheating or by circumventing the prescribed path.

Certainly the farmer who labors so diligently and faithfully ought to be the first to partake of the fruit of the harvest.

Just think about what I'm telling you for a moment. Jesus is like this and yet a whole lot more. God will add to your knowledge and understanding of the work of Jesus on behalf of the whole world, in all things!

Remember that Jesus, a descendant of good old Dave, was raised from the dead and this is the very gospel message I've been preaching. This message of God's loving grace and peace for the whole world is what has gotten me into so much trouble. Some folks obviously think I've fallen off my rocker. Perhaps others think I've pushed a bit too much on theirs, making them mighty uncomfortable. Whatever, it's landed me in this precarious position of bondage.

BUT, the promise of God is not bound by any thing, nor by any one!

So, bring it on. I'll gladly take whatever comes my way for telling folks God has chosen to gift everyone with His love. I will not stop preaching the whole world has been liberated from the slavery of self-righteousness. I will not stop from teaching the whole world they're liberated to enjoy the abundance of the eternal glory that is in Jesus!

The truth in these sayings is indisputable.

For, if we've been made participants in the death of Jesus, surely we also share in His glorious life!

If we've been made to participate in the suffering of Jesus, surely we also share in His reign!

If we deny the work of God in Jesus, it would be only natural for us to conclude Jesus would deny us. However, this is contrary to the truth of the nature of God, for even if we don't believe it, yet God remains faithful to His promise. You see, God simply cannot lie, nor can He go back on His word!

Tim, help folks to remember these incredible truths.

Exhort them, before God, to stop striving after teachings and doctrines that not only profit less than nothing, BUT, they also contribute more to the subversive poverty of those who hear the promises these deceptive illusions offer.

Concentrate your efforts on being who God has made you to be!

Who are you?

You are a servant in the kingdom of God and you need to be ashamed of absolutely nothing!

Stay on the straight path God has prepared for you in Jesus, making sure you preach and teach the word of God's truth correctly.

BUT, never get sucked into the treadmill of profane, ignorant babblings and speculations of parasites whose aim in life is to stimulate the "un-god-liness" of folks.

The self-righteous thinking they espouse is like an ulcerous gangrene that creeps insidiously in to contaminate.

Hymenaeus and Philetus are two examples of this breed of manure spreaders. Concerning the truth of God's promise, they've erred, proclaiming the resurrection of Jesus is irrelevant to those who live in the present. Their message of self-righteousness has led to the plague of confusion, overthrowing and undermining the confidence of many in God's faith and faithfulness.

Nevertheless, the foundation of God is rock solid!

God has put His indelible stamp onto His kingdom with this genuine guarantee:

"God knows who belong to him (Numbers 16:5)!"

And with this one:

"Let everyone named of Jesus depart the tyranny of self-righteousness (Isaiah 52:10,11)."

BUT, in any great house there are not only objects built out of gold and silver, BUT there are also objects constructed out of more mundane products such as wood and clay. Some of these objects are treasured with great honor while others are considered quite ordinary.

So, if a person will purge themselves from the profane and vain babblings of the self-righteous systems of mankind's wisdom (foolishness):
- they'll indeed become convinced in their own minds they are a treasure of unlimited honor,
- they'll renew their mind to know and understand they've been made absolutely right and perfect in the sight of God,
- they'll renew their mind to know and understand they truly are worthy of God's faith and faithfulness,

- they'll renew their mind to know and understand God has blessed them with everything they require to live in the abundance and liberty of God's grace and peace!

Listen to me Tim, run like stink from the youthful, inexperienced, exuberant lust for the self-righteous attempt to gain the favor of God with your own systems of belief and effort!

- BUT, live in the generosity of God's righteousness!
- BUT, live in the assurance of God's faith and faithfulness!
- BUT, live in the warmth of God's love!
- BUT, live in the sweetness of God's peace

By yourself? Oh no, there are actually many other folks out there who've renewed their minds to the knowledge and understanding God has by His own will unilaterally and universally, lovingly and faithfully gifted all mankind with His grace and peace. BUT, avoid getting into foolish debates with folks over the ignorant questions and answers based upon the wisdom (foolishness) of mankind, knowing full well these baseless discussions engender nothing more than angry confrontations to the benefit of nobody.

There's no necessity for a child of God to struggle along in the pursuit of God's acceptance!

- BUT, there is the wonderful privilege of showing the gentleness of God towards other folks.
- BUT, there is the great honor of being ready to instruct and teach other folks of the wisdom of God.
- BUT, there is the fabulous reward of dispensing patience with other folks who surely could use some.
- BUT, there is the immense challenge of humbly instructing folks who haven't got a clue how sad it is they don't even believe what they claim to believe.

Why would you do these things?

- So your gentleness, your instruction, your patience, and your humility will help others renew their minds to acknowledge and accept the truth of God's loving will for all mankind.
- So folks can recover themselves from the stupidity of their own corruptive thinking, thereby escaping the snare of the deceptive lusts of the self-righteous systems of belief and accomplishment.

207. DIRTY RATS
(2 Timothy 3:1-13)

Tim, there's something else I want you to know. It shouldn't be a surprise to anyone that, in the final days preceding the coming of Jesus into this world, perilous times came upon all mankind. The menace and danger humans posed to themselves and to each other is staggering.

- Folks became infatuated with themselves, tripping mercilessly over their egotistical attempts at self-righteousness.
- Folks, in jealous anxiety over the apparent attainments of others, stooped to covet what they could never gain on their own.
- Some folks exercised their superiority complexes and took every opportunity to brag about it.
- Others, in pomp arrogance, puffed out their chests in pride like quack doctors proclaiming cures for every disease imaginable because of the great strides they were making.
- Folks descended into a pervasive disregard and a conscious contempt for both God and their fellow human beings.
- Some folks drifted to the bottom of the barrel, becoming disobedient to even their own parents.
- Apathy and ungratefulness became the norm.
- Folks, despairing in hopeless, concluding holiness was such an illusive characteristic, refused to recognize even the very basic decencies of life.
- Compassion and affection within the family circle hit an all time low.
- Folks had no qualms about breaking agreements, or were so bitter they refused to even enter into a contract with others.
- Folks engaged in the distasteful tyranny of the slanderous deception of any truth.
- Folks became ungovernable in their desires.
- Sensitivity and sympathy were eroded to the extent some folks displayed an animalistic savagery towards others.

- Folks came to despise anything or anyone representing good.
- Folks became treacherous traitors.
- Folks got carried away by a precipitous passion and impulse to soothe their senses.
- The heads of folks was swelled by the inflated, conceited sense of their own importance.
- Folks got more wrapped up in the love of pleasure than in the love of God.
- Folks had a form of "godliness," BUT, they chose to deny the affect this had upon their lives!

The sad reality is many of these characteristics of mankind still persist to this day.

Tim, run like crazy from folks who refuse to acknowledge the faith and faithfulness of God towards humankind in Jesus.

Don't trust for a moment the irresponsible, insensitive, and deceptive nature of those steeped in their own forms and systems of self-righteous behavior. These sneaky varmints will creep into the dwelling space of others, placing into increasing bondage unwitting folks already overloaded with the anxiety, guilt, and fear of their own baggage. These dirty rats have been led astray with the diversions and lusts of the self-righteous wisdom (foolishness) of mankind, perpetuated by systems of beliefs, traditions, laws, rules, and regulations.

Don't kid yourself. They will never stop trying to learn the secrets of success, and yet, they are never able to grasp the knowledge and understanding of the simplicity and truth of the wisdom of God.

Now, as Jannes and Jambres made an attempt to stop Moses...

Perhaps, before I continue with this thought, I ought to let you in on the infamous characters I just referred to. You may recall the great incidents surrounding the attempts of Moses and Aaron to get the Pharaoh to free the people of Israel (Exodus 7:11; 8:7; 9:11). Although not mentioned by name, popular opinion has identified the magicians who tried to mimic the miracles of God as Jannes and Jambres.

Well, these confrontations with Moses are not the only ones that have been assigned to these two characters. Some believe Jannes and Jambres were the two servants who were with Balaam when he was disobedient to God (Numbers 22:22). Some figure they were a part of the great multitude who actually accompanied the Israelites out of Egypt (Exodus 12:38).

What a switch!

On the other hand, some think they drown with the rest of the pursuing Egyptians in the great sea debacle. Stories persist they helped make the golden calf, dying for their indiscretion (Exodus 32:28). There are even some suggestions they became proselytes to Judaism.

One thing is sure. The names of Jannes and Jambres have become legendary in typifying those who oppose the purposes of God, in addition to the work of those who lead His people.

...now, as Jannes and Jambres made an attempt to stop Moses, those who persist in self-righteousness resist the truth of God's loving grace and peace. The wisdom (foolishness) of mankind has done nothing less than corrupt their minds, making it almost impossible for them to renew them to know and understand the faith and faithfulness of God towards His creation.

BUT, they will not succeed in gaining the favor of God with all of their self-righteousness, in spite of what they believe or what they do!

Why?

Because the folly of the wisdom (foolishness) of mankind has been demonstrated to everyone in Jesus, just as the inability of Jannes and Jambres was revealed in their day.

BUT, you are very well acquainted with:
- **what I've come to know and understand concerning the grace and peace of God,**
- **how I live,**
- **my purpose in life to share the gospel message,**
- **the confidence and trust I have in the faith and faithfulness of God,**
- **my ability to retain hope in folks when they're stupid, or when they don't deserve it,**
- **my concern for the ultimate best of others,**
- **my patience,**

- all of the persecutions I've endured, and
- all of the sicknesses I suffered through while I was at Antioch, Iconium, and Lystra.

BUT, through thick and thin, **GOD CONTINUALLY DISPLAYS HIS FAITH AND FAITHFULNESS TO ME!**

All those who profess the sufficiency of God's will and ability through the work of Jesus, irrespective of the participation of mankind in any form, will suffer the indignity and reproach of those who seem determined to retain for mankind some hope in self-righteousness.

BUT, for those who make self-righteousness their mantra, this life will be consumed by the bondage and slavery of the seductive, evil lusts of systems of belief and accomplishment. They think it will make things better for them in the long run.

Ha!

It only will make worse things worse. In the deception, they too will be deceived even more by the fallacy and inconsistency of their own ability.

208. PREACH IT SON
(2 Timothy 3:14-4:5)

BUT, Tim, I want you to continue to have confidence in what you've already learned concerning the grace and peace of God, especially as you consider who has taught you about all these things. Since you were a little kid you've been instructed in the wisdom of God revealed in the holy scriptures. Indeed, the very recordings of God's dealings with mankind are a revelation of God's plan of salvation for all through the faith and faithfulness of Jesus!

Yes, the revelation of God's will for all mankind has been inspired by Him.
- It's profitable because everyone can know and understand the love of God.
- It's profitable because everyone can become convinced of the error and stupidity of the self-righteousness wisdom (foolishness) of mankind.
- It's profitable because everyone can be challenged to renew their minds to the incredible reality of the wisdom of God.
- It's also profitable because everyone can receive instruction concerning the impartation of the righteousness of God to all of His creation.

Why did God reveal Himself?
- So everyone would know and understand God has provided the way for all to become perfect in His sight!
- **SO WE ALL COULD GET ON WITH LIVING IN THE ABUNDANCE AND LIBERTY OF GOD'S LOVING GRACE AND PEACE,** thoroughly furnished and equipped to treat others with the compassion and servitude of the Spirit of Jesus within us.

Tim, I charge you, before God and Jesus, who've already judged the living and the dead at the time of the arrival of Jesus, and who've introduced His kingdom to all to:
- Preach the word of truth concerning the wisdom of God.
- Confidently remain planted firmly in the knowledge and understanding you have whether things go the way you like or not, or whether folks will listen to you or not.

- Convince, rebuke, admonish, exhort, and encourage folks to renew their minds with the wisdom of God in a logical, consistent way.

I'm telling you, a time will come when folks won't be able to stand the sound doctrine of God's love for all mankind! Almost sounds crazy to say it, and yet, it's true. BUT, pursuing instead their own messed up lust for self-righteousness, folks will fall all over themselves to follow after the teachings of those who think they have a better way to the righteousness of God than His gracious way.

Go figure!

With itchy, burning ears folks will turn their sensitivity away from knowing and understanding the truth of God's loving grace and peace, preferring to place their confidence in deceitful fables conjured up in the imaginations of the wisdom (foolishness) of mankind.

BUT, Tim, keep your eyes wide open. Take whatever folks dish out. Continue to do the work of preaching and teaching the wonderful message of God's love. Don't be ashamed to say what you mean and do not refrain for an instant from living in the confident assurance of the grace and peace of God.

2ND TIMOTHY

209. AS FOR ME
(2 Timothy 4:6-22)

As for me, Tim, I know I'm not exactly a spring chicken anymore. I've a gut feeling my remaining days on this old earth are numbered. I'm ready to loosen the ropes, take down the poles, pack up my personalized tent, and head off to discover a whole new campground. I'm fully prepared to unhook the mooring ropes from the dock and set my sailboat on a course to discover a whole new sea of possibilities. I'm fully prepared to unclasp the chains that have bound me, escaping to discover an entirely new kind of freedom.

Yep, I've had a few good battles along the way. I've had a pretty good run! I've enjoyed the trip. And I'm ever confidently grateful in the faith and faithfulness of God towards me.

I know God, the judge of all righteousness, anointed me with the crown of His righteousness on that day when Jesus became my portion. BUT, hey, not just my portion only, the provision for everyone who know and understand what His appearance has meant for all mankind.

Tim, please try as hard as you can to come and visit me soon. Demas has taken off for Thessalonica, preferring to find some treasure in the things of this world. Crescens has left for Galatia, while Titus has departed for Dalmatia. The only one who remains with me here at the moment is "Doc," my good buddy Luke.

Grab hold of Mark and bring him along with you when you come, for I'm sure I could really use him to carry on with the preaching and teaching of the gospel message.

Oh yes, I've sent Tychicus off to Ephesus.

I left an overcoat in Troas with Carpus. Could you please bring it along with you when you come? Bring my books too, BUT, more importantly, don't forget to collect all of my note pads for me.

Alexander, the coppersmith, hasn't exactly treated me too well, spreading vicious rumors and such. In fact, he's been downright nasty. I know it's not possible, however, I wish God would reward Alex based upon his actions.

Watch out for this character 'cause he'll stab you in the back if given the opportunity. He hasn't exactly been sympathetic to what we've been preaching and teaching.

At my pretrial examination none of my friends were permitted to serve as witnesses before the tribunal on my behalf, BUT, I still felt as if I had been abandoned by everyone simply because of the great gospel message I was sharing.

Ha, I guess I feel a little bit like Stephen did, knowing God won't hold their abandonment of me against anyone.

Notwithstanding my disappointment concerning the loyalty of my fellow human beings, I remain confident in the knowledge and understanding God continues to abound in His faithfulness towards me, providing me with the strength to handle the circumstances of each day. I'm assured of His faith in me to continue preaching the gospel of God's grace and peace to all who consider themselves outside the scope of God's love.

I've been delivered out of the jaws of certain disaster more than once. God has delivered me from every inclination to return to the bondage of self-righteousness and I'm confident He'll preserve me in His grace and peace until the day I make my eternal home in His heavenly kingdom.

To God be the glory for ever and ever!

Amen.

P.S.

Please give my love to Priscilla and Aquila and to the family of Onesiphorus. Erastus has stayed on in Corinth, BUT, I left Trophimus back in Miletus because he was just too sick to travel.

Once again, do everything you can to come and visit me before winter sets in.

Eubulus sends you greetings, as do Pudens, Linus, Claudia, and all the rest of the brothers and sisters.

REMEMBER, THE SPIRIT OF JESUS IS PERMANENTLY WITH YOUR SPIRIT!

The grace of God is with you always.

Amen.

Take care.

CONCLUSION

210. THAT'S ALL FOLKS

Well, that's it folks!

My whole life in a nutshell.

Pretty big nut mind you!

I can only hope my life will be, in some measure, an inspiration to you. I'd like to think how I've lived has made an impact somewhere along the line.

Hero in the eyes of mankind?

Considering what I've been through I guess I could live with the honor.

Hero in the eyes of God?

You bet. Unquestionably! God thinks the world of me! Always has, always will!

The story of my life ought to provide encouragement and hope to everyone. Hey, if ever there was a person engrossed in the self-righteous attempt to gain the favor of God it was I. I climbed the sanctimonious ladder of religiosity with the best of them. Oh, I was an ardent follower of God all right, or so I thought.

My goodness, how could I have been blind for so long? I had studied all the good books so thoroughly. How could I miss the blinding truth of God's eternal love for all of His creation? How could I ignore all the ways in which God pointed mankind to the truth?

And then Jesus came along!

My, oh my, this Jesus character really upset the apple cart, that's a for sure. Talk about getting in the way. Indeed He did, however, those of us who thought we had a better way to God's favor reacted with an indignation probably unsurpassed to this day. With ardent zeal it became my mission to wipe out all vestiges of His followers.

And then I saw the light!

Literally and figuratively.

No foolin'.

I want to encourage you by saying the process of renewing my mind to the truth of God's wisdom wasn't as immediate as you have been led to believe. The process is a journey. Anyone who tells you different is exaggerating.

I never stopped learning. I never stopped being amazed by the goodness of God. Coming to new knowledge and to a new understanding ought never come to an end.

I encourage you to press on in your quest for knowledge and understanding. Don't ever be lulled into apathy and contentment with where you're at. Don't accept the fallacy that questioning the wisdom (foolishness) of mankind's systems of belief and accomplishment is somehow inexcusably wrong.

One more thing, don't expect everyone to appreciate your new sense of understanding if you find it. You've got another coming if you think everyone will share your new discoveries and insights. I can testify to that.

Your search will lead you to discover more and more of God's view and opinion concerning you. You'll never know enough about God. Be assured He knows everything about you! You can never know too much about how spectacular God's love for you truly is!

Remember this: The truth will always be the truth!

God's love is an absolute. The sacrifice of His Son, Jesus, to unilaterally and universally cover every failure of mankind can't be undone. The adoption of all into the family of God is a done deal. God sealed it with the implantation of the Spirit of Jesus into all His creation.

This truth is truth whether you like it or not.

This truth is still the truth whether you believe it or not.

This truth will be truth for all eternity whether you know it or not.

This truth is truth regardless of the amount of faith you place in it.

Your belief, your faith, your knowledge, your accomplishments doesn't affect the truth. Why do I say that? Because truth is just simply truth!

Isn't it great?

It's all about God folks! It's all about Jesus folks!

God's acceptance of you has nothing at all to do with what you do. His plan in Jesus was what God wanted to do!

His righteousness was His gift to you.

His grace was His gift to you.

His peace was His gift to you.

His mercy was His gift to you.

What a bummer if it was up to me! I'd never have made it. And, with all the arrogance I can muster, if I couldn't make it with my credentials and work ethic, you wouldn't make it either!

I think I could write another book or two instead of just a few more letters.

Well, this is going to have to do for now. It's been a real slice for me to share my life with you. It's been beyond my pleasure to share with you my understanding concerning the wisdom of God's grace and peace.

It probably wouldn't even hurt you to read all of my letters a few more times to help you in the renewal process. Years and years of the mismanagement of information will not be overcome in a few hours. Give it a chance to sink in. I'm confident the renewing of your mind to this new and living way will change your life forever. You'll slowly start thinking more highly of God, of yourself, and of others.

Open your eyes to see the magnificence of God.

Start to realize your life does have value and purpose. Hey, if God loved you so much to do what He has done for you, can you not grasp hold of the psychological impact this ought to have upon how you think of yourself?

Then, begin to see other folks in a whole new light. They're no different from you. No better. No worse. We're all bathed in the righteousness of God, His children forever loved!

The abundance and liberty of God are yours to enjoy.

What's my favorite piece of advice I could leave with you from all of my writings? Let me take you back to a passage from a letter to my Roman friends.

"Therefore, since your righteousness is based solely upon the will and activity of God, not upon the resolve of your belief, nor upon the successful adherence to laws, rules, and regulations, I plead with you, my dear friends, ACCEPT THE MERCIES OF GOD FOR WHAT THEY ARE! You are living examples of the sacrifice of Jesus, not skillful players in the game of offering sacrifices of works which are as dead as doorposts."

"LIVE LIKE YOU ARE, HOLY! Live knowing you're acceptable to God the way you are! This is a very reasonable way to live."

"Don't be conformed to the wisdom (foolishness) of this world that would have you sucked into the downward spiral of performance based guilt and shame."

"BUT, be transformed."
"How?"
"By the renewing of your mind!"
"Why?"
"So you may prove what is the good, acceptable, perfect will of God!" (Romans 12:1-3)
Remember:
"the grace and peace of God is with you eternally!"
Until we meet, embrace life!

ROGER'S CONCLUSION

211. THANKS

There you have it. Something to chew on, eh!

Well, I've been chewin' on this thing for some twenty years now. My journey of discovery has taken me where I never dreamed it would. Through the various manuscripts I've not only discovered a whole lot more about what I thought everyone would like to know about God, I've actually come to discover what God thinks about everyone, ultimately the most important lesson in this massive theological piece of work.

Truthfully and confidently, my journey of discovery is far from over. If you told me ten years ago I'd someday read books about quantum physics and other eye popping stuff that Donna is discovering for us, and actually liking it, I'd have told you that you were confusing me with someone else. Quantum physics! No kidding. The study of time and space from a scientific basis is fascinating to say the least. Here's just one example of a thought that has revolutionized my understanding of God and how He has so wondrously and marvelously created me in His image.

Donna and I were on our way home from Calgary where we attended the memorial service for a very special child of the kingdom, our dear Uncle Walter Kerber. If there ever was a person who had a passionate love of his heavenly Father, his family, and his life, it was Walter. We all miss him. It was Donna's turn to drive and I was reading a section of a particular book we were tackling together. The relevance to this somber occasion where the difficult questions concerning life and death was obvious.

I've been brought up with the understanding I'm more than flesh and bones, I'm a magnificent body with a soul. That's a great thought, however, from a different perspective I really dig, it's actually much more complex than that. I'm acutely thankful to discover I'm really an eternal soul with, for the moment, a body.

Eureka!

Time and space, among other things, are just illusions which my mind play with. In the realm of God these dimensions have no significance at all. Pieces of the puzzle I've read in the scriptures since I was a little kid, pieces I didn't have a clue as to where they fit in the bigger picture, are starting to drop into place like never before.

Folks, I hope you've discovered how passionate I've become in my understanding of God's love for me as I've read, studied, and written this rendition and commentary of the writings of Paul. I trust this adventure in reading will be for you a stepping-stone to new discoveries as well.

I exhort you to step out of your comfort zone, at the very least, I'd like to encourage and stimulate you to read, to study, and to dialogue with others. We live in a world of technology and information. Be bold enough to expand your horizons. Be a sponge to absorb the manifold blessing of God.

It is His good pleasure to bless you with abundance beyond your wildest imaginations. God has liberated you to sunbathe in the radiant warmth of His great love, His limitless grace, His unfailing mercy, and His everlasting peace.

I sure am!

Until we meet...all the best!

ABOUT THE AUTHOR

Roger Rapske and his wife Donna currently reside in Sequoia Ridge at Coyote Creek, a wonderful oasis in beautiful British Columbia, Canada. They share their love of life in the abundance and liberty of God's blessing with their phenomenally creative children Richard and Mandilyn, daughter-in-law Sharla, and two precious grandchildren, Ryan and Keira.

Roger is an avid putzer, sports junkie, non-earth muffin food addict (he likes his junk food) and a very blessed husband, proud father and grateful grandpa. He loves to create things, from the challenge of being an author to the artistic pursuits of calligraphy, doodling, needlework, stained glass work, intarsia, picture framing, wood-working and constructing wooden projects from architectural drawings.

Roger has gained a wealth of experience and insight from years spent in the industries of religion and business. He holds a Bachelor of Theological Degree from North American Baptist College and has served in various capacities in a number of different church situations. He has spent over 35 years in the automotive industry, holding virtually every position possible in a car dealership from owning a Volkswagen dealership to driving a parts truck (perhaps his favorite job of all). Following a stint at retirement he currently works as a customization co-ordinator at a major automotive dealership.

Roger's other contribution to the literary world is his insightful and delightfully written work concerning the extraordinary parables of Jesus entitled, "More Than Just a Piece of Sky.

The author will consider invitations for speaking engagements and can be contacted at threescoops@shaw.ca

www.ingramcontent.com/pod-product-compliance
Lightning Source LLC
Chambersburg PA
CBHW071428300426
44114CB00013B/1355